RESEARCHING
SOCIAL LIFE

RESEARCHING
SOCIAL LIFE
Third Edition

edited by
NIGEL GILBERT

Los Angeles • London • New Delhi • Singapore

SAGE Publications Ltd
1 Oliver's Yard
55 City Road
London EC1Y 1SP

SAGE Publications Inc.
2455 Teller Road
Thousand Oaks, California 91320

SAGE Publications India Pvt Ltd
B 1/I 1 Mohan Cooperative Industrial Area
Mathura Road
Post Bag 7, New Delhi 110 044

SAGE Publications Asia-Pacific Pte Ltd
33 Pekin Street #02-01
Far East Square
Singapore 048763

Library of Congress Control Number: 2007935178

British Library Cataloguing in Publication data

A catalogue record for this book is available from the British Library

ISBN 978-1-4129-4661-2
ISBN 978-1-4129-4662-9 (pbk)

Typeset by C&M Digital Pvt Ltd, Chennai, India
Printed in Great Britain by TJ International Ltd
Printed on paper from sustainable resources

SUMMARY OF CONTENTS

CONTENTS

CONTRIBUTORS

Victoria D. Alexander is Senior Lecturer in the Sociology Department at the University of Surrey. She is author of *Sociology of the Arts: Exploring Fine and Popular Forms* and *Museums and Money: The Impact of Funding on Exhibitions, Scholarship and Management*, and co-author of *Art and the State: The Visual Arts in Comparative Perspective*. Her research interests include sociology of art and culture, organisational sociology, visual methods, and mixed methods. She teaches sociology of art, organisational analysis, and documentary analysis.

Nick Allum is a Lecturer at the Department of Sociology, University of Essex, where he mainly teaches research methods. He previously taught sociology at the University of Surrey. His research interests are primarily in public understanding of science, risk perception and social trust. He has published widely in these areas in journals and books. Nick is engaged in research on survey methods, particularly in relation to the measurement of social attitudes and factual knowledge in population surveys using latent variable models. He is also co-editor, with Bulmer and Sturgis, of a four volume book on the secondary analysis of survey data.

Sara Arber is Professor of Sociology, and Co-Director, Centre for Research on Ageing and Gender (CRAG) at University of Surrey. Sara has written over 200 journal articles on gender and ageing, and on inequalities in health. She is currently pioneering multi-disciplinary research on the sociology of sleep. Her books include *The Myth of Generational Conflict: Family and State in Ageing Societies*

(with Claudine Attias-Donfut, Routledge, 2000), *Gender and Ageing: Changing Roles and Relationships* (with Kate Davidson and Jay Ginn, 2003); and *Connecting Gender and Ageing* (with Jay Ginn, 1995), which won the Age Concern prize for best book on Ageing in 1996.

Martin Bulmer is Professor of Sociology at the University of Surrey and Director of the ESRC Social Survey Question Bank, http://qb.soc. surrey.ac.uk. His own research is concerned with the history of the social sciences, the application of knowledge to policy-making, and race and ethnicity. He is editor of the journal *Ethnic and Racial Studies*. His most recent book, jointly edited with Patrick Sturgis and Nick Allum, is a collection on the *Secondary Analysis of Survey Data* (Sage, 2008).

Geoff Cooper is a Senior Lecturer in the Department of Sociology at the University of Surrey. His intellectual interests lie within social theory and the sociology of science and technology, and his work focuses on the organisation of knowledge in contemporary societies and epistemological issues within the social sciences. He has done research on the social shaping of mobile telecommunications and, more recently, on decisions to invest in nanotechnology, and published articles in a number of journals including the *British Journal of Sociology*, *Social Studies of Science*, and *Sociology*. He is currently researching the relation between lifestyle and energy consumption and working on an edited collection on the reconfiguration of sociological theory.

Ann Cronin is a Lecturer in Sociology at the University of Surrey. She teaches sociological theory, the sociology of work and the sociology of gender and sexuality. She also runs courses on focus groups and qualitative analysis. Her main research interests are in gender and the social construction of sexual identities, narrative analysis and the sociology of story telling, integrating methodologies and sociological theory. Her work on the social networks of older lesbian women can be found in *Ageing and Diversity: Multiple Pathways in Later Life*, (Sage, 2004).

Sarah Earthy is a Lecturer in Sociology at the University of Surrey. She teaches social research methods, the sociology of health and illness, and social policy analysis. She also runs courses on qualitative interviewing and analysis. Her main research interests are inequalities in health, chronic illness, social exclusion, and the sociology of story-telling.

Mary Ebeling is an Assistant Professor in Sociology at Drexel University in Philadelphia, USA and has previously held research posts in the Department of Sociology at the University of Surrey. Her research interests span several areas of social inquiry and investigation including work in science and technology, financial markets and journalism, online political communication and exile, and media and culture, especially advertising culture. Recent research projects have focused on African political exiles and their uses of online technologies, emerging nanotechnologies and financial markets, and pharmaceutical advertising. Her work has appeared in *Sociological Research Online*, *Radical History Review* and *Science and Technology in Africa* (Red Sea Press, 2004).

Jane Fielding joined the University of Surrey in 1981 as a researcher working on part-time contracts in the departments of Sociology, Human Biology and Psychology. In 1984 she became the Departmental Research Fellow and has been involved with the teaching of computing and quantitative methods since then. She was appointed as a Lecturer in Quantitative Methods in 1994 and Senior Lecturer in 2001. She is interested in research methods, particularly mixed methods and the use of computers in quantitative and qualitative data analysis. She is currently studying the application of geographic information system techniques to an investigation of environmental inequality in the flood plains of England and Wales. She is also interested in the career pathways of men and women with science, engineering and technology (SET) qualifications. She published *Understanding Social Statistics*, (2nd Edition, Sage, 2006, with Nigel Gilbert).

Nigel Fielding is Professor of Sociology and Associate Dean of Arts and Human Sciences at the University of Surrey. With Ray Lee, he co-directs the CAQDAS Networking Project, which provides training and support in the use of computers in qualitative data analysis. His research interests are in new technologies for social research, qualitative research methods, and mixed method research design. He has authored or edited 20 books, over 50 journal articles and over 200 other publications. In research methodology his books include a study of methodological integration (*Linking Data*, 1986, Sage, with Jane Fielding), an influential book on qualitative software (*Using Computers in Qualitative Research*, 1991, Sage; editor, with Ray Lee), a study of the role of computer technology in qualitative research (*Computer Analysis and Qualitative Research*, 1998, Sage, with Ray Lee) and a four-volume set, *Interviewing* (2002, Sage, editor). He is presently researching the application of high performance computing applications to qualitative methods.

Julie Gibbs joined the Department in of Sociology at the University of Surrey 2001 as a Research Officer on the ESRC Question

Bank. Julie has since completed the part-time MSc in Social Research and is now a Research Fellow, managing the Question Bank project since April 2005. Her research interests are in survey data collection methods and she regularly teaches on this subject. Julie has published a number of articles on survey data collection methods, quantitative social research and teaching quantitative methods.

Nigel Gilbert is Professor of Sociology at the University of Surrey. His current interests focus on the computer simulation of social phenomena (*Simulating Societies*, UCL, 1994; *Artificial Societies*, UCL, 1995; *Simulation for the Social Scientist*, with Klaus G. Troitzsch, 1999, second edition 2005; *Agent Based Models*, Sage, 2007) and science and technology policy. After graduating with a degree in Engineering from Cambridge, he worked in the sociology of science (*Opening Pandora's Box: A Sociological Analysis of Scientific Discourse*, with Michael Mulkay, Cambridge University Press, 1984). He has written and edited textbooks on statistics and research methods and edited a number of other books. He is a Fellow of the Royal Academy of Engineering and an Academician of the Academy of Social Sciences.

Nicola Green is a Senior Lecturer in the Department of Sociology, University of Surrey. She joined the department in 2001 having previously held a Research Fellowship in the Digital World Research Centre. Her research interests have crossed disciplinary boundaries in work on science and technology, embodiment and identity, media and culture, and gender and everyday life. Her research projects have spanned virtual reality technologies, mobile multimedia, surveillance, Internet technologies, and web media. Her recent publications have appeared in *Surveillance and Society*, *The Information Society, Journal of*

Consumer Culture, and *Information, Communication and Society*. She is co-editor of a collection entitled *Wireless World* (Springer-Verlag, 2002), and co-author of *Mobile Communications* (Berg, forthcoming). She has been a consultant for companies such as British Telecom and Intel, and for organisations such as the Office of the Information Commissioner and the Royal Society.

Christine Hine is a Senior Lecturer in the Department of Sociology at the University of Surrey. Her main research centres on the sociology of science and technology. She recently completed an ESRC fellowship which focused on the use of information in contemporary science. This study combined ethnographic and historical approaches to understanding the role of information and communication technologies in biological research. She also has a major interest in the development of ethnography in technical settings, and in 'virtual methods' (the use of the Internet for social research). In particular, she has developed mobile and connective approaches to ethnography which combine online and offline social contexts. She is author of *Virtual Ethnography* (Sage, 2000) and *Systematics as Cyberscience* (MIT, 2008) and editor of *Virtual Methods* (Berg, 2005) and *New Infrastructures for Knowledge Production* (Information Science Publishing, 2006). Christine is President of the European Association for the Study of Science and Technology (EASST).

Paul Hodkinson is Lecturer in Sociology at the University of Surrey. His research interests focus on the role of commerce, media and new technologies in the formation of young people's lifestyles and identities. He is author of *Goth: Identity, Style and Subculture* (Berg, 2002) and co-editor of *Youth Cultures: Scenes, Subcultures and Tribes* (Routledge, 2007). He has also published a variety of articles and chapters focused upon young people's uses of online communications technologies and on the methodological implications of studying groups of young people as an 'insider researcher'. Paul is co-convenor of the British Sociological Association Youth Study Group.

Ann Lewins joined the University of Surrey in 1994. She helped to develop the ESRC funded CAQDAS Networking Project, turning it into a unique resource for researchers looking for debate, training or advice concerning the growing interest in computer assistance for qualitative data analysis. She has expertise in a number of computer based approaches to qualitative data and teaches and advises at introductory and advanced project-specific level. In 1994 she set up and still co-manages the Jiscmail Internet discussion list *qual-software* and currently maintains the project web site resource http://caqdas.soc. surrey.ac.uk. She was a co-researcher in the joint Huddersfield/Surrey project to set up the *QDA Online* resource http://onlineqda. hud.ac.uk. Former research interests have included the British Labour party, the health and welfare needs of older people and community services. Her recent publications include *Using Software In Qualitative Data Analysis: A Step by Step Guide* (Lewins and Silver, Sage, 2007).

Keith Macdonald is Visiting Professor of Sociology in the Department of Sociology, University of Surrey, where he has held various posts since 1964, including Head of Department 1984–88. He held visiting Research Fellowships at Edinburgh University (1969) and Manchester University (1970). He has published numerous articles on the sociology of occupations, especially the professions and the military; the most recent has involved the application of Bourdieu's concepts to the British military elite (*Sociological Review*, 2004). He is the author of *The Sociology of the Professions* (Sage, 1995) and

has contributed chapters on the professions to *Social Theory at Work* (OUP, 2006) and *The Blackwell Encyclopaedia of Sociology* (2006). While maintaining his interest in the sociology of occupations, he is also working on studies in historical sociology.

Jo Moran-Ellis works in the Department of Sociology at the University of Survey. Her research is primarily in two areas: childhood studies, particularly social competence, and issues involved in integrating multiple methods. She has recently completed a major study looking at practice and processes involved in integrating multiple methods, working with a team of colleagues in the Department. Jo has also co-edited (with Ian Hutchby) *Children and Social Competence: Arenas of Action* (Falmer Press, 1998) and *Children, Technology and Culture* (Falmer Press 2001), developing ideas of social competence as an interactional phenomenon embedded in social and structural contexts.

Mike Procter was a Lecturer in the Department of Sociology at the University, from which he retired in 1999. He helped to set up the MSc in Social Research in 1973 and taught mainly in the areas of quantitative research methods. He has worked on cross-national comparisons of attitudes, studies of poverty and on the social psychology of adolescence.

Christina Silver has worked with the CAQDAS Networking Project at the University of Surrey since 1998. The Project, http://caqdas.soc.surrey. ac.uk, provides information and training for a range of software packages designed to facilitate qualitative data analysis. She has supported hundreds of researchers in their use of qualitative software and taught under- and postgraduate social research methods courses at several universities. Christina also undertakes commissioned research projects for independent organisations. With Ann Lewins,

Christina has co-authored *Using Qualitative Software: A Step-by-Step Guide* (Sage, 2007), the first book to provide step-by-step support for several qualitative software packages.

Rosemarie Simmons runs Surrey Social and Market Research (SSMR) Ltd, a company carrying out social research that is linked to the Department of Sociology at the University of Surrey. She has wide research experience carried out in an academic environment within the Universities of Surrey, Manchester and Leicester where her main fields of research were on the impact of becoming blind in adult life; the effects of disability on life chances: training and rehabilitation; and adoption: the search for birth parents. Since setting up SSMR, Rosemarie has been involved in a diverse range of projects for government, local authorities, and voluntary organisations.

Patrick Sturgis is Reader in Quantitative Sociology in the Department of Sociology, University of Surrey. His research interests are in the areas of public opinion, statistical modelling and survey methodology, with a particular focus on longitudinal surveys. He teaches survey methodology and statistical modelling at both undergraduate and postgraduate level and has published widely on different aspects of survey design and analysis. He is an Associate Fellow of the Southampton Social Statistics Research Institute (S3RI) and associate editor of the journal *Survey Research Methods*.

Hilary Thomas, formerly a Senior Lecturer in the Department of Sociology, University of Surrey, is Professor of Health Care Research in the Centre for Research in Primary and Community Care, University of Hertfordshire. Her research interests include the sociology of health and illness, particularly reproduction, women's health and recovery from illness and injury. She was convenor of the BSA Medical Sociology Group (1991-94) and President of the European Society for Health and Medical Sociology (1999-2003).

Robin Wooffitt, formerly a Senior Lecturer in the Department of Sociology at the University of Surrey, is now Senior Lecturer in Sociology at the University of York. His research interests include language and interaction, especially in the context of reports of anomalous or exceptional experiences and the scientific study of parapsychological phenomena. He has been a Visiting Fellow at the universities of York (1999), Edinburgh (2001) and Adelaide (2007). Recent books include *The Language of Mediums and Psychics: The Social Organisation of Everyday Miracles* (2006, Ashgate). *Conversation Analysis and Discourse Analysis: A Comparative and Critical Introduction* (Sage, 2005) and *Conversation Analysis: Principles, Practices and Applications* (with Ian Hutchby, 1998, Polity).

ACKNOWLEDGEMENTS

We are very grateful to Karen Phillips, Stephen Barr, Patrick Brindle and Natalie Aguilera of SAGE for their enthusiastic encouragement and help during the preparation of the three editions of this book, to Caroline Eley who prepared the index, to Lu Yang who assisted with a great deal of the editing work for the third edition, and to Agnes McGill, Jon Gubbay, Geoff Payne and several anonymous reviewers who read and commented on the first edition while it was in draft.

The authors and publishers wish to thank the *American Sociological Review* for permission to use copyright material from J.M. McPherson and L. Smith-Lovin (1986) 'Sex Segregation in Voluntary Associations', *American Sociological Review*, vol. 51, pp. 61–79.

The book is dedicated to the current and past staff and students of the Sociology Department at the University of Surrey.

GUIDED TOUR

 KEY POINTS – an outline of the important points and conclusions that will be discussed in depth throughout the chapter.

 DISCUSSION QUESTIONS – assist in the focusing and application of the various theories and concepts that have been discussed.

 RESOURCES – Suggestions and information on further reading that will provide deeper understanding on the issues raised in the chapter.

 GLOSSARY – Throughout the text bolded words signify key terms and phrases that can be looked up in the glossary

2 Research, Theory and Method
Nigel Gilbert

 KEY POINTS

- Theory, method and analysis are closely interconnected. Decisions about one affect the others.
- Data are never theory-neutral: what data are collected and how they are interpreted depend on one's theoretical perspective and preconceptions.
- Theories can be constructed from concepts and relationships, and concepts measured using indicators. Indicators need to be evaluated in terms of their validity and reliability.
- Social research is a social process and can be studied sociologically.
- There is no one best research design. The choice depends on the research question and the resources that the researcher has available.

2.1 INTRODUCTION

In the previous chapter, it was suggested that **theory** is a vital part of social research, helping us to see the world in different ways and to ask new questions. In this chapter, we shall look more closely at the relationship between theory and data and at how the methodological tools that are described in the rest of the book fit into the research process. By 'theory' in this chapter is meant the 'middle-range' theories that aim to explain a range of observations, not the perspectives and world views in which they are embedded, as explained in the previous chapter.

Social research involves constructing theories, designing appropriate research methods, collecting data and analysing the data. This chapter considers the relationship between these activities and especially the link between theory and data. It describes the strategies of **induction, deduction** and **falsification**, defines **validity** and **reliability**, and distinguishes between **concepts** (the ingredients of theories) and **indicators** (the way one measures concepts).

2.2 THREE INGREDIENTS OF SOCIAL RESEARCH

There are three major ingredients in social research: the construction of theory, the collection of data and, no less important, the design of methods for gathering data. All of them have to be right if the research is to yield interesting results. We can see these three ingredients in most accounts of good research.

Goffman (1959; 1961; see also Chapter 1) spent much of his career exploring the social world of organisations. He writes about hotels, schools, prisons and hospitals. But what is *theoretically* interesting about such places? As a sociologist, his concern is with one of the fundamental problems of sociology, how social relationships are co-ordinated and regulated. He notes that in many 'establishments', there are common features in the ways employees present themselves to the 'customers' and that this presentation is not just an issue for the individual employee; it is a collective effort. He uses an analogy based on the theatre. In a theatre, a performance is given on stage, but the activity out front is only possible because of the efforts of those who work backstage. In the same way, Goffman argues, the performance of hotel porters, prison officers, mental hospital orderlies, and so on, relies on the support of other members of the staff. He cites as an example his observations in a hospital ward, where he says that the more experienced doctors are able to display their apparently superior ability because they have spent time the previous night 'studying up on the chart', and because this work is shared out between them so that they all support each other in creating a good impression for the benefit of the trainee.

> In a medical hospital the two staff internists may require the intern, as part of his training, to run through a patient's chart, giving an opinion about each recorded item. He may not appreciate that his show of relative ignorance comes in part from the staff studying up on the chart the night before; he is quite unlikely to appreciate that this impression is doubly ensured by the local team's tacit agreement allotting the work-up of half the chart to one staff person, the other half to the second staff person. (Goffman, 1959: 83)

Goffman's theories about the presentation of self in organisations are intended to be applied across many social settings, indeed, to all 'establishments'. That is, his work is not just about the behaviour of people at the Ritz Hotel or in Nether Poppleton Mental Hospital, but about these places and all similar ones. Of course, he could be wrong, but, like a good researcher, he sticks his neck out and asserts that he has found something that is to be found in all 'establishments'. There will be more to say about testing such generalisations later, but for the moment it is important to note that it is a sign of good research that it concerns itself with 'regularities' which transcend the specifics of time or place.

The second ingredient of social research is the collection of data. Theories ought to be firmly based on data if they are to be useful in understanding the social world. What does Goffman do? As the quotation above illustrates, Goffman does provide data to test his theory, much of it splendidly unexpected. He uses data from his own meticulous observations obtained during periods of study of life in institutions, and he uses data from other people's observations, including from novels and even etiquette books.

TABLE 2.2   Types of research design

			EXAMPLE
Quantitative	Cross-sectional	Case	Studies of particular organisations or settings (see Chapter 6)
Quantitative	Cross-sectional	Representative	Large social surveys (see Chapter 19)
Quantitative	Longitudinal	Case	Historical studies of nations or groups (see Chapter 15)
Quantitative	Longitudinal	Representative	Panel and cohort studies (see Chapter 19)
Qualitative	Cross-sectional	Case	Focus group studies (see Chapter 12)
Qualitative	Cross-sectional	Representative	Cross-national comparative case studies
Qualitative	Longitudinal	Case	Ethnography (observation) of small groups and settings (see Chapter 14)
Qualitative	Longitudinal	Representative	Studies of small societies and groups, by interviewing informants (see Chapter 13)

one is wanting to try to falsify a theory using a deductive research strategy. Law and McLeish (2007) compared the findings from their research on the Fife mast protest with an extant theory of protest (the 'New Irrational Actor Model') and concluded that this theory was not a good explanation of what they observed. Studies of this kind are called 'critical case studies'.

The preceding discussion has shown that there is no one best design. Each has its strengths and weaknesses. If we cross-tabulate the three dimensions of research design, we get eight possibilities. Table 2.2 lists these possibilities and typical examples of the types of research that might use each.

If you are selecting a research design, consider with the help of Table 2.2 whether a quantitative or qualitative, cross-sectional or longitudinal, a case study or a representative design is likely to yield the most informative data. In addition, you should consider practical issues, such as getting access to the sample, the costs of doing the research, and the time that would be involved. These issues are considered in more detail in the following chapters.

2.8 SUMMARY

In this chapter, we have seen that what makes social research different from mere data collection is that it is an activity conducted within a research community. This community provides a body of theory in which the research needs to be located. Sociological theory, like all theory, aims to be explanatory, answering 'Why?' questions. It also aims to be general, offering explanations that transcend the particularities of time, space, or personal circumstance.

---

analysis oriented to the gradual development of greater and greater theoretical focus and clarity as the project continues. Glaser and Strauss' work has also helped to establish that, whatever approach they take, researchers should try to outline and reflect upon the ways in which they develop concepts, explanations and theory.

DISCUSSION QUESTIONS

1   What is the difference between theory and description?

2   Why should researchers wish to take an inductive approach to the development of theory?

3   Why might grounded theory procedures assist in the inductive development of theory?

4   What is theoretical sampling and what are its implications for the structure of the research process?

5   In what ways might the detailed line-by-line coding of data be a valuable approach to analysis? Does it have any disadvantages?

6   Should researchers seek to reduce the impact on their research of existing ideas or should they openly draw upon existing theory?

7   Think of an example of a published qualitative research study and consider the approach taken by the author to the relationship between data and theory. In what ways is the approach taken similar to and/or different from grounded theory?

CHECKLIST

* Inductive researchers seek to build theory from data rather than testing existing theories.

* Grounded theory involves an iterative process characterised by an ongoing interplay of data collection and analysis.

* Through theoretical sampling, grounded theorists attempt to focus data collection on themes which have emerged from earlier data analysis.

* Grounded theorists develop theory through detailed coding of data.

* Codes are gradually refined and eventually integrated and reduced through a process of constant comparison of the data pertaining to them.

---

* During the process of constant comparison, memos are used to record hunches, possibilities and ideas.

* Existing theory and research are drawn upon only after the process of theory generation is at an advanced stage.

* Grounded theory has been criticised by some for being overly prescriptive, for lacking explanatory power and for overestimating the possibilities of researcher neutrality.

* Many qualitative researchers use selected features associated with grounded theory, without adopting the approach in its entirety.

RESOURCES

Bryant and Charmaz (eds) (2007) *The Sage Handbook of Grounded Theory*. A contemporary collection of chapters covering the various elements of grounded theory from the point of view of a range of well-known contributors from around the world.

Bryman and Burgess (eds) *Analysing Qualitative Data*. A text outlining in relation to research experience, the different ways in which scholars have approached the analysis of data, including via the use of grounded theory.

Fielding and Lee (1998) *Computer Analysis and Qualitative Research*. A valuable early contribution to discussions on the development and use of computer aided qualitative analysis software, which was designed with grounded theory in mind.

Glaser (1992) *Basics of Grounded Theory Analysis: Emergence Versus Forcing*. This book represents Glaser's impassioned critical response to Strauss and Corbin's book, which is said to have encouraged 'forced, preconceived, full conceptual description' and thereby to have betrayed the inductive principles on which the grounded theory approach were initially based.

Glaser and Strauss (1967) *The Discovery of Grounded Theory: Strategies for Qualitative Research*. Glaser and Strauss' original outline of grounded theory is both detailed and accessible. It is a must for anyone seeking to develop their understanding of the approach.

Strauss and Corbin (1998) *Basics of Qualitative Research: Techniques and Procedures for Developing Grounded Theory*. Strongly criticised by Glaser, this book, whose first edition was published in 1990, outlines Strauss and Corbin's detailed and exhaustive elaborations on the procedures grounded theorists should use in order to transform their data into theory. Although some of the techniques are complex, the book is again written in an accessible manner.

GLOSSARY

Account: a general term for the overall report or description given by an interviewee during a research interview. An account may include a variety of different forms of talk and represents the interviewee's perceptions, understanding and experiences of the issue(s) being researched.

Action research: an approach to conducting social research which aims to improve the social situation under study while simultaneously generating knowledge about it. The focus is on changing a social situation or practice as part of the research process rather than simply gathering data and generating findings which may or may not be implemented subsequently. It is a cyclical process, moving between stages of enquiry, intervention and evaluation.

Agency: the capacity of individuals to act independently and autonomously, and to make their own choices and decisions.

Antecedent variable: a variable measuring a concept that is thought to have a causal effect on some other variable.

Attitude: an enduring tendency to perceive a situation or a person in a particular way. Attitudes may have cognitive (resulting from beliefs and ideas), affective (resulting from values and emotions) and behavioural (resulting from previous action) components. Attitudes are unobservable except through their presumed effects on behaviour.

Attrition: the tendency for people responding to a **panel** survey to drop out through death or illness, emigration or refusal to continue to be involved.

Axial coding: coined by Strauss and Corbin (1990), this refers to the second stage of the coding process, in which the relationships between categories and subcategories are carefully mapped through the use of a detailed paradigm.

Biography: in the everyday sense a biography is a literary work in which an author gives an account of the life of a person, usually someone of note; such people also write their own autobiographies. Both are useful to the sociologist, who needs to be aware that the authors may have had a variety of non-sociological reasons for writing them. Diaries are in a sense biographical, but are written at the time rather than in retrospect. Biographies created by or for the sociologist or ethnographer are usually termed life histories.

Blog: short for weblog; an online diary or journal.

Brainstorming: a method of generating ideas in which members of a group are encouraged to contribute suggestions free of criticism from other group members. Once sufficient ideas have been generated, they are categorised and may be ranked for effectiveness or value.

CAQDAS: Computer Assisted Qualitative Data AnalysiS is an umbrella term referring to a broad range of software packages designed to facilitate the analysis of qualitative data, including text, graphics, audio and video. They are powerful project management tools allowing the organisation of data (according to known characteristics), ideas (according to user-defined codes) and interpretations (noted by the user in written annotations and memos). Patterns and relationships can be identified by retrieving parts of the dataset according to the presence and absence of codes in the data, among, for example, different

COMPANION WEBSITE

Be sure to visit the Companion website at http://www.sagepub.co.uk/gilbert to find teaching and learning materials for both lecturers and students:

PowerPoint slides – slides are provided for each chapter and can be edited as required by the lecturer.

Online readings – interesting and relevant journal articles that will add to your understanding and awareness of the topics covered in the book.

Links to relevant web sites – useful links are provided for each chapter.

Projects – projects for students to carry out to test their understanding of the issues covered in the text.

Online glossary – key terminologies are covered.

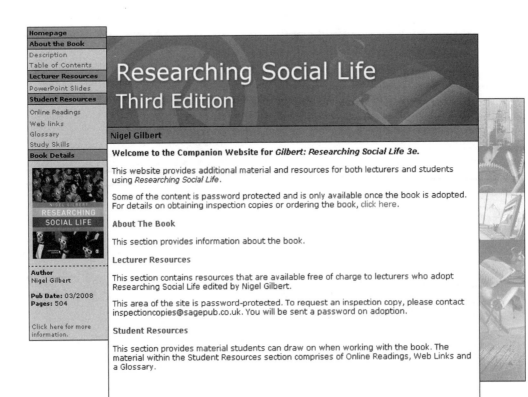

Researching social life is partly about having the right knowledge: for instance, how to design samples, when to take field notes and how to analyse interview data; and partly about practical skills: how to lay out questionnaires, how to gain access to historical archives and how to get the cooperation of an interviewee. It is because research is such a mixture that this book includes chapters that touch on philosophy and theory as well as including many down-to-earth examples of research in practice.

The book is organised around the idea of the research process – roughly, deciding what you want to find out, finding a setting or a sample, collecting some data, analysing the data and writing up the results. Thus, the book is divided into four parts, 'Beginnings', 'Into the field', 'Back home' and 'Endings'. But as the chapters make clear, the process can be a lot messier than is implied by this image of a steady progression through clear stages.

As a first step, however, it is important to clarify what counts as social research, and, in particular, how it differs from 'fact gathering'. In Chapter 1, it is argued that social research has to be embedded within a theoretical framework that offers perspectives, methods and a 'tradition'. The final chapter, Chapter 24, returns to these concerns.

Chapter 2 introduces some of the conceptual tools that a researcher will need. It is concerned with the link between theory and data – a link that continues to trouble philosophers as well as sociologists. Do data exist 'out there', waiting to be collected by the researcher? Or is what we find influenced or even determined by the theories and the methods we employ to understand the social world?

This chapter and many of the following chapters conclude with a project that can be carried out with minimal resources and in a reasonably short time. These projects are important because it is difficult to become a good researcher simply by reading about research; you need to have a go yourself. Every chapter also includes a list of 'Resources' that suggest where to look for a deeper or more extended treatment of the issues it covers.

These first two chapters offer an overview of the research process. The next group of chapters are concerned with issues that have to be considered before one starts collecting data: how to formulate a researchable question, what is already known about the research topic, and what the approach to research should be.

The first step in doing good research is to be clear about what the issue to be researched is. Formulating a 'good' research question is often surprisingly tricky, and yet it is vital to do so if the research is not to lose its way. Chapter 3 offers advice about strategies that you can use to develop an initial broad interest in a research area into a focused, researchable and answerable research question.

Chapter 4 discusses the purpose of a literature review and what one can do to find what has already been written about your topic. The emphasis in this chapter is on being systematic in your literature searching, and on being analytic when you are writing up the results of your searches.

The following three chapters discuss a range of approaches to research that will help to define what methods of data collection and analysis you will use. In Chapter 5, the idea of grounded theory is explained and its application to qualitative research discussed. In Chapter 6, the advantages and disadvantages of engaging in participatory research, in which those researched play a role in the research process, are considered. In Chapter 7, the various ways in which one can mix methods, for instance, by combining qualitative and quantitative research, are examined.

Social research is not always welcome in all quarters and this means that researchers have to make decisions about whether they conceal what they are doing from some or all of their respondents ('covert' research) or whether they will be open about their objectives but risk being repulsed. And some groups are much more capable of resisting enquiries than others. These questions of research ethics are addressed in Chapter 8.

Once these preliminaries have been settled, it is time to get down to detailed planning of the research. It is usually neither practicable nor wise to interview everyone and observe everything. Some kind of sampling of data is needed, regardless of whether the research is survey-based or involves observational or documentary methods. Chapter 9 discusses the standard ways of obtaining representative samples, and considers whether representativeness is always necessary and appropriate.

Chapters 10–17 examine various ways of collecting data. During the 1950s and 1960s, great advances were made in the 'technology' of asking standardised questions to representative samples of respondents. This had the result that the interview survey became the data collection technique most closely associated with social research. Chapter 10 discusses the current state of the art, offering advice about how to construct, not just interview schedules, but also questions for interviewing over the telephone, and questionnaires for surveys sent through the mail. Chapter 11 deals in more detail with one of the trickiest aspects of this style of research: how to measure people's attitudes.

Although using structured interviews is a common method of data collection, especially in commercial and policy-related research, less formal and more qualitative methods are also very important. Focus groups, already frequently used in market research and in politics, are becoming increasingly popular in social research as a means of gathering qualitative data. Chapter 12 describes how to organise a focus group, and how the data it generates can be analysed. Chapter 13 is about the kind of individual interview that is more like a guided conversation and deals with how to construct an interview guide, how to conduct an interview and how to transcribe a recording. Interviewing is often combined with observation of people in their 'natural' settings, a style of research called ethnography. This approach to research emerged from anthropology and Chapter 14 traces this history, considering also the practicalities of ethnographic research and, in particular, some methods of analysis of ethnographic data, since it is at the analysis stage that this style of research presents the most difficulties.

Not all social research involves asking people questions. Many of the classics of sociology were based solely on documentary evidence, the topic of Chapter 15. The documents of interest to social researchers include not only public documents such as official reports and newspapers, but also personal records such as diaries and letters, and some objects which, although they document social life, were never intended as records, for example, statutes, novels, photographs and even buildings.

A new source of data is the Internet. As the Internet and especially the World Wide Web increasingly permeate our lives, at least in developed nations, more and more sociologically interesting data become available for researchers electronically. Many of the standard techniques of social research, such as surveys, interviews and documentary analysis, can be transposed to the Internet. Chapter 16 points out that the World Wide Web allows researchers to study people who are distant, to find respondents from rare groups, and to reduce the cost and increase the speed of data collection. On the other hand, Internet samples can be biased, rapport can be difficult to establish, and the technicalities of using the Internet can be an obstacle.

Whether one has chosen a survey, an interview, observation, documentary sources or the Internet for one's data, the result is all too often a mass of material, too great in quantity to be analysed unless one is prepared and able to be systematic. The third part of the book considers how you can analyse these data.

The management of quantitative data has been revolutionised by the computer, and computers are now also beginning to be used to assist in handling qualitative data, such as interview transcripts. Chapter 17 discusses the management and coding of both types, explaining the technology and the options available. Once you have put quantitative data sets onto a computer, programs can be used to prepare tables and frequency distributions. This is illustrated in Chapter 18, which uses an example to illustrate the steps you need to go through to do simple analyses of survey data using the most widely used computer package, SPSS.

You do not necessarily have to collect survey data yourself to do quantitative research. Government departments, research companies and academic social researchers often deposit their data sets as computer files in national archives, from which copies can be obtained for further analysis. This is 'secondary analysis', which is fast becoming one of the most important forms of social research. It opens up quantitative research to those who do not have the considerable resources needed to carry out a large-scale survey. As Chapter 19 notes, secondary analysis demands some skills not needed for other forms of social research, including being able to devise ways of testing hypotheses against data originally collected for other purposes.

The next four chapters illustrate approaches to analysing qualitative data such as interview transcripts and audio and video recordings. Chapter 20 describes the computer programs that have been developed in the past few years to help with the analysis of qualitative data. While it used to be the case that only quantitative data was processed by computer, it is now common to use programs to assist with analysing interview transcripts and fieldnotes. The chapter examines what these programs have to offer and how they can help.

In many research studies, interviewees are asked to talk about their lives or, more generally, to provide 'accounts' of what they have done and why. Chapter 21 suggests one way of handling such data: in terms of narrative analysis, a range of approaches to qualitative data that explore the form of narratives and their role in the construction of identity.

Chapter 22 describes another range of approaches to analysing interview data that go under the label of discourse analysis. These include conversation analysis, critical discourse analysis, Foucauldian discourse, and discursive psychology. Chapter 23 shows how some of the same ideas and methods can also be applied to the analysis of visual materials, although analysing the visual also introduces some challenges of its own.

Research only becomes effective when it is written down and published for researchers, policy-makers and others to use and to criticise. The final chapter of the book is about writing up one's research. It examines the format of a typical research article and explains some of the historical background to publication conventions in the social sciences.

The coverage and treatment of topics in this book are based on the courses taught in the Department of Sociology at the University of Surrey for first and second year undergraduates. All the contributors are or have been lecturers and researchers in the Department and not only have had experience in carrying out research in the ways they describe, but also of teaching it, both to undergraduates and to graduate students. The book has been greatly influenced by feedback from many generations of students, a surprising number of whom have gone on to become social researchers themselves. We hope that you, like our students, will find that the skills of social research can be used both to help in understanding our society better and to support work in many professions and careers.

Throughout the book, all words in **bold** are keywords that are defined in the Glossary.

Many web addresses in this book are given in the form of a 'tinyurl', which look like this: http://tinyurl.com/2maoym. If you type these addresses into your browser, you will be redirected to the intended site automatically. The advantage of tinyurls is that they are much easier than the full address to copy.

1 Conceptualising Social Life

Geoff Cooper

- Appreciate some of the ways in which sociological theory can open up new issues and questions.

- Understand that different theoretical frameworks provide different perspectives on the object of study.

- Recognise that these different perspectives can therefore influence research questions.

- Appreciate the significance of the sociologist's membership of society, and presence in the research setting, for the way we understand the ethical and political dimensions of research.

1.1 INTRODUCTION

Good social research involves more than the identification of a worthwhile topic and the selection and competent use of an appropriate method, vital though these are. This chapter looks at the way in which research is inevitably framed by conceptual and theoretical considerations and shows how such frameworks, when properly handled, can enrich and enhance the research.

In one sense, it is not a question of choosing whether to ignore or attend to these issues, since **theory** *will* be present in the research, but it may be present in the form of unrecognised assumptions that shape what is done in an uncontrolled manner. The explicit use of concepts and theories is therefore part of good research practice, in that the researcher is more in control of the direction, meaning and implications of his or her work. However, the main emphasis of this chapter is on a slightly different point: that theoretical and conceptual frameworks can inspire fresh ways of looking at the social world, and suggest new angles of approach or lines of inquiry. The significance or purpose of particular frameworks may differ. They may, for example, provide a critical view of some feature of society; or they may show us that familiar and apparently unremarkable features of everyday life can in fact be seen as rather strange. What they share is the capacity to re-conceptualise the social world, and thereby to stimulate us to ask new questions of it.

This chapter therefore aims to demonstrate the richness and diversity of sociological theory, and the potential of different theories both to make us see the world in different ways and to open up new lines of inquiry. It also suggests that engagement with theory is invaluable for prompting reflections on the role, significance and ethics of social research.

Terminology can be rather slippery in this area. In particular, as the following section indicates, 'theory' can be used in a number of senses. Chapter 2 discusses the use of theory in research, focusing on theory as a specific hypothesis about some phenomenon which can be tested through empirical investigation. This chapter, by contrast, is mainly concerned with theory in the sense of broad frameworks that shape our view of the world.

The chapter is structured as follows. First, the different senses of theory are clarified and we see how different theoretical frameworks, largely derived from the discipline of sociology, can lead us in particular directions and illuminate particular issues. Second, we illustrate this variation with some examples. Third, we look at the way in which different theories can bring an apparently unpromising thing to life and open up a number of sociological dimensions for possible further exploration. Fourth, we consider the relationship between theoretical frameworks, empirical research and society, and indicate that different conceptions of this relationship can have important consequences for our approach. Finally, it is suggested that attending to the issues discussed in the chapter can provoke us to ask questions not only of the social world, but also of ourselves as researchers, thereby developing a more critical sensitivity.

1.2 THEORIES, CONCEPTS, FRAMEWORKS

'Theory' has become an increasingly difficult term to define with any certainty, since it can refer to quite different things in different contexts. In the natural sciences, it denotes a possible explanation which, crucially, can be tested: thus, in this context and in the most common everyday meaning of the term, a theory is something provisional, tentative and in need of confirmation. In the humanities, literary criticism or history for example, it can mean something quite different: a style of work which engages with philosophical questions (what is a text? what is history?), sometimes in a formidably abstract manner, often borrowing ideas from other disciplines in order to address them (Culler, 1987).

In sociological work both of these meanings, and others, are found. For example, the term 'social theory' can be used in the latter sense to describe work which engages with philosophical questions, and which is not confined within the boundaries of one discipline (Sica, 1998). 'Sociological theory' – clearly referring to work within the discipline of sociology, and our main focus here – can be used in the former sense to describe an explanation which takes the form of an assertion that can be tested. However, it can also denote a framework for viewing the social world that is too general, too broad and too all-encompassing to be confirmed or refuted by empirical research; indeed, the kind of empirical research we choose to do will be profoundly shaped and influenced by the framework in the first place. Similarly, one cannot compare theoretical frameworks by simply checking which one has come up with the right answer about some feature of society: for since each conceptualises society in quite different ways, they are likely to be asking quite different questions. The philosopher Thomas Kuhn (1970) uses the term **'paradigms'** to describe these kinds of broad and radically different frameworks; they can also be referred to as, for instance, 'theoretical frameworks', 'theoretical perspectives', 'sociological perspectives', or simply 'sociological theories' (although each term carries its own specific connotations).

Before we look more closely at these frameworks, it is worth mentioning that there is much more that could be said about the relationship between these very broad conceptions and specific theories that can be tested. For example, some have argued that we should think of the relationship in terms of different levels of theory, and indeed suggested that there is at least one more level that comes in between the two, so-called 'middle-range' theory (Merton, 1967). We leave this issue to one side in this chapter. One thing we can say is that sociological theories, at whatever level, all share a common general orientation: they focus on the ways in which phenomena (be they institutions, political arrangements, communities, everyday activities, beliefs and attitudes, forms of knowledge, technologies, art, media representations) are socially organised; and they assert that this social organisation has important consequences. However, it is also the case that there are enormous differences between them: for some, 'social organisation' is taken to mean the ways in which people interact, talk, and make use of gestures within particular settings; for others it may mean large-scale structures of domination and subordination which affect the whole society.

There are other kinds of differences. For example, some theoretical frameworks are more comprehensive than others in scope, that is, in the range of social phenomena they claim to explain, and in the level of detail at which they tend to operate. Confusingly, some even claim that they are not theories at all since they are committed to exploring, without preconceptions, the ways in which people interpret the world (see Rock, 1979, on **symbolic interactionism**) or the everyday methods by which people routinely achieve social order (see Garfinkel, 1967a, on **ethnomethodology**); that is, in both cases, to think about the social world on its own terms. These are important qualifications. Nevertheless, it remains the case that even these approaches have an interest in explaining features of social organisation, and are thus sociological, and have a distinctive orientation, style and conception which can be contrasted with other approaches. The key issue remains the way in which we conceptualise the social world; and it is on the basis of different conceptions or pictures of the world that we can distinguish between different theoretical frameworks.

It should be stressed that these theoretical frameworks can be crucial in shaping the ways in which we *investigate* the world. They highlight particular features of the world as significant; they direct our attention towards certain forms of behaviour; and they suggest certain kinds of research questions. Some will have a relatively direct influence on the kinds of research methods we use; for example, symbolic interactionism's interest in the ways in which people interact and construct meaning within particular settings, determines that qualitative methods which focus on behaviour in its natural context will be most appropriate (see Chapters 13 and 14). Some frameworks may have a less direct link to method: feminist research, for instance, can equally profitably use statistical methods to examine large-scale structural inequalities, look at the operation of patriarchy in the media via textual analyses, or study social interaction in particular institutional settings by the use of observational methods. The strength of the links between particular frameworks and particular methods, in other words, varies considerably. Nevertheless, each framework will, at a deeper level, exert a profound influence on the design, orientation and character of the study.

1.3 DIFFERENT UNDERSTANDINGS OF THE SOCIAL WORLD

There are many more theoretical approaches than can be listed in the space available, let alone properly explained. (Some observers regard this high level of variation as a problem, others see it as evidence of the discipline's richness; this author tends towards the latter view.) The following examples are intended to give a flavour of this variation and illustrate how these different ways of conceptualising the social world bring different facets of social life to our attention, and suggest different lines of inquiry.

That said, it is important to note that some issues and questions recur throughout more than one framework, even though they are often envisaged in very different terms. For example:

- What is the nature of the relationship between the individual and the collective?

- Is society a structure that limits and constrains the way we act, or rather the sum total of various forms of social interaction in different settings?

- How do power and inequality operate within society?

- Is society inherently consensual or riven by conflict?

- How do the informal rules and norms which seem to govern social life come into being?

1.3.1 SCHOOLS OF THOUGHT

By schools of thought we mean theoretical approaches that have achieved a degree of recognition such that a number of people subscribe to them, and that can be clearly differentiated from other approaches in terms of their key concepts and issues of concern. **Structural functionalism** sees society as a single and unified entity, almost like an organism, and for the most part sees its component parts (the family, for example) as being functional for the maintenance of equi-librium. **Marxism**, by contrast, envisages society as being structured around what it calls a mode of production: it focuses, in particular, on the capitalist mode of production, which is seen as fundamentally exploitative and unjust. Marxist theory thus places conflict centre stage, and sees its own role as helping to challenge existing arrangements. Likewise, **feminism** sees society as unjust, and seeks to challenge it, but the basis of exploitation here is seen to lie in gender relations, in patriarchy. In both of these cases, theory is closely linked to political movements. Ethnomethodology is interested in how social order is achieved but, unlike structural functionalism, sees this as something which is routinely accom-plished in everyday life by a host of 'methods' – such as knowing when to take a turn in conversation – which are both taken for granted and yet, when properly studied, extraordinarily skilful. **Rational choice theory** by contrast, to give a final example, seeks to explain social behaviour by positing the individual as a strate-gic and calculating actor who makes choices according to rational criteria.

It should be noted that the history of the discipline shows that different the-oretical frameworks come to have a more or less dominant presence at differ-ent times; some may be seen as particularly pertinent to, even influenced by, the prevailing socio-political context. This alerts us to the fact that sociology is very much a part of the society that it sets out to study, as we discuss in Section 1.5.

Theoretical frameworks are not always easily located within schools of thought. Distinctive and sometimes highly influential views of the world may be derived from the work of individual writers, who may be more or less easy to categorise in this way. Let us look at three writers, each of who casts a distinctive light on the social world.

1.3.2 ERVING GOFFMAN

Goffman – sometimes identified as a symbolic interactionist, but thought by many to be too unorthodox to be located within any school – studied a wide variety of social phenomena, using a wide variety of approaches. One strand that ran through much of his work was an interest in the details of what he called the 'interaction order', that is, the ways we behave in face-to-face interaction with others. Goffman suggests that we continually manage the impression that we make on others, that such things as gesture and gaze are crucially important for monitoring and interpreting the behaviour of others, and that this world of face-to-face interaction is patterned according to subtle but powerful norms and expectations about what is appropriate: a kind of moral order.

In city life, for example, where we are often in close proximity with others (on public transport, for instance), we routinely control the direction of our gaze and adopt what Goffman calls 'civil inattention', because direct eye con-tact may imply certain kinds of direct involvement that are inappropriate.

Even the apparently simple business of walking along the street emerges as a delicately structured and complex activity. We continually monitor the gestures and movements of others in order to interpret their behaviour; we recognise certain kinds of behaviour such as two people engaged in conversation, and take action to avoid walking in between them; and in some cases we have to balance the requirements of communicating with others and making progress. For example, if we see an acquaintance in the distance coming our way, we often feign ignorance until they are closer and only then acknowledge their presence: this avoids the awkwardness, and physical difficulty, of maintaining eye contact, and perhaps sustaining a suitable expression on the face, while simultaneously navigating through the pedestrian traffic (Goffman, 1971).

We also have ways of displaying social relationships to others which Goffman calls 'tie-signs'. Holding hands is an obvious one, but in some cases they can become more complicated. Someone on the phone to a close friend or partner, in the presence of a business colleague, may go to great lengths to keep both parties from feeling left out: talking in a friendly tone into the phone, while simultaneously making gestures of impatience to the other person present is one strategy that is sometimes adopted.

To read Goffman describing how behaviour in public places is patterned can be to recognise features of one's own behaviour but discover that they are in fact socially organised: they are general properties of social life. We experience a kind of recognition; but the world of everyday social interaction is transformed and never looks quite the same again. He draws our attention towards the ways in which people are continually controlling and skilfully interpreting the signals they give off to each other, and to the complex tissue of obligations and expectations that we observe, even in our interactions with strangers.

Goffman has provided an important resource and source of inspiration for theoretical and empirical studies. For example, Heath's studies of doctor–patient interaction draw on Goffman in highlighting such factors as the ways in which patients systematically avert their gaze in order to minimise embarrassment during intimate medical examinations (Heath, 1986). Hochschild's (1983) innovative work on the emotional dimensions of social interaction, which has provided a key foundation for the sociology of emotion, both relies on and extends Goffman's work. Her formulation of the concept of 'emotional labour', for example, has significantly facilitated understanding of the demands made of employees in service industries where the professional smile is a requirement, some of the strategies used to deal with these demands, and in many cases the gendered aspects of this kind of work.

1.3.3 MICHEL FOUCAULT

Foucault was not a sociologist, but he has had a good deal of influence within the discipline. (The same could be said of Marx, now regarded as one of the key figures in 'classical' sociology.) Often described as a 'post-structuralist', Foucault was interested in explaining how many features of social organisation which we now take for granted as normal and unremarkable have come into being; these features include our sense of self, that is, our notions of what an individual is. His work takes the form of historical studies that show that particular, widespread practices can be seen as quite recent inventions. He forces us to ask uncomfortable questions about the way that society operates, the workings of power, and even our own role as social scientists.

One strand that runs throughout many of Foucault's studies is a critical view of the role that certain kinds of knowledge have played in modern Western societies. He argues that the 'human sciences', a range of disciplines which turn people into objects of study, have played a key role in the extension of certain kinds of power. Let us look at just one example. In *Discipline and Punish* (1977), he suggests that the widespread assumption that we are now more compassionate and lenient in our treatment and punishment of criminals is misleading; as with much of his work, he attempts to turn such an assumption on its head. We may not be so visibly cruel as before, may no longer have public torture or executions; but we monitor, regulate and control behaviour with a thoroughness that could not have been dreamed of in former times, both within prisons and in the wider population. Foucault suggests that the human sciences have been central to this process. They urge that we have to 'really understand' people, and must therefore study them more closely; and they define what is normal and what is abnormal behaviour, which then provides a basis for judgements of various kinds. Moreover, they have often done so with the very best of intentions, for instance, playing a key role in prison reform. However, the effect has been to extend power throughout society to the point where surveillance of many different kinds, by institutions *and* fellow citizens, is a taken-for-granted feature of daily life.

Foucault gives us a very uncomfortable and in many ways gloomy picture of modern Western societies. Like any account, it is one that can be questioned, but its value is as a form of criticism. Foucault shows us the extent to which our society is organised and regulated according to ideas about what is normal (whether we are talking of intelligence, physical development, social behaviour or whatever). He fosters a sceptical attitude towards many different forms of expertise and claims to authority, and suggests that we should not assume that the good intentions of particular institutions will guarantee good outcomes. In so doing, he opens up new avenues of inquiry.

1.3.4 BRUNO LATOUR

Latour's main interests lie in the field of Science and Technology Studies, but the influence of his ideas and general approach, which he terms actor network theory, is becoming more widely felt in other areas of social science. Latour argues that, in spite of the fact that technologies have an obvious and undeniable presence in modern Western societies, most theories of social behaviour fail to take the role that they play sufficiently seriously. The idea, put forward particularly forcefully by Émile Durkheim, that there are distinctively 'social' things which are quite separate from technological – or indeed natural – things is something that Latour (2005) contests. Rather, to put this in terms of our earlier definition of sociology as the discipline which looks at the social organisation of phenomena, Latour suggests that such organisation is always achieved by combinations, or networks, of different categories of actor – people certainly, but also technologies, texts, natural phenomena, materials and artefacts, to name but a few.

One important element of this argument is that many social functions are now routinely performed by technologies. When we consider the centrality of computers and digital technologies in so many areas of social life, the point seems obvious but, interestingly, Latour often uses different, simpler technologies to make his argument. For example, he focuses on the ways in which moral functions are frequently handled by technological means (Latour, 1992). Hotels stop guests removing, and possibly losing, their keys by the simple expedient of attaching heavy weights to them which make them inconvenient to carry around; ineffective laws designed to prevent people driving without seat belts can be enforced by designing ignition systems which will not work until the seat belt has been fastened; and the problem of getting people to close doors behind them in institutional buildings is solved by the design of an (automatic) door closer. As Latour sees it, what is happening, in all three examples, is a process in which we delegate to technologies the task of disciplining people to act in the correct way: in each case, the technology in question appears to succeed where human interventions or written instructions on their own have failed. To understand social life today, we need to acknowledge that even some of its most trivial features involve the use of technologies, and consider the significance of this fact.

1.4 CONCEPTUALISING COMMON OBJECTS: AN EXAMPLE

Different conceptualisations of social life can mean that different kinds of things are studied: the figures we have briefly considered, for example, could be said to focus on social interaction (Goffman), the historical development of forms of power (Foucault), and the ways in which technologies become an integral feature of everyday life (Latour). At the same time, considering how the work of different thinkers can be brought to bear on a common object can be a useful exercise in highlighting conceptual differences, and illustrating the different kinds of questions and concerns that are raised by particular approaches. It can also show the richness and diversity of what C. Wright Mills (1959) called 'the sociological imagination'. With this in mind, let us return to Latour's simple example of doors in public or institutional buildings, and consider what different kinds of sociologists might have to say about them.

Latour encourages recognition of the ways in which social functions routinely become 'delegated' to technologies. In the case of doors, the problem of ensuring that people keep them closed is solved by the use of a simple technology, the automatic door closer, which performs this function and, moreover, does so in such an unobtrusive way that we take it for granted. The example is in some ways idiosyncratic, in the sense that doors (and door closers) are not normally thought of as obvious topics for sociological analysis, but its apparent idiosyncrasy serves to highlight the extent to which we do not notice the many forms of technical mediation that are woven into the fabric of everyday life.

Doors can become the focus of a rather different kind of study if we consider them with some of Goffman's insights in mind. Large doors and the areas around them, whether they are within or are the entrance to a building, are sites of quite delicately co-ordinated forms of social interaction. People not only choose whether or not to hold a door open for someone who is following them, but make such choices within the framework of sets of expectations about what is reasonable or polite behaviour; and they signal their intentions by means of subtle but discernible actions, gestures and facial expressions. Simply going through a door, in other words, turns out to be a highly ritualised form of activity; and the ritual properties of this simple activity are crucial both to the co-ordination of action and to the ways in which people manage the impression that they convey to others.

Goffman's work suggests other ways in which doors in institutional buildings can be of sociological interest. It is not the case, as we know, that all doors serve relatively neutral social purposes such as keeping out the rain and wind. Many doors open into rooms or spaces that are not accessible to everyone, and in these cases may serve as a kind of boundary beyond which different forms of behaviour take place. Goffman himself famously noted that the doorway from a restaurant to its kitchen constitutes just such a boundary, and that waiters' facial expressions, speech and general demeanour can change radically as they cross the threshold and leave the public space where politeness is required (Goffman, 1969). Here, consideration of the part played by the doorway in social life directs attention towards highly differentiated forms of behaviour, and the ways in which such factors as occupation may constrain the ways people act in particular spaces.

Foucault provides another way of thinking about such constraints on behaviour in public spaces. As for Goffman, visibility is crucial, but is conceptualised in more explicitly historical terms: here, the door is one element in a wider and developing set of forces. The disciplinary power that is characteristic of the modern era takes on a concrete form in, among other things, the architecture of institutional buildings; initially prisons, but subsequently military barracks, hospitals, schools and other institutions are designed in ways that facilitate continuous surveillance and control. According to this approach, some of the features of public or institutional buildings whose overt purpose is to ensure and enhance public safety should be seen as also controlling people: the siting of CCTV cameras at entrance doors, and at other strategic places within a building, are a good example of this duality of purpose.

A historical sociology of doors and their use could take many other forms. The fact that there has been, in recent years, an increase in the number of doors within the corridors of many large buildings appears to be the result of an increasing concern with risk and public safety. Fire doors may therefore be a symptom of wider developments that, according to some, are characteristic or even definitive features of many contemporary societies (see Beck, 1992). Elias's (1998) historical analysis of the changing functions of etiquette points to the importance of the layout of rooms and doors to the structure and form of court rituals, and he notes that the extraordinarily elaborate ceremony of Louis XIV's *levée* (getting up in the morning) could not take place in any building: rather, the arrangement of doorways and rooms had to be designed in a way that made the ceremony possible. More generally, his work illuminates the ways in which customs and conventions change, and could provide a framework for analysing the evolution of arrangements for getting through doors. One such custom, less widespread today but still observable in some settings, involves men holding doors open for women, and could provide a focus for critical feminist analysis of the gendered dimensions of behaviour and rituals in public spaces. Frye (1983), for example, argues that this practice can only be interpreted as helpful if one ignores its place within more general social relations of gendered oppression, and that an analysis which takes account of this wider system would have to conclude that the symbolic purpose of the practice is to reinforce female dependence.

We can therefore see that approaching, in this case, doors in different ways opens up different kinds of questions for investigation, and alerts us to different kinds of issues. Furthermore, even with this simple example, we can see how some of these issues connect and intersect with matters of public concern or political significance: safety, control, surveillance, social hierarchy and oppression, to name but a few. In this respect, there are further questions that could be considered – such as the ways in which door and building design might be implicated in the social construction of disability, or the energy costs of the increasing numbers of automatic doors in use – and sociological approaches which can illuminate them (see respectively Oliver, 1996 and Shove, 2003). These interconnections demonstrate that theories do not exist in a vacuum. It is therefore time to close the door on this specific example and look in more general terms at the relationship between theories, on the one hand, and society and its concerns, on the other.

1.5 CONNECTIONS BETWEEN THEORY, RESEARCH AND SOCIETY

The reader should now have some idea of how sociological theory can be used to construct distinctive views of the social world, views which suggest certain questions, issues and problems that might be explored or pursued through empirical research. The relative usefulness of these views will depend on the general area in which research is to be done, and the kinds of issues that are of interest. Further questions then arise about the nature of the links between theory, research and society.

The following chapter deals with the important issues of how exactly theory should be incorporated into the research process, and at what stage in the research it should be employed. However, there is more to the relationship between theory, research and society than this: indeed, there is a danger that focusing exclusively on how theory connects to research and research methods can reinforce a particular picture of sociological work which is, in important respects, misleading. This picture is one in which the sociologist occupies a vantage point which is quite separate from the object of study (society or some aspect of it), and from which it can be clearly viewed: to extend the metaphor, he or she merely has to select some interesting theoretical spectacles, and perhaps some appropriate measurement devices from the available tool kit of methods, before proceeding to analyse the phenomena of interest from this position of detachment. (One disadvantage of the term 'theoretical perspective' is that it can be taken to imply something along these lines.) The sociologist, according to this view, is quite disengaged from society; and the problems that arise in attempting to study it are simply technical ones (about such matters as choice and correct use of methods). In fact, however, the relationship between sociologist (whether theorist or researcher) and society is more complicated, more contentious and more interesting than this picture suggests. Indeed, some have argued that the existence and prevalence of this picture of disengaged empirical observation is itself the product of particular pernicious currents within modern Western societies (Adorno, 2000).

A key issue that needs to be considered in this respect is the obvious fact that sociologists are not the only people to construct theories about society. There are of course many different disciplines that can validly claim this to be an important part of their work; but even more importantly, coming up with theories about society is an important part of everyday life and a recurrent feature of everyday talk. These lay theories can take many forms: they may be explicit, as in statements about the relationship between poverty and crime; they may be visible in the form of the assumptions that underlie particular statements, for example, about whether one society is more modern than another; or they may be implicit in jokes and clichés such as 'it's a fair cop but society is to blame', which suggests a very specific relation between individual and society. The point here is that people studying society professionally do not have a monopoly on theories about society.

This raises the issue of the relationship between, and the relative importance of everyday theories and 'professional', that is, social scientific theories. There are different approaches to this, but I will briefly sketch out two that, though different, take the issue very seriously. Ethnomethodologists take the line that the world is already so full of theories that the last thing that is needed is for social scientists to add more: what is needed is a shift of emphasis and focus (see, for example, Sacks, 1963). Furthermore, they argue that too much sociology has set about constructing its own theory without critically examining the significance of the fact that much of this is derived from common-sense notions (Zimmerman and Pollner, 1973). Insofar as ethnomethodologists are interested in theories at all – much of their work being focused on what people do, and how they do it, rather than what they believe – it is in everyday theories as *topics* of investigation, as things that can be studied in their own right. They are vehemently opposed to the idea that social science, by virtue of its professional status, can construct allegedly superior theories which can then be the basis for criticism of 'mere' common-sense theory.

Although Pierre Bourdieu shares with ethnomethodology an interest in the understanding of the patterns and forms of everyday activities, his approach to this question is, in one respect at least, quite different. Following, among others, the philosopher of science Bachelard (1984), he argues that a true science is one which makes a radical break with common sense; and that this is the goal to which sociology should aspire (Bourdieu et al., 1991). Thus, when sociology has reached this level, it is legitimate and sometimes necessary to take a critical attitude towards everyday beliefs and attitudes, to say that they are mistaken, and to explain which particular social forces are responsible for these misunderstandings.

To summarise, in the first case the recommendation is that we shift focus and avoid accidentally incorporating everyday beliefs into our work, and trying to construct superior theories. In the second, we are urged to improve the quality of our theories (by following a number of principles of good practice) until we can claim that we have managed to break away from the limitations of common sense into true science, from which position we can engage in criticism. In both, there is a recognition of the extent to which sociology is embedded within society, and therefore of the need to think clearly about the consequences of this.

There are other positions that have been taken on this question, including ignoring it altogether! However, these two approaches illustrate, albeit in a rather paradoxical way in one case, the value of a distinctive conceptualisation of the world to be studied: for the very closeness of this world, the fact that we cannot assume that we have a clear and detached view of it, alerts us to one important function of a theoretical framework. It can help us see the social world afresh; it can help us conceptualise it in new ways, even when dealing with things that may be all too familiar to us (as we saw with the example of Goffman). Other things can do this too, notably art. Just as with art's sometimes shocking re-presentations of the world we inhabit, these new views may become commonplace as they are incorporated into mainstream culture over time; and this provides part of the force that helps produce new theoretical work. This can provide a stimulus and framework for the further investigation of the world, and can generate new topics, questions and problems.

1.6 QUESTIONING OURSELVES: REFLEXIVE SOCIOLOGY

We have seen that theoretical and conceptual frameworks have the capacity to provide new views of the social world; but we have also indicated that the social world includes the activities of sociology and social research. It therefore follows that conceptual frameworks have further value in helping us to reflect upon our position as sociologists and researchers and develop a more critical sensitivity towards the activity of social research.

We have already touched on some of these issues. What, for example, is the relationship between 'lay' and 'professional' interpretations of the world? Does one have a higher status than the other? These might be crucial issues to consider if we are carrying out an interview-based study for example. We might also ask questions more specifically of ourselves as researchers since, no matter what professional hat we have on, we are also members of society:

- Does our personal identity (thinking of such variables as class, race, gender and age) have some significance for the way people respond to us?

- Does our membership of a particular professional community predispose us to see the world in a quite different way to that of our respondents, and thus form a kind of barrier to understanding, one that we must take into account (Bourdieu, 1990)?

- Or is it the case that some styles of sociological work are themselves more closely related to certain forms of social organisation, such as the gendered division of labour, than is usually acknowledged (Smith, 1996)?

There are many such questions. What they have in common is a recognition that an adequate conceptualisation of the social world has to include the activity of researching it; the researcher is not simply observing from a position of detachment. This inclusive conceptualisation is sometimes called **reflexive inquiry** and it can be invaluable for improving the quality of our research.

Reflexive sociology also has ethical importance in that it prompts us to ask questions about what we are doing as researchers, whether we are justified in doing it, and more generally what our responsibilities and obligations are (see Chapter 8). As noted in Section 1.3.3, Foucault's work, for example, argues that the human sciences – those forms of knowledge which turn the human into something to be studied – are a relatively recent and rather peculiar invention, and have played a key role in monitoring, examining and judging the populations of modern Western societies; moreover, he suggests that in many cases they have done so with the very best of intentions. This should make us, at the very least, pause for thought before setting out to do more research, particularly in a society in which more and more research is being carried out, to the extent that one might legitimately characterise it as a research society. Reflection upon such issues, and subsequent consideration of the different ways in which our research might be designed, carried out and used, are vital to responsible, sensitive and critical research (see also Chapter 24).

Just as there is no separate vantage point from which to view and describe society, so there is no neutral space from which to describe theoretical and conceptual issues. Any text setting out to describe a range of theories will do so from some position or another, one which sees others from a particular angle, and defines the key issues accordingly. This chapter has stressed the usefulness of frameworks in helping us see the world in new ways, and avoided discussion of, for example, whether some more accurately represent the world than others: in this respect, it is in line with pragmatist thought, as articulated and defended by Rorty (2000). Other accounts will have a quite different emphasis.

1.7 SUMMARY

This chapter has argued that theoretical and conceptual issues are indispensable features of social research, and can enrich it in a number of ways. Research is impoverished if these issues are neglected; but more simply, theoretical frameworks are valuable in that they provide us with new and different conceptualisations of the social world, inspiring us to see it in new ways and ask different questions of it, and of ourselves as social researchers.

DISCUSSION QUESTIONS

Social theories – whether in the form of assertions, statements, policies, assumptions or even jokes – are all around us.

1   Can you think of any theories currently in circulation?

2   Do any of these depend on, or presuppose, wider frameworks of assumptions?

3   Do you see any problems with these assumptions?

RESOURCES

For general introductions to sociology, Lemert (2005) *Social Things: An Introduction to the Sociological Life* and Bauman and May (2001) *Thinking Sociologically* are both accessible and critical; Lemert is particularly good on the 'political' dimensions of sociology in terms of who is included and excluded. Wright Mills' classic introduction (1959) *The Sociological Imagination* is addressed to a different era, but contains much that is still pertinent.

On theoretical frameworks, Ritzer and Goodman (2007) *Sociological Theory*, 7th edn and Sharrock et al. (2005) *Perspectives in Sociology* provide informed overviews, while Abbott et al. (2005) is a good guide to feminist approaches. For readers interested in learning more about sociological understandings of technology, Sismondo (2003) *An Introduction to Science and Technology Studies* provides a useful introduction.

2 Research, Theory and Method

Nigel Gilbert

2.1 INTRODUCTION

In the previous chapter, it was suggested that **theory** is a vital part of social research, helping us to see the world in different ways and to ask new questions. In this chapter, we shall look more closely at the relationship between theory and data and at how the methodological tools that are described in the rest of the book fit into the research process. By 'theory' in this chapter is meant the 'middle-range' theories that aim to explain a range of observations, not the perspectives and world views in which they are embedded, as explained in the previous chapter.

Social research involves constructing theories, designing appropriate research methods, collecting data and analysing the data. This chapter considers the relationship between these activities and especially the link between theory and data. It describes the strategies of **induction**, **deduction** and **falsification**, defines **validity** and **reliability**, and distinguishes between **concepts** (the ingredients of theories) and **indicators** (the way one measures concepts).

2.2 THREE INGREDIENTS OF SOCIAL RESEARCH

There are three major ingredients in social research: the construction of theory, the collection of data and, no less important, the design of methods for gathering data. All of them have to be right if the research is to yield interesting results. We can see these three ingredients in most accounts of good research.

Goffman (1959; 1961; see also Chapter 1) spent much of his career exploring the social world of organisations. He writes about hotels, schools, prisons and hospitals. But what is *theoretically* interesting about such places? As a sociologist, his concern is with one of the fundamental problems of sociology, how social relationships are co-ordinated and regulated. He notes that in many 'establishments', there are common features in the ways employees present themselves to the 'customers' and that this presentation is not just an issue for the individual employee; it is a collective effort. He uses an analogy based on the theatre. In a theatre, a performance is given on stage, but the activity out front is only possible because of the efforts of those who work backstage. In the same way, Goffman argues, the performance of hotel porters, prison officers, mental hospital orderlies, and so on, relies on the support of other members of the staff. He cites as an example his observations in a hospital ward, where he says that the more experienced doctors are able to display their apparently superior ability because they have spent time the previous night 'studying up on the chart', and because this work is shared out between them so that they all support each other in creating a good impression for the benefit of the trainee.

> In a medical hospital the two staff internists may require the intern, as part of his training, to run through a patient's chart, giving an opinion about each recorded item. He may not appreciate that his show of relative ignorance comes in part from the staff studying up on the chart the night before; he is quite unlikely to appreciate that this impression is doubly ensured by the local team's tacit agreement allotting the work-up of half the chart to one staff person, the other half to the second staff person. (Goffman, 1959: 83)

Goffman's theories about the presentation of self in organisations are intended to be applied across many social settings, indeed, to all 'establishments'. That is, his work is not just about the behaviour of people at the Ritz Hotel or in Nether Poppleton Mental Hospital, but about these places and all similar ones. Of course, he could be wrong, but, like a good researcher, he sticks his neck out and asserts that he has found something that is to be found in all 'establishments'. There will be more to say about testing such generalisations later, but for the moment it is important to note that it is a sign of good research that it concerns itself with 'regularities' which transcend the specifics of time or place.

The second ingredient of social research is the collection of data. Theories ought to be firmly based on data if they are to be useful in understanding the social world. What does Goffman do? As the quotation above illustrates, Goffman does provide data to test his theory, much of it splendidly unexpected. He uses data from his own meticulous observations obtained during periods of study of life in institutions, and he uses data from other people's observations, including from novels and even etiquette books.

Which brings us to the third ingredient: the design of methods of data collection which accurately report on the social world. One of the problems with Goffman's work is that, although the data are vividly described, the methods he used to gather his data and to select his examples are not very clearly or explicitly explained. As a consequence, it is hard to be sure that his observations are typical. A second example, concerning crime statistics, will show the importance of understanding what a method of data collection involves.

Crime statistics apparently show that working-class youth commit more crime than middle-class youth (e.g., see the review in Braithwaite, 1981). A generation of sociologists tried to devise and test theories to explain this observation (e.g. Cloward and Ohlin, 1960; Quinney and Wilderman, 1977; Schur, 1971). Some suggested that working-class youth had more opportunity to commit crime and therefore succumbed more often. Others proposed they had fewer opportunities to pursue success and riches through legitimate channels and so were forced to turn to crime. Yet others argued that working-class and middle-class youth were located in different sub-cultures with different norms and that the working-class sub-culture permitted or even encouraged law breaking.

These different explanations assumed that the official crime statistics were correct. Increasingly, however, criticisms of these statistics accumulated. For example, the basis of the statistics is 'crimes known to the police'. And the police only know about crimes that they themselves have spotted or are reported to them by the victims. If the police patrol working-class areas more than middle-class areas (a reasonable strategy if the statistics show more crimes among working-class youth), they will tend to notice more crime in working-class areas. They will also find it easier to apprehend working-class youth for criminal acts. It was thought that one way around these biases in criminal statistics is to interview a sample of young people and ask them, in confidence, whether they have themselves been involved in any crimes. Interestingly, the rate of self-reported crime showed little difference between middle- and working-class young people (e.g. Short and Nye, 1958). Chapter 14 discusses crime statistics and the collection of such self-report data in more detail.

These criticisms of official statistics and the results of self-report surveys presented sociologists with a new set of data and suggested a quite different sociological problem: why working-class youth are *convicted* of crime more often than middle-class youth. Theories began to be proposed which focused not so much on 'criminal' activities, but on the activities of the police and their role in apprehending youth (e.g. Pearson, 1983). Thus new methods of data collection produced new data and new theories.

There are two alternative conclusions which we could draw from the example of crime statistics:

1   There is one right way of looking at the social world and that social research strives to find this way. If we find that crime statistics offer a biased view, other, more valid methods of data collection must be found to get us closer to the truth. Empirical reality is treated as the privileged source of our theoretical understanding of the social world. In its starkest form, this is the position known as **empiricism**.

2   The alternative position denies that one can ever read off theories from observations of the social world. What we as social researchers see as 'empirical reality' is a consequence of the theories that we bring to bear in organising our understanding of it. In short, theories are treated as the privileged source of our understanding of empirical reality. For example, we might conclude that attempts to discover the 'real' or 'true' crime rates among working- and middle-class youth will never be finally successful: different theories suggest different definitions of 'crime rate'.

2.3 CONSTRUCTING THEORIES

In this and the previous chapter, we have stressed the importance of theoretical frameworks and of middle-range theories. But what exactly is a theory?

2.3.1 WHAT IS A THEORY?

A theory highlights and explains something that one would otherwise not see, or would find puzzling. Often, it is an answer to a 'Why?' question. For example, why are some people poor and others rich; why are so many people unemployed in Western capitalist societies, and so on. Thus, one characteristic of a theory is that it can be used as an explanation.

Suppose that someone proposed a theory of unemployment – that the rate of unemployment depends on current interest rates, for example. Then the theory could be offered as a reasonable (if partial) answer to a question about why there are now so many people unemployed: interest rates are high. Of course, we might want to know quite a lot more than this in answer to the 'Why?' question. It would be interesting to know just what the mechanism connecting interest rates and unemployment rates is supposed to be, what counts as a 'high' interest rate, and whether there is anything that could be done to reduce interest rates and thus rates of unemployment. Nevertheless, the theory that interest rates and unemployment are connected does offer a

Table 2.1
Suicide rates in selected countries

Source: WHO:
http://tinyurl.com/ytvygu/

COUNTRY	YEAR	MALE	FEMALE
Bahamas	1995	2.2	0
Greece	2002	4.7	1.2
UK	2002	10.8	3.1
Italy	2001	11.1	3.3
Spain	2002	12.6	3.9
United States	2001	17.6	4.1
Sweden	2001	18.9	8.1
Denmark	2000	20.2	7.2
France	2001	26.6	9.1
Austria	2003	27.1	9.3
Finland	2003	31.9	9.8
Sri Lanka	1991	44.6	16.8
Hungary	2003	44.9	12.0

solution to what would otherwise be a puzzle and is not obvious from straightforward common sense, both characteristics of good theory.

As well as providing explanations, theories often provide predictions. For example, if the interest rate is dropping, and the theory is correct, it would be possible to predict that the unemployment rate will also fall.

One of the most famous sociological theories is Durkheim's theory of suicide. Individual acts of suicide are almost always puzzling. Often the first thing families and friends ask after a suicide is, why did he or she do it? But as Durkheim ([1897] 2002) observed, suicide is also puzzling on a wider, societal level. Overall suicide rates in different communities and countries vary widely, yet within any one community they tend to be fairly constant from one year to the next (see Table 2.1). Why is there such variation between the rates in different communities?

Statistics on the suicide rates in particular countries are available from the World Health Organisation. There has been a considerable amount of research on how such suicide rate statistics are constructed and what they mean (e.g. Atkinson, 1978). This work indicates that there is no simple relationship between official statistics on suicide and a 'real' rate of suicide; indeed, just like crime statistics, the research raises deep questions about the process of labelling certain deaths as 'suicides'. However, again just like crime statistics, the statistics themselves, however they may be constructed, are social facts that warrant sociological investigation.

Hungary, for example, has a very high suicide rate compared with other European countries. Hungary has also been experiencing rapid economic growth and a major change in cultural and political values since the break-up of the Communist bloc. We might guess that Hungary's high official suicide rate is caused in some way by these rapid social, cultural and economic changes. This statement certainly answers a 'Why?' question. But as a theory, it is still lacking.

One problem is that, as it stands, it refers only to Hungary. A statement relating to a single case, such as Hungary, would not normally be considered to be a theory. A theory needs to be able to cover a range of settings. But we could look for other countries also experiencing rapid socio-economic changes and see whether they too have high suicide rates. If we found several such countries, we would have a more impressive theory and one that represents a general pattern or 'regularity'.

For example, Sri Lanka has also been subject to major disturbances in the last few years and its suicide rate is also very high (see Table 2.1). Indeed, after some thought and some delving into suicide statistics, one might suppose that 'the rate of suicide increases in times of rapid social and economic change', a conclusion which Durkheim also proposed and which he explained using the concept of anomie. Anomic suicide, according to Durkheim, results when society's regulation of the individual through normative controls breaks down and this is likely to happen where there is social and economic instability.

2.3.2 INDUCTION AND DEDUCTION

The process that we have just worked through, of finding a single case and observing a relationship, then observing the same relationship in several more cases and finally constructing a general theory to cover all the cases, is known as **induction**. It is the basic technique for moving from a set of observations to a theory and is at the heart of sociological theory construction. Once a theory has been formulated, it can be used to explain. For example, the theory about suicide rates being high in countries with high rates of social and economic change can be used to explain why the Russian Federation has a high suicide rate (the rates for the Russian Federation are 69.3 for males and 11.9 for females (WHO, 2005)). This process, starting with a theory and using it to explain particular observations, is known as **deduction**. Deduction takes the data about a particular case and applies the general theory in order to deduce an explanation for the data. Thus induction is the technique for generating theories and deduction is the technique for applying them (see Figures 2.1 and 2.2).

For the sake of defining the terms, we have discussed induction and deduction as though they are quite distinct. Logically, that is true. But in the course of doing research they often are intertwined. First, one has an idea for a theory, perhaps by contemplating the common features of a set of cases and inducing a theory. Then one checks it out against some data, using deduction. If the theory doesn't quite fit the facts, induction is used to construct a slightly more complicated, but better theory. And so on.

Figure 2.1   Theory construction by induction

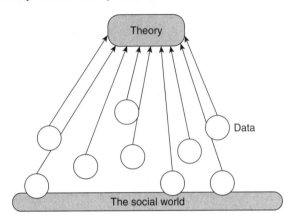

Figure 2.2   Theory use by deduction

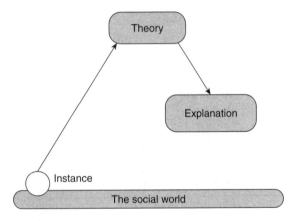

It is important to realise that *induction is not foolproof*. It is certainly possible to construct erroneous, misleading or over-simple theories by induction. For example, induction has led us straight to the theory that high suicide rates are the product of economic and social change. Unfortunately, this isn't the whole story. Finland has a high rate of suicide compared with other industrialised nations, yet it has not experienced great political or economic changes recently.

This counter-instance can be put to good use, however. The theory can be extended in scope and deepened in its explanatory power if we look to see what characteristic Finland has which might explain its high rate. The answer, as Durkheim argued from his data, is that economic and social change is only one influence on suicide rates. The degree of social integration that is encouraged by the dominant religion is also important. He suggests that Catholic countries tend to have families with closer ties, leading to more support for individuals and more disapproval by the society of suicide. This is the reason, he argues, that Protestant countries, such as Finland, tend to have higher suicide rates than otherwise similar Catholic countries.

2.3.3 FALSIFICATION

This leads to another important aspect of theory construction, the strategy of **falsification**: always look for the awkward cases. If we had stuck with the cases that fitted the original theory about the significance of social and economic change, that is, if we had looked no further than Hungary and Sri Lanka, we would not have formulated the wider theory that brought in the religious dimension.

Falsification as a strategy is important for two reasons. First, by directing attention to 'awkward cases' it helps to improve theories. Second, it has been argued that it is a useful criterion for what should count as a theory. The criterion is that it must be possible *in principle* to falsify a theory. That is, it must be possible to imagine some data which, if found, would demolish the theory.

The preceding theory about suicide rates being linked to economic and political change may not be a good theory, but by the criterion of falsification, it is at least a theory. It is possible to imagine some data that would destroy the theory: a single case of a country experiencing great changes but having a low suicide rate would do. But consider the statement, 'People who kill themselves are suicides'. This is *not* a theory. First, the statement is not an answer to a 'Why?' question. Second, it is impossible to think of data which would falsify it. In fact, this statement is a definition of suicide, not a theory.

One of the problems of research is that the search for falsifying observations is in principle never-ending. No matter how much data one collects that fits the theory, it is always possible that a falsifying instance might turn up next. The consequence is that there is an asymmetry about a researcher's confidence in theory: one can be quite sure that a theory is wrong if there are any data which falsifies it, but one cannot be sure that a theory is right, because there may yet be some data which will disconfirm it. Scepticism is therefore the right attitude to assertions that this or that theory is correct.

2.4 CONCEPTS AND RELATIONSHIPS

Durkheim writes, in *Suicide*:

> The fact that economic crises have an aggravating effect on the suicide tendency is well known ... Even fortunate crises, which have the effect of raising a country's prosperity, have an effect on suicide like economic disasters ... Every disturbance of equilibrium, even though it may involve greater comfort and a raising of the general pace of life, provides an impulse to voluntary death. (Durkheim, [1897], 1985: 108–9)

Figure 2.3   A theory about a cause of high suicide rates

Durkheim is arguing that there is a causal link between economic crises and suicide rates. Crises cause ('have an effect on') suicide. Such causal statements are often shown graphically, with arrows to mean 'cause'. Figure 2.3 illustrates Durkheim's theory in this way.

Figure 2.3 can be read as saying that there is a causal relationship between economic conditions (the occurrence or absence of economic crisis) and high or low suicide rates. We call the things in boxes **concepts** and the lines between the boxes, **relationships**. Theories are composed of concepts linked by relationships.

In this example about suicide, there are only two concepts and one relationship. But most theories are a lot more complicated. Let us turn from suicide to a rather different example, 'gentrification'. Poor housing areas become 'gentrified' when run-down homes occupied by poor people are taken over by the relatively rich. The process of gentrification has been studied in a number of urban research programmes in the US and the UK (e.g. Ley, 1996; Smith and Williams, 1986) and is interesting because it is an example of the unintended consequences of apparently beneficial social policies.

The theory goes like this. Social planners and politicians attempt to improve a poor locality for its residents, by providing favourable loans, redevelopment grants and so on. The effect is that the overall quality of the area improves. This raises the value of the housing and makes properties not yet improved particularly attractive to developers. The price of housing goes up and with it the rents charged by private landlords. If rents are controlled, landlords take advantage of rising market prices to sell their property. The rise in housing costs pushes the original, poorer residents out and they are replaced by richer owners. The poor neighbourhood has been gentrified, displacing the established residents, often to even poorer housing stock.

Figure 2.4 summarises the theory as a diagram. Each box represents a concept and each line a causal relationship. The causal effect can either be positive or negative. For example, as the quality of the neighbourhood rises, the price of housing rises also – a positive effect. As the price of housing rises, the number of poorer residents falls – a negative effect.

If you wanted to test a theory like this, it would be difficult to do it all at once. It is too complicated; there are too many relationships to consider (although some of the most recent statistical techniques, such as those mentioned at the end of Chapter 18, can help). Instead, it is best to break the

Figure 2.4 A theory of gentrification

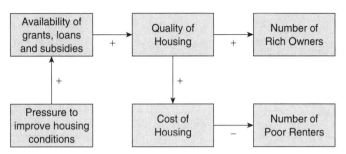

theory down into parts, each covering just one relationship. So, one might test the causal relationship between the Quality of Housing and the Cost of Housing and then, separately, the relationship between the Cost of Housing and the Number of Poor Renters. Each such part is known as a **hypothesis** and it is hypotheses that researchers generally test and try to falsify.

2.5 TESTING THEORIES

So far, this chapter has been concentrating almost entirely on theories. It has been argued that theories are things that aim to explain puzzling observations. They are composed of one or more hypotheses, each of which consists of concepts linked by relationships. Theories must be capable of being tested, or falsified. Now we must move on to examine in more detail what is involved in testing a theory.

In order to test a theory, we need to compare the predictions it makes with measurements made of the social world. For example, we need to see whether, as the Quality of Housing increases, so does the Number of Rich Owners, which is what the theory of Figure 2.4 predicts. However, this is more difficult than it seems because concepts cannot be measured directly. Before Quality of Housing can be assessed, one has to have some definition of 'quality' and some means of applying that definition to actual neighbourhoods.

2.5.1 INDICATORS

In general, in order to test theories, there must be a way of measuring each concept, that is, for each, there must be an **indicator**. An indicator is a method of measurement that aims to measure the concept accurately. If we want to test the hypothesis that the Quality of Housing was related to the Cost of Housing, we would need independent indicators for both these concepts. The cost of housing could be measured by averaging the asking price for houses for sale (but there would still be some issues to settle: What is to be counted as a 'house'? What about a property which has tenants? What if the price actually paid for property is less than the asking price? and so on). An indicator for 'Quality of Housing' is more difficult to devise. One indicator that would not be suitable is the value of the housing, for this would then be confusing measurement of the two concepts. One approach might be to consult a panel of experts, such as estate agents, surveyors or lawyers and ask them to assess the quality of the housing. Another way would be to conduct an attitude survey of the general public. A third way would be to rely on some more direct measure, such as the average number of months since the exterior woodwork was repainted. Obviously, there is room for debate and for careful thought about the right choice, and factors such as the cost of the research and the speed with which data can be obtained will need to be considered as well.

2.5.2 VALIDITY AND RELIABILITY

Naturally, researchers want their indicators to be as good as possible. That means that the measurements that they make should be **valid** (accurately measuring the concept) and **reliable** (consistent from one measurement to the next). For instance, suppose that you want to measure people's consumption of alcohol (a concept). You choose to do this using a questionnaire in which you will ask respondents to tell you how much they drank during the last month. In fact, this is not a good indicator of alcohol consumption. People tend to under-report consumption – they say that they drink less than they actually drink – casting doubts on the validity of the indicator. Also, people have difficulty remembering in detail what they were doing as long as a month ago. This means that if you were to ask someone repeatedly over the course of a few days what they had drunk during the previous month, it is quite likely that they would give you different answers, just because they were not remembering consistently. The indicator is not reliable.

In order to know whether an indicator is valid and reliable, we need to understand how it works, that is, the way the indicator measures its concept. Consider two of the indicators mentioned in the previous section. Official statistics measure suicide rates in as much as they record the decisions of coroners' courts, bodies which apply procedures laid down in legal statute for assigning causes of death. Coroners, of course, do not have direct access to the cause of death; they themselves use a set of indicators and a body of 'theory' – common sense and legal knowledge – to decide whether a particular death is the result of suicide or some other reason (Atkinson, 1978; Kitsuse and Cicourel, 1963) and this needs to be recognised when we use the indicator. The quality of housing in a neighbourhood may be measured by an indicator consisting of the average time since house exteriors were painted because houses in poor condition are rarely repainted, while houses which are in good condition and are being looked after by their owners tend to be repainted regularly, as soon as the paintwork begins to show signs of age.

2.5.3 MEASUREMENT THEORIES

As these examples show, the validity and reliability of an indicator will depend on the adequacy of the way in which it measures its concept. One way of thinking about an indicator is that it links a concept (e.g. Quality of Housing) with observable facts (e.g. average time since repainting). The adequacy of this link depends on a theoretical proposition, known as the indicator's **measurement theory**. The measurement theory for the indicator of housing quality is the proposition that 'houses in poor condition are rarely repainted, while houses which are in good condition and are being looked after by their owners tend to be repainted regularly, as soon as the paintwork begins to show signs of age'.

Like any other theory, a measurement theory can, and should be tested. The more it is tested against data, the more confident one can be in the adequacy of the indicator that relies on that theory. But like all theories, measurement theories can still eventually turn out to be wrong or incomplete. What are the consequences of using an incorrect measurement theory?

One consequence could be that we are led to draw the wrong conclusions when inducing theories from observations. This is what happened in the case mentioned at the beginning of this chapter, that working-class youth seemed to be committing more crime than middle-class youth. The measurement theory implicit in using official crime statistics to measure crime rates (that official statistics validly measure the number of criminal acts committed) turned out to be false. The effect of using the wrong measurement theory was that incorrect theories that attempted to account for a spurious differential crime rate were constructed.

Another consequence of using incorrect measurement theories is that one may falsify correct theories or fail to falsify incorrect theories, because the indicators are not measuring the concepts properly. This has the unfortunate implication that if a theory is apparently not corroborated by the data, we do not know whether this is because the theory is in fact wrong, or whether it is because the measurement theories on which the indicators rely are incorrect. Of course, the solution to this dilemma is to test the measurement theories.

However, this can lead to trouble. As a good researcher, you will want to test your hypothesis. You therefore devise some indicators for the concepts in your hypothesis. But before using the indicators, you need to satisfy yourself about the adequacy of the indicators. To do this, you need to investigate the measurement theories on which they are based. This will involve devising indicators to test the measurement theories. These indicators will themselves rely on measurement theories ... We seem to have embarked on an endless task!

2.6 SOCIAL RESEARCH AS A SOCIAL PROCESS

The answer to this conundrum comes from the fact that research is never conducted without reference to other studies. It can always rely on previous knowledge and previous experience. This means that rather than having to justify every measurement theory and thus every indicator, researchers can call on other people's work.

Social research, like other scientific work, is situated within a 'paradigm' (Kuhn, 1970), a scientific tradition. The paradigm influences research in several ways (see Chapter 1). The problems researchers tackle are derived from sociological perspectives which, although in constant flux, have been fashioned through a hundred years of sociological thought. The indicators we use and the measurement theories on which they are based have been honed by many previous researchers through thousands of projects. Instead of having personally to test every measurement theory you use and having to justify every theory you mention, you can rely on standard indicators, standard concepts and standard theories.

Linking new research to the existing paradigm is one of the functions of the 'references' that are sprinkled through journal articles. These references not only acknowledge previous work (saying, in effect, 'the idea I am mentioning is not my own invention, but was previously proposed by someone else'), but also and more importantly, borrow the authority of earlier research (saying, 'it is not just me who thinks this research method, this hypothesis, etc. is correct, but also the person I am citing'). Chapter 24 discusses the techniques of writing and referencing in more detail.

This is just one example of the way in which we, as sociologists, can examine the social processes that contribute to the construction of sociological knowledge. There is no reason to exempt sociology or science in general from investigation by sociologists (Barnes et al., 1996).

Learning about how to do social research is thus not just a matter of becoming proficient at some technical skills, although knowledge of technique is very important. It is also about learning the culture of social science so that you can become a proficient member of the social scientific community.

2.7 CHOOSING A RESEARCH DESIGN

One of the basic questions that researchers have to ask themselves is what kind of research design is appropriate to their research problem. In the following chapters, you will be introduced to a variety of research techniques commonly used by sociologists. You might wonder why this variety exists and how one can choose between the different designs. This section will review the choices and suggest which is most appropriate for which problems. But there are no hard and fast rules: as we shall see, it depends on the research question, the availability of data, and the researcher's own skills and preferences.

There are three basic choices that can be made: quantitative versus qualitative; cross-sectional versus longitudinal; and case versus representative.

2.7.1 QUANTITATIVE AND QUALITATIVE

Quantitative research is research that aims to measure using numbers. Typical forms of quantitative research are surveys, in which many respondents are asked questions and their answers are averaged and other statistics calculated; and research based on administrative data, where, for example, the number of people who have been patients in a hospital each month is counted. On the other hand, qualitative research most often describes scenes, gathers data through interviews, or analyses the meaning of documents. In both types of research, one is measuring the social world, but in quantitative designs, the aim is to create a numerical description, perhaps through a process of 'coding' (see Chapter 17) verbal or textual data. In qualitative designs, one creates an account or description, without numerical scores.

One advantage of quantitative data is its relative precision and lack of ambiguity. To use a simple example, it is quite clear what we mean when we say that a respondent is 19 years old. The qualitative equivalent, which might be the observation that 'the young man walked into the room with a swagger' is 'richer' but less precise. Another advantage is the opportunity that quantitative data affords for summarisation and analysis using statistical tools. Thus quantitative data is particularly appropriate for representative studies (see below). However, it is generally not very helpful if one is interested in testing for causes and effects. While quantitative data can be used to discover associations, such as that people who are sick are more likely than the healthy to be unemployed, quite complex designs have to be used to shed light on which is the cause and which is the effect: for instance, is it that sick people find it harder to get a job, or that people who are unemployed tend to get less exercise and eat poorer food and so become sick more often – or is there some third factor that influences both people's health and their chances of employment? Qualitative data often makes it easier to follow cause and effect, since one can track people through their lives or ask them to tell their life histories.

In practice, the distinction between quantitative and qualitative is not absolute. Even in qualitative studies, it is common to count how many informants fall into one or other category. For instance, in a study of the homeless, in which a dozen men are interviewed on the streets, one might find that about half regularly use hostels: a quantitative description of the sample. And even in large surveys, it is not uncommon to record respondent's replies verbatim when they answer questions such as 'Why did you move to this accommodation?'.

2.7.2 CROSS-SECTIONAL AND LONGITUDINAL

This distinction is about whether the data are collected at more or less one moment in time ('cross-sectional') or over a period of time, repeatedly observing or interviewing the respondents (**longitudinal**). A typical social survey is cross-sectional: all the respondents are asked the same questions at the same time (in practice, there may be differences of a few days between the first and the last responses, but the design assumes that this time period is irrelevant). A case study that, for example, follows the development of a controversial topic in science over a period of twenty years as various theories are proposed, tested and rejected (e.g. Collins, 2004) is a longitudinal design. The advantage of cross-sectional designs is that they can be completed quickly and that they can involve large samples. Longitudinal designs obviously take longer, because they extend over a time period, and it is more difficult and more expensive to involve large samples. One also has to worry about drop-out, or 'attrition', when some members of the sample withdraw from the study, die or move away. This is an important problem especially in quantitative research because a sample that had the right composition at the start of the study may become biased as a result of attrition (see Chapter 9).

Despite such problems, the great advantage of longitudinal research is that one can directly study process and mechanism: that is, how one thing is affected by or depends on another.

2.7.3 CASE AND REPRESENTATIVE STUDIES

A case study is one in which a particular instance or a few carefully selected cases are studied intensively. Usually there is no attempt to select a random or a representative sample of cases. Instead, the cases are ones that are interesting for their own sake, or sometimes are exceptional in some way ('unique case studies'). In contrast, a representative study strives to select a large number of cases or respondents who are chosen so that it is possible to infer from the features of the sample to the population as a whole. For instance, a typical opinion poll will have more than 1,000 respondents, chosen using random or quota sampling methods (see Chapter 9) so that the average opinion of the sample can be used as a good guide to the average opinion of the whole population.

The advantage of the case study design is that the research can be much more detailed than would be possible if one were studying a large sample, but the corresponding disadvantage is that it is much more difficult and often impossible to generalise the findings. For example, one cannot know whether the findings from a study of protests against the erection of mobile phone masts in Fife, Scotland (Law and McLeish, 2007) can be applied to explain a mobile phone mast protest in Surrey, still less a protest about the construction of an additional runway at a London airport. The difficulty of generalising may seem a major limitation of case studies, but they can still be valuable when

Table 2.2   Types of research design

			EXAMPLE
Quantitative	Cross-sectional	Case	Studies of particular organisations or settings (see Chapter 6)
Quantitative	Cross-sectional	Representative	Large social surveys (see Chapter 19)
Quantitative	Longitudinal	Case	Historical studies of nations or groups (see Chapter 15)
Quantitative	Longitudinal	Representative	Panel and cohort studies (see Chapter 19)
Qualitative	Cross-sectional	Case	Focus group studies (see Chapter 12)
Qualitative	Cross-sectional	Representative	Cross-national comparative case studies
Qualitative	Longitudinal	Case	Ethnography (observation) of small groups and settings (see Chapter 14)
Qualitative	Longitudinal	Representative	Studies of small societies and groups, by interviewing informants (see Chapter 13)

one is wanting to try to falsify a theory using a deductive research strategy. Law and McLeish (2007) compared the findings from their research on the Fife mast protest with an extant theory of protest (the 'New Irrational Actor Model') and concluded that this theory was not a good explanation of what they observed. Studies of this kind are called 'critical case studies'.

The preceding discussion has shown that there is no one best design. Each has its strengths and weaknesses. If we cross-tabulate the three dimensions of research design, we get eight possibilities. Table 2.2 lists these possibilities and typical examples of the types of research that might use each.

If you are selecting a research design, consider with the help of Table 2.2 whether a quantitative or qualitative, cross-sectional or longitudinal, a case study or a representative design is likely to yield the most informative data. In addition, you should consider practical issues, such as getting access to the sample, the costs of doing the research, and the time that would be involved. These issues are considered in more detail in the following chapters.

2.8 SUMMARY

In this chapter, we have seen that what makes social research different from mere data collection is that it is an activity conducted within a research community. This community provides a body of theory in which the research needs to be located. Sociological theory, like all theory, aims to be explanatory, answering 'Why?' questions. It also aims to be general, offering explanations that transcend the particularities of time, space, or personal circumstance.

Theories are generally constructed through induction, extracting the common elements of many specific instances, and are applied to explain other instances by means of the logic of deduction. Theories are made up of hypotheses, individual statements that relate together theoretical concepts.

Theories must be susceptible to falsification, that is, they must be framed in such a way that they could be proved wrong. Testing a theory involves choosing indicators for each of its concepts, using the indicators to collect data, and comparing the data with predictions made from the theory. An indicator should be valid and reliable. This can be determined by examining the measurement theory on which it is based. However, in practice, most researchers most of the time use standard indicators which have been developed and used by other sociologists before them and whose validity is largely unquestioned.

DISCUSSION QUESTIONS

1   What is the best way of measuring the amount of crime that is committed each year?

2   Give a definition of what you mean by 'theory'. Compare your definition with the definitions in this chapter and in Chapter 1, and with definitions offered by other sociological authors. Why is there such a lot of disagreement about these definitions?

3   When is it best to be inductive and when deductive?

4   Is there any connection between the 'deduction' described in this chapter and the deduction that detectives do to find criminals?

5   Give some examples of statements or propositions that cannot be falsified, even in principle (if possible, take these examples from newspapers or other popular media).

6   Describe the measurement theory that underpins the measurement of social class using a person's occupation.

PROJECTS

1   See if Durkheim's theories of suicide still fit data about current suicide rates. For this, you will need a table of suicide rates by country (see the weblink in Table 2.1), and data on changes in economic performance and on religious affiliations by country (these are produced by national

and international statistical offices and can also be found on the world wide web. For example, you can download a table of gross national product per person (GNP per capita) from http://tinyurl.com/26g32f and numerous statistics about countries for the world from the CIA World Factbook, http://tinyurl.com/jor92).

2   This chapter has suggested a particular model of social enquiry, one which proposes that social research involves theories, data, indicators and theory testing. In some ways this model can be regarded as itself a theory – a theory about social research. Like any theory, it ought to be capable of being compared with data.

For this project, you should locate in the library a recent issue of one of the major journals in your field. In sociology, this might be one of the *Sociology, Sociological Research Online, Sociological Review*, the *British Journal of Sociology*, the *American Sociological Review* or the *American Journal of Sociology*. Find an article in your chosen issue that looks interesting. Read the article closely to see the way in which the author puts forward his or her argument. Write down, in as few words as you can, the theory being advanced in the article. List the concepts that are used in the theory. For each concept, identify the indicators that the author uses. For each concept and indicator, briefly suggest what the implied measurement theory is.

For some articles, these steps are easy to carry out. In other cases, you may find the theory, the concepts or the indicators hard to pin down. Is this because there is something amiss with the research being reported in the article, or because the model of social enquiry proposed in this chapter does not fit the research in the article you have been examining?

RESOURCES

Hammersley (1993) *Social Research: Philosophy, Politics and Practice* includes a useful set of readings related to this chapter, with an emphasis on qualitative research.

Hollis (2002) *The Philosophy of Social Science: An Introduction* provides a clear introduction to the philosophy of social science.

Smith (2005) *Philosophy and Methodology of the Social Sciences* is a comprehensive collection of readings.

Two older books are also still useful: Hughes (1976) *Sociological Analysis: Methods of Discovery*, Chapters 1 and 2, addresses many of the issues touched on in this chapter in more detail, and Stinchcombe (1968) *Constructing Social Theories* is very good on forms of social theory and how theories are constructed.

PART I
Beginnings

There is much to be planned before you should venture out into the field to collect data for your research project. This Part considers how to refine a wide-ranging interest into a focused, researchable question and how to conduct a literature review to find out what is already known about the subject. It also identifies the ethical issues that need to be considered when designing a research project. You will learn about some common approaches to research, including research based on grounded theory, participatory research and research that combines several methods within the same project.

3   Formulating and Refining a Research Question

Nicola Green

KEY POINTS

● Specifying the research question clearly is central to the success of a research project.

● Formulating a research question is the first step of a project.

● The question must be researchable and answerable.

● The question should be used to guide the research.

● It is common that the research question changes as the research proceeds.

3.1 INTRODUCTION

The **research question** is central to the design of a research project as a whole, and a crucial step in the process of carrying out a research project. Initially, however, many researchers find the task of identifying their research question quite daunting, and the process frustrating. This chapter presents some clear and specific steps to follow, which are designed to assist researchers in this process: the overall objective is to examine the process of devising and refining a social research question. The chapter seeks first of all to emphasise the importance of the research question in the research process. It then explains the characteristics and qualities of a focused social research question, and describes the process of formulating a researchable question from a general topic area. The chapter goes on to consider the role of the research question in project design, the literature review, and data collection and analysis, and suggests practical strategies to assist the process of focusing and reformulating the research question throughout the research process. The chapter will argue that the formulation of the research question is intellectual *work*, and a task that is continually revisited throughout a research project.

3.2 'DEEP THOUGHT'

In Chapters 1 and 2, the importance of considering broader research approaches and theoretical frameworks at the beginning of the research process was established. The way a research question is formulated is crucial in drawing together the underlying philosophical approach and conceptualisation, with the design of a project, and its methodology and methods. It is the first step in research design (Chapter 2), and shapes the subsequent conduct of empirical investigation and other research activities of a project.

A robust and answerable sociological research question is therefore essential in any successful social research, and the absence of a researchable question may cause later difficulties – as the pan-dimensional, hyper-intelligent race of beings that built Deep Thought found, to their cost:

> According to *The Hitchhiker's Guide to the Galaxy* [Adams, 1979], researchers from a pan-dimensional, hyper-intelligent race of beings constructed the second greatest computer in all of time and space, Deep Thought, to calculate the Ultimate Answer to Life, the Universe, and Everything. After seven and a half million years of pondering the question, Deep Thought provides the answer: "Forty-two." The reaction?
>
> *"Forty-two!" yelled Loonquawl. "Is that all you've got to show for seven and a half million years' work?"*
>
> *"I checked it very thoroughly," said the computer, "and that quite definitely is the answer. I think the problem, to be quite honest with you, is that you've never actually known what the question is."* (Wikipedia, 2006)

Loonquawl's dilemma – not actually knowing what the question is – is one that often faces sociologists and other social scientists at the beginning of the research process. Social researchers often embark on the process of research with general interests in broad topic areas, which are generally sparked by a lively curiosity about the social world, and a 'sociological imagination' (Mills, 1959). Sometimes they are derived from previous reading, writing, and thinking, or are informed by a perceived social problem, or are prompted by reports in the media. At other times they may be derived from our own personal experiences, or a critically informed observation of, and participation in, the social world around us.

Dixon, et al. (1987: 25) comment that '[w]hen we want to know something, we begin formally or informally to engage in research', and suggest there are a range of starting points from which we can begin the process of sorting, refining and focusing our interests in topic areas into more systematic research questions. To extend the starting points above, for example:

- Previous reading and thinking might compel us to ask:
  'Society as a whole is more and more splitting up into ... two great classes directly facing each other – bourgeoisie and proletariat' (Marx and Engels, [1848] 1948). So does 'the proletariat' really still exist? If so, who are these people? If not, what has changed? *What recent reading has prompted your interest in particular areas of research?*

- A perceived social problem might compel us to ask:
  Is it really the case that more CCTV in city centres leads to a reduction in crime? Why is the unemployment rate higher (or lower) now than it has been recently? What are the difficulties faced by teenage mothers and fathers? What prompts ethnic conflict in neighbourhood areas? *Are there current policy-related or perceived social problems that you are particularly interested in?*

- A media report might compel us to ask:
  Why is it that newspaper headlines are now all talking about climate change (or homelessness, or biotechnology, or unemployment, or divorce rates, or health, or education, or …)? *Have there been issues in the news recently that have particularly caught your attention, and that you want to research further?*

- Personal experiences might compel us to ask:
  Why am I having such a difficult time applying for a bank account? How come there are so few people from my culture in my neighbourhood? Why is moving out of home such a big deal to my parents? Why does my grandmother seem to have so little money? Why is my friend hanging out with that guy? And how did I end up doing social research anyway? *Are there issues you want to investigate that arise from aspects of your own experience in the social world?*

- Observation and participation in our society might compel us to ask:
  Why is it that more men than women seem to play computer games? Why is population density higher in some countries than in others? Why don't people talk to each other when they are standing in queues? Why is it that people from different religions seem to be in conflict with one another? Why do people always face the doors in elevators? *What observations have you noted recently that might deserve further investigation?*

While we may have an area of general interest in mind for research, and perhaps an inkling of the kinds of topics and variables we might want to address, we rarely have a well-considered and systematic research question immediately to hand. As Schutt (2004: 28) remarks, 'So many research questions are possible that it is more of a challenge to specify what does not qualify as a social research question than to specify what does.' What is needed in a research project, however, is a research question or problem that *provides direction* for the project, that *defines* the course of the investigation, and that *sets boundaries* on the research (O'Leary, 2004).

As Chapter 2 indicates, social scientific research is generally based on the systematic gathering of empirical data to answer a question or provide evidence about a proposition (whether cast as a research question, a problem statement, or later, as more specific hypotheses – this will be discussed further in Section 3.4). The expression of a general area of interest is rarely a systematic or specific enough basis upon which to design and execute a sufficiently self-contained research project, however. To take an earlier example – Why is it that more men than women seem to play computer games? – we can immediately see that this question, while of interest, is not nearly specific or concise enough to investigate, because the question itself prompts too many further questions. For example – What men? What women? Where? Of what age group? In what context? Which computer games? (and you can probably think of several further questions). While research questions or problem statements can take a myriad of different forms, they share those characteristics of being systematic, clearly defined, and specific. As Blaikie (2000: 59) notes, it is not only 'that research questions are necessary; but ... good research needs high quality questions'.

3.3 THE CHARACTERISTICS OF SOCIAL RESEARCH QUESTIONS

In order to be sufficiently systematic, clearly defined and specific, a social research question must, first and foremost, be *researchable*. To be researchable, the research question or problem statement should have at least six properties. It should be:

- Interesting

- Relevant

- Feasible

- Ethical

- Concise

- Answerable.

> TIP
>
> **Use these terms as a checklist when you are refining your own research problem**

3.3.1 INTERESTING

The research question needs first of all to be interesting for the *researcher*, because without the ongoing motivation and enthusiasm of the researcher throughout the duration of the project, the research project risks ultimate failure. Maintaining a curiosity about the subject one is studying can sometimes become challenging, particularly when the research presents difficulties. If, however, one is 'passionate' (Game and Metcalfe, 1996) about sociology and social research, and enthusiastically curious about the issue or problem under scrutiny, maintaining momentum in the research process becomes easier, and the product more satisfying. On the other hand, having too intense an interest in what one is studying can have unintended consequences, if bias is introduced in this way.

Maintaining a critically reflexive stance while formulating one's question can therefore mitigate any effects of potential bias, as well as maintain interest in the project over its lifetime.

3.3.2 RELEVANT

While the question should be interesting for the researcher, it should also be interesting and relevant for the research community of which the research forms a part. Research is generally of interest to a research community when it makes a contribution to the collective knowledge base of a study area or discipline, so formulating a question to which the answers are likely to be significant, novel, or original is most relevant for other researchers in the area. The orientation, according to Walliman (2006: 30), is to 'find a question, an unresolved contro-versy, a gap in knowledge or an unrequited need within the chosen subject'. It should be remembered, however, that the importance or relevance of a research question is often relative to the context in which a researcher finds themselves, so the criteria for the relevance of a research question in a seminar project, may be very different to those criteria in, for example, an institutionally funded inde-pendent research project (Schutt, 2004: 30). Sometimes the problems to be researched are not entirely at the discretion of an individual researcher, and instead can be influenced by supervisors, research institutions or by organisa-tions with a specific interest in the area. It is therefore desirable to maintain a balance between the specific research interests of the researcher, and the interests of the research community as a whole.

3.3.3 FEASIBLE

The research question or problem should be stated in such a way that the project is feasible, and has specific boundaries that make the project delimited and *do-able*. There are many possible and interesting research questions to be asked, but not all of them can be answered within the timeframe and by the resources of a specific project. Consideration needs to be given to the costs of the project, the timeframe in which it is to be completed, the time and skills of the researchers undertaking the project, and whether the access to research participants, and information needed to complete the project, are likely to be available.

3.3.4 ETHICAL

As the research question is the fulcrum around which all other research decisions are made, it is essential to consider the ethical dimensions of the research ques-tion or problem from the beginning, as this will inform the ethical obligations and procedures throughout the research project as a whole (see Chapter 8). It is particularly desirable to reflect on the ethical dimensions of the research problem when institutional ethical procedures are required for project approval. Considering these issues from the outset, and embedding these considerations in your research question, will help to ensure that the research project fulfils its ethical obligations, both professionally and institutionally.

3.3.5 CONCISE

The research question should be concise. That is to say, the question should be well articulated, its terms clearly defined, with as much precision as is possible in written language. For example, many research questions make reference to specific *concepts*. As was described in Chapter 1, most research projects usually have a broad overarching theoretical framework that informs the area of interest under scrutiny. The theoretical background, however, needs to be more specifically formulated in a sociological research question, and can be articulated in terms of specific concepts (for example, 'class', 'gender' or 'power') that are derived from previous theorisations (with reference to the theorist), and defined in terms of specific words or phrases in the question. Moreover, many research questions also specify an *object* of research, sometimes several objects. The term *object* as it is used here differs from its everyday usage referring to a material 'thing' – rather, the 'objects' are the social entities, relationships and processes that are under scrutiny by the researcher. In social research questions, very often the 'objects' of research specified are particular social groups, specific social institutions, particular organisations, social contexts or sites of various kinds, or social relationships or processes, across both micro-sociological and macro-sociological scales of reference. Further discussion on introducing sufficient precision to the research question is included in Section 3.4.

3.3.6 ANSWERABLE

Finally, the research question should be answerable. Although this appears to be common sense, or self-evident (a question requires an answer), it is sometimes forgotten. In order to make a question answerable, it is often desirable in the initial formulation of the research question to use an interrogative form in the first instance (although this may later be changed to the form of a problem statement when the research focus has been refined). The most common interrogatives are those that are commonly used in everyday language: who, what, when, where, how, which, and (often most importantly) why. Using interrogatives means first of all that an answer to the question is expected, and can be provided. Furthermore, interrogatives serve to clarify the characteristics and *objectives* of the research – that is, to suggest whether the research question is *descriptive* or *analytical* in nature (see 'research objectives' in Section 3.4.3). As one might expect, a descriptive research question (beginning with such interrogatives as 'what?') seeks to *describe* a situation or case under scrutiny, in order to add to a knowledge base of what exists with respect to some aspect of the social world. By contrast, if a research question is *analytical* in nature, it seeks to *explain* or *understand* some aspect of the social world (and therefore often answers 'why?' questions). Most research projects contain both descriptive and analytical elements. Sometimes this is because in order to explain, one must first describe. At other times a *causal relationship* is being explored between related terms or variables which requires the description of the association in order to establish a causal relationship. Further discussion of the relationship between research questions, and the characteristics and objectives of the research, are given in Section 3.4.

These six properties of researchable sociological research questions are a useful checklist to keep in mind throughout the process of formulating and refining a question. It remains the case, however, that devising and clarifying social research questions remains one of the most difficult, as well as one of the most crucial, tasks to carry out in the design of a research project. Considering its importance, it is also an element of the research process that has had relatively little attention paid to it in the methodological literature (although see Blaikie, 2000, for a review of this literature). Those that have addressed this process have, however, put forward a number of useful strategies that are explored, expanded and categorised below (see Resources for particularly useful texts).

3.4 FORMULATING AND REFINING A RESEARCH QUESTION

As we have already seen, general interests in broad topic areas can be expressed in a number of ways, from the relatively limited, micro-sociological and observation-based ('I wonder why people graffiti?'), to the relatively large scale, macro-sociological and discipline-based ('I'm interested in why some people end up in prison, and others don't'), and combinations of both. There could be a range of possible answers to broad questions or problems such as these, such that they might take a lifetime of research to answer, certainly beyond the feasible scope of a single research project.

As O'Leary (2004: 11) observes, the process of devising and refining a research question involves 'the art and science of knowing what you want to know', and formulating a sociological research question is a critical research skill that must be practised in order to be perfected. The process is one of a progressive focusing and refinement of an original area of interest, and is a process based on critical thinking, involving the systematic questioning of the objectives, terms and assumptions expressed in a larger area of interest. The process involves four steps.

3.4.1 STEP 1 GO LARGE

Paradoxically, when beginning with a broad area of interest that needs clarifying and narrowing, one of the best places to start is to 'go large' – to generate all the possible research questions that you can think of (and that you are interested in) in particular research areas. This process is one of lateral thinking and will help you to identify questions that you may not have previously considered and, most importantly, test the limits of your ideas on the topic.

There are a number of strategies that can help in this process:

- Have a **brainstorming** session, where you make a first attempt to write down every interesting question you can think of about the subject, including questions of all different kinds, and different orders of magnitude. Use a notebook for this first brainstorming session, and then carry it with you to write down further questions as and when they occur to you. Recording one question will often inspire other questions, and these should also be recorded until you appear to have exhausted the limits of your ideas in the topic area.

- Test the questions against what you already know about the subject from your own knowledge, and the discipline's collective knowledge in previous social research. Compare those questions that might already have answers proposed in previous research, against those that may not have been considered before. Which existing answers might be extended, or considered from a different angle? Which new questions already have partial answers, and what is missing? What questions seem entirely new, and why?

- Consider how you could make use of '**concept mapping**', a process whereby both logical and creative visual association allows the researcher to consider links and relationships between different concepts – from the most abstract concepts to the specific and concrete, from the central thematic focus to related key words and phrases, to the specific associations or relationships between linked concepts. Concept maps can help to focus the most important elements of your questions with those that are more peripheral concern, can identify existing knowledge and gaps in it, or can identify existing relationships or generate new ones (see O'Leary, 2004).

- Think widely about your subject area, and what can be found in sources other than academic literature. The topic may be represented in many different forms, from popular films, television programmes and songs, to newspaper reports, policy documents and museum exhibits. What stories are these other media presenting, and why? What relationship do they bear to your emerging research question? (see Chapter 1 on 'lay theories').

- Brainstorm not only yourself, but talk extensively to peers, colleagues and supervisors. Often others can see the strengths and problems of a question that a researcher may miss when they are immersed in the extensive possibilities.

3.4.2 STEP 2 NARROWING THE LIST

Once you have a list of research questions that would be interesting to research, it is necessary to start the work of narrowing the list, excluding some questions and refining others. This is an iterative process, and one that will be carried out many times throughout the research project as a more rigorous order is imposed on ideas that are initially only loosely associated. It is important to try to maintain a critical reflexivity in this part of the process, and to cultivate a frame of mind in which previously treasured ideas can be excluded. Remember that not all potentially interesting questions are researchable ones, and that even when researchable, any specific project may not be possible given the constraints that inevitably attend the research process:

- It may be the case that some of your proposals for a research question are actually *sub-questions* of other, more over-arching questions, or that some questions can be consolidated together. It is likely that 'major' research questions will provide the central focus for the research project as a whole, and that 'subsidiary' questions will provide more detail and focus for particular concepts or elements (Blaikie, 2000). Often, the subsidiary questions make a more general and abstract major question more concrete, and break the major problem down into smaller components that can be more easily researched.

- Reconsider your list and exclude any questions that seem of more peripheral interest. You could try to rank your questions in their order of importance, and exclude those that are least important to you.

- At the same time, concentrate on thematically clustering those questions that seem of most central interest, and consider the relationship between them. Which questions seem more abstract, and which more concrete? What is their scope? Try to rank your questions in order of abstraction and/or scope, and consider which questions might be answerable within given constraints and which might not.

- Keeping in mind the over-arching injunction that a research question should be answerable, return to the checklist of characteristics of good social research questions. Any particular question on your list might be interesting for you, but is it also relevant for the research community, and an ethical project? Is the question feasible and do-able within the time constraints of the project, the information available, and the skills and resources of the researcher? If any particular question does not conform to these criteria, exclude it from your list.

3.4.3 STEP 3 REFINING THE QUESTIONS

Steps 2 and 3 are presented separately here, but in practice, the processes of narrowing and refining research questions often happen at the same time. This is because making judgements about what to narrow and exclude, or what to cluster together and consolidate, also relies on reflective judgements about what your questions mean – their objectives, terms, and assumptions with respect to the knowledge they are likely to produce. The process of refining a question involves paying very detailed attention to its wording and critically evaluating the assumptions that are embedded in the way the research questions are put together.

- *Research objectives*: When you have achieved a rather more narrowed list, reconsider the objectives of each research question. The **research objectives** are different from its hypotheses or data collection methods – the objectives are often embedded in the form of the research question itself, and state what purpose the collection of data will accomplish, and the types of knowledge to emerge, whether descriptive or analytical (see Section 3.3). Research objectives are often flagged by a number of key words and phrases that signal the research purpose: for example, will your research explore, will it describe, or is it intended to explain, to compare, to understand, to intervene and change, or to evaluate?

   What is your research question trying to achieve? What does the question imply are the purposes of the research project, and the types of knowledge it will produce? What does your list of questions currently suggest your research objectives are? How can they be rephrased, refined (or excluded) to better reflect the orientation of the research? Is it possible to rephrase your question as a statement of a research objective (or objectives)?

   Blaikie (2000: 60–1) suggests that there are three main types of research question: *what* questions (requiring description), *how* questions (concerned with process, change, interventions and outcomes), and *why* questions (concerned with causes, reasons, relationships and activities). Consider the relationship between the ways your question is phrased (there can be different phrased variations of what, how and why questions), and the objectives or purposes of the research. How can the question be better refined so that the objectives of the research are most closely related to the way the question is phrased? It is possible for each kind of question to be phrased in terms of the others (a 'what' question into a 'how' question into a 'why' question) depending on what the objectives of the research are.

- *Terms*: When a research question is vague and unspecified, a number of critical questions may also be asked in order to identify those terms in the question that remain imprecise. The question must be broken down into its terms, or component parts of language (words and phrases), and subjected to critical, specifying questions in order to identify how more precise language might be employed. Often, these specifying questions are interrogatives that we use in everyday language – beginning with the 'what, how and why' questions that help frame our research objectives, but also including 'who, when, where, and which' questions. These specifying questions may be asked both of the terms that specify the *objects* of the research, as well as the *concepts* included or implied in the question (see Section 3.3 for the characteristics of social research questions that make them concise).

- *Assumptions*: All research questions contain assumptions of some kind (see Chapter 1). Empirical or theoretical assumptions are an inescapable feature of research, as in each instance of research we are building on a previously existing knowledge base that confirms some existing assumptions, and challenges others. Assumptions are therefore impossible to avoid – but at the same time, it is necessary to be clear about the specific assumptions that underpin the research question, both in order to position them with respect to other research in the field, and to establish the limitations of the knowledge claims that can be made with respect to the questions asked, and data thereafter collected.

  Assumptions exist both at the level of theoretical conceptualisation (see Chapter 1) in the research question, as well as the philosophical and methodological orientation implied by the way the research question is posed (see Chapter 2).

Earlier in the chapter, an expression of general interest in a topic area was posed – 'Why do more men than women play computer games?' By breaking down this question into its component parts, it becomes immediately apparent that several terms or words are general rather than specific, and critical questions may be posed to clarify and specify those terms:

(*Why*) do (*more*) (*men*) than (*women*) (*play*) (*computer games*)?

- The *why* suggests that the objectives of the research are to understand and explain, to provide reasons for a phenomenon or set of activities.

- The *more* suggests a quantitative comparative element to the research. Is this quantitative comparison a descriptive element of the planned research? Or is it an assumption that needs to be interrogated and confirmed with reference to other, relevant research?

- What *men* and *women*? Where? Of what class, or ethnic group? Of what nationality or region? Of what age? When? (This kind of critical question is also important in the design of samples – see Chapter 9).

- If the comparative terms are 'men' and 'women', it suggests the concept of *gender* is involved. Is this an assumption that is underpinning the research? Should it therefore be made more explicit in the research question?

- How is the term *'play'* defined? What behaviours are entailed? Is 'play' an activity, an event, a relationship, or a process?

- What kind of *computer games*? Individual games? Team games? On a games console, a PC, on the **Internet**? Situated in the home, in a cybercafé, at a league meeting?

What critical questions are missing from the list above that could also be applied to the terms included in the research question?

On the basis of these critical questions, how could the question be rephrased in different ways to introduce more precision and clarity?

What words or phrases in your own research questions could be further specified and clarified in this way?

Many research questions will include specific theoretical *conceptualisation*, and wherever specific concepts are introduced to the research question, thought should be given to the assumptions being made about the concepts under scrutiny.

- In the example 'How does the concept of gender help us to understand why more men than women play computer games?', what role is being given to 'gender'? What is meant by the term? If the concept of gender is involved, then how will gender be *defined* in the proposed research? On what basis – or with reference to what theoretical framework or previous research – would you define it in such a way? As a property of a person? As a property of group activity? As a social process? (see Chapter 1 on conceptualisation).

- What concepts are implicit in your research question? Should they be made explicit?

- What concepts are explicit in your research question? What are the parameters of those concepts, and how will they be defined and deployed in the research?

In the case of theoretically-based research questions, the level of conceptualisation is high, making reference both to concepts in a general theoretical framework, as well as the conceptual work that constitutes the empirical elements of the research.

The level of theoretical conceptualisation explicitly present in the research question is closely related to whether the project is based on **induction** or **deduction** reasoning (see Chapter 2). If the project is focused on the description of a particular example of social life, which is then used to theorise a more general pattern, inductive reasoning is being used – and in this instance specific theoretically-based conceptualisation may remain more implicit in the research question itself (i.e. the question is more likely to focus on the gathering of descriptive empirical data – guided by 'what' questions – that are later theorised in the analysis). In the example – 'Why do more men than women play computer games?' – more inductive reasoning is being employed, as the research question focuses more directly towards an empirical situation. By contrast, in a research question that begins with the exploration of a specific theoretical or conceptual framework, more deductive reasoning is being used. The theoretical explanation acts as the general case, and the empirical element of the project is the particular instance that is used to explore or test the more general theory. To orient the earlier example more deductively, we could rephrase the research question to read 'How does the concept of gender help us to understand why more men than women play computer games?', as above.

In practice, most research questions contain both inductive and deductive elements, and the research questions will reflect both logics. This is because some knowledge of the empirical world is needed first to develop theories, and some theoretical knowledge is needed to decide what empirical data should be addressed (see Chapter 2).

The level of explicit conceptualisation in the research question, and the researcher's understanding of the relationship between theory and research, will also affect whether specific hypotheses will be formulated and operationalised in the research design. In Chapter 2, we learnt that an **hypothesis** is a conjecture about relationships between relevant variables, cast as a statement that is testable. It provides a clear (if tentative) proposition of what might be the case, that is then subjected to verification via empirical investigation. Hypotheses are, however, *distinct* from the research questions asked, and should not be confused. It is not always possible, appropriate or desirable to formulate hypotheses in order to guide a research project as a whole. This is generally because hypotheses seem to have a different status in different traditions of social research, and vary with respect to their role, purpose and precision. In Blaikie's (2000: 70) view:

> Hypotheses are tentative answers to 'why' and, sometimes, 'how' research questions. They are our best guesses at the answers. But they are not appropriate for 'what' questions. There is little point in hazarding guesses at a possible state of affairs.

Hypotheses, therefore, should be treated with caution, and should not be the primary guide in the research process. Rather, it is the research question (and sub-questions) that guide the research project as a whole, even in the case where it is later appropriate to formulate hypotheses in order to empirically test theories, concepts and relationships.

3.4.4 STEP 4 REVIEW

Once you have narrowed down the questions from the original list, identified your major and subsidiary questions, and refined them with respect to their objectives, terms and assumptions, you are in a position to review the process, and the narrowed list of questions. At this point, it is worth again asking further critical questions of your narrowed list:

- Are all the questions you have decided upon essential? What purpose does each serve? What is the relationship of each to the others?

- Are you able to identify the objectives of the research in each question? Are you clear about the meanings of your terms, and the assumptions that lie behind your question?

- Revisit the checklist of a researchable social research question. Is your question researchable according to these criteria?

At this point, you should have a list of no more than around five or so questions and/or sub-questions (often there may be less, but be wary of committing to too many more, as focus may be lost). After your narrowing and clarifying activities, these questions should be sufficiently clear and precise to provide a focus for the ongoing research and boundaries around it, and to then guide the design of your research.

When a researcher has hit upon a small number of related – major and subsidiary – research questions, it is tempting to assume that the process of refining a research question for a project has 'finished'. In practice, however, the refining of a research question is intellectual work that takes place again and again in the course of research. Not only is it common, but it is often desirable that the research question change (especially in the early stages of a project) as your knowledge of the field grows. Each stage of the research project as a whole will challenge the research question, and prompt a re-refining and re-narrowing process, so that the research question will be revisited many times through the research project.

3.5 THE RESEARCH QUESTION AND ...

Depending on the type of research, the research question is not necessarily complete when the narrowed list has been formulated. Rather, each further stage of the research process – including the literature review, the research design, and data collection and analysis – provides the opportunity to revisit the question. Often this is because each further investigation into some aspect of the problem will illuminate unexpected directions and new avenues of possible thinking and investigation – each stage will confirm some assumptions, and challenge others. Research is rarely linear, and the form of the research question is therefore intimately embedded with other stages of the research process in a recursive and iterative way – while the research question guides all other research activities, other research activities can cause us to critically challenge and re-examine our research questions. The difficult decisions to be made are whether further developments refine the questions you already have and enrich your research, or whether they are distractions, sending you off in ultimately unproductive directions.

While the process of re-evaluation is constant, there are three significant points where it is sensible to step back and review the focus, objectives and terms of the research question. These points are design, review and data collection and analysis.

3.5.1 RESEARCH DESIGN

The formulation of a research question underpins the design of research as a whole and implies what form the research project will take. In research design, every element of the research process is considered and planned, including the background to the problem and the review of previous research, through to the methodological approach, and the methods of data collection and analysis. It affects how populations or groups are sampled, what methods will be used to access those groups, through what means data will be obtained, and how those data will be treated once they are collected.

As O'Leary (2004: 2) comments,

> It is important to remember that particular research strategies are good or bad to the exact degree that they fit with the questions at hand. The perspectives you will adopt and the methods you will use need to be as fluid, flexible, and as eclectic as is necessary to answer the questions posed.

This implies that the strategies adopted throughout the design and execution of the research project are all informed by the underlying question. It is therefore wise, at each stage of research design, to reflect on your questions, and use the research design and question to interrogate each other:

- Are your approaches and research strategies commensurate with the question you are asking?

- Is your proposed sample consistent with the groups, organisations, relationships or processes specified in the question?

- What methodological strategies are implied by the purposes and objectives of your research question?

- What methods of data collection are most consistent with the objectives of the research, as they are embedded in the question?

- Does your question need adjusting in light of your proposed research design, or could you rework your research design on the basis of your reconsidered question?

3.5.2 THE LITERATURE REVIEW

Even before engaging in the process of formally refining a research question, it is likely you will have made some initial foray into the literature in your field of study – whether this is from previous reading, or any pilot literature review while initially exploring your research topic? Once you have formulated and refined your research question, a more formal review of the literature often follows.

As is indicated in Chapter 4, a literature review serves multiple purposes. These can include the need to explore and summarise previous research in the field to identify the research base on which your own research is to be built, to explore the theoretical and conceptual foundations of your project, to critically assess the strengths and limitations of previous research to inform the design of your own study, and to explore various methods of data collection and analysis.

As this exploration of various literatures takes place, it is again desirable to reflect on your own research question in order to re-assess its strengths and weaknesses:

- As you explore the theoretical literature, consider how you are defining the conceptual underpinnings of your question. Has any of the theoretical literature caused you to reconsider the ways you are defining the terms of your question, or the assumptions implicit in it?

- Has your summary of previous research caused you to reconsider the originality, relevance or interest of your current research question? If so, how can your question be recast to better reflect the position of your research with respect to that of others?

- Has any of the literature on data collection and analysis caused you to reconsider the scope of your project, or its design and execution? How can this be better articulated in a revised research question?

3.5.3 DATA COLLECTION AND ANALYSIS

Research questions guide and direct the selection of the most appropriate data collection and analysis techniques for your project. The terms 'quantitative' and 'qualitative' most appropriately refer to types of data, rather than types of method. Many data collection techniques can collect data of both a quantitative and qualitative nature. O'Leary notes (2004: 11).

It's just too easy to fall into the trap of selecting a familiar method, rather than approaching method as a critical thinking exercise aimed at answering particular research questions. It is amazing how much simpler it is to adopt, adapt, or create appropriate methodological approaches when you are absolutely clear about what you want to know.

The decisions you take about the most appropriate data collection and analysis techniques for your project will be based upon the underlying objectives of the research, and the types of knowledge that may be expected to result from the deployment of particular methods. As you are considering your data collection methods and analytical techniques (both in research design and research planning), consider how the resulting data might provide answers to your research question.

- What kind of data will your proposed collection methods provide? Is this the most appropriate type of data to answer your research question, and to address your research objectives? Why?

- Reconsider your type of question – what, how, why – and think about how your proposed data will address the specific type of question you are asking.

- What are your proposed methods for analysing the data you collect? Are these analytical methods likely to provide the conceptual and empirical evidence sufficient to provide an answer (or more likely several possible answers) to your question?

It may not always be possible to determine at the outset whether particular collection and analysis techniques are likely to provide the evidence needed to answer the research question. This is particularly the case in exploratory research. However, these points should all be considered, both when designing research and during the data collection process. The data collection phase offers opportunities to re-think the research question because data collection methods can sometimes unearth unexpected results. One of the reasons a research question may change is when an initial or 'pilot' phase of data collection provides data that are either inappropriate to answer the research question as it stands (or do not provide the evidence needed), or when a more fruitful avenue of investigation arises unexpectedly from the process of data collection itself.

In short, every phase of the research offers opportunities to reconsider, reformulate and refine the research question. Indeed, the formulation of the research question is *ongoing intellectual work*, a difficult and reiterative task that is continually revisited throughout the research process until the end of any given project. With continual practice, formulating and refining a research question becomes an important skill in the researcher's repertoire. It remains the case in every research project, however, that **question work** is sometimes only resolved when the question, and answers, come together at the end of the research process.

3.6 SUMMARY

This chapter has examined the process of devising and refining a social research question by examining just how important this task is in the context of the research process as a whole. The chapter began by considering the characteristics and qualities of a focused sociological research question, and indicated six criteria that might be used to assess whether any particular question posed is 'researchable'. The chapter went on to describe techniques and strategies in a four-step critical process of refining a research question from a general topic area, to a question that is both researchable, and answerable. The chapter considered the relationship between the formulation of a research question, and other elements of the research process such as research design, the literature review, and data collection and analysis. The chapter concluded by arguing that the crucial intellectual work of refining a research question is often only completed, and resolved, when, at the end of a project, the data derived from research provide answers to the questions posed.

DISCUSSION QUESTIONS

1   What are the desirable characteristics of researchable social research questions? Are any of these more important than the others? Why?

2   Why is it important to create a long list of possible research questions when you really want to narrow your choices?

3   What is the relationship between narrowing your research questions, and refining them?

4   What relationship do major and subsidiary questions bear to each other? What function does each type of question bear?

5   Why is it important to revisit the research question at each stage of the research process?

RESOURCES

Many sources for strategies and techniques with respect to formulating research questions are to be found in guides for dissertations and theses, at both undergraduate and graduate levels. O'Leary (2004) *The Essential Guide to Doing Research* provides a very useful and practical introductory text on 'doing' research, especially Chapter 3, 'Developing Your Research Question'.

Blaikie (2000) *Designing Social Research*, Chapter 3, 'Research Questions and Objectives' provides a slightly more advanced text, particularly considering the research question with respect to the logic of enquiry more generally.

Dixon, Bouma and Atkinson (1987) *A Handbook of Social Science Research*, Chapter 3, 'Selecting a Problem' is a useful starting point.

Walliman (2006) *Social Research Methods* on social research methods is a thorough introduction, considering the research problem with respect to the conditions of knowledge production (**epistemology** and **ontology**).

4 Searching and Reviewing the Literature

Mary Ebeling and Julie Gibbs

- Know what a literature review is and what purposes it serves in social science research.

- To understand how you will use a literature review in your dissertation or thesis.

- Know how to start searching for literature to include in your review.

- Understand the main databases and electronic resources for social science reviews.

- Know how to make notes and build up your references either on paper or with software.

- To be confident that you can stop your search after having covered the literature.

4.1 INTRODUCTION

In Chapter 3 on designing a research project, the stages of research were discussed – from choosing a **research question,** deciding upon the best method for your question, to more practical considerations such as respondent recruitment and planning a timetable. In this chapter, on searching and reviewing the literature, an essential component to the research process is discussed, considering both why a **literature review** is important to your research question and what the most effective methods for conducting a successful review are.

The literature review in the social sciences is an important foundation for your research project, as it will help to frame and strengthen your research question as well as help you to hone your searching and analytical skills. By writing a critical and thoughtful literature review, most importantly, you can demonstrate your knowledge of the research field and how your work fits into a larger picture.

4.2 LITERATURE REVIEWS: WHY AND HOW

Students new to the social sciences can feel some trepidation when facing the prospect of doing the literature review. 'What is the purpose of a literature review?' 'How do I write one?' 'Isn't it the most boring part of the research project?', 'I'm not sure what a literature review looks like' – these are all common questions and concerns before starting.

There are three fundamental reasons to write a literature review: (1) to learn as much as you can about your research topic; (2) to develop the searching and analytical skills necessary in a research project; and (3) to demonstrate this knowledge through a coherent and systematic text that helps to link what you have learned from previous research to what you are researching for your own project. A literature review is not simply an annotated bibliography or a series of summaries. A successful literature review is one where there is effective analysis and synthesis of previous work, one that is written with clarity and purpose, one that discusses significant controversies and challenges the researcher's own perspective.

In this chapter we will help you better understand the aims of the literature review, why it is important to your larger research question, where to start, and how to use reference resources to help you find research, and then we will provide some tips on how to write it.

4.2.1 THE AIMS OF THE LITERATURE REVIEW

Howard Becker advises students not to be 'terrorised by the literature' in his influential writing guide *Writing for Social Scientists* (1986: 186). Quite often, however, when faced with the enormity of the research field on a given subject, the prospect of writing a literature review can be daunting. However, if the literature review is understood as an opportunity rather than an onerous task, conducting and writing the review can be a very rewarding experience. It will help you learn the history of the research area that you are examining, guide you on how to think about the methods that you might use in your own research project and help you to contextualise and theorise your particular research question, through building on the works of others (Hart, 1999: 27). Seen in this way, the literature review is an opportunity for you not only to learn all that you can about your chosen research topic, but also to guide your research and to enable you to think and argue in a more sophisticated way about the subject.

Within the social sciences, the literature review serves many purposes: some goals are to demonstrate knowledge of the field, to explore controversies and to define new questions or areas for consideration. Generally, reviews of literature should achieve the following (ibid.: 27–8):

- Identify what has been achieved and what needs to be done in regards to the research area.

- Outline all the factors or variables impinging on the research question.

- Provide a contextual framework for the research question.

- Explain the methods or research processes used and their effectiveness in previous studies.

- Explore the relationships between the theories and the practices in the research field under study.

- Provide a rationale for the research question or problem under study.

- Demonstrate a deep knowledge of the history and breadth of the subject under study as well as how the intellectual field around it has developed.

- Display a knowledge and mastery of the field's vocabulary in discussing the research question.

4.2.2 WHAT IS AND IS NOT A LITERATURE REVIEW

When you think of a literature review, what first comes to your mind? Do you think of reviews published in the *London Review of Books* or your Sunday paper? A social science review of the literature serves a different purpose from a book review. In social science, the review systematically examines and synthesises previous studies and theories that have developed around a research question and helps you to build on existing knowledge and frame your research project.

The simplest definition of a literature review is that it is a piece of writing that is a systematic, critical evaluation and synthesis of existing scholarly works, studies, theories and current thinking on a given research subject or area. A review of this kind should be explicit in its **methodology**, that is, the way that decisions were made about which studies and scholarship were chosen for inclusion in the review should be explained within the review's **narrative** (Fink, 2004: 3). Good reviews are those that rely upon original, primary sources of research and studies rather than secondary sources or interpretations of original research. Sources for the literature review can come from books, journal articles, and study reports; any work that contains original research on your specific subject. Reviews are also a space where you can engage critically with the theories and arguments that have developed around your research subject. Argumentation is at the heart of most social sciences, because it helps to build knowledge and advance critical thinking within disciplines, and it is in your own review of the literature that you can interrogate these arguments to organise and frame your research (Hart, 1999: 79). Good reviews also are those that go beyond simply summarising previous research. By the end of your review of the literature, you should not only have identified the key concepts that will frame your research question, but also have teased out significant questions that are still unanswered or not considered by the literature and proposed how your research project might answer these questions. Your research might be able to suggest new directions for the field.

If it forms part of your dissertation or thesis, the purpose of your review is most likely to investigate several theories or concepts that have previously been developed on your research question, as well as allowing you as a researcher to engage with this body of scholarship (Hart, 2001: 7). Before you begin your literature review, however, you should, as far as possible, have refined your research question (see Chapter 3). Suppose that you would like to discover what factors determine marijuana use among 16–24-year-olds in suburban areas of South-East England. Through framing your question to be limited to a

Table 4.1 Areas of the literature review

LITERATURE REVIEW STRUCTURE	LITERATURE TYPE
Descriptions: What is cannabis? What effect does it have? What are you using as your definition of young people?	Books, journal articles, dictionaries and encyclopaedias
Statistics/evidence: What are the numbers of youth using cannabis? Where is the evidence that this is a topic worthy of research?	Reports and news articles
Theory: What are the main theories as to WHY young people use cannabis?	Books, journals, research reports
Methods: Are there special methods needed for the study? How have people studied this topic before?	Previous research articles

particular geographic area, age group and income bracket, you can begin to consider previous research that has focused on similar topics (Table 4.1). Once the limits and scope of your research question have been decided, they will help you to define the purpose of your literature review. Your defined research question will guide your review and will be the overall theme that will organise it. The aim of the review is not to exhaustively list all that has been written on your question, but to engage critically with a few theories and studies that will help to contextualise your own research. More importantly, however, a review of the literature helps you better understand the debates, controversies and current thinking in your research area.

4.2.3 TYPES OF REVIEWS

There are several types of scholarly reviews, however, the three types of literature reviews that are often relied upon in the social sciences (Petticrew and Roberts, 2006: 19) include:

- *systematic review*: this identifies and synthesises all relevant research on a specific topic. Often a systematic review appraises one hypothesis or links together a series of related hypotheses.

- *meta-analysis*: a quantitative review that uses statistical techniques to synthesise results into a single report.

- *narrative review*: a review that synthesises and assesses primary research into a single, descriptive account.

Systematic reviews tend to be narrowly focused, which are much less comprehensive than narrative reviews, and employ strict methods both in the selection of literature under review as well as how it is analysed. Meta-analytical reviews attempt to capture all of the findings from evidence-based, primary and current research on a particular topic and apply statistical analyses to the data in order to build an integrated, comprehensive picture of the subject under question. Meta-analytical reviews dramatically differ from narrative reviews, which are characterised by more of a qualitative analysis of previous research (Glass et al., 1981). Often meta-analytical reviews can be written as stand-alone articles or books, and although systematic and narrative reviews are also written in this way, they tend to be used to frame or explain new or continuing research or integrated into a larger text, such as a dissertation or thesis.

It is your research question as well as the purpose of your larger thesis or dissertation that will determine which of these types of literature review is most appropriate. If you are writing a literature review for your dissertation or thesis, it is likely that you will be writing a systematic review that may include elements from narrative review methods, in which you will be summarising, appraising and synthesising all the relevant studies and theories developed around your research topic, but it is best to consult with your advisor before selecting one of the three types.

You may find that as you review and synthesise the literature, your research question may change or at least be subtly altered as a result of uncovering new information and integrating it into your research framework. And you may find that the review of the literature is an ongoing process. Once you have completed your primary empirical research, you may have to search out literature in a different area that helps to frame and make sense of your own research findings. Which methodologies worked for other studies, which did not? Which findings were surprising to the researchers and which confirmed their hypotheses?

In all approaches to reviewing the literature, there is an underlying aim: to critique and build on existing social theories, to present a comprehensive overview of existing social scientific research on a given question, to synthesise primary research and studies to demonstrate where new studies can be conducted, or to justify why a particular new study should be undertaken based on previous research.

4.3 SEARCHING THE LITERATURE

Now you know why a literature review is so important to your project, what should you do next, how do you begin to search through the vast amount of sociological literature out there? Beginning a literature search is a bit like standing on a diving board at the swimming pool. How deep are you going to dive? What is at the bottom?

Starting to look at the search in a systematic way, thinking clearly about what you want to look at, what your search terms will be and where you are going to look, will help you to remain focused. Once the literature review is under way you may find that the same texts come up time and time again and you will begin to get a clear idea of the key sources of literature for your review.

TIP

Don't let yourself panic about getting started: the very act of starting, however tentative, will relieve anxiety. Just do it!

4.3.1 STARTING YOUR SEARCH

The first place to begin to look for literature is in your university library. Your project supervisor should discuss with you what you are going to look for and any key references that they know (remember, they are the experts). Try to discuss this with them before you begin.

Researching young people and their use of cannabis will lead us to explore and explain to the reader quite diverse areas, as shown in Table 4.1.

There will be different aspects to your literature review, each requiring different types of literature. If you start with descriptions, look in the library catalogue for specific key words (see below for search tips). It is good to start by looking at a dictionary to find the precise definition of the topic. You may also try typing the keyword into a **search engine** such as Google and exploring the online literature.

TIP

If you are looking for up-to-date statistical information it is better to look online. Ensure that you find a reputable source of information. Most countries have a statistical office which have current statistics on the population. Make sure that you keep a record of your search and the sites that you looked at.

4.3.2 RECORDING INFORMATION

It is worth thinking about how you are going to store and record your information before you begin your search, because you will then have consistent records that are easy to work with, rather than scraps of paper all over the desk. Making notes and keeping records is a matter we shall return to later in the chapter. Software such as the Endnote and Reference Manager programs can make the process of recording information, making notes and putting it all into a finished bibliography easier. These programs are generally free to students through their institution.

The difference between Endnote and Reference Manager is a matter of personal preference. In both programs, you create libraries for your project, adding a record for each book, article or online resource you look at. You can also store your notes in these records. Both programs allow you to 'cite as you write' in Microsoft Word and this can be very helpful and save time.

You can also use Microsoft Word or Excel to keep your notes and records in order. It is worth remembering to back up your work onto another disk, CD or hard drive to avoid pain if the work is lost.

Of course some people do not like to use IT and prefer paper records. There are two main options: a card system or notepads. The key for paper records is to be consistent in your note-taking, making sure you have the same information for each book, article or other resource that you have found. There is more on this later in the chapter.

4.4 RESOURCES FOR SEARCHING

4.4.1 THE LIBRARY

Most university libraries use a classification system called the **Dewey Decimal Classification System**. Each subject will have its own reference number, for example, Sociology books always have the classification number 301 (see Hart, 2001: 166, for the classification numbers of all subjects). By the time you are doing your dissertation, you should be well versed in the way that your institutional library works.

Once you have located an area where there are books on your topic, look at the other books in that area. When you find a relevant text, look at the bibliography and note or copy it to find key authors. Once you have a few books on the topic, you may find that you see the same names repeatedly in the reference lists. Go back to the catalogue and try to find a book by the author who is being cited. Looking at original work where possible is better than quoting from secondary sources. At this stage you will only be skim reading the books, looking for keywords. If there is a substantial amount of material in that book on your topic, keep it to read later on.

The university library may not be sufficient for your needs. If you are undertaking doctoral research, then you may need to go and find a more specialised library. Large charities often have their own research libraries. For example, Drug Scope has its own excellent library on drug research. You can often visit these libraries by prior arrangement, sometimes for a fee. You will not be able to take the books out of the library, so bear in mind that you may either have to stay and write copious notes or spend money photocopying articles to read later. These libraries are sometimes the only place where you can read specialised or rare texts.

You can search the catalogues of other libraries to see if they contain books that will be useful. Online Public Access Catalogues (**OPAC**) are free library catalogues that are available online. One example is the OPAC of the British Library, which has 12 million references fully searchable online (http://catalogue.bl.uk) and Copac is another (http://www.copac.ac.uk).

Most libraries in universities provide online access to a large number of journals where you can search for articles and download them in PDF format for free. Some specialised journals will charge a small amount for their articles. There is often a key journal for the area that you are studying and your supervisor should be able to advise you of this. If you are not aware of a specialist journal, try searching the large databases detailed below first to see what journals come up most often in your search.

4.4.2 DATABASES

There are a number of databases that contain bibliographic records of social science literature. Normally these are listed and accessed through your library web pages. The four large databases for social sciences are the International Bibliography for the Social Sciences, Ingenta Connect, Copac and the Web of Knowledge.

Before using any of these databases, you will need to register with them. In the UK, this is done through a system known as Athens registration. Athens is a secure way of gaining access to a large number of academic and educational resources that you would otherwise have to pay to use. Once you have found records of interesting articles in the databases discussed below and have logged on as an Athens user, there will be a link to the journal from which you will be able to download a PDF of the article and print it, without the hassle of leaving your desk and finding it in the library. You can find further details about Athens and a list of the institutions and contacts who use Athens at http://www.athens.ac.uk/. In most cases you log on to Athens via your library web pages which will have a link to electronic resources. Each of the resources listed below will be available as a link from your library.

Because online resources change frequently, going into detail about them is not feasible in a text book. If you get stuck using these resources, the best advice is to speak to a librarian or to use the help field on that resource.

- The International Bibliography for the Social Sciences (IBSS) is maintained at the London School of Economics and Political Science. It has over two million bibliographic references, focusing on the topics of anthropology, economics, politics and sociology. The references may be books, journal articles, and reviews dating back to 1951, including the regular indexing of over 2,500 social science journals (IBSS Quick Tips 2006). IBSS has a useful Getting Started section with tips on getting the best out of the database and this is a good starting point for your search.

- IngentaConnect is another large database that covers around 30,000 publications. However, IngentaConnect is more general than IBSS and so not all the publications are related to social science.

- Copac differs from the above databases. It is a library catalogue from merged sources where you can access the merged online catalogues of 24 major university research libraries in the UK and Ireland as well as the British Library, the National Library of Scotland, and the National Library of Wales/Llyfrgell Genedlaethol Cymru. Copac is useful if you are unable to locate a specific book or report and want to get an interlibrary loan.

- The ISI Web of Knowledge includes the Social Science Citation Index. This index can help you to find articles and other materials that have been cited by other publications. You can do a general search to find articles, or search specifically for articles which have cited a specific author. So, if you find a key text which comes up a lot in your search, you could do a citation search on that author to see who else is writing in that area.

A citation is simply a reference to another person's work. Academics use citations from other authors' work to back up an argument or to make a point. Citation Indexes such as the Web of Knowledge involve the searcher looking for an author. Results will show other published articles that have referenced that author in some way. This is very useful when you have found a key text and want to know who else has used that text and this often yields further references for your review.

TIP

Find your key texts before using the citation search on the ISI Web of Knowledge and use it to gather further material for your review.

4.4.3 SEARCH ENGINES

Using a basic search engine may seem like the fastest way to begin your literature search, but there are pitfalls to this approach that need careful consideration. Google is the most popular search engine and it can be very helpful. However,

Google can yield hundreds, thousands or even millions of hits for one search term, and that is clearly not a practical start to your literature search!

Search engines such as Google, Yahoo or Ask use 'robots' or 'spiders', that go out and search the text of web pages, in order to build the databases that you search. This means that the 'hits' that are at the top of the list are there for a number of reasons related to the engine's way of ranking pages, and it does not necessarily follow that those pages are good, reliable sources of information. Be aware when searching on the internet that there are many bogus or unreliable sites that you would not want to use in your academic work.

Having warned you of the pitfalls, it is important to say that these large search engines can be very helpful if you have found a source through reading or mentioned by your supervisor and you want to locate it. This may be at a point later in your reviewing when you have found your main literature using other means.

Searching databases or search engines can be a lot easier if you understand the way that they function. Most search facilities use Boolean logic, which allows three types of basic search 'AND', 'OR' and 'NOT'. Hart (1999) includes a discussion of Boolean logic searching.

In this chapter we have used the example of young people and marijuana in suburban locations in South-East England. To begin a search for a literature review on this subject, you might start with a list of the four main databases above. You should write down the search terms that you are going to use and be consistent in each search that you do. You might start with the following search terms and use each one once in each database:

Young people AND marijuana OR cannabis OR dope
Young people AND drugs AND South-East England
Young people AND drugs in suburbia

You may find that you are getting a number of hits that are not useful, for example, you may find records for articles about the treatment of long-term drug use which you are not especially interested in. To deal with this, you could run the search again with an additional NOT criterion:

Young people AND marijuana OR cannabis OR dope NOT treatment

Once you have a results list for each of your search terms, look carefully through them and discard any that do not look useful. The rest can be saved, usually by ticking a box next to the result and clicking on a 'save' or 'email' icon on the database page. You can then get the results e-mailed to you for future reference. At this stage, you are just gathering information and should not yet locate each reference. Using this method you will quickly find the key texts in the subject area, and the key experts who are writing in the field.

4.4.4 OTHER RESOURCES

There may be other resources that are important for your topic. For the example of cannabis use among young people, it is useful to think of other sources of information that can provide evidence for your research. These other resources generally fall into three areas:

1   *Official statistics*: Official statistics can be helpful in providing basic evidence of the importance of your research and can provide a sound start to the literature review. Most countries have their own statistical organisations: for example, in the UK, the Office for National Statistics and in the USA, FedStats. It is also worth visiting the web pages for the Government Department relevant to your research area, where you can often find and download official publications.

2   *Charities or specialist organisations*: There are often key charities or organisations working in the area that have a range of information and publications on their web pages. Large charities also often have libraries which researchers can visit for a small fee which contain rare books and articles.

3   *Other ad hoc resources*: Sometimes you will find other web resources which do not fall into the above two categories, such as the site of a particular research group or the web site of people interested in the topic. Be wary of the quality of these resources. A general guide to evaluating web resources can be found on INTUTE: http://www.vts.intute.ac.uk/

4.5 WHAT TO DO WITH THE INFORMATION

By this point you will have a large pile of books from the library, a list of key journals in the area and a number of saved searches from the databases. What do you do now?

4.5.1 WRITING NOTES

Often the best way forward is to pick up the first book or article that comes to hand and begin to skim read to find if it is useful. If you think it will be a key text, resist the urge to read it all and just make a note of its importance. Use whatever method of note-taking that works for you, i.e. a computer file or a simple notepad. Ensure that you are being consistent in your notes. Start each with the author's full name, the title, the date of the publication, where it was published, the ISBN number if applicable and the pages that you have read or you think will be useful later on. An example of a record card is shown in Figure 4.1.

Figure 4.1   Example of a note on a record card

Date: 01/01/01

Book Ref: Hart, C (2001) Doing a Literature Search, Sage, London

Found: In University Library, classification number: 025.524/HAR (only one copy)

Overview: Has chapters on the purposes of the literature review and search management. Useful following chapters on reference materials and searching for specific literature including using the internet, (although the book is slightly dated now so this may be of limited use). Also has very useful appendix on Dewey classifications and how to cite.

Keywords: Classification, searching, internet search.

This may sound tedious but when you are in a panic because your dissertation is due in tomorrow and you can't find a reference, you will be very grateful you made these notes now! You will notice in your skim reading if certain authors are coming up again and again, or if a specific article is being referenced frequently. It is probably worth going back to the databases or library to find these often cited articles. You should always try to get hold of the original of a work rather than quote from a secondary resource.

It may also be helpful to develop a list of keywords attached to your notes, such as 'cannabis', 'young people', 'dope', 'suburbs', 'methodology', and so on, to help you categorise when you come to write the review. If you are using one of the bibliographic software packages described above, there are fields for all of these notes and references built in.

Once you have reviewed all of the information you obtained in your searches, you can start to read those articles and books you noted as being of key importance. These notes will be much more detailed with quotes and the beginnings of ideas for the arguments to be included in your literature review.

TIP

Remember to note the page numbers of every quote and important point as this will save time later on.

4.5.2 BIBLIOGRAPHIES AND CITATIONS

The importance of your bibliography and the way you cite published works should never be underestimated. Supervisors and examiners will look closely at all your references for signs of plagiarism, so it is vital that every quote or argument throughout your project is properly referenced. When you use a reference for the first time, go to the end of the document and put the reference in. When you have finished, print the bibliography and go through your chapter, ticking off each reference as you read to ensure that they are all there.

Generally, social scientists use the following style of citation:

Books
Name (date) *Title*. Place of publication: Publisher.

For example:
Hart, Chris (2001) *Doing a Literature Search*. London: Sage Publishers.

Journals
Name (date) 'Article title', *Journal Title*, Journal edition (Issue): page numbers, date of publication, and if applicable the URL and date accessed.

For example:
Taylor, Nichola Jane and Kearney, Jackie (2005) 'Researching Hard to Reach Populations: Privileged Access Interviewers and Drug Using Parents', *Sociological Research Online* Volume 10, Issue 2. Available online: http://tinyurl.com/ytxu7w Accessed March 2007.

Online references
Name of web pages. Date if known. Author if known. Name of site URL. Date accessed

For example:
Cannabis (2002) Author Unknown, DrugScope, URL: http://tinyurl.com/2vu2oa Accessed March 2007

Citation style can vary between academic institutions so check your dissertation handbook or with your supervisor to make sure you are using the right style. Hart (2001) has a useful section on citations.

Throughout this chapter the importance of keeping good records has been emphasised. Records should be kept in good order so that if you have problems later on with, say, a supervisor asking to see your notes you will be able to produce them. Plagiarism is a major problem in academic settings and the best way to protect yourself is to keep clear consistent records of your reading. Do not throw your notes away as soon as the project is handed in!

Structuring your review: researching drug use among 16–24-year-olds

This is a synopsis of an actual literature review project for an undergraduate dissertation on Young People and Drugs in the Community. You can see the structure of the chapter with the official statistical evidence outlined first followed by the more theoretical arguments as to why young people use drugs and the effect that this may have on the community. This is how a draft of the literature review should be drawn up with the actual notes and data filled in later on.

Introduction
General statement as to why this review is important and what it will encompass. Definitions of terms to be used, e.g., how are you defining 'young people'.

Statistics
A review of young people and drug use. Identifying trends over the past 10 years. Use statistics from official publications, Government papers. Critique of these statistics, for example, official police statistics do not include all drug use just that identified by the authorities. What other statistics can be used? How do they help us to explain drug use?

Surveys of drug use
School surveys of drug use. What do they find? What information can we glean from them?

Regional use
We are focusing on drug use in the regions of the UK here, especially in our ongoing example of South-East England. We must demonstrate in the review that the regional differences (if there are any) in drug use have been explored. This will use official statistics and survey data as above.

Explanations for young people's drug use
This is the more theoretical part of the review which looks at theories as to why drug use is so high among young people. You should be using the key texts that you have found here from books and journal articles.

Government strategy
A look at what the government is planning on doing to control young people's use of drugs and the main targets that have been set.

Summary
Brief conclusion of the evidence reviewed in the chapter.

TIP

Remember to write your bibliography as you go along if you are not using a software package that will generate it automatically.

4.6 ENOUGH IS ENOUGH! KNOWING WHEN TO STOP

Knowing when to stop reading and looking for references can be difficult, because one always feels that an important reference has been missed. If you have completed a systematic review as outlined in this chapter and have read the key texts in the field, it is likely that you have found the books, articles and experts in the area. Once the fieldwork is finished, you are happy with the research question, and you have systematically searched the literature for each topic, you can be confident that you can stop.

4.7 SUMMARY

In this chapter, we have explored the purposes and goals that the research literature review serves in the social sciences and some methods for conducting a successful review. A good literature review examines previous research and theories on a particular research subject and systematically analyses and synthesises this work. The second part of the chapter has shown how to carry out a systematic search of the literature and how to make notes and keep a record. The example on p. 76 shows how all of this information might be brought together to structure the review.

CHECKLIST

- Do you know where the books are in the library for the subject you are looking for?

- Have you asked your advisor for their opinion on the key texts in the subject?

- Have you identified keywords for your database search?

- Do you have access to an Athens username and password through your institutional library?

- Have you thought about record keeping?

- Identify which system you will use for notes and referencing, for example, software or paper.

- Are there other organisations or charities with libraries on your topic?

- Are you sure that the web references you are using are reliable and trustworthy?

- Do you know the exact citation style for your department?

DISCUSSION QUESTIONS

1   What is the main purpose of the literature review in the social sciences?

2   How should you go about starting a systematic review?

3   What are the main resources that you could use to demonstrate knowledge of the field?

4   What are the main differences between the major databases that you might use for your research?

RESOURCES

Becker (1986) *Writing for Social Scientists* is a classic writing guide for the social sciences, Becker reassures readers on the challenges and fears faced by students embarking on dissertation or thesis writing projects by providing practical hints and sharing stories of his own uphill battles with writing.

Fink (2004) *Conducting Research Literature Reviews: From the Internet to Paper* is a very clear and concise how-to guide to searching for and reviewing literature in the social sciences.

Hart (1999) *Doing a Literature Review: Releasing the Social Science Research Imagination*, and Hart (2001) *Doing a Literature Search*. Both books serve as complements to one another and are extensive and comprehensive guides to writing literature reviews. Hart targets both books for postgraduates in the social sciences and the guides are sympathetic to the many questions and concerns students have when approaching large writing projects.

The following web pages are useful:

International Bibliography of the Social Sciences: http://www.ibss.ac.uk

Copac: http://www.copac.ac.uk

Web of Knowledge: http://wok.mimas.ac.uk/

IngentaConnect: http://www.ingentaconnect.com

DrugScope: http://www.drugscope.org.uk

5 Grounded Theory and Inductive Research

Paul Hodkinson

KEY POINTS

- Instead of testing pre-formed hypotheses, inductive researchers attempt to develop new theory from their empirical observations of the social world.

- Grounded theory provides a detailed set of procedures for the inductive development of theory, including theoretical sampling, coding and constant comparison.

- There is considerable debate among different proponents of grounded theory and also between such proponents and critics of the approach.

- Many qualitative researchers use some features associated with grounded theory without adopting the approach in its entirety.

5.1 INTRODUCTION

This chapter focuses upon the principles and procedures associated with grounded theory, which has become the best-known approach to inductive social research. Having distinguished between inductive and deductive approaches to the development of theory through research in a general sense, the chapter goes on to outline the key features of grounded theory, including the notions of theoretical sampling, coding, constant comparison, and theoretical saturation. The focus is partly on providing practical information and examples on how to carry out grounded theory research but also on understanding the justifications and arguments offered by proponents for adopting this approach. Having set out such procedures and arguments, we will examine some of the criticisms which have been levelled against grounded theory. It is suggested that, although highly influential, grounded theory is not very often followed to the letter and that – for better or worse – it is more common for researchers to adopt selected features of the approach as part of their efforts to develop theory through research.

5.2 INTEGRATING THEORY AND RESEARCH

Ultimately, the purpose of most social research is to generate empirical data that can be used to inform the development of general theories about the way society works. It is hoped that collection and analysis of data will enable a researcher to do considerably more than merely provide some interesting description of elements of the lives of a particular sample of respondents. Rather, through focusing analytically on particular themes, patterns or processes in our data, we attempt to infer conclusions about social relationships, processes or causalities that have a broader significance.

For example, having conducted extensive observation and analysis of the behaviour and attitudes of working-class school pupils in central England, Willis (1977) did not content himself with describing the specifics of the lives of these individuals. His identification of patterns and themes in the data enabled a broader analytical contribution to theoretical debates about youth culture, educational achievement, labour markets, social class and broader power relations. To take another well-known example, Goldthorpe and colleagues' (1968) collection and examination of data relating to the lifestyle and orientation of a particular sample of 'affluent workers' was used as the basis for broad conclusions about whether or not fundamental changes were taking place to the class structure of UK society.

While social research is nearly always linked to the development of theory, the precise nature of this relationship varies significantly depending upon the approach taken. Positivist approaches have often centred on **deductive** styles of reasoning similar to those which predominate within the natural sciences. As outlined in Chapter 2, deductive research starts with the development of a **hypothesis** by the researcher on the basis of existing theory. Subsequently a research project is carefully designed to enable empirical corroboration or **falsification** of that hypothesis. Goldthorpe and colleagues' study of affluent workers broadly fits with the deductive model, having been designed to test, in the UK context, theories of embourgeoisement that had been developed by US sociologists. As a result of their focus on testing a particular hypothesis, deductive studies tend to be tightly planned in advance and often are dominated by pre-structured methods such as surveys or standardised interviews. The practicalities of deductive research approaches are discussed at various points in this book (see Chapters 9, 10, 11, 17, 18 and 19).

This chapter, however, is about **inductive** approaches to the relationship between theory and research. Instead of designing research to test preconceived hypotheses, inductive researchers attempt to take empirical social phenomena as their starting point and seek through the process of research and analysis to generate broader theories about social life. The idea is that studies should begin in an open-ended and exploratory fashion, becoming more focused on particular themes and perspectives as the research and analysis develop. And although in principle the notion of inductive research does not exclude quantitative methods, in practice, the flexibility of qualitative approaches such as observation and in-depth interviews means that these are particularly suited to such an exploratory overall approach to research.

Of our previous examples, Willis' *Learning to Labour* study comes closer than Goldthorpe et al.'s work to this exploratory style of research, having used relatively open-ended participant observation and interviews to explore issues of class, culture and education and having elaborated theoretical themes as the project continued. To take a lower profile and more recent example, my own study of young people involved in goth culture involved no initial hypothesis and utilised a similarly open-ended ethnographic methodology, pursuing issues I regarded as theoretically important or interesting in a more focused fashion as the research project progressed (Hodkinson, 2002). Yet, crucially, the notion of inductive research in its strictest sense implies more than merely an unstructured, exploratory approach to research such as that taken by Willis or indeed by me, and for this reason it is questionable whether either study should be labelled inductive.

The most important practical implications of pure induction are that investigators should seek to avoid or neutralise theoretical preconceptions and that explanations should be based exclusively upon a dispassionate analysis of data. Indeed, those who favour inductive approaches often have justified their preference by criticising what they regard as the overly predetermined nature of deductive research. From their point of view, theories should be allowed to emerge from data rather than the other way around. In this sense, inductive researchers assert – or at least imply – that, through minimising the influence of preconceptions, their approach leads to explanations which are superior to those emanating from deductive research in terms of their level of fit with the realities of the social world. The best-known and influential elaboration of how social researchers might achieve the inductive development of theory in practice is provided by Glaser and Strauss' grounded theory approach.

5.3 GROUNDED THEORY

The notion of grounded theory is often taken to refer to theoretical explanations about the social world that emerge from empirical data. Before applying this label to a research project, however, you should be aware that grounded theory entails a specific set of procedures and strategies for the achievement of such empirically embedded forms of understanding. The tendency for dissertation and research students to claim the use of grounded theory in their **methodology** chapters, without any detail or reflection on the way in which they used these procedures and strategies, does not go down at all well with examiners!

> TIP
>
> When describing your methodology, provide detail and reflection on the approach you took to the collection and analysis of data – don't use a label like grounded theory without elaborating.

The approach was developed by Barney Glaser and Anselm Strauss (1967), who wanted to challenge two features of social science in the 1960s. First was a preoccupation with the use of a relatively small number of 'grand theories', such as those of Marx, Durkheim and Weber, as well as theorists more recent to their time of writing such as Parsons and Merton. Rather than being encouraged inductively to develop their own research-driven theories, students were being trained, it was argued, to 'master great-man theories and test them in small ways' (ibid.: 10). And this connects to the second feature which Glaser and Strauss found problematic: that the discipline was increasingly dominated by deductive and quantitative methodologies oriented to the verification of existing theory. In a climate favouring scientific principles, inductive and qualitative approaches were being dismissed as unsystematic and unreliable. According to Glaser and Strauss, qualitative research was in danger of becoming little more than a preliminary stage in the development of deductive surveys (ibid.).

Grounded theory represented an attempt to contest the domination of social science by grand theory and deduction and to encourage researchers to generate their own new theories from empirical data. Glaser and Strauss outlined a rigorous series of procedures for carrying out such inductive, theory-generating research. This emphasis on method was contrasted by Glaser and Strauss with previous qualitative approaches deemed either to have been rich in their data but insufficiently theoretical (as in the case of some Chicago School studies) or, alternatively, characterised by the development of 'impressionistic' theory based on a 'non-systematic and non-rigorous' use of data (ibid.: 15). By setting out clear procedures for inductive research, Glaser and Strauss sought to enable grounded theorists to contest the exclusive claims to scientific legitimacy of deductivism.

Explanations of grounded theory can often be found within books or courses dealing specifically with approaches to data analysis. In fact, the approach has implications right from the start of the research process. Notably, the underlying expectation – that theoretical preconceptions should be avoided in order to allow theory to emerge from data – has implications for the design of research questions, for the process of sampling, for the form taken by interview schedules, for strategies of observation and for the structure of the overall research plan. It also implies that the literature review – which often is regarded as the first stage of a research project – should be delayed until a much later stage (Charmaz, 1994: 47). Meanwhile, in contrast to research models characterised by distinct and separate phases of data collection and analysis, the adoption of a grounded theory approach implies an ongoing iterative process in which an initial period of analysis may precede further more focused data collection and so on. Let us have a look at this aspect in greater detail.

5.3.1 COLLECTING DATA AND THEORETICAL SAMPLING

In grounded theory, the process of data collection runs alongside that of analysis and becomes gradually more focused as the project progresses.

Initially data should be collected in a relatively open and non-prescriptive manner. The researcher may have some general interests or motivations for studying the group, institution or subject-matter and methods will inevitably be oriented towards these, but the imposition of a 'preconceived theoretical framework' should be avoided at all costs (Glaser and Strauss, 1967: 45). It is for this reason that flexible qualitative methods that maximise the potential for exploration are more suited to the grounded theory approach than rigidly structured interviews or surveys, which predetermine the agenda.

Rather than completing the entire process of data collection prior to starting a discrete 'analysis stage', the examination of data may begin as soon as the first set of transcripts or **fieldnotes** are available. The initial outcomes of this preliminary analysis will then feed back into further data collection oriented to the exploration of particular themes or hunches. At this stage, the process of data collection shifts from its initial exploratory focus towards something deliberately designed to investigate emerging theoretical concepts or possibilities. The object of such theoretical sampling is to access further instances of themes identified in the initial data. Any new instances should be compared and contrasted with existing examples in order to enable these themes to be explored and elaborated fully.

Let's look at a simple hypothetical example of theoretical sampling. As part of an interview-based study of young people's involvement in music or fashion subcultures, your analysis gradually begins to suggest that your respondents' involvement in school peer groups seems to be an important factor in the data. Specifically, negative experiences in school peer groups appear to be a significant feature in the accounts of some subcultural participants. You have identified and analysed every instance of this theme in your existing data, but need to investigate further. According to Glaser and Strauss, you should do this by going back into the field and recruiting further respondents in a theoretically targeted manner – or in other words, by employing a theoretical sampling approach. For example, you may deliberately seek out and interview members of music or style subcultures who had a particularly unpleasant set of social experiences at school, or alternatively you may deliberately seek a group of respondents with highly contrasting school experiences. In neither case would we expect such a sample to be representative, but this is not the intention of theoretical sampling. What such targeted sampling would enable is the concentrated exploration and elaboration of a factor identified in earlier data analysis.

In particular, Glaser and Strauss emphasise that theoretical sampling may be used in order to compare themes across different types of individuals and

Figure 5.1   Simplified illustration of interplay between analysis and data collection

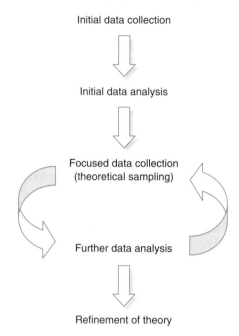

Initial data collection

Initial data analysis

Focused data collection
(theoretical sampling)

Further data analysis

Refinement of theory

groups. Researchers should therefore ask, 'What groups or subgroups does one turn to next in data collection? And for what theoretical purpose?' (1967: 47). In some respects, the emphasis on further exploration of theoretical hunches may be taken to imply the introduction of a deductive element into grounded theory – that is, an element which is focused upon the testing of a hypothesis developed during a previous stage of the project. Yet, the purpose of ongoing data collection in grounded theory is not simply to provide additional cases relating to elements of the theory that have already been demonstrated, but rather to develop the theory further by identifying and comparing cases which illustrate new variations.

After this theoretically focused data collection has taken place, the researcher should conduct further analysis, which may lead to yet more tightly focused collection and so on (see Figure 5.1). After the initial data collection phase, then, the processes of collection and analysis are closely entwined throughout the study. It is therefore neither possible nor desirable to plan all the details of grounded theory studies in advance. As Glaser and Strauss put it:

> Beyond the decisions concerning initial collection of data, further collection cannot be planned in advance of the emerging theory ... The emerging theory points to the next steps – the sociologist does not know them until he is guided by emerging gaps in his theory and by research questions suggested by previous answers. (ibid.: 47)

At first glance, such a lack of forward planning may seem to imply a disorganised or ad hoc approach whereby research decisions are selected on the basis of the most arbitrary of judgements. Yet such lack of systemisation is precisely what grounded theory seeks to avoid. The development of theory in Glaser and Strauss' formulation – from the first hunch to the final explanation – involves a rigorous and precise set of procedures for the analysis of data, centred upon coding and constant comparison.

5.3.2 ANALYSING DATA: CODING AND CONSTANT COMPARISON

One of the best-known and influential features of the grounded theory approach is its emphasis on the importance of the **coding** as its primary method of analysis. Coding refers to the ongoing process of assigning conceptual labels to different segments of data in order to identify themes, patterns, processes and relationships. Codes should be assigned by asking questions of the data such as 'Of which category is the item before me an instance?' or 'What can we think of this as being about?' and appropriate labels developed accordingly (Lofland and Lofland, 1995: 186). For an example of how this process might work, see Box below. Coding may be done by writing codes in the margin of fieldnotes or interview transcripts or through the use of note cards, but many contemporary researchers find that the process is made easier and more efficient through the use of Computer Aided Qualitative Data Analysis Software (see Fielding and Lee, 1998, and Chapter 20 in this volume).

The idea is that, in the initial stages of analysis, codes should be detailed, specific and numerous, but that as the integrated processes of data collection and analysis continue, these initial codes should be combined into larger, more generalised, categories, whose properties and relationship to one another will provide the beginnings of a theoretical explanation of the data. If the procedures are followed properly, this careful building of theory 'from the ground up' (Charmaz, 1994: 37) ensures that eventual conclusions emerge from and are traceable back to the data. According to Charmaz, this systematic building approach helps to avoid 'theoretical flights of fancy' and protects against excessive imposition by the researcher of their own personal motives and prejudices (ibid.).

Illustration of initial coding

To illustrate how the initial process of coding might work, I have coded a very short section of data from my research on the goth scene. Note the number of different categories and sub-categories generated by this short extract. You may even be able to suggest further categories beyond those I decided to settle upon.

(Continued)

Also note that, with the possible exception of the first, the categories are fairly specific and not especially abstract or conceptual. At this stage, they should remain fairly close to the actual content of the data. As the coding process continues and the researcher collects, examines, codes and compares more and more data, such rough, specific categories should gradually be refined and, eventually, reduced into a smaller number of broader concepts. For example, depending upon the data, my initial code, 'frustration at physical isolation' eventually might be broadened into a more general concept, such as 'subcultural isolation' which may act as an umbrella concept encapsulating various types of isolation and various emotional responses to it. Similarly, 'awareness of information without co-presence' may form a starting point for a broader code relating to subcultural communication processes, including different sorts of information and different channels through which it travels.

Coding	Interview data

Identification with goth 'crowd'
Frustration at physical isolation
  – size of conurbation
  – distance
Desire for co-present participation
  – public/social music consumption
  – socialising/hanging out
Awareness of information
without co-presence
	Well, in small towns and villages there tends to be no goth scene to be involved in. Being able to hang out with your crowd, listening to a goth band or at a goth disco without having to travel hundreds of miles has to be better than knowing what's going on but not being able to participate.

The precise procedures for the coding process and the terminology used for the different stages varies somewhat between different accounts of grounded theory. In Glaser and Strauss' original formulation the process begins with the researcher studying interview transcripts and/or field-notes line-by-line, assigning new codes every time a new theme emerges in the data and also reassigning existing codes wherever they reoccur. At the same time, through comparing each new instance within a category with all the previous instances, the researcher is able to build up their understanding of the properties of the category. Glaser and Strauss explain this use of constant comparison in the following way:

> The constant comparison of incidents very soon starts to generate theoretical properties of the category. The analyst starts thinking of the full range of types of continua of the category, its dimensions, the conditions under which it is pronounced or minimised, its major consequences, its relationship with other categories, and its other properties. (1967: 106)

Importantly, the process of constantly comparing instances within and across categories and defining the properties of categories often involves not just the coding of existing data but, where appropriate, the targeted collection and coding of new data through theoretical sampling, as set out in section 5.3.1. The process of coding and comparing should also be accompanied by the ongoing writing of memos, which simply means the creation of notes to oneself that are connected to particular sections of data or categories and that express ideas or hunches about properties, dimensions, comparisons and contrasts in the data. Far from being optional, the recording in this way of even the most transitory of thoughts should be regarded as crucial to the process.

TIP

Whether or not you are using a full grounded theory approach, the recording of hunches, ideas and possibilities via memos should be regarded as an invaluable tool in making sense of data.

Although this initial coding process is liable to be time-consuming, it is not necessary to code every single instance of a given category. New instances should only be coded if they demonstrate something different to the previous instances, since it is only through doing this that they contribute to the development of theory. If an instance merely replicates a feature already identified, then 'it only adds bulk to the coded data and nothing to the theory' (ibid.: 111). Eventually there will come a point when there are no further instances that add anything new to a category, at which point the category should be regarded as theoretically saturated. If it is felt, having gone through all the data, that **theoretical saturation** may not have been achieved, the researcher should consider further data collection through theoretical sampling.

As this process of coding, assigning, comparing and memo writing continues and the categories are further refined and elaborated, an *integration* of categories should gradually start to take place, whereby their relationships with one another begin to be accounted for in a theoretical manner. In other words, they gradually cease to be separate labels and become part of an integrated explanation. A further part of this process is that of the *reduction* of the large number of highly specific categories into a smaller number of broader, more overtly theoretical concepts. In other words, categories which all share a particular property or all illustrate a broader process or theme may be brought together as different instances of the same essential tendency. For example, as part of their study of terminally ill patients, Glaser and Strauss individually coded various different strategies used by nurses to maintain their professional composure when dealing with the social loss of dying patients. These different categories were eventually brought together under

Figure 5.2   Simplified illustration of how Glaser and Strauss' (1967) grounded theory process might work

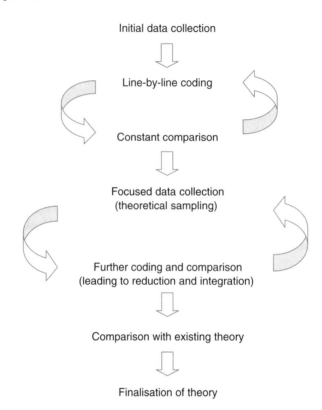

Initial data collection

Line-by-line coding

Constant comparison

Focused data collection
(theoretical sampling)

Further coding and comparison
(leading to reduction and integration)

Comparison with existing theory

Finalisation of theory

the broader theoretical concept of 'loss rationales', all of which constituted means by which nurses reassured themselves that the social loss caused by the death of patients might be preferable to the social worthlessness the patients would endure if they were to continue to live in a restricted, dependent or painful state.

It is only at this late stage, when categories have been significantly reduced and integrated, that the researcher should begin to compare the concepts and emerging theories with existing literature. Delaying the use of literature until this point is intended to ensure that existing theory is consulted and used in a manner that fits in with the patterns and processes already independently identified in the data. With reference to previous literature as well as continuing development and definition of concepts, the theory should gradually be taken to a further level of abstraction and generality where appropriate. Here Glaser and Strauss give the example of their generalisation of the notion of nurses' 'loss rationales' about dying patients into a broader means of explaining the strategy of *all* hospital staff, dealing with *all* patients. Furthermore, these value judgements on the part of staff are directly connected by the authors to another set of codes concerning decision-making processes about the allocation of care to patients. Thus it is theorised that decisions about the quantity and type of care provided to patients are closely related to judgements made by staff about social loss (Glaser and Strauss, 1967).

5.3.3 ELABORATIONS ON GLASER AND STRAUSS' MODEL

To some, Glaser and Strauss' original formulation of grounded theory may seem systematic and prescriptive. Yet the subsequent writings of Strauss and Corbin elaborate a considerably more detailed and technical set of practical guidelines for the carrying out of the process of theory generation, involving a plethora of precisely outlined procedures and techniques. There is not space in this chapter to deal with all of these, but the most noticeable development is perhaps the division of the coding process into 'open', 'axial' and 'selective' forms of coding, each of which is elaborated into a series of practical guidelines.

Open coding broadly translates to the first stages of coding in Glaser and Strauss' original account, whereby 'data are broken down into parts, closely examined and compared for similarities and differences' (Strauss and Corbin, 1998: 102). Emphasis is placed on the need to code each line of data with as many classifications as possible. As the process of constant comparison continues, such initial *concepts* should gradually be refined and reduced into broader, more meaningful categories.

If open coding involves the breaking up of data, **axial coding** represents the process of putting things back together again, through elaboration of the ways in which categories and sub-categories 'cross-cut and link' (ibid.: 124). Each category is treated as the 'axis' for its own set of related sub-categories and it is the nature of these relationships with which axial coding is concerned. A detailed coding *paradigm*, intended to act as a guide to the axial coding process, is prescribed by the authors.

Selective coding should happen towards the end of the process of analysis. The researcher elaborates the relationships between the most significant categories in order to develop broader theoretical conclusions. A *central category* should be identified, one which links together all the other major categories and which provides the basis for an overall integrated explanation of the research findings. The relationships between the central category and the other main categories should then be subject to a detailed process of elaboration and an overall theory devised and refined.

Strauss and Corbin's elaborations are not universally accepted by other grounded theorists. For example, others prefer to think in terms of just two types of coding: initial coding which equates to Strauss and Corbin's open coding, and focused coding, which encapsulates the process whereby codes are reduced, elaborated and developed into theory (Charmaz, 1983; Lofland and Lofland, 1995). More significantly, Glaser is strongly critical of Strauss and Corbin's account, arguing that the procedures outlined are so prescriptive and specific that they are liable to 'force' the researcher into focusing on certain themes and to prevent the inductive emergence of theory. Glaser's strongly worded critique accuses Strauss and Corbin's work not only of misconceptions, but also of immorality, betrayal and distortion (Glaser, 1992). It is important, then, for readers to note that in spite of many common themes, proponents of grounded theory differ among themselves in terms of exactly how the mechanics of the process should work.

5.4 CRITICISMS OF GROUNDED THEORY

Grounded theory has been enormously influential as an approach to qualitative research and in particular to the analysis of data. It is widely cited in research proposals, in methodology chapters of dissertations, in methodology courses and of course in research methods texts such as this one. And importantly, it has been used as something of a blueprint for the development of Computer Aided Qualitative Data Analysis Software such as NVivo, MAXqda and Atlas (see Chapter 20) whose use is increasingly common among social researchers (Bryman and Burgess, 1994; Fielding and Lee, 1998). In spite of its level of influence, however, grounded theory is not universally accepted by social researchers and readers should give some consideration to a number of criticisms of the approach before deciding to adopt it.

5.4.1 OVER-PRESCRIPTIVE

A number of commentators have argued that, in seeking to place so much emphasis upon methodological rigour and systematisation, grounded theory ends up being over-prescriptive. The intention is that the precise procedures enable us to have confidence that our theoretical conclusions have emerged directly from the data rather than as a result of selective or random ideas (Charmaz, 1995). Yet might such emphasis on procedural rules inhibit the human creative thinking necessary to develop useful theory? Arguing that the most valuable theories can often emerge from the most disorganised and unpredictable of processes, Thomas and James assert in relation to grounded theory that, 'one must be careful that fertility is not sacrificed to orderliness' (2006: 773).

According to some, the extent of the emphasis on proper methods and procedures may cause us to neglect assessing the value or plausibility of theories in their own right. In other words, we may come to accept or dismiss theory, not on the basis of its overall usefulness, coherence or plausibility in relation to supporting evidence, but instead, on the basis of whether the methodological procedures through which it was developed are deemed to have been the correct ones. In support of this view, Thomas and James (ibid.: 791) cite the following from Andreski: 'The overemphasis on methodology and techniques, as well as adulation of formulae and scientific-sounding terms, exemplify the common tendency ... to displace value from the end to the means' (Andreski, 1972: 108–09).

5.4.2 LIMITED EXPLANATORY POWER

A related but more specific complaint about grounded theory is that, by ensuring that every element of a theory has been systematically built up from the data itself, one places limits on the explanatory power of such theory. In other words, the approach may result in sociological explanations whose emphasis on the detail of the trees prevents us from learning a great deal about the broader context of the forest.

Thus, the discouragement of the use of existing theory and the insistence that each study produces its own new grounded theory may prompt the development of small-scale theories: explanations which usefully classify and conceptualise some elements of social life but which are limited in their broader value or application (Bryman, 2004; May, 2001). The approach is apparently biased, then, towards the relatively narrow and case-specific explanations which Glaser and Strauss (1967) termed 'substantive theory' and is perhaps unlikely to result in the development of more conceptual and broadly applicable 'formal theory'.

For Layder (1993), meanwhile, the insistence in grounded theory that concepts emerge exclusively from data serves to limit the capacity to explain social phenomena external to the specifics of the individuals or groups studied and neglects the significance of the broader world in which the respondents' lives are taking place:

> Such a focus cannot tell us about the mechanisms which may exist below the observable, sensorily detectable surface and which contribute to the formation of the observable features. Similarly, the narrowness of focus prevents us from having a real appreciation of the wider context in which people are pursuing their activities ... In this manner, theory is hedged in by our sensory limitations. (ibid.: 61)

In particular, Layder believes grounded theory is systematically biased against explanations which emphasise the impact of macro socioeconomic structures of power and inequality that impact upon individual lives but that may not be directly discernible from the data.

5.4.3 THE GOD TRICK?

A further criticism concerns the claim that, whereas other approaches privilege preconceived ideas, grounded theory procedures offer us the chance to access untainted truths about the social world. Through exhaustively following the correct techniques, it is held by grounded theorists that we can and must minimise the influence of existing theories or assumptions, nullify subjective biases and draw conclusions based only on the social realities illustrated in the data. It is assumed, then, that researchers can transcend their situatedness or that, as Bulmer has put it, 'the chicken and egg can be separated' (1979: 667). In explicitly emphasising the '*discovery* of grounded theory' (my italics), Glaser and Strauss accepted positivist premises previously associated with deductivist approaches. As Thomas and James put it, 'In grounded theory, a set of "neutral" analytical procedures replace the "neutral" controls and treatments of the experimental situation in the hope that they will provide the same guaranteed route to an uncontaminated correspondence' (2006: 779).

According to critics, such neutrality is simply not achievable and those who believe otherwise are guilty of claiming superhuman powers for themselves or, as Donna Haraway (1991) has put it, of playing 'the God trick'. Whether or not they conduct a formal literature review and develop explicit hypotheses at the beginning of a project, researchers always will hold values, assumptions and biases and these always will shape their research. As Stanley and Wise put it: 'All knowledge, necessarily, results from the conditions of its production ... and irrevocably bears the marks of its origins in the minds and intellectual practises of those ... who give voice to it' (1990: 39). Our biases affect the subjects we choose to research, the questions we ask, the places we visit, the focus of our observations, the content of our interviews and, of course, the ways in which we code, compare, write memos or otherwise make sense of data. According to this view, rather than removing or even reducing such biases, the introduction of systematic procedures for coding and constant comparison merely shapes the manner in which the subjectivities of the researcher will manifest themselves. As Phil Hodkinson and colleagues have put it, 'Any method both enables and constrains the research process, making some outcomes more likely and others less' (2005: 11).

Some supporters of grounded theory at least partially accept criticisms of Glaser and Strauss' emphasis on theory 'discovery'. Charmaz (1994: 32) distances herself from such 'traditional positivistic assumptions', accepting that interpretations will 'reflect the interaction between the observer and observed' and that 'any observer's worldview, disciplinary assumptions, theoretical proclivities and research interests will influence his or her observations and emerging categories'(ibid.: 32; also see Charmaz, 1994). Nevertheless, she argues that grounded theory is of significant use to those, like herself, who subscribe to 'interpretative constructivist perspectives' (1995: 31). Techniques such as line-by-line coding are deemed to offer the means to ensure as close a fit as possible between subjective interpretations and the data – thereby protecting against the forced or arbitrary imposition of 'preconceived ideas'. There are also indications of a movement away from pure induction in Strauss and Corbin's writings on grounded theory, in which it is acknowledged, for example, that researchers 'draw on their own experiences when analysing materials' (1998: 5). Yet at the same time, it seems clear that the detailed sets of procedures outlined in their account are intended to minimise the impact of such preconceptions.

5.4.4 OTHER CRITICISMS

There are also some other criticisms of grounded theory that merit a brief mention. Some have argued that the coding can result in a loss of the richness and depth potentially offered by qualitative data. This is because, as soon as the coding process goes beyond the 'initial' or 'open' phase, slices of data are effectively extracted from their place within the original narrative of which they were a part and are treated, out of context, as instances of a particular category. According to some, much of the meaning and significance the stories of respondents, as well as the ways in which such stories are told, can be lost in this process of extraction (Riessman, 1993).

A more practical issue is that the exploratory form taken by grounded theory research often conflicts with the need to seek approval for research proposals. Funders, supervisors, tutors and ethics committees often require a detailed methodological plan, complete with timescale, as well as a clear statement of the relationship the project has with existing theory and specific questions and objectives. Such requirements contradict what is expected in grounded theory (Bryman, 2004).

Finally, it has been argued that the notion of saturation is somewhat unclear when applied to practical research situations, making it less than certain at what point the iterative process of collection, coding and comparison should end. As Bulmer puts it: 'The constant comparative analyst is rushing hither and thither gaining new insights, while also trying to build up from data to categories and their properties to substantive theory and then formal theory. When are his categories sufficiently formed to stop the process?' (1979: 668).

5.5 FLEXIBILITY IN THE DEVELOPMENT OF THEORY THROUGH RESEARCH

Partly as a result of some of these problems, the number of studies that have used grounded theory in a complete and precise fashion is probably relatively small; certainly smaller than the number of researchers who, for one reason or another, have 'paid lip service' to the approach (Bryman, 2004). Many studies, particularly in the ethnographic traditions, take a broadly exploratory style rather than one based upon precise hypothesis testing. In so doing, such studies share at least some principles and procedures with grounded theorists. Though they were not the first scholars to champion exploratory, qualitative approaches to research and theory, there can be little doubt that Glaser and Strauss' intervention raised their profile and helped to challenge the domination of sociology by quantitative deduction. Yet rather than being adopted as a single holistic formula, selected elements of Glaser and Strauss' approach often form part of research strategies that tend to be rather more flexible about the research process and in particular about the ways in which theory is developed.

Notably, few qualitative researchers refrain from engaging with existing theory until the end of their project. Most believe that one does not have to be a strict hypothesis-tester in order to see the value of drawing upon the work of others from the beginning of the research process. Some focus intensively on previous literature at the beginning and end phases of projects, and less so during the main period of data collection. For others, engagement with existing theory is an integral and ongoing part of the iterative research process. At the same time as moving to and fro between data collection and analysis, the researcher also constantly seeks out and draws on relevant existing research or theory as a third point of 'constant comparison'. Either way, it is often recognised that, even in projects which have a relatively exploratory overall structure, existing literature is of significant value in the identification of areas of potential focus in the collection and analysis of data (Hammersley and Atkinson, 1995).

Willis' (1977) *Learning to Labour* study, mentioned earlier as an example of a research approach that took an exploratory, qualitative approach, offers a valuable case in point. He gave an account of the research he did for his study (1980). Willis' investigations took a loosely structured, ethnographic form and, in a later piece of writing, he specifically endorses the capacity of such an approach to capture the richness of everyday life and to facilitate the possibility of 'being surprised' or of 'reaching knowledge not prefigured in one's starting paradigm' (1980: 90). However, Willis rejects the notion of induction, regarding existing theory as an inevitable and also invaluable shaper of the ways in which he studied and made sense of the lives of his respondents. For Willis, researchers should avoid 'delusions' of inductive purity and instead regard existing frameworks as a necessary and useful resource. They should therefore outline their theoretical starting points and try to be explicit about the use of such preconceptions (ibid.).

Qualitative studies can also differ significantly in the approach taken to the analysis of data itself. It has already been pointed out that some researchers reject the use of coding procedures, preferring to analyse data in a more holistic fashion and as part of the context in which it was recorded. The analysis of personal biographies and narratives provide important examples, in attempting to understand social worlds through detailed presentation and analysis of individuals' stories (Riessman, 1993, also see Chapter 21). More common, however, is the use of some means of breaking up or sorting of data, but in a manner distinct from the precise coding procedures advocated by proponents of grounded theory. Many draw on existing theory or other prior ideas during the coding process. Indeed, Miles and Huberman (1994) advocate the creation before the analysis begins of provisional 'start lists' of codes, based on a combination of the research questions and existing conceptual frameworks, which will then be refined during the process of assigning the codes to data. Other variations include attempting from the start to establish and refine a limited number of broad categories or themes, rather than exhaustively compiling hundreds of highly specific line-by-line codes and deriving broader categories from these. Others use coding more as a descriptive means of organising data to make it easy to access, rather than as an interpretative means of establishing the building blocks of theory.

5.5.1 EXPLORATIVE BUT NOT INDUCTIVE? AN EXAMPLE

My own three-year study of young people involved in the goth music scene (Hodkinson, 2002) is an example of a project that used an exploratory style and structure of enquiry, but which avoided some of the more prescriptive grounded theory procedures and which rejected the notion of induction in its purest sense. The research took an ethnographic approach, characterised by an ongoing integration of data collection and analysis. Rather than designing every aspect in advance, I allowed the focus to develop and change as opportunities arose and as I began to identify what struck me as significant themes, possible explanations or key questions. It was my intention to develop a theoretical contribution to my discipline through gradually making my initially broad enquiries more focused and more analytical as the project continued. In these respects, my research was consistent with some aspects of inductive research.

Yet I have already hinted that it would not be appropriate to describe the project or its outcomes as an illustration of grounded theory – or indeed of purely inductive research. Like most PhD students, I was advised to begin my project with an extensive literature review. This engagement with existing work quickly resulted in identification of a variety of previous studies, concepts, theories and debates about youth practices and identities that seemed potentially relevant to the goths I was studying. There can be no doubt that theoretical arguments about youth cultures, popular music scenes and consumer culture influenced my ongoing decisions on where to go, what to observe, who to talk to and what to talk to them about. An additional important and unavoidable source of preconceptions was provided by my experience of having been a participant of the goth scene prior to the start of the project – something on which I have reflected elsewhere (Hodkinson, 2005).

As well as influencing the agenda of my research, these theoretical and personal preconceptions were also drawn on during my data analysis throughout the project. I gradually identified key themes in the data, using labelling and highlighting to show examples of their occurrence in printed transcripts. The production of numerous memos was crucial to this process, as were two other procedures associated with grounded theory; the rigorous comparison of themes and examples and the ongoing collection of new data. Yet the themes and eventual explanations developed were not preceded by exhaustive descriptive coding of every single line of data as intended by Glaser and Strauss and illustrated in the box on p. 87. Rather, my themes emerged as a result of an ongoing and flexible synthesis of research data with themes and priorities from existing literature and from my existing and developing knowledge, experience and assumptions with relation to the goth scene. Furthermore, although my ongoing data collection was informed by the emergence of themes from earlier data analysis, it was not exclusively targeted on the investigation of such hunches. I did not want to narrow down my enquiries or close my mind too early, so at the same time as exploring emerging themes, my sampling and interview questions tended to remain relatively broad and exploratory in their focus.

My eventual conclusions were very strongly supported by my data. Yet they did not emerge through rigid adherence to the systematic inductive building process envisaged in grounded theory or through any other process which could be described as strictly inductive. My extensive data was of course crucial to the development of my findings, but the process of generating theory reflected the ongoing integration of the data with existing theoretical and personal ideas.

5.6 SUMMARY

In this chapter, we have examined the distinction between deductive and inductive research and have focused in detail on grounded theory, which undoubtedly represents the most detailed and influential attempt to operationalise the inductive approach. We have illustrated a range of tools and procedures offered by Glaser and Strauss and other proponents of the approach, for those seeking to make analytical sense of qualitative data in an inductive fashion. And we have examined some key arguments for and against the use of grounded theory by social researchers.

The debate over the usefulness of the detailed methodological guidelines offered by the proponents of grounded theory is set to continue for some considerable time. What is undeniable, however, is the importance of the work of Glaser, Strauss and others in helping to establish the legitimacy and value of approaches to research that, instead of being entirely pre-planned to test existing theory, adopt an exploratory and iterative approach to data collection and analysis oriented to the gradual development of greater and greater theoretical focus and clarity as the project continues. Glaser and Strauss' work has also helped to establish that, whatever approach they take, researchers should try to outline and reflect upon the ways in which they develop concepts, explanations and theory.

DISCUSSION QUESTIONS

1   What is the difference between theory and description?

2   Why should researchers wish to take an inductive approach to the development of theory?

3   Why might grounded theory procedures assist in the inductive development of theory?

4   What is theoretical sampling and what are its implications for the structure of the research process?

5   In what ways might the detailed line-by-line coding of data be a valuable approach to analysis? Does it have any disadvantages?

6   Should researchers seek to reduce the impact on their research of existing ideas or should they openly draw upon existing theory?

7   Think of an example of a published qualitative research study and consider the approach taken by the author to the relationship between data and theory. In what ways is the approach taken similar to and/or different from grounded theory?

CHECKLIST

*   Inductive researchers seek to build theory from data rather than testing existing theories.

*   Grounded theory involves an iterative process characterised by an ongoing interplay of data collection and analysis.

*   Through theoretical sampling, grounded theorists attempt to focus data collection on themes which have emerged from earlier data analysis.

*   Grounded theorists develop theory through detailed coding of data.

*   Codes are gradually refined and eventually integrated and reduced through a process of constant comparison of the data pertaining to them.

- During the process of constant comparison, memos are used to record hunches, possibilities and ideas.

- Existing theory and research are drawn upon only after the process of theory generation is at an advanced stage.

- Grounded theory has been criticised by some for being overly prescriptive, for lacking explanatory power and for overestimating the possibilities of researcher neutrality.

- Many qualitative researchers use selected features associated with grounded theory, without adopting the approach in its entirety.

RESOURCES

Bryant and Charmaz (eds) (2007) *The Sage Handbook of Grounded Theory*. A contemporary collection of chapters covering the various elements of grounded theory from the point of view of a range of well-known contributors from around the world.

Bryman and Burgess (eds) *Analysing Qualitative Data*. A text outlining in relation to research experience, the different ways in which scholars have approached the analysis of data, including via the use of grounded theory.

Fielding and Lee (1998) *Computer Analysis and Qualitative Research*. A valuable early contribution to discussions on the development and use of computer aided qualitative analysis software, much of which was designed with grounded theory in mind.

Glaser (1992) *Basics of Grounded Theory Analysis: Emergence Versus Forcing*. This book represents Glaser's impassioned critical response to Strauss and Corbin's book, which is said to have encouraged 'forced, preconceived, full conceptual description' and thereby to have betrayed the inductive principles on which the grounded theory approach were initially based.

Glaser and Strauss (1967) *The Discovery of Grounded Theory: Strategies for Qualitative Research*. Glaser and Strauss' original outline of grounded theory is both detailed and accessible. It is a must for anyone seeking to develop their understanding of the approach.

Strauss and Corbin (1998) *Basics of Qualitative Research: Techniques and Procedures for Developing Grounded Theory*. Strongly criticised by Glaser, this book, whose first edition was published in 1990, outlines Strauss and Corbin's detailed and exhaustive elaborations on the procedures grounded theorists should use in order to transform their data into theory. Although some of the techniques are complex, the book is again written in an accessible manner.

6   Participatory Approaches to Social Research

Christina Silver

KEY POINTS

- There are many different ways in which people can participate in research projects, from informing the design, through collecting data, undertaking analysis and presenting findings.

- Participatory approaches emphasise the need to do research *with* and *for* participants rather than *on* them. They therefore challenge conventional dichotomies between the researcher and the researched.

- Participatory approaches generate in-depth and valid understandings of the phenomena being studied, leading to shared interpretations and grounded practical interventions.

- Lay involvement in research requires careful thought as to *how* and *why* people are involved, frequent reconsideration of progress and safeguards to avoid exploitation.

6.1 INTRODUCTION

This chapter defines and historically locates participatory forms of social research in terms of their distinguishing features. This includes discussion of the emergence of **Action Research (AR)** and **Participatory Action Research (PAR)** in response to the implicit assumption of much conventional research that lay people and research 'subjects' are not capable of 'doing research'. Using contrasting examples, a spectrum of participatory research is developed. At one end are projects where participants are only involved with one or two aspects of the research, for example, being actively involved in collecting or generating data. At the other end are projects where participants are directly involved with all aspects of the research process, from design and data collection through to analysis, interpretation, representation, implementation, and evaluation. Practical, methodological, and ethical considerations are discussed, as well as the implications of technological developments on participatory research practice. The chapter ends by posing discussion questions and listing resources.

6.2 HISTORICAL ROOTS OF PARTICIPATORY APPROACHES TO SOCIAL RESEARCH

Participatory approaches to social research are exactly that: approaches to conducting social research rather than a methodology or discipline. In the literature, several terms are used, often loosely and interchangeably, to refer to social research that is informed by similar underlying philosophies, but that have often subtly but importantly different foci. These include, among others, Participant Research, Participatory Research, Practitioner Research, Partnership Research, Emancipatory Research, Collaborative Research, Action Research and Participatory Action Research.

In unscrambling differences between Action Research, Participatory Research and Participatory Action Research, it is useful to consider the extent to which *action, participation*, or both *action and participation* are stressed. In simple terms, Action Research places emphasis on the *action*, Participatory Research on the *participation*, and Participatory Action Research emphasises both *participation* and *action*.

6.2.1 ACTION

In many senses, all social research involves a degree of action. Undertaking research inevitably has consequences and some element of change occurs for all those involved as a result. This is true for the researchers, research participants, and the research audience. If this was not the case, why would we be conducting research in the first place? That said, not all conventional social research explicitly seeks to advance measurable change.

6.2.2 ACTION RESEARCH

Action research is an umbrella term that is widely used to refer to many variations of the general approach, and that, since its first usage, has been developed and applied in many different substantive, theoretical, and empirical contexts. Originally coined by American psychologist Kurt Lewin in the 1940s, the term Action Research broadly refers to an applied form of social research that overtly aims to improve the social situation under study while simultaneously generating knowledge about it. In his seminal paper of 1946 in which he described the processes involved in his conceptualisation of Action Research, Lewin also referred to the approach as 'rational social management', a means of combining experimental approaches to social science with social action. Because Action Research is driven by the desire to improve social situations, Lewin saw it as crucial to assess the success of interventions, then revise and re-implement them, re-evaluate them, and so on. Rather than gathering information from research *subjects* and generating findings which may, or may not, be implemented subsequently, the focus is on changing practice as part of the research process. It is a cyclical process, moving between stages of *enquiry, intervention* and *evaluation*. Action Research therefore maximises opportunities to learn from practice and promotes the transferability of new ideas.

> **TIP**
>
> *Enquiry* involves collecting information and data about the research topic. *Intervention* involves implementing a change in practice which is designed to improve the situation. *Evaluation* involves assessing whether the intervention has been successful, and determining why. These stages may be carried out several times in an action research project.

Lewin's ideas have been developed in many different applied research settings. These include organisational change research, community development projects, practitioner research, and education, health and social care research. Over many decades the trend has generally shifted from Lewin's conceptualisation of Action Research as a form of rational social management to an explicitly anti-positivist approach to social change (Hart and Bond, 1995: 34). Despite the variations, it is generally considered that Action Research is achieved through collaboration between researchers and participants and by following a cyclical process of planning, acting, observing and reflecting.

Action Research projects have in common a clear underlying set of democratic, social justice, and emancipatory values. Much Action Research is undertaken in areas where research participants are oppressed or disenfranchised, for example, in the fields of health, disability, youth, education, and in the developing world.

6.2.3 PARTICIPATION

Participation is also involved in all social research; whether conducting a survey, collecting interview data, undertaking participant observation, or conducting narrative or discourse analysis on historical documents, there are participants. These participants are more or less visible depending on the method employed. It is clear that those filling out questionnaires, explaining an experience in an interview setting, or being observed, are participating in the research. However, even where the research is based purely on documents, with no active involvement from the authors of those documents at the time of the research, the researcher is influenced by a range of external participants (other researchers, authors, etc.). In such circumstances, the researcher is attempting to 'speak' for those being researched in some way and so the original authors of the documents are participating, albeit indirectly and invisibly.

Participatory research constitutes an acknowledgement of and reaction against the more traditional forms in which there is a clear division between the researcher(s) and those being researched. Traditionally, this separation has been seen as important in establishing and maintaining objectivity: the researcher is the 'expert', bringing his or her knowledge and expertise to the research problem and being seen as the person able to understand what is going on in the research setting. Those being researched usually play a relatively passive role, often not being involved again after the initial research contact (filling in a questionnaire, being interviewed, observed, etc.). In many cases, the researched are not aware of the results or outcomes of the research project.

In contrast, participatory forms of research see the active involvement of participants in the research process as beneficial and necessary. For example, participant involvement in research can be both empowering for those groups and individuals, and valuable in ensuring that the research remains grounded in the understanding and experiences of those being studied. As illustrated later in this chapter, the degree to which participants are involved varies quite considerably between research projects depending on their particular needs.

6.2.4 PARTICIPATORY ACTION RESEARCH (PAR)

Participatory action research (PAR) developed from the Action Research tradition. PAR places greater emphasis on the participation of those being researched throughout the whole process of the research project (Whyte, 1991). Like Action Research, PAR explicitly aims to change and improve the social situation being studied. However, in many cases, the research is conceived and driven by those experiencing the unsatisfactory situation. As such, PAR takes the idea of involving participants in the research a step further. 'Lay' people are the researchers themselves and are seen as the experts. The role of 'professional' researchers (working in universities or other research organisations) is thus that of facilitator rather than expert.

PAR has three main elements: people, power, and **praxis**.

- *People*: The participatory nature of PAR is its fundamental characteristic. PAR differs from other forms of research because lay people are not just involved in the research, but actively inform and direct it. Research is conducted not only for but also by the participants. In this way, PAR is people-centred. Often employed when researching sensitive topics and when the population involved is marginalised or disadvantaged, the focus is clearly on action with the goal of achieving discernible and effective changes in policy, practice or both to the benefit of the population involved.

- *Power*: A factor underlying the interest in increasing participation in social research is an acknowledgement of and reaction against the imbalance of power between the researcher and the researched in much conventional research. Proponents of PAR challenge such hierarchical power relationships, seeking to empower research participants through the process of undertaking the research. They do not see research participants as research 'subjects', as doing so objectifies and further marginalises them, but as equal partners in the process.

- *Praxis*: Praxis is the transformation of academic or purely theoretical knowledge into applied practice. One focus of PAR, therefore, is on praxis, recognising that theory and practice in research are both inseparable and iterative. Many PAR projects are explicitly informed by a political stance and set of values that aim to assert the rights and improve the social circumstances of disenfranchised or marginalised groups.

6.3 A SPECTRUM OF PARTICIPATORY APPROACHES TO SOCIAL RESEARCH

In order to reflect the differences in Action Research approaches without losing sight of their commonalities, Hart and Bond (1995) developed a typology of Action Research that outlines seven distinguishing criteria and four types of Action Research (see Table 6.1). The criteria are those which differentiate Action Research approaches from traditional or conventional social research: Educative base; Individuals in groups; Problem focus; Change intervention; Improvement and involvement; Cyclic process; and Research relationship, degree of collaboration. The types of action research are: Experimental; Organisational; Professionalising and Empowering. These types reflect both broad developments in Action Research over time and underlying perspectives on the social world. Hart and Bond comment:

> The typology can be read from left to right as representing a developmental process over time as action research has shifted from a scientific approach to social change to a more qualitative and social constructionist methodology. The framework is based on a binary opposition between rational social management, assuming a consensus view of society on the left, and a structural change and conflict model of society on the right. (1995: 44)

Although not the only attempt to differentiate between applications of Action Research, this typology provides a clear summary of the main differences, helping those involved in Action Research projects to locate their own work within a broader context.

Hart and Bond acknowledge that this Action Research typology obscures to some extent the 'fluidity and dynamism' of real-life projects. In practice, boundaries between the types are more blurred than is indicated by the typology and a given project may draw upon or incorporate elements of several types. This is illustrated later in the chapter using real-life examples of participatory research projects.

Nevertheless, a broad summary of the key components of the four main types of Action Research is useful in that it helps make sense of a rich and

Table 6.1   Action Research typology

ACTION TYPE/ DISTINGUISHING CRITERIA	CONSENSUS MODEL OF SOCIETY RATIONAL SOCIAL MANAGEMENT		CONFLICT MODEL OF SOCIETY STRUCTURAL CHANGE	
	EXPERIMENTAL	ORGANISATIONAL	PROFESSIONALISING	EMPOWERING
1 Educative base	Re-education	Re-education/training	Reflective practice	Consciousness-raising
	Enhancing social science/ administrative control and social change towards consensus	Enhancing managerial control and organizational change towards consensus	Enhancing professional control and individual's ability to control work situation	Enhanced user-control and shifting balance of power; structural change towards pluralism
	Inferring relationship between behaviour and output; identifying causal factors in group dynamics	Overcoming resistance to change/restructuring balance of power between managers and workers	Empowering professional groups; advocacy on behalf of patients/clients	Empowering oppressed groups
	Social scientific bias/ researcher focused	Managerial bias/client focused	Practitioner focused	User/practitioner focused
2 Individuals in groups	Closed group, controlled, selection made by researcher for purposes of measurement/ inferring relationship between cause and effect	Work groups and/or mixed groups of managers and workers	Professional(s) and/or (interdisciplinary) professional group/ negotiated team boundaries	Fluid groupings, self selecting or natural boundary or open/closed by negotiation
	Fixed membership	Selected membership	Shifting membership	Fluid membership
3 Problem focus	Problem emerges from the interaction of social science theory and social problems	Problem defined by most powerful group; some negotiation with workers	Problem defined by professional group; some negotiation with users	Emerging and negotiated definition of problem by less powerful group(s)
	Problem relevant for social science/ management interests	Problem relevant for management/social science interests	Problem emerges from professional practice/ experience	Problem emerges from members' practice/ experience
	Success defined in terms of social science	Success defined by sponsors	Contested, professionally determined definitions of success	Competing definition of success accepted and expected

(Continued)

Table 6.1   *(Continued)*

ACTION TYPE/ DISTINGUISHING CRITERIA	CONSENSUS MODEL OF SOCIETY RATIONAL SOCIAL MANAGEMENT ⟷ CONFLICT MODEL OF SOCIETY STRUCTURAL CHANGE			
	EXPERIMENTAL	ORGANISATIONAL	PROFESSIONALISING	EMPOWERING
4 Change intervention	Social science, experimental intervention to test theory and/or generate theory	Top-down, directed change towards predetermined aims	Professionally led, pre-defined, process led	Bottom-up, undetermined, process led
	Problem to be solved in terms of research aims	Problem to be solved in terms of management aims	Problem to be resolved in the interests of research-based practice and professionalisation	Problem to be explored as part of process of change, developing an understanding of meanings of issues in terms of problem and solution
5 Improvement and involvement	Towards controlled outcome and consensual definition of improvement	Towards tangible outcome and consensual definition of improvement	Towards improvement in practice defined by professionals and on behalf of users	Towards negotiated outcomes and pluralist definitions of improvement: account taken of vested interests
6 Cyclic process	Research components dominant	Action and research components in tension; action dominated	Research and action components in tension; research dominated	Action components dominant
	Identifies causal process that can be generalised	Identifies causal processes that are specific to problem context and/or can be generalised	Identifies causal processes which are specific to problem and/or can be generalised	Change course of events; recognition of multiple influences upon change
	Time limited, task focused	Discrete cycle, rationalist, sequential	Spiral of cycles, opportunistic, dynamic	Open-ended, process driven
7 Research relationship, degree of collaboration	Experimenter/ respondents	Consultant/ researcher, respondent/ participants	Practitioner or researcher/ collaborators	Practitioner researcher/ co-researchers/ co-change agents
	Outside researcher as expert/research funding	Client pays an outside consultant – 'they who pay the piper call the tune'	Outside resources and/or internally generated	Outside resources and/ or internally generated
	Differentiated roles	Differentiated roles	Merged roles	Shared roles

Source: Hart and Bond (1995: 40–4).

diverse research tradition which can otherwise seem overwhelmingly complex.

6.3.1 PARTICIPATORY APPROACHES IN PRACTICE

As mentioned at the beginning of this chapter, participatory approaches to social research are perspectives for undertaking social research rather than methods of conducting it. Such research projects often focus on a particular situation or programme at a specific point in time, therefore, the methods employed are developed according to the needs of the particular project.

Many research projects informed by participatory approaches employ qualitative methods, but that is not to say that quantitative methods are inappropriate; indeed, in many situations it will be necessary to generate a range of data types and employ a combination of analytic strategies in interpreting them (see Chapter 7).

We now turn to three quite different research projects in order to illustrate the spectrum of forms of participatory social research. In the first, participants are only involved in data generation; in the second, participants are involved in data collection, implementation of developments in practice and meaning-making; and in the third, participants are involved in all stages of the research process.

Participants only involved in data generation: Video Intervention/Prevention Assessment (VIA), Children's Hospital Boston

Since 1994, Video Intervention/Prevention Assessment (VIA) at Children's Hospital Boston, has conducted research with young people living with various chronic conditions including asthma, obesity, spina bifida, sickle cell disease, cystic fibrosis and perinatally-acquired HIV.

VIA define their work as 'participant-centred' rather than as a form of action or participatory research; however, it is consistent with the common principles that underlie participatory approaches to social research.

VIA grew out of an observation by founder and director Michael Rich that modern hospital-based healthcare obscures clinicians' holistic understanding of patients' illness experiences because contact between clinicians and patients occurs almost exclusively within medical settings. When it was usual for doctors to make house-visits to patients, they were able to witness both their physical and social living environments, but this is no longer the case.

The everyday lives and environments of patients have a significant impact on both their health conditions and their medical self-management. When

(Continued)

clinicians are not directly aware of the reality of patients' lives and environments, these issues can be difficult to solve. For a description of VIA, see http://tinyurl.com/ysb23m

Forms of participation

In order to bridge the gap in communication and knowledge between patients and clinicians, the VIA team has developed an innovative methodology that provides access to the realities of young people's lived experiences of chronic conditions so that clinicians can develop more realistic, sensitive, and effective medical management plans in partnership with the patient. This, in turn, may make the patient more likely to adhere to the management regime, thus, improving their overall health and well-being.

Participant-generated audio-visual narratives

VIA research participants are provided with digital video recorders and unlimited blank tape and asked to 'teach your doctor about your life and your condition'. Participants are not specifically directed to what or how they should create their videos; instead, they are asked to tell the story of their lives with a chronic condition and encouraged to show daily life activities, conduct interviews with family and friends about the impact of their condition on those around them, and create personal monologues all in the form of a visual narrative.

The participation of young people in the research process concludes when they have finished generating their visual narratives. This is negotiated between the participant and the VIA Field Co-ordinator when it is mutually agreed that the elements of the project have been satisfactorily completed. Although participants receive copies of all the video they create, they are not involved in the analysis process at all. http://tinyurl.com/ytkbhl

Summary

This participant-centred approach results in large quantities of audio-visual data generated *for* but not *by* VIA, which, after rigorous analysis by the research team, is used to inform clinical practice. Once common themes have been identified across the visual narratives generated by participants with a certain condition, they can be used for a number of purposes including the development of more effective medical management plans; educating medical students, clinicians and the general public; empowering patients to be advocates for themselves; and improving access to care, services and information. http://tinyurl.com/ytqo5e

Participants involved in data collection and implementation: More than 'just the cleaners'?

The project 'Enabling and Supporting the Integration of Non-clinical House-keeping Roles into Ward Teams', at the Centre for the Development of Healthcare Policy and Practice (CDHPP), University of Leeds took place in 2002–2004 and was informed by the then UK policy commitment to improve patients' hospital experiences by raising standards in the non-clinical aspects of ward-based health-care. These include cleanliness, food service, routine maintenance, and other elements of the overall patient environment. The research was located in a UK hospital and conducted in partnership with two quite different ward-based health-care teams: an orthopaedic trauma ward and an acute medical ward.

There were two main elements to the project; one to study the implementation, development and effectiveness of an established ward-based house-keeping model in order to provide transferable recommendations for hospitals yet to implement the model; and a second to evaluate CDHPP's Practice Development Unit (PDU) accreditation process as a vehicle for facilitating intentional, evidence-based improvements to healthcare effectively and sustainably.

The PDU model is widely recognised as a means by which to enhance innovative patient-centred care, inter-disciplinary team-working, professional development and job satisfaction (Gerrish, 1999; Page and Hamer, 2002). The programme takes approximately two years, during which time teams work towards demonstrating progress on 15 criteria. As well as a number of coaching and facilitation events provided by the CDHPP, the ward teams are required to submit written accounts of their progress at three key stages in the process. More information about the PDU model can be found at: http://tinyurl.com/2a9n2l

An Action Research approach was used because of the focus on improvement and the need to involve all team members in the process of change. The project was framed by the principle of 'bottom-up' rather than 'top-down' innovation, with an emphasis on involving practitioners from both clinical and non-clinical backgrounds, as well as members of the local public in all stages of developing new and more effective ways of delivering support services. The developmental nature of the PDU process also mirrors the focus on collaborative cycles of enquiry, intervention, and evaluation that typifies the formative style of Action Research.

Forms of participation

The research was a collaborative project between two UK universities and one National Health Service (NHS) Hospital Trust that had established a

(Continued)

ward-based non-clinical housekeeping role several years previously. A researcher, based in the hospital, co-ordinated communications between the different research participants and collected most of the data.

Although the researchers collected and analysed the various forms of qualitative and quantitative data, and were primarily responsible for writing the final report and disseminating findings, key stakeholders were involved in different aspects of the project throughout.

Steering Group membership

The collaborative research team remained grounded in the realities of the needs and experiences of the hospital patients, practitioners, managers and members of the public through regular Steering Group meetings. Membership of the Steering Group was diverse in order to reflect the key stakeholders' opinions and expertise. The Steering Group comprised the research team (members from the two universities and the locally-based researcher), the Ward Managers and non-clinical Housekeepers working on the case-study wards, two patient representatives, personnel from the hospital management team (Nursing and Facilities), and a member of the NHS Ward Housekeeping Team.

Ongoing feedback of and consultation about research results

It was important that all the stakeholders had the opportunity to be actively involved in developing changes and improvements in order to ensure effective and sustainable implementations. This was achieved through regular feedback events in which the research team not only informed stakeholders of findings so far, but asked them to discuss the implications and contribute to potential developments. These events were important in ensuring that the researchers' interpretations accurately reflected the opinions and experiences of those at the 'cutting-edge'; and that consensus was reached about implementing new ways of working.

Documenting the PDU Accreditation Process

In evaluating the PDU accreditation process, the research team drew on the written materials presented by each ward team at the interim stages of the accreditation process. Throughout the two years, the locally-based researcher attended ward team meetings where the PDU accreditation progress was discussed and informally observed the ward teams. The different forms of data generated by this multi-pronged approach were used by the research team to evaluate the accreditation process as a vehicle for delivering integrated interdisciplinary approaches to improving healthcare provision.

Summary

The Action Research approach used in this project helped to identify a range of benefits for the patients' experience of ward-based housekeeping roles from a number of perspectives: those doing the job; the clinical staff working on the wards; the hospital management teams; and patients. A number of factors that may support or inhibit the implementation of such roles in other hospitals were also identified, resulting in transferable recommendations. Following the Action Research cycle of enquiry, intervention and evaluation, findings were directly used by hospital staff to improve ward-based housekeeping roles further; both in terms of the job satisfaction of staff and improvements in service delivery for patients.

In addition, the informal observation of the two wards' PDU process revealed the challenges and rewards of following the accreditation programme as experienced by those undertaking it. The power of a truly 'bottom-up' approach to innovation in and sustainability of practice development in multi-disciplinary healthcare teams was clearly established.

Participants involved in all stages: 'Our Home': Bankside Hostel, University of Manchester

This project took place between 2004 and 2006 and was framed by the growing policy drive to take account of the views of service users in the operation and management of social services for vulnerable groups in the UK. Specifically, it developed in response to a number of UK government White Papers concerning housing provision for vulnerable groups, particularly that of people with learning difficulties. For more information about this project, see http://tinyurl.com/ytfq2q

The focus of the study was twofold. Substantively, it focused on the improvement of services for people with severe learning difficulties as they undertook the transition from living in hostels to supported housing. The project aimed to enable hostel tenants and staff to document this significant change from their own perspectives. While people with mild to moderate learning difficulties had previously been involved in consultation activities, those with severe learning difficulties had generally been excluded from such involvement. The project aim was 'to facilitate the "voice" of people with learning difficulties during the transition from group living to supported housing' (http://tinyurl.com/yp7c7f). Although the

(Continued)

authors refer to the research approach as 'Partnership Research', it has much in common with the other approaches discussed in this chapter.

The second aspect of the research was methodological: to explore factors that enabled or hindered effective participation of people with severe learning difficulties in research. The substantive research project was used to 'aid reflection on the methodological implications of conducting research in partnership' (http://tinyurl.com/27zt74). Subsequently the Partnership Education web site was developed to provide information about the Bankside Hostel project and act as a practical resource for others engaged in similar research projects.

Forms of participation

The Bankside Hostel project differs from the previous examples in that the tenants were involved in all stages of the project from research design through data collection, analysis, and presentation of findings. Such a fully inclusive approach necessitates a large amount of negotiation and the development of shared understandings at the outset, and these also need to be maintained throughout. This, in turn, requires all participants to subscribe to the idea that all those involved have an equally important opinion and that they can all learn from one another. An additional aspect of this particular project was that some tenants required extra help in participating because of the severity of their learning disabilities.

Fieldwork

The major means by which data was generated by tenants was through 'participatory photography'. Residents took photographs of the aspects of the hostel's physical environment, including buildings and artifacts, and the people with whom they lived and who worked in the hostel. Taking photographs enabled the documentation of the places that tenants liked and where they felt comfortable, and those that they did not like or where they felt uncomfortable. This provided a better understanding of the aspects of their living environment the tenants might like to change or keep the same as they moved to new types of housing and living arrangements.

Analysis

The Bankside Hostel tenants were invited to look at the photographs generated during the project on several occasions and to comment upon them. The aim was to capture the emotions and feelings evoked by different photographs and different ways of representing them, for example, different sizes, colours and the use of different media. Tenants' comments and non-verbal cues, such as paying particular attention to certain photographs, were recorded and used to produce captions and annotations of the photographs. All participants received an annotated 'photo record' of the hostel and an audiotape of the 'captions'.

Writing in partnership

A key element of this project was to provide an opportunity for those who had been involved in the other aspects to contribute also to writing up the research. This posed a number of particular challenges because of the tenants' learning difficulties. Through a process of discussion and negotiation, however, the team was able to write a joint account that incorporates pictures as well as text. A short version of this document is available on the project web site and the full version has subsequently been published as a chapter in a book (see Goodley and Van Hove, 2005). http://tinyurl.com/29szmk

On the project web site there are several different versions of written information to ensure its accessibility to as wide a population as possible. As well as reports with and without pictures and photo-stories, there are 'easy' and 'full' versions of some documents.

Summary

This project developed a unique understanding of tenants' feelings about their impending change in living circumstances, eliciting feelings of anxiety concerning the move and identifying preferences for the new living arrangements. Such understandings might not have been possible to elicit using conventional research methods because of the tenants' verbal and written communication difficulties.

It also empowered people who are often marginalised and situated in a passive role to make active statements about their own needs and desires. Photographs were found to be an accessible means by which people with learning difficulties can communicate with one another and understand each other's meanings and opinions.

The findings were incorporated in the plans for the new supported housing project and so tenants were not only able to have a 'voice' but also to have a positive impact on their own future, in which they might otherwise have had little choice or involvement.

This project resulted in a useful web site detailing the experiences and challenges involved in this project and providing access to the range of materials that were developed in partnership. The site also includes a lot of information about partnership research more generally including references to relevant literature and links to related resources.

6.4 METHODOLOGICAL AND ETHICAL CONSIDERATIONS

There are a number of methodological and ethical considerations when undertaking participatory forms of social research. Some of these are similar to those encountered when adopting more conventional methods, but some are particular to participatory approaches.

Although there are a number of benefits to adopting participatory approaches to social research, doing so is not without potential difficulties. In particular, involving lay participants in research raises a number of ethical considerations.

A sense of ownership over the research, data, interpretations and outcomes is particularly important when the aim is developmental. If interventions and improvements are to be effective and sustained, those responsible for enacting them need not only to be involved in developing new ways of working, but also be in agreement with the proposed changes.

It can seem easy to involve stakeholders in research at some level, but it is important not simply to pay lip service to the idea of involvement. If a participatory project is to be successful, involvement needs to be real. At the beginning of a project a number of questions need to be considered in detail including *who* is to be involved, *how* they are to be involved, *why* they are to be involved, *to what extent* they are involved, and how is their participation *taken into account?* Failure to consider these questions and to ensure the involvement of participants is both meaningful and maintained throughout the project can not only result in an unsuccessful research project and ineffective developments, but also result in the exploitation of participants.

TIP

Be realistic about how participants can be involved in research projects and the impact they can have.

6.4.1 PROBLEMATISATION OF CONVENTIONAL RESEARCH CONCEPTS

As mentioned earlier in this chapter, participatory approaches to social research developed in part from the idea that those involved in research are best conceptualised as 'participants' rather than research 'subjects' or 'objects'. A clear democratising motive underlies participatory approaches, challenging conventional research relationships that are seen as dichotomous, elitist and exploitative.

Depending on the nature of the particular project, the extent to which conventional roles of 'researcher' and 'researched' are challenged varies. This is clearly illustrated in the three examples discussed in this chapter. In particular are questions about who are the stakeholders, who are the observers and the analysts, and the nature of dialogue among research participants. Although participatory forms of social research do not necessarily solve these issues, they do raise a number of important issues which are relevant to many other methodologies.

TIP

Whatever type of research project you are undertaking, it is important to be clear about the roles and responsibilities of all those involved, and to reconsider them as the project progresses.

In challenging these conventional research concepts, participatory approaches encourage researchers to be more reflexive about and transparent in their practice. **Reflexivity** relates to scrutiny and reflection on all elements of the research process (see Chapter 1). Working in partnership requires a high degree of reflexivity for several reasons. The research design is often fairly loosely specified at the outset as such projects are subject to alteration depending on progress. It is also important to frequently review not only research progress but also the perceptions and involvement of all the participants in order to ensure their opinions continue to be accounted for.

Closely related to reflexivity, **transparency** refers to openness about and accountability of research methods and processes. Being open about and accountable for research processes to all partners is a key element of participatory approaches and is necessary in order to maintain the collaboration of those involved. Those conducting such projects are also often more likely to be explicit about methods and difficulties faced during the project. This is to the benefit of social research methods more generally as the transparency of methods has traditionally been somewhat lacking, especially among qualitative researchers.

CHECKLIST

- Identify and approach all possible stakeholders as soon as possible.

- Discuss and agree upon the ways in which stakeholders can contribute to the project and the effect their participation will have.

- Ensure that all those involved are participating voluntarily and that they are aware they can terminate their participation at any point.

- Negotiate individual roles and responsibilities and ensure everybody fully understands their own and others' contributions.

- Frequently discuss the project progress and revisit roles and responsibilities to ensure all participants remain actively involved and satisfied.

- Take steps to ensure all participants' contributions are equally valued and taken into account.

6.4.2 EVALUATING PARTICIPATORY APPROACHES

Participatory approaches have been criticised for being unscientific and for producing anecdotal and subjective results (see Cornwall and Jewkes, 1995; Baskerville and Wood-Harper, 1996). Those working within more positivist traditions may see the exploratory purpose and evolutionary nature of the research design as too loosely defined and therefore unscientific.

Similarly, participatory approaches have been criticised for producing results that cannot be generalised beyond the population under study. The charge arises because it is necessary to become thoroughly familiar with the research setting and its contexts and to spend time negotiating consensus among the stakeholders at various stages of the cyclical process. Interventions and outcomes are therefore to a large extent context-specific, leading to the charge of anecdotal, unreliable and ungeneralisable results. Such challenges may be compounded by the case-study nature of many action research projects.

6.4.3 VALIDITY AND TRANSFERABILITY

In evaluating participatory approaches, however, it may be inappropriate to employ criteria developed for judging conventional social research. While Action Research initially sprung from positivist experimental psychology, as discussed above, developments over time have led to a very different set of criteria for undertaking research. It is therefore more useful to evaluate such projects according to the effectiveness of the interventions and the **validity** and transferability of the research findings.

The example projects discussed earlier in this chapter illustrate that participatory approaches to conducting social research, by their very nature, are likely to generate in-depth and valid understandings of the phenomena being studied and to lead to shared interpretations and grounded practical interventions. The VIA and CDHPP examples show that the direct involvement of the population being studied can result in real and effective change in practice.

During the 1990s, many governments in industralised nations prized evidence-based policy-making and as a result participatory research projects increased in number.

As indicated by its title, Video Intervention/Prevention Assessment explicitly aims to induce discernible change in the form of health intervention and illness prevention. An underlying assumption of the VIA method is that those with chronic conditions are best placed to relate information crucial to their health. Collecting data through participant-generated audio-visual narratives has a number of impacts on the nature and quality of the data generated for VIA. The participants themselves are able to define the research agenda to a large degree. The hospital-based researchers are in fact intentionally vague about the kinds of things they are looking for the children and adolescents to video-record because they want to ensure the themes identified are patient-rather than practitioner-focused. This results in powerful audio-visual data sets that are grounded in the experiences of the young people themselves and directed by their own understandings.

The method enables children and adolescents who are disadvantaged by their youth and condition to take an active role in increasing practitioner understanding of the social and medical aspects of living with the condition being studied. In many cases, this process has not only yielded improvements in the treatment of the condition by clinicians, but has also empowered the young people so that they have been able to take more control over their own treatment and thereby improve their health outcomes.

The example of the CDHPP project illustrates that 'bottom-up' approaches to change, while challenging, can result in significant and sustained improvements. It also demonstrates that, while the findings of small-scale participatory projects may not be generalisable, they can be transferable. The ward teams engaged in the PDU accreditation programme found the early stages of the process difficult, principally in terms of how to get started, how to engage and involve a range of stakeholders actively, and how to manage the workload. In both wards, however, as they progressed, a well-defined and widely shared PDU philosophy developed and the majority of members of both multi-disciplinary ward-teams felt ownership of the process. A sense of ownership is important in ensuring that change is both effective and sustainable. In terms of developing transferable recommendations, a number of local factors were found to contribute to the timing and nature of the ward-based housekeeping role implemented at the case-study hospital. However, factors identified as supporting the development of the role or found to be problematic or inhibiting, are useful for other hospitals yet to implement the government policy.

Both these projects explicitly aimed to affect health-related practice and both illustrate that directly involving participants in the research process can significantly contribute to this aim.

6.5 IMPACTS OF TECHNOLOGICAL DEVELOPMENTS ON PARTICIPATORY APPROACHES

A number of technological developments have an impact on the ability to involve lay participants in social research. These include the rise of digital technology, the use of the **Internet** as a research tool and the role of qualitative software in research collaboration and methodological transparency.

6.5.1 THE RISE OF DIGITAL TECHNOLOGY

Digital technology has become widely available, increasingly financially accessible and as a result, an everyday aspect of life for many people. It is now commonplace and relatively acceptable to be inadvertently photographed as well as to routinely carry digital cameras and take ad hoc snapshots; often without the need to request permission (but see the warnings in Chapter 23).

As the VIA program and the Bankside Hostel project illustrate, the rise and normalisation of digital technology have had an impact on the ways in which people can participate in generating research data. For example, inspiring the creation of VIA in the mid-1990s was the observation that children and adolescents generally feel comfortable with technology such as cameras and video recorders. An appreciation of the power of video and the need to understand the realities of living with a chronic condition as a young person combined to enable the development of the VIA method. Similarly, participant-generated photography enabled access to an understanding of the meanings and feelings of people with learning difficulties in the Bankside Hostel project, which it would have been difficult if not impossible to uncover through conventional means.

However, the use of digital photography in social research does not come without methodological and ethical implications. Chapter 22 discusses some of the difficulties and debates on the analysis of visual materials, in particular, about the meaning of participation in terms of the subsequent use of research materials, and in relation to visual materials specifically, the scope of informed consent and the representation of participants (see also Chapter 8).

6.5.2 THE USE OF THE INTERNET AS A RESEARCH TOOL

The Internet is increasingly being used as a data collection tool, a means of research collaboration, and a way to disseminate the results of social research projects. As access to the Internet increases among disadvantaged groups and technological advances continue, the potential role it can play in participatory approaches to social research also widens.

As a data collection tool, the Internet can be used in several ways (see Chapter 16). Research participants can be recruited via the Internet, for example, through informal or formal **chat rooms** or web-based or email discussion forums. Data can also be collected via the Internet; interviews can be conducted by email, through chat rooms, **instant messaging**, or through audio/video link-ups. Research participants can also communicate and collaborate online, with secure web pages allowing only those involved to participate, but enabling full access to research information and data.

The Bankside Hostel project provides a striking example of how the Internet can be used to disseminate research findings and, in particular, represent the voices and experiences of disadvantaged and/or marginalised groups in society. Not only were service users involved in all aspects of the project, including writing up the results, but the web site also provides different versions of reports to make them accessible to both an academic and lay audience. The versions include information about the principles of conducting research in partnership, fieldwork questions and challenges, as well as research findings. Rather than providing one large research report combining all the different aspects of the project – from background and design through to analysis and findings – these aspects are available as separate web pages, in either 'easy' or 'full' versions. The research findings include a 'Report with Pictures and Words', a 'Report without Pictures' and a 'Photostory'. This makes the material accessible to a wide variety of audiences and clearly reflects the democratic principles of the whole project.

Projects such as the Bankside Hostel are increasing in number, as are the availability of tools for enhancing web access for hearing- and visually-challenged people. Nevertheless, a large proportion of the world's inhabitants still cannot make use of these developments, including those who cannot afford computers, elderly people who find it difficult to use computers, and the majority of the populations of developing countries.

6.5.3 THE ROLE OF CAQDAS IN COLLABORATION AND TRANSPARENCY

Software packages designed to facilitate qualitative data analysis (CAQDAS, see Chapter 20), can both facilitate collaboration among researchers and enable a higher degree of methodological transparency. Neither of these happen merely by using a software package, since software is simply a tool, not a method, but using them in certain ways can help with both.

In terms of collaboration, the number of software tools specifically designed for the collaborative analysis of qualitative data are increasing. Packages such as Transana[1] and MiMeG,[2] for example, enable geographically dispersed researchers to work on the same dataset concurrently. Although participants have to be trained to use this technology, the potential is there to enable an analytic partnership that can itself be recorded and monitored.

There are a number of methodological benefits of using CAQDAS packages that are analogous to participatory approaches. For example, using software encourages transparent analytic strategies. Analysing qualitative data using a customised CAQDAS package enables that analytic work to be saved and used to illustrate analytic procedures. Given the potential criticisms of participatory approaches discussed above, this can be a powerful means to illustrate to sceptical audiences that the analysis has been rigorous.

When working in collaboration using qualitative software, it will also usually be possible to log the work of different team members and then assess the contributions of different researchers. This can be invaluable to participatory approaches, which prize the real and meaningful involvement of participants at all stages of the research process. It also allows for diverse perspectives to be illustrated as part of the process of reaching consensus.

Even if some research partners cannot be directly involved in the analysis in this way, using a CAQDAS package will allow developing interpretations to be easily demonstrated and discussed at various stages with the wider team. This will encourage everyone to contribute, even if it is not possible, for whatever reason, for all to be involved in the analysis at the same level.

6.6 SUMMARY

This chapter has discussed participatory approaches to conducting social research, illustrating that, rather than constituting a particular method or discipline, they are perspectives on doing social research. As such, they can involve a range of methods, including qualitative and quantitative forms of data collection and analysis. These approaches are often described as being developmental, emancipatory, collaborative and empowering as they aim to change and improve social situations as well as generating understandings about them. In action research projects this is achieved through a cyclical process of enquiry, intervention and evaluation. The historical roots of these approaches were outlined and their general principles illustrated using research examples. These examples illustrate that there are many ways in which lay people can participate in social research and that their contributions can provide access to information which may not otherwise be possible. In particular, participation can result in effective and sustained improvements. Whatever the specific design or focus of a research project employing a participatory approach, the need to do research *with* and *for* participants rather than *on* them has been emphasised. The main contributions that participatory approaches have made to the theory and practice of social research and a number of important methodological and ethical considerations were considered.

NOTES

1 Transana is a software tool specifically developed for the transcription and analysis of audio and video data. It has separate single and multi-user versions. See www.transana.org
2 MiMeG (Mixed Media Grid) is a software tool specifically developed to enable researchers to analyse audio-visual data collaboratively and concurrently. See http://tinyurl.com/2efye5

DISCUSSION QUESTIONS

1 In what ways can different stakeholders participate in social research?

2 What are the common features of participatory approaches to social research?

3 What are the benefits and limitations of participatory research approaches?

4 Locate the examples of research projects presented in this chapter (and/or other studies of which you're aware) in Table 6.1. Discuss the decisions you made about each in order to situate them in the table.

5 Identify and discuss the main differences between the three example projects in terms of how they problematise conventional social research.

6 What factors need to be considered before involving lay participants in research? What problems may arise from doing so?

RESOURCES

Cornwall and Jewkes (1995) 'What is Participatory Research?' is a comprehensive overview of participatory research, including discussion of similarities and differences with conventional research. It focuses on participatory research in healthcare settings but also useful more generally.

Hart and Bond (1995) *Action Research for Health and Social Care* is an in-depth book discussing the history and application of action research, including several case-studies in health and social care which used different action research approaches.

Todhunter (2001) 'Undertaking Action Research: Negotiating the Road Ahead' is a brief but useful case-study of a real-life action research project providing a discussion of transferable lessons and is freely downloadable from the *Social Research Update* web site: http://tinyurl.com/26shwj

The Action Research entry on the Online QDA web site: http://tinyurl.com/ys43no provides definitions of action research and links to several related web-based resources and list of further readings.

The web page, Video Intervention/Prevention Assessment (VIA), http://tinyurl.com/2g24lw, describes the work of VIA program, including information on the development of the method, examples of audio-visual narratives and ways to get involved.

The official web site of the Bankside Hostel project, *Partnership Research: Negotiating User Involvement in Research Design, Bankside Hostel*, http://tinyurl.com/2bn6nz provides information on all aspects of the project, including the history and background of the project, fieldwork, data analysis, writing in partnership and presentation of findings.

7 Mixed Methods

Victoria D. Alexander, Hilary Thomas,
Ann Cronin, Jane Fielding,
and Jo Moran-Ellis

• •

7.1 INTRODUCTION

This chapter considers mixed methods, defined as using two or more research methods within a project. At the beginning of a project, researchers make decisions on crucial issues: what the research questions are (Chapter 3), what the existing literature has to say about the topic (Chapter 4), and what type of research they may undertake (Chapters 5 and 6). A key decision is the choice of method that is employed. Other chapters in the book address the purposes of individual methods. This chapter looks at the reasons why a researcher may choose two or more methods to address their chosen area of study.

The chapter starts with a discussion of the aims researchers may have in using multiple methods and briefly describes debates about what constitutes mixed methods. It presents the advantages of using a mixed methods approach and discusses a variety of ways that researchers have used mixed methods in social research. It considers how different methods may be linked to different paradigms of social research and how different types of data offer researchers different perspectives on the social world. The existence of different **paradigms** and perspectives is crucial to understanding mixed methods, because being able to see from different points of view is one of the key reasons for undertaking mixed methods research. These differences, however, are the source of some difficult aspects of mixed methods projects. Mixed methods also entail a number of practical difficulties, and these are also discussed.

7.2 WHAT ARE MIXED METHODS?

Mixed methods research seems, self-evidently, to be the use of two or more methods in a single research project (or research programme). We define mixed methods in this common-sense way. We also define the use of two or more types of data as falling under the mixed methods rubric. Nothing in social research remains self-evident, however, so we start this chapter by describing how different researchers have thought about mixed methods and we briefly describe some of the debates that occur over mixed methods.

There is a long history to mixed methods research. Sociologists have been using more than one method or source of data for as long as sociology has been a discipline. Recently, however, there has been a new interest in mixed methods as a distinct approach to social research. Several books unpack the complexities of mixed methods (Greene and Caracelli, 1997; Newman and Benz, 1998; Tashakkori and Teddlie, 1998, 2003), and the *Journal of Mixed Methods Research*, launched in April 2007, is devoted to these issues.

Many authors (e.g. Bryman, 2004, 2006; Creswell, 2003; Tashakkori and Teddlie, 1998, 2003) reserve the term 'mixed methods' for those projects that bring together qualitative and quantitative methods. We argue, however, that this definition is too limited (Moran-Ellis et al., 2006), and that 'mixed methods projects' should also include studies that bring together two different qualitative methods (Cronin et al., 2007), and perhaps, even those that bring together two different quantitative methods. For the purposes of this chapter, then, we leave the definition of 'mixed methods' open to encompass a large range of work using more than one method.

One debate among theorists specialising in mixed methods, then, is whether mixing methods necessarily entails both qualitative and quantitative methods. Other debates centre on whether research designs that have one data strand, analysed with different methods, can be considered as mixed methods, and similarly, whether studies that quantify qualitative data (e.g. through content analysis) can be included (Bryman, 2006). And some writers advocate research designs that set out with a formal plan on how data and analysis will be integrated (Coxon, 2005; Pawson, 1995) whereas other researchers are comfortable in taking 'a bit of this and a bit of that to form a more complete picture', an approach which Pawson (1995: 9) criticises. In addition, several theorists have presented more formal definitions and typologies of mixed methods approaches (e.g. Creswell, 2003; Greene and Caracelli, 1997; Moran-Ellis et al., 2006; Morse, 1991; Tashakkori and Teddlie, 1998). There are disagreements among these authors, and others, over which terms to apply to what type of multi-methods design.

7.3 WHY RESEARCHERS USE MULTIPLE METHODS

The main reason that researchers use multiple methods is that they wish to know more about the topics that they study. However, there are many different ways to 'know more'. Mixed methods have been used to increase the accuracy of research findings and the level of confidence in them (e.g. Kelle, 2001), to generate new knowledge through a synthesis of the findings from different approaches (e.g. Foss and Ellefsen, 2002), to hear different voices and bringing into play multiple constructions of a phenomenon (Mason, 2006; Moran and Butler, 2001), to reflect the complexity of a phenomenon (Boaler, 1997; Coyle and Williams, 2000; Deren et al., 2003) and to demonstrate theoretical claims that knowledge is both qualitative and quantitative (Bowker, 2001; Coxon, 2005; Nash, 2002; Pawson, 1995).

Greene et al. (1989) provide a useful typology of the purposes to which researchers may put mixed methods: **triangulation, complementarity, development, initiation,** and **expansion**. Some researchers are interested in *triangulation*. This technique involves measuring a phenomenon in two or three (or more) different ways in order to generate a more accurate measure of it. This is often done when a single, direct measure is difficult or impossible. For instance, if researchers wish to know how many homeless people there are in a given city centre, they might go out on several different nights to count people sleeping in doorways, they might interview residents at homeless shelters asking how often they have slept outside in the last few weeks, and they might interview representatives of charities and public officials to gain their estimates of shelter residents and rough sleepers. In this way, the researchers hope to get a more accurate measure of the number of homeless in the city. Bryman (2004: 544) suggests that triangulation is using two or more methods or sources of data 'so that findings can be cross-checked'. Other theorists find the concept of triangulation to be problematic because it implies that there is a singular reality 'out there' to be measured. (Triangulation has been discussed extensively; see, for example, Bryman, 2004; Campbell and Fiske, 1956; Denzin and Lincoln, 1994; Fielding and Fielding, 1986; Greene et al., 2001; Kelle, 2001; Webb et al., 1966).

Researchers may also be interested in *complementarity* (as Greene et al., 1989, call this approach). Here, multiple methods are used, not to gauge a concrete number (such as of homeless people) or a more accurate picture of a singular reality, but to reveal the different dimensions of a phenomenon and enrich understandings of the multi-faceted, complex nature of the social world. For instance, in our own work on vulnerability, we used different methods (**secondary analysis** of quantitative data, interviews, and visual methods) to examine different facets of the concept of vulnerability. The quantitative data gave us an overview of various aspects of vulnerability (e.g. crime rates), the interview data gave us an insight into how people experience vulnerability and the strategies they take to avoid risk (e.g. if they are worried about being attacked – and many people in crime hotspots are not – they may avoid walking in certain places after dark), and the visual data let us see how our participants viewed their neighbourhoods (e.g. graffiti suggested the presence of undesirable youths and dark alleyways suggested the potential for assault).

Researchers also use mixed methods in order to develop more accurate research instruments. Greene et al. (1989) call this *development*. For instance, if researchers are interested in how management can play a leadership role in decisions to downsize an organisation, they may conduct a preliminary case study in one organisation. The results of this qualitative study can help the researchers to develop a questionnaire that can be sent to a larger sample of organisations. The case study is analysed qualitatively as a preliminary step, while the survey, which may be the primary aim of the study, is analysed quantitatively.

Researchers might use mixed methods when puzzles that appear in one part of their study are explored in a subsequent part. Greene et al. term this *initiation*. For instance, researchers may conduct a survey, on the work-life balance, and discover that while people say they want to spend more time at home, they in fact spend more time at work. This may lead the researchers to conduct a second investigation, using a series of interviews to learn more about this contradiction.

Greene et al. describe one final use of mixed methods, *expansion*. In this approach, researchers broaden and deepen their inquiry by using different methods for different components of the study. Here, researchers purposefully use different methods to explore a larger number of research questions. For instance, researchers interested in the effectiveness of health services might choose to examine policy documents produced by the government, interview policy-makers, survey doctors, and run focus groups with patients. This allows for a broader understanding across a range of stakeholders than would a single method with only one group of respondents.

In deciding to conduct a mixed methods approach, the first questions to ask are:

1   What is the topic I wish to study?

2   What are my research questions?

3   What could each of the methods that I might choose tell me about this topic?

4   How could multiple methods help me answer my research questions?

5   What can I learn about my topic if I employ more than one method?

7.4 HOW RESEARCHERS HAVE MIXED METHODS

There are many different mixed methods designs. Some of the important aspects include: the sequencing of each method, the status of each method relative to the others, and the independence or interdependence of the methods. We present these issues. We also point out that mixed methods projects may mix different types of data or they may mix different means of analysing the same data set. We then give examples of studies that mix qualitative and quantitative methods, those that use different qualitative methods, and those that employ different quantitative methods.

7.4.1 SEQUENCING, STATUS AND INDEPENDENCE/ INTERDEPENDENCE

Punch (2005: 246) identifies three key points for consideration when using mixed methods: whether the methods are conducted sequentially or more-or-less simultaneously, whether one method influences the operationalisation of others, and whether all of the methods are given equal weight.

Methods can be brought into the study in different sequences (Creswell, 2003; Morse, 1991). For example, a qualitative interview method may be used to generate ideas for a questionnaire-based survey, or interviews may follow a survey, to explain apparent paradoxes that the survey brings to light. These approaches mix methods *sequentially*, as the results from one method are analysed before proceeding to the next method. In other cases, the quantitative and qualitative components may proceed in *parallel*. Here mixed methods are sometimes said to be used 'simultaneously' (Morse, 1991) or 'concurrently' (Creswell, 2003). In practice, individual researchers using parallel methods may conduct one aspect of the study at a different time than the other, but in parallel studies, each component is designed with respect to the original research questions, the results of each are analysed separately, and then compared to each other.

A related feature is the independence or interdependence of methods. This follows from examples of sequential studies where one method is used to prepare for another. Sequential studies often use the first method to help with the operationalisation of concepts in the second study. Parallel studies may proceed in an independent manner, or they may be designed from the outset to contain similar, interdependent measures.

Finally, the status accorded to each method should be considered (Greene et al., 1989; Moran-Ellis et al., 2006; Morse, 1991). Often, a qualitative method may follow after a quantitative one to 'flesh out' the quantitative findings, which are given priority. Or a qualitative pilot study precedes the design of a survey to inform the content of the questionnaire. In these cases, the qualitative component is an adjunct to the quantitative, improving its depth or quality, rather than positioned as making an equal contribution to knowledge about the phenomenon. The opposite weighting can occur, for instance, when a survey or content analysis provides a quantitative backdrop to the emerging qualitative analysis. Studies which weight each method equally are more likely to be parallel studies that aim to 'know more' through complementarity.

7.4.2 WHAT IS BEING MIXED?

It is important to realise that 'method' can refer to the style of data collection (surveys, interviews) and also to the means of analysis (statistical analysis, thematic analysis, narrative analysis). Some data collection methods imply particular analytic techniques. For instance, surveys are usually analysed statistically. But in other cases, the data do not necessarily dictate the method of analysis. For instance, in visual research, a collection of images can be analysed with a quantitative content analysis or with a qualitative semiological one (see Chapter 23), and interview techniques can generate data that are thematically coded (Chapter 13) or that are examined with narrative techniques (Chapter 21).

This suggests that methods can be mixed at different stages in the research process. The outcome of the project will at least partly rest on the stage at which this happened. Mixing may begin at the very outset of discussion about the research project. Here the part to be played by different methods will be precisely established, and any interdependence sketched. In contrast, it is possible that multiple methods are envisaged but without specific consideration concerning the relationship between them; in this case the mixing of the methods will take place at some later stage of the project, in the analysis, interpretation, or presentation of the findings.

In some studies, methods are mixed when data are collected. This results in the generation of two or more data sets (e.g. interview and survey data). But in other cases, one technique is used to collect the data, which are then analysed with methodologically distinct frameworks.

A good example of a mixed methods project that draws on one data set is that of Coxon's (2005) study of gay men's sexual behaviour. Coxon asked participants to keep diaries that had both a structured and an unstructured component. The structured format ensured that information related to Coxon's research questions were recorded, while the unstructured format enabled the participants to provide textual narratives of their sexual behaviour. The diaries were analysed both quantitatively and qualitatively, allowing Coxon to blend his findings into a coherent account.

We have already stated that mixed methods can be used to examine different aspects of complicated phenomena (e.g. different conceptions of vulnerability) or to understand the beliefs of a range of participants (e.g. different stakeholders in a policy area). In mixed methods projects, researchers can also examine different levels of analysis (Boaler, 1997; Hartnoll, 1991; Kelle, 2001; Mason, 2006; Nash, 2002). In this type of work social phenomena are seen to operate on different levels, specifically, the macro level (structure) and the micro level (agent).

Kelle (2001) mixes levels of analysis, arguing that for those empirical questions about phenomena which operate at both macro and micro levels, one method alone cannot offer a sufficient basis for sociological explanation. Using a quantitative panel study, he shows that a statistically significant correlation between access to training for workers in particular occupations in Germany and the sex of respondents indicates the existence of gender discrimination. A linked set of qualitative data enables an exploration of the micro-social processes (individual choice and action) by which the discrimination occurs. Kelle's work demonstrates how the occupational and educational system mediates social and gender stratification and, he argues, how a multiple methods approach improves our understanding of the social world, because it illuminates structure, agency and the interplay between the two.

7.4.3 USING QUALITATIVE AND QUANTITATIVE METHODS

Explicitly 'mixed methods' projects often combine the qualitative and the quantitative. (Indeed, as we have stated, some theorists define mixed methods as encompassing only this combination.) Bryman (2006) examined 232 studies in social science that had both qualitative and quantitative components. He found that the majority (57 per cent) of these projects mixed a survey instrument (a questionnaire or a structured interview) on the quantitative side with interviews (semi-structured or unstructured) on the qualitative side. He also found that in about a quarter of these studies, qualitative and quantitative *data* were collected with a single research instrument. This occurred most often when open questions were included in self-administered questionnaires or structured interviews, and less frequently, when qualitative interview or focus group data were coded to produce quantitative data.

One impressive example of a project that mixed qualitative and quantitative methods is Deren et al. (2003). Deren's team studied HIV risk in Puerto Rican injection drug users in San Juan, Puerto Rico and New York City. For each field site, they collected an array of primary data, including qualitative maps of drug-using areas, focus groups with five different types of participant, field observations, in-depth semi-structured interviews at two different points in time, and a survey of 1,200 respondents.

A notable characteristic of the Deren study is that it was a parallel, but interlocking study, in which each site and the qualitative and quantitative methods informed each other as the study proceeded – as they put it, 'both methods provided both discovery and validation for the other' (Deren et al., 2003: 10). This stands in contrast with many parallel studies in which each component is separately conducted and analysed. Alexander (1996a, b, c), for instance, used quantitative analysis (logistic regression on 4,000 exhibitions coded from museum annual reports) and qualitative analysis (interviews with museum personnel). Both of these components were addressed to the main question of how the funding of exhibitions affected their content, but each phase proceeded independently and was reported in different chapters and papers.

Sequential studies may also mix qualitative and quantitative methods. Gobo (2001), for example, employed conversation analysis to improve the response rate to a telephone survey. He used findings from the conversation analysis to redesign the survey, which improved the response rate at initial contact, and thus, the representativeness of the sample. Here quite different methods were used (conversation analysis and a quantitative survey), but not to answer the same research question.

As a final example, Rogers and Nicolaas (1998) used mixed methods in a study of how people use self-care instead of, or alongside, healthcare services when they fall ill. The authors drew on surveys and structured diaries that were analysed quantitatively. Qualitative interviews, conducted with diary keepers, were also quantified in the analysis. The qualitative data in their original form were used only as case-study examples to illustrate the statistical findings. This unequal weighting of the components is common in mixed methods studies.

7.4.4 USING DIFFERENT QUALITATIVE METHODS

There are many different qualitative methods and these may be mixed without reference to quantitative work. Interviews, focus groups, visual methods and documentary analysis all offer the potential for qualitative analysis but are derived from different ways of generating data. Some theorists prefer to call combinations of qualitative methods 'multimethod' rather than 'mixed method' designs (e.g. Tashakkori and Teddlie, 2003), as they see all qualitative methods as springing from the same 'worldview'. But qualitative methods are not all of one piece. Tesch (1990: 58), for instance, identifies 46 different types of qualitative research. This diversity allows for many different combinations.

Qualitative mixed methods studies may be comprised of different types of qualitative data, for instance, textual data from interviews of focus groups, ethnographic observations, diary entries, life histories, historical documents, or visual materials. Or they may draw on distinct qualitative analysis methodologies, such as thematic, semiotic, documentary, historical, or narrative analysis. It may be worth mentioning that some strategies of qualitative research, notably ethnography, draw on several data sources during fieldwork (Fielding and Schreier, 2001), although ethnography is not usually considered a form of mixed methods.

Bagnoli (2004), for instance, used multiple methods in a study of young people's identities in Italy and England. Research participants, who were seen as 'co-researchers', kept week-long diaries, provided a favourite photo of themselves, drew a schematic representation of their lives, and took part in two open-ended interviews. These techniques allowed the participants, along with Bagnoli, to co-create multifaceted autobiographies which were integrated into holistic 'pictures' of identity for each of the research participants. Bagnoli drew upon these to examine how identity is constructed in dialogue with others. Throughout the analysis, she established links among the types of data, as they were seen as 'different parts pertaining to the same whole' (ibid.: 6.13).

Another example is Morrow (2001), who used a mixed method approach in her study of children's 'social capital' and its effects on their well-being. Morrow asked children to write answers to questions such as 'who is important to me and why?' and 'what is a friend for?' (ibid.: 257). This produced textual data. She also asked them to photograph places in their neighbourhoods that were important to them. The children then captioned the photographs with self-adhesive notes. This produced both visual and written data. Finally, the children were asked to talk about their neighbourhoods in small discussion groups. These sessions were tape-recorded and transcribed. Morrow then used a thematic analysis to draw out themes that were found in the visual and textual data. These themes allowed her to comment in rich detail about how neighbourhood spaces affected the children's social relationships and their sense of belonging.

7.4.5 USING DIFFERENT QUANTITATIVE METHODS

Quantitative researchers routinely mix methods of analysis. They frequently use various statistical techniques to analyse data of different sorts. For instance, they may use OLS regressions, correlations, analysis of variance, and factor analysis in the course of one study. Moreover, they often generate both qualitative and quantitative data with a single data collection tool, for example, through a survey that has both closed and open-ended questions. The former are pre-coded and generate specifically quantitative data and the latter generate qualitative data, which then may be quantified or which may be used in qualitative form to illustrate the quantitative findings.

These examples of different analytic techniques and data in quantitative work are not usually considered to indicate a mixing of methods. This is because the methods are not seen as *different enough* to indicate a mixing. (Some theorists, as we have said, cannot see the use of different qualitative methods as mixing, for the same reason.) Also, using different statistical techniques is what quantitative researchers have always done. As with ethnography, which has always drawn on data from multiple sources, combining data or methods in traditional ways does not seem innovative enough, to some observers, to be called 'mixed methods'.

Keeping this in mind, we shall nevertheless mention two studies that employ multiple quantitative methods. We suggest that there are three types of quantitative methods that are distinct enough to be combined in multi-methods projects. These are: (1) secondary analysis of census, demographic, or large-scale survey data; (2) primary survey analysis through self-administered questionnaires or quantitatively coded structured interviews; and (3) content analysis of documents or media texts.

Gerbner et al. (1977) used secondary analysis of crime statistics, a content analysis of television shows coded for criminal acts, and a representative survey – the latter two which they collected themselves – to comment on the relationship between TV viewing and fear of crime. They found from their survey that heavy viewers of television perceived crime rates to be higher than they actually were; the level of crime that they thought occurred in real life matched the rate of fictional crimes on television (the levels found in the content analysis). In contrast, people who watched little television thought that crimes occurred at rates that were closer to those in crime statistics. Although dated, this study shows a particular blend of methods that is often used by students.

Another example is Fielding et al. (2007), who used both secondary analysis of quantitative data and a new survey, which was then quantitatively analysed. The researchers were interested in how people who live in flood plains respond to flood warnings. The first part of the analysis examined a survey of flood victims that had been collected for the Environment Agency after an 'event' (the November 2000 floods in the UK). The results helped the researchers to develop a new survey on how people might respond to three different levels of flood warning. The secondary analysis showed that most people in flooded areas thought that their actions were effective. Fielding et al., using a logistic regression, predicted that those 'feeling prepared' were most likely to report their actions as effective. The new survey, which asked 'at flood risk' respondents to imagine they were in imminent flood situations of varying degrees of seriousness, showed that most people who are at risk intend to act when they receive a flood warning, and the more severe the warning, the more likely they were to take action. However, 6 per cent of the at-risk population would not take action even in the event of the most severe warning. This suggests that future research is needed on people in this group, so that the government can help them prepare for a flood emergency in order to minimise the impact of flooding should it occur.

7.4.6 MIXING: COMBINING OR INTEGRATING

So far in this chapter we have used the term mixing to cover the ways in which multiple methods may be used together. But just how mixed is mixed? In the literature, words such as 'triangulating', '**integrating**', '**combining**' and 'mixing' are often used interchangeably. This tends to obscure some important differences, particularly between the *outcome* of using mixed methods and the *process* by which different data sets are brought together. The outcome of mixed methods may be more accurate measures of important variables, a multifaceted picture of a complex phenomenon, or findings on a broader range of questions. (The term 'triangulation' is an outcome term, and technically it refers only to the first type of outcome.) The process involves how data are generated, analysed and presented. (The terms 'mixing', 'combining' and 'integrating' refer to the process.)

An important distinction can be made between the *combination* of methods on the one hand and *integration* on the other (Moran-Ellis et al., 2006), and both of these are subsumed by the term 'mixing'. In studies in which data or methods are integrated, each method or data set is given equal weighting, but this is not the case in studies in which data or methods are combined.

Sequential studies usually combine methods, as one component of the study is given higher priority than the other, as in Gobo's (2001) use of conversation analysis to improve a survey.

Moreover, integration is a process that brings different methods (data sets, analyses, interpretations) into a relationship with each other to form a coherent whole, without translating one component of the study into another form. (Such a translation would occur, for instance, if narrative data were coded and presented alongside other thematically coded data, rather than being presented in their original, longer, story-like form.) Integration, as a process, requires researchers to choose a means of integration, making decisions on how a significant relationship can be created between methods, data and/or perspectives. Integration can occur from the start of a project. Here, intermeshing occurs from conceptualisation, as in Coxon's (2005) study of gay men mentioned above. Integration may also take place at a later stage at the point of analysis, interpretation or theorising, as in Bagnoli's (2004) study of identity, or Morrow's (2001) study of children and their neighbourhoods.

Integration may be achieved at the point of analysis, in situations where data have been generated by separated methods. We have described a process, which we have called 'following a thread', in which an emergent finding in one data set is identified as having resonances in others (Moran-Ellis et al., 2004). The thematic thread is explored in the other data sets. This creates a data repertoire, which can then be analysed further to generate an integrated account concerning that theme. This is then linked back to the wider research question. Mason (2006: 20) also calls for an integrative strategy, which she terms 'dialogic', in which researchers incorporate visual or sensory methods alongside those that focus on 'talk or text'.

Studies that are integrated in the sense we describe tend to be parallel studies. Parallel studies, however, are often combined, rather than integrated. It is common, for instance, that qualitative findings are presented in one chapter and quantitative ones in another, perhaps with a discussion chapter that briefly considers both.

7.4.7 CHOOSING A MIXED METHODS DESIGN

Having seen examples of how researchers have used mixed methods designs, the reader pondering whether to adopt a mixed methods strategy has a number of questions to consider:

1   Will I collect new data, or analyse existing data, using one methodology as a first step, and then use the results of this step to inform the next one? Or will I collect and/or analyse data from two different sources independently of one another and then compare the results only after each of the studies is completed?

2   How will the contribution of each method be weighted with respect to the other?

3   Will I have one source of data or multiple sources?

4   If I have multiple sources of data, will different data focus on different aspects of one phenomenon, or will they address a range of related research questions? Will they look at different levels of analysis?

5   If I use one source of data, will I analyse the data both qualitatively and quantitatively (e.g. a content analysis alongside an interpretive one, or a statistical analysis complemented by qualitative examples)? Or will I use different qualitative analysis tools (e.g. thematic analysis and narrative analysis)?

6   Which methods will I use: multiple qualitative methods (e.g. interviews, focus groups, ethnography, visual methods), multiple quantitative methods (e.g. content analysis, surveys, secondary analysis) or a combination of qualitative and quantitative?

7   How will I combine or integrate the various components of my study?

7.5 DIFFERENT PARADIGMS, DIFFERENT DATA

Having looked at a variety of ways to use multiple methods, we now turn to some of the difficulties that researchers may encounter in using them. The first set of issues has to do with the fact that different methods often come with assumptions, some of which are not commensurate with others, and that different types of data represent distinct takes on the social world and different ways of knowing.

7.5.1 PARADIGMS AND POSITIONS

It is often stated that quantitative and qualitative methods draw on different paradigms. Indeed, the failure of certain researchers to see the value in each other's work has sometimes been referred to as 'paradigm wars' (Tashakkori and Teddlie, 1998). We believe, however, that a simple dichotomy between the qualitative and the quantitative drastically oversimplifies important issues regarding the assumptions that researchers bring to their work. A paradigm, in simple terms, is a set of assumptions about how we know the world and what we do when we conduct research (see Chapter 1). One crucial paradigm distinction separates strong versions of **positivism** and strong versions of **interpretivism**. We contrast positivism and interpretivism to show that the assumptions underpinning them are incompatible. Note, however, that there are many other approaches in sociology which we do not discuss.

Researchers may differ in their assumptions about the nature of reality. This is called **ontology**. Positivists believe that the world is out there to be measured. They take a realist stance towards data, suggesting that it can be objective and that it is an index of what actually exists. They look for facts. Interpretivists, in contrast, believe that the world is socially constructed. They take a constructivist stance towards data. They argue that social research can never measure a single, external reality; it can produce only an interpretation of what researchers themselves see. Research participants provide researchers with interpretations, which researchers then reinterpret in the research process. These distinctions in ontology do not map neatly onto a quantitative/qualitative split. Quantitative data is, by its nature, realist. Qualitative data, however, can either be realist or constructivist, depending on how it is collected and viewed by the researcher.

Researchers also vary in their beliefs about what we should (or can) do with social research. This is called **epistemology**. Positivists believe that the purpose of social research is to develop abstract and general theories about how the world works. Positivists seek causality and predictability; they test hypotheses. Interpretivists, on the other hand, argue that social research can produce only local, historically-contingent meaning. They seek explanation and understanding; they tell stories. Here, again, positivists draw more commonly on quantitative research. Some positivists draw on qualitative data; however, the positivistic purist spurns studies that draw on a small number of cases because they can never be representative and therefore do not offer the possibility of generalisability. Interpretivists, on the other hand, argue that quantitative data can never produce understanding, in their terms. They therefore favour qualitative data. Purists with an interpretive bent may, however, also reject qualitative studies that aim to be exploratory inquiries that set the groundwork for causal theorising and the production of generalisable results.

These distinctions between positivists and interpretivists are more than a caricature. Strong positivists and strong interpretivists exist. These purists state that methods can not be mixed across paradigms. But the dichotomy between pure positivism and pure interpretivism is also a caricature. Many researchers take a more nuanced view and are willing to see the value of a variety of research as valuable on its own terms. There are other differences in assumptions, or **meta-theories**, that map onto the many different viewpoints that are used in social research (Burrell and Morgan, 1979; Tesch, 1990). (Other divisions in the field include differences in views of human nature and views of society: Are people atomistic actors with free will or are people's actions embedded in social structures that construct their actions? Is society more accurately characterised by consensus or by conflict?) These differences lead researchers to start with different **positions**. Positions are based on the assumptions and rationales held by researchers. These clump into groups in which distinctions are not drawn as strongly as with paradigms (Greene and Caracelli, 1997).

Differences in assumptions are an important issue in mixed methods, because it is much more difficult to mix approaches that aim for local, contingent knowledge with approaches that aim for abstract and general knowledge. If you are a purist, you would never even consider it.

In mixing methods, many researchers take a **pragmatic** approach (Bryman, 1988; Patton, 1998; Tashakkori and Teddlie, 1998) in which little attention is paid to paradigm differences in actual research practice, and different methods are not treated as exclusive to a particular perspective. Other researchers take a **dialectical** approach, which 'calls for explicitly seeking a synergistic benefit from integrating ... positivist and constructivist paradigms' (Rocco et al., 2003: 21). Here, the view is that research that explicitly mixes paradigms leads to a fuller understanding of the social world. For instance, Sale et al. (2002) suggest mixed methods in the study of complex social phenomena because complexity itself consists of both 'interpretivist' and 'positivist' aspects. Mixing methods allows researchers to tap this complexity (Cronin et al., 2008; Greene and Caracelli, 1997; Mason, 2006; Moran-Ellis et al., 2006).

Mixed methods may be used in team research, both in professional research and students' group projects. Team research can highlight the importance of positions and paradigms, as differences in the paradigmatic assumptions that are held by individual team members can lead to disagreements on how data should be collected, analysed and presented. If these issues are not resolved, some sidelining of methods and, indeed, people may result. Being the sole champion of a particular approach can prove to be a lonely business.

7.5.2 HOW DATA REPRESENT THE SOCIAL WORLD

Just as researchers may bring different assumptions to their work, data generated by different methods may provide different windows onto the social world. A statistical table, an image, and a narrative (story) each call for different types of understanding. That is, different types of data imply different types of knowledge: visual, verbal, narrative, conceptual, numerical, or statistical.

Mason (2006) argues that these different ways of understanding generated by different methods are the best reason for undertaking mixed methods. She writes, 'Our ways of seeing, and of framing questions, are strongly influenced by the methods we have at our disposal, because the way we see shapes what we can see, and what we think we can ask.' In failing to mix methods across theoretical or methodological orientations, she argues, 'social scientists may repeatedly miss whole dimensions of social experience because their methodological repertoire or tradition limits their view' (ibid.: 13).

We agree with Mason, but point out two difficulties inherent in the mixing of different types of data. The first is that different ways of knowing, as with different paradigms, are sometimes difficult to reconcile. The second is that one type of data – or way of understanding – may take precedence over others. This may be because researchers are more comfortable in thinking in a particular way, out of habit or because of a strongly held meta-theoretical position. These difficulties can be evident in mixes of numerical and textual data, but they are particularly pronounced when a type of data is less commonly used in social research or when it is hard to represent on the printed page as text or table.

This discussion leads us to several questions to think about, with reference to paradigms, positions, and data:

1   Do I have a good sense of my meta-theoretical, as well as my theoretical, aims in choosing more than one method? Have I examined my underlying assumptions?

2   Can I defend my choice of a mixed methods design?

3   If I work with a team, do we agree on underlying assumptions or have we discussed how we might resolve difficulties if we do not?

7.6 PRACTICAL ISSUES IN MIXED METHODS

The intellectual advantages of using mixed method have been explored in this chapter but such possibilities come with a number of disadvantages. We have discussed the problems that arise because different methods and data imply different research positions. Other problems are of a highly practical nature. At the top of the list is the fact that it takes more work, effort and, hence, time to undertake a mixed method project. Indeed, the use of two methods often implies more than twice the work and more than twice the time.

In a mixed methods project, each aspect of the project must be undertaken properly. Each method poses its own demands. At the beginning of a project these range from ethical clearance to data cleaning. And as the work progresses, even single-method projects provide challenges in terms of data management, analysis, and presenting results. (Here, the other chapters in this book will help with the individual methods chosen.) Then, on top of completing each separate strand, the results of the first must, in sequential projects, inform the design of the second, and in parallel studies, the results of both must be combined or integrated. The fact of using more than one method will not be enough to compensate for poor execution or presentation of the project as a whole. Keep in mind that the time available for student projects and dissertations may simply not allow for a mixed methods approach.

Mixed method designs also require sufficient facility with each method. Varying competence between methods in a mixed method project will show up in the project report, and again, being outstanding in dealing with the process and results of one method will not compensate for inadequacy in another. Another consideration is that use of two methods often implies twice the word count in the write-up. More methods usually result in further complexity of the argument and it may not be possible to write in sufficient depth to be meaningful while observing the guidelines about the length of the finished report.

Working in teams can address the need for expertise in each chosen method, as teams draw on the diversity of methodological skills of their members. Those with quantitative flair may complement the skills of their qualitatively adept peers, those confident with observational techniques may complement those with good interviewing skills, and so on. However, this may also bring to the fore any paradigm clashes within the team. And teamwork is fraught with the problems of ensuring that all team members contribute their fair share to the common effort: taking a mixed methods approach may unwittingly add to any existing difficulties.

Simply managing the data in a mixed method project provides a challenge to the organisational and intellectual skills of the researcher. We could say: twice the methods, twice the analytic notes, and (often) twice the data. As with single methods projects, researchers need a strategy for managing raw data, transcribed or coded data, analytic logs, and notes on findings. And practical decisions must be made as to how the findings from each method are presented – separately chapter-by-chapter, or integrated within parts of the report, perhaps by bringing together findings from across the methods by theme, research site, or participant.

Some researchers have found CAQDAS (see Chapter 20), helpful in multi-method analysis. These qualitative software packages hold different types of data and allow researchers to make links among them. Most versions offer aid to researchers who mix across qualitative methods, and some versions also handle visual and multimedia data. And Bazeley (2002) even found CAQDAS helpful in mixing quantitative and qualitative data. She generated various kinds of quantitative analyses of her qualitative data, while retaining the link between the original qualitative data and their quantitative forms. Technology may also help with the presentation of data. Dicks et al. (2006), for instance, describe how they used hypertext to **hyperlink** across textual, visual and multimedia data. But while hypertext offers great potential for changing the way that researchers present data, currently, most reports are printed on paper.

Researchers must also consider how they will address inconsistent results. Researchers starting from a realist position whose aim is triangulation have particular difficulties should inconsistencies occur. A key claim for triangulation is increased 'validity'. If different measures produce dissimilar results, decisions need to be made about whether one measure is flawed, and if so, which one? With a triangulation model, anomalous findings need to be addressed and explained. Along these lines, inconsistent results may lead members of a team to argue among themselves over whose results are 'better'.

In contrast, researchers from a constructivist perspective whose goal is complementarity are less troubled by disparate results. These are not seen as 'inconsistency', but rather, as an index of the complexity of what is studied. Nevertheless, these researchers must describe and address any complexity that they uncover and, preferably, connect it to their theoretical discussion.

A final consideration brings us full circle. Ideally, researchers will have a clear idea about why they have mixed methods, and their reasoning should be clearly stated in their reports. Mixing methods has come to be seen as a good thing, but why this may be so is often left unexplained. Indeed, Bryman (2006) reports that more than one-quarter of the studies he examined did not state their rationales for using mixed methods. We suggest that researchers should start their projects with a consideration of why they may wish to use more than one method. And at the end of a project, researchers having chosen to mix methods would do well to look back on the project and reflect on the benefits (or problems) this has brought them.

This discussion leads to a final set of questions that need to be considered. These questions might lead one to speculate about when not to use mixed methods:

1   Do I (or does my team) have the skills needed to conduct research using each of the methods that I might use in a mixed methods project?

2   Do I have the time to do two studies and the time to combine or integrate them?

3   Do I have a strategy for managing a larger amount of data?

4   Do I have enough space in my report or paper to write up results from more than one method? Will my word limit make it difficult to report thoroughly my findings from each method?

5   Will I report findings from each method separately, or will I integrate the findings in some way?

6   Have I considered the reasons for using more than one method, and will I make these clear in my report?

7   What would be lost if I rely on one method? Is the gain produced by multiple methods worth the cost in time, effort and word count?

7.7 SUMMARY

This chapter has discussed mixed methods in social research, describing both advantages and difficulties of taking such an approach. Mixed methods may seem a simple addition – one method plus another equals mixed methods. But we have shown that bringing together distinctly different methods, or distinctly different data, is considerably more complicated. In the chapter we have provided examples of different types of mixed methods projects, and we have set out questions that researchers should address when they consider undertaking them. We have not discussed the issues involved in conducting research from within individual methodologies – these are covered in other chapters in the book – but we have given an overview of the many ways methods can be mixed.

DISCUSSION QUESTIONS

1   What are the advantages of using a mixed method approach? What are some of the disadvantages? What topics in social research might benefit from a mixed methods approach?

2   What aspects of the research question, research design, analysis, and presentation of results are affected by a mixed methods approach? How would you design a project that was sequentially ordered? How would this differ from a design of that proceeded in parallel?

3   How can we 'know more' by using a mixed methods approach? Is it possible to reconcile different paradigms within such an approach? How might you make links among very different types of data?

PROJECTS

Here we suggest four short exercises that will give you practical experience with mixed methods. After you have completed an exercise we suggest you reflect back on your experience.

1   Choose a topic, such as people's experience of watching television or listening to music, which is not too personal or intrusive. Ask five or six people to keep diaries for a specific length of time, e.g. a week, noting events, thoughts and experiences relevant to your topic. Analyse the diaries, then follow up the diary-keeping with short, qualitative interviews with each individual. Combine or integrate the diary and interview findings in a short report.

2   Choose a subject for which quantitative data are accessible, for example, a large-scale government survey such as the General Household Survey. Examine the data for a specific topic (for example, recent use of health services). You may analyse the data yourself, or you may draw on results from the surveys that are published online. Using these results design an interview schedule that could be used to explore questions about your topic that the results bring up (for example, the circumstances in which participants choose to consult a doctor or a complementary practitioner, or to rely on self-care). How has the quantitative analysis helped with the design of the interview schedule?

3   Conduct three or four qualitative interviews with friends about a chosen topic, perhaps asking about their experiences of holidays and their ideas about what makes a good holiday. Analyse these data. Use the

emerging themes to design a structured questionnaire that could be used in a survey about your topic. How has the qualitative analysis helped with the design of the survey instrument?

4   Choose ten newspaper articles addressing the same subject. Analyse the material using different methods. (a) *Content analysis*: choose themes and develop codes to categorise these themes, based on the usage of specific words or the column inches devoted to specific themes. You may also wish to develop codes for any visual material that accompanies the article. After you have coded your sources, provide tables or graphs to display your findings. (b) *Interpretive analysis*: instead of choosing themes and coding them, you will develop an understanding of the ways the topic is presented in the articles, demonstrating these with illustrative quotes from your sources. Or you may wish to conduct a semiotic analysis of the text or visual images. How do the content and interpretive analyses compare?

RESOURCES

Recently, 'mixed methods' has emerged as a distinct methodological field. Several textbooks have chapters on mixed methods (e.g. Bryman, 2004; Creswell, 2003; Punch, 2005). Tashakkori and Teddlie (1998) provide a 'taxonomy' of mixed methods designs in their book, which sees mixed methods as a pragmatic solution to the 'paradigm wars'.

Greene and Caracelli (1997) also discuss paradigms and 'positions', but these authors see the benefit of mixed methods not as pacifying different paradigmatic warriors, but rather as a way to tap the complexity of the social world.

Along these lines, Mason (2006) argues that mixed methods can help researchers to think more creatively, and her thoughtful discussion illustrates how different data imply different ways of seeing and knowing. She points out that the use of different methods will necessarily produce tensions as they produce different understandings of the world. To manage this in research, she prefers the notion of 'linking data', which is described by Fielding and Fielding (1986).

Finally, we mention the large edited collection by Tashakkori and Teddlie (2003) who believe that mixed methods are the third 'methodological movement' of the social sciences following on from quantitative, and then qualitative, methods. While their claims that mixed methods are a new and distinct methodology may be overstated, their book nevertheless brings together 26 useful articles on a range of issues in mixed methods.

8 The Ethics of Social Research

Martin Bulmer

KEY POINTS

● Sociologists have responsibilities to the subjects of their research.

● There are a number of ethical principles that need to be considered in designing and carrying out a project, such as informed consent, respect for privacy, safeguarding the confidentiality of data, and avoiding harm to subjects and researchers.

● Publication of results can have consequences that need to be understood and considered from an ethical perspective.

● Social research is increasingly regulated and monitored. The procedures for obtaining ethical approval need to be followed when they apply.

8.1 INTRODUCTION

Ethics is a matter of principled sensitivity to the rights of others. Being ethical limits the choices we can make in the pursuit of truth. Ethics say that while truth is good, respect for human dignity is better, even if, in the extreme case, the respect of human dignity leaves one ignorant of human nature. Such ethical considerations impinge upon all scientific research, but they impinge particularly sharply upon research in the human sciences, where people are studying other people. Sociologists necessarily need to consider ethical issues that arise in the course of their research and this chapter sets out some of the issues.

The sociological research community has responsibilities not only to the ideals of the pursuit of objective truth and the search for knowledge, but also to the subjects of their research. Just as in other sciences, with human subjects in the physiological laboratory, patients in the medical school, or students in the psychological laboratory, so members of the public whom the sociologist encounters while out in the field need to be considered from an ethical standpoint. Researchers always have to take account of the effects of their actions upon those subjects and act in such a way as to preserve their rights and integrity as human beings. Such behaviour is ethical behaviour.

This chapter considers these ethical issues. When designing a research project, you need to consider ethical principles such as informed consent, respect for privacy, safeguarding the confidentiality of data, harm to subjects and researchers, and deceit and lying. It also discusses ethical issues arising in quantitative and qualitative research, emphasising the dilemmas of ethically aware research. Research ethics has been a matter of academic and public debate, and towards the end of the chapter we summarise processes of ethical regulation and review.

8.2 ETHICS IN SOCIAL RESEARCH

8.2.1 UNETHICAL BEHAVIOUR IN THE NAME OF RESEARCH

Two examples indicate the strength of feeling towards those researchers who have used unethical methods in their research. In 1919, Franz Boas, the dominant figure in American anthropology of the time, wrote to *The Nation* that

> (b)y accident, incontrovertible proof has come to my hands that at least four men who carry on anthropological work, while employed as government agents, introduced themselves to foreign governments as representatives of scientific institutions in the United States, and as sent out for the purposes of carrying out scientific researches. They have not only shaken the belief in the truthfulness of science, but they have also done the greatest possible disservice to scientific inquiry ... The very essence of (the scientist's) life is the service of truth ... A person who uses science as a cover for political spying, who demands himself to pose before a foreign government as an investigator and asks for assistance in his alleged researches in order to carry on, under this cloak, his political machinations, prostitutes science in an unpardonable way and forfeits the right to be classed as a scientist. (quoted in Weaver, 1973: 51–2)

Social science should not be used as a cover for spying. Boas argued that whereas soldiers, diplomats, politicians and businessmen might set patriotic devotion above everyday decency, the scientist's calling, the search for truth, made very special demands. Such behaviour was unethical.

Around 1950, William Caudill, an American anthropologist with interests in psychology, took part in a research project to study some of the social and medical problems of life in a mental hospital as seen from the patient's point of view. Known only to two senior members of staff, he was admitted as a bona fide patient resident in the hospital, and was treated there for two months. He did not reveal to most staff and all other patients that he was a sociological observer. The story that he invented to tell his psychotherapist (who did not know that he was there as a covert observer) was that:

> he had recently been trying to finish the writing of a scholarly book, but felt that he was not getting ahead; worry over his work drove him to alcoholic episodes ending in fights; he was withdrawn and depressed, and had quarrelled with his wife, who had then separated from him. Beyond these fictions, Caudill had given a somewhat distorted picture of his own life, in which he consciously attempted to suppress his own solutions to certain problems and to add a pattern of neurotic defences. (Caudill et al., 1952: 315)

Such duplicity on the part of the sociologist has been attacked by Kai Erikson, who believes that 'the practice of using masks in social research compromises both the people who wear them and the people for whom they are worn, and in doing so violates the terms of a contract which the sociologist should be ready to honour in his dealings with others' (Erikson, 1967: 367–8). Four kinds of wrong are involved:

1   The sociologist has responsibilities to the subjects of research. The method has potential to do (unforeseeable) harm. If subjects know they are being studied, at least they have agreed to expose themselves to possible harm. To study them secretly is ethically comparable to a doctor who carries out medical experiments on human subjects without their agreement.

2   Sociologists have responsibilities to their colleagues. Covert observation is liable to damage the general reputation of sociology and close off further avenues for research.

3   Most of those who get involved in covert observation are graduate students. Since covert research poses serious ethical problems and often results in personal stress for the observer, it is unreasonable to use a method, the burden of which will fall upon those still dependent upon their academic elders.

4   Erikson's final and strongest argument is that covert research is bad science. The complexities of human social interaction are but imperfectly understood. To believe that it is possible to conceal one's identity from others by playing a covert role is highly problematical. It is by no means clear that those who do research in this way really succeed in becoming full participants accepted as such by others. The rationale of the method therefore falls away and the quality of the data collected by its use is liable to bias, distortion and error. We shall return to these general considerations below, but the debate gives a flavour of some of the issues that are involved.

8.2.2 ETHICAL GUIDANCE AVAILABLE TO THE SOCIAL RESEARCHER

The social researcher faced with potential ethical problems in the conduct of research may have to resort to guidance from codes of ethics and ethical guidelines provided by professional associations. Two sets of guidelines are readily available in the UK, from the Social Research Association (SRA) and the British Sociological Association (BSA).

The Social Research Association's *Ethical Guidelines* point the social researcher towards good practice in the conduct of social research. Members of the Association are required to acknowledge them in becoming members, and they appear in the SRA's Directory of Members. They may also be consulted on the SRA web site (http://tinyurl.com/yqqzsw) and are reprinted in Bulmer et al. (1999: 53–68).

The British Sociological Association's *Statement of Ethical Practice* appears under the banner 'Professional Standards' on the BSA web site (http://tinyurl.com/2bwz3y). The Association has a set of Rules for the Conduct of Enquiries into Complaints against BSA members under the auspices of the Statement, and its Guidelines on Professional Conduct. The Statement is, however, primarily meant to inform members' ethical judgements rather than impose them as an external set of standards. Sociologists need to be aware of the ethical issues that can arise in their work and use the Statement of Ethical Practice to sensitise themselves to the sorts of ethical issue that can arise.

Broader guidance is also available. The RESPECT project (n.d.) was an EU-wide attempt to formulate professional and ethical guidelines for the conduct of socio-economic research in Europe.

8.3 ETHICAL BEHAVIOUR IN SCIENCE: THE NORMS

The norms of science advocate the search for truth as the driving force behind the creation of new knowledge (Merton, 1968: 591–603). According to this view, the prime objective of sociology should be the search for the truth. What is the social context in which truth is to be sought? Conventional accounts of social research stress the need to cooperate with informants, establish trust, create empathy between researcher and subject, and be relatively open about what one is doing. Such conventional procedures, it is often suggested, rest upon a consensual view of society in terms of social order. Against this, it is argued that the nature of contemporary society is best described by a conflict model.

> Profound conflicts of interest, values, feeling and action pervade social life. Conflict is the reality of life; suspicion is the guiding principle. It's a war of all against all and no one gives anyone anything for nothing, especially for the truth. (Douglas, 1976: 55)

The problems faced by sociologists are shared by many other practitioners – for example, doctors and clergymen – some of whom have very well-developed ethical guidelines for decision-making. The ethics of social research are not therefore peculiar, but they do provide an instructive case-study of some of the dilemmas that face the social scientist trying to reconcile different objectives. The complexity of ethical decision-making is indicated by the variety of views there are about the principles of ethical conduct in social research.

8.3.1 INTERVIEWS

Another perspective is provided by looking at social research from the point of view of the general public. Graham et al.'s (2007) study of how members of the public view and experience social research emphasises the crucial importance of the interviewer and trust in negotiating the subjects' participation. The differences between qualitative and quantitative studies are less than might have been expected. What seems more meaningful is how sensitive or personal the subject matter of an interview is. Rather than creating new ethical requirements, sensitive topics place particular emphasis on voluntariness in participation, being mentally prepared for the interview, the scope for self-expression, confidentiality and the option to withhold information.

An important factor in persuading members of the public to participate is that the research may be used and lead to wider benefit. This underlines that the research relationship is tri-partite, involving participant, researcher and funder. Funders also have responsibilities. Graham et al.'s research highlights the importance of returning to the research field to see what footprints the research has left, and incorporating the lessons into future research practice. There is a need for more research on participants' perspectives, using a wider range of approaches and exploring experiences of different research methods and different research populations.

8.4 ETHICAL PRINCIPLES GOVERNING SOCIAL RESEARCH

Many principles have been used to justify taking an ethical view of the activity of social research. One general principle that runs through much of the discussion is the need to strike a balance between society's desire, on the one hand, to expose the hidden processes at work in modern society and, on the other, to protect the privacy of individuals and groups and to recognise that there are private spheres into which the social scientist may not, and perhaps even should not, penetrate (Barnes, 1980: 13–24).

8.4.1 INFORMED CONSENT

A second very important general principle, which is a linchpin of ethical behaviour in research, is the doctrine of **informed consent**. This provides that persons who are invited to participate in social research activities should be free to choose to take part or refuse, having been given the fullest information concerning the nature and purpose of the research, including any risks to which they personally would be exposed, the arrangements for maintaining the confidentiality of the data, and so on.

This principle was restated following the end of the Second World War in the Nuremberg trials of Nazi war criminals. The Nazi regime had exposed many subjects, particularly concentration camp inmates, to extreme medical experiments in which subjects sometimes died from the treatment which they received. An example was immersing people for long periods in icy water to test the survival chances of downed air crew in the sea.

The notion of informed consent was embodied in 1946 in the following principle:

> The voluntary consent of the human subject is absolutely essential. This means that the person concerned should have legal capacity to give consent, should be so situated as to exercise free power of choice, without the intervention of any element of force, fraud, deceit, duress, overteaching or any other ulterior form of constraint or conversion; and should have sufficient knowledge and comprehension of the elements of the subject matter involved as to enable him to make an understanding and enlightened decision. (quoted in Homan, 1991: 69; see also Katz et al., 1972: 292–306)

Informed consent is generally taken to mean that those who are researched should have the right to know that they are being researched, and that in some sense they should have actively given their consent. In medical experiments, a signed consent form is required. This is rarely the case in social research, but the principle does suggest that some attempt should be made to explain to those being studied what the study is for. Thus in a social survey, the respondents will usually be told who is the sponsor of the survey, what in general terms is its subject matter, and what will be expected of them by the interviewer. In **ethnographic** research, it is usual for ethnographers to be open about their identity as researchers, and to give some general indication of what they are doing, for example, that they are writing a book about the group or setting being studied.

In particular, the principle acts as a constraint on those who might be tempted to conduct covert research under the guise of some other role or identity. For example, 'sugging', the practice of pretending to conduct an interview that then turns into a sales pitch, is a practice that many people object to and that the market research industry goes to great lengths to counter. The salesperson is gaining the respondent's cooperation on false pretences and is violating informed consent. Covert participant observation raises similar difficulties, which are discussed further below. A researcher who pretends to be a true participant (for example, a member of a small political party or a religious sect, e.g. Festinger, 1964) is violating the confidence of the people with whom that person is spending his or her time.

8.4.2 RESPECT FOR PRIVACY

An ethical dimension to social research that often plays a part in the public perception of social science is the extent to which sociologists are perceived to intrude into areas which are believed to be private. Why such areas are deemed private may vary. Some aspects of behaviour (for example, ownership of wealth or sexual behaviour) are often considered to be the concern of no one other than the person concerned. Sometimes the milieu (for example, the nuclear family) is considered a domain into which the researcher should not enter. Sometimes a public arena (for example, the key political power centres of central government, such as the Cabinet and ministerial offices) are preserves into which the sociologist should not expect access.

Many definitions of privacy emphasise the control by an individual of information about him or herself as a key component. In modern industrial society, information is a commodity, and given the multiple social ties in which people are involved, keeping control of information about oneself and deciding what to release and to whom is often a key means by which one's privacy is protected, and control is maintained over what others can learn about you. But the 'right to privacy' is not a simple matter, since so much information is held about individuals by organisations, and the exchange of information is often necessary for the provision of different kinds of services.

In social research, there are also complications stemming from the institutionalised nature of social life. Entry to research settings may be controlled by **gatekeepers** who are professionals or administrators in charge (see Chapter 14). Yet they may grant permission on behalf of clients or customers or patients frequenting the milieu – or may deny entry even if members of those groups are willing to grant it and cooperate in the research. The role of gatekeepers in social research is therefore a critical one, to which separate attention is given in ethical codes and guidelines. In some areas, particularly in sociomedical research, scrutiny of research proposals is institutionalised in ethical review committees where scientists sit in judgement over the research designs and procedures of fellow scientists.

8.4.3 SAFEGUARDING THE CONFIDENTIALITY OF DATA

A continuing concern in social research has been not just with the conditions under which data are collected, but with how they are stored and disseminated. Assurances are commonly given to those providing responses to questionnaires or interview questions that these data are needed for purposes of statistical aggregation and the individual will not be identifiable in the resulting analysis.

Increasingly, quantitative data sets are available for **secondary analysis** via data archives (see Chapter 19) that also control the distribution of data by requiring the registration of users and releasing data only to those who have signed a legal agreement. This provides some safeguard for the uses to which the data are put. Safeguards for quantitative data are further discussed in Section 8.5.2.

8.4.4 HARM TO SUBJECTS AND RESEARCHERS

There has been considerable debate about the ethical implications of harm in social research, involving harm to those being researched and to those who are doing the research (for a review, see Warwick, 1982). Although there are no clear conclusions to this debate, there is general awareness that social research may have consequences for those being studied.

A graphic example was provided by an ethnographic study in the USA some years ago of impersonal sex among gay men in a public setting. A sociologist, Laud Humphreys (1970), acted as a 'watch queen' in an isolated public toilet located in a park frequented by gay men, in order to carry out an observational study. He also noted down the licence numbers of cars parked near this facility. Later, he obtained the names and addresses of the owners, changed his appearance, and called on these men at home in order to carry out a supposed health survey. In fact, he was seeking information about their social and family backgrounds in order to show how a gay sample of the population compared to a 'straight' sample. When the research became publicly known, a great public furore resulted, since many considered that he had been spying on the men concerned and held information which could be used to their detriment, for blackmail and so on. Humphreys eventually destroyed the data he held identifying the men in the study, deeming the bank vault in another city, where he had stored the data, as not sufficiently safe. The essence of the argument was his potential to cause harm to the men he had studied.

It has also been argued that if sociologists use less than frank methods and pretence to gain access to settings and data, not only do they violate the principle of informed consent (Section 8.4.1) but they may also do harm to themselves. The reader may compare the (true) social psychological study *When Prophecy Fails* (Festinger, 1964) with the fictional account of a very similar set of circumstances, *Imaginary Friends* (Lurie, 1967). In both, the sociologist infiltrates a group that believes that the end of the world is about to arrive and attempts to explain how group members adjust their beliefs when the predicted event does not happen. In the fictional account, serious harm results for the sociologist. It has often been argued that the perils of role pretence, dissimulation and deception are harmful for the individual and for sociology as a profession, and this is a dimension of more ingenious research designs in sociology that needs to be kept in mind (see Warwick, 1982).

8.4.5 DECEIT AND LYING IN THE COURSE OF RESEARCH

Argument has waxed fierce at times about the use of deception in research. Lying by sociologists to gain access to data is rare, but misrepresentation has been more common, although still unusual. The extent to which the sociological researcher has an obligation to tell the unvarnished truth has been much debated. In principle the issues are not very different from truth-telling in other situations – do we always tell the literal truth to our friends?, do doctors tell the truth to dying patients?, do critics tell the unvarnished truth to artists? and there is scope for considerable moral argument about the latitude allowed to an individual in such situations (see Bok, 1978). As a general principle, the use of deception in research has been condemned, and concealment of the fact that one is a researcher has attracted criticism. But there are many situations in which it is not possible to be completely open to all participants and sometimes a full explanation of one's purposes would overwhelm the listener. So it is recognised that there are degrees of openness and concealment possible in social research. Some examples are considered briefly below.

8.4.6 ATTENDING TO THE CONSEQUENCES OF PUBLICATION

A substantial section of the British Sociological Association's Statement of Ethical Practice is concerned with relations with, and responsibilities towards, sponsors and/or funders. There are a number of aspects to this, but one of the most important concerns publication of the results of research. Researchers should try to ensure that they retain the right to publish research results without hindrance, although this is not always possible with certain types of applied research carried out for a client. Maurice Punch, who conducted a study of the independent boarding school, Dartington Hall, has written at length about the problems that can arise in this area, and that he himself encountered (Punch, 1986).

There is a more general issue about where the wider social responsibilities of the social scientist reside. Sociologists who have studied particular, disadvantaged social minority groups have often been sensitive to the consequences of publishing studies of them that make previously private information public. Self-censorship is not unknown to protect those who might be harmed by publication. Relations with the mass media also need to be handled carefully, and sociologists who have had dealings at close hand with television, radio or the print media have not always come away from the encounter feeling that their research has been fairly presented (Haslam and Bryman, 1994).

8.5 ADDITIONAL ISSUES FOR QUANTITATIVE RESEARCH

In survey research, one important area concerns what the respondent is told about the auspices and purpose of the study, what are the conditions under which the addresses and names of respondents are used, how the data will be published, how anonymity of individual respondents will be preserved, and how the confidentiality of the final dataset will be safeguarded. These are all issues to which thought will need to be given at the design and fieldwork stages of the survey (see Chapter 10).

8.5.1 WHAT IT IS PERMISSIBLE TO ASK IN SURVEYS: SENSITIVITY

How does the sociological researcher weigh the sensitivity of topics in designing a questionnaire and determine what is permissible? Consider two examples.

A policy researcher is investigating the adequacy of social security provision for persons who have recently been bereaved. How does the government grant compare to the actual cost of a simple funeral? The researcher plans to interview the spouses of recently deceased elderly people in order to assess this issue. A second example concerns the study of teenage pregnancy and the availability of contraception (see Holland et al., 1998; Lees, 1993). Researchers interview adolescents in order to throw light on these issues and test theories. What are the researchers' responsibilities in these cases? The elderly widow or widower may be upset or distressed to be asked questions about the loss of their spouse, and so the issue needs to be handled sensitively. The young person being asked about their sexual knowledge, experience and behaviour needs to be approached with care, possibly with the permission of parents. If the person is under the age of 16, particular problems arise. Lee (1993) has a good discussion of some of the approaches that can be taken to broach sensitive topics in surveys.

8.5.2 ENSURING THE CONFIDENTIALITY AND ANONYMITY OF QUANTITATIVE DATA

Social researchers also need to consider their ethical responsibilities in relation to the handling of data resulting from large-scale enquiries, such as the results of a survey. Proper arrangements for the custody of the paper questionnaires or the electronic files resulting from the survey need to be made. The implications of the survey need to be considered. (In the UK, this may involve consultation with the Data Protection Registrar, see the web site: http://tinyurl.com/25pcrs

Various methods have been used to ensure the confidentiality of large datasets. With census data (which cover the entire population), special precautions are taken: the individual data are not released outside the Census Office; in small area tabulations random error is injected into the tables; and in the individual and household samples available from the UK 1991 Census (the Sample of Anonymised Records – see Chapter 15), certain mainly geographical variables are suppressed or altered to prevent people deducing facts about individual respondents. With survey data, in addition to omitting respondents' names and addresses, their geographical location is frequently not accurately identified, thus maintaining confidentiality. In longitudinal research, where individuals and households may be followed over a period of time, special precautions need to be taken to keep secret the identities and locations of participants, and these precautions need to be re-doubled if datamatching or linking is involved. A variety of different models are available (see Boruch and Cecil, 1979: 93–126) to ensure insulation of different files from each other, and to keep the identifying links separate from the data to which they relate. Statistical methods, such as random error injection and randomised response (Lee, 1993: 82–6), have often been attempted. The most effective recent innovation is computer-assisted self-interviewing (**CASI**), in which respondents answer questions themselves on the interviewer's lap-top computer without the interviewer being involved, thus ensuring privacy in the interview and a degree of confidentiality of the resulting data (see Chapter 10).

8.6 ADDITIONAL ISSUES FOR QUALITATIVE RESEARCH

Many ethical dilemmas also arise in qualitative research and these have been discussed in a number of sources (e.g. Ellen, 1984: 133–54; Filstead, 1970: 235–80; for an example, see Fichter, 1973). In some respects, the ethical dilemmas facing the qualitative researcher are sharper and the freedom of action in research greater, so that the consequent ethical problems that may be encountered are more varied. Self-presentation is at a greater premium in much field research, and this can lead the researcher into problems and dilemmas that frequently have an ethical dimension. The general issues can be demonstrated by means of two specific examples.

8.6.1 USING COVERT OBSERVATION: IS IT EVER JUSTIFIED?

Are sociologists ever justified in concealing their identity in order to gain entry to a milieu?

In a famous Californian study, Rosenhan (1973) sent eight volunteers to seek admission to different mental hospitals, saying that they 'heard voices' but with instructions to say that the symptoms had disappeared as soon as they were admitted (see also Chapter 14). They were also told not to reveal their identities as researchers. The researchers took between seven and 52 days to be released, with a mean of 19 days, and usually with the diagnosis of schizophrenia 'in remission'. Few of the medical or nursing staff questioned the genuineness of these 'pseudo-patients', although a number of the other patients did. One experimenter, who was much exercised about whether to take notes on the ward in case it revealed his purpose, found 'engages in compulsive writing behaviour' written in his notes by one of the nursing staff. Was the director of the research justified in concealing the true identity of members of his research team in order to test the value of labelling theory?

Covert participant observation is clearly a violation of the principle of informed consent. By definition, the subjects of research are kept in ignorance of the true identity of the researcher. They have no opportunity to decide whether or not to participate. Secret participant observation is also frequently an invasion of privacy. To insinuate oneself into a particular setting on false pretences, in order to gather material for research, violates the right of the individual to be let alone and to control her or his personal sphere. On the outside, the individual can hold objects of self-feeling, such as her or his body, actions, thoughts and some of her or his possessions, clear of contact with alien and contaminating things. But in total institutions like hospitals, these territories of the self are violated; the boundary that the individual places between her or his being and the environment is invaded and the embodiment of self profaned. The same is true of staff in such settings, who are not aware that they are dealing with someone who is not as they seem.

A major criticism of covert methods is that they involve out-and-out deception. Researchers are pretending to be people who they are not. This runs counter to the usual norm in empirical research – including observational studies – of building up relations of trust with those whom one is studying. In certain highly exceptional circumstances, deception may be justified by the context in which research is carried out. Bruno Bettelheim's study on the concentration camp (1943) is an example of a covert study that was justified. Bettelheim was imprisoned in the camp. Indeed, he embarked on the study in order to try to survive psychologically in an extreme situation that was not of his own choosing. This research may be justified ethically (if it needs such justification) on the grounds that Bettelheim was held in the camp under duress. But such cases are very rare.

A common defence of the use of covert methods of research is to argue that, although some criticisms of it have force, covert methods do not cause harm to those studied if the identities and location of individuals and places are concealed in published results, the data are held in anonymised form, and all data are kept securely confidential. It is proposed that the benefits from greater social scientific knowledge about society outweigh the risks that are run in collecting data using covert methods. Apart from the problem of being unable to predict the consequences of publishing research, the central issue in any risk/benefit equation such as this is: who is to draw up the balance sheet and determine whether particular methods are justified or not?; whose causes are the right causes in social research?

A further dimension to the problem, less often considered, is what effect covert observation has on the social scientist who is doing the observing. It is noteworthy that several scholars who have used covert methods have subsequently made statements against their use, saying that they would not have used them with benefit of hindsight.

This brief summary (presented in more extended form in Bulmer, 1982) gives some indication of the dimensions of ethical debate about the use of covert observational methods.

8.7 ETHICAL REGULATION AND ETHICAL REVIEW

An increasing feature of human sciences research in western democracies is ethical review of research before it is undertaken. In the UK, universities have established Research Ethics Committees which oversee research in all areas of academic inquiry. In the National Health Service, ethical review is an established part of all research with patients and staff, whether biomedical or social and economic. In the United States, Institutional Review Boards exercise these regulatory roles over research including social science research. Increasingly postgraduate and undergraduate students undertaking empirical research for dissertations will find themselves undergoing ethical review of their research plans, with requirements to explain and justify the way in which they will conduct research, by producing a research protocol.

In 2006, the UK Economic and Social Research Council, which is a major funder of social science research, published a Research Ethics Framework (ESRC 2005) which was intended to inform the behaviour of holders of ESRC Research Grants and Research Studentships. It stated that there were six key principles of ethical research that the ESRC expects to be addressed, whenever applicable:

1   Research should be designed, reviewed and undertaken to ensure integrity and quality.

2   Research staff and subjects must be informed fully about the purpose, methods and intended possible uses of the research, what their participation in the research entails and what risks, if any, are involved. Some variation is allowed in very specific and exceptional research contexts for which detailed guidance is provided in the policy Guidelines.

3   The confidentiality of information supplied by research subjects and the anonymity of respondents must be respected.

4   Research participants must participate in a voluntary way, free from any coercion.

5   Harm to research participants must be avoided.

6   The independence of research must be clear, and any conflicts of interest or partiality must be explicit.

ESRC does not seek to impose a particular model for achieving these expectations. As well as research with living human subjects, research involving deceased people with living relatives, body parts, or other human elements will require ethical approval and a broad view should be taken of possible ethical problems arising from research. The Framework ensures that ESRC peer review of proposals addresses ethical issues, and ESRC checks institutions with awards to see that commitments to ethical review have indeed been followed through. There is thus a connection between the research council expectations and the internal procedures of institutions.

Universities and other research institutions have established appropriate procedures to monitor the conduct of research that has received ethical approval until it is completed. Monitoring is intended to be proportionate to the nature and degree of risk entailed in the research and should include consideration of best practice procedures for the secure holding and preservation of data.

The ethical review of research in the health and medical fields is particularly rigorous, because of the risks involved in biomedical research with patients. Academic ethical review bodies are typically multidisciplinary, and there are sometimes tensions between those coming from different disciplinary backgrounds. Do scientists, for example, properly understand the way in which sociologists conduct research? A further difficulty is whether such review bodies confine themselves to strictly ethical issues, or start commenting on the design and data collection methods used in a particular piece of research. The use of the controlled clinical trial as the gold standard for research in medicine, in particular, has been a source of contention. It is now recognised that there are alternative ways in which socio-medical research may be conducted which does not have an experimental or quasi-experimental design.

In recent years, some have argued that the system of ethical regulation erected in the biomedical sciences has become a threat to freedom of inquiry in the social sciences. British sociologist Robert Dingwall (2006) has put forward a trenchant argument of this kind, suggesting that once ethical review bodies are created, they tend to take on a life of their own. Even in the health services, efforts to roll back the role of ethics committees in hospitals and health trusts are resisted by such bodies, which see their self-interests threatened. Dingwall considers that institutional review boards infringe the First Amendment to the US Constitution, which protects freedom of speech and freedom of the press. In the UK, he argues that there is a danger that informed consent becomes fetishised, and regarded as the be-all and end-all of ethical review. One recent manifestation of this is the requirement by some Ethics Committees that consent forms, signed, for example, by young persons under the age of 18, and separately by their parents, should in addition be witnessed by a third party, as if the human subject or their parents were signing a will! Dingwall's argument is an extreme one, and may be consulted as part of an examination of the case for and against ethical review. There is no doubt, however, that in relation to social science research some Ethics Committees behave in an officious manner, and place obstacles in the way of completing social research.

8.8 SUMMARY

In this chapter, we have seen some of the ethical issues that can arise in social research. It is not always easy to steer a course between obtaining full and informed consent and obtaining information that would be important but concealed. Similarly, it is sometimes hard to avoid invading privacy. However, it is argued that covert research, in which the fact that research is being conducted is not revealed to subjects, is almost never justifiable. There is a possibility that behaving unethically can harm not only those being researched, but also the researcher.

There are no cut-and-dried answers to many ethical issues which face the social researcher. Very often the issues involved are multifaceted and there are contradictory considerations in play. There is not necessarily one right and one wrong answer, but this indeterminacy does not mean that ethical issues can be ignored. Far from it. The best counsel for the social researcher is to be constantly ethically aware.

DISCUSSION QUESTIONS

1   Can you think of any circumstances in which you would consider it justifiable to engage in the covert observation of a group or setting? If so, explain how you would justify such research.

2   Suppose that you were an employee of a large corporation and your manager asked you to design a questionnaire to interview the public. Your manager explained that the information gained would be used to target the respondents with special offers promoting the corporation's products. Why is this not ethical research? Which sections of the Social Research Association's and the British Sociological Association's ethical guidelines could you use to support your arguments against conducting such research?

3   If a respondent to a focused interview names and talks at length about the behaviour of their friends, is there a case for asking these friends for their consent?

4   Do you agree that, while individuals have rights such as the right to privacy and the right to decline consent to being involved in research, organisations such as business, political parties and voluntary associations have no such rights?

RESOURCES

Homan (1991) *The Ethics of Social Research* is the best, short general introduction to the subject of social research ethics. Although concerned with a slightly different topic, Lee (1993) *Doing Research on Sensitive Topics*, on researching sensitive issues, is a first-class survey of problems in the practical conduct of social research that has ethical dimensions.

A number of somewhat older works are still relevant to different aspects of the problems of ethics. Barnes (1980) *Who Should Know What? Social Science, Privacy and Ethics* is still the best general discussion of the social responsibilities of the sociologist and how to balance the right to know with the need to respect privacy. In addition to Lee (1993), Boruch and Cecil (1979) *Assuring the Confidentiality of Social Research Data* discuss the problems of safeguarding the confidentiality of quantitative data. Beauchamp et al. (1982) *Ethical Issues in Social Science Research* examine a variety of issues including harm to subject and researcher. Bulmer (1982) *Social Research Ethics: An Examination of the Merits of Covert Participant Observation* sets out the arguments for and against covert participant observation.

A case study of the nature of ethical and legal issues in research in a single area, that of AIDS research, is presented in Gray, Lyons and Melton (1995) *Ethical and Legal Issues in AIDS Research*. Foster's (2001) *The Ethics of Medical Research on Humans* discussion of the philosophical principles underlying medical research on patients has relevance to social research. Lee-Treweek and Linkogle (2000) *Danger in the Field: Risk and Ethics in Social Research* present a collection of international papers about ethical dilemmas in qualitative research and Lee and Stanko (2003) *Researching Violence: Essays on Methodology and Measurement* is a collection on researching violence that touches on the ethical implications.

Part II
Into the Field

This Part is concerned with the detailed planning of a research project, including guidance on how to design and select a sample of respondents, how to design questionnaires, and how to use surveys, focus groups, interviews, observation, documents and the internet as methods to collect data.

9 Designing Samples

Patrick Sturgis

KEY POINTS

● It is possible to make accurate inferences about the characteristics of very large populations from relatively small samples, if the sample is drawn randomly.

● The reason that we are able to make accurate inferences from sample to population is due to the known properties of sampling distributions.

● There are several different methods of drawing random samples, and the one we choose will affect the accuracy of the population estimates we are able to make.

● In surveys of human populations, nonresponse can be a considerable problem for the accuracy of estimates when those who do not respond are different from those who do, on the variables measured in the questionnaire.

9.1 INTRODUCTION

In modern life, we are bombarded with statistics: 20 per cent of people think this, 80 per cent of people do that, more people are doing more of this than they used to in the past, and so on. While the frequency with which such figures are bandied about by politicians and in the popular media may be tiresome for the average 'person in the street', the practical utility of such numbers is of undoubted importance for the development of government policy and sociological theory alike. Statistics on rates of criminal victimisation, health and morbidity, saving and expenditure, for example, are key to the development of government policy on crime and criminal justice, health, and taxation respectively. Similarly, the percentages of people with different attitudes, opinions, behaviours and beliefs underpin much of the empirical work undertaken across the social sciences.

This chapter introduces the notion of inference from **sample** to **population** by way of random sampling. Key concepts from statistical theory are discussed and some of the main practical sampling strategies reviewed. We then move on to consider some of the factors affecting the accuracy of survey estimates and the implications of nonresponse for survey error.

Given the practical importance of statistics relating to the characteristics of populations, it is essential that they are produced with as high a degree of accuracy as possible. The question of how to make accurate inferences about population characteristics by drawing samples from that population is the focus of this chapter. It begins by considering the logic underlying survey sampling before moving on to detail some of the main practical ways that samples can be drawn. It then considers the implications for survey accuracy when some of those selected into a sample, for a variety of different reasons, fail to provide information on some or all of the questions asked.

9.2 STATISTICAL INFERENCE: FROM SAMPLE TO POPULATION

The underlying motivation of sampling is to make statistical inferences from samples to populations. That is, we wish to use known facts (responses from the sample) to understand unknown facts (responses of the population) (King et al., 1994). A population is the totality of objects in the 'real world' in which we are interested. These objects may be individuals, households, organisations, countries or practically anything we can define as belonging to a single taxonomic class.

Because populations are often extremely large, or even infinite, it is usually impossible – for cost and practical reasons – to take measurements on every element in the population. For this reason, more often than not, we draw a sample and generalise from the properties of the sample to the broader population. In addition to the cost savings this entails, we are usually able to make more – and more detailed – observations on each sample element.

When we do make observations on every element in the population, we are conducting a population census and the issue of inference is not applicable, because we will know the true score of the population on the variable of interest from the data, measurement error notwithstanding.

Making **valid** and **reliable** inferences from a sample to a population is a cornerstone of science and there are many pitfalls that may crop up along the way. Because of such difficulties, we often hear researchers attempting to limit the claims they are making for their analyses by saying their results 'apply only to the sample at hand and should be generalised to the broader population with caution'. Such claims should be viewed with scepticism, for idiosyncratic characteristics of a particular sample are hardly ever of interest. Furthermore, even when this sort of statement is made, generalisation to a population is usually implicit in the conclusion being drawn.

Fortunately, however, if a sample is collected properly, it is possible to make valid and reliable generalisations to the broader population within quantifiable bounds of error. To appreciate how this is done, it is first necessary to understand the concept of sampling distributions, as this is the key that allows us to link our specific sample with the broader population.

9.2.1 PROBABILITY AND SAMPLING DISTRIBUTIONS

When we talk about distributions, we usually understand this as referring to the distribution of values on a particular variable in our sample or in the broader population. Such distributions are known as *probability distributions*, because they describe the probability of observing each of the different possible values a variable can take in the sample or population. Probability distributions have different shapes and are named according to the shape they assume. For example, the Normal distribution, or bell curve, describes how human samples and populations vary on characteristics such as height or intelligence.

Probability distributions can also be applied to statistics. A statistic is just a mathematical transformation or formula applied to a set of numerical data. The distribution of possible values of a statistic in a population is referred to as the sampling distribution of that statistic. The difference between the distribution of a variable (a probability distribution) and the distribution of a statistic (a sampling distribution) can be somewhat confusing. However, it is important to understand this distinction if the rationale of inferential statistics using random sampling is to be properly understood.

When we draw a random sample from a population, it is just one of many samples that might have been drawn using the same design and, therefore, observations made on any one sample are likely to be different from each other and from the 'true value' in the population (although some will be the same). Imagine we were to draw 10,000 (or some other very large number) random samples of individuals from a population. On each sample we calculate a statistic, say, the mean age in years, and we then plot the mean age obtained from each sample on a histogram (a histogram is a chart using bars to represent the number of times a particular value occurred). This histogram would represent the sampling distribution of the arithmetic mean of age in this population. Do not worry about the practicalities of actually drawing all these samples, as we are only talking about a hypothetical set of possible samples that could, in theory, be drawn.

Sampling distributions are useful because they allow us to make statements about how likely it is that the true population value will fall within the margin of error of the estimate we make from the sample we have drawn. This is because the sampling distribution tells us the frequency with which the statistic in our particular sample would be found in the population of all possible samples.

But how do we know the sampling distribution of our statistic without drawing a huge number of samples each time we wish to make use of it? Fortunately, we don't need actually to draw all the samples that would be necessary to plot sampling distributions because of known mathematical links between the parameters of a random sample and the sampling distribution from which it is taken.

If we draw a sufficiently large random sample from a population, all the information necessary for making inferences about the population is contained within the sample data. To understand how this is so, it is important to understand a number of additional, inter-related ideas. The first and most important of these is the concept and properties of the **Normal distribution**.

9.2.2 THE NORMAL DISTRIBUTION

The exact shape of the Normal distribution is defined by a function which has only two parameters: mean and standard deviation. The standard deviation is a

Figure 9.1   A Normal probability distribution

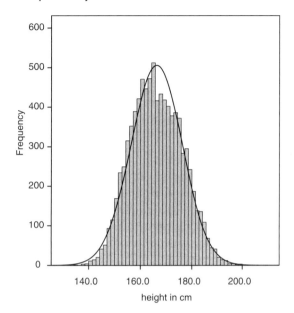

measure of dispersion and can be thought of as a measure of how much, on average, people differ from the sample mean.

A characteristic property of the Normal distribution is that 68 per cent of all of its observations fall within a range of ±1 standard deviations from the mean, a range of ±1.96 standard deviations covers 95 per cent of the scores and ±2.58 standard deviations covers 99 per cent of all the observed scores. This has the useful consequence that, when a variable is normally distributed, we are able to tell what proportion of a sample falls within a range of values around the sample mean.

For example, Figure 9.1 shows an example of a normally distributed variable. Let's imagine that this is the distribution of the variable 'height in centimetres' from a randomly drawn sample. The mean height in this sample is 166 cm and the standard deviation is 9.62. Because the data are normally distributed, we know that 95 per cent of sample cases will be within the range of 166 plus or minus 1.96, which is the range of 146 to 185.6. Another way of putting this is that the probability of a given individual being smaller than 146.4 cm, or taller than 185.6 cm is 0.05 (or 5 per cent). (Note that, had we wanted to talk about a more precisely defined group, say 99 per cent of cases, we would have multiplied the standard deviation by 2.58 rather than 1.96. This is because 2.58 standard deviations covers 99 per cent of the Normal distribution. The consequence of this is that the range of values increases to 140.2–191.8).

So, the Normal distribution is useful in that it enables us to make statements about the probability or likelihood of observing particular values. But so far, this only refers to the characteristics of our particular sample. How can we use the sample data to make statements about the whole population? This is possible because of the following links between the properties of sample statistics and their corresponding sampling distribution:

1   When the distribution of a variable is Normal in the population, the sampling distribution of the mean (and many other statistics) is also Normal.

2   Even when the distribution of the variable in the population is not Normal, Central Limit Theorem tells us that, as the sample size increases, the sampling distribution of the mean (and many other statistics) becomes Normal.

3   The sample mean (and many other statistics) is an unbiased estimator of the population mean. This means that if we draw repeated random samples (of the same size) from the population and estimate the mean, the mean of these means will itself equal the population mean when the sample of means is large enough. Sorry about the wording here!

4   Although we usually don't know the standard deviation of the sampling distribution, it turns out that we can use the sample standard deviation as an estimate of it. The standard deviation of a sampling distribution is known as a *standard error*. This is calculated by dividing the sample standard deviation by the square root of the sample size.

9.2.3 CONFIDENCE LEVELS AND CONFIDENCE INTERVALS

So, from the above points, we know that so long as the sample is random and of sufficient size, we can assume it provides an unbiased estimate of the true population mean (note that this does not mean it is equal to the true population mean, just that the sample mean is an unbiased estimate of it). We also know that the shape of the sampling distribution is Normal and that the sample standard deviation provides us with a very good estimate of the standard deviation (standard error) of this sampling distribution.

Now, rather than merely saying that 95 per cent of observations in our sample fall within ±1.96 standard deviations of the mean, we can say that if we were to draw 100 samples of the same size, we would expect only five of them to have means that fall outside our estimate of the mean ±1.96 standard errors. Another (more common) way of saying the same thing is that we are 95 per cent confident that the true population mean falls within the range of the sample mean ±1.96 standard errors.

To illustrate, if we drew a random sample of 1,000 individuals (assuming no nonresponse or measurement error) and calculated the mean age to be 45 and the standard deviation to be 10, we could say that we are 95 per cent confident that the true population mean age is 45 years plus or minus 0.62 years:

s.e. = $s.d./\sqrt{n}$ Formula for standard error of mean
s.e. = $10/\sqrt{1000}$ Put in actual values
s.e. = 10/31.623 = 0.316   Perform calculations
1.96 * 0.316 = 0.62   Multiply by 1.96 (1.96 standard error = 95 per cent
                                         of distribution)

This introduces the linked ideas of **confidence levels** and **confidence intervals**. For a given level of confidence, say, 95 per cent, we specify the interval within which the true population value is likely to fall. Although this discussion has been concerned with the arithmetic mean, the same logic applies to many other inferential statistics, such as proportions, differences between means and regression coefficients.

It is important to note that this 'magical process' linking sample to population parameters can break down at various points in the research process, predominantly during the sampling and measurement stages. However, if we are confident that our sample has been properly drawn (i.e. randomly and without nonresponse bias), the sample size is large enough (greater than about 100) and the characteristic of interest has been validly measured (i.e. without bias or random error), the logic of inference is unassailable and can be proven mathematically. It is this logic that enables us to make very definite statements about the characteristics of populations such as 'people in Britain' (which at the last count approached sixty million) based on samples of only around 1,000 individuals.

9.2.4 FACTORS AFFECTING THE PRECISION OF ESTIMATES

The width of the confidence interval determines the *precision* of the estimate we are making. The wider the confidence interval, the less precise the estimate and vice versa. From the discussion above, we can tell that the two factors affecting the precision of our estimates are the population variance and sample size. The more variable the thing we are measuring is in the population, the less precise our estimates will be, if the sample size is kept the same.

The larger the size of our sample, the more precise our estimates will be, if the population variance is constant. However, because the standard error decreases as a function of the *square root* of the sample size, there are steadily diminishing returns for increasing sample size. Thus increasing sample size from 500 to 1,000 reduces the standard error by 29 per cent, while increasing it from 1,000 to 1,500 reduces the standard error by only 18 per cent. This is why many opinion poll samples have a sample size of around 1,000, because beyond this point the gain in precision for each additional respondent becomes smaller and, therefore, more costly.

Another factor affecting the precision of estimates is the way in which a random sample is drawn. As we shall see in Sections 9.4 and 9.5, there are a number of different ways of drawing random samples and which one we choose influences the reliability of the estimates made from the obtained sample data.

9.3 NONRESPONSE

The logic of statistical inference using random sampling derives its strength from its mathematical underpinning. If all relevant theoretical assumptions are met, we can have known levels of confidence in the inferences from sample to population. In the real world of survey research, however, human populations rarely conform to the assumptions of neat mathematical laws! One of the primary areas in which the mathematical assumptions underpinning random sampling are rarely met in practice is that of *nonresponse*. Nonresponse is when some of those selected for inclusion in a sample do not provide answers to some or all of the questions in the questionnaire.

9.3.1 RESPONSE RATES

The key indicator of survey nonresponse is the response rate. The response rate is calculated by dividing the number of achieved interviews by the total number attempted (this latter number is often referred to as the 'issued sample size'). So, if we drew a sample of 1,000 households and were able to conduct interviews with only 650 of these, the response rate would be 650/1,000 = 65 per cent. Conversely, the nonresponse rate for this survey would be 35 per cent (100 per cent minus the response rate).

Nonresponse occurs for many different reasons but the most common are 'non-contact', when no contact is made with the selected unit (usually a person) for the duration of fieldwork, and 'refusals', when contact is made but the selected unit declines to participate. This type of nonresponse is referred to as unit nonresponse, as no information is obtained at all on the non-responding sample unit.

A second type of nonresponse is when a respondent provides an interview but does not complete all the items in the questionnaire. This item nonresponse might be deliberate, in the case of sensitive questions such as those relating to income or drug use. Alternatively, respondents may omit items inadvertently through haste or as a result of poor questionnaire design.

9.3.2 NONRESPONSE AND SURVEY ERROR

If some sample members fail to provide answers to some or all of the questions in the questionnaire, there is a risk that survey estimates will be biased. That is to say, the survey estimate may be systematically different from the true value in the population. Bias in survey estimates arises when there is a difference in the variable of interest between respondents and nonrespondents to the survey.

Because the precision of estimates is a function of sample size, nonresponse also results in less reliable estimates (see Section 9.2.4). This problem is not particularly serious, however, because we can build an anticipated level of nonresponse into the survey design and still achieve the required sample size by drawing a larger initial sample than would be necessary with 100 per cent response. For instance, to achieve 1,000 interviews with an anticipated response rate of only 60 per cent, you would need to attempt interviews with 1000/.6 = 1,667 individuals in the population.

While a low response rate may indicate the existence of nonresponse bias, it is important to note that a low response rate does not automatically mean a sample estimate will be biased. Bias only arises if nonresponse is correlated with the thing you are trying to estimate. So, for instance, if a survey measures annual income and richer people are less likely to respond to the survey than poorer people, the sample estimate of mean income would be biased (we would underestimate mean income in the population). However, if nonresponse is completely uncorrelated with income, the estimate would be unbiased, no matter what the response rate is.

Similarly, bias should be thought of as relating to estimates, not samples. One estimate from a sample with less than a 100 per cent response rate might be biased, while another estimate *from the same survey* may have no bias at all. What determines whether an estimate is biased or not is the correlation between the propensity to respond and the variable which is being estimated. Survey researchers are currently very concerned about nonresponse bias, as studies show that response rates around the world have been going down steadily for the past 20 to 30 years (de Leeuw and Hox, 2001).

Fortunately, high and rising rates of nonresponse can be mitigated by improving interviewer training, the timing of calls at addresses and the general design of surveys. Nonresponse *weighting*, a process whereby under-represented groups in the sample can be weighted up to match their composition in the population, can also be used during analysis to remove or reduce bias arising from non-response.

9.4 SAMPLING STRATEGIES

Thus far, we have focused on the conceptual foundations of survey sampling. In practical terms, though, how do you go about selecting a sample from a population? This decision will depend on the type of measurements you want to make, the nature of the population being studied, the complexity of the survey design and the resources available.

The first stage in any survey is to define the population from which you want to draw your sample. For example, you might be interested in the effects of youth unemployment on psychological well-being and thus need to study samples from the population of employed and unemployed youth. Or, you might have a developmental hypothesis that some cognitive abilities change around the seventh or eighth year, so you might sample from the population of children aged 6–9 years. Determining the exact population from which you wish to sample is important as you must be clear about the population to which inferences are being made.

Having an explicit and detailed description of your population is also important because for most sampling strategies you will need a **sampling frame**, which is a list of all members of the population. This might sound easy at first but practical restrictions often curb your initial ambitions. For large-scale surveys of the general population of adults in the UK, the Electoral Register and the Postcode Address File are the most commonly used sampling frames. The Electoral Register is available in libraries and main post offices and lists people eligible to vote. The register is used only rarely these days because it does not have anywhere near complete coverage (many people are not on it). Recent legislation also allows people who are registered to vote to remove themselves from the publicly available register.

The Postcode Address File (PAF) lists all UK addresses to which mail can be sent and is available in computerised form. It has very high coverage of UK addresses (approaching 100 per cent) and is regularly updated. As PAF is not a list of individuals but of addresses, contact must first be made with the household and a randomly selected household member interviewed (if the survey is of individuals, rather than households). PAF contains approximately 13 per cent non-domestic addresses, so many of the sampled addresses are considered ineligible for the survey. The proportion of addresses ineligible needs to be factored in to estimates of sample size requirements. Several companies now exist who will draw samples from PAF and other population frames at a commercial rate. We now turn to a consideration of the different ways in which samples can be drawn from the sampling frame, once the population has been defined and the list obtained.

9.4.1 SIMPLE RANDOM SAMPLE (SRS)

Although it is rarely used alone for drawing general population samples, the simple random sample (SRS) is the yardstick by which other sampling strategies are judged. A SRS gives every unit in the population an equal probability of selection. For this reason, simple random samples are referred to as *epsem designs* (for Equal Probability of SElection Method). To draw a SRS, every population unit must be assigned a unique identification number ranging from 1 to N (where N is the total population size). Random numbers between 1 and N are then drawn (using a random number table or other random number generating device) until the required sample size is achieved. If the same number is drawn more than once, it is not selected into the sample multiple times, we simply draw another number until we select one that has not already been selected. This is called *sampling without replacement* and is the normal practice in survey sampling.

In practice, SRS can be cumbersome and time-consuming. An alternative approach – systematic random sampling – is simpler and more convenient. To draw a systematic random sample, begin as before by assigning every population unit a unique number in ascending order. Next, calculate the sampling interval, i, which is the ratio of the required sample size to the population total, $i = N/n$. A random number between 1 and i is then generated, called the seed number, representing the unique identifier of the first population unit to be included in the sample. Next the sampling interval, i, is summed with the random number between 1 and i and this is taken as the second unit in the sample. The process is continued until the end of the sampling frame has been reached and the desired sample size achieved.

To illustrate, let us assume that you have a sampling frame containing 1600 names and you want a random sample of 200 to receive your questionnaire. The sampling interval here would be $i = 1600/200 = 8$. The next step is to use random number tables to select a number between 1 and 8 to give the seed number to start with. Say you get a 5. You would select the 5th person on the list, then the 13th (5 + 8), then the 21st (13 + 8) and so on. Strictly speaking, this procedure is not an epsem design, since once the 5th person has been selected, the 4th and 6th cases cannot be selected, because the order of the list determines who is now selected. However, for most practical purposes, systematic random sampling can be considered equivalent to simple random sampling.

SRS techniques are impractical when you wish to sample from large and geographically diffuse populations, such as 'adults in the UK'. Interviewers would need to be sent to all corners of the country, at great practical inconvenience and expense. For this reason, simple random sample designs are rarely used in practice for household surveys. Where sample designs diverge from equal probability of selection methods, they are referred to as complex sample designs.

9.4.2 COMPLEX SAMPLE DESIGNS

The two main ways in which sample designs diverge from equal probability of selection methods is in the use of *clustering* and *stratification*. Clustering – or multi-stage selection of sample units – is almost always used on national, face-to-face interview surveys, as non-clustered designs are both impractical from the perspective of data collection agencies and prohibitively expensive for funders of research. The basic idea of a clustered design is to select the sample in stages so that individual sample units are kept in relative geographical proximity. Consider conducting a survey of secondary school pupils. We might begin by drawing a sample of schools and then randomly select pupils within each school. This would make the interviewers' job much easier than if a simple random sample had been used as she would need to visit only one or two schools to conduct all their interviews.

For a fixed cost, clustering produces more precise population estimates than a simple random sample. However, for a fixed sample size, clustered designs are

[handwritten marginal notes: "Investigation into large national British..." "subsection this topic can wrong clean in the middle"]

subject to larger standard errors. This is because there tend to be greater similarities between members of the same geographical sub-unit on many attributes than between independently selected members of the total population. For instance, size of garden, number of bedrooms and household income are all variables that are intuitively likely to be more similar within than they are between postcode sectors. Clustering, therefore, underestimates true population variance and this is reflected in standard errors that are larger than those that would have been obtained from a simple random sample of the same size.

National probability surveys also routinely employ stratification in the selection of sample units. Stratification divides the sample into separate sub-groups and then selects random samples from within each group. These sub-samples are then combined to form the complete issued sample. Strata are created through the cross-classification of variables that are assumed to be correlated with key survey variables. So long as this assumption holds true, stratification will reduce sampling error, relative to an un-stratified sample design of the same size.

Sampling within strata can be either proportionate or disproportionate to population totals. In addition to obtaining more precise estimates, disproportionate stratification is often used to ensure that robust estimates can be made within substantively important strata. For instance, surveys of the British population might disproportionately sample within strata formed by the three countries of Great Britain. 'Over-sampling' within the Wales stratum would enable separate estimates to be produced for people living in Wales, where sample size might be too small under a proportionate stratification. To produce estimates representative of the British population from such a disproportionate allocation, however, sample units from Wales would need to be down-weighted to their correct population proportion.

When different sub-groups of the population have different probabilities of selection into the sample, post-survey weighting should be applied when analysing the data. The main purpose of this weighting is to reduce bias in population estimates by up-weighting population sub-groups that are under-represented and down-weighting those that are over-represented in the sample. Sometimes, this under- or over-representation may be a deliberate part of the survey design, such as when disproportionate stratification is used. Other times, unequal selection probabilities arise through differential nonresponse. Weighting generally reduces bias in survey estimates. A less desirable by-product is that when the variance of the weights is large, it can result in a loss of precision, that is, standard errors that are larger than they would be for un-weighted estimates.

9.4.3 COMPLEX DESIGNS AND THE PRECISION OF SURVEY ESTIMATES

The net effect of clustering, stratification and weighting, therefore, is that the standard errors of these 'complex' sample designs tend to be different (smaller or larger, but usually larger) than those of a simple random sample. The difference in the precision of the estimates produced by a complex design relative to a simple random sample is known as the design effect (**deff**). The design effect is the ratio of the actual variance, under the sampling method used, to the variance calculated under the assumption of simple random sampling. This number will vary for different variables in the survey – some may be heavily influenced by design effects and others less so.

For cluster samples, the main components of deff are the intra-class correlation or **rho**, and the number of units within each cluster. Rho is a statistical estimate of within cluster homogeneity. It represents the probability that two units drawn randomly from the same cluster will have the same value on the variable in question, relative to two units drawn at random from the population as a whole. Thus, a rho of 0.10 indicates that two units randomly selected from within the same cluster are 10 per cent more likely to have the same value than are two randomly selected units in the population as a whole. Estimation of rho is beyond the scope of this chapter but it can be easily obtained from commercially available statistical software. The design effect is calculated as follows:

$$\text{deff} = 1 + \text{rho} \, (n - 1)$$

where:

- deff is the design effect;

- rho is the intra-class correlation for the variable in question;

- n is the size of the cluster (an average is taken where clusters differ in size).

From this formula, we can see that the design effect increases as the cluster size (in most instances the number of addresses sampled within a postcode sector) increases, and as rho (within cluster homogeneity) increases.

A somewhat more readily interpretable derivation of the design effect is the design factor or *deft*, which is the square root of deff. Deft gives an inflation factor for the standard errors obtained using a complex survey design. For example, a deft value of 2 indicates that the standard errors are twice as large as they would have been had the design been a simple random sample. Deft can also be used to obtain the effective sample size, neff, of a complex survey design, which gives the sample size that would have been required to obtain the same level of precision in a simple random sample.

9.4.4 QUOTA SAMPLING

Quota sampling is a non-probability method of selection that aims to make the sample representative of the target population by setting controls on sample composition to make it match known population characteristics. For instance, we know that approximately 50 per cent of the population of Great Britain is

Table 9.1
Example of independent quota controls for a survey of women, aged 21–65

AGE	(%)	SOCIAL CLASS	(%)	WORK STATUS	(%)
21–35	34	Class I and II	30	Not in employment	36
36–50	33	Class III	50	In paid employment	64
51–65	33	Class IV and V	20		
Total	100		100		100

Table 9.2
Example of interrelated quota controls for a survey of women, aged 21–65

Notes: N = not in paid employment; W = in paid employment.

SOCIAL CLASS: WORK STATUS: AGE	I & II		III		IV & V		TOTAL
	N	W	N	W	N	W	
21–35	5	8	6	10	1	4	34
36–50	2	7	2	15	2	5	33
51–65	5	3	10	7	3	5	33
Total	12	18	18	32	6	14	100
	30		50		20		

female and around 10 per cent are from minority ethnic groups. Thus, for a quota sample where the target population is 'all adults in Great Britain', we might specify quota controls that result in an achieved sample that contains 50 per cent women and 10 per cent from ethnic minority groups. To the extent that the quota control variables are correlated with survey variables of interest, the approach may serve to reduce bias, relative to a non-random sample with no quota controls.

Quota control variables may be selected according to the topic being researched. For example, a quota control on employment status would be appropriate in a study of women's purchasing behaviour, since the shopping behaviour of full-time housewives differs from that of women in paid employment. Table 9.1 illustrates the use of three quota controls (age, social class and employment status) for a survey of 100 women aged 21–65. The numbers in Table 9.1 indicate how many of each type of women are to be included in the sample.

The independent controls shown in Table 9.1 ensure that the sample contains the correct representation on each of the three quota control variables separately. However, the resulting sample may still have an unrepresentative combination of characteristics. For example, all the class IV and V women may be housewives over age 50. To ensure that the sample has the correct combination of characteristics, interrelated (also known as interlocking, interlaced or interdependent) controls can be used (see Table 9.2). However, as quota controls become more complex and the number of variables and categories to be interrelated increases, it becomes more difficult for interviewers to find people to fill each quota cell and the costs of the research escalate.

There is a trade-off between the higher costs and the increased representativeness of using more detailed quota controls. And, no matter how many quota controls are applied, there is no guarantee that nonresponse bias will be eliminated. If we apply quota controls on gender, age, and employment status, we may well end up with a sample that is different in important ways from the target population as a result of differential nonresponse.

Quota samples are widely used in market research, opinion polling and audience research for three main reasons:

1   Interviewing costs are much lower than for probability samples because there is no need for call-backs, and travelling distances and times are much reduced.

2   Administrative costs prior to fieldwork are lower. There are no costs for obtaining a sampling frame and drawing the sample, although there may be costs in setting the quota controls.

3   The period of interviewing can be very short. For some research topics, such as opinion polls about political events and audience views about specific television programmes, it is essential that interviews are completed on the same day and the results published within a few days. A probability sample cannot be used for this kind of research, because by the time all sample members had been contacted they would probably have forgotten the event and the results would no longer be newsworthy.

A major drawback of quota sampling is that, since it is not a probability sample, it is not possible to estimate the standard error and so the researcher cannot calculate confidence intervals or use inferential statistics (see Section 9.2). A further limitation of quota sampling is that the researcher must know the proportion of people with each characteristic in the population in order to specify the quota controls. These proportions can sometimes be obtained from the Population Census or from large government surveys, such as the General Household Survey (see Chapter 19). Often, however, the population totals of many variables are simply not known. This is, after all, the main reason for conducting surveys in the first place!

9.4.5 SNOWBALL SAMPLING

Snowball or 'network' sampling is sometimes used to obtain a sample when there is no adequate list to use as a sampling frame. It is a method for obtaining samples of numerically small groups, such as members of minority ethnic groups, illegal drug users, or sex workers. It involves contacting a member of the population to be studied and asking them whether they know anyone else with the required characteristics (for example, people born in England whose parents came from Poland). The nominated individuals are interviewed in turn and asked to identify further sample members. This continues until no further sample members are obtained. This latter point is an often over-looked feature of snowball sampling; if interviewing does not continue until no further 'in-scope' individuals are identified, the procedure is likely to result in biased estimates of population characteristics.

Because the snowballing technique involves personal recommendations that vouch for the legitimacy of the researcher, it may be the only feasible method of finding a sample of people engaged in illegal activities, such as drug users. It is therefore useful when the potential subjects of the research are likely to be sceptical of the researcher's intentions. Snowball sampling can only be used when the target sample members are involved in some kind of network with others who share the characteristic of interest. This is both a strength and a potential weakness of the method. An advantage of snowball sampling is that it reveals a network of contacts that can itself be studied. A potential problem is that it only includes those within a connected network of individuals. For example, in a study of people with Polish parents, it would fail to find anyone who had no contact with other second-generation Polish people. This would be a serious source of bias if the research topic is the continued maintenance of Polish cultural traditions. In snowball sampling, as in any other method of obtaining a sample, it is essential to assess and report the representativeness of the sample and any likely sources of bias.

9.5 SUMMARY

This overview of survey sampling provides an understanding of the theory underlying statistical inference from sample to population, the main issues involved in drawing a random sample, and some of the advantages and disadvantages of the various kinds of design. When random sampling is used, a key indicator of the accuracy of survey estimates is the response rate, which is the proportion of the total sample with whom interviews were completed. Where response rates are low, survey estimates may be biased if the non-respondents are different from the respondents on the variables of interest.

Although random samples are generally preferable because they enable the use of inferential statistics, they are also considerably more expensive and time-consuming relative to non-random techniques such as quota and snow-ball sampling. Thus, choosing the appropriate sample design always involves trading off the accuracy of estimates with the requirement to stay within a fixed budget and to report the survey results in a timely manner.

DISCUSSION QUESTIONS

1   You have conducted a face-to-face household survey and achieved a response rate of 60 per cent. How might you go about assessing the presence and magnitude of nonresponse bias?

2   You are considering conducting a postal survey of the public in your local area using a simple random sample design. A pilot study indicates that the response rate is likely to be around 25 per cent. Should you consider conducting a quota sample instead? What are the factors that would influence your decision one way or the other?

3   You are analysing data from a probability survey of people in Britain, in which questions were asked about the frequency of different leisure activities. The sample size is 1,000 and the percentage of people reporting that they cycled in the previous week is 32 per cent, giving a standard error of 1.5 per cent. Calculate the 95 per cent and 99 per cent confidence intervals for the percentage of cycle riders in the population.

RESOURCES

Kalton's (1983) *Introduction to Survey Sampling* is also a thorough, yet not too technical treatment of the issues.

Moser and Kalton's (1971) *Survey Methods in Social Investigation* is widely admired as one of the most detailed although accessible works on survey design and sampling.

The more recent *Survey Methodology* by Groves et al. (2004) provides an accessible account of the fundamentals of survey sampling and survey methodology more generally.

10 Questionnaires

Rosemarie Simmons

KEY POINTS

- There are a range of ways of gathering structured data, including self-completion questionnaires, face-to-face interviews and telephone surveys.

- All these involve asking questions and, to be effective, these questions need to be carefully designed.

- Choices include those between open and closed questions, the order of questions, and selecting appropriate ranking scales.

- Ambiguous, double-barrelled, leading and hypothetical questions should normally be avoided.

10.1 INTRODUCTION

Most people have encountered survey research, in one form or another, either as participants in surveys or as recipients of information from surveys. Often surveys are used to predict outcomes, for example, the MORI polls conducted prior to elections that attempt to gauge the voting behaviour of the adult population. Surveys provide an effective aid to commercial organisations enabling them to make decisions about the development of products, pricing, market penetration and the profiles of their customers.

Social scientists also regard surveys as an invaluable source of data about attitudes, values, personal experiences and behaviour. Surveys allow researchers to gather information from a specified target population by means of face-to-face, telephone interviews, postal questionnaires, and increasingly, online surveys. One of the most important parts of any research survey is the development of the questions. The success of a survey will depend on the questions that are asked, the ways in which they are phrased and the order in which they are placed.

The challenge for a researcher is how to formulate the questions that will obtain the most valuable and relevant information. This is a skill to be learnt like any other in social research, and this chapter provides guidelines to help you devise such questions. It begins by reviewing the main methods of structured questioning, using self-completion questionnaires, face-to-face interviews and telephone surveys, and then considers the factors that need to be thought about when deciding on topics and the wording of questions. Ways of obtaining answers from respondents using open or closed questions and ranking scales, and some pitfalls in question wording are outlined. The chapter concludes with a discussion of how best to format a questionnaire or interview schedule. The chapter will also discuss the use of open-ended and closed questions; show how to avoid ambiguous, leading, double-barrelled and hypothetical questions; describe the types of questions that can be asked and the order in which they should be placed; and finally, discuss the varieties of format for questionnaires and interview schedules.

10.2 CHOOSING A METHOD OF QUESTIONING

Social research involves detective work. You begin with a problem and then ask a number of questions about it, such as, 'what?, 'who?, 'where?, 'when?', 'how?' and 'why?'. In some research, the most important question may be 'What are the consequences?'. Consider the subject of discrimination:

What constitutes discrimination?
It is necessary to begin by identifying what is meant by discrimination. A starting point would be to look at existing literature on the subject and work out ways in which the concept can be measured.

Who experiences discrimination?
You will need to focus on the particular groups that may be discriminated against, for example, people with disabilities, minority ethnic groups, or gays and lesbians. You may be interested in a certain age group, or those in a particular socio-economic group, or those living in an urban or rural environment.

Where does the discrimination take place?
Is it specific or general, for example, in the workplace, in schools, or simply on the streets?

(Continued)

When does the discrimination occur?

How regularly? For what length of time? Is it a large part of the subjects' everyday lives?

How does it occur?

This question may cover several aspects of behaviour, from investigating formal discriminatory practices to the measurement of levels of abuse. You may decide to explore ways in which institutions deal with discrimination, or concentrate on how prejudice affects the lives of those who experience related acts.

Why?

The main purpose of the study may be to seek an *explanation* for discrimination and why it occurs in certain areas and not others.

Most research studies will include questions within these categories.

At the outset of a research project, it is essential to identify the most appropriate method of carrying out the study. The method you choose is likely to be determined by the time and budget available, as well as the subject matter of your research (see Chapter 2). The following section will describe the three main types of survey data collection method: using self-completion questionnaires, face-to-face interviews and telephone interviews. Chapter 16 discusses online surveys.

10.2.1 SELF-COMPLETION QUESTIONNAIRE SURVEYS

Self-completion questionnaires are used in postal surveys, and, increasingly in web site surveys. The guidance given for producing self-completion questionnaires is similar, whether the surveys are conducted by post or by Internet or email; only the delivery of the questionnaires and the process by which individuals respond will be different.

Postal surveys are a popular way of conducting research studies where the views of large populations are needed. The questionnaires follow a standardised format in which most questions are pre-coded to provide a list of responses for selection by the respondent (coding is discussed in Chapter 17). The questions must be phrased in a way that a wide range of respondents can understand, and so that it is easy for them to see how they can record their responses.

The main advantage of self-completion questionnaires is that a large population can be surveyed relatively cheaply. Costs are lower because interviewers are not used, and pre-coding and computerisation speed up analysis. It is also possible for respondents to complete questionnaires at a time convenient to them.

The main arguments against using postal questionnaires have generally been that the response rate is low. For example, some postal surveys do not achieve more than a 20 per cent rate of return. The response rate will depend on a number of factors, including the subject matter of the survey, the target population under survey, the recipients' perception of its value, and the ease of completion of the questionnaire. High response rates are often achieved when there is a controversial issue under discussion, for example, the development of a motorway or a by-pass which may be perceived by local people as destroying local habitat or amenities. Conversely, if the survey concerns a subject which is considered remote and not having any impact on an individual's life, there may be no incentive to take the trouble to complete a questionnaire. Even when respondents do complete questionnaires, their answers may be incomplete, illegible or incomprehensible. This poses a problem for those who have to transfer the data to a computer.

Another important consideration is that the researcher generally needs information about the target population in advance of the study in order to develop survey questions that are appropriate for the recipients. As many of the questions will list pre-coded answers, exploratory research to obtain these categories will have to be done before developing the self-completion questionnaire.

With regard to web site surveys, whether this method is chosen will depend on the subject matter and the target population. Clearly there are certain groups who either do not have access to the Internet, or if they do, would not be inclined to complete a form, especially if personal information is requested.

10.2.2 FACE-TO-FACE INTERVIEWS

Some projects benefit by using face-to-face interviews. For example, a study that is concerned with household waste recycling behaviour might benefit from an interviewer visiting homes to steer respondents through a range of disposal options.

Interviewers will need to be provided with some form of document to guide questioning; this may consist of both pre-coded and open-ended questions (see Section 10.5). It is important to note the distinction between an **interview schedule** and an **interview guide**. Increasingly in social and market research circles, the interview schedule is also referred to as a questionnaire. A schedule contains set questions in a pre-determined order that is adhered to in each interview. This type of instrument is generally used in a large-scale survey.

An interview guide, on the other hand, is used for a **focused interview** and will list areas to be covered while leaving the exact wording and order of the questions to the interviewer. In some cases, the interview guide will be quite sketchy to allow for the possibility of non-directive interviewing in which the interviewee's replies determine the course of the interview.

Interviewers may record responses directly onto an interview schedule/questionnaire by pen or use a tape-recorder to record the interview for later transcription. Laptop computers can also be programmed with the questions to make recording answers easier and less prone to error.

Interviewing can have both advantages and disadvantages. Interviews can be more flexible and, in the hands of a skilled interviewer, can extract more information from the individual than a postal survey. The disadvantage is that it is expensive to carry out interviews because of the cost of paying interviewers and their travel expenses. Furthermore, some potential participants may be reluctant to take part in a face-to-face interview, while they might be happy to fill in a self-completion questionnaire.

Often, interviews are used in preliminary research to develop ideas for questions and to determine what pre-coded answers should be offered in a postal survey.

10.2.3 TELEPHONE SURVEYS

Interview schedules or questionnaires are also used for interviews conducted on the telephone. Telephone surveys have similar merits to those involving face-to-face interviews, but have the added benefit that it is possible to reach a wider population at less cost.

Although telephone surveys are less popular with social scientists than they are with market research companies, they can be an effective way of conducting social research. Developments in computer technology have now made telephone interviewing easier. A computer-assisted telephone interviewing (**CATI**) system is able to sample the specified population, provide guidance for the interviewer's introduction, display the interview schedule item by item with appropriate filter questions (see Section 10.6), and record the interviewees' responses.

Telephone surveys do have disadvantages. The main problem is that certain groups such as the poor, the young, the sick and disabled, and those who are frequently away from a telephone (perhaps in the course of their work) may be under-represented. Sensitive questions are difficult to ask at a distance, and it is less easy to offer the interviewee stimulus material such as prompt cards (see Sections 10.4.1 and 10.8).

Furthermore, telephone interviewing is very different from face-to-face interviewing and the training of interviewers in telephone technique must be thorough. Interviewers cannot interpret the reactions of the interviewee by observation so they must learn to present questions clearly and listen carefully for any signals that might indicate lack of understanding. A further problem concerns concentration; if the interview is not prearranged, the interviewer may not get the full attention of the interviewee.

It might be assumed that since all three of these methods, self-completion, face-to-face and telephone surveys, have significant deficiencies, the chances of obtaining valid and reliable data are small. This is not so, argues Dillman (2006), who claims that many difficulties can be overcome by using a 'Total Design Method'. By giving minute attention to every aspect of the survey process, from the training of interviewers to the devising of questions, from the letters asking for participation to the paper on which questionnaires are printed, the quality of response for all types of surveys can be improved. This approach is to be thoroughly recommended: giving careful attention to the planning and execution of the research project will enhance the likelihood of producing useful results.

10.3 HOW TO BEGIN

Before embarking upon any research, it is important to explore any previous studies that have been carried out on the subject. This will not only provide a framework for developing questions for the new research, but will also ensure that the project builds upon previous work. Start, therefore, by obtaining academic papers, books and reports based on related research. The use of the **Internet** is invaluable for exploratory work (see Chapter 4). Questionnaires and interview schedules that have been used in a study are sometimes included in published work and can prove a useful foundation for one's own research.

A first draft of a questionnaire should be based mainly on questions derived from previous studies and on 'brainstorming', that is, writing down all questions that could be useful. It is not enough that questions should reveal interesting information; the data obtained *must* relate directly to the study. Often, it is quite difficult to decide what the important issues are, but preliminary background reading will usually help to elaborate a set of hypotheses and sort the relevant from the irrelevant (see Chapter 3).

> TIP
>
> Keep a careful watch that your questions are relevant to your study. It is easy to slip into asking questions because the answers might be interesting. but this will make your questionnaire too long for the respondent and more difficult to analyse.

If you were to investigate whether e-mailing to friends was the most popular means of written communication, you would need to begin by defining 'popular'. Does this mean 'most liked' or 'most often carried out', or both? You would probably want to know whether different sections of the populations had different patterns of communication. A number of variables would therefore have to be considered: age, sex, marital status, employment status, educational level, social class, and so on. You may be able to think of several areas that have a bearing on the research topic, but each question must have a direct relevance to one of the variables of the hypothesis, so you need to be ruthless in weeding out questions that do not.

> **TIP**
>
> It is advisable to keep the hypothesis and the objectives of the research very firmly in mind when developing questions (see Chapter 3).

When drafting questions, you also need to consider **reliability** and **validity** (see Chapter 2). A study can be said to be reliable if similar results would be obtained by others using the same questions and the same sampling criteria. In order to make it possible for repeat studies to be carried out, first, questions should be worded clearly and unambiguously so that they can be asked in the same way in follow-up studies. Second, instructions for both administration and completion should be the same for all questionnaires or interview schedules. Third, the sample of the population under study should be well defined and the details provided in the research report.

A study can be said to have validity if it actually measures what it sets out to measure. This is more difficult than it sounds. For example, what set of criteria could be used to measure what contributes to 'good health'? Some researchers might use variables such as physiological factors, relationships or employment status, while others might choose spiritual or psychological criteria (see the discussion of measurement theories in Chapter 2).

10.4 TYPES OF INFORMATION

Four main categories of information can be obtained from a survey. These are: (1) attributes; (2) behaviour; (3) attitudes; and (4) beliefs. They are listed below with examples of how questions might be phrased.

10.4.1 ATTRIBUTES

Attributes include personal or socio-economic characteristics such as sex, age, marital status, religion and occupation. Obtaining valid and reliable information about occupation is more difficult than it might seem at first. You could ask some simple questions:

> Are you in paid employment?   Yes
>   No
>
> If yes:
> What is your occupation?   ....

However, what constitutes paid employment? Would, for example, two hours work per week in a bar put the respondent into the 'employed' or 'unemployed' category? A good example of the kind of careful and thorough questioning needed to overcome these kinds of difficulties can be found in the interview schedule used in the General Household Survey (ONS, 2005).

10.4.2 BEHAVIOUR

Behaviour constitutes what the individual has done, is doing, and may possibly do in the future. For example:

> Have you ever belonged to a political organisation?   Yes
>   No
>
> Are you a member of a political organisation at the moment?   Yes
>   No
>
> Do you intend joining a political organisation in the future?   Most likely
>   Likely
>   Unlikely
>   Most unlikely
>   Don't know

There may be difficulties in defining what is meant by a political organisation and it may be necessary for the researcher to make it clear to the respondent what is meant by the term. For example, should Greenpeace, the ecological pressure group, and the Institute for Economic Affairs, a politically committed research institute, be counted as political organisations?

10.4.3 ATTITUDES

Attitudes imply evaluation and are concerned with how people feel about an issue (see Chapter 11). Questions about attitudes usually employ scales: a statement is made and individuals are asked to indicate their level of agreement in a positive or negative direction. For example:

I think anyone with a conviction for drinking and driving should be banned indefinitely.	Strongly in favour
	In favour
	Neither in favour nor against
	Against
	Strongly against

10.4.4 BELIEFS

Beliefs can usually be assessed by asking whether something is seen as true or false. For example:

The number of people living on the streets in London has increased in the past five years.	True
	False

10.5 FORMS OF QUESTIONS

In both interview schedules and questionnaires, there are two forms of question that can be asked: **closed questions** and **open questions**. The type of study will determine whether open or closed questions are best. But it is worth bearing in mind that

> closed questions should be used where alternative replies are known, are limited in number, and are clear cut. Open-ended questions are used where the issue is complex, where relevant dimensions are not known, and where a process is being explored. (Stacey, 1969: 80)

> Their advantage is that they allow a respondent to answer on their own terms, enabling the researcher to discover unexpected things about the way people see a topic. (Seale and Filmer, 2004: 130)

In most questionnaires and interview schedules, both open and closed questions will be included. However, when large numbers of individuals are to be studied by self-completion questionnaire, it is best to use a majority of closed questions.

10.5.1 CLOSED QUESTIONS

Closed questions are developed in advance, complete with a number of possible answers that could be given. Each respondent is asked to choose from one of the listed options. For example, a closed question asking about highest level of educational attainment would ask respondents to choose from a list of categories such as basic education, degree, and professional qualifications. Other questions, such as 'Are you married?' have the appearance of open questions, but are only answerable by 'Yes' or 'No'.

Closed questions have advantages because they can be pre-coded and the responses can easily be put on a computer, saving time and money (see Chapter 17). They also have particular advantages in studies using self-completion questionnaires because they are less time-consuming for the respondent to complete.

However, such structured questions also have the disadvantage that they force the respondent to choose between the answers provided. When faced with a question such as: 'Do you enjoy your work?' the respondent may wish to say 'yes and no', 'it all depends', or 'I like the social contact'. This difficulty can be overcome to a certain extent by asking for more information. When the respondent is asked to indicate either 'yes' or 'no', this can be followed by a 'why?' or 'please provide further details' allowing for more elaboration. Where lists are given, a category of 'other' should always be provided for those who cannot find an appropriate pre-coded response.

Ranges can be given which make completion and coding easier. For example, when asking about income, the following options could be offered:

Under £5,000 per annum
£5,000–£9,999 per annum
£10,000–£14,999 per annum
£15,000–£19,999 per annum
£20,000–£24,999 per annum
£25,000–£29,999 per annum
£30,000–£34,999 per annum
Over £35,000 per annum

In face-to-face interviewing, such ranges of answers can be printed onto a prompt card and given to the respondent.

A *ranking scale* is a form of closed question that can be valuable when trying to ascertain the level of importance of a number of items. A list of choices is provided and the respondent or interviewee is asked to rank them. For example:

Which do you feel are the most important factors in staying healthy? *Please rank the following in order of importance to you. Number them from 1 = most important, to 7 = least important.*

Taking regular exercise
Having a good diet
Being in a stable relationship
Having regular health checks
Living a low-stress lifestyle
Being engaged in productive activity
Knowing about what contributes to good health

It is advisable to limit the range of alternatives because it may be difficult for the individual to rank a large number. This is particularly important when carrying out face-to-face and telephone interviews, where more than four or five items can be unmanageable. It is helpful in face-to-face interviews to allow the respondent to look at a prompt card showing the choices.

10.5.2 OPEN QUESTIONS

Open questions are those that allow individuals to respond in any way they wish. For example, asking an open question: 'What do you think can be done to improve your local environment?' will allow the respondent or interviewee to state any measure from reducing noise pollution to instituting large penalties for dropping litter.

Open questions can be most usefully employed by skilled interviewers, who can allow interviewees to develop answers much more fully than they would if they were completing questionnaires.

It is also very useful to use open questions when beginning a new research project. If investigating the ways in which students cope financially while at university, the researcher would do well to begin by asking open-ended questions of a small sample of students. From such a small-scale study, it would be likely that a list of possible answers would emerge, for example, working in a bar, borrowing from the bank, staying with relatives, and so on. If a larger study were to be carried out, answers to these open questions could then be used to devise pre-coded categories for closed questions.

Open questions do have their drawbacks. In questionnaires, it is relatively simple for respondents to tick pre-coded categories, whereas unrestricted answers require more thought. A further disadvantage of using open questions is that they produce responses that may be ambiguous, wide-ranging and difficult to categorise. Answers can be time-consuming to code, interpret and analyse and therefore expensive to deal with when conducting large-scale studies.

10.6 DEVELOPING QUESTIONS

Your choice of questions will obviously depend on the subject matter of your study. However, a number of important guidelines need to be considered.

10.6.1 RELEVANCE TO PARTICIPANTS

It is essential to assess whether respondents will have the knowledge to answer the questions, whether the questions are relevant to them and whether they wish to reveal the information.

10.6.2 CLARITY

A fundamental point is to ensure that questions can be clearly understood and are not subject to any ambiguity. Although this applies both to interview schedules and questionnaires, it is particularly important when producing a document for self-completion. If someone is interviewed and does not understand a question, he or she can at least ask for some elaboration, but when the questionnaire is the only means of communication, confusion will discourage the respondent. Furthermore, any misunderstanding will mean that any response given is invalid.

Getting the wording right may present a problem, particularly if a wide-ranging population is under study. The wording should not appear too simplistic for some, seeming to insult their intelligence; on the other hand, it must not be too sophisticated for others. If words or phrases are complicated, then misunderstanding may result. It is preferable to avoid jargon: words like 'social interaction', 'alienation' or 'socialisation' may be everyday terminology to sociologists, but their meanings may not be fully understood by others. It is worth remembering that significant numbers of the population may be functionally illiterate and that, for many, English will not be their first language. Of course, if the sample comes from a particular group, for example, engineers, medical practitioners, or lawyers, it would be appropriate to use the vocabulary common to the group.

It is important to have the same frame of reference as those under study and this is one of the most difficult aspects of producing questions. Certain words may be interpreted in differing ways, depending on individual perspectives. For example, common words like *equality* or *independence* may mean different things to different people. Other more technical words such as *fault* or *fracture* will be understood differently by tennis players, horse riders and geologists. Therefore, questions need to be developed carefully to match the sample to be used.

TIP

The important principle is to use simple words and uncomplicated sentences.

10.6.3 LEADING QUESTIONS

Television or radio interviewers' questions are sometimes preceded by 'Wouldn't you agree that ...?', or 'Isn't it the case that ...?'. The object is to *lead* an individual into agreeing with a particular statement. Researchers, however, need to take a more objective stance and avoid leading questions. For example, if you are carrying out a study of attitudes towards government policy, you should not ask: 'Don't you agree that the present government's policy on crime is an excellent one?' or 'Isn't it the case that, since the present government came into office, the life of pensioners has improved?' Rather, an open-ended question such as: 'What do you think of the government's policies on crime?' or a closed question listing various elements of the policies and asking the respondent to rate which they regard as most valuable, would yield more objective and helpful results. It is important to establish what the respondent thinks is important, without being directed by the researcher.

10.6.4 DOUBLE-BARRELLED QUESTIONS

Double-barrelled questions are those which ask two questions in one. For example, if the question: 'Are you employed, and do you enjoy your work?' is asked, it may be that the answer to the first part is yes, while the second is no, so that the respondent is not sure how to answer. The questions should be separated: 'Are you employed'; if *yes*, 'Do you enjoy your work?' Two questions in one will lead to confusion. Another example is a question in which a person is asked, in one sentence, whether they know about something and what they think of it: 'Do you know anything about the work of Greenpeace, and what is your opinion of it?'

It is also advisable to avoid double negatives. If you were to ask someone whether he or she agrees that, 'Those not over eighteen should not be allowed to drink alcohol in pubs, restaurants or at home', it is not clear what an answer 'No' is intended to mean.

10.6.5 HYPOTHETICAL QUESTIONS

For most studies, hypothetical questions are best avoided. These questions usually begin with: 'What would you do if ...?' or 'Would you like to ...?' What the respondent or interviewee says he or she might do when faced with a given situation may not be a good guide to their actual future behaviour. There are some questions that inevitably produce favourable replies: 'Would you like to have a higher income?' is unlikely to be met with a negative response.

There are, of course, instances where it may be useful to ask people to imagine what they would do in a certain situation: 'If you witnessed someone stealing a wallet, would you intercept?' Whether such hypothetical questioning is useful will be dictated by the subject matter of the study. Hypothetical questions are sometimes used at the outset of a study, as part of a focus group discussion, where such questions stimulate ideas and debate between participants.

10.6.6 SECONDARY INFORMATION

In most instances, it is inadvisable to ask respondents or interviewees about someone else's views, that is, request secondary information. An individual may not be able to state the opinions or perceptions of another with accuracy. Nor will respondents necessarily be able to describe the experiences of someone they know. However, if the other person is not easily available for interview, it is common practice to ask a member of their household for *factual* information about them (for example, their age, sex, occupation, and so on). This is called using a 'proxy' for the intended interviewee.

10.6.7 PERIODICITY

When investigating behaviour which requires the individual to specify a time or a number, supply specific categories. Thus, when asking how often the respondent attends the theatre or reads a newspaper, offer the alternatives: daily, 2–3 times a week, once a week, twice a month, and so on. Terms such as *often, frequently,* or *regularly* are too vague and should be avoided.

10.6.8 SENSITIVITY

Attention must be given to ensuring that the ways in which questions are phrased are handled sensitively so that respondents are not offended or alienated. For example, your study may be interested in the sexual behaviour of young adults and questions will, of necessity, be personal in nature. Piloting to test responses will help guide the development of acceptable questions.

A key problem with researching sensitive issues is to know whether respondents are being truthful. They may over- or under-report some activities. Sudman and Bradburn (1982) suggest that there are three main areas where over-reporting may occur:

1 'Being a good citizen', that is, voting behaviour, relationships with government officials and community activities.

2 'Being a well-informed and cultured person', for example, newspaper and book readership, and attendance at concerts and plays, involvement in educational activities.

3 'Fulfilling moral and social responsibilities', that is, contributions to charity, helping family and friends, and being in employment.

Conversely, there may be under-reporting of certain aspects of individuals' lives, such as illness and disability, criminal behaviour, sexual activities, smoking, illegal drug-taking, drinking alcohol, and financial status.

Because of the dangers of either over-reporting or under-reporting, questions need to be phrased so that they do not intimidate those taking part in the study. Careful preparation of questions, using foresight and experience to predict those which may prove to be sensitive, will ensure that you get the best response from participants.

10.7 THE FORMAT OF A QUESTIONNAIRE

A questionnaire should be designed with the respondent in mind. It is also important to include information to explain the purpose of the study.

In a postal survey, it is essential that a covering letter is included as part of the questionnaire so that it does not go adrift. For a postal questionnaire, the date by which the questionnaire needs to be returned should also be given; generally, two weeks from the distribution date. Either a stamped addressed envelope or a 'Freepost' envelope must be included. If carrying out a web survey, a similar introduction will be needed with clear instructions on the latest date for return.

The questionnaire should explain at the beginning what is needed, give clear instructions throughout, and, if necessary, provide illustrations. It is particularly important to ensure that participants understand whether a single response to a question is wanted, or the answers should include all that apply.

CHECKLIST

- All closed questions must be pre-coded, allowing space for as many alternatives as possible. Always include an 'other' category.

- For some open-ended questions, prompts may be needed.

- Ensure that you have appropriate column numbers to help with transferring the data to a computer file (see Chapter 17).

- Remember to include filter questions and provide clear directions so that the respondent need only read questions that are appropriate to his or her circumstances.

- Each question must be numbered. If appropriate, section headings and subsections are useful as guidance for both respondent and researcher. When the topic changes, an introductory sentence should be provided.

- Never split questions between pages, nor ask a question on one page and ask for a response on the other.

- An identification number must be put on every questionnaire to enable checking and reminders to be sent if questionnaires are not returned.

The questionnaire should be no longer than necessary. For most studies, it should take less than half-an-hour to complete. So, list the questions you require, edit as much as possible, and try to limit the layout to no more than six sides of paper. It is more likely that there will be a good response rate if a concise questionnaire is provided.

The order in which questions are asked is important; the questions should not jump from subject to subject. A question about marital relationships, followed by one about work experience, then one on home ownership before a return to the subject of marital relationships, would be an example of poor ordering. When positioning the questions, try to follow the same sequence one would in normal conversation, with each question arising logically from the one before.

Questions should not only fit together but also be grouped together according to subject. If the ordering of questions is unpredictable, it will frustrate respondents and make the study appear ill-considered and amateurish.

It is also essential to provide clear linking sentences, particularly when moving on to a different topic. Phrases such as: 'Moving on to ...', 'Thinking about your experience of ...', 'The next set of questions concern ...', or 'I'd now like to ask you about ...' can be used.

The interest of the respondent needs to be engaged and maintained. It is best to begin with simple and easy questions that are non-threatening. Once the individual begins to complete the questionnaire, or take part in the interview, the chances of successfully obtaining the more sensitive items of information improve. Even if the later questions are left unanswered, it may still be the case that earlier responses will be valuable for the study.

Questions concerning background and socio-economic data are normally best asked at the end of questioning. However, there are exceptions, in particular for screening purposes. For example, if you are examining experiences of children's care in hospital, you would need to ask early on whether the respondent had children, so that those who were childless could be re-directed or excluded.

Self-completion questionnaires should begin with closed questions, where responses can simply be ticked, rather than open questions which may require the respondent to give considerable thought to an answer. It is preferable to ask open questions at a point when the respondent has become committed to the questionnaire.

Both questionnaires and interview schedules usually need to include filter (or skip) questions to guide respondent and interviewer through, avoiding those questions that are irrelevant to the respondent. Interviewees who have not had a child should not be asked questions about children. This is the purpose of the instructions to the interviewer on the right-hand side.

Q.1 Do you have any children?	Yes No	*If yes, go to question 2* *If no, go to question 4*
Q.2 What ages are your children?	....	
Q.3 Do they still live with you?	....	

For postal surveys, producing the questionnaire in a booklet form looks professional and makes the document easier to handle. Generally, an A4 paper size allows questions to be well spaced and clearly printed.

Choose a font for the document that is attractive and easy to read, such as Arial, and use a range of sizes to make instructions and questions clear to the respondent. If the budget allows, use good quality paper, preferably coloured so that it stands out from the mass of other paper which might be received. Remember that the questionnaire's appearance will have a significant influence on whether respondents feel like completing the form.

A note of thanks expressing appreciation for the assistance given should be placed at the end of the questionnaire.

When each questionnaire is returned, it needs to be checked for missing information and to ensure that it is legible prior to data capture.

It may be necessary to send reminders to those who have not returned questionnaires. Plot the rate of return on graph paper and send reminders when the response rate begins to fall. The questionnaire forms will need to have identifier numbers on them to enable you to check which ones have been returned. If you think the identifiers may put people off responding, and yet you wish to send reminders, send them to everyone, saying that if they have not already done so, they should return the forms. Usually, reminders including another copy of the questionnaire are sent two weeks after the original deadline.

10.8 THE FORMAT OF AN INTERVIEW SCHEDULE

An interview schedule, or a focused interview guide, will be handled by a trained interviewer. It is important that the same guidelines are followed by every interviewer and, therefore, the instructions must be explicit.

All interviewers must carry some means of identification (with a photograph), and, if required, a letter of authority from the funding body. Here is an example:

Good morning/afternoon/evening. I am........... from the University of Poppleton.

We are conducting a survey on behalf of your local Council, to find out what people think about their services. A representative sample of people in the Borough have been selected for interview in this survey. This will give you the opportunity to 'have a say' and your taking part will make a great contribution to the study.

Everything you say will be treated confidentially. No names will be attached to any information you provide.

The interview will take about 30 minutes.

If potential agreement is shown:

Would it be convenient to carry out the interview now, or if preferred, I could come back (or telephone) at another time? When would be most convenient?

Even if the interviewee has received prior notification of the interview by letter or telephone, the interview schedule must begin with a brief introduction, stating who the interviewer is, which organisation he or she represents and the purpose of the interview. Confidentiality and anonymity should be stressed.

Interview schedules, like questionnaires, must provide filter questions to ensure that the interviewer can move smoothly from section to section. This is particularly important in telephone interviewing when silences over the telephone while the interviewer sifts through the questions may confuse or annoy interviewees. A filter question (When you first took up the tenancy what was the internal decoration like? ... If 'Poor' or 'Very Poor' (a) How did you feel about this?) and examples of other features of interview schedules are shown in Figure 10.1, an extract from a housing survey.

For some closed questions, it can be more convenient to offer grouped answers on a prompt card. For example, in most instances the exact dates of birth of respondents is not of interest, but simply their age group. Participants also find it more convenient (and, in terms of age, sometimes less embarrassing) to indicate a range, for example:

Your Age
18–25
26–35
36–45
46–55
56 and over

Figure 10.1 An extract from a public housing survey

IF HOUSEHOLD TOOK UP TENANCY IN 1996 OR LATER (IN LAST 5 YEARS)
ASK SECTION 1, *if not*, GO TO SECTION 2.
SECTION 1. INITIAL TAKE UP OF TENANCY

1. When you moved into your present house/flat (1)
    did you move:

From Council Waiting List_____	1
From temporary Hostel (Homeless)	2
accommodation	
Moved because of modernisation programme_____	3
Transfer or exchange of Council property_____	4
Other (Specify)_____	7
NA/NR_____	9

(a) Is your present house/flat temporary (2)
    (short-term) accommodation?

Yes – temporary accommodation_____	1
No – permanent home_____	2
Don't know_____	8
NA/NR_____	9

2. When you first took up the tenancy what (3)
    was the internal *decoration* like?

Very good_____	1
Good_____	2
Acceptable_____	3
Poor_____	4
Very poor_____	5
Don't know_____	8
NA/NR_____	9

If 'Poor' or 'Very Poor'
(a) How did you feel about this? (4)

Extremely upset/very disturbed/desperate_____	1
Very unhappy_____	2
Unhappy_____	3
Did not mind/not concerned_____	4
Quite happy_____	5
NA/NR_____	9

(b) Did you receive a decoration allowance (because of the (5)
    poor decorative order of the property)?

Yes_____	1
No_____	2
Don't know_____	8
NA/NR_____	9

Cards can also be used to list various alternatives from which the interviewee can choose. For example, when asking the question: 'What are the most important aspects of being employed?', the card could list:

financial reward
social contact
self-esteem
something to do
other

Cards can be used for attitude questions. For example, the responses offered for the proposition, 'The Government should reduce the tax on fuel' might be:

Strongly agree
Agree
Neither agree nor disagree
Disagree
Strongly disagree

Supplying prompts will also help respondents remember events that they might otherwise have forgotten.

If there is a long list of statements to be read or shown to interviewees, it is possible that items at the top of the list are attended to more closely than those in the middle or at the bottom. To reduce this potential bias, the items in the lists can be rearranged with some interviewers using one order and others using an alternative.

An interviewee cannot look at a card when being interviewed by telephone so an alternative technique is to read all the items and obtain a yes/no answer to each one separately. The number of items will need to be limited to three or four for this to work.

10.9 PREPARING FOR FIELDWORK

When developing a questionnaire or interview schedule, there are two preliminary steps you should take. First, try your draft out on people you know. Second, 'pilot' the questionnaire or schedule on a small sample drawn from the same population as the main study.

It can be very useful to try a questionnaire or schedule on friends and colleagues who will cast a critical eye over the questions and the order in which they are placed. This will also help to ensure that instructions and guidelines are clear. It is surprising how often a question that seems perfectly satisfactory to the author proves to be ambiguous to others. It is better to discover this before it is too late. The questions can then be revised and a working document produced.

The next stage is to conduct a pilot study; as a guide, in a proposed survey of 2000 respondents, the pilot sample should include between 10 and 20 respondents. This initial group must have similar characteristics to those of the population to be studied. From the pilot, the researcher will be able to assess whether the line of questioning is appropriate and whether the document is understandable and simple to use.

Remember that people are under no obligation to take part and will need to be encouraged and feel valued in order to comply with your request. The theory of social exchange propounded by Blau (1967), among others, argues that individuals' actions are motivated by the 'rewards' they are likely to receive from others. Although there may be certain 'costs' in performing any particular action, most individuals try to ensure that these are outweighed by the benefits they receive. In general, the material rewards offered by researchers to participants taking part in a study are likely to be low. However, if individuals feel that they have been specially selected and that their participation is highly valued, this may be sufficient reward. The costs are the time taken to provide answers and the mental effort required. If the questions make the individual feel anxious or embarrassed, these costs may in the end outweigh any rewards.

An effective introductory letter is especially important when carrying out postal studies because it helps secure the cooperation of potential participants. When an individual receives an unsolicited questionnaire through the post, his or her immediate reaction may be to ask any or all of the following questions: 'What is the study about?', 'Who is carrying it out?', 'How long will it take to complete?', 'What are they trying to sell to me?' An introductory letter may allay some of these doubts and anxieties. Begin by introducing yourself and your organisation, and briefly state the aims and objectives of the research. Emphasise why the study is important and make the individual feel that he or she will be making a valuable contribution to research by participation. You will also need to state why the individual was chosen for the study so a brief outline of the sample is useful. It is also vital to stress that confidentiality will be maintained and that information provided will only be used by those involved in the research. State that the report derived from the study will only include statistical information and unattributable quotations. Letters should be personalised by a signature. Provide a telephone number or e-mail address for obtaining more information.

10.10 SUMMARY

This chapter has provided some guidelines and offered some practical assistance so that most of the difficulties of preparing questions can be foreseen and avoided. The fundamental idea underpinning the approach outlined here is that attention must be given to all aspects of the questioning process if a satisfactory response rate and valuable data are to be obtained.

The researcher must give thought to what is to be investigated, what form and types of questions are relevant and whether the questions ask for information that is available to the participants. Questions should be clear, composed of everyday words and simple sentences, and the order in which they are presented should be logical. Questionnaires and interview schedules should be drafted, tested, edited and tested again, before being used for the survey.

DISCUSSION QUESTIONS

1   When would you use a closed question and when an open one?

2   Is it ever a good idea to use (a) hypothetical questions; (b) leading questions?

3   Review the relative advantages of postal, face-to-face and telephone surveys. Which would you consider would be best for a study of:

(a) attitudes to the redevelopment of a city centre square;

(b) experiences of opening and using a bank current account;

(c) experiences with using a sexual health clinic.

PROJECT

Put the guidelines introduced in this chapter into practice by developing a self-completion questionnaire. Imagine that you have been asked by a local authority to carry out an investigation into attitudes towards the recycling of waste. You have been asked to select a representative sample of the population (see Chapter 9) and to find out whether respondents recycle their waste, if so to what degree, if not, why not, etc. For example, what have respondents recycled during the past month? You will need to devise a working definition of what is meant by recycling activity to guide the design of the questions. The authority is particularly interested in how people might be encouraged to recycle more, so questioning along these lines will be necessary.

As this will be a self-completion questionnaire, try to include as many closed questions as possible, with pre-coded categories. So that correlations can be made when you analyse the data, choose a number of variables that may be relevant, for example: age, sex, employment status, income, marital status, housing status, and so on.

Prepare a draft, test it with a friend, and then try the final questionnaire out on a small sample (e.g. five people).

RESOURCES

A very useful book that comprehensively covers all aspects of questioning is Bradburn et al. (2004) *Asking Questions*. It is particularly helpful on the subject of designing questions on 'sensitive' issues and also addresses the problem of ensuring that the answers accurately represent the views of the respondent. Questionnaire development is also fully explored in de Vaus (2002a) *Social Surveys*.

Bulmer (2004) *Questionnaires* provides useful tips on producing questionnaires.

For the analysis of data gained from in-depth interviews, Silverman (2006) *Interpreting Qualitative Data* provides helpful guidance.

11 Measuring Attitudes

Mike Procter

11.1 INTRODUCTION

The content of many surveys can conveniently be divided into two components: 'objective' and 'subjective'. The first of these certainly needs to be printed in quotation marks, since there is a point of view according to which all social facts are social constructs (see Chapter 1).

Nevertheless, it often makes sense to distinguish between, on the one hand, the approximately objective, factual variables such as age, gender, and even social class since this is typically classified on the basis of ostensibly factual information about the respondent's occupation, and, on the other, the variables that result from asking the respondent for a subjective reaction: an opinion on a social issue, or something of the sort. This latter component is often referred to as attitudinal. ('Opinion' and 'value' are near-synonyms to attitude.)

This chapter explains what social scientists mean by an **attitude**, and how it might be measured. Attitudes are best measured by combining the answers from several indicators, each of which is a scale. Five types of attitude scale are described and the techniques used to assess their reliability and validity are explained. Correlations and factor analysis are introduced as ways of combining the results from several scales.

11.2 WHAT IS AN ATTITUDE?

An attitude is a hypothetical construct: no-one has ever seen or touched one, and its existence and properties must be inferred indirectly. This is in itself not a problem: there are plenty of other perfectly respectable examples of unobserved constructs, including not only most of social science but also large chunks of physics. What is important is that the particular concept should be linked in well-understood theoretical terms to other concepts, and that it should be possible at least in principle to make empirical observations that could produce evidence either consistent or inconsistent with those theoretical links (see Chapter 2). It has to be admitted that in practice there is not as much theory or evidence as one would like. However, the idea of an attitude is so natural that despite these failings it remains central to much research in sociology and social psychology.

What seems to be common to most definitions is that an attitude is a predisposition to behave in a particular way. If a friend eats no meat, her vegetarianism could be based on health concerns; if she attends hunt saboteur meetings, the anti-hunt stance could be due to class identification; and if she demonstrates outside the Pharmacology Department's animal laboratories, it might be part of a general mistrust of globalisation and of transnational corporations. Alternatively, you might explain all three of these behaviours in terms of a particular attitude to animal welfare. There is a tension here: Ockham's razor goes in favour of simplification, but this may be an *over*simplification. Later in the chapter, we shall show how we may be able to decide between these two hypotheses.

11.3 ATTITUDES AND BEHAVIOUR

To avoid oversimplifying, we should mention the long-standing debate sometimes referred to as the 'attitude-behaviour problem'. This refers to the common (indeed, almost universal) finding that there is no simple relationship between verbal and non-verbal indicators of an attitude.

This finding was dramatically illustrated by a landmark study published before World War II. LaPiere (1934) described how, for two years starting in 1930, he travelled extensively throughout the United States with a Chinese couple. He reported that they were received at 66 overnight lodgings and served in 184 eating establishments during their travels, and only once were denied service – by a proprietor who said he did not provide accommodation for Orientals. However, when LaPiere sent out questionnaires 6 months later asking each of the 250 establishments that served them whether they would accept Chinese guests, only one of the 128 respondents replied that they would.

The general point to be made is that if there is an underlying attitude it will not be the sole determinant of either the verbal or the non-verbal behaviour, and strong relationships can be expected only if the entire situation is very carefully analysed. In particular, it seems likely that LaPiere's restaurateurs, motivated chiefly by commercial considerations, believed that they would be less likely to lose custom by discreetly admitting a Chinese customer who was actually in the foyer than by risking a scene. The latter problem did not exist for the postal questionnaire.

In short, a verbal statement is only a *behavioural indicator* of an attitude and the attitude-behaviour problem is really just one aspect of the more general one of imperfect relationships between different behaviours.

11.4 A PRELIMINARY EXAMPLE

Before going more deeply into the theoretical and methodological problems of attitude measurement, let us consider the problem of measuring political radicalism through a questionnaire, either self-completed or administered in the course of a survey interview. A number of points will emerge to be dealt with in more detail in later sections.

You might begin by thinking of a simple question to ask: for instance, 'Do you consider yourself to be politically radical?' Respondents could be invited to simply answer 'yes' or 'no', or to choose one of, say, five answers from 'yes, very' to 'no, on the contrary'. (In principle, they could be allowed to make an open response, but in practice this would be too complicated to analyse in a typical survey sample of 1,000 or more.)

There are several objections to such an approach. The first is that the researcher is asking the lay respondent to make a social-scientific judgement: the question assumes that the respondent uses the term 'politically radical' in essentially the same way as the researcher, even when applying it to him or herself. Even if there were agreement on the beliefs that tended to be part of radicalism, a person's judgement is likely to be context-dependent: when I am with some of my colleagues (ageing 1960s revolutionaries) I might think myself a conservative; in the company of some students I might think myself a dangerous radical. Only an 'objective' observer, such as a researcher aspires to be, may be expected to apply the same criteria in a roughly consistent way across a range of individuals and settings.

It would perhaps be more reasonable to ask the respondent to answer a question that did not demand as much prior analysis on their part. For instance, we could ask which political party he or she belongs to or identifies most closely with, and then use our knowledge of the parties to classify people into radicals and non-radicals, or to locate them on a radical-conservative scale. A different problem here is that people sometimes identify with parties for non-ideological reasons – because of class identification, or family tradition, perhaps, so that you measure the wrong concept.

Alternatively, we could try to formulate a question that would encapsulate our concept of radicalism more directly. Suppose we saw it in terms of the

Labour Party's celebrated Clause Four, which called for the common ownership of the means of production, distribution and exchange. Then we would
ask our respondent to indicate an opinion of that view, either by a simple
agreement or disagreement, or on a scale from complete endorsement to complete rejection.

What are the problems now? The first is that a single item is a very unsatisfactory way of measuring an underlying attitude.

An analogy may help. Suppose that you want to get a brief message from
one mountain top to another by using teams of shouters, who are recruited in
pairs. The big difficulty is that every signal shouter, who will obediently shout
the same message in unison with the other signal shouters (the words 'Party
tonight!', say) is accompanied by a noise shouter. All the noise shouters will
shout different words. If you have just one pair of shouters the noise is just as
audible as the signal, which may well not be received. But if you use ten pairs,
the message will be shouted ten times as loud, whereas the different noises will
tend to cancel each other out, so that the signal has a much greater chance of
being correctly received. Something rather like this can be observed at the last
night of the Proms, London's summer classical music festival, where, during an
interval in the music, a small, carefully rehearsed section of the Promenaders
shouts a humorous message in unison, which is quite audible over the random
chatter of thousands.

The same analysis can be applied to measurement problems.

It is convenient to see any behaviour as being determined by an equation of
the following form:

$$B = A + R$$

Here B means an item of Behaviour (in the case of attitude measurement it will
be verbal behaviour), A means Attitude, and R means Randomness. In other
words, a particular item of verbal Behaviour (a statement of opinion, say) is
determined partly by a relevant Attitude and partly by a large number of other
influences, which can be regarded as essentially random.

If we consider two related statements (related in the sense that they may be
regarded as manifestations of the same underlying attitude), called B_1 and B_2,
then their two equations will be identical in form, though slightly different in
detail:

$$B_1 = A_1 + R_1$$
$$B_2 = A_2 + R_2$$

It is often reasonable to assume that A_1 and A_2 are essentially the same thing
(because both statements are, as already specified, to do with the same attitude),
but that R_1 and R_2 are different random influences.

Suppose, now, that we consider both B_1 and B_2 (for the same individual). This compound behaviour now contains a double dose of both the attitudinal determinant and the random influences. The difference between these is that the attitude is duplicated (like the shouted signal), and therefore reinforced, whereas the random influences (like the shouted noise) are not duplicated, and thus become diluted. So the share of the compound behaviour that is due to the attitude is greater than is the case for either of the individual statements.

To put this in more concrete terms, any single statement, intended as an indicator of an underlying attitude, will always be heavily contaminated by other influences, and thus measure the attitude rather poorly; several statements, all chosen so as to reflect the same underlying attitude, will do so collectively far more effectively.

Some technical details will be added to this observation below, under the heading of reliability and validity.

The second problem is that it is certainly unrealistic to see political radicalism solely in terms of an attitude to Clause Four. To put it in more technical terms, most attitudes are multidimensional. In the present context this means that we would almost certainly want to include in our conception of radicalism other issues that are logically unconnected with the question of common ownership. Examples that occur (though one would usually use less subjective sources, as will be outlined later) include nuclear disarmament and pacifism, redistribution of resources within a nation and between nations, racial and gender divisions, sexuality, freedom of information, trial by jury and other civil liberties, and so on. Each of these is a very broad heading, and might be represented by a range of specific statements. For instance, the redistribution area might include statements about levels of income tax and inheritance tax, and about direct confiscation of wealth; and about terms of trade and financial relations between developed and 'third world' countries.

Appropriate analysis would probably show that, rather than a single dimension of radicalism, there are several, and that, although there may be some tendency for a respondent who is in favour of reducing expenditure on armaments also to be in favour of increasing overseas aid, there will be many individual exceptions, so that, in brief, the two views may be seen as belonging to two distinct dimensions of radicalism.

All of this implies that it is always desirable, and often essential, to adopt a multiple indicator approach. This means putting together a collection of statements thought to be relevant to the concept to be measured. First, of course, the concept itself must be defined as closely as possible, with what help one can get from a search of the literature. The statements are then assembled from a variety of sources, including written materials of various kinds (the press, pamphlets, polemical books) and oral statements taken from group discussions and unstructured interviews. They are edited to try to avoid the pitfalls discussed in Chapter 10. The final versions of the items are then put to a sample from the appropriate population and the responses analysed so as to determine how best to use them to represent the attitude. In practice, one usually starts with too many statements, so as to be able to select a subset of the best.

A number of approaches have been proposed within this general framework and these are described in the next section. However, in order to understand them, it is necessary to know about a key statistical concept: correlation.

11.5 CORRELATION

The **correlation coefficient** is a number between 0 and 1 (calculated from a rather complicated formula – or by clicking the appropriate button in a computer program) that indexes the strength of the relationship between two variables. If the correlation is zero, then the two variables are completely unrelated: for instance, if there is no tendency whatsoever for agreement with one of two statements of opinion to imply agreement with the other. On the other hand, a correlation of 1 means perfect association: here it would mean that agreement with one statement would unerringly imply agreement with the other. Correlations can also be negative: a value of −1 would mean that everyone who agreed with one statement disagreed with the other. (One might get something approaching this situation because the wordings of the two statements were in some sense 'opposite ways around': one that favoured first-strike use of nuclear weapons and another that favoured immediate unilateral disarmament, perhaps.)

Of course, in practice we always find correlations of intermediate value. You can either interpret these essentially qualitatively – 'a higher correlation means a closer relationship' – or you can try something slightly more technical. To be precise, if you square a correlation coefficient, the resulting value (which must necessarily be positive, of course) can be interpreted as the proportion of the variance in one variable that is shared with the other.

11.6 TECHNIQUES OF ATTITUDE SCALE CONSTRUCTION

There are a large number of methods of constructing attitude **scales**, which will be described rather briefly in this section. Many of them are of importance more because of their frequent mention especially in the older literature than because they are still recommended.

11.6.1 LIKERT SCALING

Leo Thurstone (1928) was the first important pioneer in this field. He suggested a method that involved recruiting a panel of about three hundred judges, and asking them to sort statements into 11 numbered piles, from most to least favourable, with a middle, neutral category. The set of statements is then offered to the respondents, who are asked to indicate the ones they agree with. Their scale scores are then the averages of the endorsed items' scale values. However, this method is extremely expensive in time and other resources and is rarely used today.

Rensis Likert (1932) developed a method (**Likert scaling**) that, as well as making different statistical assumptions, had the great advantage over Thurstone scaling of dispensing with the initial large panel of judges. His method was as follows:

1. The initial collecting of opinion statements proceeds as before.
2. The statements are administered to the study sample (without a preliminary panel of judges).
3. Respondents are asked to respond to each item by placing their response on (typically) a five-point scale, most often

   > strongly agree … agree … can't decide … disagree … strongly disagree

   These are usually coded 5 … 1.

4. For each item the 'item-whole' correlation is calculated between that item and the sum of the remaining items. Items with excessively low correlations are eliminated from further analysis, on the grounds that they must be failing to tap the attitude that is measured by the other items. The computer program SPSS (see Chapters 17 and 18) includes a procedure called RELIABILITY which carries out all of these calculations.
5. Scale scores for individuals are determined by summing the retained item scores.

An important difference between Thurstone and Likert scale items should be explained. A typical Thurstone item is worded in such a way that some respondents will agree with it, some will disagree because it is too favourable to the issue in question, and some will disagree because it is too unfavourable. For instance, a statement designed to measure attitudes to the present government might say 'about half their policies have been successful'. Strong supporters and opponents would both reject this statement (and would be catered for by parallel statements attributing higher and lower success rates.) On the other hand, a Likert item would say 'the policies of the present government have been successful'. This would be rejected by all opponents of the government, but could be accepted by all their supporters, however enthusiastic.

Likert items are called **monotonic** and Thurstone **non-monotonic**. To understand these terms, think of each person as occupying a position on a vertical line extending from most 'con' (at the bottom) to most 'pro' (at the top) with respect to the government (or other social object). Statements of opinion are arranged on the same line, in increasing favourableness from bottom to top. A moderate Likert item will be rejected (for simplicity suppose we only permit two responses, agree or disagree) by all respondents positioned well below it and accepted by all those well above it. There will be individuals in the immediate vicinity of the item who hesitate: the more favourable they are, the greater the probability that they will accept. On the other hand, a Thurstone item will be rejected by respondents too far above it or below it. As we consider individuals who are close to the item, going from bottom to top, the probability of acceptance will first rise and then fall again.

In essence, monotonic means 'order-maintaining': as we go up the attitude continuum, the probability of accepting a Likert item at first remains steady at 0, then rises over its immediate vicinity, then remains steady at 1; having risen, it never falls again. A non-monotonic Thurstone item, on the other hand, first rises in probability and then falls again.

Nowadays most attitude items are constructed so as to be monotonic (and are often referred to as 'Likert items', especially if the responses form a five-point scale), although the analysis usually follows the factor model described below in Section 11.8.

11.6.2 GUTTMAN SCALING

Louis Guttman (1944) was one of a team of eminent social scientists recruited to the US Army during World War II. The method that bears his name has been extremely influential (even though it is not often used in its original form) because Guttman continued for many years to develop his methods into more general forms.

The essential idea behind his original formulation is that of a cumulative scale. One problem with, say, a Likert scale is that though a particular set of responses will always add up to the same total score, the same total score may arise from many combinations of responses.

For instance, a score of 10 on a five-item scale could come from 'disagree' (scored 2) on each item, or from one 'strongly agree', one 'disagree' and three 'strongly disagrees'. In practice, one would seldom get quite such different combinations, but clearly it would be preferable if the same score always meant the same thing.

It is easiest to give an example of such a desirable property from achievement testing. Suppose a class is given a maths test consisting of three questions which require respectively addition, multiplication and division. Each answer is scored 'pass' or 'fail'. In principle there could be eight different patterns of pass/fail ($2{\times}2{\times}2$), but in practice there would only be four: some would pass all three items, some would pass the first two but fail the third, some would pass only the first, and some would fail all three. To put it slightly differently, a score of 2, for instance, would in practice identify someone who can add and multiply but not divide: we would not expect to find someone who can divide but not multiply.

One attitude item can also be regarded as more difficult than another, in the sense that it will be endorsed only by a respondent with a stronger positive attitude. For instance, a respondent with a moderately negative attitude to smoking might agree that TV advertising of cigarettes should be banned. Someone with a stronger negative attitude, who agreed with a ban on smoking in all public places, would almost certainly also agree with the first item. There would probably be rather few individuals who would reverse this: who agreed with the public smoking ban but thought TV advertising should continue. Of course, since there is no logical connection between the two items, whether this neat relationship actually holds is an empirical question, and the development of a multi-item cumulative scale of this kind (often simply called a Guttman scale) involves a complicated statistical analysis.

In more recent years, Guttman, Lingoes and others have developed multidimensional extensions to this method, called generically smallest space analysis. In parallel with this, other groups of researchers have developed very similar analyses called multidimensional scaling. At one level these may be regarded as alternatives to **factor analysis** (see Section 11.8) that make more realistic assumptions about the measurement properties of the data. Specifically, many of these methods assume only ordinal measure(see Chapter 17), whereas Factor Analysis is usually regarded as requiring interval measure, for which the difference between 'agree' and 'strongly agree' should be quantitatively the same as that between 'strongly disagree' and 'disagree'.

11.6.3 MAGNITUDE ESTIMATION

Magnitude estimation has its origins in the attempts of psychologists to measure the relationship between the strength of a physical stimulus (the intensity of a light, the pressure level of a sound, a weight resting on the hand, an electric current) on the one hand, and the strength of the corresponding experience on the other. The same stimulus is offered at a range of different objective intensities, and the subject is asked to give a subjective numerical rating to each one. The results, averaged over a dozen subjects, are plotted. It turns out that people can handle this task in a quite consistent way, although the details differ between sense modalities.

Sellin and Wolfgang (1964) found that their respondents could give similarly consistent ratings on a social perception task. They constructed brief narratives focusing on the theft of goods worth a varying amount, other details of the offence being held constant. Ratings of the perceived seriousness of each offence were plotted on the vertical axis, with the actual amount on the horizontal. As with physical stimuli, respondents (judges, police officers and students) spontaneously gave ratings that followed a consistent curve. Emboldened by this success, Sellin and Wolfgang asked for seriousness ratings on other offences not involving a quantifiable loss, such as smoking marijuana, assault and sex abuse. It seemed reasonable to assume that seriousness was being rated in the same way as when a money amount was mentioned; if this is so, one can assign a seriousness score to any offence and estimate the aggregate seriousness of a year's offences in a way that makes far more sense than merely counting 'crimes known to the police'. For instance, there is the basis for assessing the effect of a decrease in crimes against the person and an increase in property offences.

Since Sellin and Wolfgang, magnitude estimation has been used much more widely, to obtain, for instance, quantitative measures of a candidate's political popularity. Respondents have been asked, instead of giving an oral numerical response, to draw a line whose length reflects their strength of feeling. Originally this was done on paper, with obvious inconvenience from the researcher's point of view, but respondents can now use a games joy-stick or a mouse to draw the line on a computer screen, which automatically measures the length and 'acquires' the data for instant statistical analysis.

11.6.4 EXPECTANCY-VALUE SCALING

Fishbein and Ajzen (1975) propose a method of not just measuring but also analysing attitudes, the expectancy-value (E-V) approach. This is based on the assumption that we consider a number of dimensions in evaluating any social object, and refers back to early theoretical formulations that refer to affective and cognitive components in attitudes. Respondents are asked to what extent they approve of each of a set of dimensions (the affective, or 'value' component), and then to what extent they believe each dimension applies to the issue being considered (cognitive, or 'expectancy'). Each expectancy is combined with its value to get an overall E-V score. For instance, overall preferences between energy technologies (nuclear, fossil fuel, tidal power, etc.) were evaluated by asking to what extent (in probability terms) each was characterised by low cost, risk of catastrophe, long- and short-term pollution and favourable technological spin-offs. Before this, the liking or disliking for each dimension was elicited. The contribution of each dimension to the overall evaluation was estimated by multiplying the probability score by the liking score. A technology would tend to be favoured overall if liked dimensions were seen as having high probability, and disliked dimensions had low probability. For instance, catastrophe was highly disliked, but seen as very unlikely for tidal power.

The advantages of the E-V approach are, first, a convenient format and, second, the possibility of analysing the reasons for an overall score. In the example just given, it was found that overall attitudes measured separately seemed to be far more highly correlated with negative than with positive dimensions: respondents tended to approve of a technology because of the absence of bad points rather than because of the presence of good ones. This in turn would tell policy-makers that if they wanted to gain public acceptance for nuclear power, say, it would do little good to emphasise low costs and favourable spin-offs; what was needed instead was to change perceptions of the dangers of catastrophe and long-term pollution.

11.7 RELIABILITY AND VALIDITY

A pair of key methodological concepts that have been touched on in Chapters 2 and 10 are **reliability** and **validity**. The distinction between them may be seen in these terms: reliability is about whether a measure works in a consistent way; validity is about whether the right concept is measured.

Reliability and validity are most often described in terms of correlation or some closely related concept. Validity is conceptualised as correlation between the measure (any measure, not only attitudinal) and a relevant independent criterion. The crudest version of this is called face validity, and here no formal correlational analysis is attempted, though the underlying ideas remain. For instance, an end-of-term test may consist of multiple-choice items based on statements taken from the course lecture notes or textbook. Usually no evidence for the validity of these items is offered other than that they 'obviously' measure knowledge of what the course is about. When we are trying to measure something as slippery as an attitude, this should never be regarded as sufficient justification: it is not difficult to find examples of obvious errors based on such a glib approach to the problem.

The simplest case of a proper correlational analysis is called predictive validity. For instance, the validity of an aptitude test, to be used for selecting candidates for a course of training, may be defined as the correlation between the test score and some subsequent measure of success, such as a passing-out exam or an on-the-job performance measure. The criterion measure must be assumed to be a perfect indicator of success, obviously questionable in itself.

Clearly the problem is far more severe when there is no objective external criterion – as when, for instance, we try to devise a measure of an attitude. A conceptually convincing solution (that is, however, difficult to apply) is offered by the idea of construct validity (Cronbach and Meehl, 1955). This requires that the measure being evaluated should represent a hypothetical concept that is well embedded in theory, so that the nature of the relationships between it and other concepts is well understood. Then by analysis of the statistical relationships between the various measures, and comparison of these relationships with the corresponding theoretical relationships, the appropriateness of the measures can be assessed. To give a more concrete example, if theory requires that the correlation is 1, but the correlation between measures is 0.5, then the validity of each measure (assuming them to be equally good) is 0.71. The details of the mathematical reasoning will be skipped, but notice that 0.5 equals 0.71 times 0.71. Having established the validity of a measure in this way, it can be used to help in calculating true correlations with other variables, and so on. The difficulty, of course, is in getting a sufficiently precise theoretical baseline from which to begin. In reality, a lengthy process ensues, in which an initially insecure baseline is gradually reinforced by adding more and more similarly wobbly buttresses. It is a perfectly sound engineering principle that the same strength can be achieved by a single strong component or several weaker ones, and this seems a plausible analogy to follow.

Reliability is measured without reference to external criteria. It includes two slightly different concepts: *stability* and *consistency*. Stability is usually measured by administering the same instrument twice to the same respondents, the time interval being chosen so as to minimise the effects of memory while avoiding the likelihood that 'real' change may have taken place. A stable measure will be indicated by a high test–retest correlation. A low correlation may mean an unstable measure, prone to be affected by short-term irrelevancies such as mood, distraction, or differences in the circumstances of completing the instrument; or it may mean an attribute that is genuinely very changeable, such as, apparently, voting intentions. Because of this ambiguity, the concept is seldom accorded much importance nowadays.

Consistency is generally considered more significant. An early form of assessment entailed splitting the constituent scale items into two sub-scales, computing total scores separately for the two halves, and finding the correlation between the two sub-scales. A high correlation would mean consistency between the halves. Of course, the exact value of the correlation would depend on just how the split was made: first half versus second half, odd versus even, etc. Almost universally used instead is *Cronbach's alpha* coefficient (Cronbach, 1951), which is approximately the average of all the possible split-half correlations, and thus measures the consistency of all items, globally and individually.

A conceptually very powerful approach to the problem of establishing validity is offered by Campbell and Fiske (1955). They point out that reliable variance in an item will come partly from a consistent dependence on the concept it is designed to measure, and partly from irrelevant characteristics of the method. For instance, some respondents show a consistent (hence, reliable) preference for one end of a Likert-type scale – usually the 'strongly agree' end, the so-called 'acquiescent response set'. Or the very fact that we are relying on a verbal response may mean that a respondent with literacy problems will lack confidence and thus consistently avoid the extreme categories. To avoid such problems we should use several different methods. For example, we can include essentially the same item twice, but with reversed meaning, and compare people's responses. Then the pattern of correlations

Figure 11.1   Attitudes to abortion

Please tell me whether or not you think it should be possible for a pregnant woman to obtain a legal abortion…

A. If there is a strong chance of serious defect in the baby? (ABDEFECT)
B. If she is married and does not want any more children? (ABNOMORE)
C. If the woman's own health is seriously endangered by the pregnancy? (ABHLTH)
D. If the family has a very low income and cannot afford any more children? (ABPOOR)
E. If she became pregnant as a result of rape? (ABRAPE)
F. If she is not married and does not want to marry the man? (ABSINGLE)

Source: General Social Survey, 1996, National Opinion Research Center.

between items, using the same and different methods and tapping the same and different attitudes, can yield important insights into the true validity of our measures.

In conclusion, it may be noted that it is very simple to calculate a quantitative measure of the reliability of an instrument, because it is based entirely on internal criteria, but almost impossible to do the same for validity. Perhaps the best advice is to bear the problem in mind, and find ways of improving validity, even if it cannot be definitively measured.

11.8 FACTOR ANALYSIS

If a set of attitudes is indeed multidimensional (as argued above), how is it to be analysed? There are several ways to approach this problem, but probably the most commonly used is a statistical method called factor analysis. This is generally regarded as an advanced method, but the results are not too difficult to understand, and what follows is an example of such an analysis. (You could duplicate these results using the computer program SPSS, which is described in a little more detail in Chapter 18.)

The example is rather simpler than the problem of political radicalism discussed earlier. Respondents to a general purpose survey in the USA (the General Social Survey carried out every year by the National Opinion Research Center) were asked the question shown in Figure 11.1. Respondents were invited to answer 'yes' or 'no' to each reason; 'don't know' was also permitted, but excluded from analysis.

These items are monotonic, so, although they have only two possible values rather than the traditional five-point scale, they could in principle be analysed according to the Likert model.

Figure 11.2   Correlation matrix

	ABDEFECT	ABNOMORE	ABHLTH	ABPOOR	ABRAPE	ABSINGLE
ABDEFECT	1.00					
ABNOMORE	.41	1.00				
ABHLTH	.57	.27	1.00			
ABPOOR	.40	.79	.27	1.00		
ABRAPE	.61	.39	.58	.38	1.00	
ABSINGLE	.41	.79	.26	.83	.39	1.00

The 'words' in parentheses after each reason for abortion are the names by which the corresponding variables will be referred to in the computer analysis that follows.

You may not like the wording of some of the reasons. For instance, some may find the patriarchal implications of reason F irritating or even offensive. Others might say that, realistically, even today many women (and even more women's parents) would find the idea of having a child without being married pretty aversive, and therefore it is an important hypothetical situation to ask respondents to consider. The choice of wording, like most research decisions, is not value-free. On the other hand, these questions came out of the standard process of examining spontaneous statements of opinion in open-ended discussions. In short, this example is an instance of secondary analysis, where we are dependent on someone else's decisions, with all the potential difficulties (and advantages) discussed in Chapter 19.

The items were selected so as to cover the main range of grounds that might be used to justify an abortion. By using several statements rather than just one (such as 'Do you think abortions should be legal always, most of the time, sometimes, seldom or never?') the overall reliability of a derived score will be much improved. In addition, the researchers leave open the possibility that people's attitudes in this area may be multidimensional. Of course, in a sense a person's responses to these items will be six-dimensional, since they are making six responses, but the use of factor analysis entails the assumption that the six items are not entirely independent, but can be understood in terms of a smaller number of underlying attitudes; the question is, how many?

The first thing that the factor analysis program does is to calculate the correlation between each pair of variables (Figure 11.2). You will notice first that every single correlation is positive: a respondent who approves of abortion on any ground tends also to approve on any other ground. However, the coefficients vary quite a lot, from 0.26 up to 0.83: **abpoor, absingle** and **abnomore**

Table 11.1
Factors and the variance they explain

FACTOR	EIGENVALUE	PERCENTAGE OF VARIANCE	CUMULATIVE PERCENTAGE
1	3.10	51.71	51.71
2	1.09	18.24	69.95

Table 11.2
The relationship between the factors and the attitude items

	FACTOR 1	FACTOR 2
ABDEFECT	.09	.73
ABNOMORE	.86	.03
ABHLTH	−.09	.79
ABPOOR	.91	−.01
ABRAPE	.05	.76
ABSINGLE	.91	.00

are closely related, as are **abhlth, abrape** and **abdefect,** but the correlations *between* the two subsets are smaller. From this, one might suspect that people's views tend to fall into two categories, and indeed factor analysis can be seen as a more systematic way of investigating patterns of correlation.

The factor extraction takes place in a 'black box' that it would be inappropriate to delve into in an introductory discussion. A summary of the results is presented in Table 11.1.

An **eigenvalue** is a concept in matrix theory, the area of maths that underlies all multivariate statistics. For present purposes, it can be regarded as the variance of each factor – a measure of its importance in explaining the measured items. Because there are six items, the total variance is 6.0 and the percentage of variance explained in each case is the eigenvalue divided by 6. 51.71 plus 18.24 equals 69.95, the second figure in the cumulative percentage column, so altogether these two factors successively summarise almost seven-tenths of the original variation.

But what are these factors? They are inferred from the correlations among the items, but they are understood as underlying the items. Each entry in Table 11.2 indicates the extent to which the row item is determined by the column factor. **Abdefect,** for instance, is determined largely by factor 2, whereas **abnomore** belongs almost entirely to factor 1. As you look down the columns you can arrive at an interpretation of each factor: factor 1 is to do with attitudes to abortion on social grounds, or with 'elective' termination, whereas factor 2 is to do with medical grounds, or matters outside the woman's control. (Yet again, it is impossible to express this in a value-free way: coping with this is part of the researcher's responsibility.)

Table 11.3
Attitude to abortion on 'social'
grounds: percentage approving by sex

	MALE	FEMALE	
Tend to approve	51.0%	49.8%	50.5%
Tend to disapprove	49.0%	50.2%	49.5%
Total	(728)	(922)	(1650)

Table 11.4
Attitude to abortion on 'medical'
grounds: percentage approving by
educational level

	LESS EDUCATED	MORE EDUCATED	
Tend to approve	46.5%	58.6%	48.9%
Tend to disapprove	53.5%	41.4%	51.1%
Total	(1134)	(512)	(1646)

Although there are two distinct factors, they are not independent: the factor analysis reports that there is a moderate correlation, 0.49, between the two factors. Approval on one set of grounds tends to go with approval on the other set. Common sense (which can be confirmed by further analysis) suggests that the correlation is less than perfect mainly because many people approve on medical but not on social grounds.

Of course, discovering the structure of people's attitudes is only the beginning. Having identified the two factors, a program like SPSS can assign to each respondent a score on each factor, based on their individual item scores. Then the real analysis begins. Instead of having to tabulate each of the six items by various explanatory variables, we need only tabulate the two factors, thus simplifying both the computer analysis and the subsequent interpretation. As an illustration, Tables 11.3 and 11.4 show the result of examining the relationship between factor 1 and sex, and between the same factor and level of education. (This is a simple two-category classification, divided into those who had some higher education and those who did not.)

All the variables in these tables are dichotomous: sex is naturally a two-state variable, and the others have been recast into similar classifications for simplicity of analysis. (In professional research this might be regarded as a rather wasteful way to treat data.) As far as the two factor scores are concerned, there is no natural dividing line, so for reasons of statistical efficiency they have been split into roughly equal-sized categories. As explained earlier, it is impossible to say exactly where the neutral point lies.

The creation and interpretation of tables of this kind are outlined in Chapter 18. For now, we shall focus on just a couple of figures in each table. In both tables, each cell contains the number of individuals in that combination of row and column categories, expressed as a percentage of the column total (shown in parentheses). Notice that 51 per cent of men tend to approve of abortion on social grounds, compared with 49.8 per cent of women. This is really no difference at all. First, such a difference is almost certainly not statistically reliable: simply because of random sampling variability we could easily get precisely the opposite result in another sample; and in any case, 1.2 per cent difference is not enough to get excited about. So the conclusion must be that there is no real difference in men's and women's attitudes in this respect.

But there is a substantial difference in attitudes to abortion on social grounds between less and more educated respondents: a tendency to approval is expressed by 46.5 per cent and 58.6 per cent of the respective groups. To put it slightly differently, a non-manual worker is 12.1 per cent more likely to be in the more approving group.

To summarise, then, a set of six attitude items can be successfully condensed into two factors, which can then be used as variables in their own right. The advantages are not only in simplification: it will generally be found that, because of the reduced 'noise' in the derived variables, the relationships with explanatory variables are more distinct than is the case for the raw variables. That is, of course, the essence of construct validity.

11.9 SUMMARY

The measurement of attitudes deserves great care and close attention to detail. The general point to recognise is the necessity to improve reliability and validity. At a minimum that means adopting a multiple indicator approach wherever practicable. If you are seriously interested in this area of research design you should look through some of the suggestions in Resources, and build up a repertoire of methods, so as to avoid always forcing your respondents into the same mould.

DISCUSSION QUESTIONS

1   What is a scale?

2   If attitudes are unreliable predictors of behaviour, what is the use of studying attitudes?

3   What question or questions would you use to measure students' political opinions?

PROJECT

To do something worthwhile with your own data probably means a class project. Decide on a researchable area, probably one that other students will be interested in, since you will need willing research subjects. You could, for instance, examine attitudes to participating in higher education. This may well be multidimensional: for instance, some people are more concerned with the 'pure' benefits of education: general intellectual development, self-actualisation, and so forth, whereas others will emphasise the practical advantages to the individual and to the nation. Do a bit of reading around, to get an idea of the necessary breadth of coverage. Start collecting items: keep a note of statements made in the press, especially student journals; record group discussions and extract coherent opinions. Edit your collection, bearing in mind the rules discussed in Chapter 10. Assemble between 10 and 20 items into a questionnaire, adding a few factual questions – gender, age, course of study, parents' occupations, etc. Ideally, design and attempt to achieve a proper sample – though that is a project in itself. Set everyone in the class a quota: you will need at least two hundred completed questionnaires. Put the data onto a computer and (if you know enough about factor analysis, or can get more detailed advice) use the example here as a model. For a relatively small data set you may be able to manage without a specialised package like SPSS. If you can get advice on a good spreadsheet program like Excel you won't be able to do factor analysis, but you can weed out items that don't seem to correlate with anything else, and then add together the remaining scores. Finally, look at the relationship between your scales and students' background characteristics. Which disciplines seem to be related to which justifications for education? Are there class background differences?

If you cannot collect your own data, you will find that many data sets available for secondary analysis (see Chapter 19) are particularly suitable for attitude research: as well as the NORC GSS from which my illustration was taken (see Davis and Smith, 1992), there are the annual British Social Attitudes Survey and the Euro Barometer series sponsored by the European Commission. If you have access to suitable computing facilities, you can learn a lot by obtaining one of these data sets from your national Data Archive and hunting through it for groups of connected attitude items. The British Social Attitudes Survey, in particular, is the subject of an annual report (for example, Park, 2004) that might give you some ideas on where to start.

Recently, some data sets have become available for public analysis and downloading via the Internet. To get your own copy of the NORC General Social Survey used in the Factor Analysis example, point your browser at http://www.tiny.cc/dBTqg, and follow the instructions on screen. The subset we used took only a few seconds to download from the archive in California.

RESOURCES

Many of the classic papers are brought together in Summers (1977) *Attitude Measurement*.

Oppenheim (1992) *Questionnaire Design, Interviewing and Attitude Measurement* gives a useful guide to many of the practical details of scaling.

A more technical overview is presented in Netemeyer et al. (2003) *Scaling Procedures*.

The measurement of attitudes cross-nationally and cross-culturally is discussed in Jowell et al. (2007) *Measuring Attitudes Cross-Nationally*.

To learn about factor analysis you should start from a foundation in basic statistics including correlation and regression; then Norusis (2007) gives a clear account directly related to SPSS output.

12 Focus Groups

Ann Cronin

KEY POINTS

● The generation of focus group data is dependent upon interaction between participants.

● The level of moderation adopted by the facilitator will affect the quality of interaction between participants.

● Focus groups can be used for a variety of research purposes, either on their own or in conjunction with other methods.

● The key to a successful focus group is good preparation and organisation.

12.1 INTRODUCTION

This chapter provides an introduction to the methods involved in organising and conducting **focus groups** and in managing and interpreting the data they generate. Chapter 14 examines the quantitative analysis of attitudinal data, while this chapter explores the collection and analysis of data from a qualitative perspective. As such it has much in common with Chapter 13 which focuses on interviews; however, it differs in that the unit for both data collection and analysis is the group rather than the individual.

This chapter is divided into four main sections. The first defines the term 'focus group' and provides a brief overview of its use in social research. The second examines the processes involved in preparing for a focus group. The third section provides guidance on constructing a focus group schedule followed by a step-by-step guide to running a focus group; it also considers some of the problems that may arise during the course of focus group discussion and offers possible solutions. The fourth section considers the analysis of focus group data. A general summary of the issues examined in the chapter, a student project, and suggestions for further reading finish the chapter.

12.2 WHAT IS A FOCUS GROUP?

This section begins with a brief definition of a focus group before moving to examine the type of data generated through focus group discussion and the role of the moderator. An extract from a focus group transcript illustrates the points made in this section.

A focus group is a group interview or discussion (Morgan, 1997). Elaborating on this it can be said that a focus group consists of a small group of individuals, usually numbering between six and ten people, who meet together to express their views about a particular topic defined by the researcher. A facilitator, or **moderator**, leads the group and guides the discussion between the participants. In general, a focus group lasts one and half to two hours and is tape-recorded. Sometimes a video is made as well. The tape-recording can be transcribed for the purpose of analysis.

This description of a focus group implies that both participants and facilitator will be physically co-present for the discussion; while this is generally the case, there may be occasions when this is neither possible nor desirable. For example, participants might be geographically dispersed, necessitating the use of video or telephone conferencing facilities. A researcher interested in how people use the internet might wish to run a focus group online as a deliberate part of their research strategy. Schneider et al.'s (2002) comparison between online and face-to-face groups suggests that despite qualitative differences in the type of data produced, each medium has its uses. Stewart et al. (2007) offer useful advice on the use of both video conferencing and online methods to run group discussions, while Chapter 16 in this book examines the use of virtual methods in social research.

Regardless of the medium, and akin to the individual interview discussed in Chapter 13, the focus group enables the researcher to explore participants' views and experiences on a specific subject in depth, for example people's views on recycling or the experience of being homeless. So, as with the individual interview, the focus group discussion involves the exploration of ideas and interpretation of what people say. However, it differs from the individual interview in that the focus group is dependent upon interaction between participants; as Morgan (1997) points out, it is this interaction that is the 'hallmark' of the focus group.

Thus, a focus group is not a replacement for the individual interview; the type of data generated through focus groups is very different from that generated through individual interviews. This issue needs to be given consideration if you are thinking about using focus groups in your research.

12.2.1 THE ROLE OF THE FACILITATOR

The level of interaction between participants, which ultimately has a bearing on the type of data produced, is largely dependent on the role taken by the group facilitator. A good focus group looks easy to run, but making it look easy depends on preparation and acquiring a complex set of skills. Because there is more than one way of running a focus group, it is important that you develop a style that you are comfortable with and will deliver the type of data that addresses your research aims and objectives. Puchta and Potter (2004) and Stewart et al. (2007) offer excellent advice on developing the personal communication skills needed for successful focus group moderation; to this might be added the following guiding principles:

- Show a genuine interest in all the participants.

- Be a moderator and not a participant.

- Be prepared to hear unpleasant views or views you do not agree with.

- Make a decision about the appropriate level of moderation.

Morgan (1997) talks of low and high levels of moderation, although his preference is for 'self-managed' groups. Those wishing to know more about self-managed groups should read Morgan; this section concentrates on low- and high-level moderation and offers a third position of medium-level moderation. However, as Morgan points out, it is best to view moderation of focus groups on a continuum and adopt the position best suited to your research needs.

Low-level moderation means that the facilitator's role in the discussion is kept to a minimum. In this scenario it is usual for the facilitator to introduce the broad topic, for example 'healthy lifestyles' and then withdraw from the discussion, thus preventing the group turning to the facilitator for guidance or direction. Non-involvement with the group can be demonstrated by physically withdrawing, perhaps to an adjacent room with a one-way mirror or simply by sitting outside the group. The data produced are therefore entirely dependent upon the interaction of the group members.

Faced for the first time with the prospect of running a focus group with eight to ten people, this might seem an attractive option! Furthermore, data produced in this way can be said to be free of researcher influence and, certainly, this is a valid reason for choosing to adopt this level of moderation. It is clearly useful when the aim of the research is to gain an insight into the perspective of the participants without the researcher imposing any limits on their understanding of the subject. However, be prepared for the discussion to wander away from the set topic or for the development of group dynamics not conducive for a full exploration of the subject. For example, some individuals may dominate the proceedings. This may make analysis of the data difficult. Of course, if your interest lies in the study of group dynamics, this level of moderation is ideal. However, if you are more concerned with gathering specific information, this may not be the most appropriate method.

In contrast, high-level moderation means that the facilitator assumes a high degree of control over the direction and nature of the discussion. Questions are asked in a specific order and there is little opportunity for participants to deviate from the topic or to raise issues of concern to them. This approach may be appropriate if you require information of a very precise nature, for example, feedback on the phrasing of a questionnaire (see Chapter 10). This level of moderation is not appropriate for gaining in-depth qualitative material about attitudes, behaviour and experience. It is also likely to impede rather than facilitate group discussion and interaction.

In practice, the majority of focus group facilitators opt for a level of moderation somewhere in-between these two extremes. The moderator performs a guiding role in the discussion, ready to interject, ask questions and probe for further information when necessary. In an individual interview the dialogue is largely dependent upon the interviewee responding to the questions and prompts of the interviewer. In contrast, a focus group facilitator will not ask or expect that all participants will answer every question in turn, or ensure that everyone answers each question (Krueger, 2000; Morgan, 1997). Furthermore, even with medium-level moderation, the facilitator will often 'step back' and let the discussion develop between the participants.

In contrast to low-level moderation, this approach has the advantage that as a facilitator you can maintain a greater degree of control over the direction of the discussion, hence ensuring that the data are relevant to your research question. It is this middle level of moderation that is discussed in this chapter; however, you should be able to see how it could be adapted for either high- or low-level moderation.

12.2.2 ASSISTANT MODERATOR

Many facilitators work on their own and this is certainly likely to be the case if you are a student, although you could decide to team up with another student who also wants to run focus groups and act as assistant moderator. While the success or otherwise of a focus group is not dependent upon having an assistant facilitator, if you do have one, they can help to ensure smooth running. Their role includes:

- monitoring the entrance of the participants and handling any interruptions to the focus group;

- recording the discussion;

- making detailed field notes which should include verbal comments and body language;

- debriefing the moderator;

- providing constructive criticism to the moderator about their performance;

- assisting with the analysis.

If you have never run a focus group before, being an assistant facilitator can be a useful way of learning how to moderate groups.

12.2.3 UNDERSTANDING FOCUS GROUP DATA

The type of data produced by focus groups can best be illustrated with a short extract from a transcript of a focus group discussion; in this case all the participants had experience of homelessness and were recovering from alcohol/drug dependency. The focus group, which I moderated, formed part of a mixed methods study (see Chapter 7) interested in understanding the experiential nature of vulnerability with different groups of people living in the same location.

The facilitator's words appear in bold. Prior to this point in the discussion, participants had been recounting their personal experiences of drug/alcohol recovery and the link between this and having somewhere safe to live. In order to move the discussion forward I reflected back to the group some of the issues they had raised and in doing so linked them to vulnerability.

I was just thinking about what you were saying there, one of the things we are interested in in the project is issues around vulnerability, and I was struck by what you said about being isolated, you know, suddenly shoved in this place, the drugs are across the road and feeling incredibly isolated. Also you have all talked about being in different stages of your recovery, what does vulnerability mean in relation to that?

- It means feeling unsafe.
- Yeah, in your own home. If you are unsafe in your own home, how the hell are you supposed to recover?
- I think it all depends on how confident you are that you are going to recover as well.
- Therefore they need to put you somewhere that is safe.
- But, Mike, being in a slightly worse area than say I am but at the end of the day you shut the door and it is just four square walls, isn't it? And you have got to get on with it.
- But it is being aware of where you are and if you look outside your window at night and you see what you've just come away from, you are not going to want to stay there. And you are aware that you are living in a block of flats and there is someone downstairs who is drinking, for instance, or someone downstairs that is letting people in and serving drugs up, why put someone who is in recovery and trying to get away from that back into it? It is madness. Because they are all tarred with the same brush, drink, drugs, mental health. Active or not active, they are all the same, we'll chuck them all on the edge of the city in this new block of flats and keep them out of mainstream Hilltown. That is what it boils down to in a nutshell.
- Yeah, there is an element of that not in my backyard, isn't there, wherever you go?
- Yeah. It happens everywhere.

(Continued)

> – Yeah, that's what I mean, that is what I first said, you know, I quite understand that. You are put in a town, if you were put in, say, [Block of Flats] you are right by the town, you'll get used to it you won't hear cars screeching in and out at 3 o'clock in the morning and stuff like that because you'll be used to that anyway because there will be noise going on all the time and it is like a normal, you know, a normal environment. But where that is, it is like after 10 o'clock at night or whatever you feel like you are stuck in the middle of nowhere, well, you feel like you are, I felt like I was.

Leaving to one side the interesting sociological issues in this data extract, it helps us to see the unique character of focus group data: these data were not the result of one person talking or from me as the facilitator asking each person in turn the same question, but arose through the interaction of the participants. This type of exchange is typical of focus group discussion. That is, in the normal course of a focus group, participants will raise issues relating to the subject that the facilitator may not have previously considered and comment on each other's experiences and attitudes (Barbour and Kitzinger, 1999). Finally, while I was directing the participants to focus on a particular topic, vulnerability, the topic remained sufficiently open for the ensuing discussion to raise new ideas and experiences.

12.2.4 WHEN TO USE FOCUS GROUPS

Focus groups produce qualitative data, and so we can apply many of the same reasons for conducting in-depth interviews to focus groups (see Chapter 13). Focus groups can be used either as a 'self-contained' method or in conjunction with other research methods (see Chapters 6 and 7). Their use at the preliminary stage of a project can provide insight on a topic and inform the development of an interview schedule or questionnaire. Alternatively, in the final stage of a research project, they can be useful for gaining feedback on research findings obtained through other methods. Because focus groups are useful for examining people's knowledge about a subject, they have a broad application in social research. Focus groups can also be used to test topics and the phrasing of questionnaires. However, it is important to remember that the data from a focus group will lack the depth of information that could be obtained from individual interviews, although it may be broader in content. This needs to be taken into account when selecting the appropriate research method for your research project.

Some uses of focus groups:

- to encourage people to develop their own views on a subject and to discuss their knowledge about a topic;

- to understand more about where people's knowledge has come from, that is, the sources and resources that they use;

- to extend knowledge about the dimensions and experiences of a particular process or phenomenon which the respondents are familiar with but you don't know anything about;

- to explore a subject where little research has previously been conducted.

12.3 PREPARING TO USE FOCUS GROUPS

This section examines some of the issues you will need to address prior to running a focus group. It begins with a discussion about the membership of focus groups and sampling strategy before moving to consider the optimum group size and the importance of venue and location. These issues are illustrated in the final part through examination of two research examples.

12.3.1 TOPIC AND MEMBERSHIP OF FOCUS GROUPS

As suggested in the literature (for example, Barbour and Kitzinger, 1999; Morgan, 1997), there are few topics unsuitable or too sensitive for discussion in a focus group, so long as attention is given to the composition of the group. For example, it would be more appropriate to hold single sex groups rather than mixed ones to examine people's attitudes towards the punishment of those found guilty of sexual abuse. The key factor is that groups containing people who have shared experiences or the similar social identities will be more successful than those with disparate views and backgrounds. Additionally, people often benefit from being a member of a group and having the opportunity to share experiences with people who understand them.

This raises a related issue, should focus groups always consist of strangers or is it acceptable to have people who know each other? There are no hard and fast rules and the answer to this question will often depend on the nature of the research and availability of participants. For example, if you obtain your sample from a student population, or a specific community, it is possible that people will know each other. However, you need to bear in mind that the group dynamics between groups of friends will differ from those between strangers and this may affect the quality of the data (see Greenbaum, 2000, for an extended discussion on managing group dynamics).

12.3.2 SAMPLING STRATEGY

Students considering using focus groups for the first time often ask: How many focus groups should I run and how big should they be? These questions are about sampling size and strategy. Barbour and Kitzinger (1999) identify three factors to consider:

- the nature of the research question;

- the range of people who need to be included;

- limitations imposed by time and cost.

Bearing in mind the discussion in the previous section, you also need to consider whether the focus groups will be self-contained or form part of a process of 'triangulation' with other research methods, for example, individual interviews or surveys.

Consideration of these issues leads to what Barbour and Kitzinger (ibid.: 7) term "structured rather than random sampling". In the planning stage of your research you will need to decide how to find samples from your target population (see also Chapter 9). Focus groups depend on purposive sampling in order to select participants according to the project's goals. For example, if you wish to talk to university students about their experience of higher education you might begin by asking the Student Union if you can have access to their student email list.

Purposive sampling is different from the sampling used in quantitative surveys. The goal of surveys is to generalise the findings to larger populations by collecting numerical data, and this requires a random sample (see Chapter 9). The main goal of a focus group is to gain insight and understanding by hearing from representatives from the target population. As with any research method, the recruitment of participants is one of the most important elements of the research study. In some instances, the participants need to be drawn from a cross-section of a population. To return to the example above, you might wish to include students of different socio-economic status, ethnicity and age.

Having determined the number and composition of your focus groups you need to obtain your sample. Below are a few suggestions for how you might do this:

- getting someone to nominate participants;

- sampling from an existing list;

- sending questionnaires to a population asking for participants;

- advertising for participants;

- snowball sampling.

When planning your research do not underestimate the time and effort it takes to recruit a sufficient number of participants for even one focus group. Experienced facilitators advise beginning the recruitment process at least three weeks prior to running the focus group; likewise, once participants have been recruited, do maintain contact with them. Following recruitment it might be useful to send them a letter or email confirming the details and a phone call a few days beforehand helps to ensure participation on the day. Where necessary, you may need to arrange transport or be prepared to cover the costs of travel to and from the venue, and childcare costs may need to be considered.

TIP

Remember to leave plenty of time for recruitment.

12.3.3 SIZE OF GROUPS

Ideally, focus groups should consist of between six and ten people. However, this is a matter for which there are no hard and fast rules. Very small groups of three or four may be useful, particularly if a subject is deemed sensitive or in-depth accounts are required; however, in general conversation in groups smaller than six can be very limited. Nevertheless, while the minimum number might depend on the nature of the research, it is unwise to go above ten. Running large groups poses a number of problems, resulting in data lacking both depth and substance. As a facilitator you will find it difficult to maintain control over a group with more than ten people. Furthermore, participants do not feel the need to contribute, relying on the group to carry the discussion (Morgan, 1997), a phenomenon that Latané et al. (1979) refer to as 'social floating'. The important point to remember is that focus groups provide an understanding of the range and depth of opinions, attitudes and beliefs, rather than a measure of the number of people who hold a particular view or opinion. Therefore, be prepared to substitute quality for quantity.

12.3.4 VENUE AND LOCATION

Your venue should suit both the research project and the type of participants you wish to recruit. Suitable venues may be community halls, school buildings, council offices, a room in the Student Union, or an individual's home. It should be one where people feel comfortable enough to sit and talk for a couple of hours. If possible, choose a venue which is familiar to the members of the focus group, thus aiding attendance and participation.

Green and Hart (1999) provide an interesting account of the way in which different locations can affect levels of participation. For example, 'socially disadvantaged' participants are likely to perceive their local community hall as a more suitable venue, than say, a meeting room in the local Town Hall.

It is a good policy to check the chosen venue prior to the meeting to ensure that:

- All participants will be able to see and hear each other.

- There will be a minimum of distractions and interruptions.

- Observing or recording can easily be carried out.

- It is not too warm or too cold.

- The venue is accessible to all members of the group.

Refreshments such as tea, coffee, soft drinks and biscuits should be provided. The key point to remember when choosing a location is that the venue should provide an appropriate and 'sympathetic' social setting for the group discussion. Finally, here is a checklist of equipment necessary for running a focus group.

CHECK LIST

- Cassette recorder(s) with cord/leads
- Remote microphone
- Extra batteries
- Blank cassette tapes
- Flipchart and pens (if appropriate)
- Pads/pens for moderator
- Copies of focus group schedule
- List of participants
- Pens/paper for participants (if necessary)
- Handouts (if appropriate)

12.3.5 RESEARCH EXAMPLES

Two examples from my own research will help to clarify some of the points raised in this section. The first concerns the multi-method study on vulnerability mentioned above. The research design for this part of the study consisted of two focus groups to be followed by eight in-depth interviews. The number of focus groups was determined first of all by the funding available and time constraints and, second, the purpose of the focus groups. They were used to identify issues of importance to homeless people and the findings informed the development of an interview schedule. The eight in-depth interviews supplemented the findings from the groups, adding depth and substance to the issues raised in the discussions.

In the second example, the aim of the research was to assess the extent and nature of community involvement in a large urban area with an ethnically and culturally diverse population. In order to take this diversity into account it was necessary to run 25 groups with people from different ethnic minorities, older people, young people and single parents. So in this case the need to include the voices of as many different sections of the community determined the number of focus groups. Both these examples demonstrate that the number of focus groups and the composition of those groups will be specific to your research needs and based on your research question.

12.4 RUNNING A FOCUS GROUP

This section describes the development of a focus group schedule and includes a step-by-step guide on how to run a focus group.

12.4.1 FOCUS GROUP SCHEDULE

Merton and Kendall (1946), who were among the first sociologists to advocate the use of focus groups in social research, cite four criteria necessary for a successful focus group discussion: range, specificity, depth and personal context. This section uses these criteria to highlight some issues to consider when constructing a focus group schedule and running a focus group.

Range refers to ensuring that the focus group schedule enables the maximum number of relevant topics to be covered. Although you will have a good idea of the issues you want to discuss, the questions should not inhibit the participants from raising topics of interest to them. Specificity means ensuring that the facilitator encourages participants to move beyond the abstract to situate their talk in actual lived experience. This will help to shed light on the sources of attitudes and beliefs and add clarity and depth (Merton and Kendall's third criterion) to the points being made. Finally, there is a need to take account of the personal context of participant's lives, that is, the social role they perform or the social category to which they belong. Attention to such issues provides a better insight into the social construction of people's attitudes and beliefs.

The issues raised by Merton and Kendall's four criteria relate particularly to the phrasing of questions. Much of the advice given about the construction of interview schedules in Chapter 13 is also applicable to the design of a focus group schedule. 'Think back' questions are useful for encouraging participants to provide a social context for their responses, for example, "Can you tell me about the last time you visited the doctors?" It is best to avoid using 'why' questions because they presume that people always behave in a rational manner and can account for their behaviour in this manner. They can also make people feel that they are being interrogated and judged. Similarly, while occasionally it is helpful to give an example to illustrate a point, it is best to avoid using this strategy too often. Examples can constrain answers to the topic of the example and prevent participants from talking about their own experiences. Likewise, if a participant provides a long or very complicated example to answer a question, do repeat the original question. Finally, while a focus group schedule usually consists of questions to stimulate discussion, it is possible to use other means to generate talk. For example, visual, written or audio material, a list of attitude statements or a short questionnaire can all be effective. Such stimulus material can be used on their own or in combination with questions.

12.4.2 A STEP-BY-STEP GUIDE

The step-by-step guide to running the focus group is based on a five-stage model: (1) introduction; (2) opening circle; (3) introductory questions; (4) key questions; and (5) ending questions.

1   Introduction

Begin by introducing yourself and give a brief outline of the research topic. Too much information may confuse the participants and leave them unsure about their role. Make a brief statement about what you intend to do with the data collected in the focus group, for example, that it forms the basis of a dissertation or a local government report. Assure confidentiality on your part and remind participants to respect the confidentiality of all members of the group. The aim is to provide a friendly and welcoming atmosphere in which participants will feel sufficiently comfortable and relaxed to talk. It might be an idea to let people know that you are not seeking right or wrong answers, but are simply interested in hearing what they have to say. Likewise, let them know that you might ask what could appear to be obvious questions, because you want to hear their understanding of the subject and not simply your interpretation of it. Bellenger et al. (1976) quite aptly refer to this as 'incomplete understanding'.

You might like to consider introducing 'ground rules' at this point, although they can inhibit discussion. A possible exception is when working with young people, in which case you might like to spend a few minutes at the beginning getting them to devise their own ground rules. These should be written on a large piece of paper and stuck on the wall, thus acting as a reminder when necessary. It can be useful to ask participants, regardless of age, not to hold private conversations with the person next to them but to direct all comments to the group Asking people not to interrupt each other is not advisable as this can make for very stilted conversation and inhibit discussion. If all the participants start talking at once, this is generally a very good indication of the salience of the topic under discussion.

2   Opening circle

Following introductions, begin with an opening circle in which participants say their name and other relevant personal information. If participants are not wearing name badges, make a note of participant's names and where they are sitting. This will enable you to direct questions at particular participants and to draw in the quieter members of the group. It is helpful to use the opening circle to elicit participants' views on the subject under discussion. This is useful for helping to prevent the development of **groupthink** (Janis, 1982) and enables you to make an initial judgement about areas of agreement and disagreement. Make notes of anything of interest and refer back to them in the discussion. It is quite likely that a member of the group will say something that you can use to introduce your first question, thus encouraging discussion.

3   **Introductory questions**

Following the open circle, use one or two questions to introduce the topic under discussion and to encourage participants to think about the range of issues it involves. One way of doing this is to ask participants about their understanding and definition of the subject, which may differ from your own.

4   **Key questions**

These questions will be followed by the key questions driving the study. What these are will depend on previous research, your understanding of the subject matter and the aims and objectives of your research. Ideally there should be between two and five key questions. Any more and you will not have sufficient time for in-depth discussion. Remember that you can use probes to follow up responses, which will allow you to explore the issues in depth.

5   **Ending questions**

Finally, there are ending questions which, as the name suggests, are designed to draw the discussion to a close, but can take a variety of different forms. You might like to throw out a general 'all things considered' type of question. Alternatively, you could have a closing circle. The advantage of a closing circle is that it will allow all participants to say something. This is particularly useful if the group contains quiet members who have not contributed to the main discussion. Alternatively, you might like to summarise the key points of the discussion and ask participants if they agree with this summary. Regardless of the method you use in this closing period, the main purpose is to provide people with a final opportunity to raise issues of concern that have not yet been explored and/or to make a closing statement. Do not be surprised if this closing phase goes on for some time as some people use this opportunity to say what they really think.

The model presented here is intended to be used as a guide only, so do not be afraid to adapt it to suit your own purposes. Nevertheless, remember that successful focus group discussions partly depend on the construction of a focus group schedule that does not confuse either the participants or the facilitator and allows sufficient time for in-depth discussion of all the questions. Again, further advice can be gained from any of the references cited in this chapter, although Krueger (2000) and Morgan (1997) are particularly useful for the novice facilitator.

12.4.3 DEALING WITH FOCUS GROUP PROBLEMS

This section outlines some of the problems you may encounter when running a focus group and offers solutions for dealing with them. It is quite likely that in a group of about eight people you will have one or two who are shy or reluctant to join in the discussion. These people need to be gently drawn into the discussion, for example, by directing a question at them. However, if you do this, do be prepared to give them plenty of time to answer.

In addition to the shy person, it is very common to have at least one person who will try to dominate the conversation. While their contributions might be interesting, it is important that they do not prevent other people from speaking. Although there is no simple solution to dealing with such people, the following are suggestions you might like to consider:

- Acknowledge their contribution and then ask other people what they think.

- Avoid eye contact with the dominant person.

- Directly ask them to be quiet and let others speak.

- Take a break and ask them to leave.

Other common problems include people who have a private conversation with their neighbours, people who wander off the subject and inattentive participants. Very often a gentle reminder of the purpose of the group is sufficient to correct the problem, but at other times more drastic action is required. For example, in the case of a private conversation between two individuals you might decide to call a five-minute break and ask people to sit in a different order when reconvening the group. Do not be afraid to take control of the group when appropriate. Participants will expect you to and will feel reassured by it.

> **TIP**
>
> The golden rule here is to be firm and direct, while remaining friendly and open.

It occasionally happens that the group as a whole is very silent thus making it difficult to maintain sustained discussion. One possible solution is to ask participants to discuss in pairs their ideas on a specific topic or question before feeding back to the group for further group discussion. While doing this just once is normally sufficient to encourage group interaction, do not worry if you feel the need to repeat this strategy several times during the course of the session.

> **TIP**
>
> The key here is to be aware of the group dynamics and be prepared to be flexible if necessary.

A useful exercise can be to think of the types of problems you might encounter in a focus group and devise strategies on how to deal with them, thus minimising disruption to the group.

12.5 ANALYSIS OF FOCUS GROUP DATA

A focus group generally lasts about 90 minutes and will yield a transcript of 20–30 pages. Multiply this figure by the number of groups you are conducting and you will begin to understand the enormous amount of data generated by focus group discussions. The quantity can seem daunting when it comes to analysis. However, because it has been directed by the focus group schedule that you developed, the data will include at least your initial conceptualisation of the problem you were investigating.

Focus group data can be analysed from a variety of different approaches. In addition to the more traditional thematic analysis closely associated with qualitative interview data (see Chapter 13), it can be examined using content analysis (see Chapter 23), discourse analysis, and conversation analysis (see

Chapter 22), narrative analysis (see Chapter 21) and an approach that focuses on group dynamics, although the latter is more closely associated with social psychology than sociology.

Regardless of the approach you take, the main point to remember is that the group is the unit of analysis, not the individual participants. This means that, first, your analysis needs to take into account the group context and, second, you are looking for themes, issues, areas of agreement and disagreement that arose at a group level and not simply from individuals within the group. Therefore, you need to be able to distinguish between the opinions of individuals and group opinions (Barbour and Kitzinger, 1999).

For a thematic analysis of the data, begin with the systematic coding of the data from each focus group, generating hypotheses as you proceed. In the early stages you will not be able to make comparisons between the focus groups, but this is something that will become possible as your analysis proceeds. Differences between the groups should take account of the social composition of each group. For example, in a study of adult education it is very likely that socio-economic status would have been taken into account when selecting the composition of the groups. This would need to be addressed in an analysis of, for example, the effect income has on the participation in, and completion rates of adult education courses.

The edited collection by Barbour and Kitzinger (1999) provides numerous illustrations of the analysis and write up of focus group data. As a starting point, see the chapter by Myers and McNaughton on the application of conversation analysis to focus group data. Those who wish to know more about content analysis of focus group data should consult Knodel (1993) or Frankland and Bloor (1999). Krueger (2000) offers a very good introduction to both analysis and writing up.

12.6 SUMMARY

The aim of this chapter has been to provide an introduction to the methodology of focus groups to the researcher with little or no experience of facilitating group discussions. It began by exploring what a focus group is and how the role of the facilitator can affect the level of interaction between participants and consequently, the quality of the data. It then outlined the key issues that need to be considered before embarking on focus group research. In doing so, it emphasised the importance of developing a robust sampling and recruitment strategy, as well as allowing sufficient time to organise and prepare for each of your focus group discussions. Following this, the theoretical and practical issues of devising a focus group schedule, and facilitating a group were discussed. To help you think through these issues a five-stage model for running a focus group was presented; however, with practice and experience you may wish to adapt this model to suit your own purposes and needs. The chapter concluded with an overview of the different approaches that can be used in the analysis of focus group data. There are discussion questions below, some suggestions for further reading and a checklist you might find useful if you are thinking about using focus groups to collect data. Finally, do remember that it is only through practice that you will begin to gain both the confidence and the skills which in time will help you to become a competent focus group moderator.

CHECKLIST

- Why have I decided to use focus groups? Will focus groups provide me with the most appropriate type of data to answer my research questions?

- Will I use focus groups on their own or in conjunction with other methods? At what stage of the research process will I use focus groups?

- What level of moderation do I need to adopt in order to get the type of data I need to answer my research questions?

- How comfortable do I feel about leading a group discussion? How will I encourage participants to interact with each other?

- What criteria will I use to recruit participants? Where will I recruit my participants from? How will I recruit them?

- How many focus groups do I need to run?

- Have I allowed sufficient time to organise the focus groups and recruit participants?

- Is the focus group venue the most appropriate one? Is it both physically and socially accessible for participants?

- What equipment do I need to take to the focus group?

- Does my focus group schedule cover the maximum number of relevant topics that need to be covered? Does my focus group schedule enable participants to raise their own topics and ask questions? Are my questions open-ended?

- Does my focus group schedule consist of an appropriate number of questions for each stage of the process?

- What sort of problems might I encounter in a focus group? What strategies will I use to deal with them?

- How will I analyse my data?

DISCUSSION QUESTIONS

1   Briefly describe the key characteristics of a focus group discussion.

2   Outline the relation between moderation and the type of data generated in a focus group discussion.

3   What factors need to be taken into account when devising a sampling strategy for a research study involving focus groups?

4   How important are venue and location for ensuring participants attend a focus group?

RESOURCES

Barbour and Kitzinger (1999) *Developing Focus Group Research: Politics, Theory and Practice* is an edited collection which draws on a range of different disciplines to examine both the advantages and disadvantages of using focus groups in social research.

Bertrand et al. (1992) 'Techniques for analysing focus group data' offer three different methods for analysing data and also offer advice on writing up the data generated from focus group discussion.

Greenbaum (2000) *Moderating Focus Groups: A Practical Guide for Group Facilitation* provides a practical overview of the different stages involved in using focus groups. Facilitators will find the inclusion of new and advanced techniques particularly helpful.

Krueger (2000) *Focus Groups: A Practical Guide for Applied Research* provides a practical step-by-step guide to running focus groups.

Morgan (1997) *Focus Groups as Qualitative Research* provides a brief but thorough introduction to focus groups. It is particularly good for its discussion on using focus groups in conjunction with other research methods.

Putcha and Potter (2004) *Focus Group Practice* offer excellent advice on subjects such as managing group dynamics, energising a tired group and keeping both yourself and the group focused on the subject.

13 Qualitative Interviewing

Nigel Fielding and Hilary Thomas

- The different formats of research interviews.

- The ways in which interview data are used.

- Issues and techniques of communication during interviews.

- The process of designing an interview guide.

- The practicalities of recording and organising interview material.

13.1 INTRODUCTION

This chapter surveys the varieties of research interviews currently in use and the contemporary applications of interview data, highlighting the ubiquity and adaptability of interview methods. Interviewing is a very widely used research method: the chapter draws on methodological and substantive literature to illustrate the issues involved in this approach. The practicalities of interviewing are given due consideration. The chapter concentrates on non-standardised interviewing and considers the processes of generating data in this way and the value of such data. It goes on to explore the process of preparing an interview guide, to identify the practicalities of recording, transcribing and organising interview material and finally to consider analytic stances towards the data.

13.2 VARIETIES OF RESEARCH INTERVIEWS

Interviewing has a strong claim to being the most widely used research method. Whenever we are getting our bearings, whether as a researcher or a new arrival in a foreign land, the quickest, most instinctive method is to ask a question. It is therefore no surprise that interviewing takes many forms. The usual way of differentiating types of interview is by the degree of structure imposed on their format.

In the **standardised** or **structured interview** the wording of questions and the order in which they are asked are the same from one interview to another. The piece of paper the interviewer holds is called the **interview schedule**, and that word 'schedule' seems to convey the formality of this type of interview. It is most familiar from market research; most of us have been stopped in the street or visited at home by an interviewer bearing a schedule to be completed by ticks in the boxes corresponding to our answers.

The next type of interview is **semi-standardised**; here the interviewer asks major questions the same way each time, but is free to alter their sequence and probe for more information. The interviewer can thus adapt the research instrument to the respondent's level of comprehension and articulacy, and handle the fact that in responding to a question, people often also provide answers to questions we were going to ask later.

The endpoint of this typology is the 'non-standardised' interview, also called **unstructured** or **focused interviews**. Here interviewers simply have a list of topics which they want the respondent to talk about, but are free to phrase the questions as they wish, ask them in any order that seems sensible at the time, and even join in by discussing what they think of the topic themselves. The paper the interviewer holds is called an **interview guide**, and once again the second word, 'guide', conveys the style of this approach, where interviewers take their own path within certain guidelines.

This chapter is mainly about non-standardised interviews. The standardised types are discussed in Chapters 10 and 11. Non-standardised interviews best fulfil the Loflands' (1995) case that the essence of the research interview is the 'guided conversation'. Because of its simple design and correspondence to conversational procedures that are routine in social life, it is often the type of interview that students conduct in their research projects.

After examining the uses of interview data, the chapter considers the conduct of interviews, the design of an interview guide and the practicalities of transcription, coding and analysis. The second part covers problems of interview methods and the ways these can be overcome, with an emphasis on the perspectives on validity found in different theoretical traditions.

13.3 CHARACTERISTIC USES OF INTERVIEW DATA

Like other qualitative methods, non-standardised interviews are valuable as strategies for discovery. Standardised interviews are suitable when you already have some idea of what is happening with your sample in relation to the research topic, and where there is no danger of loss of meaning from asking questions in a standard way. However, if you are on new ground a more flexible approach is best. Lofland summarised the objective of the non-standardised format as being

> to elicit rich, detailed materials that can be used in qualitative analysis. Its object is to find out what kinds of things are happening rather than to determine the frequency of predetermined kinds of things that the researcher already believes can happen. (1971: 76)

Interviews can be administered either one-to-one or to a group. In the former, respondents are seen individually, while in the latter the interviewer, or a group leader, guides discussion among a small group of respondents. Market research has embraced what Merton and Kendall (1946) called **focus groups** as a way of studying consumer preference and the method has spread to the study of political and policy preferences (see Chapter 12). To social scientists, the strength of group discussions is the insight they offer into the dynamic effects of interaction on expressed opinion.

Many studies begin with 'pilot interviews', to gather basic information about the topic before imposing more precise and inflexible methods; this is why interviews are the most often used research method. But the flexibility of non-standardised methods is a major attraction and many influential and sophisticated analyses have been based entirely on interview data.

This versatility is apparent in the uses to which interview data can be put. Interviews can be used to identify the main behavioural groups to be sampled, and to provide insight into how they should be defined. Interviews can be used to get acquainted with the phrasing and concepts used by a population of respondents. Interviews are often used to establish the variety of opinions concerning a topic or establish relevant dimensions of attitudes. Interviews are also used to form hypotheses about motivations underlying behaviour and attitudes.

Non-standardised interviews have other important uses. For those who accept that motivations can be studied this way, interviews can also be used to examine non-motivations, why people do not do certain things. For instance, in London, postal surveys were conducted on why people failed to apply for welfare benefits for which they were eligible. The surveys had poor response rates, perhaps for reasons similar to the low take-up of benefits themselves. A research organisation commissioned to pursue the matter discovered that interviews were the best way to elicit response from the semi-literate, the frail, the aged and the plain suspicious – the main target groups for the campaign to maximise benefit take-up. Another subsidiary use is when we need detailed and extensive data, such as case histories of patients, or detailed records of behaviour, such as criminal careers. The 'life history' interview is also important, particularly in feminist research (Devault, 1990).

The non-standardised approach is valuable where the subject matter is sensitive or complicated. For instance, a research agency had to establish attitudes to nuclear waste disposal, but reaching an informed view required complex technical information. No survey questionnaire or standardised interview could provide the information in sufficient depth or attune it to the varying levels of comprehension present in the population. Non-standardised interviews allowed the researchers to fine-tune explanations and satisfy themselves that respondents had sufficient grasp to reach a considered view. Of course, care must be taken that the technical explanations are not biased.

Similarly, the flexibility of this approach is helpful where topics have varying salience within the sample but it is difficult to anticipate which will register with particular respondents using only broad indicators such as age. When the applicability of research instruments cannot be predetermined by sampling assumptions, non-standardised interviews can help. This is how Robb (1954) compiled his sample of East Enders who were anti-Semitic. Aware that East

Enders were reputed to be anti-Semitic he used interviews to identify such views and select a sample.

13.4 COMMUNICATION IN INTERVIEWS

Two principles inform research interviews. First, questioning should be as open ended as possible, in order to gain spontaneous information rather than rehearsed positions. Second, questioning techniques should encourage respondents to communicate underlying attitudes, beliefs and values, rather than glib or easy answers. The objective is that the discussion should be as frank as possible.

Frank discussion can be impeded in several ways. There may be attempts at *rationalisation*. Respondents may offer only logical reasons for their actions, withholding evaluative or emotional reasons that may give a truer insight. We have already noticed the problem of a *lack of awareness*; as well as a lack of information, many people are not used to putting their feelings into words. Respondents may fear *being shown up*. People often avoid describing aspects of behaviour or attitudes that are inconsistent with their preferred self-image; examples include questions about personal hygiene or involvement in deviant behaviour. Respondents may tend to *over-politeness* to the interviewer. Being shy or anxious to impress can distort response. A common problem is where respondents give answers they anticipate interviewers want to hear. There is good reason to be careful about your initial explanation of the interview's focus.

There are several solutions to these obstacles. The interviewer's manner is important. Relaxed, unself-conscious interviewers put respondents at ease. Research on interviewer effects suggests that interviewers should not be drawn from either extreme of the social scale, that their demeanour should be neither condescending nor deferential, that they should display interest without appearing intrusive (Singer et al., 1983). Another tactic is to personalise the discussion to get at underlying attitudes. For example, do not talk about 'police policy' in the abstract, ask respondents to tell you their experiences with the police.

There are special questioning techniques to deal with particular communication problems. When perceived relationships are to be investigated the **repertory grid** is useful, particularly in measuring attitude change over time. Initially dimensions of attitude – 'constructs' – are identified. The researcher presents three stimuli to the respondents (a 'triad'), and asks them to say which two are most alike and how they differ from the third. The procedure is repeated with a number of triads. Let's say we are studying attitudes to noise. Presented with traffic noise, aircraft noise and noisy children, the respondent may say noise from aircraft and children is intermittent, whereas traffic noise is continuous where they live. Thus, 'continuity of noise' emerges as a salient dimension of opinion. This has the virtue of eliciting constructs (like 'continuity of noise') directly from respondents rather than supplying constructs which may be meaningful to researchers but not to respondents. Respondents then relate the set of constructs to each other to form a grid, and, if the procedure is repeated over time, changes can be identified (Norris, 1983). For example, a constable's identification with the triad of detective, patrol officer and inspector can be measured at different stages of training.

Projective questioning techniques are designed to encourage respondents to give views indirectly. There is *sentence completion*, for example, 'The noise from the motorway _____'. Another is *indirect questioning*, which works on the basis that people are more prepared to reveal negative feelings if they can attribute them to others. You might ask, 'How do you think other young people feel about noise?' Not knowing others' views, respondents will offer their own. Another technique is *personalisation of objects*, in which emotions or other qualities are attributed to inanimate objects. For example, 'If your house were a person, how would it feel about re-development?' The technique was developed for child respondents but is surprisingly effective with adults.

13.4.1 PROBING AND PROMPTING

Prompting involves encouraging respondents to produce an answer. In standardised interviews care is taken to get a response without putting words in the respondent's mouth. The mildest technique is merely to repeat the question. If this fails, the interviewer may be permitted to re-phrase the question slightly; interview schedules will often list acceptable re-phrases. It is thought more important that the stimulus (question) be delivered in precisely the same way to each respondent than to allow the interviewer to improvise to get an answer (Foddy, 1993). In standardised interviews failure to elicit a response after such attempts will result in missing data. In non-standardised interviewing, interviewers have more latitude.

Probing involves follow-up questioning to get a fuller response; it may be non-verbal or verbal. An expectant glance can function as a probe as much as a direct request like 'please tell me about that'. Probes are entirely acceptable in non-standardised interviews, because we probe frequently in normal conversation and our objective is to have a 'guided conversation'. However, probes should be as neutral as possible.

The less standardised the format, the more flexible these injunctions. Life history and other discursive interview formats may contain prompting of a kind which is heresy in standardised interviews (Atkinson, 1997b). It may take the form of the interviewer's comment that they have heard others express some view or other, and what does the respondent think of that. Sometimes interviewers will even say what they think or have experienced. The fact that non-standardised interviewers, especially in feminist methods, talk about 'sharing' their view with the respondent gives an idea of the opposition between those who prefer stimulus-response conventions and those who believe interviewing should involve genuine interplay between researcher and respondent. What is permissible ultimately depends on the analytic task to which the data will be applied.

Probing is a key interviewing skill. It is all about encouraging respondents to give an answer and as full a response as the format allows. Probing is especially important in open-ended questions, and even highly standardised formats will usually include a few of these. To get respondents to expand their answers the following probes may be used, in increasing order of imperativeness:

- an expectant glance

- um hm, mm, or yes, followed by an expectant silence

- what else?

- what other reasons?

- please tell me more about that

- I'm interested in *all* your reasons.

That last one would probably make most respondents uncomfortable and is best kept for the truly evasive! Burgess offers a scale to evaluate the interviewer's degree of directiveness, allowing interviewing styles to be calibrated to the interview situation (Burgess, 1982: 111–12). The rule of thumb is to probe whenever you judge that the respondent's statement is ambiguous. Generally, anything that would make you wonder what the respondent meant in a normal conversation would be worth probing. So responses like 'This is important' should always be probed, perhaps by asking 'What do you mean by "important"?' The interviewer's task is to draw out all relevant responses, to encourage the inarticulate or shy, to be neutral toward the topic while displaying interest. Probing needs skill, because it can easily lead to bias. The best way to acquire this skill is to practise interviewing, initially with someone prepared to help you review your performance and later in pilot interviews with people like those who form your sample. Videoing can help in honing your interviewing skills.

13.4.2 THE VALUE OF GROUP DISCUSSIONS

Group discussions are especially valuable for assessing how people work out a common view, or to elicit the range of views. Most research interviews are one-to-one, but researchers interested in consensus formation, interactional processes and group dynamics find the group discussion useful. They allow you to see how people interact in discussing topics, and how they react to disagreement. They also help identify attitudes and behaviours that are considered socially unacceptable.

Apart from these uses, group discussions are quicker and cheaper than individual interviews with the same number of respondents. However, they have their own disadvantages. Not everyone who has been invited will attend, but if some of them have shown up, you will have to run the session regardless. The elderly, disabled and members of elites are particularly unlikely to attend. If these groups feature in your sample, you may need to target them individually.

Group discussions are also rather unwieldy; it helps to share the running of the session, or split the roles so that one person maintains the discussion while the other looks ahead to new topics and introduces them, or to alternate taking the lead on topics (see Chapter 12). Getting a clear recording takes care; you will need more than one microphone, and should check that your equipment can handle people speaking at different volumes and distances from the microphones before conducting the actual session.

This may make it sound like discussions are too difficult to bother with. However, their value was demonstrated when one author (Fielding) was helping students convene a group discussion on domestic violence.

Women from a refuge were invited and eight came. Several students – males and females – shared the running of the session, and one concentrated on the equipment. We found that the women were prepared to share emotionally intense information about harrowing experiences we regarded as deeply private and had thought we would be unable to address in interviews. Because they all shared the experience of having been abused, once one respondent launched a line of discussion the others were willing to join in. We were certain we would not have got the amount and depth of data using one-to-one interviews, particularly as we could not have matched genders without denying some students the experience of interviewing. It was difficult to end the session. The women wanted to continue, and were generating their own topics, which led us on to new and relevant ground. The session finally ended when the building was locked up for the night.

13.4.3 TELEPHONE AND ONLINE INTERVIEWING

Technological developments have added to techniques available to interviewers. The first is the heavy market penetration of telephone ownership in Western societies, accelerated by the popularity of mobile phones. The second is the emergence into the consumer domain of computer-mediated communication. As the proportion of population accessible by telephone has risen, telephone interviewing has become a more important research tool. Telephone interviews have the advantage of generally being cheaper than interviewing face-to-face, and some testify that useable data is more forthcoming because people tend to stay focused on the topic. Except for the most evident characteristic, gender, interviewer matching will not usually be an issue. Where there is time pressure, telephone interviews may be an efficient alternative to field interviews (see Chapter 10).

But telephone interviews have drawbacks. Special recording equipment is needed (a 'bug' attached to the interviewer's handset) if the interview is to be in semi-standardised or non-standardised format (respondents are particularly unlikely to tolerate note-taking during a phone call). Interviewers need very effective communication skills to make the interaction 'natural' while keeping an eye on the interview guide and helping respondents stay on topic. Important nuances may be lost because we communicate by body language as well as speech. You may have to make preliminary calls to arrange the interview. It will not be possible to show the respondents materials that might inform their response. Because of the ubiquity of market research interviews – and their misuse as a disguised sales pitch – potential respondents may be suspicious and refuse to participate. Nevertheless the technique can be particularly useful where the interviewer already has an 'in' with respondents, such as when conducting research with employees of the organisation sponsoring or endorsing the research (for example, with police in Home Office research). The technique seems to be particularly successful when collecting factual information as compared to matters of attitude and feelings. In a national survey of social work and police practice in child sex abuse investigations we pre-circulated the interview schedule so respondents could gather necessary information from files before the interview (Moran-Ellis and Fielding, 1996).

There is now increasing experience with online 'interviewing' (see Chapter 16), although some still dispute whether it is interviewing at all. Nevertheless this emergent method already has its advocates, particularly for interviews administered via e-mail (Mann and Stewart, 2000). A recent addition to interview modes is virtual interviewing using video-teleconferencing technologies like the 'Access Grid' or web cameras. 'Real-time' interviews can take place with respondents remotely located from the interviewer and digital audio-video recordings made.

13.5 HOW TO DESIGN AN INTERVIEW GUIDE

The best way to learn the ins and outs of a research procedure is to try it out for yourself, provided you recognise that your first efforts are practice rather than the finished product. To get you started on refining your interview technique we borrow from the Loflands' discussion of the basics of designing a non-standardised interview guide (Lofland and Lofland, 1995). Having identified a topic which is appropriately researched by interviewing, the first step is thinking over what you find problematic or interesting about it; the Loflands call these things 'puzzlements'. Jot down questions expressing each puzzlement. Spread the range of inquiry by asking friends what they find puzzling about the topic, too. What you are doing is teasing out what is puzzling about the phenomenon in the context of your particular 'cultural endowment'. We are all located in particular social contexts, with particular biographies. Our point of departure is always what is puzzling relative to our own cultural perspective. Chapter 3 offers further advice on defining research questions.

The next step is to write each puzzlement, or research question, on a separate sheet of paper. Now sort the sheets into separate piles that seem to be topically related. These clusters may have to be arranged several times to obtain an order that captures the phenomenon. In the process, some puzzlements will be discarded; growing knowledge means you can see they are irrelevant to the phenomenon. Others will emerge as being related and so can be amalgamated. The puzzlements, expressed as questions, can then be decanted from the sheets of paper onto one list. It should display a logical, orderly sequence, taking the form of an outline.

The last step before piloting your interview guide is to design probes. Since this is a non-standardised interview, probes may be couched informally or written flexibly so the exact words you say to each respondent can be fine-tuned to your estimation of their comprehension and ease of response. Devising probes is as important as generating the main questions.

Let's take the example of a study by Lyn Lofland of urban careers, how people get on when they move to a new city. The outline of the interview guide looked like this:

1   Pre-residence images

2   Initial contact

3   Subsequent career

4   Experience of the city.

As you can see, the outline is minimal. Nearly all the work goes on in the detailed probes. We can see this when we look at the main question featuring in 2, 'initial contact'. The question, whose informal wording is typical of the non-standardised style, was:

> Can you tell me exactly how you went about finding a place to live, how you got your first place, and so forth?

Such a question would not measure up to standardised requirements. It asks more than one question at once, and ends with a non-specific clause. But if the interviewer has gained rapport such questions are fine in a non-standardised format. So here are the probes:

Probe for: Conception of city areas; Areas would not consider; Contacts with landlords, real estate people (estate agents); Financial constraints; Any need to find a place quickly; Internal or external conflicts and compromises; Network involvement (e.g., friend found place, relatives, etc.).

Clearly the probes are in 'sociologese' and would confuse respondents if spoken exactly in these words. They are instructions to pursue particular sub-topics, reminders to the interviewer to be sure to check on each. They don't have to be put into the exact words you will use because the non-standardised format is discursive, letting respondents develop their answers in their own terms and at their own length and depth. So the interviewer has to keep all the probe sub-topics in mind as the respondent talks, mentally ticking off the ones the respondent mentions and remembering to ask about the ones the respondent does not mention. The idea is to have a list of things to be sure to ask about. Often probes will emerge spontaneously, as in any conversation. One may even know so little about the phenomenon that probes cannot be devised in advance. Remember, the non-standardised interview tries to be a guided conversation, and the paper you hold is only a guide.

13.6 INTERVIEWER EFFECTS

As we noted, the standardised and non-standardised approaches vary greatly in the role they permit interviewers to play in the interaction with respondents. Methodological research warns of the many effects interviewers have on the respondent's statements. While advocates of non-standardised interviewing value and analyse the part played in the discussion by the interviewer, proponents of standardised approaches regard these effects as undesirable and maintain quality controls seeking to reduce the interviewer's impact on what the respondent feels able to say. Whatever the approach, it is sensible to note some key findings of research on interviewer effects.

The classic study dates from 1954 (Hyman), but in 1974 Sudman and Bradburn published a definitive review of what was already a considerable body of literature. There was an early concern with whether the demographic characteristics of interviewers and respondents should be matched; this literature, being largely American, displayed a preoccupation with race. Hyman found that white interviewers received more socially acceptable responses from black respondents than from white respondents. Similarly, black and Oriental interviewers obtained more socially acceptable answers than did white interviewers, with the differences predictably being greatest on questions of race. Such findings were borne out by many subsequent researches. In fact, as well as race, characteristics such as age, sex, social class, and religion proved to have an impact which has to be allowed for. Socially acceptable responses are particularly likely to represent convenient ways of dealing with interviewers rather than expressing the respondent's actual view. Standardised interviews thus try to match interviewers to the characteristics of the research population wherever possible.

Another body of findings concerns the effects of the interviewer's behaviour and conduct of the interview. One study showed that variations in respondent 'verbosity' resulted from the interviewer's willingness to probe (Shapiro and Eberhart, 1947). Aggressive interviewers elicited more information. It has also been shown that response rates and extensiveness of response are different between experienced and inexperienced interviewers, which suggests that, as well as matching, it is important to practise your techniques and include pilot interviews in your research design. These are vital in helping you to get acquainted both with your interview schedule or guide and with respondents of the sort you will encounter in your main data-gathering.

While interviewer effects must be controlled if they endanger the validity or reliability of response, there are limits to the extent of matching that can be achieved. There are also limits to interviewers' ability to conduct interviews the same way every time, and differences in respondents and the interview context may make it less meaningful to think in terms of similarity. It could be argued that it may be easier to confide in a stranger, that female interviewers may be less threatening to both female and male respondents and that deference may encourage rather than inhibit response. Such doubts about matching suggest why it is crucial to have as full and accurate a record of the interview as possible, for scrutiny during analysis. The record is not only the foundation of analysis but the best index of the interviewer's effect on the respondent's testimony. This brings us to the business of transcription.

13.7 TRANSCRIPTION

Technologies for interview transcription are increasingly sophisticated. Computer software for transcription has improved considerably. Software like 'Dragon Dictate' and 'IBM ViaVoice', which convert audio files into text, can now achieve accuracy rates as high as 90 per cent. However, to achieve this, the software must be 'trained' to a particular voice. This is acceptable for its primary application – replacing secretaries who take dictation – but means that when used for transcription, users have first to train the software and then read back the interview recording to the software, because training the software to all the respondents' voices is impractical. Also, though it sounds good, 90 per cent accuracy still leaves you correcting one word in ten.

A more appealing approach may be to use qualitative data analysis software (see Chapter 20) with a direct coding capability. Software such as Code-A-Text and C-I-SAID enables users to apply codes representing the themes of the

analy...   ...leo file. Th... ...t transcription altogether; when
you wa... ...dent 8's comm... ...ss you use the feature
and it pla)   ...of the interview. ...s is a significant shift from
working with   ...ugh, and may have implications for analytic
work. With both ... ..., and transcription software there is a further
point: as discussed b... ..., when you transcribe you get analytic ideas. Cutting
out or cutting down transcription may save on tedium but could be at analytic
cost. Hereafter we will focus on conventional transcription of one-to-one non-
standardised interviews.

The first choice is whether to transcribe everything respondents say: the
choice between verbatim and selective transcription. Verbatim transcription
offers the advantage that all possible analytic uses are allowed for. You may
not know what will be the most significant points of analysis when you are
doing the transcription; verbatim transcription means you have not lost any
data that may later become significant. But the disadvantage is that it is labori-
ous and time-consuming.

TIP

The advice is that even if you plan to be selective with most of the interviews you should
still transcribe the first few verbatim.

Verbatim interviews will help guide your analysis and probably reveal themes
you had not thought of. You may even decide to adjust your guide for subsequent interviews to pick up on things your transcription reveals as unexpectedly
important. Whether to transcribe verbatim may also depend on how many interviews you are doing. If your sample is small, say, 20 or less, you should probably
transcribe the lot verbatim.

Another decision is whether to record the interview or write notes. If you are
doing a standardised interview using a highly pre-specified schedule, you will
probably not need to record but develop the skill of completing what is in
effect a questionnaire as the respondent talks. But if you are conducting non-
standardised interviews you will be joining in too, and without recording you
will inevitably lose data as well as have to engage in a stilted and peculiar interaction as you pause every few utterances to write down what the person says.
The advice is to record whenever possible.

Most people worry about negotiating recording of interviews with respondents. But recording does convey that their responses are being taken seriously.
In most cases it is worth pushing hard to record. Note-taking is not only slow
but open to doubts about validity. When British police interviews went from
contemporaneous note-taking to recording, average interview times fell

dramatically. An interview that took four hours with note-taking took half an hour. Responses also became more factual, and accusations of 'verballing', putting words in the respondent's mouth, fell to virtually nil (Irving and Mckenzie, 1988). Nevertheless, researchers should ensure that the request to record is explicit, that confidentiality is offered, and that respondents know they can ask for the recorder to be switched off while giving a particular answer. Special care should be taken over recording when interviewing members of vulnerable groups. The researcher needs to weigh up any possible harm to respondents should they be identifiable as a result of doing recorded interviews and in some cases whether they may become distressed or feel threatened by being interviewed 'on the record'. Discuss the matter fully and ensure the final decision is one with which both parties are satisfied.

Recording can be made more palatable by offering to supply respondents with a transcript so its accuracy can be checked (of course, this commits you to full transcription). This is a useful 'foot-in-the-door' device too, because you will then have a further contact with the respondent to discuss the transcript, which often yields more data, including comments on what the respondent thought of the interview. This can be useful both analytically and in gauging the validity and reliability of responses. If respondents are worried about the uses to be made of the interview data you can also offer to anonymise quotes used in the final write-up and to destroy recordings once transcribed.

If the respondent is really reluctant, you may be able to get recording accepted by starting to write notes. This will be unbelievably slow. After a few minutes you can ask whether they still object to the recorder! Also, because many people now use recordings in their work, and because many occupational groups are now more accountable, it may be that your respondent not only assents to recording but pulls out their own recorder to make an independent record of the session. Don't be shy.

Transcribing is slow work, a typical ratio being four to six hours of transcription per hour of interview, but if undertaken by the researcher has the advantage of familiarising you with the data. Type your questions in a different font or in upper case to help distinguish between yourself and respondents. Set generous margins to allow space for coding and analytical notes. Number lines or sections for referencing purposes. Do not 'tidy' your respondents' language or grammar; where clarification is required, identify your additions, for example, by enclosing them in brackets. Jotting down thoughts about the data during transcription contributes to subsequent analysis and relieves the tedium of transcription. Checking each transcript against the recording is particularly important if the transcription was done by someone other than the researcher.

Transcription services are available in many towns, and some people have secretaries who can transcribe for them. It is still worth transcribing at least some of the interviews yourself. We have ideas as we transcribe, and transcribing makes you very familiar with the data. It helps you to start making connections and identifying analytic themes.

> **TIP**
>
> Keep a pad handy when you transcribe to write down these thoughts as they occur to you.

13.8 PRACTICALITIES OF ANALYSING INTERVIEW DATA

Key to successful qualitative analysis is the need to become thoroughly familiar with the data and to devise a practical system that enables rigorous comparison to be made between interviews while retaining the context of data within each interview.

It is useful to listen to each recording as soon as possible after the interview. This provides opportunities to make brief notes about content, especially information such as age, marital status, occupation, etc. which was collected systematically and which will form the sample characteristics. These notes might be held in a card index. It is easier to calculate, for example, the mean age of a sample from a card index than from transcripts. Note the length of the interview, if this was not done at the time. Listening to the entire recording at this stage exposes any difficulties with the quality of the recording when unclear material can still be replaced by notes from memory. Notes about the setting, conduct of the interview, the interviewee, and so on, will help to bring back the context of the interview later in analysis.

13.8.1 CODING AND ANALYSIS

Qualitative analysis involves systematic consideration of the data to identify themes and concepts that will contribute to our understanding. Themes and concepts that are identified in one interview are compared and contrasted with similar material in the other interviews. New themes that emerge in subsequent interviews necessitate further analysis of previously coded interviews. The analytical and practical issues of this process stem from a need to both compare and contrast segments of data from different interviews and to maintain the chronological integrity of each interview. The analytical challenge is the identification of thematically similar segments, both within and between interviews. The practical counterparts are the labelling and subsequent retrieval of similarly coded segments together with a reference to their original location (interview/line number).

Codes may have a number of origins. Themes, topics and subject areas may be generated *a priori* from the research questions or the interview guide. These may be supplemented by field notes, jottings during transcription and transcription checking, and of course the transcripts themselves. Where coding is done on paper, some means of identifying codes, for example, with different coloured pens should be used. It may be most practical to develop the set of codes in the margins and later, when the coding frame is established, to outline the exact text area pertinent to each code. Codes may well overlap in the text so keep the eventual coding frame as simple as the analysis allows. Note where potentially useful material for quotation overlaps the boundaries of a particular coded segment, for example, by starring the relevant section.

Having identified and noted codes, a system enabling the researcher to retrieve all instances of each individual code is needed. This may involve listing the instances on separate sheets, perhaps with the addition of a grid or matrix. If the transcript is to be cut up, ensure that a whole version of each transcript is retained. Ensure that each cut segment is referenced to the particular location (interview/line number). Cuttings can then be reassembled into thematic sections by code or group of codes. Merging of codes may happen at this stage. Qualitative software greatly facilitates these procedures (see Chapter 20).

A useful way to capture thoughts from systematic comparison and contrast of data within themes is to write up a particular theme to develop a feel for presenting the analysis. This will incorporate descriptive findings but also tap into the emerging analysis. Relationships between themes and linkages between types of respondent will emerge, and counter-trend data. Keep asking *why* differences are emerging. Use examples to illustrate and unpack your emerging analysis but do not depend on 'favourite' quotations and evidence from particular respondents.

13.9 SOME PROBLEMS OF INTERVIEW ANALYSIS

Critics worry about the effects interviewers have on validity and reliability of data. The charge of interviewer bias has been levelled at non-standardised interviews. Active commitment to a particular perspective certainly affects interview data. On the other hand, Selltiz and Jahoda showed that 'much of what we call interviewer bias can more correctly be described as interviewer differences, which are inherent in the fact that interviewers are human beings and not machines' (1962: 41). Social scientists depend on data collected by oral or written reports and these are 'invariably subject to the same sources of error and bias as those collected by interviewers'. In dealing with bias, the advice of eminent sociologist Robert Merton still holds true (Merton and Kendall, 1946: 555):

1   Guidance and direction from the interviewer should be at a minimum.

2   The subject's definition of the situation should find full and specific expression.

3   The interview should bring out the value-laden implications of the response.

As Merton's carefully balanced advice suggests, we cannot simply ignore interviewer bias. So far we have identified bias from carrying out the method badly: misdirected probing and prompting, ignoring the effects of interviewer characteristics and behaviour, neglecting the cultural context in which the researcher is located, and problems with question wording. These are susceptible to quality control measures. But, more profoundly, the logic in analysing interviews makes challengeable assumptions, and we must anticipate the criticisms.

The first is the assumption that language is a good indicator of thought and action. Attitudes and thoughts are assumed to directly influence behaviour and language is presumed to accurately reflect both (see Chapter 11). Such assumptions make social psychologists cringe (Potter and Wetherell, 1987; Potter, 1996). Expressed attitudes are problematic indicators of what people have done, or will do. The relationship between attitude and action always has to be empirically tested, so collecting information about people's attitudes is only one part of any study concerned with explaining or predicting behaviour. There is value in documenting attitudes provided we do not claim that by doing so we have proven what they do, nor provide a basis for prediction. A classic reference for those interested in tightening the fit between expressed attitude and actual behaviour is Deutscher (1973).

It is easy to compile reasons to doubt what people say to us in interviews. It is hardly a revelation that people sometimes lie or elaborate on the 'true' situation to enhance their esteem, cover up discreditable actions or for any of a whole gamut of motives. A good case is 'self-report studies' in deviant behaviour. Social scientists have long been aware of the many deficiencies of crime statistics (see also Chapter 2). Ambiguities abound. For example, would you consider the theft of a chequebook with 30 cheques left in it to be one theft or 30? In one system, if all 30 cheques are fraudulently 'passed' it counted as 31: the theft of the chequebook plus each fraudulent encashment. The government issues 'counting rules' to help police decide how to report the statistics. For such reasons criminologists have long worried about the so-called dark figure of crime.

In the 1960s, social scientists thought they had solved the problem with a technique called 'self-report' based on interviews, usually with young people, who were shown lists of offences and asked if they had committed any in the last year. The results were staggering, typically showing up to 99 per cent of crimes going unreported. The difference between known and admitted crime was especially acute in the case of middle-class youths (Empey and Erickson, 1966). Because crime theories are largely based on official statistics, which suggest crime is a lower-class phenomenon, the results were important. But doubt set in. Most studies were of juveniles, for reasons of easier access (often through schools). Could one generalise to adults? Most of the studies were in the mid-Western United States, because this is where most of those using the technique worked. Were the results valid for city kids? But, most important, there were no checks on response validity. Respondents might exaggerate offending to impress interviewers, but is equally likely they would minimise their involvement, fearing interviewers would inform police. There was a flurry of further tests. Some used polygraphs to try to see if respondents were lying, others checked what respondents said against school records and parent views to see if what was reported was plausible, and others told respondents they changed their answers prior to such validity checks to see if they changed their claims. The conclusion was that self-report is not an adequate substitute for official statistics. Subsequently another technique supplanted it, victim surveys. Self-reporting is not straightforwardly wrong, and in conjunction with other methods it is still used. But anyone using it must be aware of the methodological problems arising from the question of the fit between accounts and action, and allow for it in the analysis.

We have already noted problems with 'social desirability' as an influence on response validity. Admitting to involvement in some socially disapproved behaviour is influenced by cultural factors and can give false data. Take rates of mental illness in different cultural groups. In New York, it was found that, holding class constant, Puerto Ricans had a higher apparent rate of mental illness than did Jews, Irish-Americans or blacks. However, on subjecting the mental health inventory to a social desirability rating it was found that Puerto Ricans regarded the items as less undesirable than did the other ethnic groups and were more willing to admit to them (Dohrenwend, 1964).

Cross-cultural research is especially susceptible to problems in interpreting interview responses. It is hard to establish equivalent meaning in work involving translation, especially if material is attitudinal (is my repudiation of public drunkenness as fervent as a teetotal Muslim's?). Faced with the Marathi language group in India, who have no concept of the generalised other (e.g., 'people', 'they'), most researchers would despair. But there are different cultures in every society. The classic culture-based term is 'democracy', whose meaning varies tremendously according to cultural nuances.

There are even more straightforward problems to wrestle with. Some people consistently answer 'yes' or 'no' independently of question content. Also, people are woefully inaccurate. One study found 30 per cent inaccuracy in whether respondents had voted in an election held a few weeks previously, and similar problems have been found in studies of birth control, social welfare and health information (Gorden, 1980).

Thus, the hardest problem is assuming correspondence between verbal response and behaviour. We can overcome most technical problems, by interviewer training, careful question design and probing, and comparison with results using other methods. But we need better theories of why people do and do not act as they say they do. So to our final topic.

13.10 ANALYTIC STANCES TOWARDS INTERVIEW DATA

Sociologists disagree in their assessment of the status of interview data. This section reviews several perspectives, but is not exhaustive (see also Chapters 2 and 5). The discussion draws on Silverman (1985; 2006).

The first approach is **positivism**, the longest-established perspective on social science methods (see Chapter 2). It is geared to a statistical logic mainly based on survey research. Interview data are regarded as accessing 'facts' of the social world, accounts whose sense derives from their correspondence to a factual reality. Where accounts imperfectly represent that reality, checks and remedies must be applied.

For positivists, the idea that responses might be an artefact of the interview setting or its conduct challenges validity. Positivists aim to generate data that hold independently of settings and interviewers. They prefer standardised interviews and dislike non-standardised approaches. Interviews follow a standard protocol, asking each question precisely the same way each time and in the same order. Interviewers should not show surprise or disapproval, offer impromptu explanations of questions, suggest possible replies or skip questions. If care is taken the 'facts' will be established, affording a reliable and valid basis for inference.

The second approach is that of **symbolic interactionism**. For interactionists, interviews are based on mutual participant observation. The context of the production of interview data is intrinsic to understanding it. No distinction between research interviews and other forms of social interaction is recognised. The data are valid when mutual understanding has been achieved between interviewer and respondent. Most interactionists reject standardised interviews in favour of open-ended interviews. These let respondents use their own way of defining the world, assume that no fixed sequence of questions is suitable for all respondents, and allow respondents to raise considerations interviewers did not think of.

Interactionism has a relativist tinge (seeing the meaning of social action as relative to the researcher's perspective) but retains an orientation to the validity threats that worry positivists. For example, Denzin (1981) lists as problems to which non-standardised interviews are a solution: 'self-presentation'; fleeting encounters to which respondents are uncommitted, leading to possibilities of fabrication; the relative status of interviewer and respondent; the interview context. These are problems if it is assumed there is a truth which lies behind them. It is a kind of positivism-plus, where the plus is full attention to the interactional context of the interview.

But some, so much doubt the status of interview data that they abandon a concern with the content of responses in favour of examining their form. For ethnomethodologists, interview data do not report on respondents' external reality but on the internal reality constructed as both parties contrive to produce a recognisable interview. They treat interview data as a topic and not a resource (see Chapter 22). For them, when standardised, multi-interviewer studies produce invariant data but this does not establish credibility but the practical accomplishment by which intrinsically variable stimuli were made to produce the same results (Cicourel, 1964: 75). This approach is indifferent to power differences between interviewers and respondents, preferring to see them as co-operatively engaged in producing the interview. The problem of 'facts' is solved, since the issue of truth is marginalised, it being a matter of content, not form.

Postmodern perspectives emphasise that analysis of interview data is relative to perspective. Postmodernism 'de-centres' the subject, shifting attention from respondents to researchers and to the interview context. Some postmodernists take this to the conclusion that interview data has no bearing on reality, and even moderate postmodernists reject researchers having any privileged insight into the meaning of interview response. Post-positivists accept relativist and context-based considerations, and agree that the researcher's voice should not be alone in interpreting interview data. However, rather than see these things as fatally undermining interview data, they treat them as things to take into account in designing interviews and analysing the results.

While these are important positions on analysis of interview data, they are not the only ones. Research can also be informed by more than one perspective. We cannot say one is 'better' than the other, but what we must acknowledge is that they are tied to very different theories of the social world (see Chapter 1). Your choice of which approach to take will reflect not only your theoretical orientation but your thoughts on what most fairly reflects your data.

13.11 SUMMARY

Interviewing is a very widely employed research method. This chapter has identified and explored issues that researchers need to consider when contemplating a qualitative interview study. These include communication in interviews, especially the value of prompts and probes, and the variations that may emerge from different contexts such as group discussions and interviews conducted via the telephone or online. The practicalities involved in designing an interview guide, in making decisions about recording interviews and in organising the resulting data have been identified. The problems inherent in analysis of qualitative interview data and the debates about analytical stances taken towards data have been discussed. The chapter emphasises that there is no one 'right' way to interview and that each researcher should consider the implications of the chosen approach.

DISCUSSION QUESTIONS

1   What should a researcher consider when planning an interview?

2   How would you begin an interview with one of the following: a teacher, a doctor, a policeman?

3   Choose a topic on which you might conduct qualitative interviews. What puzzlements can you identify that would help you construct an interview guide?

PROJECT

Everyone has been to school. In this exercise you will pair with a partner for an interview. Each acts as interviewer and respondent in turn. The exercise takes about an hour. Begin by thinking over your school experiences and choose some aspect of school about which to ask questions. It could be relations with teachers, how people prepare for exams, the value of religious education, or many other things.

Since you will only be interviewing for 10 minutes, you only need to prepare for the beginning stage of the interview. Write down several questions addressing the research issue, and a standard 'project explanation', a general statement of the research issue which you can say to your respondent to get the interview going.

Take 10 minutes to design your questions.

Now choose who will be interviewer first. Do your interview in 10 minutes. There is no need to take notes on the respondent's replies.

The next stage is debriefing. The interviewer should write down skills they managed well and those needing work. Discuss it with your respondent. This should take 5 minutes.

Now swap roles, do another 10-minute interview and another 5-minute debriefing.

When you have finished, discuss with your partner your experience of interviewing and the accuracy of your debriefing notes. Allow 15 minutes.

RESOURCES

Arksey and Knight (1999) is a comprehensive source with a wealth of useful tips, examples, project ideas and other resources.

Gorden (1980) is a comprehensive book with good attention to problems of communication.

Mishler (1986), a social psychologist, emphasises the need to take account of reflexivity and the interaction between interviewer and respondent in analysing interview data.

Norris (1983) offers a beginner's guide to repertory grid.

Rubin and Rubin (1995) provide a good overview of non-standardised interviewing incorporating recent perspectives.

Silverman (2006) is particularly good on theoretical approaches to interview analysis.

14 Ethnography

Nigel Fielding

KEY POINTS

● Ethnography is a form of qualitative research usually combining interviewing and observation.

● Ethnography involves becoming a member of a setting, and this may mean learning the 'language' used in the setting.

● The researcher will produce fieldnotes to record accurately and systematically what happens.

● There are several procedures for analysing fieldnotes, including sequential analysis and grounded theory.

14.1 INTRODUCTION

This chapter concerns **ethnography**, a form of qualitative research combining several methods, including interviewing and observation. Ethnography originated in the classical tradition of anthropology which evolved during the colonial period of the British Empire, although elements of the method date back to antiquity. The ruling principle of Thucydides' *History of the Peloponnesian War* (Grene, 1959) was strict adherence to carefully verified facts. But it was not only a matter of chronicle, because the speeches making up a quarter of the *History* shed a vivid light on Greek political thinking, the motives of contemporaries and the arguments they used. Balancing detailed documentation of events with insights into their meaning to those involved is an enduring hallmark of ethnography. We can already discern its characteristic mix of observation, documentation and speech (usually interviews). However, for these concerns to be separated from the discipline of history and become a distinctive method for studying unfamiliar cultures we must await the time of the British Empire.

Early anthropologists sometimes accompanied scientific expeditions, but the armchair approach was more common. British colonial administration used district commissioners, local representatives who dealt with anything affecting British interests. They were ideally located to document the way of life of the indigenous peoples. Yet they were men of action and hardly 'intellectuals' by training or inclination. A system grew up whereby scholars in Britain effectively used district commissioners as fieldworkers, collecting data that was sent home to analyse. It had a standard format enabling the so-called 'man on the spot' to ask similar questions of native informants in any colonial society, and was called the 'notes and queries' approach (Van Maanen, 1988: 15).

The chapter begins with an overview of ethnographic method, discussing how it compares to other methods and how the method is used in contemporary research. It then explains the ethnographer's role in fieldwork, discussing the emphasis on immersion and context, and the problems of going native and of too fleeting a fieldwork engagement. Documenting fieldwork is next considered, covering types of **fieldnotes** and their contents, and advising on how to compile reliable, interesting fieldnotes. Analytic and ethical considerations are then introduced. Finally, there is a project you can use to try out your ethnographic skills.

14.2 ETHNOGRAPHIC PRACTICE

Despite the dwindling number of cultures which can truly claim isolation from the outside world (a fact which has seen the emergence of 'the new urban anthropology', which adapts ethnography to the study of the anthropologist's own society, and of 'virtual ethnography', which treats cybersociety as uncharted territory), there is a lot of continuity in ethnographic practice. Consider this summary of Caroline Humphrey's study 'Karl Marx Collective: economy, society and religion in a Siberian collective farm' (1983):

> This book, the first ethnography based on fieldwork in a Soviet community by a Western anthropologist, describes the contemporary life of the Buryats, a Mongolian-speaking people in Siberia, through a detailed analysis of two collective farms. After describing Buryat historical traditions and ethnic relations, Dr Humphrey sets out the official theoretical model of the Soviet collective farm, its statutes and forms of social control. She then analyses how far the reality conforms to the model; in what respects it does not; and how the Buryats respond to the inconsistencies between theory and reality. (Humphrey, 1983: Publisher's catalogue, CUP, 1983: 60)

Ethnography is often path-breaking, and Humphrey's study is no exception, exploring a hitherto obscure niche of social life. It is not a rule that ethnography must study the unknown, but, as we shall see, some of the constraints on it as a method can be excused by its value as a 'method of discovery'. As a means of gaining a first insight into a culture or social process, as a source of hypotheses for detailed investigation using other methods, it is unparalleled.

The second thing to notice about Humphrey's study is that it involved a small sample, just two collective farms. Ethnography does not have to be limited in sample size, but because of its emphasis on 'depth', 'context', 'intensity', and so on, it usually is. Gathering detailed material is demanding, and few ethnographers are able to devote such effort to more than one or two settings. But notice also that, by focusing on two farms, Humphrey is able to employ a key element of sociological analysis: to compare and contrast between settings in which similar activities occur.

Also a characteristic emphasis is Humphrey's mention of 'the official theoretical model'. That word 'official' is very revealing. It implicitly signals that things could well be otherwise than they appear on paper: there must be an 'unofficial' reality, too. Sociologists make an important distinction between 'formal' and 'informal' organisation; for instance, the law in the books and the law as practised on the streets. Thus, Humphrey explores the fit between the official model and the reality of the collective farm. Finding the fit less than perfect, she shows how the Buryats handle the breakdown between theory and reality. Ethnography is often a debunking exercise, especially when used to shed new light on the darker corners of our own society.

14.3 THE MEANING OF ETHNOGRAPHIC RESEARCH

Contemporary ethnography has another important precursor, the social reformist sociologists of the Chicago School, who had backgrounds in journalism and social work, and were keenly aware of the failings of their own society. They brought to ethnography a campaigning, critical edge, and a sympathy for the powerless who were the principal subject of their studies. The idea of 'appreciation' was a key part of their naturalistic stance, which emphasised seeing things from the perspective of those studied before stepping back to make a more detached assessment. These early sociologists followed the Native American adage that one should 'never criticise a man until you have walked a mile in his moccasins'.

Also within the spirit of the adage is to argue that ethnographers must be involved in the ongoing, daily world of the people being studied. As Goffman put it:

> any group of persons – prisoners, primitives, pilots or patients – develop a life of their own that becomes meaningful, reasonable and normal once you get close to it, and … a good way to learn about any of these worlds is to submit oneself in the company of the members to … [their] daily round. (1961: ix–x)

Goffman believed every social group had something distinctive and the best way to understand it, to see how it was normal no matter how zany it may seem to outsiders, was to get close. He was just following the Chicagoans who taught generations of students to 'get the seats of their pants dirty' in real research which, naturally, had to take place in the real world, not the library.

We can derive from this the principle that ethnography always involves studying behaviour in 'natural settings', as opposed to the experimental settings of clinical psychology. Further is the idea that an adequate knowledge of social behaviour cannot be grasped until the researcher has understood the symbolic world in which people live. By 'symbolic world' we simply refer to the meanings people apply to their own experiences, meanings developed through patterns of behaviour which are in some way distinctive. To understand these special meanings the researcher must adopt the perspective of the members, in an effort to see things as they do.

Ethnography has been referred to as 'a curious blending of methodological techniques' (Denzin, 1989a). According to McCall and Simmons, it includes:

> some amount of genuinely social interaction in the field with the subjects of the study, some direct observation of relevant events, some formal and a great deal of informal interviewing, some systematic counting, some collection of documents and artefacts; and open-endedness in the direction the study takes. (McCall and Simmons, 1969: 1)

That last point is important in suggesting a preference for adapting the research focus to what proves available and interesting rather than imposing an outsider's sense of what is going on. But whether the ethnographer is a Brit in Borneo or a professor on an assembly line, the techniques to record and make sense of the experience are likely to include interviews (usually more like a conversation than a standardised interview, and often involving key informants), the analysis of documents, direct observation of events, and an effort to think oneself into the perspective of the members, the introspective, empathetic process Weber called *verstehen*.

Thus, my ethnographic study of the National Front, a racist political party, combined participant observation at marches, demonstrations and meetings, where I passed as a member, plus interviews with party officials and opponents, content analysis of party documents, and reflection on the differences between my beliefs and those of members (Fielding, 1981).

Ethnography involves becoming a (temporary) part of the natural setting. To do this, ethnographers have first to learn the language in use; this not only means jargon and dialect, but special meanings and unfamiliar uses of familiar words. This will give sufficient purchase on action in the setting to allow the compilation of fieldnotes. From these, and reflection in the field, the researcher can begin to identify the rules which govern relationships in the setting and discern patterns in members' behaviour.

Recent years have seen ethnography turn to new fields of study, such as online communities. Baym's (1995) study of a discussion group for soap opera fans was among the first. She argues both that it should be defined as a community and that ethnography was appropriate to its study. Her ethnography, following several years of regular membership of the group, certainly bears the hallmarks of standard ethnography, from learning the argot through to flexibility in the study's direction. For a full account of virtual ethnography, see Hine (2000). When such work is **internet**-based, the technical foundation is as accessible as any internet application but newer technologies periodically emerge, such as the form of video teleconferencing called Access Grid Nodes, and the use of sensing devices. Both can be used to do 'virtual fieldwork' without leaving one's desk (Fielding and Macintyre, 2006).

14.4 FRONT MANAGEMENT AND FINDING A ROLE

The process of participation necessitates impression (or 'front') management. Ethnography has an inescapable element of deception and this can present ethical dilemmas. Like many others, Lofland and Lofland (1995: 94) argue that, before choosing ethnographic methods, we should ask ourselves 'am I reasonably able to get along with these people? Do I truly like a reasonable number of them, even though I disagree with their view of the world?'. If we cannot answer 'yes', fieldwork becomes too much a matter of masking one's feelings. In special circumstances detailed below, covert observation may be acceptable; this will entail considerable front management, particularly where covert work is chosen because the group is hostile to research. It is best left to those comfortable with deception; several ethnographers who have used this technique have an acting background. A useful observational tactic is the cultivation of an impression of naïveté, so that members feel obliged to explain things that seem obvious to them; the literature even speaks of taking on the role of the 'acceptable incompetent' (Daniels, 1975). Would-be ethnographers could well consider adopting a role allowing them to ask naïve questions, such as the apprentice or new convert.

An important problem ethnographers face is that of 'going native', a term with an obvious origin in anthropology. It has to be remembered that adopting the perspective of members is a methodological tactic. One is participating in order to get detailed data, not to provide the group with a new member. A certain detachment is needed when interpreting that data. But another less remarked problem may be more common, that of 'not getting close enough', of adopting a superficial approach which merely provides a veneer of plausibility for an analysis to which the researcher is already committed. Virtual ethnography is particularly vulnerable to this problem, as it affords opportunities for lurking. Although lurking offers the advantage of observing without affecting the setting, it lacks the engagement from which ethnography derives its in-depth understanding (Beaulieu, 2004). It may help as reconnaissance but may not be a basis for a full-fledged ethnography, an issue which also relates to applied research, where time pressure often prevents full ethnography.

In deciding how close to get, ethnographers must choose a role somewhere between the 'Martian' and the 'convert' (Lofland and Lofland, 1995). The most basic choice is whether to tell members of the setting what you are up to. Those that accept the need for covert observation usually justify it on the basis that some groups would otherwise be closed to research (Fielding, 1982). I justified my use of covert observation in the National Front research on the basis of the group's hostility to research. However, covert fieldwork is almost always inappropriate in anthropology, where the deceptive role is frowned upon and may represent a breach of professional ethics. Whatever their discipline, researchers should remember that deception is not required in most circumstances.

There are many problems in covert ethnography. The first is that you must play the role which warrants your presence in the setting; if you are masquerading as an industrial worker, you will have to spend most of your time actually working on the assembly line. Your freedom to wander and observe, and to ask questions, is limited to what is appropriate for the role which has gained you entry. You may be interested in the management canteen, but as a shop floor worker that is closed to you. Also, unless your role includes writing, it will be difficult to take notes in the setting.

Why, then, choose covert observation? Apart from the justifications mentioned above, actually occupying the role you are studying offers an intimate acquaintance with it. There is probably no better way to understand the experiences of members, and the meaning they derive from their experiences. Further, provided you are proficient in the role, you are much less likely to disturb the setting, avoiding the risk of studying an artefact of your presence rather than normal behaviour. But it must be emphasised that covert observation is an intensely demanding method and that you must be able to satisfy yourself that breaking the ethical objections to it is warranted by your research problem.

Choosing an overt approach does not solve all the problems. It is increasingly accepted that the most faithfully-negotiated overt approach inescapably contains some covertness, in that, short of wearing a sign, ethnographers cannot signal when they are or are not collecting data. Nor is even the most scrupulous researcher entirely able to anticipate the purposes to which the data will be put. In reality, overt and covert approaches shade into each other, so that most observational research involves a 'delicate combination of overt and covert roles' (Adler, 1985: 27).

In overt observation, access is accomplished through negotiating with a **gatekeeper**. The gatekeeper will be interested in what your research can do to help – or harm – the organisation. Be prepared to have to sketch in some likely findings. If access is offered, remember that the organisation may have an interest in letting you in. This should be taken into account in deciding what information to provide. Avoid promising too much through gratitude. In particular, if you are preparing a dissertation or report, think carefully before committing yourself to providing a separate report for the organisation. Also allow for the possibility that the gatekeeper's permission may be given without the knowledge or consent of others being studied.

It is normal to accomplish access through some established contact; my study of police training (Fielding, 1988) came about because the police academy director had been a student of my PhD supervisor. In gaining access this way one also gains a sponsor in the organisation, to whom one is accountable. After all, if things go badly you can leave, but the sponsor will remain. Access-givers often serve as key informants. Informants are the unsung heroes of ethnography: it is usual to develop several key informants with whom you discuss your research. While they can help you avoid analytic errors, you should remember that they may have ulterior motives in cooperating, such as influencing your account. It should also be remembered that their cooperation may endanger their own position (Fielding, 1982; 1990).

Overt observers are able to move about the setting more freely, to ask questions which are clearly research-related and to withdraw to write notes whenever they like. The role still presents problems. Most organisations contain factions and when people know research is taking place they will be keen to discover whether the researcher is affiliated to one or other faction. It is recommended to maintain neutrality relative to internal divisions. Researchers may become scapegoats for things that go wrong; in evaluation research, where budgets stand or fall on the findings, this may be a realistic perception! Where neutrality proves impossible to sustain, researchers typically align with the single largest grouping in the setting while trying to remain aloof from internal disputes. Another problem is that of personal involvement. Observers often feel obliged to help members in exchange for access, ranging from giving lifts and stuffing envelopes to illegal activities; in one case, the observer agreed to hide a gun in his house for a criminal expecting a visit from the police (Polsky, 1971).

These problems all relate to the issue of marginality, the idea that the ethnographer is in this social world, but not of it. It leads to fears about whether one has been accepted, and to feelings of loneliness. In covert research there are also worries about whether the deception has been discovered. It is possible to deal with these by observing on a team, so there are others to share the experience. If this cannot be done, regular meetings with other researchers who know what it is like can help. Remember that this sense of marginality is actually crucial for the success of the work. The experience of being simultaneously an insider and an outsider generates creative insight. In constructing our analysis we reflect on the self that we had to become in order to pass in the setting, and how that temporary, setting-specific self differs from the person that we are normally. Identifying things that are distinctive about the people inhabiting the setting is an important basis for our analytic categories. Mention of analysis brings us to fieldnotes.

14.5 RECORDING THE ACTION: FIELDNOTES

Producing fieldnotes is the observer's *raison d'être*: if you do not record what happens, you might as well not be in the setting. In order to take good fieldnotes it is sensible to gradually develop your powers of observation (Emerson et al., 1995). Fieldnotes take three forms: mental notes, jotted notes and full fieldnotes. Before looking at each, note that memory decay is not related to time so much as to new input. It is a good idea, then, to write up fieldnotes after a round of observation before engaging in further interaction. It may be possible to sleep before writing fieldnotes but it would not be sensible to end the day by going to a party!

Taking mental notes is a skill journalists develop; they do so by practice, sometimes quizzing each other. Good reportage and observation are marked by accurate description of how many people were present, who in particular was present, the physical character of the setting, who said what to whom, who moved in what way, and a general characterisation of the order of events (Lofland and Lofland, 1995).

Reporters have one obvious aid, the notepad. In sensitive settings it may not be feasible to scribble notes, which partly accounts for journalists developing the capacity to take mental notes. But as soon as possible these will be transferred to writing. Jotted notes do not record everything that took place, but key words, phrases or quotations which represent more extensive chunks of verbal and non-verbal behaviour, and which will stimulate the memory when you have time to reconstruct the events as comprehensively as possible.

Jotted notes may be most useful in covert observation, but even when subjects are well aware they are being observed it can be disruptive for the ethnographer to be busily note-taking. It is sensible to jot notes at inconspicuous moments. A stock ploy is to develop a reputation for a weak bladder, enabling frequent retirements to scribble notes. The object of jotted notes is to jog the memory when writing full fieldnotes. It is worth including items from observation on previous occasions which one forgot to record at the time. Often the process of observation stimulates recall of such things.

There is a widely accepted standard procedure for taking systematic full fieldnotes. First, it is essential to write up observations promptly. It should be delayed no later than the morning after observation. Most people lose good recall of even quite simple chains of events after 24 hours; detailed recall of conversation sufficient to enable quotation is lost within a couple of hours. Second, writing fieldnotes requires discipline; you should expect to spend as much time writing fieldnotes as in the observation.

A third matter is the question of recording versus writing. While recording speeds things up, it has the disadvantage of leading to a less reflective approach. Being slower, writing often leads to a better yield of analytic themes. Most researchers find the process of writing fieldnotes productive not just of description but of first reflections on the connections between observed events.

A fourth routine matter is that it is essential to produce several copies of the full fieldnotes or to hold them on secure computer files. One set forms a complete running commentary. The others will be cut up (sometimes literally, when employing the 'cut and paste' approach to analysis) or marked with outline codes during analysis.

There is considerable consensus among methodologists on the contents of fieldnotes. The several rules applying to content are based on the idea that fieldnotes should provide a running description of events, people and conversation. Since different analytic uses may be made of them, it makes sense to maximise the elements of description. Consequently each new setting observed and each new member of the setting merits description. Similarly, changes in the human or other constituents of a setting should be recorded. Fieldnotes should

Figure 14.1   Example of fieldnotes

Summarised or over-generalised note
The new client was uneasy waiting for her intake interview.

Behaviouristic or detailed note
At first the client sat very stiffly on the chair next to the receptionist's desk. She picked up a magazine and let the pages flutter through her fingers very quickly without really looking at any of the pages. She set the magazine down, looked at her watch, pulled her skirt down, and picked up the magazine again. This time she didn't look at the magazine. She set it down, took out a cigarette and began smoking. She would watch the receptionist out of the corner of her eye, and then look down at the magazine, and back up at the two or three other people waiting in the room. Her eyes moved from people to the magazine to the cigarette to the people to the magazine in rapid succession. She avoided eye contact. When her name was finally called she jumped like she was startled.

Source: Based on Patton (1987: 93)

stay at the lowest level of inference and be directed to the concrete, rather than use abstractions. Such abstractions and analytic ideas that occur – and it frequently happens in the field – should be recorded separately or in a column on the margin of the page. They should be 'behaviouristic' rather than seeking to summarise (see Figure 14.1).

Any verbal data which is included should be identified as verbatim or otherwise. A system of notation should be adopted; one convention is that full quote marks (") denote verbatim quotation, while single quote marks (') indicate a précis.

Finally, it is essential to record your personal impressions and feelings. Doing fieldwork has emotional costs, and data on one's own attitude helps document one's evolving field relationships. Among other things such information helps compensate for shifts in perspective due, for example, to 'going native'. Covert observation poses special problems in recording, leading to various ploys – the use of hidden recorders, note-taking in toilets, or hasty exits when something important has to be written up precisely. These problems may lead to effects on the setting. Note should therefore be taken of memory distortion, confusion of issues and speakers, and field fatigue (Bruyn, 1966: 106).

14.6 COMES THE CRUNCH: ANALYSIS

While there are several approaches to analysing ethnographic data, the mechanical procedures researchers use are straightforward and readily summarised, as in Figure 14.2.

Appreciation of the meaning of events to members is not gained by simply 'telling it like it is' for them. One gains insight from comparing the participant observer's normal and setting-specific self, appreciating the difference in such a way as to understand on what separate assumptions about reality both are founded. Meaning emerges, then, from experience of the tension

Figure 14.2   Analysis procedure

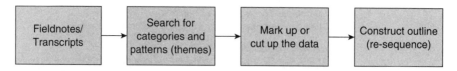

between distinct selves (Spiegelberg, 1980: 42). To appreciate the procedure of analysing ethnographic data it can be useful to compare different analyses made of the same data; Coffey and Atkinson (1996) and Cresswell (2007) offer such accounts.

Leaving the setting occurs when one is confident that one has identified the chief assumptions and themes of this particular world-view. Before this, observations will have become increasingly selective in focus.

14.7 VALIDATION

Critically assessing the reality of some unknown area of social life places a heavy responsibility on ethnographers. They must make sense of something which will remain unknown to most of their readers; precisely because the method is one of discovery it is unlikely that the audience will have any direct way of validating what the ethnographer claims. But the concept of relativism tells us that the ethnographer is never a fully detached observer: our view is inescapably relative to our own perspective.

Given that objective observation is impossible, what are the grounds for the credibility of the ethnographer's account? The participating observer is involved, not detached. Understanding is derived from experience. Sharing in the member's world enables one to gain access to one's own personal experience. Clearly such knowledge is introspective. Followers of the method have therefore pursued a **test of congruence** or principle of verifiability (Hughes, 1976: 134). The idea is that in any natural setting there are norms or rules of action in which members are competent. Understanding is achieved when the observer learns the rules and can provide others with instructions on how to pass in the same setting. Following such a recipe one should be able to have similar experiences and hence personally appreciate the truth of the description.

A more sophisticated approach is that of Glaser and Strauss' (1967) grounded theory (see Chapter 5). It requires

> the development of a systematic understanding which is clearly recognizable and understandable to the members of the setting and which is done as much as possible in their own terms; yet it is more systematic, and necessarily more verbal, than they would generally be capable of expressing. It uses their words, ideas and methods of expression wherever possible, but cautiously goes beyond these. (Douglas, 1976: 124–5)

Without such symbolic interpretation one's ethnographic description is hollow, a mere catalogue of events and constituents.

Douglas (1976) takes the matter of verification to what some regard as its illogical conclusion. Much ethnography is orientated to 'naturalism', with observation informed by a stance of appreciation, of trying to see things from the member's perspective. This tends to honour the knowledge of members on the basis that they, not outsiders, are the experts about their natural setting. But Douglas is preoccupied with the ways members can deceive outsiders. He suggests procedures like comparing member's accounts with 'the most reliable ideas and generally patterned facts the researcher has from his prior experience' (ibid.: 146) and 'comparing what one is told by others against what can be experienced or observed more directly'. Among his many examples is the case of massage parlour proprietors. Ethnographic interviews with them suggested that their popularly supposed sideline offering illicit sex (sometimes called 'relief massage') was false. Douglas just could not believe this; their expensive possessions did not seem consistent with the volume of legitimate trade. So Douglas sent graduate students in search of a massage, a device which soon undermined what the proprietors had been telling him. For Douglas, the proper 'investigative' research attitude is 'tough-minded suspicion', a position contrasting utterly with that of naturalism.

The problem is that Douglas' hard-bitten scepticism obstructs the attempt to construe the world as members do, with a view to gaining an understanding of its distinctive characteristics. Yet Douglas' concentration on the delicate balance between appreciation and being conned, between the participant persona and the observer role, does remind us that the effects of the researcher's presence on the setting are as inevitable as they are hard to gauge.

A case in point is Van Maanen's study of urban policing (1982). Van Maanen trained as a police officer for the research but his esteem among his police colleagues was dramatically improved when, after witnessing the beating of a man in the back of a police van, he refused to comply with a subpoena of his fieldnotes on the incident. Luckily for him, the case brought by the victim was settled out of court, because there are no legal grounds for refusing to surrender fieldnotes. Two years later he returned for more observations. He initially did not realise that some of what the police did on his return was for his benefit; they were, if you will, playing to camera. He suddenly realised this when they did something that contradicted his previous knowledge of their demeanour:

> I ... witnessed a bizarre encounter in which a young boy, perhaps 10 or 11 years old, was verbally assaulted and thrown to the pavement because he had aimed a ceremonial upright third finger in the direction of a passing patrol car – a gesture from a child that would have been routinely ignored or returned in my previous experience. (1982: 137)

When he had been with them every day, he could maintain a role that did not disturb their routines. But when he returned, the action did not flow from the logic

of the situation but from what the police thought he might appreciate, as someone apparently sympathetic to street justice. As he put it,

> in the abstract, relations in the field are such that the researcher is provided with
> trusted information of the sort necessary to both understand and empathize
> with the observed, but the researcher's presence itself creates little change or
> disturbance … concretely, however, such relations wax and wane over the course
> of a study, approach or exceed the upper and lower limits with different individuals
> on the scene, and vary according to the practical situation. (Van Maanen, 1982: 138)

Such considerations weigh heavily with **feminist** and postmodernist ethnographers.
Rather than seeking to satisfy what they see as the outmoded criterion of objectivity
which they associate with **positivism**, they seek validation in criteria of 'empower-
ment'. Feminist ethnographers value the way ethnographers work closely alongside
those being studied, and seek to produce analyses which can improve the lot of the
women they research. An emphasis is put on the ethnographer's 'standpoint'. Many
postmodernist ethnographers are also preoccupied with the issues of relativism and
subjectivity, the idea that what we see and report depends on our own perspective
and social location (Brettell, 1993). Rather than seeking to control for this, they act
as advocates of those they study. Here a successful analysis may not be one that
meets challenges to validity but which impacts positively on the situation of those
researched (Denzin and Lincoln, 2000). There are dangers in this. If the aim is to
'empower', this begs real questions about affecting the social world we study. It also
means that groups with whom researchers do not sympathise may be under-
researched; it could, for instance, obstruct research on elites.

Ethnography underwent a crisis of representation when the argument
gained ground that, through its presentation as a written account, ethnography
was necessarily a textual construction of social reality rather than tapping
directly into that reality (Burawoy, 2000; Clifford and Marcus, 1986).
Researchers affect settings by their presence and informants can only inform us
to the extent of their own understanding and expressive abilities. We now more
fully appreciate the challenge in producing authentic accounts. As a criterion,
truth is more than researcher or informant sincerity. A sensible middle-of-the-
road perspective is that we should still try to be accurate, even while recognising the limits of our ability to do so.

All this challenges our established canons of verification. The test of congruence may comprise the ideal check on the validity of observations, but it has to
be recognised that few research users have time to perform it. In fairness to
them, and to satisfy ourselves, observers still need to be self-critical. Lofland
and Lofland (1995) identify seven ways of evaluating the quality of ethnographic observation. First is the directness of the report; direct observation is
more reliable than second-hand observation. Second is the spatial location of
the observer. Proximity may be social as well as spatial. Third, problems arise
from skewing of reported views by the informants' social location. Informants
may not have said the same to other members of the setting. Fourth, one needs

to guard against self-serving error by asking whether the observations fit rather too neatly into one's analytic schema. Fifth are plain errors in description of events; one may not be an accurate observer. Sixth and seventh are problems of internal and external consistency. One's analysis needs to cohere around the themes identified, while external consistency is evaluated by checking agreement of key aspects against independent studies.

The Loflands' concerns are ably dealt with in the criteria of subjective adequacy suggested by Bruyn (1966). It is worth keeping a notebook evaluating one's observations, using Bruyn's criteria after writing each set of fieldnotes. Bruyn's first index of subjective adequacy is time; the more time spent with the group, the greater is the likelihood of adequacy. Second is place; the closer the observer works to the group, the greater is the likelihood of adequacy. Third, Bruyn takes account of social circumstances, on the grounds that the more varied the status opportunities within which the observer relates to the members and the more varied the activities witnessed, the more likely the interpretations will be true. Fourth, is a sensitivity to language, on the argument that the more familiar the observer is with the argot, slang or jargon in use, and with ordinary phrases which bear a setting-specific meaning, the greater is the accuracy of observation.

The fifth index is intimacy. Here Bruyn suggests observers record how they experienced and negotiated social openings and barriers. Intimacy, or how close one is allowed to get, can be constrained by one's own reserve as well as by members. In the sixth index, 'social consensus', the criterion of adequacy is fulfilled by maximising confirmation of the group's expressive meanings, either directly – by checking interpretations with members – or indirectly – by observing what members say about an interpretation.

14.8 SEQUENTIAL ANALYSIS

The analysis of ethnographic data is demanding, not least because ethnography produces a mass of data. One of Miles and Huberman's studies of a school system produced over 3000 pages of fieldnotes (1984). Not all the detail you have arduously gathered can be regarded as equally precious. If your procedure fulfils the various criteria of adequacy, you should have faith in your ability to select the most significant data. These materials must then be compressed so they cohere around several manageable themes or, formally, analytic schema (Agar, 1986). The essence of the procedure is that one works up from the data, rather than selecting some theory by convenience, whim or prejudice and then dipping into the data for fragments that support it.

Becker has suggested a procedure termed **'sequential analysis'** (1971), similar to Simmel's (1950) *Zirkel im verstehen*, in which one continually checks data against interpretation until satisfied one has grasped meaning. In Becker's approach the analysis is carried out sequentially in the sense that analysis begins while one is still gathering data. Between observations one may step back from the data to reflect on their possible meaning. Further data-gathering is then directed to matters to which the observer has become sensitive by provisional analysis. Subsequent observation may oblige the researcher to abandon the original hypothesis and pursue one more consistent with the setting. Thus, hypotheses, or, if you prefer, hunches, about the functioning of natural settings, are gradually refined. This is a distinct advantage over methods like surveys, where, once the instrument is designed, analytic interests cannot affect the data collected.

The evaluation of hypotheses hinges, then, on indices of the adequacy of data such as those suggested by Bruyn, plus consideration of the fit of one's observations to theory. Ethnography generates hypotheses for further testing through the researcher's ability to apply a theoretical perspective to observations and pick up uniformities and irregularities in the data. As McCall and Simmons note:

> these uniformities and departures, which provide theoretical richness, are seldom manifest in the data themselves but are obtained only through carefully designed theoretical sampling and analysis based upon the researcher's frame of reference ... data are not rich in and of themselves but may be *enriched* by proper use of discovery techniques (1969: 142, emphasis in the original).

Three kinds of conclusions result from ethnographic studies. First, and most demanding, the observer may be able to produce complex statements of necessary and sufficient conditions for a particular pattern of action or setting. Second, the observer may typify some of the observed phenomena as basic to the studied activity, on the grounds that they exercise a persistent influence on diverse events. Third, the observer may identify a situation as an example of a phenomenon described in abstract terms in a theory, the least demanding application.

Towards the end of fieldwork the observer draws up an outline comprising his or her current idea of the principal themes to emerge from the data, along with any analytic ideas which have accumulated during fieldwork. The data, such as fieldnotes or interview transcriptions or documents collected in the setting, are then indexed to the points on the outline. All the data should be indexed in this way. When compiling a first draft, one may then discard the weaker or simply repetitive data relating to particular points on the outline.

A somewhat more rigorous procedure is to compile the outline itself from ideas emerging only from the data. The data are read for analytic themes, which are listed. This list is then ordered by placing related items together in compounded items and, when condensed as much as possible, put in order according to an overall theme which seems to relate all the individual items. Because the selection of data pertinent to one of several analytic themes requires its separation from the rest of the data, so that it may be collated with the other data on the theme, this procedure is sometimes called 'cut and paste'. Nowadays this operation can be performed using qualitative data analysis software (see Chapter 20 for a detailed explanation).

Good qualitative analysis is able to document its claim to reflect some of the truth of a phenomenon by reference to systematically gathered data. Poor qualitative analysis is anecdotal, unreflective, descriptive without being focused on a coherent line of inquiry. It is important not to misrepresent the generalisability of findings from one setting. Ethnography's demanding nature means you are seldom in a position to claim that findings generalise to all such settings. The compensation for this is the depth of understanding gained of that one setting, which can be a rich source of ideas for work using other methods that can claim generalisability.

14.9 ETHICAL ISSUES

The decision to use ethnographic methods must be ethical as well as practical. Some consider it unethical to conduct any research not giving subjects the right to refuse to be studied, while at the other extreme are those who maintain that 'any investigation that does not deliberately damage the reputation of those studied is ethically justified' (Denzin, 1981: 33). Many professional bodies use the criterion of informed consent; in agreeing to research, subjects must be told its likely consequences. Yet it may not be feasible to predict the use to which research can be put. For example, a detailed ethnography of a group of mountain villagers may seem innocuous until, years later, the region is engaged in revolt and the agents of a foreign power develop a keen interest in the group's beliefs so they can be won to its side. Are we to desist from our study when harm *might* result at some unknown future time?

What goes in the balance against potential harms is the value to knowledge. This value may be obvious, as when a group is powerful and little is known about it. But it can be hard to guess. It is doubtful that Rosenhan (Bulmer, 1982) could have predicted the enormous impact of his team's research on mental hospital diagnoses, for the simple reason that no one would have guessed they were so abjectly unreliable. The study involved placing 'pseudo-patients' in mental hospitals. On arrival they feigned hearing voices, but once admitted and diagnosed they ceased simulating any symptoms. All but one was admitted with a diagnosis of schizophrenia. Not one was caught out, providing crucial evidence about the reliability of psychiatric diagnosis and the labelling of patients. Nor were their diagnoses changed when they switched to normal behaviour, despite many of their fellow patients guessing that, as one put it, 'You're a journalist or a professor, you're checking up on the hospital'. One case file contained perhaps the ultimate description of compiling fieldnotes – 'patient engages in writing behaviour'! But he was never questioned about what he was doing. The staff of a hospital Rosenhan was in touch with were so appalled at the results that they agreed to the same being done at their hospital. Staff were told to expect impostors and to rate all admissions with this in mind; 23 out of 193 were suspected by at least one psychiatrist. In fact, Rosenhan had not sent in a single pseudo-patient.

Tough cases like this give some idea of what is at stake. No one could seriously doubt the value of this work, but nor could they deny its dangers. It is not hard to imagine that the psychiatrists' professional competence would be severely undermined, and their effectiveness with real patients affected negatively. The reaction of some mental health systems to such studies has been to ban social research of any kind from their institutions (Bulmer, 1982). What these ethical complications do is to support the case for *situation ethics* attuned to the specifics of the case, in preference to broad, general principles which collapse when confronted with dilemmas.

While dramatic, such problems only hint at the host of fieldwork issues which provoke ethical complications. There are cases where it has emerged after the study has been published that relationships between researcher and researched go beyond the published account. In one, it turned out that a research participant who had taken destructive action against 'his' ethnographer had been motivated by a sexual relationship with the ethnographer, a relationship not acknowledged in the original published account. In another, ethnographers who studied high-level drug dealers only acknowledged some years later that they had themselves been participants in the dealing operations. Neither revelation necessarily undermines the insights of the original work, but would certainly lead us to weigh the evidence differently. Perhaps the most glaring example, though, is that of Margaret Mead's famous studies of sexuality among Pacific islanders. This research was of fundamental importance in the development of American policy on sex education and other aspects of sexual behaviour, it being used as a key comparison case to establish the nature of sexual mores in 'simple' societies. Decades later it emerged that Mead's informants had deceived her, partly to maintain the flow of rewards she used to encourage their participation. Sensing her own prejudices and inclinations, they fed her accounts consistent with those (Freeman, 1999).

These difficult cases do not mean we are left without rules of thumb. Here are some guidelines. First, all researchers should be honest enough to report their mistakes and failures, and do so as part of their overall analysis. Second, researchers should not spoil the field for those who may follow. Third, researchers must acknowledge that some groups are especially vulnerable and have a right to not be researched, an example being one ethnographer's decision not to publish a study of American draft resisters during the Vietnam War (contextual details could have revealed their location). Fourth, unless there is a danger of reprisals threatening the ethnographer's physical security, subjects should be given the right to comment on findings, by being provided with transcripts of data and/or draft publications. It should be clear to subjects what comments are legitimate; it is normal to allow points of accuracy and information to be added, while reserving the analysis to yourself.

14.10 SUMMARY

Ethnography is one of the most important methods of social research. It originated in anthropology, but has now become a basic technique in sociology. Ethnography requires the researcher to become involved in the daily world of the people being studied, observing them, recording what they do and say and, often, interviewing them, in order to understand the meanings that people apply to their own life and world. To enter into an ethnographic setting, one has to choose a suitable role and decide whether to reveal that one is a researcher (as an overt observer) or conceal it. Overt observation has a number of advantages over covert observation, including making it easier to record fieldnotes. Careful recording is vital because one's analysis is founded on this written record. Even so, questions have been raised about the validity of ethnographic observation. Analysis usually proceeds iteratively, developing interpretations and then checking back against further data. Although ethnography sometimes raises ethical issues because it involves getting close to informants and the worlds in which they live, it is often a highly effective way of understanding social life in specific settings.

DISCUSSION QUESTIONS

1   List two or three settings that are familiar to you where it might be interesting to conduct an ethnographic study.

2   Choose one of these settings and consider how you might set about doing an ethnography and describe the problems you might encounter.

3   Would you encounter any ethical issues in researching this setting? How would you resolve them?

PROJECT

This project is an exercise in collecting observational data. The emphasis is on developing your skills of observation and gaining experience of the techniques of recording social events. First, think about a research design before your fieldwork. Decide what research topic is appropriate to study through observation. For instance, you might be interested in the unstated rules that govern queuing behaviour, and so watch people lining up for buses. Or you might be interested in how people interact when they are engrossed in video games, and find your way to the Student Union to watch them. Another idea is to watch how people order drinks in the pub, noting gender differences. Several students might work on the same topic so that they can (literally) compare notes.

Second, carry out field observation. Record your observations by writing fieldnotes. Now write a description of the research procedure and the sort of data you gathered. Mention any problems in using the method and evaluate how it went.

The exercise works best if there is someone with whom you can discuss it and who has also tried it out. When you are thinking over the experience, or discussing it, here are the sorts of questions you need to ask to assess the adequacy of your observations:

1   How accurate an observer am I of sequences of action? of dialogue?
2   Have I the ability to write 'concretely' or do my notes contain generalisations and summaries?
3   Was my research aim realistic? Was it adequately specified at the outset? Was it interesting? Was it sociological?
4   Was I comfortable doing the observation? Did I tell anyone I was researching? If I did not tell anyone I was researching, do I think anyone guessed?
5   What other methods could I have used to get this data? Now that I have tried observation, was it the best available method to get this data?

RESOURCES

Burgess (1991) *Field Research* is a comprehensive edited collection which serves well as a sourcebook and field manual. It is particularly good on naturalistic and American sources.

Denzin and Lincoln (2000) *The Handbook of Qualitative Research* is an eclectic and comprehensive resource with particularly good attention to post-modern approaches.

Emerson et al. (1995) *Writing Ethnographic Fieldnotes* offers much advice on the vital activity of preparing fieldnotes.

Fetterman (1998) *Ethnography: Step by Step* offers guidance about every step in the process of conducting an ethnography.

Hammersley and Atkinson (2007) *Ethnography: Principles in Practice* is a thorough treatment of ethnography with particularly good attention to issues of analysis and writing up.

Patton (2002) *Qualitative Evaluation and Research Methods* is good on sampling in ethnography and on the practical application of observational methods.

Seale (1999) *The Quality of Qualitative Research* gives a stimulating, pragmatic account of epistemological foundations of ethnography and ways of handling challenges to its validity, and Yin (2003) *Case Study Research* provides an excellent introduction to the case-study approach.

15 Using Documents

Keith Macdonald

KEY POINTS

● What is included in the definition of 'documents' and where they may be found.

● How to understand, interpret and evaluate documents.

● Classic examples of documentary research, and how later researchers have evaluated and built on them.

● Guidelines for documentary researchers.

15.1 INTRODUCTION

Documentary research may not be as prominent in contemporary sociological work as the survey or field research, but it has a longer history and is of no less importance. Many early sociologists – Marx, Durkheim and Weber, for example – used documentary research, and it remains an important research tool in its own right, as well as being an invaluable part of most schemes of **triangulation** (Denzin, 1970: 86).

Documentary research has an affinity with **ethnography** and fieldwork rather than with survey research. Survey and questionnaire research (see Chapter 10) collects information from a predefined situation and population, to answer fairly specific questions or to test hypotheses, and is analogous to the work of natural scientists, with a concern for controlling for variables, with known parameters. In documentary research you may not know what you are looking for, or what you are looking at, until the investigation starts. It is much closer to the detective work of field research (see Chapter 14), with all the excitement of the detective story and all the hard graft of checking reams of evidence. A **document**, like an untrustworthy witness, must be cross-examined and its motives assessed. How was it written, what was it really, why did it take place in that way, what was the point? Who had a motive? Who benefited? Who was in a position to write and disseminate it? Who was it intended to deceive and why? (see Gumilev, 1987: xvi, 10, 43, 362).

Documentary research tends to be a rather general inquiry, guided by the overall question, favoured by **symbolic interactionists**, 'What is going on here?' (Glaser and Strauss, 1965).

15.2 WHAT IS A DOCUMENT?

Documents are things that we can read and that relate to some aspect of the social world. Some documents are intended to record public matters – official reports, for example – but there are also private and personal records such as letters, diaries and photographs, which may not have been meant for the public gaze at all. But in addition to the written record, there are those things which may be overtly intended to provoke amusement or admiration or pride or aesthetic enjoyment – songs, buildings, statues, novels – but which also tell us something about the values, interests and purposes of those who commissioned or produced them. Such creations may be regarded as documents of a society or group which may be read, albeit in a metaphorical sense.

While public monuments and official art can readily be seen as social products, documents which are intended to be read as objective statements of fact are also *socially produced*. This is not to imply that all official documents are some kind of propaganda. But they are produced on the basis of certain ideas, theories or commonly accepted, taken-for-granted principles, which means that while they are perfectly correct – given certain socially accepted bases – they do not have the objectivity of, say, a measure of atmospheric pressure recorded on a barometer. This view of official records has been shown clearly in the case of suicide verdicts (Atkinson, 1978), which cannot tell us exactly how many people killed themselves, but only how many were socially defined as having done so in accordance with the array of social rules and practices used by coroners and police to arrive at a socially acceptable judgement. In a very different context, Hindess (1973: 30) has shown how official census statistics may be compiled on the basis of categories that are derived from a particular theoretical viewpoint. If these categories do not reflect the conceptions of the census-takers and their informants, the census results may be quite misleading. So, a set of minutes, the accounts of a public company, or official statistics are produced in a socially acceptable form that gives a 'reasonable' account: but when one reads that between 1979 and 1991 the bases for collecting British unemployment statistics were changed 30 times (*Independent on Sunday*, 11 August 1991), it becomes clear just how unstable this 'reasonableness' can be. Furthermore, decisions about the storage of an archive are also socially produced – what is to be kept, how, where and for how long they are to be kept, and what is to be thrown away.

But in addition to social production the documentary researcher has to bear several other points in mind. There may be more than one set of documents, with different orientations. They may ignore the social context. The documents may be at variance with how the events are held in social memory, and therefore with the social significance of the matters they relate to. A classic example of the latter is how the folk memory in the United States (and elsewhere) of the uncovering the Watergate scandal that led to the resignation of President Nixon in 1974, diverges significantly from what occurred according to the documentary evidence (Schudson, 1992).

15.3 TYPES OF DOCUMENTS

The term documents includes a vast range of materials to be found in all sorts of places and all that can be done here is to give a review of five broad categories, which, although necessarily brief, will exemplify the nature of the materials and the problems encountered by the documentary researcher.

15.3.1 PUBLIC RECORDS

The oldest writings in existence are public records. Writing was devised by officials in the ancient civilisations to record the taxation and tribute that the state received and the rations it issued to its servants. The modern state generates fiscal and economic records, which because they deal with quantifiable matters are assumed to have an objectivity that other kinds of documents may lack, whereas in fact a financial or statistical record is a social product just as much as any other. Every effort may have been made to ensure the reliability and validity of these figures, but any indicator of economic performance or incidence of crime, or any other statistic is based on working assumptions, some of which, at least, could have been decided otherwise.

One must also be aware of the distortions that can arise as a result of the actions of the people to whom the statistics refer; so, for example, certain categories of person may be under-recorded in the Census. Recent immigrants, for instance, may not understand the purpose of the Census and evade being recorded because they assume it to be connected with some piece of legislation under which they might have offended.

Public documents available to the social researcher include the Census and the Electoral Registers, and annual reports on the vital statistics of the nation. Government departments produce their own national statistics – industry, education, crime, housing, and so on, summaries of which are published monthly or annually. There are also reports from government departments and boards of inquiry, local authorities, health authorities, nationalised industries and many other public sector bodies. Likewise, at the international level, statistics are published by organisations such as the United Nations, the International Labour Organization, the European Commission and numerous others.

Another important kind of official record is the verbatim account of legislative bodies: Parliaments, Assemblies and Local Authorities in Britain, Congress and State legislatures in the United States. One can consult *Hansard* in Britain and the Congressional Record in the US and reports of Parliamentary or Congressional Committees: a good example is Boylan and Kedrowski (2004). Verbatim reports of judicial proceeding are also kept. There are also the unpublished papers of government departments, which only become available after a period of years. In Britain, some records are subject to the Official Secrets Act, and these may be kept secret for longer than others. Before the mid-twentieth century the construction of these archives depended on the idiosyncrasies of departmental officials, which can prove extremely frustrating for the researcher, even if there is no attempt to hide things from public gaze.

15.3.2 THE MEDIA

The media are selective in what they publish. This is a matter of editorial policy and it may be possible to discern that policy, at least in regard to what they print. What they leave out is another matter altogether and requires much closer study of the media and current events generally, and it may be harder to perceive the selectivity imposed by a particular editor. The bias and selectivity imposed by editorial policy are only one of a number of areas in which the researcher *must* be on guard: newspapers are subject to:

- Errors: these may be technical, such as spelling, typing, or printing, when lines or longer sections of print get transposed, or they may be matters of fact.

- Distortion: this may stem from the preferences of the proprietor or editor or from the journalist producing the copy, or it may arise at source, as when an account of events is given by a participant in them, or when a journalist relies on an organisation's press release. The most fundamental form of distortion is, of course, that of propaganda, where the wholesale creation of a particular view of events is undertaken in what is perceived to be the national interest or with the object of systematically deceiving an enemy.

- Audience context: this is an aspect that may be easily overlooked. The production of any medium of communication is undertaken with an audience in mind, and unless one knows how that audience perceives the content, it is possible that the researcher will fail to grasp the message. Not only cultural norms, but jokes, deliberate mistakes, irony and so on depend on the existence of a common frame of reference between writer and reader, which may deceive the researcher who is unaware of them.

Finally, the researcher must remember that in many cases it is not the original document that is under scrutiny, but some form of copy, such as a photocopy, microfilm or microfiche and that its reliability depends on the work of a copyist. Omissions and transpositions are not unknown.

15.3.3 PRIVATE PAPERS

The documents of a private individual are also open to distortion and manipulation, especially if the person concerned is a public figure or an author whose work is so widely read and discussed as to put them in the public sphere.

For example, Seymour-Smith (1990) in his biography of the writer, Rudyard Kipling, examines several earlier biographies and shows that they contain serious distortions and omissions that resulted from the pressures and deceptions of Kipling's widow and family. This reached such a pitch that they eventually destroyed a sizeable part of the archive of material on which a biographer might wish to work. Such attitudes are even more likely to be present in the case of a politician, whose private papers refer not only to matters of interest to critics and academics, but to events that were of consequence to the nation or even to the world. So, some private papers deal with public matters.

There are also private papers that refer to private lives and personal careers but which can sometimes throw considerable light on the times in which they live, as in the case of the Paston Letters (Bennett, 1922); these come from just one family in the fifteenth century, but provide one of the best sources of material on the late Middle Ages. The researcher is at the mercy of the creator of such an archive, but it is possible to improve on this state of affairs if one is dealing with the recent past, because then one can purposefully collect the diaries and letters of people in a certain category as in the case of *The Polish Peasant in Europe and America* (Thomas and Znaniecki, 1958). One can take this a step further by soliciting material from informants and asking them to search their memories and give accounts of past events. An example of this method is the work of Middlebrook (1978; 1983), who selected for study particular events in the First and Second World Wars. Starting from the official records and histories, he then sought out the participants still surviving by, for example, advertising in the local papers of the regions from which the regiments involved were drawn and thus obtained first-hand accounts.

15.3.4 BIOGRAPHY

The accounts that Middlebrook (1978; 1983) obtained from the participants in particular events are examples in miniature of another kind of document, namely biography and autobiography. The term 'biography' is employed in two differing senses by sociologists. One is to refer to an account obtained by a particular style of interviewing, in which the informant is encouraged to describe how their conception of self, identity and personal history has changed and developed over time (Chamberlayne et al., 2000). Most of that volume is concerned with the biographical interview, but one contributor ranges wider, and all his quotations are from poets, novelists and playwrights (Rustin, 2000). There is some justification for this, for, as he says:

> Works of 'fiction' have paradoxically come closer to the truths of subjective experience than either generalizing works of science, which fail to capture the particuliarity and immediacy of lived lives, or factual descriptions of individuals, whose common defect is a lack of coherence or connectedness, a sufficient sense of 'the essential'. (ibid.: 39)

It is important to be aware that fiction and biography can overlap: but on the other hand, some sociologists argue that works of fiction are produced for and by an educated social elite and therefore

> to some extent reflect the values and interests of those groups ... They are therefore an unreliable guide to the realities of the social life they write about ... relations between literature and society are both more complex and subtle than can be conveyed by the idea of a straightforward, mirror-like reflection. (Filmer, 1998: 278)

But Filmer goes on to propose what he terms the *intrinsic* approach to the sociological study of literature, operating on the premise that literature is a *reflexive* feature of the society, which may be a critical reflection on social practices, as much as an endorsement; and that it is quite possible to determine which it is. He illustrates these techniques in an analysis of Charles Dickens's *The Pickwick Papers*.

The other use of the term biography is the conventional one. An account of this mode of documentary research may be found in *Sociology* (1993, 27(1)), a special issue on 'Biography and autobiography in sociology'. This volume places more emphasis on auto/biography in the everyday sense, and on accounts that may have been invited by an investigator, but which are written by the informant unaided and unprompted. The contributors put a high value on this source of data, for example,

> In looking, therefore, at biographies, social scientists might find rich material for the way in which the formal categories of social life are given human meaning. The use of biography is not just to illustrate a social theory but to explain its meaning. (Evans, 1993: 12)

> C. Wright Mills sees the interaction between life-experience and history as the definition of sociology. From such a viewpoint accounts of lives are more or less interesting, depending on how effectively they are able to distil both social structure and a story of an individual life without, in the process, either swamping the personal or subjectivising the social. (Erben, 1993: 15)

Later in this chapter we consider the problems of reliability in documentary research, but it is worth mentioning at this point that auto/biography may well have aims other than the presentation of objective truth.

15.3.5 VISUAL DOCUMENTS

Examples of treating literary work as a document are provided by Fussell (1975), but his work is particularly interesting because he later went on to combine this technique with the analysis of visual documents. In *Wartime: Understanding and Behavior in the Second World War,* Fussell (1989) quotes from a comparative analysis of posters in the two World Wars, and thus moves into the study of visual documents.

Interpretation seems to be a more obvious requirement when dealing with visual materials, such as photos, advertisements, paintings, posters, statues, buildings, films, and so on. Photographs are particularly problematic, because in addition to the usual problem of interpretation, the photographer can leave things out of shot, and negatives and prints can be doctored in various ways (Becker, 1979).

It is often necessary to have some knowledge of the circumstances in which an object was produced before it can be interpreted as a social document. This need is nicely exemplified by Berger (1972: 82–112), who examines a number of seventeenth- and eighteenth-century paintings to show the way in which patrons of painting of that period were concerned with their possessions, and how this trend can be associated with the emerging power of capital (ibid.: 86). Berger successfully makes his point, but it is not done on the basis of the paintings alone. This raises the problem of what tests of reliability and authenticity must be applied to the supporting data, a matter that will be considered below (see also Antal, 1962; 1987; Cohen, 1989; and Chapter 23).

15.3.6 VISUAL PRESENTATION OF DATA

Visual materials can be used as methods of presenting social data as well as being documentary sources. Harper (1979) carried out research, which combined photography, interviewing and participant observation in America on Skid Row. Commenting on Harper's work, Becker writes: 'He believes strongly that the basic working unit of sociology is text and image as an indivisible whole: that the long narrative accompanying these photographs informs them, just as it is illuminated by them' (1979: 86).

The research reported by Macdonald (1989) on the cultural significance of the buildings used as the headquarters of English professional bodies made use of photographs. With research of this kind it is scarcely possible to make a convincing case without the use of visual material, because there is no other guarantee that the text accurately describes the objects in question.

Visual materials, however, are an important topic in their own right, and are therefore the subject of a full treatment in Chapter 23.

15.4 EVALUATION AND INTERPRETATION

Many of the problems that the documentary researcher may encounter are about how to evaluate material and can be grouped under four headings: authenticity, credibility, representativeness and meaning. Scott (1990) gives a valuable treatment of these issues and what follows draws on his ideas.

15.4.1 AUTHENTICITY

'A CHECK MAY BE WRITTEN ON A COW' ran a headline in the *Memphis Press-Scimitar* in 1967, and the article claimed to refer to a nineteenth-century case in England, where this practice was said to be permitted, and quoted as authority the Chase Manhattan Bank. In fact, the original source was the dramatisation on BBC television of one of A. P. Herbert's (fictional) *Misleading Cases in the Common Law,* originally published in the 1930s (and set in that period, not the nineteenth century). Herbert (1977) recounts a number of occasions in which his fictitious characters escaped into real life, thus illustrating one of the problems of authenticity in documentary research, namely that writers (or copyists) may well quite innocently, or perhaps carelessly, convert fiction into fact or perpetuate the errors or deceptions of others.

While deliberate falsehoods are rare (Scott, 1990: 43, 175), it is possible that records or factual accounts may have been falsified for the author's own purposes at the time, and the researcher must always be suspicious of unexpected changes of paper, ink, typeface, handwriting, and so on, and must check consistency and plausibility, internally and externally. Platt (1981) encountered the problem of deliberate deception in documentary research and proposes a set of questions for deciding on the authenticity of a document. These include:

- Does the document make sense or does it contain glaring errors?
- Are there different versions of the original document available?
- Is there consistency of literary style, handwriting or typeface?
- Has the document been transcribed by many copyists?
- Has the document been circulated via someone with a material or intellectual interest in passing off the version given as the correct one?
- Does the version available derive from a reliable source?

15.4.2 CREDIBILITY

Credibility refers to the question of whether the document is free from error or distortion. The latter may occur when there is a long time between the event and the account of it being written down, or when the account has been through several hands and the author of the document was not present at the event. Credibility can be affected by the interest of the author, which might, for example, be financial, to enhance a reputation, or to please the reader. Such possibilities should always lead the social researcher to ask who produced the document, why, when, for whom and in what context?

15.4.3 REPRESENTATIVENESS

Do the documents available constitute a representative sample of all the documents as they originally existed? If the archive appears to contain all the material produced in that category, then the problem does not exist. But once it is established that there is something missing, the questions of what is missing, how much, and why it is missing become important. When the survival of documents is quite haphazard, as it is with the material from ancient civilisations, conclusions must always be tentative or at least historians must be prepared to revise their accounts if fresh evidence is unearthed. With more recent archives it must always be a matter of judgement, based on the amount of missing material, whether the blanks have any pattern to them and whether anyone could have had an interest in destroying certain documents. In this, as in the questions of authenticity and credibility, the researcher's approach must be essentially that of the detective, in the sense that everything is potentially suspect and anything may turn out to be the key piece of data, including things which ought to be there but are missing.

15.4.4 MEANING

Establishing the meaning of a document is usually seen as working at two levels: the surface or literal meaning, and the deeper meaning arrived at by some form of interpretative understanding or structural analysis. Although there is a clear difference between the extreme forms of these two modes, it is possible to see the two as merging in some instances; for form is only conceptually distinct from content, or the message from grammar, and human beings habitually handle both without any trouble.

Understanding the surface message may depend on becoming familiar with the language used by different groups, cultures and periods. The deeper meaning of a document or a text may well prove more troublesome. The simpler kind of question about meaning is exemplified by the problem of how important particular themes are to the author (or the newspaper, or whatever is the unit of investigation) and the answer to this question is usually sought through quantification, by means of content analysis (Krippendorf, 2004; Weber, 1990). The importance of a topic is measured by the number of times it is mentioned, the number of column inches devoted to it, the square inches of the photographs displayed, the number of times it appears in the index, the number of readers' letters that the editor decides to publish, and so on. This method, being a quantitative one, carries with it a number of technical issues to do with sampling, representativeness, coding and statistical reliability, which, for reasons of space, we must leave to one side (but see Chapters 9, 17 and 18).

The measurement of the relative salience of a theme by the frequency of its occurrence is a fairly simple or even simplistic notion, and in dealing with anything more complex than newspapers, content analysis on its own does appear rather unsubtle; so sociologists have searched for something more sophisticated that would do justice to the more complex kind of document. In the early twentieth century, the notion of interpretative understanding, following the ideas of Dilthey (see Rickman, 1961) achieved some importance. More recently, textual analysis has drawn on the semiotic approach to be found in the structural linguistics of Saussure, especially as developed by Barthes (1967). The former defined **semiotics** as 'a science that studies the life of signs within society', the object of which is to get to the underlying message of the text. This is to be found, not only in the words and phrases, but in the system of rules that structures the text as a whole. It is therefore this underlying structure and the rules it embodies that can tell the researcher what its cultural and social message is. The analyst seeks to connect a *signifier* (an expression which may be words, a sound or a picture) with what is *signified* (another word, description or image). The distinction between content analysis and semiotics is concisely set out by Slater (1998) and the whole topic is dealt with fully in Chapter 23.

Examples of research which explicitly reject content analysis in favour of semiotics is to be found in two studies of weekly magazines aimed at teenage girls (McRobbie, 1978; 1991). The author describes magazines as 'specific signifying systems where particular messages are produced and articulated'. Quantification is rejected in favour of the understanding of media messages as structured wholes. From the large range of codes operating in the magazines, McRobbie identifies four around which to organise her study, and from this analysis delineates 'the central feature of *Jackie* insofar as it presents its readers with an ideology of adolescent femininity'.

While this method undoubtedly provides a more coherent set of guidelines for the analysis of text than its predecessors, Scott (1990) argues cogently that semiotics still does not give us a means of judging between rival interpretations of a text. He draws on the work of Giddens (1976) and his view that a text, taken in isolation from its social context, is deprived of its real meaning. This is provided by a socially situated author and audience who are necessary for the text to have any meaning at all. 'Texts must be studied as socially situated products' (Scott, 1990: 34). A graphic example is provided by Garfinkel's (1967b) paper, ' "Good" Organizational Reasons for "Bad" Clinical Records'. This research started out as a study of a population of patients attending a psychiatric clinic, but Garfinkel found that the data in the clinicians' files were sadly deficient as a means of showing the characteristics of the patient population and how patients had been selected for treatment. Garfinkel concludes that the clinic's records are kept so as to serve the interests of medical and psychiatric services rather than to serve the interest of research. Therefore the 'expressions that the documents contain will have to be decoded to discover their real meaning in the light of the interest and interpretation that prevails at the time' (ibid.: 126). This kind of work may be regarded as closer to **discourse** analysis (DA). Although this sounds as though it concentrates on language and possibly even speech, DA may be applied to 'official documents, legal statutes, political debates and speeches, media reports, policy papers, maps, pictorial and exhibition materials, expert analyses, publicity literature and press statements, historical documents, tourist guides, interviews, diaries and oral histories' (Tonkiss, 2004: 369). Tonkiss gives a useful outline of this method, which is also covered in Chapter 23 in this volume: another good example may be found in Gilbert and Mulkay (1984).

15.5 EXEMPLARS OF DOCUMENTARY RESEARCH

As noted above, the work of early sociologists relied heavily on documentary research. This section will review briefly research that has followed up the themes of Durkheim's *Suicide*, Weber's *The Protestant Ethic and the Spirit of Capitalism* and Marx's concept of the labour process that appears in *Capital*, as part of the logic of capitalist development. The object is to illustrate the points discussed above, such as the importance of the social construction of documents, and their evaluation and interpretation.

15.5.1 *SUICIDE* AND THE SOCIAL CONSTRUCTION OF STATISTICS

Durkheim (1952) was one of the first to use statistics to support a theoretical position in sociology (see Chapter 2), and in so doing displayed considerable ingenuity and innovation. However, there are a number of problems with his data and with his argument, although in fact these act as an object lesson in the pitfalls to be avoided in this kind of work.

Durkheim argues that the causes of suicide are social, not individual or psychological. He then provides the data to support his sociological explanation and typology of suicide, using official statistics from a number of countries and provinces within them. These figures may be taken as an accurate record of judicial pronouncements of death; but the difficulties start with a problem that

Durkheim himself identified in disposing of psychological explanations, when he writes that one cannot rely on coroners' attribution of motive to classify suicide (1952: 148–52). This is indeed true but overlooks the fact that it is the attribution of motive that leads to the definition of the death as suicide in the first place. Durkheim's definition of his subject matter is those deaths where people have deliberately taken their own lives, (1952: 44) but more recent research, for example, Taylor in *Durkheim and the Study of Suicide* (1982) and *The Sociology of Suicide* (1988) recognises that there are those who intend to kill themselves, and those who merely wish to 'attempt' suicide as a cry for help or moral blackmail, get it wrong and die; and possibly some intermediate categories. Furthermore, the court's definition of a suicide depends on whether the deceased can be classified as likely to commit suicide – for example, whether they were perceived as depressed or isolated – and if there is no reason why they should have committed suicide, then the death will probably be classed as an accident (Taylor, 1982: 87). For example, in the case of 'persons under trains' on the London Underground, an important factor in a coroner's verdict is the 'normality of place'. A death that occurs at a station where the deceased travels normally took them tended to be regarded as an accident, whereas if they were miles from their usual station it was seen as suicide. London Transport employees were rarely thought to have killed themselves, wherever they were found (ibid.: 119).

While suicide statistics are authentic and credible in their own terms, they do not tell exactly how many people killed themselves. It is now generally acknowledged that suicide statistics (and indeed official statistics in general) are socially constructed, but equally important is the realisation that while Durkheim's causes – the 'suicidal currents' running through a society or sections of it – have considerable plausibility, they must be seen as functioning on the psychological, as well as the sociological, level. 'Suicidal actions will not be satisfactorily explained without reference to the actor's intentions and the micro-sociological context' (Taylor, 1982: 194). By analysing the accounts that lie behind the decisions that define a death, one may arrive at the description and understanding advocated by Taylor, and by Abbott (1998), in his detailed analysis of causality statements in Durkheim's *Suicide* (Douglas, 1967; Fullagar, 2003; Hindess, 1973; Robertson and Cochrane, 1976).

15.5.2 *THE PROTESTANT ETHIC* AND THE SEARCH FOR MEANING

Marshall's (1980; 1982) examination of certain problems arising from Max Weber's essay *The Protestant Ethic and the Spirit of Capitalism* (1930) may be regarded as a master class in documentary research.

Weber's work is based on documentary research, as well as drawing on a great range of secondary sources. It stems from his analysis of capitalism and his conclusion that what was missing from earlier treatments, such as that of

Marx, was any consideration of the motivation of the people involved. He believed that, in addition to the effects of economic, technical and political factors, the new entrepreneurs must have held very powerful convictions about their innovative activities to have overcome the inertia of traditional economic attitudes and behaviour. His hypothesis is that a number of interrelated features of Calvinistic theology provided the underlying impetus for the capitalist spirit and he presents a wide range of documentary material in evidence. Studies of this thesis hinge on the attribution of meaning by Calvinists to their theology as it evolved during the seventeenth century, and the historical fit between the presence of Calvinists and capitalist development.

Marshall's first point is the need to make clear the concepts with which the research topic is to be analysed and presented. Many critics of Weber failed to appreciate the nature of a conceptualisation using 'ideal types', and in a case like this the formulation of the concepts that underlie the problem assume considerable importance. So Marshall reviews not only what Weber wrote himself, but also the comments and criticism that others have made, in order to be quite explicit about what his thesis involves, and hence what documents need to be researched and how their meaning may be evaluated.

Marshall then shows how Protestant doctrine developed, from its original formulation by Luther and Calvin in the sixteenth century to the form it took a century or more later, which Weber argues stimulated the original spirit of capitalism. The next stage was to follow the doctrine's transformation into an ethic of everyday behaviour, and on to its final form as a secular work ethic. These phases required the examination of the writing of Puritan divines of the first period, and the views expressed by the merchants and manufacturers of the later stages. Marshall has gone to great lengths to find the original theological writings and to find the letters and diaries of the later entrepreneurs. In order to show the applicability of Weber's thesis to Scotland, he also collected data on eighteenth-century Scottish enterprises. These documents were to be found in a large number of libraries and archives, ranging from the Scottish Record Office, though municipal records to the proceedings of learned societies.

Although Marshall is cautious in the presentation of his conclusions, there is good reason to regard his work as confirming the main features of Weber's thesis and its applicability to Scotland in the seventeenth and eighteenth centuries.

15.5.3 *CAPITAL* AND THE LABOUR PROCESS

In Marx's theory of the development of capitalism, the process whereby labour becomes a commodity is an important theme, one which sprang into prominence with the publication of Braverman's *Labor and Monopoly Capitalism* (1974). This book, stimulating and insightful though it was, seemed to many to be short of the detailed research work that would actually confirm the validity of this part of Marx's thesis. There was a lack of precision, and even inaccuracy, about the depiction of skilled, craft and unskilled kinds of work, about their control and about the periods at which the nature of work and its control changed and developed. There was also debate about employers' strategies and the patterns of opposition to them, and a failure to locate these themes in the context of the labour market.

The Development of the Labour Process in Capitalist Societies (Littler, 1982) goes a long way to remedying these defects by a comparative study of the changes in work and skills and in management controls, in Britain, Japan and the USA. In particular, he uses documentary research to show that the development of the labour process in Britain came about through the application by managements of the Bedaux system of work measurement and control, and by worker and trade union resistance to it. He focuses especially on two firms in Britain for which there are documentary records available in the Bedaux Archive, company records and histories, trade union archives and even the records of the Chancery Division of the Law Courts. The Law Courts became involved because the workers at one of the firms sued their employers on the grounds that as piece-workers they were entitled to control their own work and working practices, without interference from management.

Littler goes a long way towards remedying the deficiencies in Braverman's account of the labour process and his triangulation of documentary sources in the British case play a significant part in this achievement.

15.6 GENERAL PRACTICAL GUIDELINES

15.6.1 THE NEED FOR TRIANGULATION

In documentary research it is sound practice to check things from more than one angle. Nothing can be taken for granted. A document may not be what it appears to be, the archive may have been collected for motives we do not understand, and the context may be crucial in determining the nature of the object before us. This makes documentary work very different from, say, survey research, where validity and reliability are secured within the method itself. But in other modes of research, the notion of triangulation has become a salient feature of research methodology (Denzin, 1970; 1978) (see Chapter 14). In this framework, validity is seen as having both external and internal aspects and the achievement of validity, and indeed of the research task as a whole, requires a triangulation of research strategies.

The general approach that Denzin advocates, and to some extent the actual methods he suggests, provide sound guidance for the documentary researcher. It is however, rather more difficult to give a toolkit for this kind of work, because the data materials are so various. But hopefully the principle is clear and its practice can be appreciated from the following quotation from *Belfast in the '30s: an Oral History*:

In the first place we carried out ... 'investigator triangulation'. That is, each transcript was checked by two or three researchers to ensure that it said what people had meant to say. In the second place, we systematically did a cross-method triangulation, in that every piece of oral evidence that could be was checked against a range of written sources: newspapers, parliamentary reports, documents etc. Finally, there was a considerable amount of data triangulation possible within the oral sources themselves. (Munck and Rolston, 1987)

15.6.2 SEARCHING AND COMPARING

Researchers using data on collective events need to be aware that different collections of documentary records may not have been assembled on the same bases. For example, police agencies and news sources have their own logics, producing both incomplete and selective records of collective events. Furthermore, different strategies for searching newspapers for stories about events yield very different results. News items about events do not occur at the same time as the events but are dispersed around them, so the patterns that emerge vary greatly from source to source and locale to locale. This means that a search has to start before an event takes place and that references to it may appear long after it occurred. So the results of such research need to be explicit about the nature and scope of the procedures used and any comparisons with other research findings must explicitly consider their selection methods (Maney and Oliver, 2001).

15.6.3 SOCIAL CONTEXT

Journalism often is described as the first draft of history, and while official trial reports often may be regarded to be seen as a more definitive record, neither is a wholly reliable source. Journalistic accounts can prejudge and stereotype an event and judicial reports may depict them in legally authoritative but restricted and misleading ways. Hagan et al. (2002) show that the press and the judiciary gave differing accounts of a particular urban school shooting, but neither saw it as specifically urban. They fitted it into the same frame as deadly school shootings in rural and suburban settings, as well as expressing their accounts in individualistic terms. The real social context of the event was thereby obscured, inhibiting a broader theoretical understanding.

15.7 SUMMARY

Documentary research takes a variety of forms and used a wide range of sources. Unlike survey or questionnaire research, the data are not shaped by the researcher's questions. They are whatever has been committed to documentary form, for purposes that may have little to do with the researcher's objectives. This means there are problems of selection and interpretation, and of assessing authenticity, credibility, representativeness, and meaning. Documentary resarch is a valuable way of studying new topics and of adding new dimensions to existing ones. It may even uncover hitherto unexamined subjects. It can contribute triangulation to projects based on other means of data collection, and therefore has links with, for example, ethnography (Chapter 14) and visual methods (Chapter 23).

DISCUSSION QUESTIONS

1   Present the pros and cons of the view that the study of a topic by means of newspaper reports tells you more about the opinions of the editor or proprietor than about the topic itself.

2   'There are three kinds of lies; lies, damned lies and statistics.' How would you respond to this remark (supposedly by Mark Twain)?

3   Diaries, personal letters, autobiographies and memoires have been used as data for sociological research. What are the problems of evaluating and interpreting such materials?

PROJECT

A photo that appeared in more than one British newspaper showed a group of people in an anteroom in Number 10 Downing Street, waiting for the Prime Minister to summon them for the crucial meeting at which the decision was taken to invade Iraq in 2002. Most of the people in this photograph are members of the British Cabinet. Two of them – a man and a woman – are not; they are high ranking civil servants. The man is in close conversation with the government ministers: the woman is outside the circle, looking at their backs.

This photo was accompanied by no reference to the gender of those depicted, nor to the placing of persons in relation to one another, but to a student of social interaction it would appear that a group of powerful men – cabinet ministers – conversing informally are excluding one of the two people of a lower status and including the other. The first is a woman, the second is a man.

The project is either:

1 To explore ways in which possible evidence of patriarchy is displayed pictorially in documents (in relation to a particular area of life such as politics or in a particular medium such as advertisements) and how such visual evidence is referred to in accompanying text.

Or

2 To investigate this kind of data in a particular organisation. Professional bodies might well be fruitful cases, because professional journals, newsletters and even the media print the pass lists, including prize winners, of professional qualifying exams. Their names usually enable one to determine gender and by following up members over time in membership records etc, one could determine the relative importance of ability and gender. Reports and photos of conferences and similar occasions can provide further evidence.

RESOURCES

Becker (1974) 'Photography and Sociology' is a very stimulating article, which examines the relationship between sociology and social documentary photography.

Krippendorf (2004) *Content Analysis* is a clear introduction to the principles and techniques of content analysis, including the use of computer aids.

Platt (1981) *Evidence and Proof in Documentary Research* is a pioneering article that highlights the problems of handling documentary evidence.

Plummer (1983) *Documents of Life: An Introduction to the Problems and Literature of a Humanistic Method* is a readable introduction to the importance of personal documents such as letters, diaries and life histories in social research.

Scott (2006) *Documentary Research* is a comprehensive, four-volume collection of articles on documentary research and Scott (1990) *A Matter of Record* is an essential book for anyone interested in doing documentary research. It provides a particularly valuable introduction to the problems of evaluating and interpreting documentary materials.

Sociology Special Issue: Auto/biography in Sociology (1993, 27(1)) provides valuable illustration of the potential of such work.

16 The Internet and Research Methods

Christine Hine

KEY POINTS

● The Internet is a useful tool for social researchers, but care must be taken to avoid inadvertent sample bias.

● Surveys, interviews, ethnography and documentary analysis can all be carried out online. Each requires some adaptations to make sure that data collection and analysis are as effective as possible.

● Social researchers need to pay particular attention to the development of trusting research relationships online. Researcher web sites and publication of research results online can help.

● Existing ethical research practices apply to online data collection, although there are some distinctive issues relating to the negotiation of informed consent.

16.1 INTRODUCTION

The **Internet** offers rich possibilities for collecting data and contacting research participants. As more and more people have started to use the Internet in their daily lives, it has come to seem natural that social researchers will use the Internet to carry out their research projects. This chapter builds on the previous chapters about interviews, **focus groups, ethnography** and documentary analysis, asking how these methods change when carried out via the Internet.

The Internet has some major advantages for social research, including the possibility of accessing geographically dispersed groups of respondents and locating samples to address rare topics. The searchable nature of the Internet, and the 'born digital' qualities of online interviews are big attractions for social research. Web sites and discussion forums are stimulating sources of data on an array of social phenomena. Nonetheless, there is need for caution in relation to the bias that using Internet data can introduce and the ethics of online research, and researchers will need to develop new skills in building online rapport if useful qualitative data is to be collected. It is sometimes assumed that Internet research will be quick and easy, and this often turns out not to be the case. This chapter therefore focuses on some specific advice that should help researchers to capitalise on the potential of the Internet for collecting data while being aware of the pitfalls.

16.2 THE INTERNET SAMPLE

The first issue to consider about social research on the Internet is whom, exactly, can we contact in this way. As Chapter 9 indicated, it is very important for social researchers to exclude inadvertent biases from the samples that they use. If we are using the medium of the Internet to contact research participants we need to think very carefully about who might be excluded, and whether this is a significant issue for the particular research question that we want to ask.

The Internet is a network of networks of computers that are able to communicate with one another. All the computers connected to the Internet share an agreed way of packaging the information they send to each other, and all have unique addresses that enable information to be directed across the network of networks from one to another. The information that is sent might be an email, an instant message or a web page, or it might be a contribution to a discussion forum or a request to buy a product from an online shop. The Internet encompasses all of these diverse forms of communication and many more besides, all sharing the same basic agreement about how to package and send information. To use the Internet you need to have an appropriate computer that understands this protocol, to be connected to a communication network, for example, by broadband or phone, and to have the necessary skills to use whatever form of communication you choose to carry out.

The Internet was developed in the 1970s from earlier means of connecting computers together, most famously the ARPANET developed by the US Department of Defense. The early network was limited in access to the military and to researchers doing related work in universities. Gradually in the 1970s and 1980s access to this way of communicating between computers spread to universities more widely and to some commercial organisations, and international connections became common. Still, however, the Internet of the 1980s was very much a specialist phenomenon, mostly used by university researchers and by the computing industry. In the late 1980s Internet Service Providers were set up to sell access to the Internet to the public and in the 1990s, the Internet became a steadily more widespread social phenomenon.

The Internet also gradually became easier for non-specialists to use and its potential uses multiplied. While email was available very early on, the **World Wide Web** was not developed until 1991 and the kind of graphical web browser widely used today only became available in the mid-1990s. In the 2000s, new ways of communicating became popular, as the World Wide Web became host to social networking sites such as MySpace, Internet diaries known as **blogs** became a popular outlet for personal reflections, and venues for people to share their own multimedia content such as YouTube became popular. The Internet also developed into a mainstream means for buying and selling, with auction sites hosting transactions between individuals such as eBay becoming popular in addition to the many major online retailers.

The Internet has therefore developed from a very specialised medium for a particular set of researchers into a widespread service used across society. It is still, however, not uniformly accessible to everyone and this does have an impact on its usefulness in social research. Various surveys have attempted to work out who is using the Internet and how it impacts upon their lives. In the

UK, the Oxford Internet Survey (http://tinyurl.com/yotlm2) tracks developments in the use of the Internet. In the USA, the Pew Internet and American Life project (http://www.pewinternet.org) explores various aspects of the changing demographics and implications of Internet use. On a global basis the International Telecommunication Union has developed a Digital Opportunity Index (http://tinyurl.com/yrjzek), which tracks differences between countries according to their access to telecommunications, infrastructure availability and the actual use of the Internet. According to these surveys, both national and international, it is clear that access to and use of the Internet are biased in some ways that are very significant for social researchers.

Internationally speaking, there is a significant **digital divide** which approximately reproduces the division between richer and poorer countries. According to the Digital Opportunity Index for 2005, no country had complete access to the Internet for everyone, represented by a DOI of 1 (International Telecommunications Union, 2006). The top 25 countries, including the UK and the USA, scored above 0.6, but no country in Africa scored more than 0.5 and most scored less than 0.3. Across nations, therefore, the chance that a randomly chosen individual will be an Internet user varies markedly. The Internet can provide a social researcher with a potentially global sampling frame, but the sample will be biased towards particular countries unless steps are taken to stratify it.

On a national basis, too, access to the Internet is unevenly socially distributed. In the UK the 2005 Oxford Internet Survey (Dutton et al., 2005) found that while 61% of the population said that they had access to the Internet at home, Internet access was more likely among men, younger people, those who left education later, and those from higher income brackets. A piece of social research which used an Internet-based sample in the UK might therefore risk under-representing women, older people, those with less formal education and the less economically privileged. It would be for the researcher to decide whether this bias mattered for a particular research question, or whether the sample could be stratified in some way to address the bias.

According to Pew Internet and American Life Project, in the USA, there is also an uneven social distribution of Internet access, along broadly similar lines. In 2006, their survey found that 70% of adults said they had Internet access. In addition to age, educational experience and income, ethnicity also had a significant impact on the likelihood of being an Internet user. Although white non-Hispanics had access levels of 71%, only 60% of black non-Hispanics and 56% of Hispanics reported being Internet users (Fox and Livingston, 2007). Inequalities of Internet access for different ethnic groups were also found in the UK, although the pattern varied: a 2006 report (OFCOM, 2006) found that home access to the Internet was higher for minority ethnic groups than for the population as a whole.

The Internet is, therefore, in many ways a mainstream technology that is widely available across society. For a social researcher the Internet can be used to access a broad sample of people across the world. There are, however, considerable doubts about the extent to which an Internet sample can be taken as representative of the population as a whole. In addition to the demographic factors affecting access described above, it is important to remember that the way that different social groups use the Internet will vary, and that one person's idea of using the Internet will be very different to another's. These different ways of using the Internet may mean that even among Internet users some will be more pre-disposed to take part in your study than others. Linguistic issues are also important: if you carry out your research in English alone you will inevitably be limiting your sample. Research over the Internet therefore means often relying on a self-selecting sample that may be biased in a variety of ways that can be hard to identify. This having been said, the Internet is still a very powerful way for social researchers to reach people. The next sections of this chapter look at ways in which it can be used, examining surveys first before moving on to interviews and focus groups, observational studies and documentary analysis.

16.3 QUESTIONNAIRES AND SURVEYS ONLINE

One of the most popular ways to use the Internet to collect social research data has been the online survey. There are some clear advantages to using the Internet in this way:

- Saving on postal costs. While sending out a postal questionnaire and chasing up responses can be expensive, an Internet questionnaire can be sent out to many people for no additional cost.

- Ability to reach a widely geographically dispersed target population. By contrast, a postal questionnaire, or one handed out personally by the researcher, is often limited geographically.

- Ability to target a particular population. If the right mailing list or discussion forum is used to send out the questionnaire, the survey can be targeted at people with a very specific set of characteristics or interests.

- Automatic generation of computer-readable output. It can be possible to upload results automatically into formats readable by statistical packages, thus reducing the time and potential errors involved in inputting data from paper questionnaires.

- Enhanced design. Depending on the format of the questionnaire, it may be possible to route people to particular questions depending on previous answers, or to provide automatic checks and warnings if answers are incomplete or invalid (for example, impossible dates).

There are, however, some disadvantages which need to be weighed against these positive aspects of Internet surveys:

- Sample bias. Unless it is sent to named individuals by personal email address it is very hard to assess how many people have seen an Internet survey, and how non-response might be patterned.

- Self-completion. Internet surveys are generally completed by the respondent without help from the researcher: this means that they may have little motivation to complete the questionnaire, and if they have problems they may give up.

- Design skills. Although a simple questionnaire can easily be designed for sending out by email, more complex designs will need technical skills in order to get the most from the possibilities.

Researchers need to weigh how far each of these factors apply to their particular research situation. Some find that low response rates or biased samples undermine the usefulness of the online survey. Others have found it a powerful approach: Coomber (1997), for example, found the Internet a very useful way to conduct a survey with dealers in illicit drugs.

Having decided that for a particular research question the advantages of an Internet survey outweigh the disadvantages, there are still a number of decisions to be made about the way in which the questionnaire should be delivered. Key issues include the identification of the target sample, the mode of delivery of the questionnaire, and the means of announcing the questionnaire in order to maximise response.

It would be possible to generate responses to an online survey simply by emailing details out to as many mailing lists and discussion forums as you can think of, and waiting for people to react. This is a rather difficult strategy to justify in terms of sampling, however: you have no idea who might have seen the questionnaire, and little means of assessing how representative the resulting sample is. You also risk upsetting people by appearing to send them irrelevant spam. It is usually better, both in terms of knowing your potential sample and in terms of responsible Internet practice, to have a more specific sample who are likely to find your survey relevant to them. This might involve spotting a particular mailing list that deals with a topic close to your interests, or targeting a club or organisation that keeps a list of members' email addresses. Alternatively, you may be able to persuade a relevant web site to host a link to a survey. In each case, you will need to seek permission from relevant list owners or web site owners. This could also be an advantage, in that their endorsement could improve the credibility of your survey to potential respondents.

The form of a survey can vary and this will have implications for the features that you can include and the extent to which it will be accessible to different populations. A simple survey can be included in the body of an email message.

Respondents send their answers by replying to the email and editing in their own responses to the questions. Since almost all Internet users are familiar with responding to an email, this is the simplest means of implementing an online questionnaire, but it loses out on many of the potential benefits since it is harder to process automatically and will not contain automatic checking or routing. A survey sent as an **email attachment,** for example, as a Word file, can be slightly more sophisticated and elegantly presented. Unfortunately security concerns or lack of relevant skills mean that many people will not open an email attachment. It may also not be appropriate to ask people to return survey responses as an attachment: according to the Oxford Internet Survey in 2005, 92% of their Internet-using sample used email, but only 66% sent email attachments (Dutton et al., 2005).

A survey hosted on a web site can contain many automated checking and routing features and can also be elegantly presented and supplemented by links to extra information. People also sometimes feel more secure about confidentiality if they can submit responses via a web site rather than by email. The main problems for the researcher include finding both a suitable web site to host the survey and someone with the necessary skills to build it, and also attracting people to visit the site and complete the survey. A publicity campaign using emails containing links to the survey, or a link from a popular web site can be used to attract respondents. However, response rates tend to be quite low for all forms of Internet survey. Short questionnaires which people can identify as clearly relevant to their interests are likely to be most successful. Joinson (2005) has also carried out some useful research on factors which encourage people to complete surveys online and encourage greater self-disclosure in responses to surveys. He found, for example, that it was useful for the researcher to include some information about themselves and to tailor the invitation to specific potential respondents. It is important, therefore, to think not just about the design of the survey itself, but also how to design the initial approach to potential respondents.

16.4 ONLINE INTERVIEWING AND FOCUS GROUPS

One of the key uses of the Internet is for communicating. It is therefore quite natural that social researchers have begun to use the Internet to communicate with research subjects, and that in addition to quantitative surveys online approaches to qualitative research have been tried. In particular, it has become common to talk about 'online interviews', usually meaning contact with research subjects via email or **instant messaging.** Researchers have had mixed experiences of conducting interviews in this way. The aim of qualitative interviewing (as described in Chapter 13) tends to be to gain a rich perspective on an aspect of someone's life, aiming for as spontaneous and unstilted an interaction as possible. By contrast, some online interactions can seem too terse, stilted or shallow. Nonetheless, there is a growing body of researchers who have found that online interviewing or focus groups can be an effective means to collect qualitative data. Careful planning and attention to rapport building may be useful to elicit the kind of accounts that qualitative researchers hope for. It is also possible that online interviews are more effective for some populations than others.

The first issue to consider when contemplating online interviews is whether this is likely to be a comfortable medium for your target population to use. If the people that you wish to interview are not regular email or instant messaging users, or do not have easy access to networked computers, it would be best to avoid online interviewing. The goal is to find a medium which enable people to communicate in as easy a way as possible, so that they can concentrate on the topic being discussed. Different groups will find different ways of communicating more straightforward: an older target population may prefer email, while younger interviewees may prefer instant messaging. For online focus groups you again need to find a medium that your participants will be happy to use, whether that be a chat room or a more specialist piece of software such as Mann and Stewart (2000) describe. It is possible to conduct an online focus group asynchronously in a discussion forum, or in real time in a graphical environment, if that should suit participants (Stewart and Williams, 2005).

Online interviews and focus groups have the advantage that people can take part from home, and thus may be able to fit in an interview even though they would not travel to a face-to-face meeting. Madge and O'Connor (2002) were able to use online methods to interview new and expectant mothers. Another potential advantage can be that people may feel more comfortable discussing sensitive subjects online: Illingworth (2001) found that online interviews were successful with people experiencing fertility problems. Where people are comfortable with the idea of communicating online, it can be possible to use email to collect rich qualitative data, as Orgad (2005) found in her research with people who had experienced breast cancer. People being interviewed can feel that the online interaction puts them more in charge than they would be face-to-face, allowing them to think carefully and reflect on their answers, and also to respond only when they feel able to cope with the interaction. Data that are collected online can, therefore, be very useful to the qualitative researcher and can sometimes provide insights that face-to-face methods do not. Researchers with experience of transcribing taped interviews will also be very pleased to note that online interviews do not need to be transcribed.

CHECKLIST

- Select a comfortable medium for research participants. Try not to impose your own preferences upon interviewees.

- Focus on building a relationship. You should aim to put people at their ease, by telling them something about the research and giving them enough information about you for them to feel comfortable opening up to you. Especially if your research topic is sensitive, offer them a way of checking that you are who you say you are, such as an official university email address and a web page.

- Try to avoid long lists of questions. Sending too many questions at once tends to encourage people to give very short answers. Instead, encourage people to tell you about their experiences and build an ongoing interaction with them in which you ask further questions and seek clarification.

- Give explicit acknowledgement and encouragement when you receive answers. Without this, people may feel their responses are not useful, and lose interest. You need to make a point of encouraging people to replace the nodding and signs of interest you would display in a face-to-face interview.

- Online interviews are not necessarily quick. Expect interviews to take some time, as people may choose to reflect on their answers or may not prioritise your research over their other activities. Instant messaging is often combined with other activities, and email interviews can extend over long periods of time. Encourage response by polite reminders and by offering different phrasings of questions.

16.5 FIELDWORK IN ONLINE SETTINGS

Online interviews involve an interaction designed specifically for the researcher to explore a particular topic. There is, however, a large quantity of naturally occurring data on the Internet that allows a researcher to observe what people do under less controlled circumstances. There have been numerous studies that involve observation of pre-existing online discussion groups. Sometimes these groups can be sustained and cohesive, and develop their own distinctive cultures, to the extent that they have been described as online communities (Baym, 1995; 2000). It has become possible to think of the Internet as a field site for ethnographic research (Hine, 2000), in which the researcher uses some familiar techniques from more conventional ethnography to explore the culture in the online setting.

The field site for an online ethnographer might be a discussion forum used by the target group, a **chat room** or a **social networking site**, or a role-playing game. Finding an appropriate field site can be a matter of luck: an online search looking for a particular topic of interest might lead you to stumble across an interesting group of people. If you find a place where people are discussing topics relevant to your research interest, ethnography can be a useful way to explore the practices and beliefs that characterise this group of people. You may be interested in studying online culture for its own sake, or because it gives you a window on the way that people talk about a particular topic that interests you. Alternatively, you may already be carrying out a piece of research using more conventional methods, and find that people tell you about a particular online site that they use. Offline research can sometimes lead you online and offer different field sites to explore in combination. Constable (2003), for example, studied the phenomenon of 'mail-order brides' through a combination of face-to-face interviews with the people involved and observation of mailing lists and web sites that they used. Miller and Slater (2000) studied the way that people in Trinidad interpreted the Internet, looking at both offline and online field sites.

As described in Chapter 14, ethnographic research involves a combination of techniques. When carried out online, ethnography usually includes observation through reading messages or being present in interactions, together with online interviews. Sometimes face-to-face interviews may be carried out, particularly when participants themselves have face-to-face meetings in the normal course of events. Online ethnography can also involve more quantitative studies. Because data are often available in large quantities, such as in the archives of messages that are available for many discussion forums, it can be possible for the researcher to look back in time as well as observing interactions in real time. This can often best be done by developing forms of content analysis to make observations on a systematic basis. Baym (2000) carried out her study of an online soap opera discussion group by a combination of observation, participation, online interviews and surveys and a systematic textual analysis of message content. Online ethnography has to adapt itself to the particular circumstances that it finds: Williams (2007) describes some interesting challenges a graphical game world poses for an ethnographer, who has to find appropriate ways to appear to and interact with other participants.

16.6 ANALYSIS OF ONLINE DOCUMENTS

In addition to its status as a place where diverse cultures are played out, the Internet can also be seen more prosaically as a source of documents. A number of researchers have carried out studies that take advantage of this aspect of the Internet. A web search on your research topic can quickly yield a large sample of material that can be used to explore key concepts and constructs related to the topic. Many of the issues which Chapter 15 discusses also apply to online documents, in particular the questions of evaluation and interpretation. Online documents can often be less than explicit about who created them, when and how, and this can lead to some particular problems in assessing their authenticity, credibility, representativeness and meaning. Nonetheless, the sheer volume of online documents that are available (one recent estimate suggested there were 11.5 billion publicly available web pages online in 2005 (Gulli and Signorini, 2005)) means that the web is a rich source of documents to allow exploration of almost any topic of interest to social researchers.

The first concern when designing a study using the Internet as a source of documents is to define the sample. It may be appropriate to analyse a set of documents identified through interviews or in an observational study. Alternatively, a researcher might start from scratch and try to find documents relating to a particular topic by using a **search engine** (such as Google or

Yahoo). It is important not to think of this as a random sample of documents. Search engines have ways of ranking web pages in order to maximise the chance of giving you the result you were looking for. In particular, Google tends to place well-linked, popular sites high on its lists of results. This might be what you want in your sample, but it is important to realise that the basis for selecting the sample that a search engine offers you is outside your control. In your searches you will need to be as specific as possible about the kind of site that you are interested in analysing, in order to avoid including too many irrelevant sites and to enable you to stratify your sample appropriately, where relevant.

Once you have a sample of web pages to explore, it is necessary to decide exactly what it is that you want to find out, and on what basis. The techniques of documentary analysis as described in Chapter 15, and **semiotic** and **content analysis** as described in Chapter 23 can all be applied to web pages. There are, however, some additional possibilities which take advantage of the special features of the web. Many web pages contain dynamic or interactive features and it can be important to take account of these in analysis. In addition, the way that web pages are linked together offers a different way of analysing the web as an inter-linked network rather than simply as isolated pages (Thelwall, 2004). Schneider and Foot (2004) describe some different ways in which the web can become an object of social research. In much of their own work they have collected large corpora of web sites relating to a particular issue of interest (they call these collections web spheres), and have systematically analysed the features that they contain. They have, for example, studied the use of web sites in political campaigning in the USA (Foot and Schneider, 2006). Online data, including the inter-linking patterns of web sites, have also been used to explore social networks (Garton et al., 1997). People leave traces of their interactions and connections in the ways that they use the Internet, and social researchers have been able to exploit those traces in order to study the patterns of everyday social life in an unobtrusive way.

16.7 MAKING RESEARCH OUTPUTS AVAILABLE

So far the discussion has focused on ways of acquiring data from the Internet. There are, however, many possibilities for communicating in the opposite direction. The Internet offers rich opportunities for making the outputs of research available to the participants and other interested parties. The forms in which research can be reported on the Internet vary widely. Using a conventional model of the research process, a researcher might make a final report available on the Internet. This can be a very useful way of giving access to research reports to people who might otherwise not be able to get hold of a restricted circulation publication, or might not have easy access to a university library or expensive journal. Where there is a final report in the form of a dissertation, article or presentation it can be very simple to make it available on a web page, and then publicise it to a known list of users who might be interested in reading it, in addition to anyone who might happen upon it through a search engine.

Increasingly, publicly funded researchers are being expected to make their research accessible in this open way. Many institutions are developing online repositories for researchers to make their publications available free of charge, and many funding bodies are beginning to recommend or require that researchers who accept their money also undertake to make the products of their research freely available on the Internet. There are as yet no large centralised repositories for social science research, of the kind that exists for physics, mathematics, computer science and quantitative biology in the form of arXiv (http://arXiv.org). Many individuals do, however, lodge their research reports online on individual web pages or institutional repositories, and their reports can often be found using standard search engines.

Traditionally social researchers have been somewhat cautious about telling participants too much about the research in advance, often for fear that we might shape their answers and bias outcomes if we tell them too much about what we expect to hear. Alternative approaches that view research participants as potential partners in the research project are, however, increasingly accepted (see Chapter 6). The **feminist** tradition, in particular, has pioneered participatory approaches that, instead of viewing research participants as mere sources of data, see them as partners. Similarly, various forms of **action research** seek to transform people who would otherwise be research subjects or consumers of final research reports into more involved participants. In these situations the Internet offers considerable possibilities for giving people access to the research at various stages. In particular, research **blogs** have become a means that researchers employ to open up the research process to participants and to other researchers and also as something that they can reflect upon themselves (Mortensen and Walker, 2002). Just like a personal diary, a blog can become a tool for reflection.

A blog can help to make the process of research more transparent, revealing the twists and turns that a project takes as the researcher tries to make sense of emerging data. It can also help to include research participants and users in the process of enquiry. This opening up of the research process does not have to come to a stop, however, with the final report. Hypertext and **multimedia** have been used by a number of researchers to make their research outputs available for re-interpretation by readers (Dicks et al., 2005). Foot and Schneider (2006), for example, have created a parallel web version of their book on political campaigning via the Internet. This web site allows readers to look at the raw data on which the book is based, pursuing their own thoughts and making their own judgements. Such novel forms of publication do take a considerable effort to produce and may raise issues in terms of copyright. However, they are an interesting example of the way in which the Internet and other digital media are encouraging researchers to reflect on their research processes and outcomes and explore different ways of doing things.

There are some points for caution when making research outputs available online. The first issue, as hinted above is, that it takes considerable time and effort to do well. A hypertext or multimedia dissertation needs to be very carefully prepared, using appropriate skills, and may need to be accompanied by a more conventional written text in order to satisfy readers' expectations or institutional requirements. To justify this effort it is useful to have a clear idea of the potential audience and their needs, rather than producing a novel form of research output simply because it is possible.

There are also some reasons to be cautious about putting every fragment of data and passing thought about research into an accessible online format. Some forms of data might allow research participants to recognise themselves or be recognised by others, and it may therefore be better not to make all data openly accessible. Instead, more restricted forms of distribution may be appropriate. Online data could also be used in unforeseen ways, and the less 'polished' the form of research report that is made available, the more open it may be to what the researcher could see as misinterpretation. There are therefore some reasons to be cautious about seizing the opportunity for complete openness that the Internet seems to offer.

16.8 THE ETHICS OF ONLINE RESEARCH

In addition to the argument for restraint in reporting research online there has also been considerable discussion of the need for a cautious approach to collecting data online. While much of this chapter has been about what you *can* do as a researcher online, it is therefore important to finish on a note of caution about some things that you *should not* do. The very accessibility of data on the Internet relating to every social phenomenon and social problem imaginable has led some commentators to fear that researchers could be tempted to use it as a research playground, scooping up interesting data without due regard for the concerns of the people involved. There has been a particular debate around the circumstances in which informed consent applies to the use of data collected via the Internet.

The emerging position on the ethics of using Internet research data is not clear-cut. As in any form of research, those using Internet data are expected to be sensitive to the possible concerns of research participants and develop appropriate responses to each situation. The Association of Internet Researchers (Ess and AoIR Ethics Working Committee, 2002) has published a code of practice for research using the Internet, which consists of questions for the researcher to ask themselves rather than specific guidance on forms of data that can and cannot be used. The questions are, however, based on the premise that the ethics of Internet research are very like the ethics of any other research approach. Internet researchers are expected to adopt a 'bottom line' position that foreseeable harm to research participants should be prevented and that deceit of research participants is rarely justifiable.

There are circumstances where informed consent may not be appropriate. If a researcher can be confident that no foreseeable harm could accrue to people from use of publicly available data, such as a web site or a contribution to a discussion forum, that the topic is not particularly sensitive and that the kind of research they are doing is not particularly intrusive or troubling, were the person to recognise themselves in a research report, then it might be justifiable to go ahead and collect data without seeking informed consent. In many cases, however, approaching someone for their consent to use data is more appropriate, and it can actually be a useful part of the research process and lead to interesting insights that help in interpreting the data.

If the research focuses on a chat room it may be simply impractical to gain informed consent from everyone involved, since to do so would interrupt the flow of chat and as people join and leave the chat it would be unclear exactly who had consented to what. In such circumstances Hudson and Bruckman (2004) suggest that it may be necessary to adapt the research to involve a specially set-up chat room that is obviously a research site to all participants. Alternatively, it may be appropriate to apply for a waiver of informed consent requirements on the basis that the research poses no threat to participants. Most researchers will need to apply for ethical approval of their research to an institutional committee or funding body: it will be necessary to develop a careful statement about the reasons why an informed consent waiver is appropriate for a particular case.

Where informed consent is needed, the practicalities again vary. Often if interviewees are being contacted by email, it will be appropriate to send them an initial statement explaining the research process and the confidentiality of the data, informing them of any potential risks of participating and giving appropriate contact details for the researcher. Interviewees may be asked to 'opt in' to the research by stating that they have read and accept this statement. Rarely is it felt that interviewees need to print out and return a signed copy of a consent form, although this may be appropriate if the research topic is particularly sensitive or if minors are involved. Individual consent of this kind may be impractical for studies of chat rooms, and it may be necessary to rely on the agreement of chatroom moderators and an announcement when people join the chat room. Similarly, when a discussion forum is being observed, it may be necessary to gain the consent of the forum owners and post announcements periodically about the ongoing research to the forum itself. In addition, a researcher would be expected to make their identity clear in any interactions they might have with individuals in the forum.

The ethics of using Internet data are thus closely related to the position social researchers are expected to adopt in relation to any form of data: wanting to know, and being able to get hold of data are not in themselves enough reason to go ahead. There are, however, some specific qualities of Internet data that pose special problems. One particular concern relates to the searchability of Internet data. As soon as a direct quote is used in a research report it becomes potentially possible to use a search engine to find the source of that quote. It can therefore be very difficult to give the usual assurances of confidentiality to research participants. Identifying details can be changed, but this becomes pointless if identities can be confirmed by entering a phrase from a fragment of data into a search engine. It is therefore important to be very clear about what informants can be promised in the way of confidentiality, and to be cautious about the use of direct quotations in research reports.

16.9 SUMMARY

Although many forms of research can be conducted online, the Internet brings some considerable challenges for social researchers. It provides many different ways of accessing research subjects and observing social phenomena, but it needs to be used with caution in order to avoid introducing inadvertent biases. Design of online questionnaires, conduct of online interviews and focus groups, observation of online field sites and analysis of web sites all require the researcher to develop new skills in order to make the most of their potential. The technical possibilities that the Internet offers can sometimes lead us to imagine research projects that on ethical grounds we should not carry out. While the novelty of the Internet has stimulated the imagination of researchers, it is important to think carefully about the bottom line: what are we trying to achieve with the research, and how far does use of the Internet take us towards that goal? As the Internet becomes a mainstream medium it will also become a more routinely used tool for social researchers. This routine use should not be at the expense of careful consideration of the benefits and drawbacks that it brings.

DISCUSSION QUESTIONS

1 Is the Internet ever likely to reach saturation point, or will the digital divide persist with some people more likely to have access than others? Why are some people more likely to be online than others?

2 Choose a web site that you visit frequently. What aspects of this web site might a social researcher be interested in analysing? How could you build a sample of web sites to explore these aspects more systematically?

3 How much information about their research should social researchers make available on the Internet?

4   For the following possible research projects, would you consider informed consent necessary? If it is necessary, how would you go about negotiating informed consent? Are there any projects you would advise against carrying out?

(a)   A comparative study of blogs produced by girls discussing their experiences of eating disorders.

(b)   An interview-based study with people using the Internet to discuss their experiences of cancer.

(c)   Observation of a discussion forum used by fans of a popular band. The observation will include some participation, and one-to-one interviews via instant messaging.

PROJECT

Imagine that you have been commissioned to use the Internet to study attitudes to alternative medicine among university students. You can decide whether the study will be a qualitative piece of research using interviews, or a quantitative survey using a questionnaire. Develop a detailed design for the research project, addressing the following issues:

- How will you identify a suitable sample of students?
- What kinds of bias might this sample involve, and how might this affect the generalisability of results?
- How will you identify students and recruit them for interviews or questionnaires? Is there anyone whose permission you should ask (note: it may be important to clear use of institutional mailing lists with someone in authority first)?
- Would you use email interviews or would you conduct interviews in real time using instant messaging? Would you send surveys in the body of an email or as an attachment, or would you place the survey on a web site?
- How will you frame your initial contact with potential research subjects? What would your approach be to informed consent? How, practically speaking, would you expect people to signal their consent?
- What response rates might you expect? What means could you use to encourage response?

RESOURCES

Thurlow, Lengel and Tomic (2004) *Computer Mediated Communication* provides a good introductory text to get you started on thinking about the Internet as a social phenomenon.

Mann and Stewart (2000) *Internet Communication and Qualitative Research* offers a practical and comprehensive guide to the use of various social research techniques online. The Internet has developed fast, but many issues covered by Mann and Stewart remain relevant, as do those covered in a wide-ranging collection by Jones (1999) in *Doing Internet Research*. Mann and Stewart focus on social research using the Internet, while the collection by Jones focuses more explicitly on researchers who want to understand the social phenomenon of the Internet for its own sake.

A more recent collection, *Virtual Methods* by Hine (2005), covers both of these aspects of the Internet in social research, exploring the research sites that the Internet offers and the prospects for developing research relationships online.

Another recent collection, *Online Social Research Methods* by Johns et al. (2004) places particular emphasis on research ethics online.

Dillman (2006) *Mail and Internet Surveys* provides a comprehensive introduction to online surveys, while Best and Krueger (2004) in *Internet Data Collection* offer more recent advice on sampling and instrument design for online data collection.

A very useful web site offering an online tutorial for those contemplating an online study involving interviews or questionnaires is *Exploring Online Research Methods* at http://www.geog.le.ac.uk/ORM/

PART III
Back Home

Data collection is only half the story in a research project; there is also the analysis of the data. This Part offers an overview of the most common ways to analyse sociological data. For quantitative data, there is guidance on how to manage survey data, how to analyse data using statistical computer programs, and how to analyse data that has previously been collected by others. For qualitative data, there is a guide to the computer programs that can be used to store and code interview transcripts, fieldnotes and multimedia data, and introductions to narrative analysis, conversation analysis and discourse analysis.

17 Coding and Managing Data

Jane Fielding

17.1 INTRODUCTION

After you have collected your research data, you will need to start the process of making sense of the material, whether it is a pile of completed questionnaires, a bulging notebook or a stack of interview tapes. This chapter sets out to help you explore and break down your raw data into either variables, if it is quantitative data, or manageable segments, if it qualitative data, and apply labels or codes for further analysis. The next step involves organising the information into a form that will facilitate your understanding of its meaning, using whatever modern technology is appropriate.

First, we will review the paths you could have taken to arrive at this point.

1   You designed a questionnaire, which may have been self-completion or interview-aided or even administered over the telephone (see Chapter 10). Hopefully, you gave some thought to how your respondents might answer your questions and you may have pre-coded the questionnaire so that they have already ticked appropriate boxes. If that is the case, then your next task, coding your questionnaire, is almost complete. However, you may have only just picked up this book, hoping to find a way out of a sea of completed questionnaires which have not been coded in any way. Or maybe you have something in between these two scenarios. In any case, if you have collected more than 20 questionnaires and have asked more than five questions, you should be using a computer to help analyse the results.

2   You conducted an in-depth face-to-face interview and either recorded it on cassette tape or made notes (see Chapter 13).

3   You observed a social situation or setting and made covert or overt field-notes (see Chapter 14).

4   You collected administrative details from records (Chapter 15), possibly noting the information on a questionnaire.

5   You collected articles or newspaper cuttings about yoι discussed in Chapter 15).

6   You decided to perform a content analysis on visual mε

7   A combination of these methods.

17.2 WHY CODE THE DATA?

However you collected the data, whether the data is quantitative or qualitative, you will now be faced with a sorting task which by its very nature will impose a discipline on this stage of the research. As Silvey (1975: 16) says, 'Research ultimately must be based on comparisons, whether it be comparisons between different groups of cases, between the same cases at different points in time, or even between what is and what might have been.' In order to make comparisons, you will have to access your data and organise it into categories or instances of occurrence. This is called **coding** the data. You will find that even a quantitative survey has qualitative elements and a qualitative transcript has quantitative aspects. For instance, many questions in a pre-coded survey will resort to a catch-all 'other, please specify' category as a safety net for those responses not anticipated in the original questionnaire design. Very often these responses are the most interesting, because they are exceptions to the rule, and will need particularly careful consideration and coding. A common type of question is one which explores why a particular response was chosen for a previous question. For instance, respondents may be asked to pick one answer from a list and then the next question may be 'Why did you choose that answer?' This 'open response' will also have to be coded. With qualitative data such as an interview transcript, preliminary analysis may benefit from quantitative methods such as frequency counts of occurrences of certain phrases or words or the codes that you have assigned to your data.

The discussion that follows begins by considering the quantitative coding of a questionnaire with pre-coded questions, followed by a discussion of the coding of **open questions**. Coding of open questions may be seen as qualitative coding and many of the considerations for this activity apply equally to the coding of interview transcripts. The difference lies not in the activity of coding but in the treatment of the resulting categories or codes.

The primary purpose of coding a quantitative survey is to 'translate' your respondents answers into numbers for subsequent statistical analysis. The result of coding a survey questionnaire is a data matrix stored in a separate computer file or within statistical software. In contrast, the coding process in qualitative research involves not only translation, but also analysis. Traditionally, the result of coding an interview transcript has been a stack of file cards each containing a segment of the text. The file cards are then sorted manually in various ways to generate and explore theoretical categories. However, computer programs for qualitative research are now widely available to aid the coding and sorting processes and the chapter concludes with a discussion of qualitative coding using an example of this software.

17.3 QUANTITATIVE CODING

In order to put the coding process into perspective, let us consider the following survey question: 'Do you agree or disagree that nuclear power should be used to generate electricity?' Respondents are also to be asked how old they are, whether they are male or female, and if they are married or single. In the following sections we will explore what is involved in coding these questions, but first I will describe the result of such a quantitative coding exercise and then go through each step of the process. The steps are:

1   Developing the coding frame for both pre-coded and open questions.

2   Creating the code book and coding instructions.

3   Coding the questionnaires.

4   Transferring the values to a computer.

5   Checking and cleaning the data.

17.3.1 THE RESULT: THE DATA MATRIX

A survey questionnaire is designed to gather information from a number of cases about various topics of investigation. By **cases**, we typically mean people, but a case could equally be a country or a school or even an observed incident. The information that we collect about each case, such as the sex and age of an individual, birth and death rates in a particular country, time of incident and number of people present, are the *variables*. The aim of coding is to assign a value to each piece of information. Each individual case will then consist of a complete set of values for each of the variables.

The result of such a coding exercise will be the production of a data file which should consist of numbers (or sometimes letters and spaces) such that the rows correspond to each case and the columns correspond to each variable (see Table 17.1).

Notice how the boxed part of Table 17.1 will form a block of numbers and/or letters once each variable has been assigned values. Even if the respondent has not replied to a particular question, or the question was 'not applicable' to the respondent, a value is still usually assigned to the variable for that

Table 17.1   A data matrix

		VARIABLES (COLUMNS)			
		QUESTION 1	QUESTION 2	QUESTION 3	QUESTION 4
	Case 1	Age of person 1	Sex of person 1	Marital status of person 1	Attitude to nuclear power of person 1
Cases (rows)	Case 2	Age of person 2	Sex of person 2	Marital status of person 2	Attitude to nuclear power of person 2
	Case 3	Age of person 3	Sex of person 3	Marital status of person 3	Attitude to nuclear power of person 3

case. This data matrix may be the 'spreadsheet view' you see of your coded data in your chosen statistical software package (e.g. SPSS) or it may be the contents of a data file.

17.3.2 DEVELOPING THE CODING FRAME

The coding frame for quantitative variables is a list of all possible responses to a question and their accompanying numeric codes, and in some cases, the column location of the codes. As you develop the coding frame, you need to understand the different kinds of variables that you may come across. If you ask people how much they earn in a year you could compare someone earning £10,000 with someone earning £20,000, since this variable is measured on an interval or continuous scale. The former earns half as much as the latter.

If you ask the question, 'How well do you manage on your income?', allowing the respondent to tick one of a selection of answers ranging from 'not at all well' to 'very well', you would have some basis for comparing someone who said they were managing 'very well' with someone who said they were managing 'not at all well'. However, you would not know the difference between 'doing very well' and 'doing well'. And one person who thinks that they manage 'very well' may not mean the same as another who gives the same answer. This variable is being measured on an ordinal scale since the responses are ordered.

If you ask what religion someone belongs to, you would receive a response that merely nominates a particular religion (or no religion). There is no intrinsic ordering between religions. Religion is being measured on a nominal scale.

There is a special kind of nominal variable, called a dummy variable, where the measurement is either the presence of an attribute or its absence. For instance, instead of asking people what religion they belong to, creating a nominal variable, you could ask people if they are Protestant. All those who said they are Protestant could be coded with the value 1 and all the rest with the value 0.

Similar dummy variables could be created if you asked people if they are Catholic, or if they are Jewish, and so on. The essential feature of a dummy variable is that it is a binary coded variable, having a value of either 0 or 1.

The sequence of levels of measurement is from nominal, the lowest, through ordinal, to interval. Each higher level possesses all the properties of the lower levels. With the increase in level of measurement comes greater flexibility and power in the statistical methods that can be employed in analysis.

In Table 17.1 there are four questions corresponding to four variables that illustrate these levels of measurement. Age is measured at the interval level, Attitude to nuclear power is measured at the ordinal level, as we shall see in the next section, and Sex and Marital Status are measured at the nominal level. The shaded part of Table 17.1 forms the data file.

We will start by coding the pre-coded questions. This should ideally be carried out before the questionnaire is administered so that the anticipated responses and their codes can be printed on the questionnaire.

It is usual to assign a unique ID or case number to each questionnaire, so that, if necessary, you can refer back to the original questionnaire once all the data is on the computer. This is very often the first variable.

If the questionnaire asked people how old they are, you could use their actual age as the codes, thus creating age as an interval variable. However, you may decide you do not need to retain all this information and are only interested in distinctions between age groupings. In other words, you could code age as an ordinal variable with codes corresponding to young, middle-aged and old, for instance. Another reason why you might code age as an ordinal variable is that people are often reticent about telling their age and feel happier if they just have to tick an age range on a questionnaire (see Chapter 10). So your coding frame for age as an ordinal variable may resemble Table 17.2.

Some people in your sample may have refused to answer this question and you need to decide what code to assign to these 'non-responses'. By convention, 9, 99 or 999 are reserved as **missing values** to be used to code non-responses, although minus codes are also useful for this purpose. The code 9 would be used for variables coded with only up to nine categories (codes 0–8) and 99 for those variables exceeding nine categories but less than one hundred. If you code age as a continuous variable, you should assign the value 99 to those people who did not respond. If there is a possibility of a respondent being 99 years of age, you could use the value 999 or –1 for the missing value, or you could use 98 for all those who are 98 or older. If you decide to code age into a smaller number of age groups, you could use the code 9 as the non-response code.

While on the subject of missing data, there are other possible reasons for data to be missing for a particular case. For instance, a respondent may not know the answer to a particular question and respond with a 'don't know'. Or a question or set of questions may be inapplicable. For instance, one would not ask for the salary of an unemployed person. Again there are conventions to follow. 'Don't know' responses are often coded with an 8 or a 98 and 'not applicable' responses

Table 17.2
Coding for the variable, Age

AGE	CODE
Under 20	1
21–35	2
36–50	3
51–65	4
66–80	5
Over 81	6

Table 17.3
Coding for the variable,
Marital Status

MARITAL STATUS	CODE
Married	1
Living as married	2
Separated/divorced	3
Widowed	4
Not married	5
No response	9

are often coded with a 0. If you have a large number of non-responses in your questionnaires, it is acceptable to leave blanks in the data file.

You might assign the value 1 for those who responded 'male' and a 2 for those who responded 'female' to a question about the respondent's sex. You could equally well have coded 'female' as 1 and 'male' as 2, but, whatever you decide, you must stick to it for the rest of your cases. You could have coded sex with letters, e.g. 'm' and 'f', but it is more usual to use numbers since the use of alphabetic coding sometimes imposes restriction on subsequent analysis.

A possible coding scheme for marital status is shown in Table 17.3. Marital status is a nominal variable. It is important that when the questionnaire is administered, it is made clear that this question refers to the current marital status of the respondent, and that 'married' means married at the moment, rather than 'ever been married'.

A common method of coding attitudinal questions is seen in Table 17.4. Coded in this way, this variable is an ordinal variable. Note that the coding could have been reversed with 'Strongly disagree' coded one and 'Strongly agree' coded five. For a fuller discussion of this kind of coding, see Chapter 7.

After coding, the data file for three respondents might look like Table 17.5. Here case 1 is a 23-year-old man who is living as married and agrees that nuclear power should be used to generate electricity. Once again, the data file is shaded.

Table 17.4   Coding for the variable,
Attitude to Nuclear Power

ATTITUDE TO NUCLEAR POWER	CODE
Strongly agree	1
Agree	2
Neither agree nor disagree	3
Disagree	4
Strongly disagree	5

Table 17.5   The coded data matrix

			VARIABLES			
		ID	QUESTION 1 (AGE)	QUESTION 2 (SEX)	QUESTION 3 (MARITAL STATUS)	QUESTION 4 (ATTITUDE TO NUCLEAR POWER)
	VARIABLE TYPE		CONTINUOUS	NOMINAL	NOMINAL	ORDINAL
Cases	Case 1	0 0 1	2 3	1	2	2
	Case 2	0 0 2	4 1	2	1	3
	Case 3	0 0 3	9 9	2	4	5

17.3.3 RULES FOR CODING

There are some basic rules for coding:

1   Codes must be mutually exclusive. Any particular response must fit into one, and only one category. Someone cannot be both married and single at the same time.

2   Codes must be exhaustive. You must have covered all possible coding options and allowed for them in your scheme.

3   Codes must be applied consistently throughout.

You should be consistent within your questionnaire for the values you use for similar responses in different questions. For instance, if you decide to code a 'yes' responses with the value 1 and a 'no' responses with the value 2, use those values throughout the questionnaire for other yes/no questions. Similarly, code all non-response categories with a –1, 9, 99, or 999, all 'don't know' responses with the values 8, 98, or 998 and all 'not applicable' categories with either a blank or a zero.

Table 17.6   The UK social capital measurement framework

DIMENSION	EXAMPLE OF INDICATOR
Social participation	• Number of cultural, leisure, social groups belonged to and frequency and intensity of involvement • Volunteering, frequency and intensity of involvement • Religious activity
Civic participation	• Perceptions of ability to influence events • How well informed about local/national affairs • Contact with public officials or political representatives • Involvement with local action groups • Propensity to vote
Social networks and social support	• Frequency of /friends/neighbours seeing/speaking to relatives • Extent of virtual networks and frequency of contact • Number of close friends/relatives who live nearby • Exchange of help • Perceived control and satisfaction with life
Reciprocity and trust	• Trust in other people who are like you • Trust in other people who are not like you • Confidence in institutions at different levels • Doing favours and vice versa • Perception of shared values
Views of the local area (See Table 17.7)	• Views on physical environment • Facilities in the area • Enjoyment of living in the area • Fear of crime

Source: Harper and Kelly (2003), Table 1.

17.3.4 COMPARABILITY

When selecting categories for closed questions it is a good idea to be consistent with the codes that have been used in other surveys. The *Standard Occupational Classification* (ONS 2000a; 2000b) is a manual that indexes occupations according to qualifications, training, skills and industry and is widely used by labour market researchers (http://www.tiny.cc/GIYkh). There is an online tool to help code occupational categories (see Computer Assisted Structured COding Tool (CASCOT), developed at the Warwick Institute for employment research) (http://www.tiny.cc/Qx6wy). Other sources of coding for standard variables such as household composition, education, age, gender, race and leisure are described by Stacey (1969) and Burgess (1986). Using the same codes as other surveys makes it easier to compare results.

In recognition of the value of asking the same questions in the same way, in 1995 the UK government introduced a scheme to harmonise question wording

Table 17.7   Problems in the neighbourhood (Views about the area)

Now I'd like to ask you a few questions about your immediate neighbourhood, by which I mean your street or block.	1 Very likely
	2 Quite likely
	3 Not very likely
1. Suppose you lost your (purse/wallet) containing your address details, and it was found in the street by someone living in this neighbourhood. How likely is it that it would be returned to you with nothing missing?	4 Or not at all likely
	5 Don't know
2. How much of a problem are people being drunk or rowdy in public places?	1 Very big problem
	2 Fairly big problem
3. How much of a problem is rubbish or litter lying around?	3 Not a very big problem
	4 Not a problem at all
4. How much of a problem are vandalism, graffiti and other deliberate damage to property or vehicles?	5 It happens but it's not a problem
5. How much of a problem are people using or dealing drugs?	6 (SPONTANEOUS) Don't know
6. How much of a problem is people being attacked or harassed because of their skin colour, ethnic origin or religion?	
7. How much of a problem are teenagers hanging around on the street?	
8. How much of a problem are troublesome neighbours?	
Coding note: Q1 coded 1–4 and Q2–Q8 coded 1–6 as indicated	

Source: The Social Capital Question Bank http://www.statistics.gov.uk/about_ns/social_capital/default.asp accessed 5th January 2007.

for large-scale government surveys (and subsequently coding of responses) in order to standardise the ways in which basic information is collected in government social surveys (see http://www.tiny.cc/96mCJ). One sociological concept whose measurement has been developed in such a standardised way for the use of UK government social surveys is that of **social capital** (see http://www.tiny.cc/lolsj). Social capital, defined by Putnam (1995) as 'networks, norms, and trust that enable participants to act together more effectively to pursue shared objectives', is considered to comprise many dimensions and it was this uncertainty of what was being measured that necessitated a consensus of the conceptualisation and standardisation of measurement. Table 17.6 outlines the different dimensions that make up social capital with examples of indicators that make up each dimension. The actual questions, wording and coding for one dimension, 'views of the local area', are shown in Table 17.7. (For further information about harmonised questions and question wording, see http://qb.soc.surrey.ac.uk/ and http://www.tiny.cc/gAnEH).

Figure 17.1   Sample questionnaire with pre-codes

Questionnaire

ID number:

Please can you provide the following details:

Q.1   Age:

Q.2   Sex:

Please tick one box:

Male ☐ 1   Female ☐ 2

Q.3   Marital status:

Married ☐ 1

Living as married ☐ 2

Separated/divorced ☐ 3

Widowed ☐ 4

Not married ☐ 5

Q.4 What is your opinion about using nuclear power to generate electricity?

Strongly agree ☐ 1

Agree ☐ 2

Neither agree or disagree ☐ 3

Disagree ☐ 4

Strongly disagree ☐ 5

So far we have discussed the coding of **closed questions** in which codes have been assigned to each of the responses. It is often a good idea to type these codes on to the questionnaire so that respondents only have to tick boxes or circle numbers when filling out the form. This often leads to a better response because it is quicker for someone to tick a box than write out their response. Also, the next stage of transferring the data onto a computer is considerably quicker if as much pre-coding as possible has been done beforehand. The above set of questions could have been laid out as shown in Figure 17.1.

17.4 QUALITATIVE CODING

Often a pre-coded question in a survey questionnaire will offer the option of an 'other (please specify)' category to act as a 'safety net' to catch additional responses which may be encountered infrequently. There are also questions that qualify previous responses such as 'Why did you say that?', for which pre-coding is not possible. These represent qualitative elements in an otherwise quantitative analysis. Whether one is coding these kinds of questions, open questions in which verbatim responses are recorded, or interview transcripts or fieldnotes, the initial process of coding is the same. The purpose of the first step is to reduce the data into analytic categories prior to analysis. However, while this 'code then analyse' sequence is unproblematically the case with the processing of open survey questions, it may not be such a rigidly sequential process while coding an interview transcript or fieldnote. Strauss (1987), in fact, identified three kinds of coding processes for qualitative data. The first pass through the data involves open coding the data into analytic themes in order to apply initial codes or labels to segments of the data. This step may be seen as comparable to coding open questions in a survey. However, the second and third passes through the qualitative data, also described as 'coding' by Strauss, should strictly be seen as part of the analysis. There will be more discussion about these stages of qualitative coding later in the chapter but the section that follows concerns itself with the first open coding stage.

The first set of categories into which the data will be coded is the equivalent of the coding frame for closed questions. The categories derived may come from theory or some other aspect of the literature, intuition or from the data themselves. If the research is designed to test a hypothesis, the categories should be derived from the theoretical framework and the data made to fit the categories. This is termed 'coding down'. However, if the aim is to describe data in order to generate theory, you can develop the categories from the data: 'coding up'.

17.4.1 STEPS IN 'CODING UP' FOR QUALITATIVE ANALYSIS

The development of categories during coding up involves the following steps:

1   Either take the first 20 or so questionnaires or the interview transcript or fieldnotes.

2   Use filing cards to note down each response from the questionnaire or each significant feature or quote from the interview/fieldnote. Use a new filing card for each new response or concept:

   (a)   With survey questionnaires, code question by question (i.e. across all 20 questionnaires), not case by case. This leads to greater consistency in coding each variable. It also reduces the possibility of building up a preconceived picture of the respondent, which could lead to a bias in the coding of any ambiguous response.

(b)   For an interview or transcript, it is important to code in semantically meaningful units. These may be words, phrases, sentences or paragraphs, depending on the analysis being developed. If you are planning using software to help with analysis (see Chapter 20) then the coding unit may be defined by the software.

3   Sort the filing cards into related categories.

4   Continue with another 20 questionnaires or another interview/fieldnote.

5   Repeat the sorting exercise.

6   Repeat the last two steps until no new categories are generated.

7   Create coding instructions in order to define category membership.

Deciding *what* to code in an interview transcript or fieldnote is a question of deciding what is or isn't important and is usually guided by the purpose of the study.

Krathwohl (2006) has developed a useful list of the steps involved in the coding process during qualitative analysis and these are presented in Table 17.8. Note that the shaded steps are strictly analysis steps rather than preliminary coding steps but illustrate the blurring between coding and analysis when coding up.

17.4.2 AN EXAMPLE OF CODING A FIELDNOTE

Turner (1981) offers a clear example of coding up a fieldnote. In the example shown, in Figure 17.2, the fieldnote describes an aspect of the queuing system at a cement factory. Turner generates a number of potential ways of coding the fieldnote through a 'brainstorming' session where as many plausible accounts of its meaning are listed as possible. These form possible codes which are then compared to other fieldnotes in the set. Some will be discarded because they do not resonate with the other data, while others will be seen to relate to each other and so will be combined. Thus, several codes are likely to end up being applicable to the fieldnote shown. For each code an attempt is made to 'define' it by writing it up in formal, abstract terms. Another important aspect of the procedure is that, once stated in formal terms, an effort should be made to identify parallel codes or processes in other, documented social phenomena. For example, if 'power' emerges as a code applicable to the data, you should try to think of other situations in which 'power' governs the course of interaction. This will help to identify elements of the operation of power which you can then look for in your own data. The competitive elements in the cement factory example may be related to the way tenants in a shared household work out who will get to use the bathroom first in the morning, and so on.

Table 17.8   Steps in the qualitative coding

Steps	Task
1. Find what is significant	Read the data, search for significant phrases, make notes about initial impressions (see memoing in Chapter 20)
2. Load your mind	Read and re-read the data – search for patterns, relationships and repetitions – identify commonalities across individuals and conditions in study. Also identify unusual individuals/situations
3. Let your unconscious process the data	Do something else but be prepared to make a note of anything as it pops into your mind
4. Begin initial codes	Make an initial coding list of categories and use this list with your data
5. Check consistency of title with coded material	Check that the codenames you attach to segments late in the coding process still have the same meaning as those segments you initially coded with the same codenames
6. Adjust code titles to fit data better	Combine and rename codenames to fit data upon re-reading
7. Recode at an interpretive level	Identify themes, casual links – software may help you find co-occurring codenames to help identify patterns in the initial coding
8. Develop and test hypotheses	Develop working hypotheses about repeating patterns – test these patterns with other data – develop principles and explanations – does the proposed explanation work well with other data?
9. Develop and test descriptive types	Gather together best examples of these types and describe common features – are there any individuals that don't fit these types? Will any modification of the initial descriptions allow inclusion of these 'outsiders'? If not, then these are new types. Continue until there are no new types
10. Consider developing graphics to examine code relationships	This may reveal hierarchies of codenames or maybe highlight weaknesses in the coding structure/relationships which may call for more data
11. Develop explicit definitions for each codename	Create a code book – including examples of the text attached to each codename. This activity often leads to a further refinement in coding

Source: Developed from Krathwahl (2006).

17.4.3 CODING OPEN QUESTIONS IN A SURVEY QUESTIONNAIRE

Having created a workable coding frame for the closed questions in a survey, there are several points to consider before you can go ahead and code the rest of the questionnaires. For a survey questionnaire, you will be converting responses to numbers that are to be collated later by a statistical computer program. Each

Figure 17.2   Coding a fieldnote

A. First paragraph from a Set of Fieldnotes

Paragraph 1
A row of lorries varying between 30 and 50 queue up every morning in front of the factory to obtain cement. All lorry drivers and owners place great importance to be first in the queue as this means getting served first. This has added importance in times of cement shortages when the cement outflow from the factory to the private sector is rationed and when the prices of cement are high. In addition to cement customers, there is also a set of lorry owners stationed at H... who act as transport agents for other customers. Porcelli is one of these transport agents.

Source: Former factory manager who is embarking here upon a discussion of Porcelli's activities in the area.

B. Categories Generated (to be placed on cards)

Cement shortage
Competitive behaviour among lorry drivers
Many agents transporting cement
Greater intensity of competition caused by cement shortage
Customers transporting their own cement
Role of factory
Significance of queue system as a means of distributing scarce resources
Economic context of scarcity
Porcelli's role
Significance of time in relation to the queue
Routinised pattern for the distribution of goods
Importance of priority position in queue

Source: 14 Turner(1981)

---

response category could be assigned a different value, the first category coded 1, the second coded 2, and so on. So if 15 categories were developed from the responses, the values will range from 1 to 15. However, before you decide on this scheme you need to consider how many answers to each question you will accept. For instance, to the question 'Why did you say that?', the respondent may offer one reason or many. You will need to decide whether to accept only the first mentioned reason or several. For instance, you may decide to code the first three mentioned reasons. In this case, you will need to allow three variables, one for each reason. Of course, data from some respondents may be missing for one or more of these variables. Alternatively, you may decide that you want to code all responses, each one as a separate variable, in which case you would have as many variables as categories. Each variable would then be coded as either, 'yes, the reason is mentioned' and given the value 1, or 'no, not mentioned' and given the value 0. These points are considered in the example below.

In 1982, Social and Community Planning Research conducted a national survey of 1195 members of the public about their attitudes to industrial, work-related and other risks. The respondents were asked the following, rather cumbersome question:

> Thinking of all the sorts of risks there are, at the present time what risks are you particularly worried or concerned about because they could happen to you or a member of your family?

The interviewers were instructed to 'probe and record fully' and therefore each individual might have mentioned more than one risk (SCPR, 1982). With such an open question you cannot possibly anticipate all responses and therefore need to develop a coding scheme after the questionnaires have been filled out. In the original survey the answers to this question were left uncoded and unanalysed. The opportunity arose of carrying out a secondary analysis of this and other open questions from the survey (Brown et al., 1984). This involved designing a coding frame for the first 72 questionnaires and trying to define theoretically relevant distinctions between responses. A list of 23 different risks were elicited, although nearly 25 per cent of respondents did not proffer a risk at all. This list formed the basis of the coding frame used to code the rest of the questionnaires.

Because respondents could mention more than one risk, there was a problem in deciding how to code the answers. Table 17.9 outlines three possible solutions.

We could have decided to code only the first mentioned answer on the assumption that it would be the most important. (See coding scheme 1 in Table 17.9.) However, we would have lost a lot of information from respondents who made multiple answers. Alternatively, we could have decided to code the first three responses from each respondent, each with the same coding scheme. (See coding scheme 2 in Table 17.9.) However, this might still lead to a loss of information from those respondents offering more than three responses. The third coding scheme in Table 17.9 involved creating 23 different variables, each one coded either 1 to indicate that it was mentioned or 0 to indicate that it was not. This scheme coded all the data, but the data may be more difficult to analyse.

The choice of which coding scheme to adopt should depend on the needs of the subsequent analysis. Schemes 1 and 2 lend themselves to a more descriptive account of people's responses. Scheme 3 would be more appropriate if the data were going to be analysed further. In fact, scheme 3 was employed in the study and the data were analysed using Smallest Space Analysis computer software. This provided a two-dimensional 'map' of people's responses such that those risks most frequently mentioned were located towards the centre of the 'map' and those risks mentioned together were located close to one another. From such a two-dimensional map, clusters of risks were identified as conceptually similar and given group names.

Another common method of dealing with multiple responses in open questions is to code only one that satisfies certain criteria. For instance, if you ask respondents what qualifications they have, perhaps offering them a list of

Table 17.9 Three coding schemes for risk responses

TYPE OF WORRY	CODING SCHEME 1: FIRST MENTIONED RISK ONLY CODED IN ONE VARIABLE CALLED RISK	CODING SCHEME 2: CODE THE FIRST THREE MENTIONED RISKS INTO THREE VARIABLES CALLED RISK1, RISK2, RISK3			CODING SCHEME 3: EACH RISK MENTIONED IS A VARIABLE AND CODED WITH A 1 IF MENTIONED, OTHERWISE 0. THEREFORE 24 VARIABLES ARE REQUIRED		
	VARIABLE NAME	VARIABLE NAMES					
	RISK CODE	RISK1 CODE	RISK2 CODE	RISK3 CODE	VARIABLE NAME	CODE IF MENTIONED	CODE IF NOT MENTIONED
None	1	1	1	1	RISK1	1	0
Car	2	2	2	2	RISK2	1	0
Crossing road	3	3	3	3	RISK3	1	0
Fire	4	4	4	4	RISK4	1	0
Other specific hazards	5	5	5	5	RISK5	1	0
Traffic	6	6	6	6	RISK6	1	0
Other health	7	7	7	7	RISK7	1	0
Falling	8	8	8	8	RISK8	1	0
Steam	9	9	9	9	RISK9	1	0
Work	10	10	10	10	RISK10	1	0
Electric current	11	11	11	11	RISK11	1	0
Children in traffic	12	12	12	12	RISK12	1	0
Military nuclear power	13	13	13	13	RISK13	1	0
Mugging	14	14	14	14	RISK14	1	0
Vandalism	15	15	15	15	RISK15	1	0
Other crime	16	16	16	16	RISK16	1	0
Unemployment	17	17	17	17	RISK17	1	0
Lightening	18	18	18	18	RISK18	1	0
Pollution	19	19	19	19	RISK19	1	0
Uneven pavements	20	20	20	20	RISK20	1	0
Civil nuclear war	21	21	21	21	RISK21	1	0
Smoking	22	22	22	22	RISK22	1	0
Stress at work	23	23	23	23	RISK23	1	0
Poor housing	24	24	24	24	RISK24	1	0

pre-coded responses, they may tick more than one box. You may in this instance decide only to code the highest education qualification.

17.4.4 STORING VERBATIM RESPONSES

You may prefer to use the open responses as verbatim comments in your report to illustrate certain points, rather than reducing them to numerically coded categories. Obviously, if you have not quantified them, you will not be able to do any statistical analysis on these responses, but you will still have to read and sort them. You could just type a list of responses and then pick those that are useful for a particular point. Or you could use a database program to store the verbatim comments. For example, Microsoft Access 2003 will allow you to store textual comments (not exceeding 65,535 characters each) as memo fields. Database programs have the advantage that you can save certain 'face-sheet' variables, such as the age and sex of the respondent, along with the verbatim comments. This would enable you to select, say, only those quotes for a particular question from all females over 65.

Some statistical packages, such as SPSS, can also store textual comments. However, many statistical programs limit the length of each comment. For example, with SPSS, quotes can be no more than 255 characters in length.

17.5 CREATION OF THE CODE BOOK

Having created your coding frame and written your coding instructions, you can now create the *code book*. This is best done before you carry out coding of the questionnaires. A code book is a form in which the following information is recorded for each variable:

*   question number and wording;
*   variable name for use by computer programs to refer to the variable (often restricted by the analysis software to 8 characters);
*   column location of that variable (usually not necessary for direct data entry to a statistical software package);
*   values that the variable can take and what these values represent;
*   missing value(s);
*   range of valid values.

An example of a code book for a survey questionnaire is shown in Table 17.10.

Table 17.10   The code book

QUESTION/VARIABLE LABEL	VARIABLE NAME	VALUES	VALUE LABELS	MISSING VALUES	RANGE OF VALID VALUES
Identification number	ID	-	-	-	1–450*
Age	AGE	-	-	99	18–91
Sex	SEX	1	male	9	1,2
		2	female		
Marital status	MARSTAT	1	Married	9	1–5
		2	Living as married		
		3	Separated/divorced		
		4	Widowed		
		5	Not married		
		9	No response		
Attitude to nuclear power	ATTNUC	1	Strongly agree	9	1–5
		2	Agree		
		3	Neither agree or disagree		
		4	Disagree		
		5	Strongly disagree		
		9	No response		

Note: * assuming no more than 450 completed questionnaires.

While a code book is mandatory with quantitative analysis, it is also good practice to create some form of code book in qualitative research. Here, the code book is important in providing a list of codes generated during *open coding*. The development of such a document is especially important for consistency if you are coding data over an extended period of time. These codes have several component parts which should be documented in the code book (Neuman, 2000):

- a 1–3 word label;
- a definition;
- any qualifications or exceptions;
- an example.

Code books created during both the qualitative and quantitative coding process are then used as the guide to the subsequent application of the codes to the data.

This means that researchers could work in teams coding data for the same project guided by the code book instructions.

17.5.1 CODING THE QUESTIONNAIRES

Having created the coding frame, written the coding instructions and created the code book, you are now ready to code the rest of the questionnaires. This means going through each questionnaire and writing on the ID number, if it is not already marked, checking for missed questions, marking the appropriate missing value, and marking the values for each open question.

At this stage, the importance of a pilot survey becomes apparent. Any unanticipated responses to your questionnaire may lead to the reorganisation of the coding frame. For instance, you may find during your pilot that you had not anticipated a frequent response that should be added to the pre-coded answers in the main questionnaire.

17.6 CODING THE DATA USING A COMPUTER

This section outlines how either quantitative or qualitative data can be directly entered into a computer analysis package. With quantitative data, the numeric codes themselves are entered into the software package while with qualitative data, the text file is imported or opened into the package for subsequent coding.

17.6.1 CODING QUANTITATIVE DATA USING SPSS

If you have more than about 20 questionnaires in which you asked more than five questions, it makes sense to use a computer to do the analysis. The analysis software that you use will often depend on what is available or within your budget.

There are many statistical programs for analysing survey data. The most popular and widespread is SPSS. There is also a cheap 'studentware' version (see http://www.tiny.cc/i4Kvy) which only allows you to use 50 variables and has fewer statistical routines than the full version. The INTUTE web site publishes an Internet guide to social research which is a useful resource (http://www.tiny.cc/ZutCF). And Harvard University publishes an electronic copy of 'The Impoverished Social Scientist's Guide to Free Statistical Software and Resources' (http://www.tiny.cc/FmRn1).

Whichever software you use, you will need to set up the program to recognise your variables. This usually involves giving a name to each variable, telling the program whether its values are numeric or alphanumeric and stating how many columns it occupies. In SPSS version 15, this preparatory work is carried out in the *Variable View* of the *Data Editor*. Figure 17.3 shows such a window after

Figure 17.3   Variable view of the Data Editor in SPSS

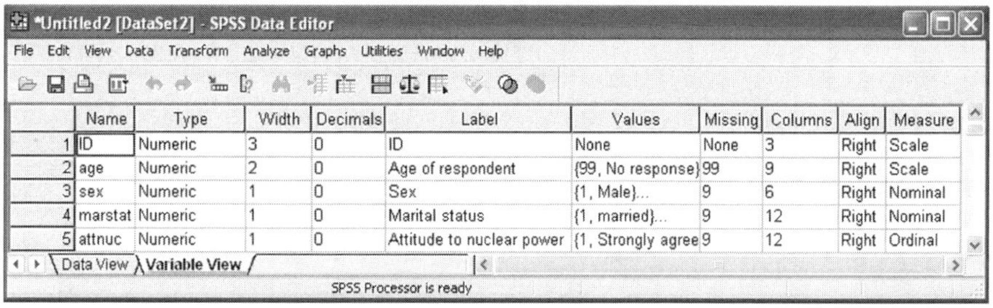

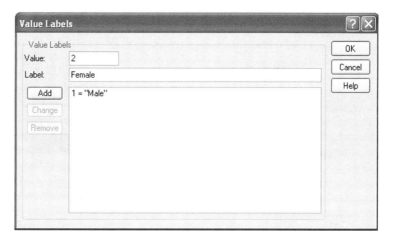

Figure 17.4   The values labels dialog box in SPSS

completing the definition of the five variables seen in Table 17.9. The words in the *Values* column are called *Value Labels* and are labels that describe the codes that have been assigned to each response. For instance, the labels for the variable SEX are 'Male' for code 1 and 'Female' for code 2. They are added by clicking the appropriate grey square in the *Values* column to see the dialog box in Figure 17.4. Figure 17.5 is the *Missing Values* dialog box which appears when you click the grey square in the appropriate *Missing* column in Figure 17.3. Since all responses are usually assigned a code, even if the respondent refused to answer or if the question is not applicable, there has to be a way to indicate that you want these codes treated differently. Once a code has been flagged as a *Missing Value,* then that code is ignored in any subsequent analysis. For instance, you may assign the code 99 to all those people who refuse to tell you their age. You do not want this code treated as a valid code, age 99, and need to indicate that 99 is a *Missing Value.* The final column in Figure 17.3, headed *Measure*, is where you indicate the level of measurement of each variable (see Figure 17.6). Note that *Scale* measurement is the same as interval measurement.

Figure 17.5   The missing values dialog box in SPSS

Missing Values   [?][X]

○ No missing values

◉ Discrete missing values

[ ] [ ] [ ]

OK

Cancel

Help

○ Range plus one optional discrete missing value

Low: [ ]   High: [ ]

Discrete value: [ ]

Figure 17.6   Defining the level of measurement in SPSS

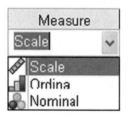

Measure

Scale

Scale
Ordina
Nominal

TIP

Always be aware of which responses (i.e. the 'non-responses' or the 'not applicable' responses) should be coded and identified as missing values when using SPSS to help analyse the data. If you get any unexpected results, check the missing values first for any problems.

Having set up the program with this initial information you can then enter the data by changing to the *Data View* screen. The codes are then entered in each cell of the data matrix to appear as in Figure 17.7. An alternative view of your data could be obtained by clicking on **View, Value Labels,** to see Figure 17.8.

Note that you can create a code book in SPSS by selecting **File, Display Data File Information, Working File...,** see Table 17.11.

Once all the data has been entered, but before serious analysis can begin, you must spend some time checking the data for obvious errors. This process is called data cleaning. The first step of cleaning is obtaining a frequency count for each variable. For instance, this will tell you for the variable SEX, how many men and how many women there are in your sample. The purpose of this frequency listing is to alert you to any 'wild codes' in your data. These are codes that may have been

Figure 17.7   The Data View in SPSS

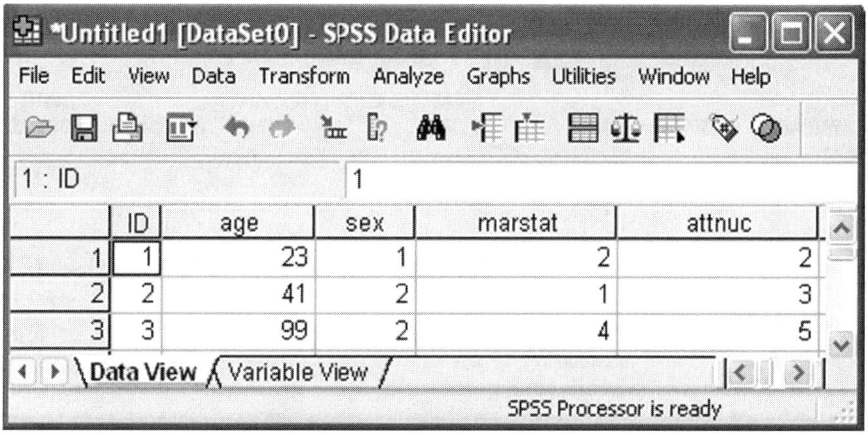

Figure 17.8   The Data View in SPSS showing value labels

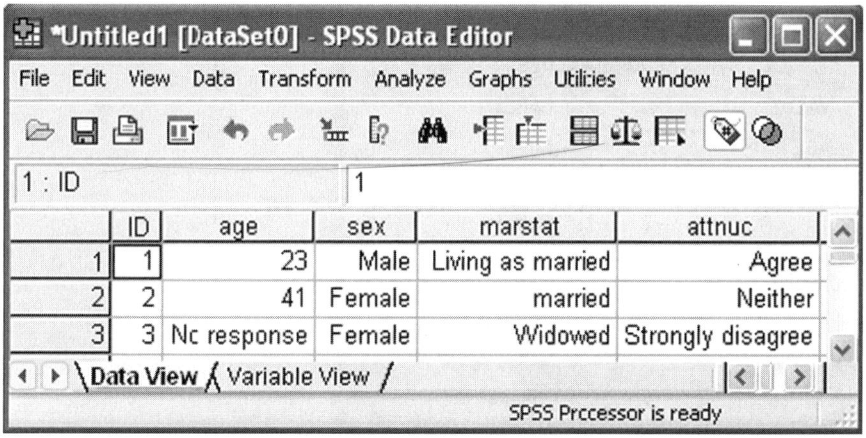

miscoded during the coding operation or been wrongly entered at the data entry stage. For instance, you might find there were some respondents coded with the value 3 for sex. You should check the frequency listing for such inconsistencies and then identify the cases where these problems occur. Then you must return to the questionnaire to check the original coding. Chapter 18 discusses how to perform frequency analysis on your data.

17.6.2 CODING QUALITATIVE DATA USING A COMPUTER

As mentioned previously, Strauss (1987) defined three stages of qualitative coding in which the data is reviewed using a different coding process in each of these

Table 17.11   Creating a Code book in SPSS

VARIABLE INFORMATION									
VARIABLE	POSITION	LABEL	MEASUREMENT LEVEL	COLUMN WIDTH	ALIGNMENT	PRINT FORMAT	WRITE FORMAT	MISSING VALUES
ID	1	ID	Scale	3	Right	F3	F8.2	
AGE	2	Age of respondent	Scale	9	Right	F2	F8.2	99
SEX	3	Sex	Nominal	6	Right	F1	F8.2	9
MARSTAT	4	Marital status	Nominal	12	Right	F1	F8.2	9
ATTNUC	5	Attitude to nuclear power	Ordinal	12	Right	F1	F8.2	9

Variables in the working file

VARIABLE VALUES		
VALUE		LABEL
AGE	99(a)	No response
SEX	1	Male
	2	Female
MARSTAT	1	Married
	2	Living as married
	3	Separated/divorced
	4	Widowed
	5	Not married
	9(a)	No response
ATTNUC	1	Strongly agree
	2	Agree
	3	Neither
	4	Disagree
	5	Strongly disagree
	9(a)	No response

Note: (a) Missing value

passes. During the first stage, codes are developed and a code book is created. Applying these codes to the data – in qualitative research, usually text – is greatly facilitated by using Computer Assisted Qualitative Data Analysis Software

Figure 17.9   Coding data in Atlas-ti

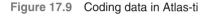

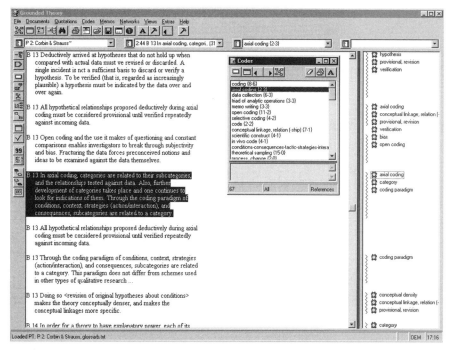

(CAQDAS). As explained in Chapter 20, there are many CAQDAS packages on the market today and, like many statistical packages, they are often designed to perform specific and different analytic functions. For a full review of software packages and their different capabilities, see Lewins and Silver (2007). Nevertheless, the application of codes to text is similar in many of these packages. An example is seen in Figure 17.9 which demonstrates the *open coding* process in the program, Atlas-ti. Text is imported into the program. Then, segments of text are highlighted by dragging the mouse over a phrase, sentence or paragraph and a pre-defined code is selected to apply to that segment.

The second pass through the data creates the **axial codes**. During axial coding the researcher concentrates on the codes created during the first (open coding) phase. In particular, the relationships between categories and subcategories are considered, with tentative relationships being examined against data. The researcher looks for categories or codes that cluster together while thinking about such things as the causes or consequences relating to the processes the data refers to, and which may inform the analysis. Other questions the researcher may ask is whether similar categories can be grouped together into a more general category or do some categories need to be subdivided. Can any categories be arranged into a sequential or time-ordered pattern? While open coding can be seen as fragmenting the data, axial coding may be conceived of as bringing it back together in a web of relationships.

Strauss and Corbin (1990) describe a useful paradigm to bear in mind while axial coding. They describe the questions you ask of the data in order to describe meaningful relationships between your initial open codes. These questions relate to:

1   the nature of the specific phenomenon;

2   the conditions that relate to it;

3   the strategy the people involved used to handle the phenomenon;

4   and any consequences of these strategies in relation to the phenomenon.

This 'Paradigm Model' is outlined in Table 17.12, illustrated by their example of someone breaking their leg and the subsequent process of pain management. Thus, while the central idea and research topic is concerned with pain, this open code in the data is linked to the code, 'breaking a leg' through a causal or antecedent condition relationship. These codes are set in context and ultimately related to the strategies used to deal with the phenomenon and the consequences of such strategies. It is often an aid to conceptualisation if the researcher considers whether these relationships can be represented by a map or network view of the analysis. Figure 17.10 shows such a network view in the Atlas-ti software. The example used, created by the developer of the software, is based on the Paradigm Model developed by Strauss and Corbin, once again illustrated by the pain example used above.

The final pass through the data occurs after the text has been coded and main themes and concepts have emerged from the text. This final coding phase, referred to by Strauss (1987) as **selective coding**, involves the researcher scanning both the codes and the data and then selecting cases to illustrate major themes uncovered during axial and open coding. This phase provides the researcher with quotable material for her final report.

Steps involved in qualitative coding

1   Development of codes and the creation of a code book.
2   Open coding: application of codes to segments of text.
3   Axial coding: development of relationships between codes created in step 2 and the identification of themes.
4   Selective coding: case selection for quoting to illustrate themes discovered.

Finally, we will mention another important activity that researchers may carry out while coding data. Analytic memos are notes the researcher writes to him or herself about the coding phase. Their aim is to help to develop new themes and

Table 17.12   The Paradigm Model

CODING PARADIGM	DESCRIPTION	EXAMPLE
Causal conditions	Events leading to the development of the phenomena	Breaking a leg
Phenomenon	What the action is about, the central idea	Pain

Context	Specific set of properties pertaining to the phenomenon	The break:
		    time since accident?
		    how did it occur?
		    number of fractures?
		Pain management:
		    duration
		    location
		    intensity

Intervening Conditions	Broad conditions bearing on the action/interaction strategies	Time phenomena occurred Location phenomenon occurred Age of person Past history of pain
Action/interaction	Action directed at managing, handling, carrying out, responding to phenomenon	Splint the leg Go for help Taking pills
Consequences	Outcomes or results of actions/ interactions	Pain relief

Source: Adapted from Strauss and Corbin (1990).

to facilitate elaboration of the coding scheme. They show the development of thinking during any phase of the coding and analysis work and in effect provide an audit trail of the whole coding exercise. Many CAQDAS packages provide for the addition of memos to segments of text.

Although the methods used in quantitative surveys and qualitative fieldwork are often seen as fundamentally different, there are many areas of overlap, especially, as we have seen, in the process of coding. Of course, although the process of coding may be similar, the objectives of coding are different. With a quantitative survey, we try to allocate a value to each category which can then be manipulated statistically, even if only by a simple frequency count. However, categories obtained from interviews and fieldnotes are not normally allocated values but maintain their contextual position. Co-occurrences of categories are explored and themes elicited. Chapter 20 reviews software specifically designed for the analysis of such data.

Figure 17.10   Network view in Atlas-ti showing relationships between open codes

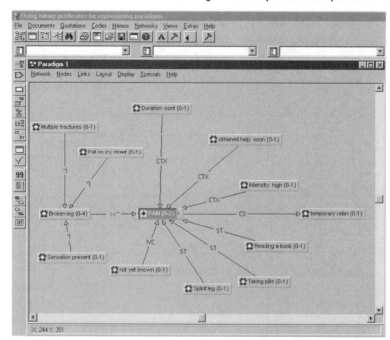

17.7 SUMMARY

This chapter has shown the steps involved in coding data from survey questionnaires and unstructured interviews. The methods used for both types of data collection are similar in many ways and emphasis has been placed on the similarities at
this stage of the research process. The differences between 'quantitative' and 'qualitative' methods are more marked in the treatment of the resulting coded data.
Chapter 18 discusses in detail how to go about the analysis of quantitative data. The
analysis of qualitative data has often been seen as being dependent on the approach
of the individual researcher and is certainly not as formalised as the analysis of
quantitative data. However, with the emergence of new computer software, even the
process of qualitative analysis is becoming more amenable to formalisation.

DISCUSSION QUESTIONS

1   Is coding necessary

    for quantitative analysis
    for qualitative analysis?
    (Think how coding can help structure the data and help analysis).

2   Does using a computer help or hinder the coding process

for quantitative analysis

for qualitative analysis?

(Think of the computer as a tool to save time – or does the complication of learning new software outweigh the advantages?)

3   What are the similarities and differences in coding a survey and coding an unstructured interview?

PROJECT

You have been asked to investigate people's beliefs in the paranormal through administering a questionnaire in the street to the general public. From such a study you can begin to investigate people's understanding of scientific knowledge.

   Decide whether you are going to administer a survey questionnaire or carry out a structured interview. Design your interview schedule or your interviewer-administered questionnaire to include the following questions. Try to pre-code the questions where possible and mark your questionnaire with response codes and column numbers in order to simplify data entry:

1   What kinds of things come to mind when you think of the paranormal? *This is an open question to which people may offer more than one answer. Allow several lines on the questionnaire in which to write the answers.*

2   Do you think that any of the following are true:

   (a) It is possible to make someone turn round just by looking at them.
   (b) Prayers can sometimes be answered.
   (c) It is possible to know what someone else is thinking or feeling even if they are hundreds of miles away and out of touch by ordinary means.
   (d) Some houses are haunted.
   (e) The Earth has been visited by beings from outer space.
   (f) Dreams can sometimes foretell the future.
   (g) Some people can remember past lives (i.e. reincarnations they may have lived).
   (h) It is possible to get messages from the dead.

You should expect people to respond with either a positive or negative answer, although it is likely that there will also need to be a 'Don't know' category.

3   Are you a religious person?

Decide whether to use a yes/no answer or an ordinal scale with responses ranging from very religious to not at all religious.

4   Age

Decide whether to use age ranges or to ask people their actual age.

5   Sex

6   Social class

7   Ethnic group

Remember to include columns for an identification number.

After designing your questionnaire, select a small sample to interview and administer it to them. Create a code book and then code the open question. Finally you could create the data file.

RESOURCES

- For a discussion of coding survey questionnaires, Silvey (1975) *Deciphering Data: The Analysis of Social Surveys* is an early but comprehensive text.

- For a brief overview of using SPSS in statistics, see Chapter 2 in Fielding and Gilbert (2006) *Understanding Social Statistics*. Chapter 3 includes a discussion about collecting and coding data for computer analysis.

- Coding qualitative data is covered by Strauss and Corbin (1990) *Basics of Qualitative Research: Grounded Theory Procedures and Techniques*, Neuman (2000) *Social Research Methods: Qualitative and Quantitative Approaches* and Krathwohl (2006) *Methods of Educational and Social Science Research*.

- Computer analysis and qualitative research are discussed by Fielding and Lee (1998) *Computer Analysis and Qualitative Research*.

- For a discussion about the classification of social class, see Rose and O'Reilly (1997) *Constructing Classes: Towards a New Social Classification for the UK* and Rose and Pevalin (2003) *A Researcher's Guide to the National Statistics Socio-economic Classification*.

18 Analysing Survey Data

Mike Procter

18.1 INTRODUCTION

Statistical analysis is seen as one of the more frightening and mysterious (some would even say 'mystifying') stages of the survey research process. This reputation is unfair to the other stages. At least as much intellectual effort is needed to conceptualise the problem, to design the sample, and to devise the interview schedule, not to mention the often enjoyable but always demanding task of writing the final report. Perhaps the reason for the special status of data analysis is that you *know* when you do not understand the technical details.

To try to take some of the fear away, this chapter goes through a small-scale example of a real-life analysis. 'Real-life' means real data, which in turn means more than you could hope to deal with equipped only with a pencil and paper and a calculator. It is not sensible to try to analyse a survey of a reasonable size except with a computer and a suitable program. The most commonly used computer software for survey analysis is SPSS (see Chapter 17). Most academic institutions in the UK, and in many other countries, subscribe to a site licence that allows them to distribute SPSS at very little cost to staff and students.

18.2 PROGRAMS FOR MANIPULATING DATA

A program like SPSS, http://tinyurl.com/4as45 and comparable products such as

- SAS, http://tinyurl.com/woz7

- Minitab, http://tinyurl.com/yvg44b

- P-Stat http://tinyurl.com/229vz5

- Stata http://tinyurl.com/2a9ted

- BMD-P http://tinyurl.com/2xp25y

have two main components: the statistical routines, which
calculations that produce tabulations and summary measures ⌐₁ various kinds,
and the data management facilities. This is best clarified by a few examples.

The General Household Survey (GHS) is an annual survey carried out by a
UK Government agency, the Office for National Statistics. The basic unit of
analysis is the household: roughly, a group of people who live together and
share catering arrangements. Variables that describe the household include the
kind of housing tenure (private rented, public rented, owner-occupied, etc.)
and whether it has features such as central heating. Information is also gathered about each individual in the household: his or her age, sex, health record,
smoking habits, etc. Chapter 19 describes the GHS in more detail.

Age is information about individuals that is collected in almost all surveys
and is usually measured by asking respondents their date of birth because
this is harder to misremember. Then 'age last birthday' is calculated from
date of birth and the date of the interview using a special formula. This con-
verts each date into the number of days since 15 October 1582 (the first day
of the Gregorian calendar), and the difference is converted back into whole
years. So far so good; but for many purposes you may want to use broader
categories of age than whole years, for example, the two categories 'up to 39'
versus '40 or over'. All these manipulations count as simple kinds of data
management.

Looking at the relationship between central heating and housing tenure is
also fairly straightforward (presumably we would find that owner-occupiers
are more likely to have the benefit of this feature than are public sector housing tenants) because both measures are household-level characteristics.

It is just as easy to see whether smokers have more respiratory disease than
non-smokers – this time both measures apply to individuals

But determining whether central heating is good for your lungs involves
looking simultaneously at variables from different **levels of analysis**, household
and individual. This would be done by copying the information about central
heating down from the household to all its individual members. Even more
complicated, the question whether you can suffer from the smoking of other
people in the household involves first carrying each household member's
smoking up to the household level and aggregating it, and then transferring
household smoking back down to the individual and relating it to his or her
health. All of this would be extremely difficult to do without the right kind of
data management tools.

Having pointed out the importance of data management, there simply is not
space to say anything more about it here. You can start to acquire the necessary skills by reading Norusis (2006) or a corresponding guide to another data
management program.

Figure 18.1   Printout from SPSS: marginal frequency distribution for 'DEGREE'

RS HIGHEST DEGREE				
	Frequency	Percent	Valid Percent	Cumulative Percent
Valid 0 LT HIGH SCHOOL	1072	35.0	35.2	35.2
1 HIGH SCHOOL	1482	48.4	48.6	83.8
2 JUNIOR COLLEGE	68	2.2	2.2	86.0
3 BACHELOR	278	9.1	9.1	95.1
4 GRADUATE	148	4.8	4.9	100.0
Total	3048	99.6	100.0	
Missing 8 DK	4	.1		
9 NA	8	.3		
Total	12	.4		
Total	3060	100.0		

18.3 AN ANALYSIS

18.3.1 FREQUENCY DISTRIBUTIONS

The first stage in the analysis of a new data set is almost always to get the **marginal frequency distributions**. The origin of this term will be explained later; all that it means is that for each question we count the number of respondents who answer in each of the possible ways. This is not quite accurate: as Chapter 17 explains, sometimes answers will be processed before they are entered into the computer – for instance, a verbatim answer to a question about the coded categories rather than the verbatim responses that will be tabulated.

Here, interspersed with a lot of commentary, is some printout from SPSS, showing the frequency distributions for three variables: educational qualification, marital status and age (Figures 18.1, 18.2, 18.3). Other programs will produce similar tables. The data is based on an American survey, the General Social Survey (GSS) carried out every year by the National Opinion Research Center (NORC).

The information reported here came from a sequence of four questions that asked the respondents whether they had graduated from high school and, if so, what higher qualifications they had. The highest qualification mentioned was then coded, so that, for instance, someone with a first degree and a Master's would be put only in category 4. The original researchers have chosen to call this variable 'DEGREE', so that subsequent analysts will have a reasonable chance of remembering the name without having constantly to look it up in a manual. The other labels have been assigned in the same way: the program uses all of this information without 'knowing' what any of it means.

Figure 18.2   Printout from SPSS: marginal frequency distribution of 'MARITAL'

MARITAL STATUS				
		Frequency	Percent	Valid Percent	Cumulative Percent
Valid	1 MARRIED	1950	63.7	63.7	63.7
	2 WIDOWED	330	10.8	10.8	74.5
	3 DIVORCED	206	6.7	6.7	81.2
	4 SEPARATED	124	4.1	4.1	85.3
	5 NEVER MARRIED	450	14.7	14.7	100.0
	Total	3060	100.0	100.0	

Figure 18.3   Frequency distribution of 'AGE'

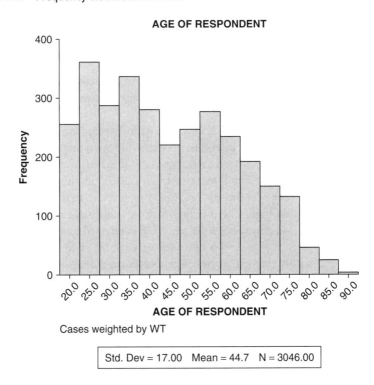

Cases weighted by WT

Std. Dev = 17.00   Mean = 44.7   N = 3046.00

We can read from the printout in Figure 18.1 that the code '0' occurs with a frequency of 1072: these are all the people who didn't graduate from high school. (LT here means 'less than'.) A rather larger number, 1482, did graduate from high school but got no further, and so on. Each of the 'Percent' figures is the corresponding Frequency divided by the total, 3060. Notice that 12 respondents are coded as 8, DK (don't know) and 9, NA (not applicable), which are grouped as missing. Data can be missing for a variety of reasons, and specific numerical codes are set aside to mark it (see Chapter 17); then the program is told that cases with those codes are not normally to be included in numerical calculations. For instance, the code for a missing income figure will not be used in the calculation of the average income. In the present example the total for percentaging should not include individuals for whom no data are available: hence the column headed 'Valid Percent', which is based on 3048 not 3060. Of course, it makes very little difference to the calculations here, but if there were more missing data it would be a different story.

Finally, the 'Cum Percent' (short for Cumulative Percentage) column gives partial sums of the previous one: 35.2 + 48.6 = 83.8, + 2.2 = 86.0, and so on, down the column. Thus we can see immediately that 95.1 per cent have a qualification up to and including a first degree. For this accumulation to make sense, the order of the categories must be meaningful: DEGREE is an example of an *ordinal* scale variable.

Marital status (see Figure 18.2), on the other hand, is said to be measured at the nominal scale, because there is no intrinsic order: it would be hard to argue that 'widowed' is intermediate between 'married' and 'divorced', for instance. Here the cumulative percentages are not meaningful, although SPSS calculates them regardless.

Age has not only a meaningful order (from youngest to oldest or vice versa) but equal scale intervals: (as Gertrude Stein might have said) a year is a year is a year, and the difference between 27 and 28 is numerically identical to that between 33 and 34. This is not true of DEGREE: despite the numerical values (chosen for convenience) there is no reason to suppose that the difference between junior college and high school is in any sense equivalent to the difference between a doctorate and a bachelor's degree. AGE is referred to as an *interval scale* variable.

Age is also a *continuous* variable, whereas the others examined here have discrete categories. Age as recorded does in fact have a limited number of categories, since we content ourselves with 'age last birthday', but even this has so many categories that the form of frequency distribution table presented so far is rather cumbersome. As a special option SPSS displays a histogram, in which the almost continuous variable is split into a number of convenient groupings, and the relative frequency is represented by the length of a bar (see Figure 18.3). The class midpoint of 25, say, represents ages of 23, 24, 25, 26 and 27. Altogether this figure looks like one half of a population pyramid.

There are two main reasons for 'getting the marginals'. As mentioned in Chapter 17, the first is to look for errors in the data. The second is that this is generally the best way of keeping tabs on the state of the data set, which necessarily gets modified during the process of analysis. This becomes especially necessary as research in general and data analysis in particular become co-operative enterprises: the costs of the fieldwork phase of a survey are so great that it makes sense to get the resulting data thoroughly analysed, often by a whole team of social scientists. As was explained earlier, practically every data set will go through repeated modifications as the analysts conceptualise new variables and new analytical frameworks. Of course, it is essential that these modifications be carefully documented, especially if a derived variable is to be used by workers other than the one who has created it. One way to do this is to keep a logbook (either a physical volume or else in the form of a text file on the computer system being used). But in addition it makes sense to generate a frequency table for every new variable and add it to the set you will have made at the beginning of the analysis process. Some programs will produce an alphabetical index to the marginals, and this makes it worthwhile to generate a complete new indexed set from time to time. Another useful feature is the ability to store general textual information in the data file itself, which can then serve as the logbook.

Finally, the most obvious reason to get a frequency distribution is because it gives you your first look at a new variable. It may be that the focus of your analysis is on the differences in health between smokers and non-smokers, but in your preliminary analysis you will certainly want to know simply what proportion of your sample smoke, and what proportion smoke less than ten a day, between ten and nineteen, and so on.

18.3.2 CROSS-TABULATION

The real analysis starts when you examine variables, not one at a time, but in pairs or more complex combinations: **cross-tabulation**. The point of this is to look at the relationship between variables, usually in order to explain differences on one variable in terms of differences on the other. As a simple example, if we find that workers with different jobs tend to have different health records, whereas workers with the same job are similar in their health, then we might say that differences in occupation at least partly explain differences in health or, more concisely, that occupation explains health. 'Explains' is here being used rather differently than in everyday language: it refers to a statistical relationship that may or may not lead to increased understanding.

What follows is the record of a run using SPSS. I make no attempt to define systematically what this requires; luckily, it is not difficult to acquire a reading knowledge of SPSS, so you should be able to follow what is going on. The main thing to understand is that the researcher types in commands that look like a version of English, and the program displays the results on the computer's screen or on a printer. The method of use and the output from other programs will differ, but the general principles of analysis are the same.

Most readers will be more accustomed to controlling a program by a point and click sequence – now practically universal in Windows applications, including SPSS. However, SPSS was originally written thirty years or so ago, and its internal architecture reflects this. This means that pointing and clicking actually generates a sequence of English-like instructions for the program to parse and obey. These instructions are displayed in the output window, and can be stored for later modification and recycling. Though most users never really notice the command language, the old-fashioned way of working can have certain advantages, one of which is that the logic of the procedure is easier to explain in a teaching situation like this chapter.

The question I have chosen to explore is: to what extent is a man's occupation determined by his father's? This is perhaps one of the central questions in the study of social mobility. A legitimate preliminary question is: why only men? The simple answer is because our society is patriarchal, and the patriarchy pervades sociology just as it does other spheres of life, so that this survey doesn't ask about the respondent's mother's work.

The first command to SPSS is to fetch the General Social Survey: thus

```
get file 'gss'.
```

A small subset of the data is provided as an example data set with the SPSS program, but I have chosen variables from the full list. In creating an SPSS-readable file, NORC provided standard variable names, and the two principal variables I used are called **occ** and **paocc16**. The first of these is formed by asking an elaborate series of questions designed to find out exactly what job the respondent does (or did, if they are retired), and then classifying every employed person into one of nearly 1,000 occupational categories defined by the US Bureau of the Census. The second is formed in the same way, except that the questions are asked about the respondent's father 'while you were growing up'; the mnemonic name suggests that this means 'when you were about sixteen'.

Social mobility usually means occupational mobility, which in turn means roughly 'having a job of a different status than your father'. A number of different status rankings have been suggested, but the simplest possible one, which I adopt here, simply differentiates between non-manual and manual occupations. Census codes 1 to 399 are non-manual occupations; 400 to 995 are manual. So in order to restrict the analysis to men (the variable **sex** is here coded 1, male and 2, female) and then divide the occupation variables into two groups, I typed in:

```
select if (sex = 1).
recode occ, paocc16
   (0 thru 399 = 1)
   (400 thru 995 = 2)
   into occ2 paocc162.
```

The mnemonic names used in SPSS are chosen arbitrarily – you could call the new variables *nigel* and *jane* if you wanted to. However, it is good practice to use meaningful names, and since the new variables are two-category versions of the old ones, I chose simply to add a '2' to the end of the name.

SPSS will print helpful labels on output tables, provided it 'knows' what labels to print. So I gave the program the necessary information by typing in:

```
value labels occ2 paocc162
    1 'non-manual'
    2 'manual'.
```

Finally, I typed in the instruction that would actually generate the table of results:

```
crosstabs tables = occ2 by paocc162
    /cells = count, column.
```

The first line specifies the variables to be used in forming the table. The only thing that needs attention is the order of declaring the variables. The customary procedure is to ask if we can establish a causal order between the variables. Here it is straightforward: a father's job can influence his son's, but not vice versa (except, no doubt, in a few eccentric cases where, for instance, junior becomes a tennis star or rock singer and takes on Dad as manager). This being so, **occ2**, which is dependent on **paocc162**, is called the dependent variable, while **paocc162** is referred to as the independent variable. Then the order is conventionally *dependent* by *independent*, which SPSS interprets as instructions to lay out the table as it appears in Figure 18.4, that is, with the dependent variable as the rows and the independent as the columns. The second line, beginning with the '/' symbol (called 'slash' by computer users) is a subcommand: what it does will be explained in a moment.

Figure 18.4 is a typical cross-tabulation as produced by SPSS. To understand the table we must first name the parts. The total number of 'cases' (in this context, people) on which the table is based is printed at the bottom right: it's 1,210. Above this are the numbers in each of the categories of the variable that defines the rows of the table: there are 768 respondents with manual occupations and 442 with non-manual jobs. The relative numbers are given, too, in the form of percentages: 63.5 per cent of respondents are manual workers. The column totals give the corresponding numbers for the respondents' fathers.

The first substantial point to notice is that the respondents (442) are more likely to be in a non-manual occupation than their fathers were (306). This is an example of **structural mobility:** the occupational structure has changed, so necessarily some sons must be in a different occupational group than their fathers. However, this could have been discovered by examining the simple frequency distributions, without arranging them in this sort of table. Here we see why those simple distributions are called marginals: they appear in the margins of a cross-tabulation.

Figure 18.4   Respondent's occupation by father's occupation

OCC2 * PAOCC162 Cross-tabulation				
		PAOCC 162		
		1.00 non-manual	2.00 manual	Total
OCC2 1.00 non-man	Count	194	248	442
	% within PAOCC	63.4%	27.4%	36.5%
2.00 manual	Count	112	656	768
	% within PAOCC	36.6%	72.6%	63.5%
Total	Count	306	904	1210
	% within PAOCC	100.0%	100.0%	100.0%

The special interest of a table of this sort comes when we examine the conditional distributions: the distributions of one variable under particular conditions of the other. Here, we are interested in the distribution of respondents' occupation under different conditions of the fathers' occupation. The findings are clearest in terms of the percentages. Specifically, among the 306 respondents whose fathers had non-manual jobs, 112, or 36.6 per cent, were in manual occupations and therefore the remainder, 63.4 per cent, were in non-manual jobs. On the other hand, if the father was in a manual job there was a 72.6 per cent chance that the respondent would be a manual worker, too, and only a 27.4 per cent chance that he would be in a non-manual job.

The subcommand /cells count, column can now be explained: it means 'each cell is to contain a count of the number of respondents with that combination of characteristics, together with that number expressed as a percentage of the column total'.

This is already quite a lot to take in, so we can concentrate on just two numbers: for manual fathers 72.6 per cent of their sons were in manual jobs; for non-manual fathers it was 36.6 per cent. An even simpler summary might be: the chance of being in a manual job was 36 per cent (i.e. 72.6 – 36.6) greater for sons of manual workers. Notice that it does not matter which row you choose: 63.4 – 27.4 = 36, just as before. In bigger tables (with more rows and columns) it is impossible to summarise the findings quite so simply, but in a 2 × 2 (two rows and two columns) table the standard procedure can be summed up as follows:

- If possible, decide on the causal ordering of your variables.

- Then tell your data analysis program to produce a table of the dependent variable against the independent variable.

- Ask for column percentages.

- Compare a pair of percentages in the same row.

More concisely, percentage down and compare across.

18.3.3 INTERPRETING THE FIGURES

What do these figures really mean? Simply that your father's occupation seems to have a substantial influence on your own, at least if you are an American man. One other reservation is necessary: we have only sample data, but we want to be able to make statements about the population as a whole. The justification for doing this – the general idea is called statistical inference – is a complicated one, although some of the issues are introduced in Chapter 6. It can be proved that, provided we really have got a random **sample**, the best guess for any percentage in the population is the corresponding sample percentage: in the USA as a whole, as in this table, about 63.5 per cent of all men will be in manual jobs. Why 'about'? Because if we took another sample just as carefully we would not be surprised to find a slightly different set of numbers, simply because of random sampling variability. The obvious consequence of this is that we should not draw strong conclusions from small differences based on small samples. Here, though, we have a reasonably large sample (the public opinion polls whose results are discussed with such interest by politicians are typically based on a thousand interviews or so), and the difference is very large, so common sense suggests that the influence must be real, even if not necessarily of precisely the magnitude that we have found.

What about 'provided we really have got a random sample'? Almost certainly we do not have one. NORC designs its sampling procedure to produce a random sample, but a problem with all survey research is non-response: people who were included in the sample design but not actually interviewed, because they were never at home when the interviewer called, or because they thought the details of their life were no business of the survey organisation's (see Chapter 9). These non-respondents are almost bound to be different in interesting but often unknowable ways from those who did take part. At best, then, we have a random sample of those adult male Americans who are not always out and who are not hostile to pollsters. This must introduce some distortion into the results, which is another reason for caution, and which is potentially more dangerous than the intrinsic sample-to-sample variability that the theory of statistical inference is all about. Nevertheless, half a century or more of experience by thousands of researchers suggests that we get more useful results than we are perhaps entitled to expect. So from now on, I shall interpret the results still to be presented without constantly worrying about what may have gone wrong.

18.3.4 CORRELATION AND CAUSATION

To what extent are we justified in making causal statements, such as that one's occupational status is influenced by one's father's, on the basis of statistical findings alone? The simple answer is that we are not. For instance, there is no statistical reason why we should not consider **paocc162** as the dependent variable and **occ2** as the independent. The reason I have not done this so far is that there is a good non-statistical reason against it: a father's occupation 'happens' before his son's, and it is universally accepted that an effect cannot precede its cause. So although **occ2** cannot (except exceptionally) influence **paocc162**, **paocc162** can influence **occ2**. 'Can', not 'must'. Another possibility is that both may be influenced by a third variable.

A good example of this is the discovery of a marked correlation between the price of rum in Barbados and the level of Methodist ministers' salaries: in any given year either both are high or both are low. There are two simple explanations of this, according to what you think the causal direction is. One says that ministers have a (secret) addiction to rum; when they get a pay rise, they can afford to buy more liquor, and the price goes up in response to the increased demand, as can be predicted from elementary economics. The alternative version is even more conspiratorial: the Methodist Church is secretly financed by the distillers of rum, and when the distillers' finances improve they can afford to give a bigger subvention.

Do not read on without trying to find a more sensible explanation in terms of a third variable that could reasonably be expected to influence both salaries and rum prices. It is general price levels, or the result of inflation. Over time the value of money falls, so both the price of rum and ministers' salaries have to rise to compensate. Here general price level is referred to as the **antecedent variable** that accounts for the primary relationship between the price of rum and salary.

In other circumstances it is useful to introduce a third variable, not in order to explain away the primary relationship, but in order to explain how it works. This is what I shall do with the occupational mobility table. It would be quite legitimate to look for an antecedent variable, but I prefer for present purposes to think about an **intervening variable**. This time we start by assuming for the time being that a father's occupation really does influence the son's, and ask how it exerts that influence. The two possible general answers are, first, that the influence is direct (a nepotistic mechanism) or, second, that some third variable acts as a causal link.

Of course, nepotism does operate to some extent. A large proportion of 'company directors' get their start from Dad's position. The best way to get to be a farmer, or a doctor, or even a docker may still be to arrange to be born to a father in the same line of work. But these are special cases, which cover only a relatively small number of workers. So it may make more sense instead to look for a third factor that is influenced by a father's occupation and in turn

Figure 18.5   Causal model to explain occupational mobility

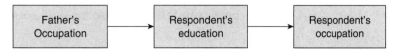

influences the son's. An obvious candidate is education. A father in a higher status job is likely to improve his son's educational chances in a number of ways: by paying for private schooling, or by moving house to a good school district, or just by knowing the ropes and pushing hard. And, of course, on the whole, the better the son's education, the higher the status of his eventual job.

Figure 18.5 represents the causal model implied by this (see Chapter 2). In an ideal world (ideal from the point of view of a power-crazy social scientist, that is), we would set up a randomised controlled trial to check this idea. A cohort of children would be assigned to schools at random, so that the causal flow would be interrupted: father's occupation would no longer influence education, so that this path would no longer be available for transmitting an effect from father's job to son's job. If this were indeed the only path through which father's occupation influenced son's, then the apparent effect of **paocc162** on **occ2** would disappear; if other paths were operating, then the effect would persist.

Alas, such a research design is hardly practicable. However, we can simulate at least part of what it implies. Instead of artificially assigning children to schools at random, we can examine sub-groups in which there is *naturally* no variation in schooling. If there is no variation then, necessarily, there can be no co-variation, so the causal flow is interrupted. Then, if we find that within these subgroups there is a reduced relationship (or even none at all) between father's and son's occupation, we can conclude that the relationship was at least partly a result of the flow through differences in education.

To do this with existing survey data we tell SPSS to repeat the original tabulation within all education level groups – those who had one year of schooling separated from those with two years, three years, etc. (This seems to assume that everyone completes a whole number of years at school, which is no doubt not true, but the inaccuracy seems unlikely to be of crucial importance.) With any practicable sample size this will not quite work, because the sample will have to be divided across too many sub-groups, so we compromise by using broader education categories. In my example I compromise by using only three categories and, since this is US data, I divide the men into those who had at least some college education, those who have a high school diploma but no more, and those who did not graduate from high school. Where to make that split will depend on what the investigator knows of important thresholds in the local education system.

First, then, I had to create my education variable. You have already seen the distribution of the variable, DEGREE (Figure 18.1). The three highest categories (2 Junior College; 3 Bachelor; and 4 Graduate) contained quite small numbers of

Figure 18.6   Respondent's occupation by father's occupation controlling for education

				PAOCC162		
DEGREE2				1.00 non-manual	2.00 manual	Total
.00 < high school	OCC2	1.00 non-manual	Count	10	40	50
			% within PAOCC162	23.8%	10.7%	12.0%
		2.00 manual	Count	32	334	366
			% within PAOCC162	76.2%	89.3%	88.0%
	Total		Count	42	374	416
			% within PAOCC162	100.0%	100.0%	100.0%
1.00 high school	OCC2	1.00 non-manual	Count	64	104	168
			% within PAOCC162	50.0%	25.9%	31.7%
		2.00 manual	Count	64	298	362
			% within PAOCC162	50.0%	74.1%	68.3%
	Total		Count	128	402	530
			% within PAOCC162	100.0%	100.0%	100.0%
2.00 college	OCC2	1.00 non-manual	Count	120	104	224
			% within PAOCC162	88.2%	83.9%	86,2%
		2.00 manual	Count	16	20	36
			% within PAOCC162	11.8%	16.1%	13.8%
	Total		Count	136	124	260
			% within PAOCC162	100.0%	100.0%	100.0%

Table title: **OCC2 * PAOCC162 * DEGREE2 Cross-tabulation**

men, so I decided to group them into a single one. The following SPSS commands did the grouping, labelled the variable, and requested the necessary tables:

```
recode degree
  (0 = 0)
  (1 = 1)
  (2 thru 4 = 2)
  into degree2.
value labels degree2
  0 '< high school'
  1 'high school'
  2 'college'.
crosstabs tables occ2 by paocc162 by degree2
  /cells = count column.
```

The crosstabs command produces an **occ2** by **paocc162** table for every category of **degree**: three separate tables in each of which education is 'held constant'. It may help to think of this as a three-dimensional table: a stack of two-dimensional tables, in which the stacking axis is the third variable. What you actually get is Figure 18.6.

What are we to make of this? First, note a caveat: some of these conditional tables are rather short of cases, especially in certain sub-groups. In particular, there are only 42 non-manual fathers in the table of non-high school graduates. This really means that we should be quite cautious about drawing firm conclusions.

Next, some further points of terminology. The variable **degree2** is called the control variable, and we are investigating the relationship between occupation and father's occupation controlling for education. You will recall that the distribution of **occ2** on its own is called the marginal distribution, while the distributions of **occ2** within categories of **paocc162** are called the conditional distributions. By analogy, the original **occ2** by **paocc162** table is called a marginal table, and the three new tables are called conditional tables: they show the relationship between **occ2** and **paocc162** under specific conditions of **degree2**. Similarly, we sometimes speak of marginal and conditional relationships; and the process of elaborating a table, as it is classically called, consists in essence of comparing a marginal relationship with its conditional counterparts. Sometimes the several conditional associations are summarised into a single partial association; in practice this is done by calculations based on the **correlation coefficients** (see Chapter 11), rather than by working on the conditional tables.

The marginal association here can best be summarised by the percentage difference already established: 36.6. In the marginal table it really didn't matter (apart, perhaps, from convenience in the wording of the verbal description of the findings) which row we chose to make the comparison. Now, however, it is important that we be consistent with that earlier decision: since we used the second row of the table and subtracted the first column from the second we must treat each conditional table in the same way; otherwise we might not notice if the sign of the difference (positive or negative) changes between marginal and conditional tables. In practice, this will seldom happen, but it would not do to miss it.

So we find the same percentage difference in each conditional table, and get respectively

$$89.3 - 76.2 = 13.1$$
$$74.1 - 50.0 = 24.1$$
$$16.1 - 11.8 = 4.3.$$

The sign does, in fact, remain positive, so in every conditional table there is still a tendency for manual fathers to have manual sons. However, in every case the conditional association is weaker than the marginal 36.6. So the overall conclusion is that when education is held constant, the relationship between father's and son's occupation is substantially weaker. A plausible causal interpretation is that, if non-manual fathers were not able to get a better education for their sons, there would be greater inter-generational mobility. But beware: there may be other variables involved whose inclusion in the analysis would lead to a quite different conclusion – for instance, IQ is quite highly correlated with education, and it is consistent with the results obtained here (though we have no direct evidence whatsoever) that non-manual fathers tend to have genetically brighter sons, who get better education through meritocratic selection rather than through father's efforts. (For an attempt to throw some light on this question, see Jencks (1973).)

Of course, almost as obvious as the difference between marginal and conditional associations is the variation *among* conditional associations, a phenomenon known in the traditional literature as specification, because education specifies the conditions that determine whether and to what extent the primary relationship holds. (In more recent literature, the term *interaction* is used in exactly the same sense.) In the present example, the association remains quite strong among those who just graduated from high school (the second conditional table), but is considerably weaker in the other two, especially among those who have some college education. My interpretation of this would be along the following lines.

- Without a high school diploma, having a non-manual father doesn't help very much.

- Once you have a college education, a manual father is no longer an important handicap.

- If you are in the middle band of education, your father's occupation can have more influence.

It has to be recognised that all this is at best true only in terms of the rather crude educational and occupational classifications that I have used. These have been to an extent necessitated by the rate at which multidimensional tables can generate cells if they have too many categories per variable, but a measure of education which fails to take account of the *quality*, both real and perceived, of the school is hard to justify as a basis for 'holding constant'. Probably if a better measure of education were available the conditional associations would be even weaker – but the opposite is possible. The problem of too many cells can sometimes be solved by using a different statistical method (multiple regression, for instance); the problem of measurement demands a constant alertness on the part of the researcher, so that measures can be developed that more closely approximate the often carefully explicated theoretical constructs. But the basic logic of causal analysis remains the same, however technically advanced the methods used to implement it.

18.4 A GENERAL APPROACH TO SURVEY ANALYSIS

In the words of Poul Anderson, the science fiction writer, 'There is no situation, however complex, which on careful examination does not become more complex.' The main application of this idea to the analysis of survey data is that the world is multivariate: every effect has not one but several causes. So to find a relationship between two variables is not the end but little more than the beginning of the analysis. It is the researcher's job to be sceptical about the causal interpretation that might be made from such a relationship, to think carefully, in a theoretically sensitive way, about what 'nuisance factors' might be involved in the system of variables, and to find ways of testing alternative explanatory hypotheses. The approach exemplified in this chapter has a long and distinguished history, and incorporates the logical principles – in particular, the idea of holding constant the suspected nuisance factors – which underlie more statistically advanced methods, such as multiple regression and log-linear analysis.

18.4.1 STATISTICAL INFERENCE

Traditionally, statistics textbooks are divided into two sections: *descriptive* and *inferential*. **Descriptive statistics** is about the best way to describe or summarise the data on your desk; **inferential statistics** explicitly recognise that the data on our desk are a finite **sample** (assumed to be representative) of a *universe* that the analyst is really interested. The universe is often referred to as a **population**, whether or not it actually consists of everyone living in a particular country or other location (see Chapter 9).

Chapter 2 noted that modes of reasoning are often divided into *deductive* and *inductive* argument. Deduction goes from the general to the particular (all men are mortal; Socrates was a man; therefore Socrates was mortal). Induction goes from the particular to the general (on every occasion (though only a finite number of occasions) that I (Isaac Newton) have observed an apple released in mid-air, it has fallen to earth; from which I derive the Law of Universal Gravitation). You will see that statistical inference uses inductive reasoning.

Now statistical inference is in turn divided into two categories: *estimation* and *hypothesis testing*. To see the difference between, albeit in caricature, consider the work of a psephologist. In analysing a 'voting intentions' survey, she examines the responses to the simple question, if there were a general election tomorrow, would you vote for the Bigendian candidate (Swift, 1726) or for the Littlendian? She concentrates on the difference between the two percentages, $d = b - l$; where b is the percentage intending to vote Bigendian, etc. The difference could be negative if there is a majority for the Littlendians.

Estimation starts from the position that the psephologist has no idea what to expect, and wants to report the most likely result in the population, using only the sample difference. In fact, the best *point estimate* in most situations is found by simply using the sample value to represent the population equivalent – the sample difference in percentages is the best estimate of the population difference. Best, but not perfect: almost certainly the sample difference will stray from the true, population value, just because of sampling processes. So her next step will be to calculate an *interval estimate*: the range within which the true value is likely to fall, given the sample value. 'Likely' is usually taken to mean '95 per cent of the time'. In pre-election polling the point estimate is usually declared to have a margin of error of 5 or 6 per cent.

Hypothesis testing approaches the problem rather differently. Now the analyst has an advance expectation about the result, based on theory, or perhaps on last year's result. Often, this expectation, or **hypothesis**, is that the two parties get the same support, so that $d = 0$. Of course, even if it is exactly 0 in the population, it is unlikely to be exactly that in this sample. The statistician's job now is to decide whether the observed result could plausibly have been found if the hypothesis is true, or whether it casts too much doubt on the hypothesis for a rational person to continue to believe it. The scientist often sees her job as trying to reject the hypothesis – rather like Popper's ideas of **falsification**, though, many would argue, different in subtle but crucial ways (see Chapter 2).

18.5 SUMMARY

This chapter has shown by example the first steps in carrying out a statistical analysis. Although it may seem complicated, a lot of the drudgery of data management and analysis is taken care of by the computer. However, learning to use data analysis programs such as SPSS, and the statistical tools they provide, does take time and effort. The rewards are considerable, because knowing the basics and developing confidence in statistical analysis will give you access to a host of datasets and interesting research possibilities.

DISCUSSION QUESTIONS

1   Explain what a marginal frequency distribution is.

2   What is structural mobility? Give some examples of the changes in occupational mobility over the past 30 years. What consequences are these changes likely to have had on the proportion of people in 'manual' and 'non-manual' occupations?

3   One of the difficulties in using random samples is dealing with non-response. This can cause a problem if the non-respondents differ in some systematic way from those who do respond (see also Chapter 9). List some of the relevant ways in which non-respondents might be different from respondents, and assess how important these differences are likely to be for a survey such as the US General Social Survey or the UK General Household Survey.

PROJECT

If you have access to a computer with almost any version of SPSS you will almost certainly be able to use the small subset of the General Social Survey which is included with the package. Ask your local SPSS coordinator how to do this, and how to get a frequency count for all the variables. Having got this far, browse through the variables until you find one that looks interesting as a dependent variable: you could start with **satjob**, **hapmar** or **life** (roughly satisfaction with job, marriage and life generally). Try to find out what sort of people are happiest with their lot. What marital status is most conducive to general life satisfaction? What truth is there in the assertion that men get more out of marriage than women? All these questions can be addressed by cross-tabulating a satisfaction variable by one or more background factors, possibly after recoding.

RESOURCES

An excellent introduction to SPSS, which will also get you started in statistics, is Norusis (2006) *SPSS 14.0 Guide to Data Analysis*. There are hundreds of books on statistical methods for social scientists, but relatively few of them deal adequately with cross-tabulation methods.

By all means browse through the shelves of your library and bookshop; one of the best is Fielding and Gilbert (2006) *Understanding Social Statistics*, which shows how to perform a range of analyses in SPSS. More advanced is Agresti and Finlay (1999) *Statistical Methods for the Social Sciences*.

A very clear treatment of survey methods in general, from problem formulation to finished report, is to be found in De Vaus (2002) *Surveys in Social Research*.

Finally, when you get seriously interested in quantitative methods, Sage have a comprehensive series of short books called *Quantitative Applications in the Social Sciences* which is often an excellent starting point.

19   Secondary Analysis of Survey Data

Nick Allum and Sara Arber

KEY POINTS

- Before thinking about collecting new data, explore the possibility of using existing sources.

- The quality and representativeness of large-scale, mainly government, datasets far exceed what the typical student could collect for a dissertation project.

- Obtaining data is easy and free for students in higher education.

- A 'sociological imagination' is needed to make interesting and insightful inferences from secondary data sources.

19.1 INTRODUCTION

This chapter discusses the practical issues and considerations that students need to take into account when selecting and analysing data from existing survey datasets. A discussion of what is meant by 'secondary' analysis and why one might want to undertake such a thing is followed by a summary of the major types of survey dataset that are available. Differences between **panel**, cross-sectional and continuous surveys are highlighted and examples of these are discussed. There then follows a discussion of some of the advantages and also the pitfalls of using secondary data sources for sociological analysis, followed by a guide to locating and obtaining datasets. The chapter concludes with a brief discussion of methods that can be used for the analysis of survey data and some ideas for student projects.

Government and other large surveys, as well as the increasing number of panel/longitudinal studies, provide very rich sources of data for **secondary**

analysis. Many of these are under-analysed, from both a statistical and a theoretical viewpoint. This chapter argues that secondary analysis requires sociological imagination and that the secondary analysis of large, primarily government, surveys has untapped potential as a source of sociological insights.

British students are usually encouraged to collect their own data for final year undergraduate projects, Masters dissertations and PhD theses. This contrasts with the USA, where most sociology students conduct secondary analysis of existing large-scale survey data, much of which has been collected by government. The lack of use of secondary analysis in Britain is surprising given that a large number of high quality national survey datasets are readily available and that expertise in the analysis and data management of large surveys is in great demand by employers.

19.2 WHAT IS SECONDARY ANALYSIS?

Secondary analysis is the re-analysis of existing survey micro-data, collected by another researcher or organisation, for the analyst's own purposes. Survey *micro-data* are the original data available in an anonymised electronic datafile (De Vaus, 2002).

In fact, the term 'secondary analysis' is really rather misleading, as in most cases the secondary analyst is analysing the data in a way that has not been done before. It really is a shorthand way of referring to survey research that involves no primary data collection. The secondary analyst is most often addressing quite distinct conceptual and theoretical issues from those of the original data collector. So, one of the challenges of secondary analysis is to use one's sociological imagination to construct theoretically informed research questions that can be addressed by somebody else's data – data that may have been originally devised and collected for very different purposes. In the case of government surveys, these purposes are almost invariably descriptive rather than analytic.

The proliferation of survey research means that more and more data are available for secondary analysis. However, according to the principle of 'garbage in, garbage out', it is important that the data to be used meets appropriate criteria of reliability, validity and representativeness. In most cases this is not too much of a problem, as the integrity of large-scale public domain datasets far exceed anything collectable by a lone researcher. Aside from the reliability of the data, a further issue relates to the conceptual assumptions embedded in surveys. These are often implicit, reflecting the underlying conceptual framework of the organisation or individuals who collected the original data, and need to be subjected to critical scrutiny. Only certain types of questions will be asked, and whole areas that the analyst may be interested in may not be covered. For example, British government surveys contain detailed questions to measure income and poverty, but rarely collect data on wealth, e.g. the value of houses and other assets.

One of the creative and intellectually satisfying aspects of secondary analysis is deciding how to measure concepts of theoretical and/or empirical interest. One needs to search through the questionnaires and codebooks of government and other surveys to identify variables that might stand as indicators of concepts of interest. These variables might be combined into multi-item scales or indices at the discretion of the researcher in order to obtain more reliable and valid measures of underlying unobserved constructs. It may be that the relevant data have been collected but not analysed or published previously (this is all too common), or analysed only in a certain way that reflects particular theoretical standpoints. For example, during data collection, it may have been assumed that the husband's occupation is an appropriate measure of married women's social class. Secondary analysts can apply alternative conceptual assumptions in their own analyses, for example, classifying women by their own rather than their husband's occupation or characterising the household by the characteristics of the highest income earner rather than the Head of Household (Arber, 1989; 1997).

Secondary analysis is now easier than ever, since nearly all students have their own personal computer and the average PC can store and process very large datasets containing thousands of records and variables without difficulty. Statistical packages, such as SPSS, STATA or SAS can often be saved onto the student's PC as part of an educational licensing agreement with the student's higher education institution. These statistical packages are now, for the most part, very user friendly, are capable of handling complex survey data structures, and can produce high quality graphical output and tables for direct export into word-processed documents and spreadsheets.

A recent development is the possibility for analysts to do simple analysis of some of the datasets available interactively via the web. This is possible for quite a few of the datasets mentioned in this chapter, including the European Social Survey, the UK Census and SARs, the US General Social Survey and others (see Section 19.3.6).

19.3 TYPES OF SURVEYS AVAILABLE FOR SECONDARY ANALYSIS

There are a vast range of survey data suitable for secondary analysis. It is likely that whatever your area of sociological interest, several survey datasets could be used to help answer your analytic questions. In fact, given the resources expended by governments on these datasets, and their quality, you should really only think about collecting your own data for a student project if there is really

Figure 19.1   Examples of British survey data available for secondary analysis

Major cross-sectional and continuous government surveys

Annual Population Survey
British Crime Survey
British Social Attitudes
Census Microdata (SARS)
Continuous Household Survey (Northern Ireland)
Expenditure and Food Survey/National Food Survey
Family Expenditure Survey
Family Resources Survey
General Household Survey
Health Survey for England
Integrated Household Survey (Continuous Population Survey)
Labour Force Surveys
National Travel Survey
Northern Ireland Family Expenditure Survey
Northern Ireland Labour Force Survey
Northern Ireland Life and Times Survey (and the former Northern Ireland Social Attitudes)
ONS Omnibus Survey
Scottish Crime Survey
Scottish Health Survey (SHeS)
Scottish Social Attitudes
Survey of English Housing
Time Use Survey
Vital Statistics
Welsh Health Survey
Young People's Social Attitudes (periodic offshoot of the BSA)

Major longitudinal surveys

1970 British Cohort Study (BCS70)
British Household Panel Survey (BHPS)
English Longitudinal Study of Ageing (ELSA)
Longitudinal Study of Young People in England (LSYPE)
Millennium Cohort Study (MCS)
National Child Development Study (NCOS)

Cross-national surveys

E-Living: Life in a Digital Europe
Eurobarometer Survey Series
European Election Study
European Social Survey
International Social Survey Programme
European and World Values Surveys

nothing available already in the public domain. This section discusses some of these public domain sources of data available in Britain. Survey data can also be obtained from other countries, often but not always as part of cross-national datasets, where the same questions were asked in two or more countries simultaneously. Figure 19.1 provides an outline of the main types of British survey data and some cross-national examples.

19.3.1 MAJOR CROSS-SECTIONAL AND CONTINUOUS GOVERNMENT SURVEYS

Central government collects a wide range of cross-sectional survey data about the characteristics of the population that are of interest to sociologists. Some government surveys are annual, containing many of the same questions each year, other government surveys are repeated every few years and some are one-off (or ad hoc) surveys conducted to provide representative data to address specific policy issues. Some of the annual surveys such as the GHS or Labour Force Survey (LFS) are actually in the field more or less continuously, with interviews being carried out during most of the year. The longitudinal datasets are derived from either panel or cohort surveys. Panels contain a sample of individuals who are repeatedly interviewed over time at intervals of between one and five years. **Cohort** surveys are similar except that all members of the sample are the same age, and are generally followed from birth, as in the NCDS and BCS, or slightly older, as in the MCS. Cross-national survey data are not generally collected directly by central government, although most of the funding will come from government indirectly. The ESS and Eurobarometer surveys are cross-sectional surveys fielded in all European Union member states. The ESS is biennial and the Eurobarometer is fielded several times per year.

Information on and access to all of the major survey datasets are provided by the UK Economic and Social Data Service (ESDS), http://www.esds.ac.uk

The *General Household Survey* (GHS) has interviewed all household members aged 16 and over in about 10,000 households every year since 1971, although there were no surveys in 1997 and 1999. Core data are collected each year, including housing characteristics, ownership of consumer goods, employment, educational qualifications, health, use of health services, income and marital and family history. Some topic areas are asked on alternate years, e.g. smoking and drinking and others are asked less regularly, e.g. sections on leisure activities, informal care and older people. A list of the topics covered in each year can be found at the back of the GHS annual reports (Bennett et al., 1996; ONS, 2005). The GHS is one of the surveys that is incorporated into the new Integrated Household Survey (IHS) from 2008. This new survey replaces the Continuous Population Survey and also incorporates the Labour Force Survey, Expenditure and Food Survey and ONS Omnibus survey, as well as the GHS. The advantage of integration of this kind is that it enables the analyst to make links between variables previously measured within different households or individuals. Developments of this kind will lead to more opportunities for interesting sociological questions and hypotheses to be addressed via secondary analysis.

The descriptive data collected in government surveys such as the GHS or FES reflect the policy concerns of specific government departments at particular times, as well as continuous tracking of some issues. For example, during the late 1980s, Conservative government policy was to expand share ownership and increase the uptake of personal pensions and private medical insurance, and questions were asked in the GHS about these topics at this time.

Another government survey of interest to secondary analysts (see Figure 19.1) is the *Labour Force Survey* (LFS), which collects data from all adults in 80,000 households per year. It focuses particularly on the social and demographic characteristics of the employed, self-employed and those seeking work. Although the LFS has a panel element (see Section 19.3.4), in which members of the same household are interviewed five times at three monthly intervals, this panel element is rarely used by secondary analysts. This is probably because methods for analysing panel data are more complex than cross-sectional methods and also because the panel extends over a relatively short period of time. The *Health Survey for England* (HSE) has been conducted annually on a sample of about 8,000 households since 1993 (Sproston and Primatesta, 2003). It collects data from all adults and in recent years also from children. An unusual aspect is that respondents are examined by a nurse, who also takes a blood and urine sample. The results of these laboratory tests provide additional indicators of health status.

The *British Crime Survey* (BCS) is another example of a repeated survey, one which has surveyed a representative sample of adults every two to four years since 1982, but which became annual in 2001. As is usual with any repeated cross-sectional survey, there are both common features and differences between each of waves. Another widely used repeated survey is the *British Social Attitudes Survey* (BSA), for which a representative sample of adults are interviewed about a range of contemporary social and political attitudes. This is not a survey funded directly by central government but relies on public funding via the research councils as well as other funders for particular 'modules' of questions. Some topic areas are only asked about in certain years while others, e.g. political orientation, or voting behaviour are asked about every year. The BSA has been conducted annually since 1983 by the National Centre for Social Research (NatCen, formerly called SCPR) (Jowell et al., 1998). It therefore provides a major time series that enables researchers to document changes in attitudes over the past 25 years.

19.3.2 OTHER LARGE CROSS-SECTIONAL SURVEYS

As well as the major established cross-sectional surveys, there are a number of irregular or one-off government-funded surveys that are available for secondary analysis. There have been four national surveys of ethnic minorities in Britain conducted over a span of 30 years. The most recent was the 1994 Fourth National Survey of Ethnic Minorities (Modood, et al., 1997). Each survey was designed to cover distinct topics, reflecting changes in the concerns and conceptual frameworks relating to the Black and minority ethnic population in Britain. These surveys provide important data on the socio-economic characteristics and health of Black and minority ethnic groups in Britain.

Surveys may be designed because of a perceived lack of information about an area of policy interest. The 1991 National Survey of Sexual Attitudes and Lifestyles (NATSAL) was conducted because of concerns about the spread of HIV/AIDs and the lack of knowledge about the sexual behaviour of adults. Nearly 19,000 men and women aged 16–59 were interviewed with funding provided by the Wellcome Trust (Wellings et al., 1994). Recently the Department of Culture, Media and Sport (DCMS) has commissioned two 'Taking Part' surveys that ask citizens about their involvement in sporting and cultural activities and their reasons for participating or not participating. In the 2006 survey an ethnic boost sample was included that makes it possible to make reliable inference about patterns of participation among ethnic minority groups (Austin and Vine, 2007).

19.3.3 CENSUS MICRODATA

The decennial population census provides benchmark data about the social characteristics of the population, the extent of geographical migration and housing conditions in local areas (Rees, et al., 2002). A description of UK census materials can be found at http://www.census.ac.uk/

Secondary analysis can be conducted on 1991 and 2001 population census data using the Samples of Anonymised Records (SARs), which comprise a 3 per cent (2 per cent in 1991) sample of individuals and an independent 1 per cent sample of households. The individual level 2001 SAR contains 1.75 million individuals living in both private households and institutional establishments. The SAR is particularly relevant for studying minority ethnic groups (Dale et al., 2000), since detailed analyses about members of different minority ethnic groups based on national sample surveys are often unreliable because of the relatively small numbers found even in large government surveys such as the GHS. Dale et al. (2000) provide a guide to analysing census microdata including examplars of analyses using the SARs. For further information, see http://tinyurl.com/om78q

In the USA, public use microdata samples were made available following each census from 1960 onwards (Marsh et al., 1991), and have provided a major source of data for sociological research on issues such as occupational attainment and residential segregation according to ethnicity. They are available as 5 per cent and 1 per cent samples, depending on the level of geographical detail required. The US Census Bureau web site shows the vast amount of census data available for secondary analysis (http://www.census.gov/). Past US censuses (since 1850) have been made available as micro-data that can be accessed via IPUMS (Integrated Public Use Microdata Series run from the University of Minnesota – http://www.ipums.org).

The ONS Longitudinal Study (LS) contains microdata on 1 per cent of the population of England and Wales. The LS links census records from 1971, 1981, 1991 and 2001 for the same individuals and other members of their household, as well as linking data about deaths, births and other vital events (Brassett-Grundy, 2003). For reasons of confidentiality, LS data are not available from the Data Archive at Essex, but can only be analysed in association with the Centre for Longitudinal Study Information and User Support (CELSIUS), accessible at http://tinyurl.com/2g84jz

Aggregate census data for local areas such as enumeration districts, electoral wards and local authority districts are extensively used by geographers. These Small Area and Local Base Statistics (collectively called Area Statistics) consist of a large number of cross-tabulations based on all enumerated people in the 2001 (and earlier) censuses. The information contained includes age, sex, occupation, qualifications, ethnicity, social class, employment, family structure, amenities and housing tenure. The area statistics are aggregated to a hierarchy of geographical units and are available electronically via CASWEB (http://census.ac.uk/casweb).

19.3.4 MAJOR LONGITUDINAL SURVEYS

Time can be taken into account in cross-sectional surveys by asking respondents about their past work, family and homes. This is called *retrospective* data. However, accurate data on many issues of interest to sociologists cannot be obtained retrospectively, for example, an individual's attitudes five years ago, their domestic division of labour prior to marriage, their income in the past, and their health or behaviour as a child. These issues can only be studied using a panel or **longitudinal design**, which collects information about the individual's current attitudes or behaviour, and periodically re-interviews them. Panel, longitudinal or cohort studies are conducted by collecting data at a number of points in time from the same set of people, that is, *prospectively*.

Cross-sectional surveys can demonstrate associations but cannot reveal the causal ordering of variables. For example, unemployment is correlated with poor health, but the theoretical and policy implications of this association depend on the direction of causation: whether being unemployed causes poor health, or poor health leads people to lose their jobs and have difficulty finding new ones (Bartley et al., 2004; Fox et al., 1985). The direction of causation can never be fully resolved with observational (as opposed to experimental) data, but panel or longitudinal studies, which measure health status prospectively at different points of time, provide much stronger evidence for the direction of causality. This is because for X to cause Y it must be the case that X precedes Y in time. In cross-sectional surveys, even where people are reporting on events that occurred in the past, we can never be sure that, for example, recall of event X is not influenced by the respondent's current experience of Y. If this were true, then we could not be sure that X really preceded Y.

Britain is fortunate to have four birth cohort studies, based on births in one week in March 1946 (National Survey of Health and Development), in

March 1958 (National Child Development Study, NCDS), and in March 1970 (the British Cohort Study, BCS, formerly Child Health and Education Study) and on a sample of children born in 2000/2001 (Millennium Cohort Study, MCS). In each case, survey data have been collected at intervals from the mother and the child, as well as from teachers and health professionals, and subsequently data have been collected during adulthood. The 1946 and 1958 studies have also surveyed the next generation, collecting data about the children of cohort members. The 1991 wave of NCDS collected data from the partners of cohort members (Ferri, 1993). The BCS and NCDS have been harmonised now in that data collection sweeps take place during the same years and many of the variables are matched, making it possible to make direct comparisons between the cohorts. The Millennium Cohort is a new cohort study of babies born during 2000–01 which is based on a sample collected over an approximately one-year period, rather than a 'census' of every birth in a particular week.

Secondary analysis of these birth cohort surveys is a highly cost-effective method of answering a host of policy and theoretical research questions, many of which were never dreamed of by the data originators. For example, the three British birth cohort studies were not originally designed to clarify the direction of causation in relation to inequalities in health, but have been used extensively to address this and many other issues (Wadsworth, 1986: 1991; Power et al., 1991).

Another important longitudinal source of data for secondary analysis is the British Household Panel Study (BHPS), which began in 1991 and interviews all adults in about 5,000 households annually (Buck et al., 1994). The BHPS is a panel survey that now has 15 waves of data. One of the aims of the BHPS is to provide a 'basic resource for both strategic, fundamental research in the social sciences and for policy-relevant research' (Rose et al., 1992: 6). BHPS data are of high quality and are made available rapidly to users; comprehensive and user-friendly information about the BHPS is available at http://tinyurl.com/yveul2

Some surveys begin as one-off, and only later is it decided to add further waves of data collection from the same individuals. This occurred for the Retirement and Retirement Plans Survey which interviewed people aged 55 to 69 in 1988 (Bone et al., 1992) about their retirement intentions and financial circumstances around the time of retirement. It was planned as a one-off survey, but later there was a follow-up interview, so it became a panel survey (Disney et al., 1997). The DSS/PSI Programme of Research into Low-income Families (PRILIF) has involved several separate inter-linked studies (Ford et al., 1998; Marsh, 2000), beginning in 1991 with a postal survey of all parents. All the lone parents were followed up each year until 1996. Alongside this were repeated cross-sectional surveys of parents in 1993 and in 1994.

19.3.5 ANNUAL LARGE SURVEYS FOR QUASI-COHORT ANALYSIS (SYNTHETIC COHORTS)

Secondary analysts can use annual and repeated cross-sectional surveys as quasi- or synthetic cohorts to address some of the policy issues that require an understanding of the impact of period, cohort and age (Harding, 1990; Waldfogel, 1993). Pseudo-cohorts can be constructed by using successive years of cross-sectional surveys such as the GHS or BSA to track a particular birth cohort through time. Although the same individuals are not surveyed each year, a sample of individuals from the same birth cohorts are. Thus, the characteristics of one cohort can be compared with those of a sample that represents them demographically five or ten years later. This approach is limited in that it focuses on average group characteristics or behaviour, rather than those of individuals, and does not capture the various changes in individuals' circumstances over time. However, it is a very useful method for examining in more detail how observed changes in an entire population can be explained by generational replacement, ageing or period effects. For instance, one could try to see if an observed decline in racial prejudice over time is due to older generations being replaced by younger, less prejudiced, ones, or whether all age groups have changed their beliefs during the same period (Rothon and Heath, 2003).

19.3.6 SURVEYS FROM OTHER COUNTRIES

Along with the increase in availability of UK data for secondary analysis, there are also more international data available. Some of it is country-specific, but increasingly cross-national comparative data are available. The USA in particular has a vast number of high quality datasets for secondary analysis. These include repeated cross-sectional surveys such as the General Social Survey (GSS), which has been conducted annually since 1972. By 2004, the combined GSS datafile contained over 46,000 individuals and over 3,500 variables. It is easily accessible and used extensively in the USA for teaching. More information about the GSS and access to the data can be found at http://gss.norc.org

There are a number of important US panel studies, particularly the Panel Study of Income Dynamics (PSID) and the Health and Retirement Survey (HRS). HRS began in 1992 as a national survey of 12,000 people aged 51–61, interviewed biannually. Since 1998 it has been extended to cover a US nationally representative sample of 22,000 people aged 50 and over – see http://tinyurl.com/yrwy9t. Countries often develop a specific study because of the insights gleaned from a comparable study in another country. For example, elements of the BHPS were modelled on the PSID and English Longitudinal Study of Ageing is modelled on the HRS.

Some studies are designed for cross-national comparison and aim to ask equivalent questions in different countries. The British Social Attitudes Survey (BSAS) is linked to the International Social Survey Programme (ISSP), which began with four countries in 1984 (the USA, the UK, Germany and Australia) and now conducts annual surveys in around 40 countries. Each year a different module of questions is asked simultaneously in each country, for example, on social support and social relations in 2001 and citizen and state in 2004 (see http://www.issp.org/ and http://tinyurl.com/26ty2r). By combining cross-time and cross-nation research, this provides a powerful research design to study social processes (Jowell et al., 1989; 1998). There is now a European Community Household Panel Study, Europanel, which takes place annually in 15 European countries. Since 1999, collection of the British data for Europanel has been merged with that for the BHPS. Another major survey is the Eurobarometer series. These surveys are carried out in European Union member states, with the most recent surveys now having 25 countries included. The Eurobarometer regularly taps European social and political attitudes, as well as having special topic modules each year such as attitudes to science and technology (European Commission, 2005). Access to Eurobarometer questionnaires, codebooks and data for UK users is at http://tinyurl.com/yomhjg. The European Social Survey is a relatively new biennial survey series that collects high quality data on European social attitudes. Unlike most major studies, the data are available to download directly from the ESS web site, rather than access coming via ESDS or the Data Archive. There have been three waves of data collection so far. The survey has a number of core questions as well as rotating modules on particular issues. Recent topics covered include attitudes towards immigration, trust and civic engagement, happiness and well-being. See http://www.europeansocialsurvey.org for access and documentation.

19.4 THE VALUE OF SECONDARY ANALYSIS

Several types of research are only practicable using secondary analysis, because appropriate primary data would be too expensive to collect or cannot be obtained. Some examples will be discussed in this section.

19.4.1 STUDYING SMALL OR RARE SUB-GROUPS

Many issues of sociological interest focus on proportionately small sub-groups of the population, e.g. a specific age group, ethnic minority group or type of family. It is usually impossible to identify a complete sampling frame for such groups in order to draw a representative sample, so research is often biased in significant ways (see Chapter 9). An alternative is to use large surveys, if necessary combining data from consecutive years to increase the sample size of the sub-group of interest. For example, sociologists may be interested in comparing lone fathers with lone mothers. Cooper et al. (1998a; 1998b) combined three years of the GHS to obtain a sufficiently large sample to analyse the health of children of lone parents and the health of children from minority ethnic groups, of which there are relatively few relative to the general UK population.

Even for research that does not involve proportionately small population sub-groups, it is often beneficial to combine a number of years of survey data. The greater the sample size, the more chance the analyst has of detecting associations between variables in the population, even when these associations are weak.

19.4.2 STUDYING HOUSEHOLD RELATIONSHIPS AND SOCIAL CONTEXTS

A key concern of many sociologists is to analyse how an individual's behaviour may be influenced by the characteristics of significant others and by the wider groupings of which they are a part. Many government datasets collect data on all adults in the household, allowing the researcher to analyse the interrelationships between the characteristics of different household members (Dale et al., 1988). For example, household surveys, such as the GHS, allow analysis of young people's unemployment and how this is related to whether their fathers and/or mothers are unemployed, and analysis of the effect of the smoking behaviour of parents on children's health. Another use for household data is to be able to adjust statistically for household or family effects on child outcomes (e.g. health or educational attainment) that would be impossible to do using only individual level data (Sieben, 2004).

19.4.3 COMPARATIVE ANALYSIS

Government surveys have grown in number in most industrialised countries. This opens up the possibility of cross-national analysis that addresses social policy or sociological issues. For example, Finland conducts a Level of Living Survey which is very similar to the British GHS. In Finland, women's employment rate is comparable to that of men, with nearly 90 per cent of women employed full-time during their child-bearing years; this contrasts with British women's high rate of part-time employment and lower overall employment participation rate. Arber and Lahelma (1993) compared the impact of employment participation on the nature of inequalities in women's health in these two societies. The ISSP, ESS and Eurobarometer series are designed for cross-country analyses, as discussed in Section 19.3.6. For instance, Gaskell et al. (2000) examined differences and similarities in attitudes towards biotechnology in Europe using Eurobarometer surveys.

19.4.4 TREND AND HISTORICAL ANALYSES

Annual surveys allow the analysis of trends over time, for example, to monitor the impact of policy changes on poverty and attitudes towards welfare and moral issues. Many of the surveys discussed in Section 19.3 have been running for several decades: the GHS since 1971, the Family Expenditure Survey (FES) since 1957 and the British Social Attitudes Survey (BSAS) since 1983, and can therefore be used in this way.

Researchers may collect their own survey data and use secondary analysis to examine changes between an earlier survey conducted by another researcher and their own survey. The contemporary survey may be designed to include the same questions as earlier survey(s) to allow analysis of changes in attitudes or behaviour over time. It is also possible to check for bias in estimates from a small scale non-probability sample survey (e.g. a quota-controlled or convenience sample) by comparing with estimates from a large-scale high quality government survey.

19.5 POTENTIAL PITFALLS OF SECONDARY ANALYSIS

Before undertaking secondary analysis, it is important to be aware of a number of potential pitfalls.

19.5.1 ASSESSING THE VALIDITY OF THE DATA

When considering a potential survey for secondary analysis it is necessary to subject its methodology to critical scrutiny, including the quality of developmental and pilot work, interviewer training and fieldwork control, the method of sample selection, nature of the sampling frame and response rate. The secondary analyst needs to obtain as much documentation as possible about the collection of the survey data and be aware of any potential data limitations. An absolutely crucial task is to read and become familiar with the questionnaire and detail of wordings and response alternatives in the original survey. It is all too easy to begin to analyse variables in a dataset without really knowing exactly what the numbers represent.

19.5.2 THEORY, ANALYSIS AND DATA

One **paradigm** in survey research is 'theory-testing'. That is, the primary researcher designs a research instrument and collects data in order to test theoretical hypotheses. These are operationalised into empirical hypotheses, and questions are developed to validly measure the theoretical concepts that constitute the various elements of the researcher's theory (see Chapter 2). However, the secondary analyst has to work with someone else's survey questions and assess whether these questions adequately measure the concepts used in the **theory** they wish to test. It may not be possible to measure the key theoretical concepts because appropriate questions have not been asked in the survey or the questions may not be valid indicators of the relevant concepts. In this case, the analyst has to be **pragmatic** and to evaluate how well available variables could stand in for those that he or she would ideally like to have, and to write a justification of this in their results.

Alternatively, appropriate questions may have been asked but the existing coding categories do not provide theoretically meaningful analytic distinctions. For example, the 1991 GHS asked a series of questions about childcare for children under 11, distinguishing between different sources of paid care. However, all forms of unpaid care were combined into a single category of 'family and friends', with childcare by partners or others living in the same household explicitly excluded. This **coding** meant a researcher could not assess how much childcare was provided by grandparents or other relatives while mothers were at work. In Eurobarometer surveys on attitudes towards science and technology (2001) and biotechnology (2002), many attitude questions were asked in a binary agree/disagree format, meaning that techniques like linear regression are not possible with attitude items as dependent variables. Also, it is likely that measurement error is large, in that respondents were forced to respond in one of two definite categories rather than on a quantitative scale.

19.5.3 TIMELINESS OF DATA

Government surveys are usually at least two years old before they are made available for secondary analysis, typically after the publication of the relevant government report. Only a few surveys are released more quickly. For example, the Labour Force Survey collects data on a quarterly basis and the datasets become available from the Data Archive 14 weeks after the end of each period of data collection. However, since most sociologists use secondary analysis to address analytic questions that are not highly time dependent, a lag in the release of data is not a major constraint. For example, the theoretical insights from analyses of class inequalities in health are likely to be the same irrespective of whether the survey data are one or four years old.

19.5.4 SIZE AND NUMBER OF VARIABLES

Many datasets have large sample sizes, which is valuable because analyses can be based on a sample large enough to produce robust conclusions. However, there is a possible pitfall here in that many associations between variables will be statistically significant but could also be very small in terms of their magnitude. This underlines the need for analysts to think about what is substantively interesting and what constitutes an effect size of practical importance rather than focusing on statistical significance. For instance, if we are comparing the attitudes of men and women towards nuclear power on a 10-point attitude scale, a mean difference of 0.2 may be statistically significant but be practically trivial and of no consequence. However, results from a large epidemiological study that show a tiny, but statistically significant, effect of aspirin on mortality rates from heart disease may lead to several hundred lives saved per year if acted upon. So, as these examples show, there is no substitute for careful thinking by the analyst to decide what constitutes a substantially important effect from one that is trivial but nevertheless statistically significant.

Survey data often contain a large number of raw and derived variables. For example, the full NCDS dataset contains about 13,000 variables! Often the raw or derived variables are not in the form that the analyst needs and so further recoding is required. For example, in many UK datasets a 9-point Goldthorpe-Heath social class schema variable is derived from hundreds of raw categories of job occupation. Nevertheless, it might be necessary to recode even this simplified version of a social class variable to binary dummy variables. All of this takes time and some facility with the relevant software for managing the data.

19.5.5 COMPLEXITY OF DATA STRUCTURE

Household surveys generally interview all adults in the household, and so the amount of data collected from each household varies according to the number interviewed. For each respondent may also vary the amount of data depending on responses to certain questions. For example, the GHS asks for details about all doctor consultations in the last two weeks; most respondents have none but some will have six or more. The Data Archive supplies the GHS as an SPSS file based on either individuals or households, which is straightforward to use but may not contain all the needed linkages between household members. A panel survey inevitably has a more complex data structure than a cross-sectional survey. Data can be organised in either 'long format' or 'wide format'. These two formats are depicted in Figure 19.2. In wide format, each record (or row of data) represents a single individual. Repeated observations on the same variables (e.g. monthly income and spending) are stored as additional variables (columns) – income1, income2 etc. In long format, each record represents an occasion of measurement so that each individual will be represented by as many records as there are occasions on which they were interviewed. The analyst may need to reformat the data according the type of analysis that is planned.

19.5.6 MISSING DATA

Another issue that affects all types of data and particularly longitudinal data is missing data and sample attrition. Sometimes people answer some but not all questions in the interview. This is known as item-missingness. This is the problem that is encountered in cross-sectional secondary analysis. For longitudinal

Figure 19.2   Relationship between long and wide formats for panel data

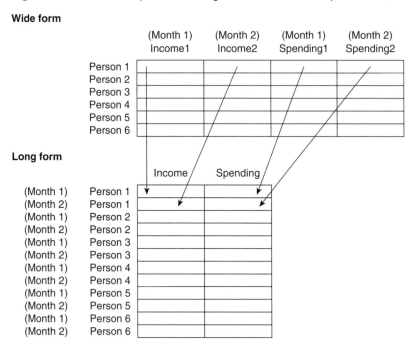

data, the analyst has to make decisions about how to handle cases where there are missing data in one or more waves of data collection. Sometimes respondents leave a panel and are never reinterviewed (**attrition**). In other instances, a respondent misses one or more waves of interviewing but returns on a subsequent wave. Missing data almost always pose a threat to the validity of the inferences that can be drawn from analysis. A simple example of why this might be is to think about trying to estimate the mean income in a population. If richer people are less likely to be available for interview, or are more likely to refuse to answer questions about their income, then our estimate of population income will be biased downwards. A full discussion of the problems of missing data and what to do about them is beyond the scope of this book, but a good place to start is http://www.missingdata.org

19.6 HOW TO OBTAIN DATA FOR SECONDARY ANALYSIS

The Economic and Social Data Service and the Data Archive at the University of Essex jointly provide access to data for secondary analysis in the UK. The Data

Archive distributes almost all British government-funded surveys for secondary analysis. Datasets are supplied free of charge for unfunded research and educational uses. The only charge is for supplying printed documentation about the survey, such as interview schedules and codebooks, but these are often freely available electronically. The Data Archive also holds overseas datasets and provides a gateway to non-UK data for UK researchers and vice versa.

19.6.1 CHOOSING A DATASET

If you are considering analysing a large dataset, a good place to start looking for more information is the ESDS (http://www.esds.ac.uk). Another key resource is the Social Survey Question Bank. Questionnaires for the main government surveys and other key surveys, such as the BHPS and BSA are available online through the Question Bank. The Question Bank (qb.soc.surrey.ac.uk) aims to increase the sharing of good practice on ways of designing questions to measure social scientific concepts, to document data collection instruments and to provide insight into underlying conceptual and design issues. The full questionnaires are online and can be easily downloaded for use by students and researchers.

The most comprehensive source of information about available data is via the ESDS Data Catalogue facility. Searches can be performed on study descriptions, keywords and geographical locations relating to all the studies in the Archive's collection. Detailed information is available about each deposited study, including names of data collectors, details of the purposes of the research, the populations sampled, data collection methodologies, and references to publications and reports based on the data. The Data Catalogue also provides access to online user documentation for the datasets in the Archive, as well as searchable lists of variables, including variable labels and value labels (response codes) for the more popular datasets, such as most years of the large government surveys. For some datasets there are links to online data analysis tools.

Once you have narrowed down your search for a suitable dataset, you should read as much as possible about the dataset before placing your order. This includes reading thoroughly the online documentation (which can be downloaded), information about the sample design, response rates and data collection methodology, and reports and publications based on the dataset. You can review the lists of publications based on the dataset provided by the Data Catalogue, or you may be able to obtain further information about publications from the data originators' web site or through direct contact. It is essential to do this background reading first, for otherwise you may find that another analyst has already used the dataset to answer the same research questions as you were planning to study. Of course, you may disagree with their results, analysis or interpretation of data, leading you to a closer refinement of your research questions.

19.6.2 ORDERING DATA

Once a suitable dataset has been identified from the Data Catalogue, the dataset can be ordered electronically by completing an order form online. The form requires information on the data and documentation requested, the format of the data, and how the data is to be supplied to the user, e.g. on a CD-Rom or downloaded via FTP.

Before a copy of a dataset is released by the Data Archive or permission is given to access the data online, the user must sign an undertaking on conditions of use. Most datasets are covered by a standard Undertaking Form, but government and some other surveys require further information, including the submission of a short proposal outlining the research purposes for which the data is to be used, as well as a special Undertaking Form which must be signed. Publications are not vetted in advance, so the secondary analyst's work is not controlled in any way. The only requirement of some depositors, e.g. government departments, is that two copies of any publications using the data must be submitted to the Data Archive, one of which is forwarded to the data depositor.

19.6.3 DATA ANALYSIS SYSTEMS ONLINE

Increasingly, data are becoming available for online analysis. Links to online analysis through an interface called NESSTAR, where this is available, are shown in the Data Catalogue search results at ESDS or by going directly to http://tinyurl.com/yrga85. The ESS has online data analysis facilities through its web site. Using NESSTAR, the user can generate frequencies and cross-tabulations as well as perform correlation and regression analysis. Online analysis can provide quick answers to basic questions and can also serve as an exploratory stage in choosing a final dataset to work with in more detail.

19.7 PROCESS OF ANALYSIS

The secondary analyst works in a much more iterative way, moving between existing survey questions and theory, than is suggested in the 'theory-testing' model of social research (see Chapter 2). In fact, the actual process of most survey analysis, be it primary or secondary is in practice a combination of exploratory data analysis and theory-testing or confirmatory analysis, (Bryman, 2004).

The main task for the secondary analyst is to become familiar with the dataset and in particular the variables that will potentially be used for analysis.

This will include examining the distribution of variables and summary statistics such as means, medians or modes (see Chapter 14). It is particularly important to understand the questionnaire routing that determines who has been asked each question. Close attention should be paid to the various missing data categories and the numbers of missing cases. The analyst will also need to be fully informed about the range of derived variables available in the dataset. In some datasets, there will be detailed information about how each variable was derived, but this may not be available for all. Information about the construction of derived variables will probably be in the form of syntax commands for SPSS, or whatever program was used to derive the variable.

Following a review of existing research literature, the analyst should be able to develop a theoretical model that they wish to explore. It may be useful to draw this out as a conceptual model (or path diagram) which shows how each concept is related to the others and the expected causal direction of the relationships. The variables that can be used to measure each of the concepts within the conceptual model then need to be examined. This phase of exploratory data analysis is likely to involve the production of a range of cross-tabulations, graphical analyses and descriptive statistics. The analyst needs to try out different indicators of the concepts and alternative ways of constructing various new derived variables to measure the relevant concepts (see Dale et al., 1988). Only at this stage will the analyst finalise which variables and derived variables are most appropriate to use for their own analytic purposes. Finally, it will be necessary to decide which statistical techniques are most appropriate to use.

19.8 SUMMARY

The challenge and opportunity of secondary analysis are to apply theoretical knowledge and conceptual skills to use existing survey datasets creatively to address sociological questions. In most cases the term 'secondary analysis' is a misnomer, since the process of secondary analysis of large datasets is more akin to 'primary analysis'. The researcher may be analysing the dataset in new and novel ways both theoretically and statistically. A key value of secondary analysis for students is to develop their skills in data analysis and managing data, while at the same time creatively applying and developing theoretical ideas by translating survey questions into analytic concepts and drawing and testing conceptual conclusions from statistical analyses. Finally, by using high quality representative data for secondary analysis in their projects and dissertations, students can produce work that may even be publishable and of interest to the wider research community.

DISCUSSION QUESTIONS

1   You are considering doing a project on racial prejudice among the British public. Where might you find some data to analyse and what kind of research questions might you be able to investigate with these data?

2   In secondary data analysis, we are compelled to use questions that other investigators have decided to include in the survey. Discuss some of the ways in which you could try to evaluate how valid these questions are as indicators of theoretical concepts that you are interested in analysing.

3   Discuss the advantages and disadvantages of doing secondary analysis. Under what circumstances would it *not* be a good idea to use secondary data?

PROJECTS

1   Compare the advantages and disadvantages of conducting secondary analysis of a large government survey with carrying out some focus groups for a research study of the reasons for gender differences in earnings.

2   Think of a research problem that can be examined using secondary analysis. For example, what is the extent of racial prejudice in Britain and what kinds of people are more or less likely to hold such attitudes? Then undertake the following:

(a) Find out what surveys could be used to address your research problem by using the ESDS Data Catalogue.

(b) Having identified a relevant survey, select questions to measure the concepts needed to address your research problem. Provide a critical appraisal of the adequacy of these questions as measures of the concepts to be studied.

(c) Draw a conceptual model of the inter-relationships between each of your concepts, including the direction of any expected causal relations.

3   Conduct secondary analysis using a subset of the 2002 General Household Survey, which can be downloaded from http://tinyurl.com/ 2fpdhr. For example, elaborate a two-variable relationship by controlling for one or more theoretically relevant control variables and draw conclusions about the direction of relationship between these variables. Your analysis could be conducted using cross-tabulation or graphical techniques. Your analysis will be easier if you first recode all the variables to be analysed into either two or three categories.

RESOURCES

Dale, Arber and Procter (1988) *Doing Secondary Analysis* provide a comprehensive discussion of secondary analysis including examples and practical guidance on how to conduct secondary analysis and derive variables using both SPSS and SIR. Dale et al. (2000) *Analyzing Census Microdata* provide an excellent overview of the use of the Sample of Anonymised Records (SAR) for secondary analysis, including examples.

Fielding and Gilbert (2005) *Understanding Social Statistics* is a clearly written guide to the statistical analysis of social science data, which refers to the use of a web site containing datasets for secondary analysis, including a sample from the 2002 GHS.

Marsh (1988) *Exploring Data: An Introduction to Data Analysis for Social Scientists* is an excellent introduction to exploratory data analysis, which should be the first stage in any secondary analysis.

See also the various web sites mentioned in the chapter, in particular:

Economic and Social Data Service http://www.esds.ac.uk

European Social Survey http://www.europeansocialsurvey.org

Inter-University Consortium for Political and Social Research http://tinyurl.com/2atun5

Missing Data http://www.missingdata.org.uk

International Social Survey http://www.issp.org

German Social Science Infrastructure Services http://www.gesis.org/en

20 Computer Assisted Qualitative Data Analysis (CAQDAS)

Ann Lewins

KEY POINTS

● Researchers can make use of many types of qualitative data and efficient management of the data requires care and systematic techniques.

● Projects may incorporate specific methodological approaches for individual elements of the research process.

● Software packages (CAQDAS) have been developed to support work in varied ways and beyond that, the user can discern which tools within each software will enable the researcher to work the way he or she wants with the data.

● CAQDAS will not do the thinking or the analysis for the researcher. CAQDAS may not even save time overall since many more sophisticated tasks of data management and interrogation are made possible.

20.1 INTRODUCTION

Using computer assistance in qualitative data analysis (CAQDAS) has become a widely accepted strategy for the management of qualitative data. This chapter refers to several categories of CAQDAS software. It will focus mainly, however, on a particular group of software packages, the 'code-based theory builders' (Weitzman and Miles, 1995) and some of the ways they seek to assist the researcher work with large volumes of qualitative information and data. Theory-building software programs will help you manage the data and to manage your ideas about them. They have a dominant place in many academic and applied social research settings as well as an increasing presence in arts and science disciplines. In addition to the analytic and clerical assistance they offer, these programs can assist in the wider management of general information about a research project. A brief overview of the categories of software which handle qualitative data, whether from a qualitative or more quantitative analytic approach, and a little of their historic development put this broad category of software in context. The range of tools in different software packages and the ways of working with them have some similarities but also distinct differences. Lewins and Silver (2007) reviewed seven programs and describe the wide range of commonly available functions and how they help the user.

The chapter begins with a general account of what is meant by qualitative data analysis, in the context of the development of Computer Assisted Qualitative Data Analysis Software (CAQDAS). Types of data and types of tasks are enabled by software listed and described. Six case study examples show how some of the basic tasks and dilemmas of qualitative data analysis are managed when using CAQDAS software. A resource section provides contact details for various programs including freely available software, sources of support, discussion lists etc.

Figure 20.1   MAXqda2 users interface: an example of a CAQDAS program, showing data storage, code and retrieve and memo functions – improving access to data

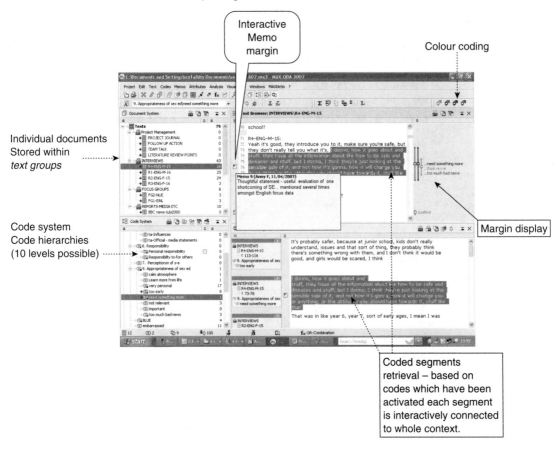

20.2 WHAT IS QUALITATIVE DATA ANALYSIS?

Qualitative data can include transcripts of interviews, fieldnotes, descriptions, narratives, biographical data, abstracts, lists and much more in the form of text and, increasingly, multimedia material. Handling such data can be disorganised and messy. When interpreting and recording significance, commonality, exceptions, or tracking a story, it is difficult to remember all the ideas you may have about the data. You need to keep in touch with examples of the data that demonstrate those ideas and the connections between those ideas. Whether the data are in textual, audio, video, or graphic format, ideas nearly always relate to parts of them. In essence, CAQDAS software seeks to maintain an easy contact between the ideas and those parts, while allowing an overview of the whole. Figure 20.1 shows the user interface of MAXqda, demonstrating how some elements of the analytical process are accessible all the time, for example, data storage, codes, the text of individual data files and retrieved segments.

Chapter 19 discusses the secondary analysis of survey data. CAQDAS may be used to analyse open-ended questions incorporated in surveys in a more qualitative way. The added value of triangulation and enhancement of the understanding of the survey population are benefits which are reflected in the expansion of mixed methods research (see Chapter 6) and in participatory approaches to social research (see Chapter 5) and CAQDAS can add new possibilities for the collection and analysis of such data.

Time and probably some support are needed to familiarise oneself with software to the point where the full range of tools can become useful rather than an extra burden. The availability of support, and the ease with which a software package can become useful are important considerations. The package should not become an obstacle to getting on with 'real work' with data. Do not be taken in by a vague recommendation to use software just 'because it's better' especially if you have a very short time frame, and even more importantly if there is no local support. Tips are included below to provide an idea of what can be done without placing too much of a burden on the user at the outset. Try to use the online help which is usually available or even better get at least a day's training from a reputable source. To enhance the quality of qualitative research it is important to know and to understand your methodological standpoint first, and then *to* bring a methodology to the software, rather than see the software as being the architect of your method.

20.3 THE DEVELOPMENT OF CAQDAS

CAQDAS software developed largely from work by academics who were involved in qualitative data analysis during the late 1980s (Fielding and Lee, 1991/1993). The CAQDAS acronym itself was solidified in the label given to a unique project (CAQDAS Networking Project – funded by the UK Economic and Social Research Council) founded by Fielding and Lee to support users in their exploration of 'Computer Assistance In Qualitative Data Analysis'. Since then, the project has continued to support researchers while the range of software packages has increased together with a similar increase in the range and sophistication of the tools within each program. As packages have been developed to handle textual data in various ways, typologies have been developed to categorise the programs (Weitzman and Miles, 1995). The major groups of packages concerned with the analysis of textual or other qualitative data are:

- Text Retriever and Text-based Managers are mainly concerned with the quantitative 'content' of qualitative data and automatic generation of word/phrase indexes, statistical information on word frequency and the retrieval of text in context. They will often have internal dictionaries and thesaurus facilities. They fall into a wider category sometimes referred to as content analysis packages. Examples include Sonar Professional, WORDSTAT and SIMSTAT.

- Code and Retrieve and Code-based Theory Builders have been more concerned with the thematic analysis and interpretation of textual data. These programs have greater usage amongst social and health sciences, and increasingly by other disciplines such as architecture, history, archaeology, dramatic and fine arts, pharmacology and management. Commercially supported software packages of this kind include NVivo, ATLAS.ti, HyperRESEARCH, KWALITAN and MAXqda QDA Miner. QUALRUS is from a slightly different generation of software and lacks some of the data management tools of the other software but has an artificial intelligence element which brings together the automatic identification of words, strings and patterns in the data with a coding device tool that learns from how you code to enable a code suggestion tool. Examples of free or low cost software include Weft QDA, TAMS Analyser, AnSWR and Transana (the latter emphasising video analysis and transcription).

The Code and Retrieve packages have caught up with the range of tools available in the Theory Builders so these categories have merged. Such packages use the database structure of the software to enable the assignment of 'codes' or labels to chunks of text, and the subsequent 'retrieval' of text segments according to selected code labels (see Chapter 17). Subsequent interrogation of codes, and their co-occurrence, proximity (or not) etc., in the data, allow researchers to test relationships between identified themes and concepts within or across subsets of data. This extra functionality allows the 'code-based theory building' label to be applied to an increasing range of programs. The label 'theory builders' must not be misunderstood. No theory is built by such packages themselves. Any theory or conclusions that are drawn are the result of the researcher's own thinking and actions in the software.

Increasingly packages do not fit neatly into these software typologies. ATLAS.ti5 and KWALITAN, MAXqda with MAXdictio and NVivo7 all provide code-based theory building tools but can also produce quantitative word frequency information formerly unusual in this category of program. QDAMiner has strong links with the Text Retrievers, the family of programs that provide a much more sophisticated level of statistical analysis of the content of textual data, yet it also provides an easy-to-use set of code and retrieve tools. Transana, a low-cost program provides transcription function keys allowing the researcher to synchronise the transcript or commentary to a digital video file, but it also has coding tools that will perform retrievals similar to ATLAS.ti and HyperRESEARCH.

The incorporation of multimedia data into a working project is now possible in different ways. In ATLAS.ti and HyperRESEARCH, multimedia data are

Figure 20.2   Integrating multimedia files into a project in Hyper RESEARCH and ATLAS.ti

In HyperRESEARCH (MAC and PC Windows compatible) the Movie Source Window displays movie files (with their audio tracks, if any) using Apple's Quicktime software

You may select and code any number of frames, to be replayed when recalling the source material from the Study Window or in a hyperlinked report

Digital video of the moonlanding of 1969

In ATLAS.ti - starting to mark clips of a video file as the cursor progresses along the frame counter, prior to assigning a thematic code to the marked clips or 'quotations' in ATLAS.ti terminology. Retrieve all themed clips/quotations later, by double clicking on the thematic code

directly analysable in the software (see Coding Tasks below). In NVivo and MAXqda, the use of hyperlinks to whole audio or video files provides a looser level of connection to the rest of the analysis. WEFTqda (free software) and QDA Miner both enable the use of the PDF (Portable Document Format) documents. Although the incorporation of multimedia data into projects has increased (Figure 20.2), the great majority of projects still consider text transcripts of interviews etc., as the best way to access large amounts of data quickly. This is the case even though the transcription of data is a very lengthy process.

20.3.1 TRANSCRIPTION SOFTWARE

Transcription of data has been aided to some extent by technological developments. Recording of interviews etc. is very often achieved via digital recorders. There are packages, mostly free or low cost, which assist the routine processes of transcription of digitised sound or video files. Transana, Transcriber, HyperTRANSCRIBE and F4 can all assist in the transcription of digital audio-visual files. They do not do the transcription for you, but they provide keyboard shortcuts and auto-structuring of the textual files you are creating. There are several Voice Recognition (VR) software packages that enable one voice (you must train the software to recognise your voice) to dictate text which the software then transcribes into machine readable format. Many computer users who have wrist and hand problems such as repetitive strain injury, which severely affect their ability to use the mouse, use VR software. Because VR software can only recognise speech by the person who has trained it, to use the software for interview transcription involves listening to sections of the recording then and reading back the sections in your own voice.

> ### TIP
>
> If you are preparing to transcribe data and you are expecting to use a CAQDAS package to manage and help analyse the data, try to get hold of a transcription protocol which fits the package. Each CAQDAS package has different requirements. See Resource section.

20.4 ANALYTIC PARADIGMS USING QUALITATIVE DATA

Qualitative researchers approach projects, the analysis of data, and the use of software from a range of methodological and epistemological perspectives. Many specifically refer to **grounded theory**, a 'general method of constant comparative analysis' (Glaser and Strauss, 1967; Strauss and Corbin, 1994). Alternatively, your approach might be heavily influenced by **theory**, so you are likely to work deductively, testing or measuring the data against the theory (see Chapter 5). Generally, CAQDAS software programs do not dictate which approach you take. You can open-code the text as you work through it, or you can create codes in advance which focus your attention on theoretical issues and their occurrence in the data. You might work with a mix of both ways. It is important to be explicit about the way you have worked and to be able to justify your choices, but the software will allow you to work in whatever way suits you.

On the other hand you might want to make use of aspects of theory or existing explanations but also want to work inductively on the data. In Layder's (1998) 'adaptive theory', for instance, he suggests that the process of coding can begin by sensitising concepts and ideas, as 'orienting devices'. These concepts are selectively plucked from existing theories to 'crank up' the theory

Table 20.1   The general tasks of analysis, assisted by code-based theory building software

Note: most tasks based on researcher's own actions and thought processes
• Storing textual data – providing immediate access to data files.
• Exploration and Discovery by searching (for strings, words, phrases in verbatim content).
• Adding memos or annotations anchored to text.
• Emergent coding (bottom-up).
• Theory-based coding (top-down).
• Flexible coding scheme structures (the organisation of codes).
• Collection of detailed codes into more abstract broad brush concepts.
• Retrieval of coded segments.
• Memo on a more abstract basis, free of text.
• Mapping connections between codes – creating graphic models/networks.
• Organising data, i.e. to enable interrogation.
• Linking to and between parts of text and other files.
• Searching the database and the coding schema, testing ideas, interrogating subsets.
• Generating reports/output (print-outs or readable files in other applications).

building process, while always retaining 'theoretical openness' to new concepts arising from the data. He suggests that since there is a general acknowledgement that any observation and interpretation is theory laden, starting the coding process from a 'clean slate' or *tabula rasa* is difficult. It is better therefore to be explicit about any theories that are contributing *a priori* to your ideas.

20.5 HOW 'CODE-BASED THEORY BUILDING' SOFTWARE CAN HELP

Theory-building CAQDAS software packages do not dictate the way in which you perform tasks, but they can influence you in terms of the complexity of the tasks you undertake and your readiness to perform them. Furthermore, they will encourage you to feel that you can be flexible in revisiting, rethinking or redoing some of the processes of analysis. Some of the tasks that they can help with are listed in Table 20.1.

20.5.1 STORING DATA AND IMMEDIATE ACCESS

Programs differ in the way they store data. Some have project databases that contain the data while others link to the data stored outside the project. The user creates a 'project' and then imports or assigns individual data files to the project database.

20.5.2 EXPLORATION AND DISCOVERY BY TEXT SEARCHING

(See point 2 in Table 20.1). Discovery achieved by reading and re-reading is likely to be the most thorough method of exploring qualitative data. With very large amounts of data this may be impracticable without using the software to locate words and phrases that signal particular topics of interest. Conventional searching works only with textual data, and varies slightly from one program to another. The differences, contexts and debate concerning the use of this tool are discussed at length by Fisher with reference to both the Code-based and Text Retriever categories of software (Fisher, 1997: 39–66).

20.5.3 ANALYTIC MEMOS

The ability to write analytical or procedural notes while working is provided in a number of ways. In some programs you can place annotations at points in the data. In others you can create one memo per data file. In most packages you can also write comments or memos to explain codes and concepts, how they are defined and how they change. Memo writing is an important aspect of the management and continuity of analysis. Insightful ideas can quickly be forgotten. It is useful to write them down as soon as you have them, especially if they require follow-up action on another day.

20.5.4 CODING, CATEGORISING INTERPRETING, IDENTIFYING CONCEPTS

Even if you were working with transcribed data on paper, you might want to annotate the data, write notes or scribble in the margin. You might highlight sections of the text in different colours to signify different themes or topics. If working with textual data in e.g. Microsoft Word, you might copy these sections of the text under different headings or into different files. Usually you will reduce the amount of text that you are dealing with and in the latter case you will be lifting those copied and pasted sections of text out of their context.

Code-based retrieval packages will allow you to apply keywords or phrases (codes) to passages of text and put a label on the significance of a section or segment of the data. This process links codes with certain segments of data rather than copying and pasting data into different headings. Retrieving coded text activates these links. You can usually apply as many codes as you like to the same segments of text. The methodological approach being taken will affect how codes and themes are drawn out from and applied to the data. Codes might be created early on as part of a coding framework that arises from the objectives of the project and are then assigned to data where relevant (a 'top-down' method of coding). If your project is defined by theory, you may establish codes that contain the main elements (for example, sensitising concepts) from that theory, before you begin to code the text. Or codes might only be created from, and be assigned to, segments of text during close work with the data (a bottom-up approach to code creation that is sometimes called **emergent coding**). The coding strategy is not a software issue, although the flexibility with which you can create, modify and refine the coding schema will be improved by the use of software. Subsequently, codes may be collected together or sorted to encompass more abstract concepts by combining issues and themes that seem to be related in some way. Very often such combinations are useful, not just because they are part of a refinement process, but because getting all the coded segments together in different ways in various reports may help in seeing new elements or dimensions in a topic.

20.5.5 ORGANISING DATA

Other categorisation processes will also allow you to organise the data if there are already significant known values that can be ascribed to the respondents; the sex and age of the respondents may be important, for instance. In Speller's example (which we look at in some detail shortly) it was important to compare data across the five time phases of her longitudinal dataset. The five time phases were values of the variable, *Time*. Each time phase value had to be assigned to the relevant data files. Such organisational categorisation of data can be a very important aspect of project management in any longitudinal project or where comparison across the sources of data or types of respondent will be useful.

> TIP
>
> Knowing how to 'organise' the data (as Speller did, by time phase) may not be obvious right from the outset. Discovering that you need to ask a particular question may be the trigger for creating a particular subset, so organisation of data for this purpose can happen at any stage.

20.5.6 THE CODING SCHEME

Most 'theory-building' programs allow for an inherently hierarchical organisation of the coding schema, though none of the CAQDAS software packages

Figure 20.3   Interrogation of subsets in Young People's Perceptions project (Silver, 2002) in MAXqda2007

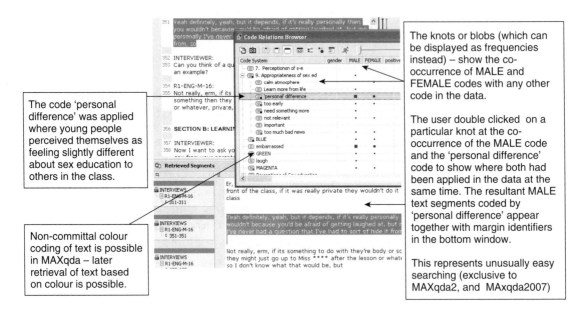

The code 'personal difference' was applied where young people perceived themselves as feeling slightly different about sex education to others in the class.

Non-committal colour coding of text is possible in MAXqda – later retrieval of text based on colour is possible.

The knots or blobs (which can be displayed as frequencies instead) – show the co-occurrence of MALE and FEMALE codes with any other code in the data.

The user double clicked on a particular knot at the co-occurrence of the MALE code and the 'personal difference' code to show where both had been applied in the data at the same time. The resultant MALE text segments coded by 'personal difference' appear together with margin identifiers in the bottom window.

This represents unusually easy searching (exclusive to MAXqda2, and MAxqda2007)

mentioned force you to organise codes in this way. In a few programs, such as ATLAS.ti and HyperRESEARCH, the default structure of the coding schema is not hierarchical. Hierarchies or the appearance of hierarchies can be imposed in some windows, and collections of codes can be made, but in the main 'code-lists', codes will be listed at the same level. Some programs (ATLAS.ti, MAXqda, and NVivo) provide alternative ways to collect codes, by allowing the user to place short-cuts to codes together in *sets* or *families*. This enables the user to re-arrange codes, possibly into more theoretical collections, without re-arranging the coding scheme, see Figure 20.3 (Gulati, 2006).

20.5.7 RETRIEVAL

The software enables the retrieval of passages of text based on the presence of codes assigned earlier. You can then examine the retrieved segments, thus reducing the amount of data and stepping back from the dataset as a whole in order to focus on certain aspects. Retrieval can be done within the program enabling, for example, the re-coding of segments or memoing. Usually there is good contact from the coded segment back to the context it came from. Retrieval can be sent to output or report files that can be opened in other applications (e.g. a word processor, and spreadsheet applications).

> **TIP**
>
> Researchers working under severe time constraints for analysis may use only the Coding, Retrieval and Memo function. It needs very few tools to improve efficiency in managing the data.

20.5.8 TEXT SEARCHING WITH AUTOCODING

In most programs, you can search for several 'strings', words or phrases, at the same time. The 'finds', or 'hits' can often be saved, and then coded or autocoded with some surrounding context (this varies with the program). In such cases, all textual references containing the finds will be stored in the coding schema. Autocoding in this way may be useful for certain recurring structures, e.g. headings or speaker identifiers but if you are looking for topics, themes and **concepts** in the data you cannot rely on the finds to be exhaustive. Your respondents may have talked at length about a topic and never used any of the key words you have searched for. For a fuller debate concerning these tools, see Fisher (1997: 39–66).

> **TIP**
>
> Do not rely on autocoding techniques to be the only way you code unless the level of work on the data is to be deliberately rather superficial. Usually the aim in generating qualitative data is to perform an in-depth analysis of them.

20.5.9 SEARCHING, MAKING QUERIES – TESTING IDEAS AND THEORIES

The software can help you to ask questions about the relationships between codes as they occur in the text. Do particular codes appear together? Does one code always appear close to a particular other code? How do they compare across different sets of data and across the different groups of respondents? See Figure 20.3 for an example of such a search. Before this type of searching and question asking can occur, you must have arrived at the point where you have achieved enough consistent coding to rely on the results of the queries you make. For examples of such searches and illustrations in the example projects, see Speller (2000) and Silver (2002).

20.5.10 MAPPING

Some programs such as Mind Manager and Inspiration have been specifically developed to draw maps and models and have sophisticated graphic representation tools. Another program, Tinderbox, uses hypertext and mapping to allow the researcher to plot a summarised map, e.g. of notes about a work of literature or an aspect of society or work, and then create specific relationships between elements in the map. However, these programs do not include the other features of CASDAS programs. In CAQDAS packages, although the mapping facilities are less sophisticated, they do have integration and interactivity with the qualitative data within the project.

> **TIP**
>
> Mapping is close to writing; see it as just another way to make notes to yourself.

20.6 EXAMPLES: HOW THE SOFTWARE HELPED

The practice of drawing on different strategies to analyse data is very common. Examples of different but combined approaches are included below.

The Relocation of Arkwright

Speller (2000) examined the relocation of an entire mining community of 177 householders (the village of Arkwright) to a new village (because of subsidence and methane). The longitudinal project involved the comparative study of 25 villagers interviewed at five points in time. She managed the data in NUD*IST 4, a precursor to the current NVivo7 software. Speller's strategy of code creation was initially based entirely on grounded coding, working inductively from the data; yet the entire project was derived from a significant existing theory, Identity Process Theory (Breakwell, 1986; 1992) and the related concept of Place Attachment (Brown and Perkins, 1992). Since there was little empirical work to support Place Attachment, Speller's intention was to begin work in a grounded and open way but to keep the concept in mind while refining her coding scheme.

She describes a part of her coding processes as follows:

I printed out participants' responses in a concentrated form according to the codes generated. This highlighted complexities within a category, including nuances or differences which frequently resulted in splitting the category through re-coding or merging codes with one another.

(Continued)

From this scrutiny she built categories contributing to her understanding of Place Attachment, including:

Sense of security
Sense of autonomy
Optimal levels of internal and external stimulation.

The process of searching for relationships between themes and the identification of emerging patterns often showed up inconsistencies in participants' accounts:

These often represented or were an indication of the process of adaptation to a new environment and were therefore considered an important element for inclusion in the analysis. (Speller, 2000: 147–148)

Using the software, she was able to interrogate her data and the codes across and within time phases, e.g. how did talk about 'Previous rituals' feature in data for Phase 5 for all respondents?

Speller's work involved much more complexity than is captured here. What we see here as in other cases is the sense that complete immersion in the data and then in the coded data was necessary to further develop her ideas and existing theory.

Understanding knowledge construction in online courses

If you are adopting one of the discourse approaches to qualitative data (see Chapter 22), you may be interested in language, conversation or discourse as social constructions or cultural expressions. Gulati (2006) was interested in how students constructed meaning in online and blended courses. She used ATLAS.ti and a combination of methods to analyse data. Coding of the qualitative data was initially developed in a grounded, 'bottom-up' way. As she developed in her analysis she used Kelly's personal construct ideas to shape, label and order the codes (Kelly, 1970). See Figure 20.3 for illustrations of Gulati's coding schema and the various ways she organised her coding.

Codes originally developed a grounded way from the data were prefixed according to personal construct concepts and these helped her to group and make sense of the way she listed codes e.g.

(Continued)

(relate) – feelings of belonging,

(relate) – confidence in others,

(power) – what I say doesn't matter,

(power) – what others say matters,

(power) – when others are dominant, and

(comm) – meaningful participation.

She then needed different combinations of codes to help her think about how individual instances of concepts related to other ones – so she created Families of codes consisting of shortcuts to codes plucked from such above groupings (see Figure 20.4). She was able to retrieve all data in one Code family, or interrogate across different types of respondent.

The Networking tool in ATLAS.ti is used in Figure 20.4 to illustrate the collection of code shortcuts in the 'Trust in online communication' code family.

Figure 20.4 Part of the coding scheme for 'knowledge construction in online courses' (Gulati, 2006): prefixes, code families and a network view of one code family in ATLAS.ti

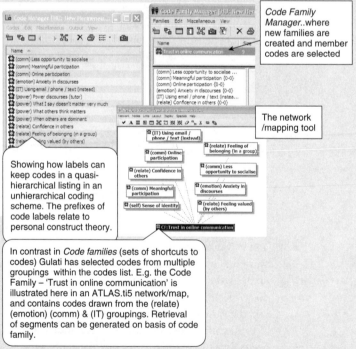

Gulati imaginatively made use of what she could see were the shortcomings of her coding scheme by tidying her list of codes in a way that made sense bearing in mind her theoretical orientation. She went further in grouping her codes in other ways to get different outputs and enable different interrogations of data.

TIP

Judge what might be useful to you in a software package and try not to be distracted by using every function available.

Distinction: Consumption and Identity in the People's Republic of China

Michael Griffiths's PhD project at the University of Leeds looks at the social effects of advancing consumerism in a provincial town in Liaoning Province, Mainland China. He uses Nvivo 7.0 to make sense of 'the strategies, or core logic, with which Chinese consumers cultivate the individual self and make themselves distinct from one another'. The theoretical roots of the project are in social anthropology and in poststructuralist approaches to meaning and power. Griffiths collected a massive amount of data in both English (fieldnotes) and in Mandarin Chinese (transcripts) as he lived and worked in the community as a participant researcher. This example helps to illustrate how software can provide flexible management in the face of considerable complexity, but also how software cannot answer all the dilemmas a researcher faces in making analytic decisions. Griffiths is still working towards his final analysis, but some of his frank descriptions of the stages of coding and the complex processes of generating insights are interesting. Griffiths's work also demonstrates that qualitative data analysis is not the easy option that it is sometimes thought to be by students shying away from statistics.

- His initial steps in coding were to be open to anything – this rapidly produced more than 200 codes within the 'Free node' area of NVivo 7.0.
- Quite often during the coding process he changed gear to flick fast through his data using the Text Search query options of NVivo 7 to find other occurrences of particular words, or Mandarin characters (see Figure 20.5).
- He began to apply theoretical notions to rationalise his codes into hierarchies within the 'Tree nodes' of NVivo 7.0:

Under my supervisor's guidance, I derived a number of larger constructs from my impressions of all the free nodes. In keeping with the aims and objectives of the research, these pertained to the strategies or dynamics employed in discourse about consumption.

(Continued)

… Though it was already clear that there were relationships between some of the codes – for example, some were dialectically opposed, others could clearly be made to fit 'within' another, larger code – it remained unclear as to how to proceed.

- Some of the emergent codes listed within the 'Free nodes' area were seen to be not relevant;

Or at least not *structurally* relevant, to aims and objectives of the research and thus could be ignored, at least for now, in the anticipation that, later, after further analysis had elucidated the core structural paradigms in the discourse, these redundant codes could be revisited to inform still further analysis.
… However, equally as clear at this stage, were that there were many free nodes which seemed clearly relevant to the objectives of the research that did not obviously seem to fit under any of the tree node constructs.

- He saw that this rationalising into hierarchical structures helped only partially.

Forming tree node hierarchies remained, however, wholly insufficient to handle the complex relationships between codes and larger constructs, despite my attempts to write memos illustrating the links and boundaries between them.

What his story tells us is that there are many demanding dilemmas of interpretation to be negotiated during qualitative analysis. As he says, 'NVivo is useful, but really it all gets done in the head. I find writing is the real key to analysis.' Although software does not perform the analysis for you, it can help to achieve a systematic process through which data can be efficiently organised and revisited, minor and major analytic changes of direction can be taken, and the relations between multiple seemingly unconnected strands of inquiry can be explored and built upon.

TIP

At an early stage of work get as familiar as you can with software in terms of how to manipulate, change and move codes when mistakes can be made when it doesn't matter.

Figure 20.5   'Distinction: Consumption and Identity in the People's Republic of China' (Michael Griffiths, PhD) thesis in progress) shows how text searching can find key words or phrases in NVivo 7

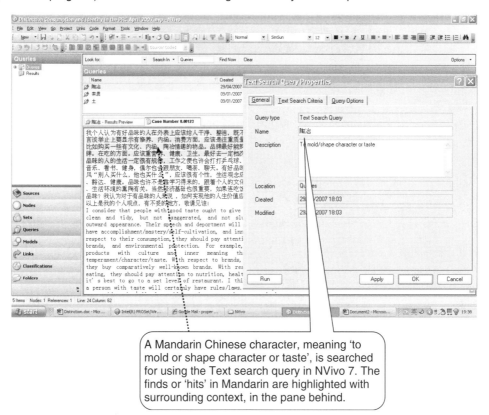

A Mandarin Chinese character, meaning 'to mold or shape character or taste', is searched for using the Text search query in NVivo 7. The finds or 'hits' in Mandarin are highlighted with surrounding context, in the pane behind.

National Child Development Study (NCDS)

In other discourse approaches, for example, in some approaches to the analysis of narrative, there may not be a very large dataset and the use of special software may not be necessary. However, if the dataset is large, it might be better managed with the improved access to data that CAQDAS offers. An example of using CAQDAS to manage a large dataset is the National Child Development Study (NCDS). This project started in 1958 as a perinatal mortality study with 17,000 cases. The birth **cohort** was followed up at ages 7, 11, 16, 23, 33, 42 and 46 years. The project became a mixed method project as different agencies peripheral to the lives of the children were interviewed and surveyed. Essays written by the children themselves at age 11 imagined what their

(Continued)

lives would be like at 25. In the qualitative part of this study Elliott uses **narrative analysis** on 560 essays written by the children. She also used the data management aspects of NVivo software to be able to interrogate the data. Coffey et al. (1996) consider the suitability of code-based theory building packages for analysing narrative data, where reduction or fragmentation of the data can be unhelpful. Coding processes are often concerned with the reduction of data. Elliott used NVivo tools and coding sparingly:

- to manage occurrences and contexts of certain words, like 'husband' and 'wife' to explore aspects of gendered identity in the essays;

- to categorise data according to quantitative information on demographic circumstances using the attribute tool in NVivo, for example, housing, and employment as an adult;

- to filter and select work for further in-depth study based on various parameters by interrogating on the basis of attributes.

Elliott's particular focus has been on gendered identity. Since the work has already gone into transcribing the handwritten essays, and inputting them and the quantitative information about the writers into an NVivo database, the potential to explore other aspects of the data is extensive.

Younger People's Perceptions of Sex Education

The research for Silver's (2002) PhD thesis comprised a comparative exploration of the historical development, provision and experience of school-based sex education in England and Wales and the Netherlands. The data, originally managed by a much older program NUD*IST v.4, were reworked significantly in ATLAS.ti 5, MAXqda 2, and NVivo 7 for the purposes of exploring and illustrating step-by-step processes for another publication (Lewins and Silver, 2007). Large amounts of various forms of primary and secondary data were used. Primary data were collected by questionnaires, focus groups and interviews, and secondary data were derived from various forms of documentary evidence. The reason for using this example is that Silver used tools in both MAXqda 2 and ATLAS.ti to redraw maps she originally drew by hand on paper in the original project. It seemed also an ideal project to illustrate a major advance in searching or interrogating the data across subsets without actually having to 'build a search/query dialogue box':

- She used the Code Relations browser in MAXqda to check gender relationships. Figure 20.3 is an illustration of how easy the process of comparing coding across subsets can be in MAXqda. This tool is a major development in making such interrogations easier.

- In MAXqda she also used a device for making layers in a map to deconstruct the learning processes of young people into different aspects, Learning from School and Learning from Friends, and to compare the modes of learning of those growing up in each country.

- The codes in the map are interactively linked to the data in various ways to enable the checking and validity of the connections being made.

- Her use of the network (mapping) tool in ATLAS.ti 5 to replicate the theoretical model she had earlier drawn by hand is illustrated in Figure 20.6. Giddens's *Theory of Structuration* (1984) (which argues that neither structure or agency should be given primacy in sociological explanations, viewing the relationship between them as a 'duality') was used in the Younger People's Perceptions project as a theoretical lens through which to view the body of empirical data and to help make sense of the interconnections. The map in ATLAS.ti was created retrospectively, but reflects the earlier hand-drawn maps. The difference when created in software is that all the material associated with the items in the map are interactively connected to it.

The figures in this chapter show the possibility of these programs for illustrating ideas and connections for presentation. The added value of having data 'sitting behind' the maps (possible in MAXdqa 2, ATLAS.ti 5 and NVivo 7) is a bonus to the researcher while still in the analysis stages of work.

20.7 SUGGESTIONS FOR PREPARATION AND PLANNING

When thinking about making use of CAQDAS software it is useful to prioritise a list of requirements that suit the way you will prefer to work. You may have very general needs or more particular requirements may strongly influence your choice of software.

Figure 20.6   Young People's Perceptions project (Silver, 2002), using a map to illustrate a theoretical model incorporating memos (see book icons incorporated in the map) to develop interpretation in ATLAS.ti

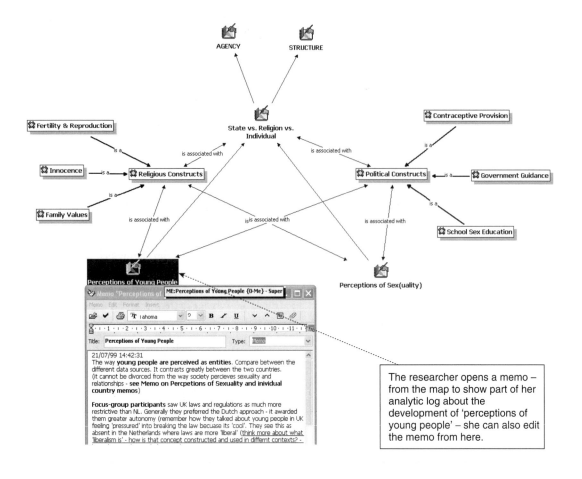

CHECKLIST

- If it is most important for you to be able to 'mark' the data as you analyse it, make sure the package you choose will give you full and unproblematic 'edit' rights on your data files. However, if you are working in a team project, it may be very important that you do not mark or change the data in any way.

- If you are engaging in a team project, prepare properly by finding out how work will be divided up, and how the software packages support that. Remember that as yet there is little software available at an affordable price which allows users to tap into one CAQDAS database and work from different workstations at the same time.

- If you have special types of data, e.g. audio-visual, find out the real extent of the support that software will give you for handling and cross-referencing the data. To prepare, generate video with the equipment you are about to use, and download the free trial CAQDAS software you are thinking of using and find out if there are any complicating factors which stop the software from seeing the data.

- Plan how you will transcribe data efficiently: if using digital recording techniques, investigate the transcription aids and software referenced earlier in the chapter.

- Investigate what the chosen CAQDAS software expects in the way of data format. The programs handle text only format (WEFT QDA, HyperRESEARCH), Rich Text format (MAXqda), all of those formats (ATLAS.ti and NVivo), or pdf (WEFT QDA, QDA Miner and shortly ATLAS.ti 6).

- Find out what units of text are used by the software chosen – paragraphs are used by all programs; sentences identified by full stops, colons, question and exclamation marks are used in ATLAS.ti; heading levels creating sections are used in NVivo.

- Allow enough time (and money) for preparation of data and familiarisation with the software.

TIP

The sooner you start using a CAQDAS program, the sooner you will start to feel more secure about what the program and its style feel like and you will gain the confidence to try out new things.

20.7.1 LIMITATIONS AND CONSTRAINTS

Not all analysis can or should happen within a software package. This may be obvious, but it is important to make the point since so much of our lives revolve around the expectation that computers are part of the way we work. The example projects and the aspects of software used in each of them have emphasised how CAQDAS has added to researchers' flexibility and ability to revisit and change ideas. Part of the flexibility gained is the immediacy of access to data.

Table 20.2   Free or low cost software

PROGRAM	SOURCE
CAQDAS Networking Project Offers support to world-wide research community. Seminars – Training workshops	caqdas@surrey.ac.uk http://caqdas.soc.surrey.ac.uk Bibliography – Articles – Events – Courses Tel: +44 (0) 1483 68 9455 Based at University of Surrey, Guildford UK
Online Resources Provides platforms for debate, information Advisory help-lines Download demo versions of software Links to free and commercial software developer pages Links to other related resources Links to data conversion/transcription software programs Links to free and low cost software	http://caqdas.soc.surrey.ac.uk/links1.htm
Online QDA and CAQDAS Resources, methodologies, references, QDA advice, step by step processes, Links	http://onlineqda.hud.ac.uk
Internet Discussion List qual-software Forum for debate about use of technology and software for QDA	http://www.jiscmail.ac.uk/lists/qual-software.html
Message archives for qual-software	http://www.jiscmail.ac.uk/lists/qual-software.html
Sociological Research Online Methodogical, political, cultural topics and debates.	http://www.socresonline.org.uk/
FQS – Forum Qualitative Social research Online quarterly journal (in English and German)	http://www.qualitative-research.net/fqs/fqs-eng.htm

Many people still have good reasons for not using CAQDAS software. They feel that the tactile processes of working with paper and the larger view of data it gives them bring them closer to data. However, there is nothing to stop you working in a combination of ways with whatever software you use. Why not work with the software for certain tasks but have paper versions of the data on hand? Generate segments coded in the software but print them out on paper? Speller (2000) describes printing out codes and scrutinising them to make progress towards code refinement.

Some of the problems of using computers are the result of a lack of adequate hardware, money, time to familiarise and local support. The most common constraint is time, especially since many of the problems associated with effective use of software are linked to the problems of qualitative data analysis itself. In too many projects, the data collection and data preparation phases spread into the time allotted for analysis. Aggravating these difficulties is the lack of formally prescribed techniques for analysing qualitative data as a result of the variety of analytic paradigms and the personal nature of the relationship between data and the researcher. These issues, when added to the need to choose and become familiar with a program, combine to make the researcher's problems more complex. As a student or researcher finding your way through a project or a module in a degree course, you need to be realistic about whether using software will add anything, given that you need to familiarise yourself with the software in order to feel secure about using it. The CAQDAS Networking Project and the Online QDA site are two sources of support that can be helpful (see Table 20.2). Make the most of the support available and use software if you feel it will help. Always stay in control.

TIP

Always remember that you are the one who does the thinking. The software is only your clerical assistant.

20.8 SUMMARY

This chapter has shown how computers can assist in the analysis and especially in the inductive development of theory from qualitative data such as field observations and interviews. The value of using CAQDAS computer programs is that they can help you manage large volumes of data systematically and make it easier to develop analyses. They do this by allowing you to code and then retrieve data segments using searches that can be quite complex. CAQDAS makes strategies such as analytic induction and grounded theory more practicable to apply to large amounts of data.

DISCUSSION QUESTIONS

1   What, in your opinion, would be the key benefits and disadvantages of using a CAQDAS package?

2   How would a CAQDAS package support either:

(a) a grounded theory approach to the analysis of data or

(b) a project designed to enrich or challenge an existing theory?

3   Expand on what you think your role is as the researcher when using a CAQDAS package and how the current limitations of CAQDAS impact on this.

PROJECT

The sooner you start using a CAQDAS program, the sooner you will start to feel more secure about what the program and its style feel like and you will gain the confidence to try out new things.

- Download a free trial version of the software (see resources section).

- Create a new project in the software.

- Find out what formats the software accepts data in – see online help menus and information in the checklist above.

- Experiment by importing or assigning documents (data files) or literature abstracts or anything textual.

- Experiment in the creation of memos to map out elements of future work.

- Explore main menus – and try out right button context menus with various things selected.

- Try out various tasks such as code creation, apply codes to selections in the textual documents you have assigned or imported.

- Nothing you do at this stage is dangerous – make mistakes and learn from them.

- Delete codes or rename them.

- Find out what you can't do!

- Find out how to save your work, close the project and try to re-open it.

RESOURCES

Gibbs et al. (2002) *The Use of New Technology in Qualitative Research* takes a broad view of the quality and potential of qualitative data analysis in the light of technological developments.

Kelle (1997) *Capabilities for Theory Building and Hypothesis Testing and in Software for Computer Assisted Qualitative Data Analysis* is a short paper on some of the methods underpinning the development of CAQDAS.

Lewins and Silver (2007) *Using Software for Qualitative Research: A Step by Step Guide* provides step-by-step graphic instructions for ATLAS.ti, MAXqda and NVivo7 and Comparisons of seven software packages.

INTERNET RESOURCES

(SEE ALSO TABLE 20.2).

- CAQDAS Networking Project (2007) http://www.tiny.cc/TNDCF Provides platforms for debate, information – advisory help-lines – download demo versions of software – links to free and commercial software developer pages – links to related resources – links to data conversion/transcription software programs.

- Internet Discussion List *qual-software* http://www.tiny.cc/IMFau is a forum for debate about use of technology and software for QDA (Message Archives http://www.tiny.cc/tzTRZ).

- Online QDA and CAQDAS http://onlineqda.hud.ac.uk Qualitative data analysis advice, resources, methodologies, glossary, links, references and checklists.

21 Narrative Analysis

Sarah Earthy and Ann Cronin

KEY POINTS

- Story telling is a natural part of social life – we all tell stories in different situations and different ways.

- Stories are not created in a social vacuum but are moulded by a social context and interactions between the story-teller and audiences.

- Social researchers are interested in the kinds of stories people tell, how stories are presented and why they are told.

- There are different approaches to narrative analysis but a common starting-point is the rejection of traditional realist assumptions about research data in favour of a social constructionist position.

21.1 INTRODUCTION

Social research has a long tradition of using qualitative methods to gain an insight into people's lives and to understand the meaning that people attach to their lived experience. Chapter 12 examines how focus groups can be used for this purpose, while Chapter 13 provides an introduction to qualitative interviewing. This chapter builds on these previous discussions by focusing on qualitative data as **narrative** and the implications for both data collection and analysis. In doing so, we explore how narrative analysis enables us to explore the socially constructed nature of the research process and the role 'stories' play in the construction of identity.

The chapter is divided into six sections. The first section provides an overview of **narrative analysis** and its use in social research. The second section examines the social production of the **story**. The third section explores how to use a narrative approach in qualitative interviewing while the fourth section focuses on data analysis. The fifth and final section provides a summary of the main points discussed in the chapter followed by discussion question, an outline of a student project and suggestions for further research. Finally, while the main focus in this chapter is on data collected through individual interviews, it should be borne in mind that narrative analysis can be as useful in the analysis of **focus group** and documentary data.

21.2 WHAT IS NARRATIVE ANALYSIS?

This section begins by examining the traditional status accorded qualitative data before moving to consider how narrative analysis challenges this. It then explores what is meant by narrative analysis and discusses some of the reasons why social researchers might choose this method to collect and analyse qualitative data.

21.2.1 THE TRADITIONAL STATUS OF QUALITATIVE DATA

The **accounts** people tell us about their lives form a fundamental part of social inquiry; that is, as social researchers we gather accounts about people's lives, which we subsequently use to produce our own accounts of issues of concern to us. For example, an interest in exploring homelessness would probably involve interviewing people who have experience of living on the streets and homeless shelters about their lives. The data collected would subsequently be analysed, possibly using thematic analysis (see Chapter 13) and the findings written up – perhaps for an undergraduate dissertation, a public report or even for publication in a journal or book.

However, for the purposes of this chapter the important issue to consider is the epistemological status accorded data collected in this manner. Traditionally it has been assumed that an individual account can be regarded as representational of a real life. In other words, the social researcher can, through appropriate use of the appropriate method, discover the 'real subject who is present in the world' (Denzin, 1989b: 14). Thus, in the case cited above, the individual accounts of homelessness would be regarded as accurate representations of the participants' experiences of homelessness.

This understanding of data is most often associated with a methodological realist paradigm. Within this paradigm, the account as a subject of social scientific interest in and of itself is overlooked in preference to the information or understanding it may yield on a given topic. In contrast, narrative analysis, located within a **social constructionist** paradigm, first of all challenges this realist position and, second, offers an alternative approach to the understanding of both the production and the analysis of qualitative data.

21.2.2 NARRATIVE ANALYSIS

Although narrative analysis has its origins in literary theory and is closely associated with media and cultural studies, social scientists have become interested in using it as a means to gain greater understanding of the social world and the production of data (for example, Bruner, 1986; Denzin, 1989b; Geertz, 1975; Riessman, 1993; Rosenweld and Ochburg, 1992). Perhaps reflecting its multidisciplinary use, the term narrative analysis can refer to a variety of different approaches to data collection and analysis, including biography, autobiography, life history, oral history, autoethnography, life narrative and the sociology of story telling. We take a closer look at these different methods of data collection in Section 21.4. While not dismissing the differences between these approaches, all share a common aim, namely to explore the different ways in which both the production and analysis of qualitative data can be understood as processes whereby different groups of people engage in 'story telling' and in doing so produce narrative accounts of their lives. As a result of this, those using narrative analysis prefer to use the terms 'narrative' or 'story' rather than 'account'; this convention is used throughout this chapter (see Section 21.2.3 for definitions).

Rosenweld and Ochberg suggest that narrative analysis disrupts the traditional social scientific analysis, which has realist assumptions and a focus on information collection. Instead the focus shifts to look at the very construction of narratives and likewise the role they play in the **social construction** of identity. 'Personal stories are not merely a way of telling someone (or oneself) about one's life; they are the means by which identities may be fashioned' (Rosenweld and Ochburg, 1992: 1).

This interest in narratives is a part of a wider move within social sciences towards a more 'interpretive turn' (Rabinow and Sullivan, 1979). This can partly be explained by a growing mistrust in the empiricist agenda, part of which urges the researcher to adopt a more reflexive approach. As discussed below, inclusion of the researcher in the production of data raises further doubts about the traditional claims that our research findings can ever represent the 'truth' of people's lives. The use of a narrative analysis approach with its focus on the social construction of the story, means that uncovering the 'truth' no longer becomes the object of analysis; there has been a move away from the 'what' to the 'how'. This in turn deconstructs the realist position that assumes that life stories can be regarded as 'mirrors of life events' (Rosenweld and Ochburg, 1992). Before looking more closely at narrative analysis we want to raise the issue of terminology and provide a couple of examples of narratives and stories.

21.2.3 DEFINITIONS

Account: a general term for the overall report or description given by an interviewee during a research interview. An account may include a variety of different forms of talk and represents the interviewee's perceptions, understanding and experiences of the issue(s) being researched.

Narrative: a term widely used in social theory and social research to describe either: (a) a tale or story; or (b) a form of talk or writing that aims to tell a story and may be structured according to classical ideas of plot.

Narrative analysis: an approach taken to interview data that is concerned with understanding how and why people talk about their lives as a story or a series of stories. This inevitably includes issues of identity and the interaction between the narrator and audience(s).

Story: the description of an event or series of events in a manner that conveys meaning as well as factual information. Traditional stories or myths serve a number of purposes including entertainment, instruction and the formation of a collective worldview. When research participants tell a story or a series of stories, the researcher will want to consider what purpose the story serves and why the interviewee has chosen to present their account in this way.

21.2.4 EXAMPLE: NARRATIVES OF CHRONIC ILLNESS

An understanding of the term narrative can be found from the following example which involves sociologists who are interested in exploring people's experience of health and illness. Sociologists who have interviewed people with a chronic illness such as rheumatoid arthritis have noted that these conversations often take the form of a narrative of both the illness (how it began, possible causes, interactions with health professionals, significant developments, day-to-day living, changed priorities, and so on) and the impact of illness and disability on the person's social roles and hence sense of worth (Frank, 1995; Williams, 1984). Bury (2001) has distinguished between narratives of chronic illness that try to make sense of the experience of illness ('contingent narratives') and those that address a changed self ('moral narratives') but in practice these may be combined. These insights into the purpose of narratives told by interviewees can be applied to many other interview topics, particularly where the experience being described is problematic, unresolved or associated with stigma.

21.2.5 EXAMPLE: STORIES OF HOMELESSNESS

Likewise, a study conducted with people who have experience of homelessness illustrates the way in which people tell stories about their lives and the meanings they attach to them. This small-scale study formed part of a larger mixed method study (see Chapter 7) exploring the experiential nature of vulnerability among different groups of people living in the same location.

The original intention had been to run two focus group discussions and use the findings to inform the development of an individual interview schedule for use with a further five participants. At this stage a decision to use narrative analysis had not been taken. However, after running the first group it was apparent that the members of the group were not simply supplying information on homelessness but were telling us stories about their experiences and in the process 'doing' identity work. Homelessness carries with it social stigma and thus the participants used the focus group as an opportunity to provide an alternative account of homelessness that explored among other things causal factors, structural factors and issues of personal agency.

Furthermore, the story telling was occurring at two levels: first, the individual stories of homelessness and, second, a collective story of homelessness. This second level of story telling occurred in several ways, for example, the participants might validate or support the stories told by other members of the groups, or they would add to the story of one participant by offering their own story on a similar subject. Recognition of the participants' desire to tell individual stories led to a decision not to run a further focus group but to extend the number of individual interviews from five to eight and to use a narrative analysis approach both to collect and to analyse the data.

21.3 THE SOCIAL PRODUCTION OF THE STORY

Although narrative and story have slightly different meanings, the terms are often used interchangeably. Furthermore, as illustrated below, the use of either 'narrative' or 'story' can also signify different disciplinary conventions and interests. Regardless of these differences, the use of these terms is not meant to imply that people produce fictional accounts of their lives, rather it is to draw attention to three interrelated issues: the social production of accounts; some of the work performed by the use of stories or narratives; and finally, the narrative-like qualities that are often present in personal accounts of life.

As discussed above, an awareness of the 'narrative potential' in qualitative accounts will lead the social researcher to attend to its social production. Indeed, this in itself is a valid reason for choosing to use narrative analysis. However, narrative analysis is not a homogenous entity and within its broad remit there are a variety of different models available to help make us aware of the social production of the story. Models closely aligned with literary theory or cultural and media studies, for example, concentrate on the narrative structures present in stories. This might involve a focus on identifying the story's plot, setting and characterisation, which will in turn help draw attention to the way in which a story is constructed and developed through the selective inclusion (and hence exclusion) of past events.

The sociologist Ken Plummer (1995), while retaining an interest in narrative structure, examines stories as both **symbolic interactions** and political process. His interest lies in producing a sociology of story telling concerned with: '[t]he social role of stories: the ways they are produced, the ways they are read, the work they perform in the wider social order, how they change, and their role in the political process' (ibid.: 19). In both symbolic interaction and political process we will see the importance of representation.

21.3.1 STORIES AS SYMBOLIC INTERACTIONS

Symbolic interactionism suggests that all human behaviour is social, involving social interaction and the development of shared meaning. Plummer locates the production of stories firmly within this framework and examines the way in which the telling of stories is a central part of this symbolic interaction. This enables stories to be viewed as joint actions involving three groups of people: the *producers*, the *coaxers* and the *consumers*. This shifts the emphasis away from seeing a story as representative of an individual life to a focus on the social production and consumption of the story.

The first group is composed of the *producers* of stories, those people who tell the stories of their lives. This might be the participants of a chat show programme, the published autobiographical 'coming out stories' told by lesbian and gay men; or the participants of a research project. In each of these cases (and many others) it is important to be aware that the story is simply a selective reconstruction or version of a life; it is not the life itself. This is the first step away from regarding the story as representative of a life, an event or experience and seeing it as a creation in itself. This approach can help us to identify issues or events that are significant to the individual telling their story.

The second group of people consists of the 'coachers' or 'coaxers' who play a fundamental role in the production of the story. Plummer points out this can include an array of people: from the chat show host to the social researcher. These people coax, persuade, and provide a forum for people to become storytellers. The role is not a passive one; the researcher is actively involved in the production of the story. An obvious example is the story that results from an interview: the questions asked limit and shape the story told. This increases the distance between the lived life and the story told about that life. The researcher's role is explored in detail in Section 21.4.

While the teller and the coaxer are involved in the production of a story, of equal importance in this model of stories as joint actions are the *consumers* of the stories. Furthermore, the consumers are involved in the active consumption of these stories. Just as those in media studies (for example Bobo, 1995; Gammon and Marshment, 1988) have highlighted the interpretative and active role of the television watcher or filmgoer, so it is with those who consume stories. Plummer argues that this means that any analysis of stories must pay attention to the social location of the consumers. If we accept the idea that individual consumers may construct different meanings from the same story, this shows the weakness of the link between the life and the story told about that life. However, this analysis of the role of the consumer would not be complete without an understanding that the producers – the tellers and coaxers – are also consumers of other stories.

21.3.2 STORIES AS POLITICAL PROCESS

To claim that stories can be understood as political process alerts us to the power mechanisms or structures that permit certain stories to be told while silencing others. An example drawn from Plummer's work on the telling of sexual stories will help to illustrate this point.

Among the stories that Plummer examines are those told by women and men who identify as lesbian or gay. Plummer observes that, over the past one hundred years of Western culture, at different times talking about being lesbian or gay would have (and has) resulted in different consequences. Thus for much of this century the personal stories of being lesbian and gay have either been silenced or told in secret. It is only since the 1970s and the growth of the lesbian and gay movement that these stories have started to be told in public. This has changed the stories from being about personal shame and pain to ones of pride and strength. This is a clear demonstration of the practice of power, both its repressive and productive qualities.

This provides us with another reason why social scientists might be interested in adopting a narrative approach within their research: it can be particularly useful with either marginalised groups or people who have a discreditable or stigmatised identity.

21.3.3 REPRESENTATION

From the discussion so far it will be apparent that one of the issues that narrative analysis is interested in is the issue of **representation**. It is of paramount importance in Plummer's sociology of story-telling; likewise it is an issue that Riessman (1993) addresses in her discussion of narrative analysis and the role of the researcher. Riessman argues that representation is ambiguous and hence open to multiple interpretations, and identifies five levels of representation that are present in the collection and analysis of data: attending, telling, transcribing, analysing and reading. At each level the researcher is engaged in a process of interpretation of a life to which they have no access:

> Meaning is ambiguous because it arises out of a process of interaction between people: self, teller, listener and recorder, analyst and reader. Although the goal may be to tell the whole truth, our narratives about others' narratives are our world creations ... Meaning is fluid and contextual, not fixed and universal. All we have is talk and texts that represent reality partially, selectively, and imperfectly. (Riessman, 1993: 15)

Hence narrative analysis, whether it is undertaken using models more commonly associated with literary theory, or using Plummer's approach, offers the social researcher a new way of looking at and understanding accounts. Instead of viewing an account as simply representative of an individual life, it directs attention to the 'joint actions' involved in the production of the story. Moreover, it indicates the way in which the meaning of the story and hence its consequences are always dependent on first of all the social location of those involved in the production and consumption of the story and, second, the wider social context in which the story is told. Plummer's examination of the important role of 'communities' who hear and receive the story, again highlights the way in which different communities over time will receive the story in different ways. This helps us to understand the way in which stories can be understood as political processes that involve power relations.

21.4 USING A NARRATIVE APPROACH

A narrative approach is concerned not only with the story-telling components or characteristics of an account, but also with the social interactions between interviewer and interviewee that encourage and influence the way that an account is presented. To adopt a narrative approach is to choose to understand and analyse interview or other data from that perspective rather than, for example, focusing solely on the content of what interviewees are saying or the conversational forms and rules that underlie the interaction (e.g. conversation analysis, described in Chapter 22).

The same section of interview data can be analysed in different ways. For example, an interviewee might describe a traumatic event involving someone close to them, such as a delay in seeking help for what turned out to be a serious illness. A thematic approach to such data would involve comparing accounts from a sample of interviewees with similar experiences to explore the reasons why those involved either sought or did not seek advice or the nature of encounters with health professionals. An ethnomethodological approach might concentrate on the language used and how conversational devices add emphasis, enhance credibility, deflect possible criticism, or convey the researcher's sympathy. A narrative approach will take account of both the content and the form of the interviewee's account and interactions with the interviewer. More importantly, a narrative approach will ask questions such as 'Why is the interviewee narrating this incident in this particular way?', 'What is the purpose of the story?', 'Why does it occur at this point in the conversation?', 'How have the researcher or others present influenced the narration?', or 'How does this excerpt fit with other parts of the interviewee's life story as narrated during the interview as a whole?'.

21.4.1 PLANNED AND UNPLANNED GENERATION OF NARRATIVE DATA

Some social researchers adopt a narrative analysis approach from the outset of their research and design their interview schedule accordingly. Other researchers do not set out to collect narratives or stories, but instead discover the presence of story-like qualities in an interviewee's account during the analysis stage of a study. An example of this last position was given above in the discussion of the study with people who have experience of homelessness.

These two styles of interviewing are not as different in practice as this distinction implies. Even in the case of apparently spontaneous narratives, a close examination of the transcript will reveal that the framing of questions and signals of interest and encouragement from the researcher (non-verbal as well as verbal) precede story-telling and shape how the narrative is presented. On another occasion with different people present, the same event or life story might be related in a different way. This is what is meant when narratives are described as being 'co-authored'. As we develop our interview questions, we need to be aware that we are occupying the role described by Plummer (1995) as that of a 'coaxer' who may either facilitate or inhibit the act of narration.

> The following interaction provides an example of how the researcher's likely interest may be tested before a story is told:
>
> RESEARCHER: Whereas here seems better...?
> SUE: It's not too bad. It has its moments.
> RESEARCHER: Does it?
> SUE: When we first moved in, it was terrible, very rough and ready. Moved here September 25th '92.
> RESEARCHER: What sorts of things were happening?
> SUE: Fights ...

Since story-telling is a natural part of conversation, it is not surprising that research methods focused on accessing an 'emic' perspective (i.e. an insider's understanding of a social situation or experience) will allow and even encourage the telling of stories. Particular topics – for example, those relating to difficult circumstances or issues closely connected with a person's sense of identity and self-worth – are likely to involve story-telling and, as we have seen, certain types of question and interactions between the interviewee and 'audience' may give tacit approval for a narrative to unfold.

However, as Riessman notes (1993: 56), narratives also occur when the line of questioning seems uninviting. The resulting narrative may be more disjointed than those encountered in narrative-orientated interviews but are nevertheless still present because the interviewee has a story to tell. It is then up to the interviewer to choose whether to include considerations of narrative in the analysis.

21.4.2 ORAL HISTORY AND LIFE-STORY RESEARCH

There are a number of research topics that lend themselves to narrative enquiry. These are often experiences or events shared by a number of individuals that tell us something about the nature of society as well as being significant to those involved.

Oral history aims to explore what it was like to live in a past era and to capture and preserve the memories of a cohort while they are still alive. An example of this is Paul Thompson's interviews with people born during the Edwardian era in Britain (Thompson, 1992; 2000). Many public libraries and some museums have local history collections in which interviews with older residents form a core resource and provide rich information about aspects of day-to-day life such as childhood, family, work, religion, shopping, transport and leisure as well as insights into social values and meaning. Such research aims to record the experiences of 'ordinary' people and thereby give them a collective voice; an objective shared by many types of qualitative social research.

Life-story research more generally is concerned with the link between personal biography and social processes, past and present. These might involve the transformation of a place, an industry or a way of life. Chronology is a key element in how we naturally tell stories and it is equally important to social researchers mapping personal and social change. This is evident in the enduring usefulness of the concept of 'career' in sociological research (Becker, 1961; Thomas, 2003). A similar concept is present in life-story interviews that focus on how people are socialised into a particular occupation or social class ('becoming' a doctor, a factory worker, a drug dealer, a member of an elite) or adapt to a radical change in circumstances (such as parenthood or illness). Other types of life-story interview concern broader aspects of identity including the enduring effects of trauma and stigma. The oral history section of the National Sound Archive at the British Library in London (http://www. tiny.cc/7yqYE), for example, includes collections of recorded interviews with Jewish survivors of the Holocaust and their children, and with people living with HIV and AIDS. Increasingly, research-funding bodies are encouraging researchers to archive their recordings so that these are available for secondary analysis by other researchers. While this has obvious practical merits, it does have ethical implications particularly in respect of informed consent (see Chapter 13).

21.4.3 MULTIPLE INTERVIEWS

A characteristic common to both oral history and life-story interviews is that they tend to last longer than other forms of in-depth interviews and may involve several sessions with the same person. These might take place over a couple of weeks or several years. For example, Robert Bogdan's ground-breaking autobiography of a transsexual, Jane Fry (Bogdan, 1974) and Kathy Charmaz's study of the relationship between self and time in chronic illness (Charmaz, 1991) are both based on multiple interviews with the same individuals conducted over an extended time period.

Interviewing a research participant on more than one occasion can have several advantages:

- It may assist the development of trust and rapport between the researcher and interviewee.

- It may be less exhausting for both parties, particularly in comparison with a single attempt to capture a person's life story.

- For interviewees who are unwell or who find aspects of the conversation distressing, the possibility of ending the interview knowing that the conversation can continue on another day may be particularly valuable.

- The gap between interviews provides an opportunity for both the interviewee and researcher to reflect.

- Aspects discussed in one interview can be clarified and explored in greater depth in a subsequent conversation.

The biographic narrative interpretive method (Wengraf, 2001) provides an example of a narrative approach that uses three separate interviews with different formats and purposes. In the first interview, the interviewee is invited to tell the story of their life. In the second interview, the interviewee is asked to talk more about parts of their life discussed in the first interview and encouraged to tell further stories. On both occasions, the researcher is concerned to minimise their influence on how the narrative is related. In the final interview, the researcher takes the lead and asks prepared questions based on the emerging analysis. The data generated in the three interviews is analysed in two distinct ways: as an objective account of a 'lived-life' and as a subjective 'told-story'. These separate stages of analyses are then brought together to explore why the person has chosen to narrate their life in the particular way that they have. The central idea is that the narrative presented in the interviews not only records the most significant events and experiences in the person's life and does so in greater detail than would be generated by other methods but also reveals the interviewee's emotions, values and beliefs during the act of narration.

While the staged process of interviewing involved in the biographic narrative interpretive method may not be feasible for small projects with limited time, it is worth considering whether two interviews with the same individual might produce richer and more insightful data than a single interview, even if it requires a reduction in the size of the sample. Real rapport is not always easily established, especially when the subject matter is sensitive. Jocelyn Cornwell, in her community study of health and illness in East London (Cornwell, 1984), described the difference between 'public accounts' – those that reflected collective norms and presented the community in a positive way – and 'private accounts' that disclosed information about more difficult subjects such as domestic violence. For some research topics, multiple interviews may offer a way of crossing from one type of account to the other.

21.4.4 ASKING NARRATIVE QUESTIONS

In both ordinary conversation and research interviews, we often ask questions that relate to chronology and time. This is particularly true when we are trying to get to know someone, we are asking about an experience that is unfamiliar to us, or wanting to explore similarities with our own experience (or the experience of other interviewees). Examples of interview questions that specifically refer to time might include: 'When did you first...?'; 'Starting at the beginning, tell me about...'; 'Thinking back over the last week...'; 'Looking ahead...'; 'Comparing your experiences with those of children today ...' Similarly, when we tell a story, we tend to structure it in a way that makes sense as a chronological sequence. We will return to the issue of narrative structures later in this chapter but in the meantime we should note that these kinds of questions lead the interviewee to believe that chronological order is important to us and this may influence how their account is presented.

Most researchers who conduct interviews that are pre-designed to invite narratives recommend the use of a combination of very broad questions ('tell me about your life') with prompts that encourage the relating of specific examples ('tell me what happened'; 'have you ever experienced...?'; 'can you think of a time when ...?'). Such questions may differ from those used in other types of in-depth interview if they point clearly to the type of response wanted; that is to say a narrative or story rather than an opinion or interpretation. Even closed questions may produce a storied response if the subject matter lends itself to story-telling or the interviewee has a story that needs telling.

Thompson (2000: 309–23) suggests one way of structuring oral history interviews is to start with family members (grandparents and their generation, parents, siblings and other relatives) before asking about each life stage and related experiences (for example, memories of childhood might invoke descriptions of family life, neighbourhood and school). Comparisons with contemporary life and perceptions of change will be recurring themes throughout the conversation.

It is also considered good interviewing practice for the researcher's involvement to be minimal so that the interviewee's narrative can flow. The interview transcript will provide a guide to the extent and content of the researcher's verbal contributions but not intonation or other sounds, facial expressions or body language. These can be equally influential and are much harder to quantify except by means of notes taken shortly after the interview and during the process of transcription.

21.4.5 TEXTUAL SOURCES OF NARRATIVE DATA

We have mainly focused in this chapter on story-telling in the context of in-depth interviews. However, a wide range of sources can provide access to narrative data that is already in the form of text. These include autobiographies, biographies, newspapers and magazines, **Internet/blogs** and discussion forums, and fiction. Although such data have not been generated through interaction with a researcher (except perhaps in a discussion forum), the three roles identified by Plummer of producer, coaxer and audience continue to be relevant.

One advantage of textual sources of narrative data is that it may be feasible to include a much larger sample size and to use random methods of selecting cases for study. Narrative analysis can then more easily be combined with quantitative methods such as content analysis.

21.5 ANALYSING DATA AS NARRATIVE

Having outlined some of the theoretical ideas that underpin narrative analysis and the research situations in which narratives and story-telling may occur, this section considers methodological issues involved in narrative analysis. The first step is to decide what aspect of narrative to explore and how the data will help to do this. These considerations will be influenced by our ontological and epistemological standpoints (see Chapters 1 and 2).

21.5.1 UNIT OF ANALYSIS: CATEGORICAL VERSUS HOLISTIC

Lieblich et al. (1998) have identified two intersecting dimensions of approaches to narrative analysis. The first dimension concerns the unit of analysis and whether this is a category (for example, a particular type of event or experience) or the narrative as a whole. Categorical approaches to narrative analysis compare all references to the selected phenomenon within one interview or across several interviews, while holistic approaches seek to understand how a particular section of text is part of a life story narrated during the course of a single interview or several interviews with the same individual. As Lieblich and her colleagues describe, categorical analysis tends to be used when the research is concerned with an experience that is shared by a group of people (for example, the process of migration) whereas holistic analysis will explore significance and change in the context of one person's life (for example, the effects of migration on identity).

21.5.2 FOCUS OF ANALYSIS: CONTENT VERSUS FORM

The second dimension of difference is between analytical approaches that are concerned with the *content* of a story/narrative and those that focus on the way it is structured (its *form*). The content of the narrative may include the surface content (what happened?, who was present?, how did different parties react?) and the underlying or latent content (what were the motives or intentions of participants?, what might particular items symbolise for the narrator or others?, what is the meaning and importance of this story for the narrator?). In contrast, if we are interested in the form of the narrative, we concentrate on aspects such as how the plot is structured, the sequence of events, and the language used. For example, particular words or phrases may have the effect of making the story seem more convincing or protecting the narrator from being criticised.

21.5.3 COMBINATIONS OF UNIT AND FOCUS OF ANALYSIS

Different choices about the unit and focus of analysis will produce one of four possible combinations: holistic-content, holistic-form, categorical-content and categorical-form (Lieblich et al., 1998: 13). Labov's interest in the structural elements of a core narrative (Labov, 1972), discussed below, is an example of a holistic-form combination. Other studies are more difficult to categorise. For example, Riessman's research on narratives of divorce (Riessman, 1990; 1993) explores the narrative form and language used by interviewees *and* the political contexts in which such narratives arise.

An example from our own research illustrates how these choices may be influenced as much by the nature of the data as the research questions.

21.5.4 EXAMPLE: A STORY OF HARDSHIP

The following story about the shame of poverty was part of the interview data generated during a study of contemporary community. The research comprised of ethnographic observations in two localities and 49 in-depth interviews involving 69 participants. Although there was nothing in the interview schedule that specifically invited stories, it became clear during fieldwork and analysis that there was something about the subject of place and its significance for people's identity that produced stories that frequently concerned the past, despite a research focus on the present.

> The only time I felt poor and I did feel this. Because the war had started in 1939 and I was thirteen and the school had left to be evacuated they allowed me to leave school at thirteen although the school age was fourteen. But there was no school to go to. And my mother (LAUGHS) went and got, found me a job at Smith's, the tailors. Can you imagine going to a top quality shop as poor as a church mouse? Oh, and she was told that the uniform, you had to provide the uniform for shop work in those days. And I was told the uniform was black. So Lillian arrives at Smith's, a shop where all the people from Park Road used to get their clothes on appro and send them back if they didn't like 'em. … And Lillian arrives from X in her black crêpe dress cut down. Uneven hem because the crêpe in those days wasn't crêpe as it is now and in this shop with all the ladies or all the assistants that were well trained assistants because you had to go forward and say 'Can I help you madam?' in those days. And I've never felt so embarrassed in all my life cos they made me feel so (pause) I dunno. But my mother, because of the area we come from, didn't see anything in this. She didn't see what she'd done to a young girl who, erm, (pause). Cos, er, that's how life was in those days. (Lillian, aged 75)

This story can be analysed in a number of ways. First, if our unit of analysis is categorical and our focus is the content rather than form of the story, then we will begin by looking at the surface and latent content of this story before looking for similar stories elsewhere in the dataset.

Lillian's story of her first day of work fits with Bury's description of a 'moral narrative type' (Bury, 2001). The act of walking into a 'top quality' shop wearing a dress with an uneven hem fundamentally challenged Lillian's identity, which until that point had been within a social environment in which her family's economic circumstances were unremarkable. The cut-down crêpe dress, which was presumably someone's best, was inadequate for a shop devoted to clothes and in which all the other assistants were to Lillian's eyes 'ladies'. She cannot find words to describe how the shop assistants made her feel or the personal impact of this experience, including her mother's inability to comprehend its significance. The final sentence of the extract 'that's how life was in those days' provides a partial resolution by emphasising the gulf between then and now. Nevertheless the fact of recounting the story more than sixty years after it occurred suggests that the sense of shame remains present in Lillian's view of herself.

When we look for other examples of this kind of story in the dataset, it becomes clear that two types of story occurred frequently in the accounts of older interviewees such as Lillian. These were stories of a golden past and stories of material hardship from the narrator's childhood or youth. Both types of story aimed to explain and illustrate a different way of life when community bonds were stronger and people behaved better, despite having fewer material possessions and less economic security. Most of the hardship stories concerned insufficiency in food or clothing or harsh working conditions, but Lillian's story of her first day at work differs from the majority since it addressed the social and moral consequences of such hardship.

An alternative approach would be to focus on the form or structure of the story as an example of a particular type of talk and social interaction. In so doing, we might explore the similarities in type between a told story and the classical story-forms (such as epic, tragic, comic, romantic, etc.). We might examine how the narrative progresses: do things get better, worse or remain much the same? We might also look for evidence of cultural resources in the language used or meanings attributed to the words. Such questions have been applied to the narratives of chronic illness discussed earlier (Bury, 2001).

In *Language in the Inner City* (1972), Labov identified five elements that he argued were present in all narratives. In addition to these five elements, a narrative might be preceded by an abstract alerting the audience to the nature and meaning of the story to be related. Whether or not an *abstract* is included, all stories begin with an *orientation* outlining who is involved in the story and when and where the event takes place. This is followed by the description of a *complicating action* that is the core of the narrative, followed by an *evaluation* of the significance of what has happened and some form of

Figure 21.1   An illustration of the application of Labov's narrative structure to Lillian's story of her first day at work

Labov's narrative structure (1972)	Elements in Lillian's story of her first day at work
1. Abstract	*'The only time I felt poor ...'*
2. Orientation	Wartime, evacuation, leaving school at 13, Lillian's mother getting her a job. Smith's the tailors as a shop and a social environment.
3. Complicating action	Lillian arrives in a home-made crêpe dress, embarrassment.
4. Evaluation	How the event made Lillian feel, her mother's lack of understanding
5. Resolution	??
6. Coda	*'Cos that's how life was in those days ...'*

resolution before a *coda* signifying that the narrator has relinquished the conversational lead.

As summarised in Figure 21.1, Lillian's story fits well with this outline structure with one important exception. The exception is that Lillian's story contains no apparent resolution that might explain why she could recollect it so clearly after a passage of 62 years. In order to understand the story better, we have to look at its place within a broader narrative comprising of two elements. The first element was Lillian's own sense of identity. The second element was the narrative co-produced by Lillian and her husband George concerning their respective childhoods and whether people living in their locality in the 1930s and 1940s had 'felt' poor since everyone was similarly deprived.

The lead-up to Lillian's story of her first day of work, reproduced below, provides further insight into the meaning of this story and its effects on the conversation that followed it:

> LILLIAN: But we were all like that.
> GEORGE: Oh yes, yes, we were.
> LILLIAN: This is what I'm trying to say. We weren't really poor because we were all like it. We were fed, well, country fed, you know. We were filled. ... But talking like that, I didn't feel poor because everyone was poor. The only time I felt poor and I did feel this ...

In the act of remembering and recounting the story, Lillian changes her stance towards poverty from something that was hardly felt, to a source of great shame. As she relinquishes the conversational lead at the end (Labov's 'coda'), she prompts George to talk about his experiences at a school attended by children from much wealthier families. This reiterates the theme of class divide. Towards the end of the interview, George voiced the opinion that if given the choice between going forward or going back 80 years, he would go back 'like a shot'. However, Lillian disagreed:

> I think people were nicer in those times. They helped each other. But I don't think I personally could live in [those times]. I'm talking about now what I see of London and that, and how this area was. I don't like squalor. That hurts me how I read how X was. If you read that book on X, it's disgusting and I don't like that. I don't think I could have lived with that.

Lillian's description of her reaction to a book containing photographs and descriptions of physical poverty is contradictory. She says that she does not think that she could live in conditions of squalor but the researcher, George and Lillian herself are all aware that her family was particularly poor even compared with others in a deprived area. The significance of the story of the first day at work is that it marked a transition from a state of unaware deprivation to an acute consciousness of difference. That process was, however, incomplete and it is in Lillian's later life that the enormity of having been connected with squalor impinges on her moral consciousness: 'That hurts me ..., it's disgusting'.

The significance of the story of the first day at work occurs at different levels. It provides an example of lived experience of social marginalisation. It illustrates how ordinary people tell stories in similar ways to great works of fiction and in so doing reveal dimensions of meaning and interpretation that other research methods may not access. Finally, it illustrates that the very act of storytelling may change the direction of an account as the people once again re-evaluate what has happened and seek some form of resolution. If narratives that relate to sensitivities concerning personal identity are often rehearsed, it may be because no single telling can provide a complete account of something so important and complex.

21.5.5 VALIDITY AND TRUSTWORTHINESS

Riessman (1993) argues that the starting point for evaluating the credibility of a narrative analysis must be an explicit acknowledgement by the researcher that their analysis is the production of particular discourses or theoretical frameworks. This enables the researcher first of all to dismiss criteria for **validity** based on realist assumptions, and, second, to acknowledge that a different theoretical framework might produce a different analysis. Therefore, as Riessman points out, the basis for assessing the validity of an analysis no longer resides with the impossible task of representing the 'truth' but instead focuses on the notion of 'trustworthiness'. An analysis should not claim to be any more 'truthful' than another, but rather render transparent the process by which the interpretation of the narrative and stories has been reached. Then we can argue that there is a high degree of trustworthiness in the analysis and any conclusions drawn from it.

21.6 SUMMARY

This chapter has provided an introduction to both the theoretical assumptions and the practical methodological issues concerned with narrative analysis. Although there is no single answer to questions such as 'What is a narrative?' and 'How do we analyse them?', there are a number of shared assumptions that will help guide our analysis and which can deepen our understanding of social research as a social activity.

As discussed throughout this chapter, narrative research is concerned not only with the content of a narrative but also the social context in which stories are told and the influence of different groups (Plummer's 'producers', 'coachers'/'coaxers', and 'consumers') on the act of narration. Stories that are narrated publicly (which may include a research interview) are often concerned with the individual's sense of self and are used to establish or negate an aspect of identity. People often tell stories or talk in a storied form about experiences that are socially stigmatised, traumatic or unresolved and so narrative research can offer insights into deeply held cultural values and assumptions. Although this chapter has focused mainly on the analysis of narratives present in interview data, the principles presented apply equally well to narratives identified in textual material, focus group interactions and other types of data. Different research questions will influence decisions about the unit of analysis (categorical or holistic) and its focus (content or form). However, whatever our research question and focus, the theoretical assumptions underpinning narrative analysis will challenge the more traditional realist approach to data collection. This in turn renders problematic the realist assumptions of reliability that are often used to assess the validity of a researcher's work and we will need to find other ways to render transparent the process of analysis and establish the trustworthiness of the analysis presented.

DISCUSSION QUESTIONS

1. What does narrative analysis mean?

2. What do you think about the challenge narrative analysis poses to the traditional assumptions underpinning the collection of qualitative data?

3. What can be gained from focusing on the social production of the story?

4. What are the advantages and disadvantages of carrying out interviews designed to elicit narratives in comparison with the unplanned generation of narrative-like data during qualitative interviews?

5. What is the basis for judging 'good' narrative research?

PROJECT

You have been asked to carry out narrative interviews on the subject of childhood with three people of different ages. Ideally, at least one of the interviewees should be aged 70+ and no interviewee should be younger than 25. The interviews should last approximately one hour. You need to develop an interview guide consisting of six or seven main questions together with subsidiary prompts. One of the interviewees should be interviewed on two occasions so that you can explore the advantages (and any disadvantages) of multiple interviews with the same person.

RESOURCES

Plummer (1995) *Telling Sexual Stories* provides an excellent introduction to a sociology of story-telling.

Riessman (1993) *Narrative Analysis* and Lieblich et al. (1998) *Narrative Research: Reading, Analysis, and Interpretation* also offer clear introductions to the nature of narrative research and the different techniques used in narrative enquiry.

The collection edited by Andrews et al. (2000), entitled *Lines of Narrative: Psychosocial Perspectives*, offers examples of studies that have used narrative approaches, either in isolation or in combination with other methods.

Articles by Atkinson (1997a) and Frank (2000) in the journal *Qualitative Health Research* provide a lively entry into the debates surrounding narrative research.

22 Conversation Analysis and Discourse Analysis

Robin Wooffitt

22.1 INTRODUCTION

There are now a range of methodological techniques that can be used in the analysis of verbal data, such as face-to-face interaction and interview data: conversation analysis, discourse analysis, **critical discourse analysis**, **Foucauldian discourse analysis** and **discursive psychology**. To the student new to the field, these methods can seem very similar. However, the relationships between these approaches are complex, and there are some deep differences in the methodological and epistemological assumptions on which these methods rest. The first part of the chapter, then, provides an overview of these diverse and occasionally competing methodologies, focusing on the basic analytic procedures distinctive to each approach.

What is common to all the approaches, though, is the view that accounts and descriptions cannot be treated as neutral representations of an objective social or psychological reality. Instead, language is examined as a dynamic, constructive and constitutive medium. This analytic focus is illustrated in the second half of the chapter, in which data from a research interview are analysed to show how the various components of the respondent's account are designed to address subtle inferential and interpersonal matters.

22.2 TALK, ACTION AND SOCIAL INTERACTION

Traditionally, the use of language has been viewed primarily as a vehicle of information transfer between people. This view is enshrined in academic disciplines such as psychology, and in 'common sense' or lay assumptions about how we use language. In the past thirty years, however, this view has been questioned by scholars in social sciences and philosophy. As a consequence, it is now accepted that language use is a form of social action. In this section we trace the emergence of the idea of language as social action and describe some features of one of the key methods for the study of verbal communication.

Two philosophers – working in very different traditions – advanced the idea that language is not merely a set of symbols for conveying information.

Initially, Ludwig Wittgenstein examined language to explore how it represented objects and the state of affairs in the world. But he came to argue that it is wrong to view language as a medium which merely reflects or describes the world, and emphasised instead the importance of language *use* (Wittgenstein, 1953). He urged that we consider language as a tool box, and focus on the ways that people use these tools. His primary contribution was to propose that language is a central feature of the social and cultural milieu in which it was used, and not merely a logical system of symbols with which we can represent the world 'out there'.

The British philosopher J.L. Austin also emphasised the social and dynamic character of language, but his work focused on instances of specific types of sentences. He began by distinguishing between two types of **utterances**: constative utterances, which report some aspect of the world; and performative utterances, which perform a specific action. An example of a performative is 'I suggest you do this', where saying these words is to perform the action of suggesting. Other examples are promises, warnings, declarations, and so on. He termed such utterances, **speech acts**. Austin subsequently rejected the distinction between performative and constative utterances: his investigations convinced him that all utterances could be treated as performative. He concluded that any use of language, regardless of what else it might be doing, was a series of actions (Austin, 1962).

A renewed interest in the sociological study of language was stimulated by the sociological approach that came to be known as **ethnomethodology**. Pioneered by Harold Garfinkel (1967a), the fundamental tenet of ethnomethodology is that the sense of social action is accomplished through the participants' use of tacit, practical reasoning skills and competencies. (These skills are referred to as 'tacit' and 'practical' because they are not the kinds of 'rules' or norms of behaviour which we could consciously articulate, or on which we would routinely reflect. Instead, they inhabit the very weave of social life, and thereby become invisible and unnoticeable.) As so much of social life is mediated through spoken and written communication, the study of language was placed at the very heart of ethnomethodology's sociological enterprise.

22.2.1 THE EMERGENCE OF CONVERSATION ANALYSIS

Harvey Sacks was a colleague of Garfinkel, and their work shares many concerns. However, Sacks was specifically interested in describing the communicative skills by which people construct utterances to perform specific social actions in ordinary, everyday conversation. He and his colleagues, Gail

Jefferson and Emanuel Schegloff, conducted detailed and repeated analyses of recordings of face-to-face and telephone conversation. This research led to the discovery of systematic properties in the way that conversation is organised. The study of the structure of conversational organisation has come to be known as conversation analysis, or CA, and is one of the pre-eminent contemporary approaches to the study of language use. Although this method is known as *conversation* analysis, it is relevant to the study of any form of naturally occurring social interaction.

To illustrate some features of CA, we can go back to the work Sacks was doing which led to the development of conversation analysis. He was studying recordings of telephone calls to the Los Angeles Suicide Prevention Center. The Center's staff found that if they gave their name then callers would give their name in reply. But in some cases, callers seemed reluctant to disclose their identity. While pondering the callers' apparent reluctance to disclose their names, Sacks began to wonder 'where, in the course of the conversation could you tell that somebody would not give their name' (Sacks, 1992, vol. 1: 3). With this puzzle in mind, Sacks became interested in the following opening section from one of the calls, in which the caller (B) seemed to be having trouble with the agent's name. (There is an explanation of the transcription symbols in the Appendix to this chapter.)

A: this is Mr. Smith, may I help you
B: I can't hear you
A: This is Mr Smith
B: Smith
(Sacks, 1992, vol. 1: 3)

Instead of treating the caller's 'I can't hear you' as a straightforward account of hearing difficulties, Sacks examined it as a form of social action: as a device designed to perform a specific task at that stage in the call. He argued that this utterance was designed to allow the caller to avoid giving his name, while not explicitly having to refuse to do so.

Sacks argued that there are norms concerning where in conversation certain kinds of activities should happen. In conversation between strangers names tend to be exchanged in initial turns. Sacks reasoned, then, that the caller is using the utterance 'I can't hear you' to fill the slot in the conversation where it would be *expected* that he return his name.

However, the caller has not had to refuse to give his name. Instead, he has used that slot to initiate what is called a **repair sequence**, which is a short series of turns in which a problem in communication (in this case, 'not hearing') is identified and resolved. By doing 'not hearing', the caller has been able to move the exchange on from that point at which he might be expected to give his name. In this case, then, the caller's expression of an apparent hearing difficulty is *methodical*: it allows him to perform the action of 'not giving a name' without having to engage in the interpersonally uncomfortable act of explicitly refusing to do so.

Based on his observations on calls to the suicide prevention agency, Sacks and his colleagues began to examine recordings of everyday conversation. The style of analysis they established has developed a distinctive methodological approach. Analysis emphasises the *sequential organisation* of interaction. Turns at talk are analysed as activities which are designed to be responsive to prior turns, and which also constitute the immediate context for subsequent turns. The primary data for research are audio (and, where necessary or appropriate, video) recordings of naturally occurring interactions. Artificially produced data (such as recordings obtained from laboratory simulation of interaction) are rejected. Transcripts assist the analysis of audio and video materials. The transcription system focuses on speech production and turn-taking organisation. It captures the details of spoken communication, including features of talk which are usually ignored in social science research, such as speech dysfluencies, 'ums' and 'errs', false starts and overlapping speech. Their work was ground-breaking, because it revealed that naturally occurring, mundane interaction had very orderly properties: a structure which can be formally described in terms of the relationship between the actions performed by utterances.

Conversation analysis is highly empirical but not experimental. Analytic claims about the properties of interaction emerge from close examination of large collections of individual cases. In this, the approach is more like that of the scientific naturalist than the laboratory scientist.

The goal of analysis is not to produce an analysts' interpretation of the data, but to describe how participants themselves are making sense of their on-going interaction. Consequently, there is a strong reluctance to engage in premature theorising. Any pre-analytic guesswork might only lead the analyst to overlook some detail, which, although significant, does not fit in with intuition, theory or speculation about 'what is really important'.

Researchers working in this tradition have examined a range of interactional procedures and phenomena. Turn-taking is fundamental to social interaction, and has been extensively studied in CA research. There is now a very clear understanding of the properties of the sequential organisation of interaction: the robust and recurrent properties of activities in talk. There have been studies of repair mechanisms by which interactants identify and address a range of problems in communication, such as misunderstanding, false starts to turns or words, or errors of reference. There has been extensive analysis of talk in institutional or work-related settings, such as courtrooms, broadcast news interviews, and doctors' surgeries. These studies have revealed how everyday interactional practices, such as turn taking or person reference, may be modified or adapted to allow participants to perform work-related tasks.

22.3 DISCOURSE, VARIABILITY AND SOCIAL CONSTRUCTION

Discourse analysis is an analytic method which grew out of the sociological study of scientific knowledge (Gilbert and Mulkay, 1984), but which developed principally in social psychology (Potter and Wetherell, 1987). Unlike conversation analysts, who focus exclusively on talk in interaction, discourse analysts examine all forms of verbal and textual materials: spoken and written accounts, letters, scientific journals, newspaper reports, and so on. The object is to describe the way that such **discourse** is constructed, and to explore the functions served by specific constructions at both the interpersonal and societal level.

In the early 1980s, two sociologists, Mulkay and Gilbert, were interested in a scientific dispute in an area of biochemistry about the correct way to understand the mechanisms by which chemical and other kinds of energy are stored within cell structures. To study this dispute, they collected taped interviews with the various biochemists involved in the dispute, read relevant research papers and obtained informal communications between the participants, such as letters and notes. However, these data presented them with a problem: within these accounts there were a variety of plausible and convincing versions of the dispute. Furthermore, they noted that any one feature of the debate, such as the significance of a series of experimental studies, could be described and accounted for in a number of different ways.

Although Gilbert and Mulkay were working in the sociology of scientific knowledge, they realised that the variability they had observed was not peculiar to their project, but is a constituent feature of any sociological (and social psychological) research which relies on verbal or written accounts of behaviour, events, mental states, attitudes, beliefs, and so on. Of course, there are customary procedures by which sociologists can produce a single 'definitive' analytic version from the multiplicity of accounts which constitute their data. They can examine their data to look for similarities between the statements, and any similarities between accounts can be taken at 'face value', that is, as if they reflect accurately 'what really happened'.

However, Gilbert and Mulkay argued that this methodological strategy rests on the assumption that any social event has one 'true' meaning. This assumption is false because the 'same' circumstances can be described in a variety of ways to emphasise different features: events, social activities – anything we might describe – are repositories of multiple meanings. Consequently, there is no privilege for the analyst's decision about what constitutes an 'objective' or 'accurate' version of the world, simply because any state of affairs can be described in a series of different ways. They concluded that it is imperative to attend directly to the variability in accounts, and not simply to employ techniques which purge it from the data.

Consequently, they advocated the study of participants' discourse (or use of language) to reveal the discursive practices by which accounts of beliefs and actions are organised to portray events in a certain way. They explicated the 'interpretative repertoires' through which scientists constructed their accounts. Interpretative repertoires are 'recurrently used systems of terms used for characterising and evaluating actions, events and other phenomena' (Potter and Wetherell, 1987: 149), and may consist of distinctive lexical, grammatical or stylistic features, and particular figures of speech, idiomatic expressions and metaphors. They began to examine the ways that accounts are organised through certain sets of descriptive practices to construct and warrant particular versions of 'what actually happened'. This focus on the rhetorical or persuasive use of language has been influential in the subsequent development of discourse analysis.

Although discourse analysis was developed initially as a new way of doing sociology, it has had more influence in British and European social psychology, especially among psychologists who were critical of the discipline's experimental methods and its assumption that cognitive processes determine social behaviour.

For example, during the 1980s, psychologists Derek Edwards and David Middleton developed a discourse analytic approach to memory and verbal recollections. They argued that, as experimental studies of memory were mainly concerned with variables that affect recall, they were of little value to our understanding of everyday remembering in real-life situations, in which a range of other issues come into play. For example, recollections are produced in talk as part of a series of discursive activities. They argued that the discursive basis of recollections, and their role in social actions, are rarely explored in cognitive psychological research.

In a series of studies, they asked people to discuss their recollections of a recently released film (Steven Spielberg's *E.T*). Their objective was to explore remembering as a situated and social activity. Their analysis revealed that the participants' accounts and recollections were oriented to various functional or situational issues: for example, the establishment of criteria for what counted as an appropriate recollection, and the production and negotiation of consensus about the topic under discussion.

In this way, Edwards and Middleton were able to show that everyday informal recollections are not merely expressions of cognitively stored information, but occasions in which participants engage in various kinds of discursive activities to ensure the appropriate-for-the-context accomplishment of memory. Moreover, they offered a **social constructionist** argument, that memories were produced as socially organised discursive accomplishments (Edwards and Middleton, 1986; 1987; 1988).

Discourse analytic work on the relationship between language and what are conventionally taken to be inner mental entities or processes (such as 'memories') has come to be known as *discursive psychology* (Edwards and Potter, 1992).

Discursive psychologists ask: What does a 'memory' *do* in some interaction? How is a version of the past constructed to sustain some *action*? Or: what is an 'attitude' used to *do*? How is an evaluation built to assign blame to a minority group, say, or how is an evaluation used to persuade a reluctant adolescent to eat tuna pasta? (Potter, 2000: 35. Original italics)

In this sense, discursive psychology is like conversation analysis, in that it seeks to describe the action orientation of discourse – what it is being used to do. However, like discourse analysis, it also focuses on the way that language is used persuasively – to warrant a particular version of events. To illustrate a discursive psychological analysis, we can make some observations on the ways in which issues of agency and responsibility are managed in discourse during courtroom cross-examination.

Atkinson and Drew (1979) studied the organisation of courtroom interaction. Some of the data they considered came from the proceedings of a tribunal established to investigate the actions of the police in their attempts to manage disturbances between Protestants and Catholics in Northern Ireland in 1969. Their analyses revealed how witnesses being cross-examined may design their answers in such a way as to anticipate, and thereby address, the counsel's version of 'what really happened' in which they are deemed to have acted inappropriately, and which thereby provides the basis for subsequent blamings or atttributions of professional error. 'C' is the counsel and 'W' is the witness.

```
1   C:   You saw this newspaper shop being bombed on the front
2        of Divis Street?
3   W:   Yes.
4   C:   How many petrol bombs were thrown into it?
5   W:   Only a couple. I felt that the window was already
6        broken and that there was part of it burning and this
7        was a re-kindling of the flames.
8   C:   What did you do at that point?
9   W:   I was not in a very good position to do
         anything. We were under gunfire at the time
```
(From Atkinson and Drew, 1979: 137)

As Atkinson and Drew point out, the apparently uncontentious questions, 'How many petrol bombs were thrown into it?' and 'What did you do at that point?' are heard by the witness as building to a version of events in which he would be seen to be culpable of not preventing certain actions by sections of the people on the streets. Consequently, his answers have a defensive quality about them. Note that in response to the first question about the number of petrol bombs being thrown, the witness replies 'only a couple', a characterisation which minimises the significance of the incident.

In that context, consider the witness's response to the second question 'What did you do at that point?'. Instead of providing a literal reply, the witness's turn displays his understanding that the question seeks to advance the claim that he was remiss in not pursuing a certain course of action. 'I was not in a very good position to do anything. We were under gunfire at the time.' Here the speaker displays that his ability to act was constrained by gunfire; and insofar as gunfire can be fatal, he establishes the strongest possible defence against the anticipated accusation of professionally inappropriate conduct.

22.4 DISCOURSES, TEXTS AND POWER

A third approach to the study of discourse and communication can be characterised by its primarily critical orientation and its concern with the political or ideological consequences of the organisation of language. There are two main types of discourse analysis which pursue a critical agenda: critical discourse analysis (CDA) and Foucauldian discourse analysis (FDA). Although these share many features, it is important to recognise that there are some subtle differences.

22.4.1 CRITICAL DISCOURSE ANALYSIS

Critical discourse analysis is concerned to analyse how social and political inequalities are manifest in and reproduced through discourse. In this it has an overt political stance, both in terms of the kinds of topics it studies and the role it sees for the results of research. It sets out to reveal the 'role of discourse in the (re)production and challenge of dominance' (van Dijk, 1993: 249). It also has an emancipatory stance, in that it is argued that analysis should intervene 'on the side of dominated and oppressed groups and against dominating groups' (Fairclough and Wodak, 1997: 259).

Empirical work draws heavily from linguistics, in that analysis often focuses on sentence structure, verb tense, syntax, lexical choice, the internal coherence of discourse, and so on. Research is also often informed by a clear **Marxist** perspective. For example, Fairclough (1989; 1995) uses CDA to analyse how inequalities and conflicts which arise from the capitalist mode of production are manifest in discourse.

22.4.2 FOUCAULDIAN DISCOURSE ANALYSIS

Foucauldian discourse analysis (FDA) draws, as its name suggests, from the writings of Michel Foucault. Broadly, he tried to identify the regulative or ideological underpinnings of dominant vocabularies that constrain the way in which we think about and act in the world. But there are many other theoretical influences, such as postmodernism and psychoanalysis (Burman, 1996).

Like critical discourse analysts, workers in the Foucauldian tradition begin with clear political intent. For example, Parker (1990) argues that language is structured to reflect power relations and inequalities in society. However, Foucauldian discourse analysis did not emerge solely as a response to social and political inequalities; at least in part it developed from a critical engagement with the academic discipline of psychology and its largely experimental procedures. Indeed, its origins can be traced back to what has come to be known as the 'crisis' in psychology during the latter part of the twentieth century (Parker, 1989; 1992).

Unlike conversation analysis, which focuses on the sequential organisation of talk-in-interaction, and critical discourse analysis, which focuses on how social inequalities are reflected or maintained in linguistic features of discourse, Foucauldian discourse analyses tend to examine the properties and role of **discourses**. A discourse is 'a system of statements which constructs an object' (ibid.: 61). To illustrate, we can examine Parker's example, which illustrates how single discourses work.

> If you say 'my head hurts so I must be ill', you will be employing a medical discourse; if you say 'my head hurts so I cannot really want to go to that party', you will be employing some sort of psychodynamic discourse; and if you say 'my head hurts but not in the way that yours does when you are trying it on in the way women do', you will be employing a sort of sexist discourse. (Parker, 1994: 94)

Discourses shape how we might participate in social life because they furnish subject positions, roles or parts with expectations about the behaviour of incumbents. Thus, FDA examines how 'discourses facilitate and limit, enable and constrain what can be said (by whom, where, when)' (Parker, 1992: xiii). Discourses also construct objects: that is entities or processes which acquire an objective status through the use of particular vocabularies.

It is argued that because discourses make available subject positions and construct objects or processes, they have a regulatory function. For example, Cameron et al. (1992) note how the concept of 'pre-menstrual syndrome' may be invoked to explain some acts of women's aggression. Furthermore, they also identify how the concept of 'foetal alcohol syndrome' is used to promote the view that women should not drink alcohol during pregnancy. Although these terms are presented as objective and value-free, they constitute a form of social control over women in that they provide a vocabulary through which we come to view women as particular kinds of beings: at the mercy of biology, or morally responsible agents during pregnancy. The vocabularies we have for describing the world bring into play a range of expectations and constraints. These medical discourses about women tie into wider discourses that perpetuate sexism. Dominant discourses thus privilege ways of seeing and acting in the world that legitimate the power of specific groups.

In FDA, the focus is on the discovery and examination of the effects of discourses. Discourses, however, cannot be observed directly. This is because they are said to be 'carried out or actualized in or by means of *texts*' (Marin, 1983, quoted in Parker, 1992: 7; italics added). Texts are not merely written documents, but are any meaningful events, processes or objects that can be interpreted. Within FDA, anything, then, can be analysed as a text: government policy documents and television programmes, web sites and footwear design; religious rituals and board games; and song lyrics and bus tickets. Parker (1994) has illustrated the analysis of discourses by examining toothpaste packaging as a text. His first step is to look for categories of people, or proper nouns which represent objects. So, he finds words like 'professionals', 'children', 'parents' and 'night', 'breakfast', 'intake', and '0.8 per cent Sodium Monofluorophosphate'.

Parker identifies four discourses which inform this text. The text establishes the importance of daily dental care, suggests the proper use of the product, and defers to the authority of health care professionals. This, then, is a *rationalist* discourse. There is evidence of a *familial discourse*, in that ownership of 'your' child is implicated in supervision, care and the daily events connected to dental hygiene. There are recommendations about the importance of teaching children good dental care habits, and this he names as a *developmental-educational* discourse. Finally, because the text provides information about hygiene and the ingestion of chemicals, there is said to be a *medical* discourse.

Parker argues that these discourses constitute and re-affirm a set of normative expectations about 'appropriate' or 'natural' ways of categorising human beings, the relationship between these categories of people, and moral expectations about behaviour attendant upon those categorisations and relationships, for example, that it is inappropriate to question the advice of professionals; or that parents are responsible for implementing and monitoring their children's hygiene regime, and so on.

In FDA, then, discourses have **agency**, because they constitute the objects which populate social life, and make available subject positions which constrain individual participation. In this sense, the concept of discourses is different to the concept of interpretive repertoires , which are taken to be discursive resources which people can use flexibly to attend to specific kinds of interactional or interpersonal concerns (Potter, 1996: 131).

22.5 ANALYSIS OF AN EXAMPLE: AN INTERVIEW WITH PUNK ROCKERS

In this section we examine some data from an informal interview conducted as part of a study of adolescent youth subcultures: punks, skinheads, rockers, goths, hippies, and so on (Widdicombe and Wooffitt, 1995). The analysis is presented to illustrate some of the empirical issues explored in conversation analysis, discourse analysis and discursive psychology. So, we will be looking at the way descriptions display robust and recurrent properties; we will also examine how the account has been constructed to be a persuasive or warrantable version of events, and finally we will make some observations about the way in which identity is constructed and negotiated throughout the account.

The extract comes from an interview between two punk rockers and a research colleague, recorded on the pavement in a back street of London's Camden Market area. The main speaker, a male punk, has been describing in general terms the police's hostile attitude to the concerts of punk rock bands. In this sequence he begins to describe what happened at the end of one specific concert.

22.5.1 THE INTERVIEW

(From Widdicombe and Wooffitt, 1995: 126. 'MR' is a male respondent. 'FR' is a female respondent. This extract has been transcribed according to conversation analytic conventions; these are explained in the Appendix. Please note: the transcription tries to capture the broad Scottish accent of the main speaker.)

```
 1   MR:   and the police were all outside there,
 2         (.) (ehr) at the co:ncert,
 3         there wasnae a bit of trouble 'part fro(m)'nside
 4         one or two wee scra:ps, you know? (0.2) But that
 5         happens=ev'ry one– every gig [there's a scrap?
 6   FR:                                [°mm°
 7   MR:   >(th)'s all's< somebody doesnae like somebody else.
 8   FR:   Mm:
 9   MR:   dunna mattah w:ha:t it is (0.4) i's always happenin',
10         'hh y' know you cannae sto:p that?
11         (0.6)
12   MR:   an' (.) we go outside. and there they are.
13         (0.8)
14   MR:   fucking eight hundred old b'll,(0.2) just wai:tin' for
15         the cha:nce, (0.3) riot shields truncheons (0.2) and
16         you're↑not doin' nothin' you're only trying to get
17         doon to the tube and gae hame 'hh so what do they
18         do?=you're walk(n) by 'en they're pushing you wi'tha'
19         (.) truncheons an' 'h they star(t) hattin' the odd
20         punk here and there, (0.3) and what happens?=the
21         punks rebe-rebel, they don' wanna get hit in the face
22         with a truncheon ↑nobody does 'hhh so what do you
23         do,=you push yer copper back and (>then<) wha'
24         happens? ten or twelve of 'em are beatin'
```

```
25              the [pure hell out of some poor bastard
26   FR:         [mm
27   MR:    who's only tried to keep somebody off his back,
28              (0.7)
29   MR:    Now: that started a ↑riot.
```

22.5.2 ANALYSIS: CONTRASTIVE STRUCTURES AND NORMALISING PRACTICES

Let us reconsider the punk's description of some incidents following a punk rock gig.

In lines 3 to 10 there is a short sequence in which the speaker describes some violent incidents which happened at the concert. Then the speaker begins a series of descriptions of the actions of the punks, and the actions of the police. In lines 12 to 17 the speaker says 'an' (.) we go outside. and there they are. (0.8) fucking eight hundred old b'll, (0.2) just wai:tin' for the cha:nce, (0.3) riot shields truncheons (0.2) and you're not doin' nothin' you're only trying to get doon to the tube and gae hame'. Note that the first reference to the punks' behaviour is a very minimal description of what they did after the concert: 'an' (.) we go outside'. The second reference provides a further characterisation of the unexceptional nature of their behaviour: 'doing nothing' and simply 'going home'. It is interesting to note that the speaker's reference to the punks changes in the course of the segment. He says, first, that 'we go outside' but then he reports their subsequent behaviour as 'you're only trying to [go home]'. There is a sense in which 'we' performs identity work, clearly marking the speaker as a member of a specific group. But the characterisation of their attempt to go home as 'you're only trying …' does not invoke such a clear affiliation. Indeed, it appeals to 'what everybody does' or 'what anybody would do'. Initially, we might assume that this is simply an idiosyncratic and 'one-off' way of engendering a recipient's sympathy for the events that befell the punks on the night of the concert. As we progress through the rest of this account, however, we shall see that the character of this specific segment is tied to the broader organisation of the whole account of the incidents.

Identity work is implicit throughout the account in the ways that the speaker formulates the actions of the punks and the police. There is a contrast between the way that the behaviour of the punks is described, and the way in which the speaker reports the presence of the police. The speaker provides a numerical evaluation of the police officers in attendance after the concert, which, regardless of its accuracy, portrays the police presence as excessive. Furthermore, he reports that the officers came equipped for violent confrontation. So, he builds a contrast between the actions of the punks and the subsequent response by the police: the behaviour of the punks is portrayed as quite unexceptional and routine, whereas the response of the police is portrayed as extreme.

In lines 18 to 20 the speaker reports 'you're walk(n) by 'en they're pushing you wi'tha' (.) truncheons an' 'h they star(t) hattin' the odd punk here and there'. Again, there is a description of the punks' behaviour and then a description of the actions of the police. And, like the previous segment, the behaviour of the punks is reported in minimal everyday terms: they are simply 'walking by'. By contrast, the police are portrayed as initiating violence in that they start 'hitting the odd punk'. Note also that the violence is portrayed as being indiscriminately inflicted, rather than directed at specific individuals, or as part of the police response to a particular contingency. This serves to undermine the warrant for such police behaviour. Furthermore, it portrays the police's actions as being propelled not by any 'rational' motives or plan of action, but as an irrational and prejudiced response. Thus, the speaker's description in this segment further emphasises the contrast between the behaviour of the punks and the police.

In lines 20 to 29 the speaker then recounts the events that culminated in what he describes as 'a riot', and provides a characterisation of the punks' contribution to the escalating violence. Note that this issue is raised via his posing the rhetorical question 'And what happens?' as a consequence of the police indiscriminately hitting the punks. Note also that the use of the verb 'rebel' portrays the punks' first active involvement in the violence as being responsive to, and a consequence of, police provocation, oppression, and so on. Furthermore, this response is warranted by an appeal to 'how any one would respond in these circumstances': '[the punks] don' wanna get hit in the face with a truncheon ↑nobody does'.

Finally, the speaker provides the first reference to violent actions actually perpetrated by the punks after the concert: 'you push yer copper back'. It is clear that he is not describing one specific event, or any number of specific incidents; rather, he describes a general response, which is again warranted by an appeal to what 'anyone would do in this situation'. There are two interesting features of the description of the punks as 'pushing back'. 'Pushing' is not a particularly aggressive act, and its use here portrays the punks' behaviour as being defensive, rather than offensive. Also, the characterisation of the punks as pushing back demonstrates that their actions are a form of resistance to an ongoing physical assault, rather than any attempt to initiate conflict.

Even from these preliminary observations, then, some interesting differences are emerging. So, for example, the behaviour of the punks is described as entirely mundane: they are characterised as simply doing what any 'ordinary' person might do. They are also portrayed as passive recipients of violence, rather than aggressive perpetrators; even when they are actively involved in violence, the punks are portrayed as using physical force to effect the most minimal form of self-defence. The description of the behaviour of the police, however, is couched in terms of their orientation to, and pursuit of, aggressive confrontation: their presence is excessive and they engage in random physical assaults. Thus, the speaker portrays the ordinary and mundane activities of the punks, but formulates the behaviour of the police through a series of descriptions which emphasise the aggressive and extraordinary behaviour of the police.

We have noted that the speaker builds a series of contrasts between the behaviour of the punks and that of the police. In this, the speaker is using a rhetorical and interactional resource that occurs in a variety of occasions of natural language use. For example, they occur regularly in political speeches (Atkinson, 1984; Heritage and Greatbatch, 1986), in market pitchers' selling techniques (Pinch and Clark, 1986), and in an account of mental illness (Smith, 1978). These studies have shown that contrast structures are employed as a persuasive device. In this case the speaker uses contrastive organisation to emphasise the extreme nature of the police response. The inference that the presence of the police and their subsequent behaviour were unwarranted in part rests upon the juxtaposition of police action with the seemingly inconsequential and ordinary behaviour of the punks.

It is important to remember that we are not assessing this account to try to discover whether the speaker's description is accurate, or whether he is distorting 'what really happened'. Rather, we are interested in the descriptive resources that are used to construct this version, and to sketch what dynamic and functional properties this version has.

22.5.3 ANALYSIS: ASSEMBLING DESCRIPTIONS

In this section we are going to develop a more detailed, conversation analytic treatment of the segment: 'one or two wee scra:ps,' (line 4). A short utterance like this seems an unpromising target for detailed examination. To indicate why even apparently minor statements such as this merit close attention, we need to discuss some salient features of the practice of 'describing'.

The first step in examining descriptive sequences is to ask why these specific words have been used in this specific combination. Initially, this might seem a trivial task with a self-evident answer: this description has been provided because it captures, represents or reflects the state of affairs in the world being described. But we have seen, that there are a variety of philosophical and sociological arguments that suggest that descriptions are designed not merely to represent the world, but to do specific tasks in the world.

Similarly, it is important to keep in mind a point we raised earlier: that any actual description, however sensible or accurate it may appear, has been assembled from a range of possible words and phrases. Schegloff (1972) has illustrated the necessary selectivity of descriptions by writing some of the various ways that one state of affairs could be reported.

> Were I now to formulate where my notes are, it would be correct to say that they are: right in front of me, next to the telephone, on the desk, in my office, in the office, in Room 213, in Lewisohn Hall, on campus, at school, at Columbia, in Morningside Heights, on the upper West Side, in Manhattan, in New York City, in New York State, in the North East, on the Eastern seaboard, in the United States, etc. Each of these terms could in some sense be correct ... were its relevance provided for. (Schegloff, 1972: 81)

The point is that any description or reference is produced from a potentially inexhaustible list of possible utterances, each of which is 'logically' correct or true. So when we pose the analytic question 'why this specific description?' we need also to ask 'what tacit practical reasoning informs the design of this description?'

Let us consider the word 'scrap'. Of all the ways that could be used to describe two people hitting each other – 'fighting', 'violence', 'a punch up' – the word 'scrap' clearly minimises the seriousness of the incident. Indeed, 'scrap' evokes images of schoolboy tussles in playgrounds rather than incidents in which people may incur severe physical damage. The characterisation of the incidents as 'wee scraps' further portrays the relative insignificance of the incidents.

Consider also the numerical evaluation 'one or two wee scra:ps'. A first point is that 'one or two' clearly registers the 'occurring more than once' character of the incident being described. Referring to a number of violent incidents could easily be used by a sceptic to undermine the general thrust of the speaker's claim that the police presence after the concert was unwarranted. However, 'one or two' provides the most minimal characterisation of 'more than one'. Second, note that the speaker does not say 'one' or 'two', but 'one or two'. In one sense, this marks the speaker as 'not knowing' the precise number of incidents. More important, however, is that the display of 'not knowing' marks the precise number as not requiring clarification, and therefore as being relatively unimportant. Third, in this sequence the speaker concedes that violent disturbances occurred at the gig. Thus the speaker makes an admission that could be damaging to his overriding claim that the punks were not to blame for the subsequent 'riot'. However, conceding such a potentially delicate point is one method by which the speaker can minimise the likelihood that his account will be seen as a biased version of events. This in turn augments his implicit claim to be an accurate reporter of 'what really happened'. So, although the speaker does reveal that indeed there were some violent incidents at the concert, he does so in such a way as to portray the 'more than one' number of incidents as minimally as possible, while at the same time registering the relative insignificance of these events, and portraying himself as an 'honest observer' (see also Potter, 1996: Chapter 5).

22.5.4 ANALYSIS: THE ORGANISATION OF DESCRIPTIVE SEQUENCES

In this section we will consider the main speaker's description in lines 4 to 9: 'But that happens=ev'ry one- every gig -there's a scrap? >(th)'s all's< somebody doesnae like somebody else. dunna mattah w:ha:t it is (0.4) i's always happenin'. It will become apparent that here the speaker's description is delicately designed to address and counter potentially negative inferences about the role of the punks in the confrontation with the police.

A first preliminary observation: note the instances in which the speaker uses the words 'always' and 'every'. Pomerantz (1986) has studied the use of words like 'always' and 'never' in ordinary conversation. She provides a technical identification of this, referring to such words as extreme case formulations. Other examples are 'never', 'brand new', 'nobody', 'everybody', 'completely innocent' and 'forever'. Such formulations serve to portray the maximum (or minimum) character of the object, quality or state of affairs to which they refer.

Initially these items might appear to be a case of simple exaggeration, with little indication that there is something systematic about their use. But Pomerantz's analysis of extreme case formulations in everyday conversation revealed that speakers use them to influence the judgement or conclusions of co-interactants, especially in circumstances in which the speaker may anticipate that the account, story or claim being made will receive an unsympathetic hearing.

With this in mind, we can now return to the instances of extreme case formulations in the punk extract. Recall that the speaker has just revealed that there was a spate of violent activity at the concert he had attended. He then says:

every gig– there's a scrap? >(th)'s all's< somebody doesnae like somebody else. dunna mattah w:ha:t it is (0.4) i's always happenin'

'Every gig there's a scrap' portrays violence as being related to a general kind of social occasion, namely, rock concerts. Note that he does not say that these violent incidents occur at every punk rock gig. Rather it is the 'gigs' that are associated with the disturbance, and not the gigs of bands whose following comes from a specific youth subculture. The second extreme case formulation 'there's always somebody that doesn't like somebody else' characterises violence as arising inevitably from interpersonal conflict. Such conflicts are portrayed as having their roots in idiosyncratic clashes of personality, irrespective of the social groups to which individuals may belong. Finally, 'it's always happening' marks such conflicts as a recurrent and consistent feature of human existence, and not peculiar to specific sections of the community.

In reporting the violence that occurred at the concert, the speaker makes no reference to the fact that the combatants were punks. Indeed, he has done considerable work to portray the incident as something which occurs routinely at rock gigs generally, or which arises from two people's dislike for each other, and which is endemic in human society. In so doing, he minimises the relevance of the social identity of the combatants as 'punk rockers', and thus implies that their subcultural membership is merely incidental to this violence and not the reason for it.

Throughout the passage, the speaker is making the claim that the 'riot' which followed the concert was a consequence of the unwarranted presence of the police, and their subsequently provocative behaviour. However, the occurrence of a spate of violence at the concert could easily be interpreted in the light of negative stereotypical knowledge about punks: namely that their lifestyle and attitudes lead them to seek rebellion, confrontation with authority and violence. The mere fact that there was some disturbance could warrant the inference that the violence was another instance of 'typical punk behaviour'. Clearly, such a conclusion would severely undermine the validity of the speaker's (implied) claim that the problems after the concert were a consequence of the police presence. The design of the speaker's descriptions in lines 6 to 9 displays his sensitivity to precisely these kinds of alternative interpretations. He uses extreme case formulations as a rhetorical device to minimise the likelihood that his account of the violence following a punk rock concert may be called into question by reference to 'what everyone knows about punks'. This sequence, then, has been designed to warrant the factual status of the account in the light of potentially sceptical responses.

22.5.5 CONCLUSIONS: WHAT THE ANALYSIS HAS SHOWN

This has been a brief examination of three features of the data extract: the asymmetrical description of the behaviour of the punks and the police; the speaker's description of some actual violent incidents; and the use of extreme case formulations. There are many further points that could be investigated in this extract. However, this exercise has been useful in that it has revealed some of the design features of the speaker's descriptive reports, and has indicated the kind of work his words are doing. In short, he is guarding against potentially sceptical responses to his account of the events following the punk rock concert, and warranting the authority and factual status of his own version of those events.

22.6 SUMMARY

In this chapter, we have considered three approaches to the study of language:

1   Conversation analysis, which treats talk as social action, and focuses on recurrent properties of the sequential organisation of talk in interaction.

2   Discourse analysis and discursive psychology, which focus on the variability of language use, and which examine the rhetorical or persuasive orientation of spoken and written discourse.

3   Critical discourse analysis and Foucauldian discourse analysis, which seek to establish the political or ideological functions served by the linguistic properties of communication and discourses.

DISCUSSION QUESTIONS

1   Is all talk persuasive?

2   In what sense can we understand talk as social action?

3   What are the main differences between conversation analysis and approaches which study political or ideological functions of language?

PROJECTS

1   Analysing devices or structures in talk. Collect a video or tape recording of a discussion between representatives of the major political parties, or an in-depth interview with one politician. Examine the ways in which specific positions and policies are described. What are the devices used to make specific policies seem reasonable and sensible? How do these devices work? (Atkinson's 1984 study of political rhetoric will be helpful for this project.)

2   Analysing the factual orientation of discourse. Tape-record interviews with friends who believe they have had a supernatural or paranormal experience. Ask them to describe what happened. Then transcribe their account, and try to identify how the account is organised to establish that the event actually happened, and was not, for example, an hallucination, dream or misidentification. (Wooffitt, 1992, describes some of the descriptive practices through which speakers build robust accounts of extraordinary experiences.)

3   Analysing the discourses in household objects. Collect everyday bathroom products that come in packaging: shower products, shampoos, soap dispensers, bathroom cleaning materials, and so on. Concentrate primarily on the written words. Following Parker's method outlined above, look first for proper nouns, and then try to identify the categories of person referred to or invoked on the object. What kind of consumer is being constructed? What kind of person is this? What kind of 'proper' or normatively acceptable behaviour is being reinforced? On the basis of this analysis then try to describe the broader discourses that inform these texts. What do these discourses do? Who benefits?

RESOURCES

CONVERSATION ANALYSIS

Introductory accounts can be found in Hutchby and Wooffitt (1998) *Conversation Analysis: Principles, Practices and Applications*, and ten Have (1999) *Doing Conversation Analysis: A Practical Guide*. Heritage's (1984) *Garfinkel and Ethnomethodology* offers an excellent introduction to CA in his account of ethnomethodology and its origins. An accessible introduction to Sacks's work can be found in Silverman's (1998) *Harvey Sacks: Social Science and Conversation Analysis*. Atkinson and Heritage's (1984) *Structures of Social Action: Studies in Conversation Analysis* is the best single collection of conversation analytic studies, and contains two chapters which are based on lectures given by Harvey Sacks.

DISCOURSE ANALYSIS AND DISCURSIVE PSYCHOLOGY

Potter and Wetherell (1987) *Discourse and Social Psychology: Beyond Attitudes and Behaviour* provides a clear introduction to discourse analysis, and its implications for social psychology. Potter (1996) *Representing Reality: Discourse, Rhetoric and Social Construction* provides a comprehensive overview of the interest in factual discourse across a range of social science approaches and subjects. Edwards' (1997) *Discourse and Cognition* is a critique of cognitivism in psychology and an extended argument for discursive psychology. It is, however, fairly complex in places, and knowledge of psychology will be helpful.

CRITICAL APPROACHES TO DISCOURSE

Introductions to critical discourse analysis can be found in Fairclough (1995) *Critical Discourse Analysis: The Critical Study of Language*, Fairclough and Wodak (1997) 'Critical discourse analysis', and Wodak and Meyer (2001) *Methods of Critical Discourse Analysis*. Gill (1996) 'Discourse analysis: practical implementation' and Willig (2001a) 'Foucauldian discourse analysis' provide useful accounts of ideologically engaged discourse analysis. Hepburn's (2003) textbook *An Introduction to Critical Social Psychology* also provides a good overview of a range of perspectives in the study of language in the context of social psychology.

Finally, Wooffitt (2005) *Conversation Analysis and Discourse Analysis: A Comparative and Critical Introduction* offers a critical assessment of the relationship between conversation analysis and various strands of discourse analysis.

APPENDIX TRANSCRIPTION SYMBOLS

The transcription symbols used here are common to conversation analytic research, and were developed by Gail Jefferson. The following symbols are used in the data.

(.5)	The number in brackets indicates a time gap in tenths of a second.
(.)	A dot enclosed in a bracket indicates pause in the talk less than two-tenths of a second.
˙hh	A dot before an 'h' indicates speaker in-breath. The more h's, the longer the inbreath.
hh	An 'h' indicates an out-breath. The more 'h's, the longer the breath.
(( ))	A description enclosed in a double bracket indicates a non-verbal activity. For example ((banging sound))
–	A dash indicates the sharp cut-off of the prior word or sound.
:	Colons indicate that the speaker has stretched the preceding sound or letter. The more colons, the greater the extent of the stretching.
( )	Empty parentheses indicate the presence of an unclear fragment on the tape.
(guess)	The words within a single bracket indicate the transcriber's best guess at an unclear fragment.
.	A full stop indicates a stopping fall in tone. It does not necessarily indicate the end of a sentence.
,	A comma indicates a continuing intonation.
?	A question mark indicates a rising inflection. It does not necessarily indicate a question.
*	An asterisk indicates a 'croaky' pronunciation of the immediately following section.
Under	Underlined fragments indicate speaker emphasis.
↑↓	Pointed arrows indicate a marked falling or rising intonational shift. They are placed immediately before the onset of the shift.
CAPITALS	With the exception of proper nouns, capital letters indicate a section of speech noticeably louder than that surrounding it.
° °	Degree signs are used to indicate that the talk they encompass is spoken noticeably quieter than the surrounding talk.

Thaght	A 'gh' indicates that word in which it is placed had a guttural pronunciation.
> <	'More than' and 'less than' signs indicate that the talk they encompass was produced noticeably quicker than the surrounding talk.
=	The 'equals' sign indicates contiguous utterances. For example:
S2	yeah September [seventy six=
S1	[September
S2	=it would be
S2	yeah that's right
[	Square brackets between adjacent lines of concurrent
]	speech indicate the onset and end of a spate of overlapping talk.

A more detailed description of these transcription symbols can be found in Atkinson and Heritage (1984: ix–xvi).

23 Analysing Visual Materials

Victoria D. Alexander

KEY POINTS

● Techniques for studying existing images.

● The use of photographs or videos as part of interviews or focus groups.

● The production of visual data for sociological research.

● Difficulties that may be encountered in the analysis of visual materials.

23.1 INTRODUCTION

Everywhere we look in the social world there are visual images. They are on television, in movies, on the **Internet**, in our photo albums. Modern technology has caused their proliferation; indeed, some observers believe that the contemporary world is dominated by the visual (Gombrich, 1960; Johnson, 1997; Mirzoeff, 1999; Sturken and Cartwright, 2001). Sociologists and other social researchers increasingly take advantage of this 'visuality'.

Early sociologists used photographs in their research, but the visual was set aside during most of the twentieth century (Becker, 1974; Stasz, 1979). Although **visual methods** have returned in recent years, they are still relatively uncommon and considered by some to be marginal, unimportant, or unscientific. Visual methods will continue to grow in importance, as technologies such as digital scanning and printing, and the Internet make it cheaper and easier to include visual results in essays and publications. Current research using visual methods is a vibrant, growing, and interdisciplinary endeavour (Barnard, 2001; Prosser, 1998; van Leeuwen and Jewitt, 2001), with contributions from anthropologists (Banks, 2001; Pink, 2007), geographers (Rose, 2001), and art historians (Mitchell, 1992), as well as from sociologists (Ball and Smith, 1992; Chaplin, 1994; Emmison and Smith, 2000; Evans and Hall, 1999; Wagner, 1978).

'Visual sociology' and 'visual research methods' are broad terms that encompass many techniques and assumptions. Visual materials come into play in varying aspects of the research process, creating four categories:

1   the analysis of *existing visual materials* (e.g. looking at the portrayal of gender or race on television);

2   the use of visual materials to *generate data* (e.g. showing photos to an individual during an interview or a film to a focus group);

3   the *creation* of new visual data to analyse (e.g. filming business people in meetings to learn about interaction and negotiating styles);

4.   the use of images to *present results*.

Cross-cutting these distinctions is the familiar divide in **meta-theory** (see Chapters 1 and 2): is sociology a systematic search for generalisable facts or is it an interpretive venture where one seeks local, historically contingent meaning?

23.2 ANALYSING EXISTING VISUAL MATERIALS

A researcher can analyse existing **visual texts** – television shows, advertisements, paintings – to learn about the social world. This form of visual research, dominated by media studies, is well established in sociology. Existing visual materials are, in fact, **documents** (see Chapter 15). To analyse visual documents in this framework, you examine four aspects of each text – its authenticity, credibility, representativeness, and meaning (Scott, 1990). Authenticity can be ignored for most analyses of media and art. An advertisement in *Cosmopolitan* does not pretend to be anything else, and museums have already done the hard work of dating artworks and detecting forgeries. There are, however, occasions where the authenticity question is important. For instance, in studying old postcards portraying 'exotic' people, it is crucial to determine when and where they were taken, and if the scenes depicted are staged (Banks, 2001). Credibility is a key issue in analysing visual materials. It is important to consider who made the image and why. Though pictures, especially photographs or videos, ask to be taken at face value, they cannot be. Photos are easily altered, retouched, or cropped; one image is picked from many. These acts affect what you see, as does the original choice of framing. Most visual images, from photojournalism to advertisements, and even family photos, are highly constructed by their creators. For instance, some of the postcards Banks discusses were taken to highlight differences between 'us' and 'them' or to depict, in what we now consider outmoded or offensive ways, different racial 'types' (Banks: 2001, 28–33, 42–7). Representativeness, which implies sampling, and Meaning, the most difficult question, will be addressed below. As with written documents, **triangulation** of findings from visual materials is often desirable.

Two other ways to study visual documents are **content analysis** and interpretive analysis. Content analysis is often based on reflection theory, and interpretive analysis on **semiotics**, though this is not always the case.

23.2.1 REFLECTION THEORY

Researchers who study visual documents, especially media texts, often rely implicitly on '**reflection theory**'. They believe that visual documents mirror, or tell us something about, society. If television dramas portray ethnic minorities negatively, for instance, as criminals but not police officers, it might reasonably be assumed that the society producing the shows is itself racist. According to the theory, skinny models in today's advertisements reflect our society's belief that women should be slim, whereas Rubens's plump ladies show his society's preference for a little more flesh. And if we want to know what Dutch houses looked like in the seventeenth century, we need only look at old paintings of everyday life in Holland.

Reflection theory leaves a number of important questions unanswered (Albrecht, 1954). What, exactly, is reflected – reality, values, or fantasies? And whose ideas are reflected – those of the whole society, ruling elites, media executives, or subcultures? Indeed, social 'facts' might be present in media texts because they are commonplace, or precisely because they are not (Laslett, 1976), as the unusual captures our attention better than the mundane. Despite these problems, many researchers, especially in media studies, are interested in how visual materials indicate underlying social factors, especially around issues of race, ethnicity, gender, class and sexuality (e.g. Cortese, 1999; Dines and Humez, 2003; Entman and Rojecki, 2002; Jewitt, 1997).

23.2.2 SEMIOTICS

Alongside reflection theory, semiotic analysis is a key method of analysing visual texts (see especially Barthes, 1977; Bignell, 1997; Hawkes, 1992; Kress and van Leeuwen, 2006; Rose, 2001: Chapter 4). Semiotics is a method which draws inspiration from Ferdinand de Saussure's (1915) theory of language. The basic ideas are: (1) **Signs** are composed of a **signifier** (a word, say, 'dog') that points to a **signified** (the object or concept the word refers to, in this case, a four-legged thing that barks). (2) The relationship between words and concepts are arbitrary. We might just as well call the barking thing a 'chien' or a 'perro' or a 'woof-woof' – or for that matter, a 'cat' (so long as we then agree to call those meowing things something else). The point is that, as part of a language, we agree that certain signs match up with certain meanings. Furthermore, (3) signs do not stand alone. Instead, they become meaningful because they work in concert with other signs in the system. So, for instance, if I say 'hawk and dove', you will probably think 'belligerent and peaceful', noticing the contrast more than their common ability to fly. The idea is that meaning comes from binary opposites, and clear meanings come from sharp contrasts. It is less certain what I have in mind if I say 'hawk, tiger, and jaguar', since three concepts cannot stand in opposition. Meaning is built up by adding opposites together.

Finally (this makes point 4), there is a distinction between *langue* and *parole*. *Langue* refers to the language itself – its grammar, its system of binary oppositions, its meanings. *Parole* refers to speech, or 'utterances', and can mean either spoken words or written ones. The reason to make this distinction is that we can see language working only through *parole*. We have to infer how the utterances work together. We figure out the rules, the *langue*, by observing those utterances.

How do Saussure's ideas apply to visual materials? Metaphorically, visual systems are languages. The goal is to look at images – these are the utterances, so to speak, the *parole* – and from these deduce the *langue*, the grammar of the image system. Semiotics tells us to uncover signs and figure out how they work. Semioticians pay attention to a range of instances from one particular type (or genre) of visual image, to discover the relationship among signs and how they create meaning in the whole system.

Williamson's (1995) semiotic study of British advertisements shows how messages are *encoded* into advertisements by the interior logic and structure of individual advertisements and the system of advertisements as a whole. The overarching message of advertisements is, not surprisingly, to encourage consumerism. In individual advertisements, advertisers use a variety of codes to this end. For instance, putting their products next to desirable people or places suggests there is a correlation between the two and this serves to characterise their product as desirable. Williamson also posits how people might *decode* these messages to get meaning out of them. She shows a variety of techniques used by advertisers to capture our attention and draw us in, such as visual and textual puns and puzzles, or the 'absent participant' into whose shoes viewers step. Often the meanings of advertisements are not seen on their surface (the manifest content), but are hidden (the latent content).

There are some difficulties in applying semiotics to visual materials. Using Saussure's ideas by analogy can be fruitful, but they do not map neatly onto image systems. For instance, we can easily differentiate language systems: French versus English, for example. Finding different systems, or genres, for images is more difficult. Do Renaissance paintings (Baxandall, 1988) use a different visual language than modern advertising images? Certainly they do! But sometimes modern advertisers draw on codes from Renaissance art. Are advertisements used in women's magazines a different genre from those used in news magazines? Well, certainly advertisements in *Cosmopolitan* look very different from those in *The Economist*, and they draw on knowledge from different sectors of society, but they also draw on ideas from the wider culture. Advertisers can expect that, to a great extent, readers of *Cosmopolitan* understand *Economist* advertisements and vice versa. In other words, genres of visual codes are multiple and overlapping. Members of a given society are familiar with a large number of them, from both past and present, while they might only know one spoken language fluently. This means that you cannot deduce a grammar for images in the same way that you can for a spoken language. And unlike linguistic signs, visual signs do not always relate to their signified in an arbitrary way. A picture of a dog somehow resembles real dogs. Peirce (1958) calls this kind of sign 'indexical'. As a result, images seem more direct than words. This can create problems when we forget that images are constructed.

23.2.3 CONTENT ANALYSIS

A key way of analysing visual information sociologically is **content analysis** (Ball and Smith, 1992: Chapter 2; Rose, 2001: Chapter 3). In this, you choose a question that can be measured with variables and decide on a coding scheme to capture them. Chapter 14 describes how to choose codes and develop **coding** rules, and emphasises the importance of a code book. The usefulness of a pilot study, to test your research instrument (in this case, your preliminary codes), is highlighted in Chapter 9. Books on general (textual) content analysis (Holsti, 1969; Weber, 1990) can also provide useful insights into coding visual data. Codes must be explicit, unambiguous, and mutually exclusive. You can code on sheets of paper, in a Word document, or an Excel spreadsheet. Alternatively, software programs, as described in Chapter 20, can help you code visual or multimedia data.

Next, you make a sampling frame, choosing cases to analyse that are representative and unbiased (see Chapter 9). Most sampling procedures are designed to reduce the number of cases; you select a sample from a larger population of possibilities. Others, however, help you build up your sample from a limited number of possibilities; you search for relevant cases in contemporary or historical archives. Finally, you code all cases and analyse the resulting data. With a large number of cases you can produce quantitative results using cross-tabulations, charts, or graphs. With fewer cases, tables are useful. Content analyses are usually reported in a standard 'scientific' format.

I used this technique in a study of children in advertisements in my undergraduate honours thesis (later published as Alexander, 1994). I wanted to know if the portrayal of children in American magazine advertisements had changed during the twentieth century; specifically how the relationship between parents and children might have shifted. I chose a sampling procedure that I hoped was representative and unbiased, and developed a coding scheme to record interactions between children and adults. I coded hundreds of advertisements picturing children and presented my results in a series of graphs. For instance, one graph showed that the proportion of American advertisements picturing children is strongly related to the fertility rate in the USA, with one caveat: during times when child-rearing was strict there were fewer advertisements showing youngsters than when child-rearing was permissive.

Macdonald's (1989) study of the headquarters of professional associations is a good example of a content analysis of a smaller number of cases. The study asked how these groups literally 'built' respectability. Macdonald carefully chose his cases to be representative and illustrative, and thoroughly researched each key variable. He examined six headquarters, three from accountancy organisations (his focus point) and three from comparable professional bodies in law and medicine. Each building was coded on eleven variables that measured its prestige. The codes ranged from minus one ('inappropriate or lacking') to plus 3 ('outstanding'), and were summed to give a single 'conspicuous consumption rating' to each case. Macdonald presents these findings in a table.

Content analysis has a number of advantages. It is formal and systematic, which lends structure to your research. It can give a good overview of your subject. If critics disagree with your interpretation of the data, they must still address the findings you presented. But there are some disadvantages as well.

The main difficulty is that content analysis requires codes to be clear and well defined. It is designed to categorise variables in a precise manner, to see each case separately and to weight them equally. It strips down and fragments content in order to count it. But visual images are usually ambiguous and they often make reference to other images. Content analysis ignores context and the potential for multiple meanings, and it often disguises, through the coding procedure, the investigator's input.

23.2.4 INTERPRETIVE ANALYSIS

Interpretive analysis, often based on semiotics, is used to capture hidden meaning, ambiguity, and intertextuality (the interrelationship among images) in visual objects. For instance, Barthel (1988) analysed American advertisements, specifically looking at gender. She was interested in such issues as how women can be portrayed as 'fair maidens' and also as 'dark ladies' – sometimes in the same advertisement. These signs reflect, but also construct, concepts of gender in the wider society.

Interpretive studies can also rely on other theoretical frameworks. A classic example of a structural study is Goffman's (1979) work on gender advertisements. He examined a large number of advertisements to demonstrate structural relationships between men and women. To uncover these 'gender displays', he analysed only the photos in the advertisements, ignoring the text. This approach stands in contrast to that of Barthel (1988) and Williamson (1995). They were also interested in underlying, latent meanings, but specifically included the words. Semioticians posit that textual elements in advertisements are integral components of their meaning. Goffman, on the other hand, argues that the structural relationships in which he is interested are more easily seen if the manifest content of the advert, often conveyed in the words, is ignored. (Along these lines, Jhally, 1990, argues that stripping music videos of their soundtracks makes it easier to discover important aspects of their meaning that are otherwise hidden.)

In sum, interpretive analysis can capture richness of meaning, and often deals with wholes rather than fragments. It can uncover latent meanings, rather than sticking to surface appearances only, and can give more weight to important cases. Yet research conducted using this framework is often accused of being unsystematic, unobjective, and 'just the researcher's opinion'. Unlike the examples presented here, interpretive analysis often rests – by necessity, justified choice, or laziness – on only a few images. Even when the samples are large (Goffman presents about 500 images, and must have looked at many more), the analysis usually proceeds without a stated sampling frame or coding scheme. These criticisms are the obverse of those of content analysis.

23.2.5 COMBINING CONTENT AND INTERPRETIVE ANALYSIS

Students often wish to combine a content analysis with an interpretive one. This is good if you can do it – indeed, it seems daft to ignore interpretive information that comes along in a content analysis, and content analysis can provide empirical strength to a more interpretive frame. For instance, I did not code for the portrayal of gender or ethnicity in my content analysis of children in advertising. But being close to the data, I had observations on these issues.

It is not always possible to combine the two types of research, however, partly because doing so properly means completing two studies (see Chapter 7 on mixed methods). Because the assumptions underlying content analysis and interpretive analysis are quite distinct, combining the two is not as easy as it sounds.

If you wish to examine existing visual materials, you may choose among a variety of techniques:

1   You may consider issues of authenticity, credibility, representativeness and meaning, as in the analysis of textual documents.

2   You may study visual materials on the assumption that they reflect aspects of society. Such a reflection approach is often useful, but can also be problematic because it is not clear exactly what is reflected.

3   If you choose a semiotic approach, start by looking for binary opposites and recurrent signs. These will help you uncover the visual grammar of the images to learn about how they create meaning.

4   If you choose to do a content analysis, you will need a coding scheme with mutually exclusive categories and a sampling frame by which you choose the images to analyse. Content analysis is particularly useful in showing trends and giving an overview of a large body of materials. However, it does not effectively capture ambiguity and multiple meanings.

5   An interpretive analysis aims to uncover hidden meanings in visual materials. Semiotics can form the basis for an interpretive analysis, but visual materials can be analysed interpretatively without reference to semiotics.

6   It can be useful to combine a content analysis with an interpretive one, but it is more difficult to do this than it might first appear.

23.3 GENERATING DATA WITH VISUAL MATERIALS

Visual materials are evocative, and can serve as stimuli in interviews and focus groups. Research based on this idea is called **photo elicitation** (Collier and Collier, 1986). Items such as ethnographic, historical, or family photos are shown to research participants, in individual or group settings, to learn about a research question. Often researchers choose existing visual information, but you can also create visual materials for this purpose, either making them yourself or, in a more complicated research design, asking respondents to make or choose them for you. I provide three examples, one using moving images and the others, photos.

Shively (1992) was interested in why Native Americans enjoy Western movies so much, given that cowboys are invariably the good guys and the Indians the bad guys. In what we might call 'film elicitation' she showed a classic Western film to two focus groups, one made up of Native Americans and the other, of 'Anglos' (white Americans). She discovered that the meanings the two groups took from the film varied tremendously. The Anglos thought of the movie as part of their cultural heritage, as an authentic portrayal of the Historical West. The Native Americans saw the stories as utter nonsense in terms of their historical value, but appreciated the depicted ideals of being at one with your horse, the range and nature.

Eck (2001; 2003) was interested in how men and women interpret and receive visual images of nudes. In a study based on photo elicitation, she interviewed 23 men and 22 women, showing them a variety of images depicting unclothed males or females from different sources (old master paintings, *Penthouse* and *Playgirl*, medical textbooks, *National Geographic*, and advertising). Her respondents readily classified female nudes into three 'frames' – art, pornography and information (e.g. medical or ethnographic images). Younger respondents found advertising images using nudes to be acceptable, though older ones did not. And while both men and women felt relatively comfortable viewing images of nude women (albeit with different interpretations of them), both groups found it more difficult to look at and classify images of nude males as these images are not strongly linked to existing cultural frames. These findings lead Eck to conclude that 'men are much harder'.

In a different type of research, Twine used photo elicitation in a larger ethnographic study of interracial families. She interviewed white women about family photos chosen by the women themselves in order to learn how they negotiate their 'racial profiles' in their roles as partners in an interracial marriage and mothers of African-descent children. The photographs present family life as positive and successful, both a love story and a story of respectability. Other stories, however, are not depicted in the photos. Through her interviews, Twine learns about suffering and difficulties, and she shows how one participant 'simultaneously "erases" race and racializes herself' as she 'constructs and reconstructs the narrative of her interracial life' (ibid.: 496–7).

If you want to use visual materials to spur respondents, you need to be mindful of a few things:

1   You must choose your visual materials carefully. Images convey information along a multitude of lines, so pictures that appear similar at a quick glance may differ markedly in important details.

2   Consider what you wish the respondents to think about and be prepared to defend your choice of materials.

3   If your respondents choose, or create, the images, be aware that each respondent will discuss a different set of materials, and this will affect the way you analyse your interviews.

4   You will need to develop an interview schedule, or the key questions you will use as the facilitator of a focus group. You will also need a strategy for analysing the interview/focus group data you collect. Chapters 12 and 13 can help with these aspects of a photo elicitation project.

23.4 CREATING VISUAL DATA

Researchers can use photography or video to collect data on people or objects. This visual data can be analysed in a systematic way. For instance, Heath (1986) videotaped people in doctors surgeries. He carefully analysed short clips in the close manner of **conversation analysis** (see Chapter 22). The minute details of motion of doctor and patient, which along with their talk teach us about social interaction, would be missed by non-visual methods.

In his study of the architecture of professional associations, Macdonald (1989) took photographs of buildings. These photos allowed Macdonald to strengthen the validity and reliability of his codes through a process of triangulation: He showed his data (the look of the buildings) to a panel of experts, who confirmed his own coding.

Visual data may also be collected as part of an **ethnography** (Banks, 2001; Pink, 2007). Twine (2006), for instance, worked with a professional photographer in her ethnographic work with transracial mothers. Chaplin (2005) took photographs of the people who lived in her street (36 households), at their front doors. She used these photos, not only as a systematic record of her neighbourhood at the turn of the millennium (the photos were taken in May 2000), but also as a way to think about what photographs mean. And Dicks et al. (2006) collected 'multimodal' evidence – fieldnotes, photographs, video – in their ethnography of a science discovery centre in Wales. They were interested in how children learn about 'science' in this setting. They also explored how the different ways that researchers collect data on, or 'represent', the social world (their notes, photos, and moving images) can afford different understandings of it. Chapter 14 provides help on conducting ethnographic research.

Researchers often tape-record interviews and focus groups. You may wish to videotape them instead. As with audio-tapes, the resulting information can be coded or 'transcribed'. CAQDAS (see Chapter 20) can be helpful, as the video can be clipped and quoted digitally, preserving the visual component of the data. You can reduce visual information, moving or still, to text, through content analysis. You can document movement with complex transcription systems, for instance, those developed for dance (Heath, 1986: 20–1). Or you can analyse your visual data through an interpretive framework. Often, visual data are collected as an adjunct to more traditional means of data collection and are not systematically analysed.

If you wish to generate visual data as part of your research, there are some things you should consider:

1   An obvious starting point is to be sure you know how your camera or camcorder works and to practise using it before you start collecting data.

2   You will need to decide how you will analyse your visual data (e.g. with content analysis, thematic coding, conversation analysis, or ethnographic techniques). Alternatively, you may decide that your visual images are only a small part of a larger project which uses other methods, and that they will be used mainly for illustration.

23.5 PRESENTING RESULTS WITH A VISUAL COMPONENT

One way to use visual information in reports and publications is to include images as decoration. This is the most common, and perhaps least interesting, mode of visual presentation. It occurs in undergraduate textbooks, especially introductory ones, where photographs of people, cartoons, advertisements, movie posters, and the like are reproduced. They enliven the narrative, and take up space so that reading seems less onerous. The illustrations, however, are often not tightly connected to the text and have a random feel to them.

More important is the use of visual materials for the illustration and elaboration of research findings. Halle (1993), for instance, studied pictures in people's homes. He looked at all the pictures – art works, religious iconography, family photos – displayed in houses in four neighbourhoods around New York City, varied by social class. The findings are brought to life in the book through photographs of the respondents, their rooms, and the objects that they keep. Halle also included floor plans of their houses, to convey a sense of their spaces. The illustrations are closely connected to the research findings and enhance the written material.

Goffman (1979) used photographs of the advertisements he analysed to present his data. Indeed, his article is unusual in that it has relatively little text with a large number of images. He argues that the images are not just his raw data but, organised systematically, they are actually his findings, analogous to a table showing multiple regression results. His work literally lets you see his argument.

Berger's (1972) book on how we see, like Goffman's article, uses pictures as an integral part of a textual argument. Indeed, the book, a melange of social theory and art historical analysis, would not really make sense without its pictures. It is no coincidence that Berger's book started as a television series and was later converted to print. Photo essays in Becker et al. (1981) tell stories about society, as in ethnography. The photos and text, created by academics in several fields, are a mix of social research and art – some would say more art than research. In fact, the book is an exhibition catalogue, that is, a publication which accompanied a temporary exhibition in an art gallery. Becker (1998) goes further by claiming a book made by an art photographer, Robert Frank (1959) as a beautiful example of social research. Photographs in *The Americans* have short captions telling where they were taken, but otherwise there are no words in the book at all. While many sociologists might agree that it is beautiful, far fewer would say it is sociology.

The best visual social science melds words and images. Because pictures are information-rich, worth at least a thousand words, they can save a lot of description. However, because they are information-rich, they are also ambiguous. Regardless of whether the goal of sociology is to study a phenomenon objectively, to make an argument, to posit a knowledge claim in a discourse, or to tell a story, the researcher must put forward the scientific findings, argument, claim, or story with clarity. Perhaps statistical tables speak for themselves (though this is arguable), but visual data clearly do not.

This is demonstrated in Berger's book in which text and image are interwoven in odd numbered chapters, but visual images with no text comprise the even numbered ones. As Berger himself points out, the visual chapters raise questions, but it is not certain what, exactly, Berger had in mind when he chose the images. In contrast, the written word serves to anchor the meaning of the images in the written chapters. Similarly, although Becker argues that Frank's book makes its themes clear through repetition and careful choice of images, these themes might be unavailable to readers who do not have training in aesthetics and photography.

Some writers have theorised that writing is privileged over seeing in sociology (Chaplin, 1994). This is often asserted in the form of a complaint that visual images are not valued on their own. While I see great potential for visual methods, I do not expect that sociology will give up writing any time soon. So the challenge for the researcher using visual materials is to incorporate the visual with the text to bolster the thrust of the argument, or to describe the visual data in words, not to use pictures without a supporting written analysis.

In using images to present results, you will need to think about the following points:

1   If you use images merely for decoration, they will enliven the text but not add to your arguments.

2   Visual images are best when they are chosen carefully to support arguments that you make in the written part of your report.

3   Ideally, visual images will work best when they include captions or descriptions that clarify their meaning with respect to the arguments you wish to make.

23.6 SOME PROBLEMS IN USING VISUAL MATERIALS

Using visual materials in research is not without its problems, practical, ethical, analytical, and theoretical.

23.6.1 PRACTICAL CONCERNS

Issues surrounding data collection include the standard problems of access, such as securing permission to videotape people, to photograph objects in private collections, or to use personal images (such as family photographs) in the course of research. There is also the expense of collecting visual data, including photocopying fees, the price of film or videotapes, and the cost of equipment (cameras, digital scanners, or playback devices).

More difficult are the practical problems in getting images published (or reproduced in unpublished works). A common irony of much writing on visual sociology is that it is in words with no pictures, even as decoration! The most tricky issue involves copyright: existing images may be owned by individuals or organisations. You cannot, however, 'quote' a visual image under fair use rules, as you can quote a passage from a book. Also, if respondents take pictures as part of your research, copyright of those pictures resides with them. You will need to gain their consent to use those images.

To publish a proprietary image, you must secure written permission, cover the cost of providing a transparency to the publisher, and often pay a fee as well. Further, copyright holders have been known to refuse permission if they do not like the use to which you put their image, and they can even sue you, as Dubin (1995) discovered when he tried to portray as gay two Ken dolls driving Barbie's pink convertible. Strict attention to copyright is not crucial for unpublished essays or dissertations, as most advertisers, artists, museums, television executives, movie studios, and the like are not on the lookout for illegal photocopies, clips, or stills taken from their advertisements, paintings, sculptures, broadcasts, films, or webpages when used for such purposes. Technically, though, permission is required for all uses of visual images that are not created by the researcher.

Finally, including images in published or unpublished works involves some costs for photocopying or printing images. Colour costs much more than black and white, but can convey important information. Most publishers expect authors to bear the expense of providing illustrations, and are often unwilling to use large numbers of images due to the cost of printing them. Many publishers will print only black and white images, and others, especially print journals, refuse images altogether. Indeed, Macdonald's was the first article in the history of the journal *Sociology* to include photos. Moving images are not possible to reproduce in print formats – unless your book or paper is accompanied by a DVD or a webpage, which add their own difficulties. Print journals, however, are increasingly willing to publish still images, and advances in electronic publishing and digital imaging have made publishing and presenting visual information of all sorts much easier. Researchers are also using technology innovatively. Dicks and Mason (1998), for instance, have explored the use of hypertext environments to integrate written, aural, visual and multimedia data.

Another practical concern is that visual research can produce a large amount of data. This is similar to the situation in qualitative or historical studies where you end up with large files of transcribed interviews, fieldnotes or piles of government documents. You will need a research strategy to handle this. When you present results visually, use representative examples as you would use quotes in an interview study or ethnography. Editing is important. Not only are there practical obstacles to reproducing a large number of images, but you also must take care not to overwhelm your reader.

Finally, while theoretical ideas about visual sociology may be clear, what, exactly, are you supposed to do when confronted with an image? Or when you have to decide what to study and how to study it? It is hard to get concrete answers to these questions from books. Some authors suggest you learn-by-doing, others that you take an apprenticeship (as you do when you write a dissertation or thesis under supervision). Becker (2000) proposes that photography courses should be included in sociology degree programmes. It is also useful to look at examples of the type of work you wish to do, and imagine yourself doing those studies.

23.6.2 ETHICS AND SAFETY

If you do create images yourself, or if you draw on private images such as family photos or pictures taken for the project by your participants, there are important ethical considerations, even for unpublished studies. Chapter 8 discusses ethics in social research, the Study Group on Visual Sociology of the British Sociological Association provides a statement of ethical practice (BSA Visual Sociology, 2006), and Gross et al. (1988) offer detailed considerations on image ethics.

The most important issue is the confidentiality of your respondents, as you cannot just change their names as you can with textual data. In all cases, you must ask respondents to sign consent forms giving permission to use pictures taken of them, taken by them, or owned by them. If the photographs will allow them to be identified, you must make respondents aware of this. Respondents can give permission for these images to be shown, but you must not use identifying photographs if this will bring harm to your respondents. To maintain confidentiality, you could digitally, or otherwise, blank out faces – although Banks (2001: 130) points out that using this technique brings up ideas of criminality. You could use software to convert photographs into line drawings. Heath (1986) rendered his respondents anonymous by using an artist to draw the interactions he recorded in doctors' surgeries. Or, in promising confidentiality, you may simply agree never to release your visual data.

Consent is required to photograph in private locations, e.g. corporate reception areas, shops and schools, and is customary in research settings. It is legal to photograph structures, objects and people in public settings, but people can object, sometimes violently. Do not put yourself at risk! In addition, taking photos can be obtrusive, especially if you use a flash or stand near to your subjects.

Harper's (1981) visual ethnography of American hobos raises issues of safety, intrusion and ethics. He took photographs, as a participant observer, of tramp life on the fringes of American society. His fieldwork put him at risk of theft and assault (perhaps by the tramps he travelled with, but more likely by people who target tramps) and of injury while illegally riding freight trains. In a sensitive discussion, he describes how, early in his research, he intruded by photographing people on Skid Row. Later in the project, he travelled with tramps as a participant observer, making fewer images less obtrusively. He also discusses his decision to publish pictures of people who make up a group that is considered by outsiders to be deviant. While experienced researchers may make a case for morally complex studies, students should not undertake research which poses ethical dilemmas, nor should they study topics that might compromise their safety.

23.6.3 AMBIGUITY AND MEANING

Visual images present problems to researchers because they are ambiguous. They can carry multiple meanings and are therefore called 'polysemic' or 'multivocal'. Chaplin (2005) demonstrates this in her photographic study of her neighbourhood, by showing how different meanings can be taken from the same photographs when they are looked at in different ways. Furthermore, as Gombrich (1972) points out, pictures are better at conveying a mood than a specific argument. If this is the case, how can the researcher possibly assert a single interpretation of an image? Does this mean that all research in visual sociology is, by definition, subjective?

To a great extent, these problems are not unique to visual data (Becker, 1974; Wagner, 1978: 20–1). Sociologists have always worried about how to measure their ideas validly and reliably and how to choose unbiased samples or representative cases. These problems are no less applicable to visual than other types of data, and can be solved for the visual with similar levels of success. Sociologists studying the reception of culture recognise that taking meaning from words is problematic, and that all texts allow some leeway for interpretation based on readers' own horizons of expectations. Further, postmodern sociologists have questioned the possibility of objective research, regardless of the source of data.

While every source of data implies problems with measurement and objectivity, these problems are more easily seen, so to speak, in visual images. This is because science, including social science, relies on a rational intelligence which is primarily verbal. Images draw on other forms of intelligence which do not set out to create clear, linear arguments. Whether your research draws inspiration from modernist or a postmodernist thinking, it is worth constructing a clear argument about the images you use and bolstering it with evidence; images must be accompanied by a text that reduces their possible meanings. As Becker (1986) argues, if your writing is clear, others may disagree with you, but you will make a stronger contribution than if you ramble, fudge, obfuscate, or try to have it both ways.

23.6.4 AUDIENCES AND CREATORS

People look at visual images. Looking creates meaning. In analysing existing visual materials in isolation, you cannot know how audiences actually receive and make meaning from them. One way to reduce this problem is to pay attention to the *intended* audience (e.g. readers of *The Economist* are, on average, more likely to be middle-aged, business and management-orientated, and male than readers of *Cosmopolitan*), and point this out in your research. But the only way to get at how people receive images is to ask them (as is done in photo elicitation). Nevertheless, there are situations where you may wish to study just the images and not branch out into interviews (e.g. media representations of social groups), and those where interviews are impossible (e.g. studies of historical images, where the original viewers have long since died).

A similar difficulty is that the creators of visual documents always have reasons for making them, as was mentioned with respect to a **document**'s credibility. Some of these reasons are political or ideological, others commercial. There are also reasons relating to the conventions of the genre of representation. It can be useful to speculate about the motives of creators, though this is not always necessary. It is also useful to consider the original context of your images, not mixing examples from different 'frames' without good reason.

Along these lines, Rose (2001) suggests that the meanings of images are generated in three 'sites': the sites of production, the image itself, and the audiences. 'Many of the theoretical disagreements about ... visual objects', she writes, are 'disputes over which of these [sites] is more important and why' (ibid.: 16). (For an extended discussion of the production and consumption of cultural objects, see Alexander, 2003.)

23.6.5 REFLEXIVITY

Reflexivity denotes a style of research whereby one addresses how the research process affects the results. It requires precision about the analytical methods and data collection procedures used, and emphasises the researcher's own assumptions and beliefs through explicit statements of how the researcher's very presence affects what he or she is investigating. It is research that looks back at itself. At its best, it makes for better work (everything is stated, nothing, such as the researcher's personal political beliefs, is left hidden), and it can create a useful humbleness in researchers. At its worst, especially when researchers spend the entire write-up talking about themselves rather than their respondents, it can lead to intellectually boring work.

Students are often quite aware of the fact that when they analyse a visual image, they are starting from their own point of view. 'It's only my interpretation,' they worry. Here are three possible solutions:

1   You can add a disclaimer that acknowledges the multivocality of your data, but leaves it aside for further research.

2   You can interview actual audiences about your material.

3   You can be reflexive in your empirical study (Banks, 2001).

In any case, make an argument which can be supported by your data, but do not apologise or look inward. Make your study a true one, but not the last word. As Becker (1974: 15) says, 'The answer lies in distinguishing between the statement that X is true about something and the statement that X is all that is true about something.'

There are a number of difficulties with visual images, and these should be kept in mind:

1   Think about how you will address such practical issues as copyright fees and the cost of reproducing images in reports and published works.

2   The issues of confidentiality and anonymity, when these are promised, need very careful consideration. This means that extra care is needed when securing permission for research which generates visual materials.

3   Be sure that you make images only where you will be safe and where you have permission to photograph or film.

4   Visual images are always ambiguous. People produce them, usually with a particular purpose in mind. They are consumed by other people (including researchers) who may make alternative interpretations. You may wish to address these issues by paying attention to intended audiences, or by making your own interpretation clear in your analysis. A reflexive approach may be useful in this regard.

23.7 SUMMARY

Visual sociology is increasingly recognised as an important area of social inquiry. This chapter has highlighted some techniques, both qualitative and quantitative, of analysing visual data that is collected or generated by the researcher. Visual data are a category of documentary data, and as such, some of the tools used for the analysis of written documents can be applied to visual material (such as content analysis or semiotic analysis). But visual data can also function in ways quite different from written documents, and therefore, call for different research techniques (e.g. photo elicitation or making images in ethnographies). The chapter also pointed out some of the difficulties and debates in the analysis of visual data. These include the ambiguity of visual information, the disjuncture between the materials themselves and the views of the creators and users of such images, and the fact that some researchers see visual materials as data in and of themselves, where as other researchers use visual material to indicate underlying social factors. The chapter highlighted the importance of ethical considerations in studies which either create images of research participants or make images in collaboration with them. And it discussed how visual data may be included in written work.

DISCUSSION QUESTIONS

1   When should you promise confidentiality and anonymity to participants in visual research? How can you protect participants if anonymity is promised? Is it ever acceptable to show identifiable people or places in your work?

2   What steps would you take if you were designing a content analysis of visual images? What would you do in a semiotic one? A photo elicitation?

3   To what degree are visual images ambiguous and multi-faceted? How can you manage to study and write about visual images, given their complexity? Is all research in visual sociology necessarily subjective?

PROJECTS

This chapter may have helped you see social research in a different light. Now go out and take a *good look* at society!

1   *Media analysis*: Choose a research question, for instance, how a social group (either a broad one, like mothers or young people, or a narrower one, like motorcyclists or police officers) is depicted. Choose a type of existing visual data – movies, newspaper photographs, advertisements, illustrations in children's books, television programmes, historical paintings or something else – which might portray your group. Analyse your data using one of the methodologies mentioned. In your write-up, defend your choice of method and sampling. Think about how to present the visual component in your essay.

2   *Photo elicitation*: Choose one of these projects – or create your own. (a) Ask your grandparents, or a few elderly neighbours, to show you photographs from their youth. Interview them about consumption patterns (what did they buy, make, or do without?) or social rituals (how did they celebrate birthdays; what did they do and where did they go with their friends?). (b) Pick a controversial topic, for instance, 'Fashion models encourage girls to be anorexic'. Gather a number of images (e.g. ten advertisements or pictures of famous people from newspapers, showing different body composition), or find a movie or TV show, on video, that captures the issue. Organise a focus group of your friends and lead a discussion using your visual material as prompts. Consider how best to convey the content of your images to your readers.

3   *Envision data*: Use your camera or camcorder to gather data. (a) Show how gravestones and cemeteries preserve memory, prestige and power. (b) Study what the buildings that house different kinds of organisations say about their occupants. (c) Examine behaviour in shopping districts, asking how shoppers browse, circulate and queue, or what people communicate by their dress and speed of walking. In all of these, be scrupulous about research ethics. It is acceptable to photograph cemeteries and the outsides of buildings, but you will need permission to shoot inside offices and stores. You may find this permission difficult to obtain, but do not be tempted to cheat. You will be more unobtrusive, and safe, if you choose a busy high street in tourist areas. 'Quote' your data, or describe them, in your report.

RESOURCES

Three overviews of visual methods in anthropology and sociology are well worth reading. Ball and Smith (1992) *Analyzing Visual Data* give a concise overview of visual ethnography, content analysis, and semiotics. Banks (2001) *Visual Methods in Social Research* is a more comprehensive discussion of the use of photographs and film in social research, covering such areas as photo and film elicitation, creating documentary images and film, and working collaboratively with participants. He considers such issues as representation (what images mean) and a range of ethical concerns. Rose (2006) *Visual Methodologies* discusses the three sites of meaning (production, image, audience) and provides chapters on content analysis and semiotics, as well as art-historical, psychoanalytical and discourse approaches to images.

Two edited collections, Prosser (1998) *Image-based Research: A Sourcebook for Qualitative Researchers* and van Leeuwen and Jewitt (2001) *The Handbook of Visual Analysis* bring together useful articles on differing approaches. Research on 'the visual' can encompass more than the media images and photographs mentioned in this chapter. Emmison and Smith (2000) *Researching the Visual: Images, Objects, Contexts and Interactions in Social and Cultural Inquiry* take up this idea in their book.

This chapter introduced a number of exemplars of empirical research incorporating the visual: (in alphabetical order) Alexander (1994), Barthel (1988), Becker (1981), Berger (1972), Chaplin (2005), Cortese (1999), Dicks et al. (2006), Dines and Humez (2003), Eck (2001; 2003), Entman and Rojecki (2001), Goffman (1979), Halle (1993), Heath (1986), Jewitt (1997), Macdonald (1989), Shively (1992), Twine (2006), and Williamson (1995). These show the methods at work and are intended to provide inspiration.

Three journals specifically publish visual research: *Journal of Visual Culture, Visual Communication*, and *Visual Studies*. Articles drawing on visual methods are often published in *Sociological Research Online*, and increasingly, in mainstream sociology journals. In addition, visual methods engage concerns in general sociology.

Part IV
Endings

This final Part is about writing up one's research and publishing it. It offers an 'insider's' view of the publication process, interesting not only when you are writing a dissertation or thesis, but also when you are reading sociological research literature, to see how journal articles and books are socially constructed and why academic writing takes the form it does.

24   Writing about Social Research

Nigel Gilbert

KEY POINTS

● Publishing the results is an essential final step in doing social research.

● A research report needs to persuade the reader of the significance of the work that it presents. This is easiest if it is written using a standard style and structure.

● Decisions about what to write, where to publish and who will contribute to the writing need to be taken early in the course of a research project.

24.1 INTRODUCTION

Until research has been published, available for all to read, it barely counts as social science at all. In science and social science, publication is an essential final step of the research process. There are good reasons for this. First, knowledge is itself a social creation. If you believe something, it remains a mere belief until you can persuade others that it is true, then it becomes knowledge that is shared. Second, as you will probably already have experienced yourself, it is not until you try to write down the results of your work in a way that is accessible to others that things become clear. Writing is a process of discovery as well as a process of clarification and of communication.

This last chapter is about writing and publishing social research. In the first section, we discuss some ways of thinking about the communication of research findings. The next section examines the origin and form of the research literature. This is followed by the dissection of a journal article published in the *American Sociological Review* to show how such articles are organised, with some hints about how you can create effective reports when writing research papers and dissertations.

24.2 TRUTH AND PERSUASION

There are several ways of thinking about social science writing. At first sight, you might think that such writing merely records the facts for all to see. The ideal social scientific paper or book should be objective, setting out as clearly and precisely as possible what has been discovered. However, this view of scientific writing does not stand much scrutiny. It leaves unexamined several crucial questions: what do we mean by 'objective'? What counts as a 'fact'? Why do research reports contain arguments as well as statements of fact (see also Chapter 1)?

A more sophisticated view of scientific writing recognises that writing is a form of rhetoric; that is, writing aims to persuade the reader of a position. It can be done well or badly. Over the years, writers have evolved stratagems for persuasion and have devised 'tricks of the trade'. Good writing is persuasive partly because of its use of these rhetorical devices, but also because it dares to go beyond them to invent new ways of putting arguments together.

A third view of scientific writing locates writing within the social structure of science. Sociological articles and books are written for and mainly read by other sociologists, who form a community with its own customs and beliefs. The shape of a journal article or the ways in which arguments are presented in sociological books are designed by writers for this community and in turn modify the community and its beliefs. Individually, sociologists write for the community because they prize the rewards it offers them, not financial rewards (often minimal or non-existent) but rewards of status, or 'recognition' of their labours and their abilities.

Understanding the sociology of the research literature is interesting for its own sake, but it is also important both for appreciating how the academic work we base our studies on comes to be written and published, and for understanding the conventions that influence the form of social science articles, dissertations and other publications. In the next section, we shall describe the origins of scientific writing, showing how innovations made in the seventeenth century have had profound effects on current social science literature.

24.3 THE RESEARCH LITERATURE

One way to get a better understanding of the social science literature is to look at the history of the research paper in the natural sciences. The sociological literature has grown in much the same way as the scientific literature. This history has been well documented by Bazerman (1988). We shall see that even though current science looks like a calm and professional activity, the origins of the scientific paper were forged in bitter disputes between amateur scientists.

24.3.1 THE HISTORY OF THE SCIENTIFIC PAPER

The first scientific journal to be published in English, *The Philosophical Transactions*, was founded in 1665 by the Secretary of the Royal Society. It had its origins in the correspondence which members of the Royal Society wrote to each other to record their observations and ideas on topics of mutual interest, mainly about what today would be called natural science. Initially, the editor treated the journal much like a club newsletter: picking out interesting tidbits from the correspondence and inviting the readers to send in further information. Gradually, however, the contributors were left to speak for themselves, and within a few years, the editor was reprinting letters verbatim, with only a few lines of editorial introduction.

The editor had to have a steady flow of correspondence coming to the journal to keep it afloat. Among the lures for authors were recognition of ideas, public acknowledgement of who was first to propose an idea or make a discovery, and the feeling that one was cooperating in a significant undertaking.

Over time, members began to write their letters, not as private correspondence to the editor which then happened to get published, but as public documents with an increasingly formal structure. Although many of the readers of the early *Transactions* were attracted by the tales of the curious and extraordinary which were reported there, there was a central circle of contributors who tended to be much more knowledgeable and much more sceptical, comparing what they read with what they believed and observed. As the journal also printed critical commentary, scientists for the first time had to defend themselves and their opinions in public.

According to Bazerman (1988), this led to role conflict for the authors, who were torn between publicising their own work in the terms which would most appeal to the general reader, and defending their work from the criticisms of knowledgeable fellow scientists. A strategy for avoiding disputes with the other scientists was to present the work in the clearest possible way, anticipating possible objections. Gradually, standardised methods for presentation evolved.

Over the next century, several other scientific journals were started. These had to compete for readers and contributors. One way to get subscribers was to publish articles that were more carefully tuned to the particular interests of their readers. In addition to *The Philosophical Transactions*, which covered the whole of science, more specialised journals appeared for particular disciplines. In order to maintain its position in the face of this competition, there were increasing efforts to improve the articles in the *Transactions*, as first the editor excluded information only of interest to amateur scientists, and then kept out work judged to be of relatively low quality.

The use of the editor as a 'gatekeeper' who rejected some articles as unsuitable for the journal imposed obvious strains on the post holder who had to fend off the disappointed contributors. After conflict erupted in the 1750s, an Editorial Board was created and later, the editor's decisions began to be made on the recommendation of 'referees', scientists chosen for their specialist knowledge who read and commented anonymously on papers.

Nowadays, when a paper is sent to an academic journal for publication, the editor first scans it to see whether the subject matter fits within the journal's scope. Then the editor sends it to two or three referees who write a commentary on it, indicating any weaknesses, and recommend whether it should be published as it stands, revised to take account of the criticisms, or rejected as unsuitable for publication. The editor, acting on this advice, writes back to the author, usually enclosing the referees' comments. If the verdict is that changes need to be made, the author is invited to resubmit and, depending on the scale of the amendments required, may either have the revised paper accepted forthwith or sent to referees again for further consideration. In the social sciences somewhere between 50 and 80 per cent of articles submitted are rejected, depending on the journal (although rejected articles may then be accepted by other journals which have less rigorous standards) (Hargens, 1988).

As the quality and prestige of the early scientific societies and their journals increased, so the advantages for the scientists of publishing in them increased also. Presenting work before the Royal Society and contributing to the *Transactions* identified one as a natural philosopher, as scientists were then called.

The task of natural philosophers was to persuade the scientific community of the truth and originality of their discoveries. In the earliest days, this was a matter of showing other scientists what one had found, in a public demonstration before the assembled Royal Society; later it depended on persuasion through the written word. Various rhetorical devices for increasing the persuasive power of scientific writing were invented. These included de-emphasising the presence of the scientist by writing in the passive, so making it seem that the results could have been obtained by 'anyone', and using plain, rather than literary language, to emphasise the objectivity of the research.

One way of defending one's procedures and arguments against potential criticism was to make it clear that they were the same procedures and arguments which others, more illustrious than oneself, had themselves already used. As Newton once said, 'If I have seen further, it is by standing on the shoulders of giants' (This famous quotation is the starting point for a fascinating book by the sociologist, Robert Merton (1965)). This is one of the functions of citations, references to previously published work which gradually came to be a standard ingredient of scientific papers. Thus, by the late nineteenth century, the 'scientific paper', a social invention of enormous significance, had been born.

24.3.2 THE MODERN SOCIOLOGICAL LITERATURE

The sociological literature is not as dominated by the research paper published in an academic journal as the natural scientific literature is, although journal articles are an increasingly important method of communication. Sociologists also write books, reports and conference papers, as well as making occasional contributions to the mass media. Books are getting harder to get published as publishers merge and publishing is increasingly big business. Academic books, such as you might find on a reading list, rarely sell more than two thousand copies and specialised monographs often sell only a few hundred. The economics of publishing in such small quantities means that the books tend to be very expensive (reducing sales still further) and publishers are choosy about what they will take on. Thus considerations about the size of the potential market become much more important than the originality or quality of the research being reported.

The process of selection of books to be published is very different from that of the selection of articles to be printed in a journal. An author will approach a publishing house (or, often, several at once) with a brief proposal for a book. If the publisher likes the idea, they will usually ask for a sample chapter, to see whether the tone and style of the writing are to their liking. This may be sent out to 'readers', academics who are paid a small fee for commenting on the proposal and estimating the likely market for the book. If the publisher's editor is happy with the readers' advice, a contract will be issued which specifies when the complete manuscript is to be delivered, the length of the book in words and the percentage of the revenue which the author will receive (the 'royalties', usually between 7 and 10 per cent for an academic book). When the publisher gets the manuscript, it is copy-edited by a professional who checks it for grammatical and spelling errors and it is then sent to the printer. Between six months and a year after the manuscript arrives at the publisher, the book is released to bookshops.

At the other end of the continuum in terms of time to publication is the conference paper. All professional societies, such as the British Sociological Association in the UK, organise conferences and there are many sub-groups that arrange meetings on specific topics. Researchers are invited to submit papers to these conferences and attend them to 'read' (or more usually, lecture on the general topic of) the paper. Sometimes the papers are collected together and published as a book, but more usually, they are only available as photocopied typescript by writing to the author. The time lag between writing and circulation is much shorter for such papers, but they are of course not so readily available as reports which have been more formally published.

Most journals are now available online as well as in hardcopy (see Chapter 5) and this is another way in which journals have an advantage over books, which are not often accessible online, although some sites such as Amazon.com will make portions of a book available as a sample of what is inside. Many academics also provide pre-publication versions of their research as electronic files that can be downloaded from their personal or university web sites. Putting material online can be a very rapid method of publishing, but from the reader's perspective, the disadvantage is that the work has not been peer-reviewed and so its quality cannot be guaranteed. It is the quality assessment that journals and book publishers carry out that will ensure that the traditional processes of scientific publication will endure, despite the fact that the Internet means that anyone can publish anything on a web page at almost no cost.

24.4 ORGANISING WRITING ABOUT RESEARCH

We have seen that writing is an essential part of the research process, and that the object of writing is both communication and persuasion. This and the next section will offer some advice about how to organise writing about social research. Suppose that you were just embarking on a research project – it might be for a dissertation as part of a course, or a thesis for a postgraduate degree, or a full-time, large-scale funded project. What preparations are needed for reporting such work?

Getting down to writing is difficult for almost everyone, but particularly for researchers, because research is a mixture of very sociable activities (organising access, interviewing, and so on) and the very unsociable act of writing. Once one has got used to the sociable side of research it is sometimes hard to move to the writing up stage, where one is often working alone, just you and a word processor. A consequence of the differences between these two kinds of activity is that many people put off writing until it is far too late.

You should be thinking about the organisation of your research report at the very beginning of the project. As the project continues, the shape of the report ought to become clearer. Some parts can even be written before any data is collected – accounts of the previous work on which your research is based and the theoretical grounding of your own work can both be drafted before data collection has been completed. One advantage of writing as you go along is that if you spend a long time not writing you can get 'rusty'. The act of writing, of trying to put down your thoughts as clearly as possible, can suggest new issues and new ideas and these can go back to influence data collection and analysis.

There are several steps you need to take before setting pen to paper. First, if you are working with colleagues, you need to decide who will be listed as the authors and the order of names. This may seem a trivial point, but some excellent research teams have come to grief because this issue was not settled before the writing began. Second, it helps if you can map out the reports, papers and other publications you hope to write about the project and where these will be published. If you think your work would best go into an academic journal, you will need to think about which journal is most appropriate and look through some back issues to see the style and type of article it publishes. If you are writing a thesis or dissertation, or to satisfy course requirements, it is worth looking at previous dissertations to see what length, style and format are expected.

Once you have decided where to publish, there are further decisions to make about what to write. Usually, the temptation is to put too much in, so that the overall message gets confused. A single paper (or a chapter in a thesis or book) should only carry one message. It requires great skill to keep even two balls in the air at once and unless you are an expert, you should decide before you start what *the* one point you want to make will be, and then stick to it ruthlessly. Of course, to arrive at one specific conclusion, you will need to cover many supporting issues. But everything should be there because it is needed to argue the one basic message; if there is anything in the paper that cannot be justified in that way it should be cast out (perhaps to become the seed of another publication).

A journal article in sociology is normally between four and seven thousand words in length and this is also the typical length of a book chapter (the chapters in this book average about 7000 words). But no one other than undergraduate course tutors ever worries about a report being too short; it is much more likely that the complaint will be that it is too long. Perhaps this is because clarity and conciseness are harder to achieve than verbosity. Length also comes from the writer not having a clear plan of how the report will be organised before the writing starts, so making yourself an 'outline' of the structure of the report (as you may have been taught to do at school when writing essays) is an excellent way of preparing to start writing.

Even if you take this advice and begin writing drafts as early as you can, you may find it hard to get started. It is not necessary to write a chapter or article by starting at the beginning and working through to the end, although some people do that. Try beginning with whatever section seems easiest to get you started. The Introduction and Conclusion are best written last because they need to be composed with knowledge of what the rest of the piece is about, and this may change and develop as you write.

It often helps to have someone in mind to whom you can aim your writing. For an academic paper or dissertation, you should be writing for another researcher, but not one who is a specialist in your area. For more popular work, you will need to decide what kind of person is likely to read your report, what they are likely to be interested in and what they are likely to know already. No matter who you are writing for, however, keep your sentences short and straightforward and, whenever you can, use ordinary words in preference to technical terms. Convoluted sentences and complex constructions merely confuse the reader (and might lead to the suspicion that you, the writer, are not thinking clearly, either).

The first draft is often the hardest. After it is completed, you should put it away for a few days and then read it through critically, trying to look at it from the point of view of someone who is coming to it fresh. You will certainly find much that is wrong, from sentences that need phrasing more clearly to major omissions and repetitions. These problems should be put right in a second draft. This second draft can then be shown to colleagues with a request for comments. Their suggestions can be incorporated into the third draft. As this sequence suggests, writing about research always involves much re-writing and refinement and you should plan for at least three times round the comments and re-drafting loop.

24.5 EXAMINING THE STRUCTURE OF A JOURNAL ARTICLE

When writing a report, it helps to know how other people have organised their work, so that you can see what arrangements are clear and persuasive. In this section, we examine in some detail how one particular article published in the *American Sociological Review* was constructed. There is nothing special about this

Table 24.1
The conventional
structure of a sociological
research paper

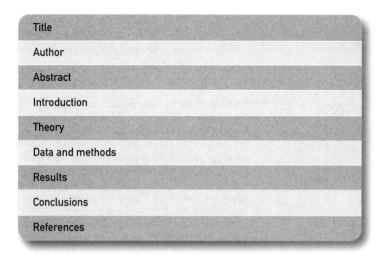

| Title |
| Author |
| Abstract |
| Introduction |
| Theory |
| Data and methods |
| Results |
| Conclusions |
| References |

article; it is typical of a particular style of quantitative sociology and there are many hundreds of similarly structured papers in the sociological literature. It does, however, have the merit of displaying its structure especially clearly. Other papers written in a more discursive style and those based on ethnographic data often do not reveal their structure so immediately, but you will usually find that more or less the same types of material are included in more or less the same order.

This section will therefore be about the standard, conventional structure for an article. Almost the same structure is typically used in project reports, Masters and doctoral theses and in research reports written for sponsors and funders, rather than for publication. It is a structure that has been devised through much experience and it will usually serve you well. But it is just a convention. If, when you come to report on your research, you find that the conventional structure does not fit what you have to say, no one will stop you from breaking the convention (at least not in sociology; other disciplines are rather stricter. For example, it is almost impossible to get articles published in certain psychology journals unless they precisely follow the conventional structure).

So what is this structure? The main sections of a research paper are listed in Table 24.1.

Let us look at each of these sections in turn and see how the authors of the *American Sociological Review* article dealt with them (Figure 24.1).

The **Title** (in Figure 24.1, 'SEX SEGREGATION IN VOLUNTARY ASSO-CIATIONS') is the best advertisement that the article will get. Most readers will be attracted to the article by noticing the title on a journal's Contents page or in the list of references in another paper. The same applies to book titles: remember how often you have picked up a book in a bookshop just because the title made it seem interesting. The title needs to be short, snappy and above all, accurately descriptive of the content.

Figure 24.1   The first page of the McPherson and Smith-Lovin (1986) journal article

SEX SEGREGATION IN VOLUNTARY ASSOCIATIONS*

J. MILLER MCPHERSON   LYNN SMITH-LOVIN

University of South Carolina

We analyze the sex composition of 815 face-to-face voluntary associations in 10 communities to determine the extent of sex integration produced by voluntary affiliation. The sex segregation in these groups is substantial; nearly one-half of the organizations are exclusively female, while one-fifth are all male. Instrumental organizations (business-related and political groups) are more likely to be sex heterogeneous, while expressive groups are likely to be exclusively male or female. From the point of view of the individual, the typical female membership generates face-to-face contact with about 29 other members, less than four of whom are men. Male memberships, on the other hand, produce contact with over 37 other members on the average, nearly eight of whom are female. Men's contacts are both more numerous and more heterogeneous. We conclude that there is little support for the sex integration hypothesis in these data, although the sex heterogeneity of instrumental groups (especially those which are job-related) indicates that this pattern may change as women move into the labour force in increasing numbers. The paper explores some consequences of segregation for the organizations and the social networks they generate.

The integration hypothesis has been a main theme of research on voluntary organizations since Toqueville (1969) first raised the issue in the nineteenth century. From Durkheim's (1902) and Kornhauser's (1959) notion of voluntary organizations as mediators between the mass and the elite, to Babchuk and Edwards' (1965) view of voluntary groups as multi-level integrators, researchers have argued that voluntary groups serve as a sort of interstitial glue. Yet the details of exactly what is integrated with what has remained remarkably unclear over the years. What emerges from the literature is a picture of voluntary groups which may represent the emergent interests of unspecified publics in the political domain,

provide resources for useful contacts in the economic domain, allow the expression of altruistic impulses in the charitable domain, and provide a variety of peripheral and ephemeral services (Smith and Freedman, 1972).

In contrast to this integrative view of voluntary groups, many of the early community studies emphasized that voluntary associations were sorting mechanisms (Hughes, 1943; Anderson, 1937). As Gans (1967: 61) noted, the groups "divided and segregated people by their interests and ultimately, of course, by socio-economic, educational, and religious differences". Of course, the integrating and sorting perspectives on voluntary associations are ...

*Address all correspondence to J. Miller McPherson, Department of Sociology, University of South Carolina, Columbia, SC 29208. Work on this paper was supported by National Science Foundation grants SES-8120666 and SES-839899, Miller McPherson, Principal Investigator. The authors would like to thank John McCarthy of Catholic University and the members of the structuralist group at the University of South Carolina for their helpful comments: Charles Brody, Michael Kennedy, Bruce H. Mayhew, Patrick Nolan, Jimy Sanders, Eui-Hang Shin, and John V. Skvoretz. Data were collected through the facilities of the Bureau of Sociological Research of the University of Nebraska, Helen Moore, Director. The authors bear full responsibility for the interpretation of the data.

The **Abstract** ('We analyze the sex composition ... networks they generate') is expected to summarise the content of the paper. Abstracting journals (e.g. *Sociological Abstracts*) will reprint just the abstract, together with those from all the other articles which have been published that quarter, under a subject classification which makes it fairly easy to track down articles on a particular topic. The abstract therefore has a double function: it serves as an overview for people who are reading the article in a journal and as a self-standing summary for people who are reading an abstracting journal. Because for most readers the most interesting part of an article is the conclusion, it is wise to put this near the beginning of the abstract. Then specify the sample or setting to indicate the scope of the findings. Finish with a brief account of the method used to collect and analyse the data. Abstracts should never include citations to other work.

A dissertation or thesis will normally have an abstract of 200 to 300 words, while the abstract of a journal article will usually be shorter – about 100 words. Reports for policy-makers often have a section called an 'Executive Summary' which takes the place of an abstract and includes the same content, as well as any policy recommendations that the researchers are proposing. Books do not have abstracts at all.

The **Acknowledgements** ('Work on this paper was supported ... for the interpretation of the data.') It is conventional to acknowledge the assistance of the people who funded the research, anyone who made a significant contribution to the research but is not an author, and colleagues who commented on drafts of the paper and helped to improve it. If you are a student writing a dissertation, it may be appropriate to acknowledge your supervisor.

The paper proper starts with an **Introduction** that should indicate the topic of the paper, demonstrate why this topic is interesting and important, and show how the approach taken in the paper is an advance on previous work. In brief, the purpose of the Introduction is to get the reader hooked. That means starting from the reader's present knowledge and leading him or her on to see that the topic is worth spending time investigating. Notice how McPherson and Smith-Lovin in their introduction locate their research immediately into 'classical' sociology, with references to Toqueville and Durkheim in the first sentences. Notice also how in the space of two paragraphs they introduce a potentially interesting controversy in the existing literature – is the function of voluntary groups that of integration or sorting? One of the objects of the paper is to offer evidence which might resolve this controversy. In these few lines of introduction, the authors have mapped out a domain of research, have suggested that there has been much sociological interest in the domain, have identified a gap in the research concerning the integrative versus sorting issue, and have implied that the paper will go some way towards filling that gap.

The hallmark of a good introduction is that it locates a 'hole' in the research literature that the rest of the paper will fill. This particular paper offers a very good example. But the same principle applies generally, not only to papers, but also to books and theses. A thesis or dissertation usually begins with a chapter intended to 'review the literature'. But in writing such a review, one needs to remember that the purpose is not to catalogue the available literature for its own sake, but rather, as with this introduction, to show that there is some research which has yet to be done – and here it is!

Notice also that, as a matter of convention, the text starts without any preceding sub-heading: there is no heading, 'Introduction'.

On the page after the one shown in Figure 24.1, the authors observe that the integrative and sorting mechanisms are not as opposed as they might seem, because both may operate simultaneously, producing homogeneity on some dimensions and heterogeneity on others. They argue that the question then becomes 'which social dimensions are integrated and which are sorted, and in what types of organisations?' (McPherson and Smith-Lovin, 1986: 68). They then move on to discuss sex segregation in voluntary organisations, which has previously been considered mainly in terms of the sorting view, and review the literature on this topic. This brings them to the second major section, headed 'Network Implications of Sex Segregation in Organizations', which is as close as this paper gets to a section devoted to 'theory'.

The **Theory** section is the place to introduce the concepts you will be using in your analysis. Although called the Theory section, it is not 'grand theory' that is needed here, but what Merton (1968) called 'Middle range theory': the specific concepts and ideas that you will use to explain your findings (see Chapter 1). In McPherson and Smith-Lovin's paper, this leads to the statement of a number of propositions which they then go on to test later in the article. For example, they write:

> Based on our earlier discussion of the changing rôle of women, we would expect that working women, more highly educated women, and younger women would be less likely to participate in organizational environments which are single sex (all women's clubs) and more likely to participate in mixed sex groups (although they may often be in the minority there). (McPherson and Smith-Lovin, 1986: 63)

This is a proposition that they will compare with the data they have collected. But before we reach these results, there is a section on Data and Methods.

The **Data and Methods** section is often the most standardised and least interesting part of a research article, because it has to convey a lot of strictly factual information. The ideal is to provide just enough detail that another researcher could find everything needed to repeat the work. That means that you must specify here the decisions you made about matters such as how you selected the respondents, how you collected the data and any special methods you used. Table 24.2 lists the important characteristics which you should consider mentioning in this section; include only those which are relevant to the research design you have chosen.

In the McPherson and Smith-Lovin study, the design was complicated by the fact that they wished to sample, not individuals, but voluntary organisations. This they did by asking a representative probability sample of adults from ten communities in Nebraska about the organisations to which they were affiliated. They write, in the section headed 'Data and Methods':

Table 24.2
Items for inclusion in the
Data and Methods section

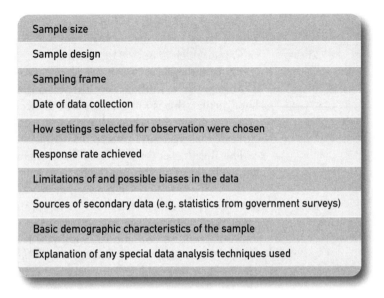

Sample size

Sample design

Sampling frame

Date of data collection

How settings selected for observation were chosen

Response rate achieved

Limitations of and possible biases in the data

Sources of secondary data (e.g. statistics from government surveys)

Basic demographic characteristics of the sample

Explanation of any special data analysis techniques used

> In the first stage, a representative probability sample of 656 non-institutionalised adults was interviewed from the 10 communities. In the interviews, we obtained a list of all the organizations with which each individual was affiliated. We used a technique known as aided recall (Babchuk and Booth, 1969) to insure that all organizations were reported. Respondents were encouraged to report even small, relatively informal groups if these groups had an identifiable membership. A total of 2091 organizational names were generated, representing an affiliation rate of about 3.2. (in smaller communities, of course, some names represented multiple reports of the same organization). Of the 2091 organizations, 815 groups which met face-to-face in the local community constitute the sample for this analysis.

In this brief excerpt from a much longer description of their methods of sampling and data collection, note how the authors take pains to be precise about the way in which their sample was obtained and the criterion (face-to-face meetings) which they used to select those organisations chosen for further study. Note also how, rather than describe in detail the way that they maximised respondents' recall of all the organisations they belonged to, they just reference another article (Babchuk and Booth, 1969) where the technique is described.

After describing the methods used to collect data, the typical paper discusses the **Results,** which in the McPherson and Smith-Lovin article are described as the 'Analyses and Findings'. When writing this part of the paper, the problem is usually to know which of all the analyses you have done should be included and which should be left out. The primary rule is: be relevant. Remember that the Introduction has already stated what the paper is about and that the purpose of this Results section is to provide the findings on which your conclusions will be based. This means that data which may be very unexpected or significant, but which is not related to the point of the paper, should be excluded (it could form the basis of another paper). For a similar reason, this section needs to focus on your findings, not the way in which you came to reach the results. In particular, this is not the place for an account of the process of research, nor of all the dead ends which all researchers encounter, nor the disasters and difficulties which you have overcome.

The Results section will probably contain summaries and analyses of the data you have collected, in the form of statistical tables (if your data are quantitative) or characteristic quotations or descriptions of observations (if your data are qualitative). McPherson and Smith-Lovin use the statistical technique called regression and present the results in tables which summarise the relative importance of marital status, employment status, education and age on being involved in voluntary organisations. They find overall that the voluntary groups they have studied are very segregated: almost one-half are all female and one-fifth are all male. Large organisations are less likely to be all female and those that recruit from the labour force are likely to be mixed, while those which are expressive in character are more likely to be segregated. Their Results section concludes:

> At the individual level, single males are more likely to belong to sex-segregated groups, while widowed or separated women are more likely to be in all-female groups. The effects of work status are quite different for men and for women. Employed women are very much less likely to belong to all-female groups than employed men are to belong to all-male groups. (McPherson and Smith-Lovin, 1986: 75)

Notice that these results are closely tied to the data and are more or less devoid of theory. The above quotation consists of little more than the output of the statistical analysis put into words. In this article, the interpretation of these results is left to the next section. However, it is usual to link the results and their theoretical interpretation more closely together than they are here, with both data and interpretation included in the Results section.

Relating the results back to the issues raised in the Introduction and the Theory sections is the job of the **Conclusion**. In the McPherson and Smith-Lovin article, the Introduction posed the question of whether voluntary groups fulfil a sorting or integrative function. Now is the time for the authors to answer that question. In the previous section they reported that, overall, voluntary associations are very segregated. In this section they conclude that these organisations reaffirm sex distinctions rather than creating ties between the sexes. 'The sorting function, then, clearly dominates the integrative function with regard to sex' (McPherson and Smith-Lovin, 1986: 75). This is a good example of the way in which the Conclusions should relate back to the issues raised in the Introduction, thus closing the circle and tying up the article neatly.

This is also the section in which you can speculate a little, going beyond the strict confines of the data, and where you can point to further issues that the research has raised.

The last paragraph of the Conclusion is one of the most difficult to write because it ought to summarise what the main findings of the research were, in a succinct and interesting way. This is because many readers will look first at the end of the article to see whether it has anything interesting to say, before they start at the beginning. And it is as well to anticipate this.

Lastly, there is the list of **References.** This is a list of the full bibliographical details of the books and articles cited in the text. ('References' are the list of details at the end of an article; 'citations' are the (Author, Year) pairs in the body of the text). Citations are important in a sociological article for a number of reasons. First, they situate the article within existing research. We saw citations used in this way in the Introduction (Figure 24.1) where the particular topic of this paper is located within the sociological literature. Second, references act as a kind of shorthand. It was pointed out that in the Methods section, instead of describing the technique of 'aided recall', a citation to Babchuk and Booth (1969) was provided. This sort of citation saves space, because the details of the technique need only be printed once in the original article, rather than being rolled out again and again in reports of every piece of research that uses it. Third, citations to reports which have come to the same or similar results can help to give an article some authority, for the citations imply that the conclusions reproduce those found elsewhere by independent investigators.

For all these reasons, sociological books and papers are always sprinkled with citations. Each citation must be linked to a reference that provides the full details about where to find the work cited. There are several standard conventions for references. Sometimes the citation is a superscript number in the text, leading to a numbered reference at the end (the Vancouver convention). More usually, as in this book, citations are given as the name of the author and the year of publication, and the references are listed alphabetically at the end. This is known as the Harvard convention and is probably the easiest for authors to use.

Ensuring that all the necessary details are correct and included in the References is part of intellectual good manners. It means that, for example, if you read a book that you might want to refer to later, you should take careful note of:

- the author

- the author's initials

- the date of publication

- the title

- the city of publication

- the publisher.

With articles in journals, you should note:

- the author
- the author's initials
- the date of publication
- the title of the article
- the name of the journal
- the volume number of the journal in which the article is printed
- the starting and ending page numbers of the article.

Keeping a record of these ought to become second nature. They are the standard data which librarians will want if you need to find the book or article again. One more item is needed if you copy out a direct quotation from a book or paper: the page number from which the quote is taken (how else will you be able to check that you have got the wording exactly right if you do not have the page number?).

24.6 BREAKING THE RULES

So ends our tour of one sociological article. The general shape of this article is a good one to follow, not only for research papers, but also for more informal reports and for dissertations and theses. Often when research is funded by an agency or is commissioned, those sponsoring the research will demand a specially written report about the results. Such reports can keep to the conventional structure which we have seen in the previous section, but with some modifications to suit the audience for which it is intended. The Abstract is often replaced by a somewhat longer preliminary section headed 'Summary', in which the findings of the research are laid out as clearly as possible, perhaps as a list of the main conclusions. If the sponsors of the research are mainly interested in social policy, the summary might also indicate the policy implications of the research. Within the body of the report, it is usual to have less about the research design than is needed for an academic article, with further details relegated to an Appendix.

Dissertations written as part of a degree also often follow the standard structure, modified slightly. A Masters or doctoral thesis will typically have at least one chapter corresponding to each of the main sections of Table 24.1. The Abstract will again be replaced by a Summary, usually about one page in length. The Introduction will probably include a rather more exhaustive literature review than would be appropriate for a published report. An undergraduate dissertation can also follow this structure, although if the research on which it is based does not include the analysis of primary or secondary data, the Methods and Results sections may be omitted.

McPherson and Smith-Lovin's paper was chosen for detailed examination because it follows the standard and conventional shape of a social research article very closely. It is a good example of following the 'rules'. But, of course, not all sociological articles do keep to the 'rules' and they are none the worse for that. Breaking the rules is fine, so long as the message you want to convey is nevertheless communicated effectively. There are some rules you should break only with the greatest of caution and others that should not give you a moment's worry. For example, it is almost always a bad idea to miss out either the Introduction or the Conclusion. These two sections tell the reader what to expect and what to take from the research. A rule that *can* be broken for many research reports is the one that says that you should divide the middle of the report into separate 'Theory', 'Methods' and 'Results' sections. Often, some other form of organisation will suit what you have to say much better. For example, it is possible to interweave theory and findings by telling a 'story' about your respondents (Thody, 2006), or select themes which emerge from your data and devote one section to each theme. The best way of learning about these alternative structures is to look carefully at how the books and articles which you think communicate effectively have been constructed by their authors.

24.7 SUMMARY

This chapter has emphasised that social research is only completed when its results have been published. Most research is published in the academic literature, in journals or in books aimed at the academic reader. This literature has very specific characteristics, the result of an evolution over several centuries from the beginning of 'natural science' in the seventeenth century. In order to write successfully for this literature, it helps to understand why it has these characteristics. Even if one is only a student reading the literature, it is important to understand the social processes of publication and quality control that shape its form.

PROJECT

Every academic paper is reviewed before publication by at least two referees, chosen from among the academic community by journal editors for their knowledge of the paper's topic. Referees (who are rarely paid for their labours) receive a copy of the paper in typescript and a letter (or

(Continued)

sometimes a form) from the editor that requests them to comment on the paper's suitability for publication in terms of its clarity, originality and the adequacy of its argument. The referee has between two and six weeks to respond with a verdict (one of: accept, accept with minor revisions such as spelling or stylistic errors, accept but require major revisions, or reject) and a report. The report, which is always anonymous and will often be forwarded to the author, explains the referee's verdict, commenting on the overall strengths and weaknesses of the paper and making suggestions for improvements.

The first step in this project is to identify a research area in which you have an interest (the sociology of health, or deviance, for example). Look through the Library Current Journals shelves and find a recent issue of a journal publishing in your area. Choose one paper from that journal. If possible, make a photocopy of it or download a copy from the Internet.

You should imagine that you have received a typescript copy of this paper from a journal editor to referee. Examine the paper closely. Is it clear? Is it well organised? Can one quickly identify the main conclusions? Are the justifications for those conclusions soundly based? Are the data appropriate to the topic of the paper? Are the methods of data collection and analysis described in sufficient detail that someone else could repeat the study? Are there plausible alternative interpretations of the data or of the results that the author has not noticed? Does the abstract adequately describe the contents of the paper? Are there passages that could be rewritten to make them clearer? Has the author referenced all the relevant literature?

It is surprising how often even published papers will wilt under careful scrutiny of this kind. In about 300 words, write a report about the article. Your criticisms should be phrased so that they are constructive, polite and encouraging – the aim of a referee's report is to encourage the author towards a better article, not to damage the author's ego.

CHECKLIST

- Start organising writing early – at the start of the research if possible.

- For team research, agree who will be shown as the authors and who will write what.

- Decide on the intended publication outlet and discover their requirements for content, length and format.

- Decide on the primary theme or message of the report.

- Create an outline to show the structure of the report.

- Start writing the easiest section first.

- Use short sentences and avoid jargon as much as possible.

- Put the first complete draft aside for a few days and then reread and edit it carefully.

- Enlist the help of colleagues in commenting on drafts.

RESOURCES

Becker (1986) *Writing for Social Scientists* is excellent on writing about social science.

Mulkay (1985) *The Word and the World* is a fascinating exploration of the textual forms that are, or could be, used by sociologists to report on the social world.

Wolcott (2001) *Writing up Qualitative Research* concentrates on the particular problems of reporting on qualitative research.

If you are writing a dissertation for a research degree, Phillips and Pugh (2005) *How to Get a PhD* should be essential reading.

GLOSSARY

Account: a general term for the overall report or description given by an interviewee during a research interview. An account may include a variety of different forms of talk and represents the interviewee's perceptions, understanding and experiences of the issue(s) being researched.

Action research: an approach to conducting social research which aims to improve the social situation under study while simultaneously generating knowledge about it. The focus is on changing a social situation or practice as part of the research process rather than simply gathering data and generating findings which may or may not be implemented subsequently. It is a cyclical process, moving between stages of enquiry, intervention and evaluation.

Agency: the capacity of individuals to act independently and autonomously, and to make their own choices and decisions.

Antecedent variable: a variable measuring a concept that is thought to have a causal effect on some other variable.

Attitude: an enduring tendency to perceive a situation or a person in a particular way. Attitudes may have cognitive (resulting from beliefs and ideas), affective (resulting from values and emotions) and behavioural (resulting from previous action) components. Attitudes are unobservable except through their presumed effects on behaviour.

Attrition: the tendency for people responding to a **panel** survey to drop out through death or illness, emigration or refusal to continue to be involved.

Axial coding: coined by Strauss and Corbin (1990), this refers to the second stage of the coding process, in which the relationships between categories and subcategories are carefully mapped through the use of a detailed paradigm.

Biography: in the everyday sense a biography is a literary work in which an author gives an account of the life of a person, usually someone of note; such people also write their own autobiographies. Both are useful to the sociologist, who needs to be aware that the authors may have had a variety of non-sociological reasons for writing them. Diaries are in a sense biographical, but are written at the time rather than in retrospect. Biographies created by or for the sociologist or ethnographer are usually termed life histories.

Blog: short for weblog: an online diary or journal.

Brainstorming: a method of generating ideas in which members of a group are encouraged to contribute suggestions free of criticism from other group members. Once sufficient ideas have been generated, they are categorised and may be ranked for effectiveness or value.

CAQDAS: Computer Assisted Qualitative Data AnalysiS is an umbrella term referring to a broad range of software packages designed to facilitate the analysis of qualitative data, including text, graphics, audio and video. They are powerful project management tools allowing the organisation of data (according to known characteristics), ideas (according to user-defined codes) and interpretations (noted by the user in written annotations and memos). Patterns and relationships can be identified by retrieving parts of the dataset according to the presence and absence of codes in the data, among, for example, different sub-sets of data (e.g. comparing male and female respondents).

Case: the unit of analysis. A case can be an individual, or a group of individuals, such as a family. Or a case could be a school, a country or even an event, such as a police incident.

CASI: Computer-Assisted Self-Interviewing. Respondents are given a laptop or handheld computer on which survey questions are displayed, and use the computer to record their answers. In this way, data can be collected confidentially, without the interviewer knowing what the respondent's answers are.

CATI: Computer-Assisted Telephone Interviewing. To assist telephone interviewing, the interviewer reads out questions displayed on a computer screen and types the respondents' answers directly into the computer.

Chat room: an **Internet** forum where people communicate in real time with one another.

Closed question: a survey question that can be answered by selecting from a set of previously specified answers. For example, the question, 'Did you vote in the last election?' is a closed question if the possible answers are only 'Yes', 'No' or 'I do not remember'. See also **open question**.

Code book: a document that lists the dictionary information about all the variables in a data file. In a quantitative survey this usually includes the original question text, the SPSS variable names if appropriate, and the value labels for each coded response. A code book may also contain information about derived variables and notes given to interviewers or coders when preparing the data file. In a qualitative study, the code book usually consists of a 1–3 word label and definition for each code developed, any qualifications or exceptions and an example.

Coding: the process by which numbers are ascribed to responses to a survey questionnaire

in preparation for computer analysis. For example, to the question 'Are you male or female?', male may be coded with the number 1 and female with the number 2. In a qualitative study, coding is the process by which segments of text are labelled with code words or phrases. These codes can be predefined or be developed during the coding process.

Cohort: a cohort survey is one where repeated observations are made of its **sample** members, all of whom belong to the same age group.

Combining methods: a term for a mixed methods design where one method takes precedence over the other, as opposed to an integrated design where all methods or data sets contribute equally to answering the research questions.

Complementarity: a term for the relationship between two or more different methods in a mixed methods research design where each method contributes a different way of knowing about the subject and thus complements the knowledge generated by the other methods.

Concept: a term used in a **theory** or theories.

Concept map: a visual tool to assist researchers when considering logical and creative **relationships** and associations between different **concepts**.

Confidence interval: an estimate of a population parameter (for example, the proportion of people who are out of work because of sickness) expressed as a range, e.g. 10.3–10.7 (sometimes written as 10.5 ± 0.2). A 95 per cent confidence interval means that it is estimated that if many random samples were drawn and measured, there is a 95 per cent probability that the population parameter would fall within the interval. The width of the confidence interval gives an indication of the standard error of the measurement: the smaller the interval, the lower the standard error.

Confidence level: the probability that a **confidence interval** will include the true population value. The 95 per cent confidence level is the most commonly used.

Congruence (test of): a method of validating ethnographic data. The idea is that in any natural setting there are norms or rules of action in which members are competent. Understanding is achieved when the observer learns the rules and can provide others with instructions on how to pass in the same setting.

Constructivism: a perspective that views all knowledge as constructed, and not necessarily reflecting any external realities. In this view, knowledge depends on convention, human perception and social experience.

Content analysis: a method by which textual or visual documents are analysed to produce quantitative data. A **sample** of documents is chosen and aspects of these are systematically coded into different categories, producing variables, which can then be presented using figures, charts, graphs or tables, or can be analysed with statistical techniques.

Conversation analysis: founded by Harvey Sacks and his colleagues, Gail Jefferson and Emanuel Schegloff, conversation analysis is a formal, qualitative method for the analysis of naturally occurring communication that treats talk as a sequentially organised (that is, highly patterned) form of social action.

Correlation coefficient: a measure of the strength and direction of a **relationship** between two variables. The most widely used coefficient is the Pearson product-moment correlation coefficient, appropriate for use when the two variables are both measured at the interval level of measurement.

Critical discourse analysis: an interdisciplinary approach to the study of discourse, which focuses on the ways social and political domination is reproduced by text and talk. It is based on the idea that there is structured, unequal access to linguistic and social resources.

Cross-tabulation: a table displaying the joint distribution of two or more variables. Sometimes called a contingency table, it is a table in which each cell shows the number of cases or respondents having a particular combination of characteristics.

Deduction: a method of reasoning in which the conclusion is necessitated by, or reached from, previously known premises. If the premises are true, the conclusion must be true. For example, a conclusion might be reached by deduction from the combination of a theory and some facts about a specific case.

Deff: stands for 'design effect'. It defines the factor by which features of a sample design such as clustering, stratification, and weighting increase or reduce the variance of a survey estimate, relative to what the variance would be under a simple random sample design.

Descriptive statistics: statistics that are used to describe or summarise the characteristics of a **sample**.

Development: in mixed methods research, the use of one method to develop a different method used subsequently in the project. Results from the first method allow researchers to improve or enhance the second method.

Dewey Decimal Classification System: a cataloguing system used in libraries to order their records. Developed by Melville Dewey in the 1870s, the system has numbers for each subject area, with sub-divisions. For example, in libraries that use the Dewey system, Sociology books will always be catalogued under the number 301.

Dialectical: in mixed methods, this is a position that brings together ideas that are in conflict with, or in contradiction to, each other in order to generate new ways of thinking about the topic.

Digital divide: a term used to describe the persistent division and social inequality between those who do and those who do not have access to modern information and communication technologies.

Discourse: in disciplines that study communication and interaction, discourse is used generically to refer to forms of communication, such as verbal interaction and written language.

Discourses: in critical discourse analysis and **Foucauldian discourse analysis**, the term 'discourses' has a specialised meaning, referring to conventional vocabularies and forms of expression that perpetuate and legitimate ideological or political orthodoxies.

Discursive psychology: a form of **discourse** analysis that focuses on the way in which people construct versions of psychological concepts such as memory, attitudes and beliefs and how these are used and displayed in social situations.

Document: is used either in the restricted sense of something that is written or in the wider sense of any human production that is thought to convey meaning. Written documents range from a shopping list to an Act of the legislature. Visual documents include works of art, photographs (from newspapers, family albums, museums or images produced for research purposes), media texts (television shows, documentaries and news broadcasts, movies) and many other forms of visual material. Documents may be classified as personal or official, and if official they may be private (an internal business memo) or public (government statistics). Accessibility can range from open, through various degrees of restriction, to those which are closed to a researcher. Semiotic studies regard a document as anything that is seen to convey meaning: official documents, political debates and speeches, media reports, pictorial and exhibition materials, advertisements, tourist guides, interviews, diaries and oral histories.

Eigenvalue: a term used in **factor analysis**. Eigenvalues indicate the relative importance of factors in modelling the data.

Email attachment: a file sent with an email message.

Emergent coding: the process of reading and developing ideas about data that results in new codes that may later get assigned to other data segments. These codes are called emergent because they did not originate as theoretical concepts informing the initial design of the project and the coding scheme.

Empiricism: a perspective on the **theory** of knowledge that assumes that there is an objective external reality and that this should be the privileged source of understanding the social world.

Epistemology: the **theory** of knowledge, that is, theory about what is true and how we come to believe that knowledge is true.

Ethnography: the observation of an organisation, small society, or social setting and its analytical description. Ethnographic researchers gather data by living and working in the setting, seeking to immerse themselves in the participants' activities, while keeping careful records of what they experience.

Ethnomethodology: is interested in how social order is achieved, but unlike **structural functionalism**, sees this as something which is routinely accomplished in everyday life by a host of 'methods', which are both taken for granted and yet, when properly studied, are revealed as extraordinarily skilful.

Expansion: in mixed methods research, the use of different methods for different components of the study. Researchers purposefully use different methods to explore a larger number of research questions.

Factor analysis: a statistical data reduction technique used to explain variability among observed variables in terms of fewer unobserved variables called factors. The observed variables are modelled as linear combinations of the factors and an error term.

Falsification: the strategy of trying to disprove a theory. Because even a very large number of confirming examples cannot definitely prove that a theory is correct, but a single counter-instance can prove that a theory is incorrect, it is argued that falsification is the appropriate strategy for researchers to use.

Feminism: a perspective that sees society as unjust and seeks to challenge patriarchy. The basis of exploitation is seen to lie in gender relations. Feminist theory is closely linked to political movements.

Fieldnote: a description of events observed during fieldwork in a social setting and recorded at the time of observation, or shortly thereafter.

Focus group: a group interview or discussion. It consists of a group of individuals, usually numbering between six and ten people, who meet together to express their views about a particular topic defined by the researcher. Generally a focus group lasts one and half to two hours and is tape-recorded. The tape-recording can be transcribed for the purpose of analysis.

Focused interview: an interview conducted on a topic or topics, in which the questioning is prompted by an interview guide, but the interviewer is free to alter the wording and the order of questions to suit the interaction.

Foucauldian discourse analysis: a form of **discourse analysis** that is influenced by the work of Michel Foucault and that aims to identify the regulative or ideological underpinnings of dominant vocabularies that constrain the way in which we think about and act in the world.

Gatekeeper: a person who controls access to a research setting, for example, a manager in an organisation.

Groupthink: a type of reasoning shown by group members who try to minimise disagreement and conflict by not adequately testing, analysing and evaluating their ideas.

Hyperlink: a connection between two pages on the World Wide Web. Clicking on a hyperlink on one page causes the linked page to be displayed.

Hypothesis: a candidate for an explanation, which needs to be tested to see whether it is true or false. Hypotheses can consist of **concepts** linked by **relationships**. Causal hypotheses are ones that propose a causal link between two or more concepts.

Indicator: a method of measuring a **concept** by gathering and analysing empirical data.

Induction: a method of reasoning that derives generalisations by seeking the common aspects of a number of specific cases.

Inferential statistics: statistics that are used to infer the characteristics of a population from a sample.

Informed consent: the consent given by a respondent or informant to participation in data collection, when that consent is made in full knowledge of the implications of his or her involvement.

Initiation: in mixed methods research, the use of a second method to explore results from a first method, especially when the first method has produced puzzles, or uncertain or inconsistent findings.

Instant messaging: a form of **Internet** communication which allows people to chat privately via text in real-time.

Integration: a term for a mixed methods design where all methods or data sets contribute equally to answering the research questions, as opposed to a combined method design where one method takes precedence over the others. Integration may occur at different stages of the research process.

Internet: a network of computer networks that can communicate with one another via a common protocol.

Interpretative repertoires: 'recurrently used systems of terms used for characterizing and evaluating actions, events and other phenomena' (Potter and Wetherell, 1987: 149) that may consist of distinctive lexical, grammatical or stylistic features, and particular figures of speech, idiomatic expressions and metaphors. Unlike **discourse/discourses** as used in **critical** and **Foucauldian** forms of **discourse analysis**, interpretative repertoires do not signify a political or ideological component, but point to the constitutive and constructive functions of language use.

Interpretive understanding: a method of ascertaining meaning that focuses on social action and stands in contrast to the structural nature of semiotics. Its origin lies in Max Weber's work on *Verstehen* (understanding) in relation to social action, which can be seen as having the two levels of *what* a person does, or says, in regard to another, and *why* – that is, their motive. Weber's position was that any sociological account must be understandable at the level of social action, and this depends on being able to achieve an interpretive understanding of that action. The idea has been followed and developed by other schools of sociology, such as the Chicago School, ethnomethodology and hermeneutics.

Interpretivism: an approach that places emphasis on empirically establishing the meanings that people use to make sense of the world. It assumes the possibility of multiple realities and is often linked with qualitative research.

Intervening variable: a variable measuring a **concept** that is thought to be causally influenced by another variable and which in turn affects some third variable.

Interview guide: a list of the areas to be covered in a **focused interview**.

Langue: a concept from semiotics, referring to the language itself (its grammar, its system of binary oppositions and its meanings). *Langue* cannot be observed; it can only be deduced. It stands in contrast to *parole*.

Levels of analysis: a term to describe the different degrees of aggregation of data. A macro-level of analysis examines phenomena at the level of society or groups, and micro-level examines phenomena at the level of individual action or meaning.

Likert scaling: a method of collecting attitudinal data using a survey questionnaire. The respondent is presented with a statement and asked to agree or disagree with the statement by choosing one of the items: Strongly disagree, Disagree, Neither agree nor disagree, Agree, or Strongly agree.

Literature review: a text written to catalogue and assess the current state of research and knowledge on a research question or subject.

Longitudinal design: a general term covering any research design that involves making two or more observations over time.

Marginal frequency distribution: a table of the frequencies of occurrence of each value of a variable.

Marxism: a theory that envisages society as being structured around what it calls a mode of production. It focuses, in particular, on the capitalist mode of production, which is seen as fundamentally exploitative and unjust. Marxist theory thus places conflict centre-stage, and sees its own role as helping to challenge existing arrangements.

Measurement theory: a **theory** about why an indicator is a reliable and valid measure of a concept.

Meta-analysis: an analysis of the findings of several previous studies on the same topic. Because it is based on data from all the studies, the power and reliability of a meta-analysis can be much greater than that of any of the individual studies it draws on.

Meta-theory: assumptions that are often based on **paradigms**, and often unexamined, that shape the way researchers see their research questions and conduct their research.

Methodological triangulation: this has two sub-types: within-method, for example, using, in a questionnaire, a combination of attitude **scales**, **closed** and **open questions**; and between-method triangulation, such as a combination of participant observation, interviews and **documents**.

Methodology: the study of research methods. Often wrongly used to mean the research methods used in a project.

Middle-range theory: Robert Merton's (1968) term for **theory** that can be operationalised in research to facilitate understanding of particular phenomena, avoiding the pitfalls of either collecting and analysing data without reference to theory (**empiricism**) or using theories that are too general to be of empirical value.

Missing value: values are assigned as missing values when the researcher wishes to exclude those values from statistical analysis. For instance, some respondents may have refused to answer a question about their age. In quantitative analysis, every response must be given a **code**, so this 'no response' might be coded with the number 999. However, this code should not be treated as a valid age response. If it were, the average age for the sample would be incorrect.

Moderator: someone who leads and guides a **focus group** discussion. Also called a facilitator.

Monotonic: two variables are monotonically related if larger values of one are associated with larger values on the other, or smaller values of one are associated with smaller values of the other.

Multimedia: data presented in a variety of formats including sound, animation, video and graphics.

Narrative: a term widely used in social theory and social research to describe either: (a) a tale or story; or (b) a form of talk or writing that aims to tell a story and that may be structured according to classical ideas of plot.

Narrative analysis: narrative analysis of interview data is concerned with understanding how and why people talk about their lives as a story or a series of stories. This includes issues of identity and the interaction between the narrator and audience(s).

Non-monotonic: two variables are non-monotonic if larger values of one are associated with smaller values of the other, or vice versa.

Normal distribution: a 'bell-shaped' probability distribution that is symmetrical around its mean. It has the useful feature that 68 per cent of values drawn from a normal distribution are within 1 standard deviation of its mean, 95 per cent of values are within 1.96 standard deviations of its mean and 99 per cent of values fall within 2.58 standard deviations of its mean.

Ontology: the study of the categories of existence and of the existence of particular kinds of objects, such as numbers or social types.

OPAC: Online Public Access Catalogue. A library catalogue that is accessible online to the general public.

Open coding: the first stage of the **coding** of qualitative data, during which data is broken down, line by line, into as many concepts as possible and these concepts are gradually reduced into broader categories.

Open question: a survey question where the respondent is permitted to answer using their own words. Often the answer is written in a box on the schedule, either by the interviewer or the respondent. For example, 'What are the names of your children?' is an open question.

Panel: a study design that involves making repeated observations on its sample members. Typically, a panel survey will follow a representative sample of its target population over a period of months or years.

Paradigm: Thomas Kuhn (1962) used the term to describe frameworks for understanding the world that are powerful, self-contained and radically distinct. Since each paradigm contains its own criteria of evaluation, it is not possible to make judgements about the relative value of findings in different paradigms.

Parallel study: a term for a research design where two or more methods, addressing the same research questions, are used independently to collect and analyse data. They may be used at the same time (concurrently) or with a time lag between them. In contrast, in a **sequential study**, one method depends on and follows on from the use of another.

Parole: a concept from **semiotics** referring to speech, or **utterances** (either spoken words or written ones). It is from observing *parole* that *langue* can be deduced.

Participatory action research (PAR): a form of action research, PAR combines generating knowledge about a social situation by collecting data about it, and changing or acting on that situation. The conventional division between the researcher and the researched is challenged so that those directly involved in the social situation have an active role in some aspects of the research process.

Photo elicitation: a visual method in which individual respondents are interviewed about images (often photographs) shown to them. The images can be historical or contemporary, and they can be images that already exist or images created for the interview either by the researcher or by the participants. Photo elicitation can also be used with focus groups. 'Film elicitation' is the term applied when interviews or focus groups are conducted with respect to moving images (e.g. television clips, Hollywood movies, or ethnographic films).

Population: the collection of all the people living in a defined geographical area, or belonging to a category such as asylum seekers. Usually, in order to find out about a population, one selects a **sample**, studies the sample, and then infers from the sample to the population.

Position: a collection of meta-theoretical assumptions that are held in common by a group of researchers. A position is similar to a **paradigm**, but is not as strongly bounded. There are more positions than paradigms.

Positivism: an approach that places emphasis on establishing cause and effect relationships empirically and sees the role of theory as generating generalised explanations of the social world. It assumes there is a single measurable reality.

Pragmatic: in mixed methods, a pragmatic approach sets aside paradigm or position differences between the methods used; practical considerations are given priority in the research process.

Praxis: the transformation of academic or purely theoretical knowledge into applied practice, or the practice of acting upon observed conditions in order to change them. It is a key aspect of **participatory action research**, which seeks to achieve critically informed and committed action through the direct involvement of the people who experience an unsatisfactory social situation.

Projective questioning: an approach used in interviews to encourage respondents to give their views indirectly.

Purposive sampling: subjects or participants are selected for inclusion in a study on the basis of a particular characteristic or identified variable. It is particularly useful when the population under study is either unique or shares very specific characteristics, for example, individuals with a chronic illness aged 50–65 or parents of children with a learning difficulty. Purposive sampling is a popular method of selecting participants in qualitative research, where the focus is on gaining insight and understanding by hearing from representatives from a target population.

Question work: the critical intellectual work undertaken to formulate and refine a research question at each stage of a research project.

Rational choice theory: seeks to explain social behaviour by assuming that the individual is a strategic and calculating actor who makes choices according to rational criteria.

Realism: the position that social reality has an existence independent of people's conception or perception of it.

Reflection theory: an assumption that researchers make, sometimes implicitly, that visual documents such as art works or media texts mirror, or tell us something about, society.

Reflexive inquiry: an approach to social research that aims to question not only the claims about what is true that others make, but also holds up for examination one's own research methods and findings. The approach assumes that the meaning of all research claims are constructed in a dialogue between researchers, the researched and the users of research and rejects the idea that there is an objective reality to which research can refer to.

Reflexive sociology: reflexivity can refer to the structural property of being part of something, or to the cognitive property of awareness. A reflexive sociology recognises the significance of the fact that it is itself part of the social world that it seeks to describe and explain.

Reflexivity: a style of research that makes clear the researcher's own beliefs and objectives. It considers how the researcher is part of the research process and how he or she contributes to the construction of meaning on the topic under study. Reflexive research is often said to 'look back on itself'.

Relationship: a connection between objects, entities or concepts, for example, social relationships between people, causal relationships between events, and theoretical relationships between variables. A relationship may be causal, that is, representing a causal linkage, or associational, meaning that the entities co-vary, but without one being the cause of another.

Reliability: data are reliable when repeated measurements of the same item are consistent.

Repair sequence: a term used in **conversation analysis** to describe talk that displays mechanisms through which certain 'troubles' in interaction are dealt with.

Repertory grid: a method of assessing personality or beliefs, consisting of two stages. In the first, a respondent is asked to list a number (usually between 7 and 15) of people in their life, such as their mother, father, best friend, admired male. The respondent is then asked to place the nominated people into groups of three and to invent a descriptive term or 'construct' that distinguishes one of the three from the other two. It is assumed that the constructs are the units with which people ascribe meaning to their experience.

Representation: an image or model of what is perceived about the external, objective world.

Research objectives: the purposes for which the research is being carried out (to describe, to understand, to explain, etc.).

Research question: the overarching question that defines the scope, **scale** and conduct of a research project. The research question focuses research design and methods towards the provision of evidenced answers.

Rho: the intra-class correlation coefficient. In a survey context it provides information about the degree of homogeneity on a survey variable within a cluster, relative to the population as a whole.

Sample: a subset of the members of a **population**. Usually, the population is very large, making a census or a complete enumeration of all the members in the population impractical or very expensive. Statistics collected from a sample can be used to make inferences to the population. The process of selecting a sample is referred to as sampling. Sample members may be selected randomly, to yield a random sample, or in some other systematic way to obtain, for example, a **purposive**, quota, or **snowball** sample.

Sampling frame: a list intended to include every member of a **population**. A sampling frame can be used to select a random sample. Examples of sampling frames are the Postal Address File, and the register of a school.

Scale: a way of ordering or measuring respondents according to their responses to a survey or using other information. For example, people may be measured on scale of political opinion from left to right, on a scale of happiness according to their answers to opinion statements, and on a scale of prejudice from unprejudiced to very prejudiced.

Schedule: a list of questions, arranged in order that an interviewer must adhere to precisely, both in the exact question wording and in the order of questioning (compare with an **interview guide**).

Search engine: software provided by a web site that allows users to locate web pages that interest them by searching using key words, for example, Google and Alta Vista.

Secondary analysis: the analysis of data for a purpose other than that for which they were collected. Normally this also means that the analyst and data collector are different people or agencies.

Selective coding: the final stage in the process of developing **theory** from qualitative data. It involves elaboration of the most significant categories identified in the **coding** process and identification of a central category, which should form the basis for the theory.

Semiotics: is the study of signs and sign systems. A sign is seen as a combination of *signifier* (the marks on paper or a sound) and the *signified* (the concept with which it is associated). Social life is regarded as permeated by such systems or structures, and their study can reveal underlying ideology or what is termed mythology. At a formal level it can show how sign systems work, but needs to draw on other sociological ideas to connect those workings to the wider social world.

Semi-standardised interview: a type of interview in which the interviewer asks questions in the same way but may alter their sequencing and may probe for more information.

Sequential analysis: a process of continually checking data against interpretations. The process is begun before data collection has been completed, and yields a provisional analysis. This analysis may be used to guide further data collection.

Sequential study: a term for a research design using two or more methods in which one method depends on, and follows on from, the other. This is the opposite of a **parallel study** where two or more methods, addressing the same research questions, are used independently to collect and analyse data.

Sign: in semiotics, a sign is composed of the **signifier** and the **signified**.

Signified: in semiotics, the concept or object that appears in the mind when one hears or reads a word (the **signifier**).

Signifier: in semiotics, the form that a sign takes, for example, the letters that spell out a written word, or the phonemes that compose its sound.

Simple random sample: a simple random sample is a sample design in which every **population** unit is given an equal probability of selection into the **sample**.

Snowball sampling: a method of recruiting a sample by initially selecting a few members and then asking them for the names of their acquaintances. The named people are recruited and are asked about *their* acquaintances, and so on until enough people have been added to the sample. The advantages of a snowball sample are that no sampling frame is required and that it can be used for hidden populations such as drug users. The disadvantage is that population members who do not know other members can never be included in the sample, while those who have many friends are disproportionately likely to be recruited.

Social capital: this is defined by Putnam (1995) as 'networks, norms, and trust that enable participants to act together more effectively to pursue shared objectives'. In other words, social capital measures the degree to which people or communities cooperate or collaborate through social networks, mutual trust or shared values to achieve a common end.

Social construction: in relation to a document is the view that what it records is not a direct transcription of social reality, but the outcome of a number of processes of collection and recording of information; processes that are governed by the conventions, norms, objectives and implicit understandings of those involved. It is the application of **social constructionism**, a long-standing theoretical strand in sociology and psychology.

Social constructionism (social constructivism): a theory of knowledge that considers how social phenomena develop in particular social contexts. A **social construction** (social construct) is a **concept** or practice that may appear to be natural and obvious to those who accept it, but is regarded by the sociologist as an invention or artefact of a particular culture or society.

Social networking site: an **Internet** site that allows users to create personal profiles, link to friends and communicate with one another.

Speech act: an **utterance** that performs some action. For example, 'Hello' performs a greeting; 'Be careful!' performs a warning and 'Order! Order! Order!' performs a command. The theory of speech acts considers that all natural language **utterances** are actions of some kind.

Standardised (structured) interview: a type of interview in which the interviewer asks questions with the same wording and the same order in each interview.

Story: the description of an event or series of events in a manner that conveys meaning as well as factual information. Traditional stories or myths serve a number of purposes including entertainment, instruction and the formation of a collective world view. When research participants tell a story or a series of stories, the researcher will want to consider what purpose the story serves and why the interviewee has chosen to present their account in this way (see **Narrative**).

Structural functionalism: this theory sees society as a single and unified entity, almost like an organism, and its component parts (the family, for example) as being functional for the maintenance of equilibrium.

Structural mobility: occupational mobility resulting from a change in the number or proportion of jobs in different categories.

Subjective adequacy: a set of criteria for evaluating the adequacy of an ethnographic analysis: the time spent with a group; how close the ethnographer was to the group; the degree of variation in the activities observed; how sensitive the ethnographer has been to the language used in the setting; the degree of intimacy with members achieved by the ethnographer; and the extent to which the members agree with the ethnographer's interpretations (Bruyn, 1966).

Symbolic interactionism: a school of sociology which focuses on the ways in which meaning is constructed, attributed, sustained and developed in the course of everyday social interaction and communication.

Theoretical saturation: associated with grounded theory, this term refers to the point at which researchers are unable to find any new or different variants of a code or concept in their data. New instances of the concept may be identified, but if these merely replicate an already identified element rather than adding anything which is conceptually different, then the concept is said to be theoretically saturated.

Theory: either a provisional explanation, sometimes in the form of a hypothesis that can be tested; or a broad framework of concepts and ideas that provides a basis for interpreting the world.

Transparency: being explicit about all aspects of the research process in order that others can evaluate methods and processes. Usually used in reference to qualitative methodology and often discussed in reference to the use of qualitative software, which provide tools enabling an audit trail of analytic procedures to be tracked.

Triangulation: a means of achieving of validity, which has three forms:

1. Data triangulation, which has three sub-types: time, space and person; that is, data should be collected at a variety of times, in different locations and from a range of persons and collectivities.

2. Investigator triangulation uses multiple rather than single observers of the same object.

3. Theory triangulation consists of using more than one kind of approach to generate the categories of analysis. This is the most difficult kind of triangulation to achieve and is possibly an aspiration rather than a practical proposition.

Unstructured (focused) interview: a type of interview in which the interviewer uses a list of topics but can vary the phrasing and sequencing of questions.

Utterance: a complete unit of speech in spoken language. Sometimes also used in an analogous way for written text.

Validity: data are valid when they provide accurate measurements of a concept.

Visual methods: a range of techniques in social research that examine an area of sociological interest visually. Researchers may study existing visual materials, use images in interviews, **focus groups** or **ethnographies**, or create new visual materials that serve as data or that are created as part of a broader study.

Visual text: a term used in semiotics to refer to a visual document that is 'read' (analysed) semiotically.

World Wide Web: a collection of documents, connected by **hyperlinks**, stored on computers connected to the **Internet** around the world.

BIBLIOGRAPHY

Abbott, A. (1998) 'The causal devolution', *Sociological Methods and Research*, 27(2): 148–81.

Abbott, P., Wallace, W. and Tyler, M. (2005) *An Introduction to Sociology: Feminist Perspectives* (3rd edn). London: Routledge.

Adams, D. (1979) *The Hitchhiker's Guide to the Galaxy*. London: Pan Books.

Adler, P.A. (1985) *Wheeling and Dealing: An Ethnography of an Upper-Level Drug Dealing and Smuggling Community*. New York: Columbia University Press.

Adorno, T. (2000) 'Sociology and empirical research', in O'Connor, B. (ed.), *The Adorno Reader*. Oxford: Blackwell.

Agar, M.H. (1985) *Speaking of Ethnography*. Beverly Hills, CA: Sage.

Agresti, A. and Finlay, B. (1999) *Statistical Methods for the Social Sciences* (3rd edn). Upper Saddle River, NJ: Prentice Hall.

Albrecht, M.C. (1954) 'The relationship between literature and society', *American Journal of Sociology*, 59: 425–36.

Alexander, V.D. (1994) 'The image of children in magazine advertisements from 1905 to 1990', *Communication Research*, 21: 742–65.

Alexander, V.D. (1996a) 'Pictures at an exhibition: conflicting pressures in museums and the display of art', *American Journal of Sociology*, 101: 797–839.

Alexander, V.D. (1996b) 'From philanthropy to funding: the effects of corporate and public support on American art museums', *Poetics: Journal of Empirical Research on Literature, the Media and Arts*, 24(2–4): 89–131.

Alexander, V.D. (1996c) *Museums and Money: The Impact of Funding on Exhibitions, Scholarship, and Management*. Bloomington, IN: Indiana University Press.

Alexander, V.D. (2003) *Sociology of the Arts: Exploring Fine and Popular Forms*. Oxford: Blackwell.

Andreski, S. (1972) *Social Science as Sorcery*. London: Andre Deutsch.

Andrews, M. and NetLibrary, Inc. (2000) *Lines of Narrative [Electronic Resource]: Psychosocial Perspectives*. New York: Routledge.

Antal, F. (1962) *Hogarth and His Place in European Art*. London: Routledge and Kegan Paul.

Antal, F. (1987) *Florentine Painting and Its Social Background*. Cambridge, MA: Harvard University Press.

Arber, S. (1989) 'Opening the "black box": inequalities in women's health', in Abbott, P. and Payne, G. (eds), *New Directions in the Sociology of Health*. Brighton: Falmer Press.

Arber, S. (1997) 'Comparing inequalities in women's and men's health: Britain in the 1990s', *Social Science and Medicine*, 44(6): 773–87.

Arber, S. and Lahelma, E. (1993) 'Women, paid employment and ill-health in Britain and Finland', *Acta Sociologica*, 36: 121–38.

Arksey, H. and Knight, P.T. (1999) *Interviewing for Social Scientists: An Introductory Resource with Examples*. London: Sage.

Atkinson, J.M. (1978) *Discovering Suicide*. London: Macmillan.

Atkinson, J.M. (1984) *Our Masters' Voices: The Language and Body Language of Politics*. London: Methuen.

Atkinson, J.M. and Drew, P. (1979) *Order in Court: The Organisation of Verbal Interaction in Judicial Settings*. London: Macmillan.

Atkinson, J.M. and Heritage, J. (eds) (1984) *The Structures of Social Action: Studies in Conversation Analysis*. Cambridge: Cambridge University Press.

Atkinson, P. (1997) 'Narrative turn or blind alley?' *Qualitative Health Research*, 7: 325–44.

Atkinson, R. (1997) *The Life Story Interview*. Thousand Oaks, CA: Sage Publications.

Austin, J.L. (1962) *How to Do Things with Words*. Oxford: Clarendon Press.

Austin, R. and Vine, L. (eds) (2007) *Taking Part: The National Survey of Culture, Leisure and Sport: Annual Report 2005/2006*. London: Department of Culture, Media and Sport.

Babchuk, N. and Booth, A. (1969) 'Voluntary association membership: a longitudinal analysis', *American Sociological Review*, 34(1): 31–45.

Bachelard, G. (1984) *The New Scientific Spirit*, trans. A. Goldhammer. Boston: Beacon Press.

Bagnoli, A. (2004) 'Researching identities with multi-method autobiographies', *Social Research Online* (9): 2. http://tinyurl.com/2lj5ag

Ball, M.S. and Smith, G.W.H. (1992) *Analyzing Visual Data*. Newbury Park, CA: Sage.

Banks, M. (2001) *Visual Methods in Social Research*. London: Sage.

Barbour, R.S. and Kitzinger, J. (1999) *Developing Focus Group Research: Politics, Theory and Practice*. London: Sage.

Barnard, M. (2001) *Approaches to Understanding Visual Culture*. Houndsmills: Palgrave.

Barnes, B., Bloor, D. and Henry, J. (1996) *Scientific Knowledge: A Sociological Analysis*. London: Athlone Press.

Barnes, J.A. (1980) *Who Should Know What?: Social Science, Privacy and Ethics*. Cambridge: Cambridge University Press.

Barthel, D.L. (1988) *Putting on Appearances: Gender and Advertising*. Philadelphia, PA: Temple University Press.

Barthes, R. (1967) *Elements of Semiology*, trans. A. Lavers and C. Smith, London: Jonathan Cape.

Barthes, R. (1972) *Mythologies*. London: Cape.

Barthes, R. (1977) *Image, Music, Text*. London: Fontana.

Bartley, M., Sacker, A. and Clarke, P. (2004) 'Employment status, employment conditions, and limiting illness: prospective evidence from the British Household Panel Survey 1991–2001', *Journal of Epidemiology and Community Health*, 58(6): 501–06. http://tinyurl.com/3492e9

Baskerville, R. and Wood-Harper, T. (1996) 'A critical perspective on action research as a method for information systems research', *Journal of Information Technology*, 11: 235–46.

Bauman, Z. and May, T. (2001) *Thinking Sociologically* (2nd edn). Oxford: Blackwell.

Baxandall, M. (1988) *Painting and Experience in Fifteenth Century Italy: A Primer in the Social History of Pictorial Style* (2nd edn). Oxford: Oxford University Press.

Baym, N. (1995) 'The emergence of community in computer-mediated communication', in Jones, S. (ed.), *Cybersociety*. Thousand Oaks, CA: Sage.

Baym, N. (2000) *Tune in, Log on: Soaps, Fandom and Online Community*. Thousand Oaks, CA: Sage.

Bazeley, P. (2002) 'The evolution of a project involving an integrated analysis of structured qualitative and quantitative data: from N3 to Nvivo', *International Journal of Social Research Methodology*, 5(3): 229–43.

Bazerman, C. (1988) *Shaping Written Knowledge*. Madison, WI: University of Wisconsin Press.

Beauchamp, T.L., Faden, R.R., Wallace, R.J. and Wallace, R.J. (eds) (1982) *Ethical Issues in Social Science Research*. Baltimore, MD: Johns Hopkins University Press.

Beaulieu, A. (2004) 'Mediating ethnography', *Social Epistemology*, 18(2–3): 139–63.

Beck, U. (1992) *Risk Society: Towards a New Modernity*. London: Sage.

Becker, H. (1979) 'Do photographs tell the truth?' in Cook, T. and Reichardt, C. (eds), *Qualitative and Quantitative Methods in Evaluation Research*. London: Sage.

Becker, H.S. (1961) *Boys in White: Student Culture in Medical School*. Chicago: University of Chicago Press.

Becker, H.S. (1971) *Sociological Work*. London: Allen Lane.

Becker, H.S. (1974) 'Photography and sociology', *Studies in the Anthropology of Visual Communication*, 1(1): 3–26.

Becker, H.S. (1981) *Exploring Society Photographically*. Evanston, IL: Mary and Leigh Block Gallery.

Becker, H.S. (1986) *Writing for Social Scientists*. Chicago: University of Chicago Press.

Becker, H.S. (1998) 'Visual sociology, documentary photography, and photojournalism: it's (almost) all a matter of context', in Prosser, J. (ed.), *Image-Based Research* (pp. 84–96). London: RoutledgeFalmer.

Becker, H.S. (2000) 'What should sociology look like in the (near) future?' *Contemporary Sociology*, 29(2): 333–6.

Becker, H.S. and Richards, P. (1986) *Writing for Social Scientists: How to Start and Finish Your Thesis, Book, or Article*. Chicago: University of Chicago Press.

Bellenger, D.N., Bernhardt, K.L. and Goldstucker, J.L. (1976) 'Qualitative research techniques: focus group interviews', in Bellenger, D.N., Bernhardt, K.L. and Goldstucker, J.L. (eds), *Qualitative Research in Marketing*. Chicago: American Marketing Association.

Bennett, H.S. (1922) *The Pastons and Their England*. Cambridge: Cambridge University Press.

Bennett, N., Jarvis, L. and Haselden, L. (1996) *Living in Britain: Preliminary Results from the 1994 General Household Survey*. London: HMSO.

Berger, J. (1972) *Ways of Seeing*. Harmondsworth: Penguin.

Bertrand, J.T., Brown, J.E. and Ward, V.M. (1992) 'Techniques for analysing focus group data', *Evaluation Review*, 16(2): 198–209.

Best, S.J. and Krueger, B.S. (2004) *Internet Data Collection*. London: Sage.

Bettelheim, B. (1943) 'Individual and mass behaviour under extreme situations', *Journal of Abnormal and Social Psychology*, 38: 417–52 (reprinted in B. Bettelheim, *Surviving and Other Essays*, London: Thames and Hudson, 1979, pp. 1948–73).

Bignell, J. ([1997] 2002) *Media Semiotics: An Introduction* (2nd edn). Manchester: Manchester University Press.

Blaikie, N. (2000) *Designing Social Research: The Logic of Anticipation*. Cambridge: Polity Press.

Blalock, H.M. (1969) *Theory Construction*. Englewood Cliffs, NJ: Prentice Hall.

Blau, P.M. (1967) *Exchange and Power in Social Life*. Chichester: John Wiley & Sons, Ltd.

Boaler, J. (1997) 'Setting, social class and survival of the quickest', *British Educational Research Journal*, 23(5): 575–95.

Bobo, J. (1995) *Black Women as Cultural Readers*. New York: Columbia University Press.

Bogdan, R. (1974) *Being Different: The Autobiography of Jane Fry*. New York: Wiley.

Bok, S. (1978) *Lying: Moral Choice in Public and Private Life*. Hassocks: Harvester Press.

Bone, M., Gregory, J., Gill, B. and Lader, D. (1992) *Retirement and Retirement Plans*. London: HMSO.

Boruch, R.F. and Cecil, J.S. (1979) *Assuring the Confidentiality of Social Research Data*. Philadelphia, PA: University of Pennsylvania Press.

Bourdieu, P. (1990) *In Other Words: Essays Towards a Reflexive Sociology*. Cambridge: Polity.

Bourdieu, P., Passeron, J-C. and Chamboredon, J-C. (1991) *The Craft of Sociology: Epistemological Preliminaries*. New York: Aldine de Gruyter.

Bowker, N.I. (2001) 'Understanding online communities through multiple methodologies combined under a postmodern research endeavour', *FQS (Forum: Qualitative Social Research)* (2): 1. http://tinyurl.com/2s3bzb

Boylan, T.S. and Kedrowski, K.M. (2004) 'The Constitution and the war power: what motivates Congressional behavior?' *Armed Forces and Society,* 30(4): 539–70.

Bradburn, N.M., Wansink, B. and Sudman, S. (2004) *Asking Questions: The Definitive Guide to Questionnaire Design, for Market Research, Political Polls, and Social and Health Questionnaires*. San Francisco: Jossey-Bass.

Braithwaite, J. (1981) 'The myth of social class and criminality reconsidered', *American Sociological Review,* 46: 36–57.

Brassett-Grundy, A.J. (2003) *LS User Guide 20: Researching Households and Families Using the ONS Longitudinal Study*. London: Centre for Longitudinal Studies, Institute of Education, University of London.

Braverman, H. (1974) *Labor and Monopoly Capitalism*. New York: Monthly Review Press.

Breakwell, G.M. (1986) *Coping with Threatened Identities*. London: Methuen.

Breakwell, G.M. (ed.) (1992) *Social Psychology of Identity and the Self Concept*. Guildford: Surrey University Press.

Brettell, C.B. (1993) *When They Read What We Write: The Politics of Ethnography*. Westport, CT: Bergin and Garvey.

Brown, B.B. and Perkins, D.D. (1992) 'Disruption in place attachment', in Alman, I. and Low, S.M. (eds), *Place Attachment*. New York: Blenheim Press.

Brown, J., Fielding, J. and Lee, T. (1984) *Perception of Risk: A Secondary Analysis of Data Collected by the Social and Community Planning Research*. London: Health and Safety Executive.

Bruner, J. (1986) 'Life as narrative', *Social Research,* 54(1): 11–32.

Bruyn, S.T. (1966) *The Human Perspective in Sociology: The Methodology of Participant Observation*. Englewood Cliffs, NJ: Prentice Hall.

Bryman, A. (1988) *Quantity and Quality in Social Research*. London: Routledge.

Bryman, A. (2004) 'Secondary analysis and official statistics', in Bryman, A., *Social Research Methods* (2nd edn). Maidenhead: Open University Press.

Bryman, A. (2006) 'Integrating quantitative and qualitative research: how is it done?' *Qualitative Research,* 6(1): 97–113.

Bryman, A. and Burgess, R. (1994) 'Development in qualitative data analysis: an introduction', in Bryman, A. and Burgess, R. (eds), *Analysing Qualitative Data*. London: Routledge.

BSA Visual Sociology (2006) 'Statement of Ethical Practice for the British Sociological Association – Visual Sociology Group', retrieved 1 March, 2007, at http://tinyurl.com/376nw2

Buck, N.H., Gershuny, J., Rose, D. and Scott, J. (1994) *Changing Households: The British Household Panel Survey, 1990 to 1992*. Colchester: University of Essex, ESRC Research Centre on Micro-Social Change.

Bulmer, M. (1979) 'Concepts in the analysis of qualitative data', *Sociological Review,* 27: 651–77.

Bulmer, M. (1982) *Social Research Ethics: An Examination of the Merits of Covert Participant Observation*. London: Macmillan.

Bulmer, M. (2004) *Questionnaires*. London: Sage.

Bulmer, M., Sykes, W. and Moorhouse, J. (1998) *Directory of Social Research Organisations in the United Kingdom* (2nd edn). London: Mansell.

Burawoy, M. (ed.) (2000) *Global Ethnography*. Berkeley, CA: University of California Press.

Burgess, R.G. (1982) *Field Research: A Sourcebook and Field Manual*. London: Allen and Unwin.

Burgess, R.G. (1991) *Field Research: A Sourcebook and Field Manual* (new edn). London: Routledge.

Burgess, R.G. (2007) *Key Variables in Social Investigation*. London: Routledge.

Burman, E. (1996) 'Psychology discourse practice: from regulations to resistance', in Burman, E., Aitken, G., Aldred, P., Allwood, R., Billington, T., Goldberg, B., Gordo-Lopez, A., Heenan, C., Marks, D. and Warner, S. (eds), *Psychology Discourse Practice: From Regulations to Resistance* (pp. 1–14). London: Taylor and Francis.

Burrell, G. and Morgan, G. (1979) *Sociological Paradigms and Organisational Analysis: Elements of the Sociology of Corporate Life*. London: Heinemann Educational.

Bury, M. (2001) 'Illness narratives: face or fiction?' *Sociology of Health and Illness*, 23(3): 263–85.

Cameron, D., Frazer, E., Harvey, P., Rampton, M.B.H. and Richardson, K. (1992) *Researching Language: Issues of Power and Method*. London: Routledge.

Campbell, D.T. and Fiske, D.W. (1955) 'Convergent and discriminant validation by multitrait multidimensional matrix', *Psychological Bulletin*, 56: 81–105.

Caudill, W. et al. (1952) 'Social structure and interaction processes on a psychiatric ward', *American Journal of Orthopsychiatry*, 22: 314–34.

Chamberlayne, P., Bornat, J. and Wengraf, T. (eds) (2000) *The Turn to Biographical Methods in Social Science*. London: Routledge.

Chaplin, E. (1994) *Sociology and Visual Representation*. London: Routledge.

Chaplin, E. (2005) 'The photograph in theory', *Sociological Research Online* (10): 1. http://www.socresonline.org.uk/10/1/chaplin.html

Charmaz, K. (1991) *Good Days, Bad Days: The Self in Chronic Illness and Time*. New Brunswick, NJ: Rutgers University Press.

Charmaz, K. (1993) 'Loss of self: a fundamental form of suffering in the chronically ill', *Sociology of Health and Illness*, 5(2): 168–95.

Charmaz, K. (1994) 'Grounded theory: objectivist and constructivist methods', in Denzin, N. and Lincoln, Y. (eds), *Handbook of Qualitative Research* (2nd edn). Thousand Oaks, CA: Sage.

Cicourel, A.V. (1964) *Method and Measurement in Sociology*. New York: Free Press.

Clifford, J. and Marcus, G. (eds) (1986) *Writing Culture*. Berkeley, CA: University of California Press.

Cloward, R.A. and Ohlin, L. (1960) *Delinquency and Opportunity*. New York: Free Press.

Coffey, A. and Atkinson, P. (1996) *Making Sense of Qualitative Data: Complementary Strategies*. London: Sage.

Coffey, A., Holbrook, B. and Atkinson, P. (1996) 'Qualitative data analysis: technologies and representations', *Sociological Research Online*, 1(1).

Cohen, W. (1989) 'Symbols of power: statues in nineteenth century France', *Comparative Studies in Society and History*, 30(3): 491–513.

Collier, J. and Collier, M. (1986) *Visual Anthropology: Photography as a Research Method* (rev. edn). Albuquerque, NM: University of New Mexico Press.

Collins, H. (2004) *Gravity's Shadow: The Search for Gravitational Waves*. Chicago: University of Chicago Press.

Constable, N. (2003) *Romance on a Global Stage: Pen Pals, Virtual Ethnography and 'Mail Order' Marriages*. Berkeley, CA: University of California Press.

Coomber, R. (1997) 'Using the Internet for survey research', *Sociological Research Online*, 2(2). http://tinyurl.com/2ldmpm

Cooper, H., Arber, S. and Smaje, C. (1998a) 'Social class or deprivation? Structural factors and children's limiting longstanding illness in the 1990s', *Sociology of Health and Illness*, 20(3): 289–311.

Cooper, H., Smaje, C. and Arber, S. (1998b) 'Use of health services by children and young people according to ethnicity and social class: secondary analysis of a national survey', *British Medical Journal*, 317: 1047–51.

Cornwall, A. and Jewkes, R. (1995) 'What is participatory research?' *Social Science and Medicine*, 41(12): 1667–76.

Cornwell, J. (1984) *Hard-earned Lives: Accounts of Health and Illness from East London*. London: Tavistock Publications.

Cortese, A.J. (1999) *Provocateur: Images of Women and Minorities in Advertising*. Lanham, MD: Rowman and Littlefield.

Coxon, T. (2005). 'Integrating qualitative and quantitative data: what does the user need?' *FQS (Forum: Qualitative Social Research)* (6): 2. http://tinyurl.com/2s3bzb

Coyle, J. and Williams, B. (2000) 'An exploration of the epistemological intricacies of using qualitative data to develop a quantitative measure of user views of health care', *Journal of Advanced Nursing*, 31(5): 1235–43.

Creswell, J.W. (2003) *Research Design: Qualitative, Quantitative, and Mixed Method Approaches* (2nd edn). London: Sage.

Creswell, J.W. (2007) *Qualitative Inquiry and Research Design: Choosing among Five Approaches* (2nd edn). Thousand Oaks, CA: Sage.

Cronbach, L.J. (1951) 'Coefficient alpha and the internal consistency of tests', *Pychometrika*, 16: 297–334.

Cronbach, L.J. and Meehl, P.E. (1955) 'Construct validity in psychological tests', *Psychological Bulletin*, 52: 281–302.

Cronin, A., Alexander, V.D., Fielding, J., Moran-Ellis, J. and Thomas, H. (2008) 'The analytic integration of qualitative data sources', in Alasuutari, P., Brannen, J. and Bickman, L. (eds), *Handbook of Social Research Methods* (pp. 572–84). London: Sage.

Culler, J. (1987) 'Criticism and institutions: the American university', in Attridge, D. and Young, R. (eds), *Post-Structuralism and the Question of History*. Cambridge: Cambridge University Press.

Dale, A., Arber, S. and Procter, M. (1988) *Doing Secondary Analysis*. London: Allen and Unwin.

Dale, A., Fieldhouse, E. and Holdsworth, C. (2000) *Analyzing Census Microdata*. Oxford: Oxford University Press.

Daniels, A.K. (1975) 'Feminist perspectives in sociological research', in Millman, M. and Kanter, R. (eds), *Another Voice*. New York: Doubleday.

Davis, J.A., Smith, T.W. and National Opinion Research Center (1992) *The NORC General Social Survey: A User's Guide*. Newbury Park, CA: Sage Publications.

De Leeuw, E. and de Heer, W. (2001) 'Trends in Household Survey non-response: a longitudinal and international comparison', in Groves, R., Dillman, D., Eltings, J. and Little, R. (eds), *Survey Non-response* (pp. 41–54). New York: John Wiley & Sons, Ltd.

De Vaus, D.A. (2002a) *Social Surveys*. London: Sage.

De Vaus, D.A. (2002b) *Surveys in Social Research* (5th edn). London: Routledge.

Denzin, N.K. (1970) *The Research Act in Sociology*. London: Butterworths.

Denzin, N.K. (1978) *Sociological Methods: A Sourcebook* (2nd edn). New York: McGraw-Hill.

Denzin, N.K. (1989a) *The Research Act: A Theoretical Introduction to Sociological Methods* (3rd edn). Englewood Cliffs, NJ: Prentice Hall.

Denzin, N.K. (1989b) *Interpretive Biography*. London: Sage.

Denzin, N.K. and Lincoln, Y.S. (1994) *The Handbook of Qualitative Research*. London: Sage.

Denzin, N.K. and Lincoln, Y.S. (2000) *The Handbook of Qualitative Research* (2nd edn). London: Sage.

Deren, S., Oliver-Verez, D., Finlinson, A., Robels, R., Andia, J., Colon, H.M., et al. (2003) 'Integrating qualitative and quantitative methods: comparing HIV-related risk behaviors among Puerto Rican drug users in Puerto Rico and New York', *Substance Use and Misuse*, 38(1): 1–24.

Deutscher, I. (1973) *What We Say, What We Do: Sentiments and Acts*. Glenview, IL: Scott, Foresman.

Devault, M. (1990) 'Talking and listening from women's standpoint: feminist strategies for interviewing and analysis', *Social Problems*, 37(1): 96–116.

Dicks, B. and Mason, B. (1998) 'Hypermedia and ethnography: reflections on the construction of a research approach', *Sociological Research Online* (3):3. http://tinyurl.com/ 2jacuw

Dicks, B., Mason, B., Coffey, A. and Atkinson, P. (2005) *Qualitative Research and Hypermedia: Ethnography for the Digital Age*. London: Sage.

Dicks, B., Soyinka, B. and Coffey, A. (2006) 'Multimodal ethnography', *Qualitative Research*, 6(1): 77–96.

Dillman, D.A. (2006) *Mail and Internet Surveys: The Tailored Design Method* (2nd edn). Chichester: John Wiley & Sons, Ltd.

Dines, G. and Humez, J.M. (2003) *Gender, Race, and Class in Media: A Text-Reader* (2nd edn). London: Sage.

Dingwall, R. (2006) 'Confronting the anti-democrats: the unethical nature of ethical regulation in social science', *Medical Sociology Online* (1): 51–8. http://www.medicalsociology online.org

Disney, R., Grundy, Emily, M.D. and Johnson, P. (1997) *The Dynamics of Retirement: Analyses of the Retirement Surveys*. London: The Stationery Office.

Dixon, B., Bouma, G. and Atkinson, G.B.J. (1987) *A Handbook of Social Science Research: A Comprehensive and Practical Guide for Students*. Oxford: Oxford University Press.

Dohrenwend, B. (1964) 'A use for leading questions in research interviewing', *Human Organization*, 23: 76–7.

Douglas, J.D. (1967) *The Social Meanings of Suicide*. Princeton, NJ: Princeton University Press.

Douglas, J.D. (1976) *Investigative Social Research: Individual and Team Field Research*. London: Sage.

Dubin, S.C. (1995) 'How I got screwed by Barbie: a cautionary tale', *New Art Examiner*, November, 20–3.

Durkheim, É. ([1879] 1985) *Suicide: A Study in Sociology* (trans. K. Thompson). London: Routledge and Kegan Paul.

Dutton, W.H., di Gennaro, C. and Millwood Hargrave, A. (2005) *Oxford Internet Survey 2005 Report: The Internet in Britain*. Oxford: Oxford Internet Institute. http://tinyurl. com/7zexq

Eck, B.A. (2001) 'Nudity and framing: classifying art, pornography, information, and ambiguity', *Sociological Forum*, 16(4): 603–32.

Eck, B.A. (2003) 'Men are much harder: gendered viewing of nude images', *Gender and Society*, 17(5): 691–710.

Edwards, D. (1997) *Discourse and Cognition*. London: Sage.

Edwards, D. and Middleton, D. (1986) 'Joint remembering: constructing an account of shared experience through conversational discourse', *Discourse Processes*, 9: 423–59.

Edwards, D. and Middleton, D. (1987) 'Conversation and remembering: Bartlett revisited', *Applied Cognitive Psychology*, 1: 77–92.

Edwards, D. and Middleton, D. (1988) 'Conversational remembering and family relationships: how children learn to remember', *Journal of Social and Personal Relationships*, 5: 3–25.

Edwards, D. and Potter, J. (1992) *Discursive Psychology*. London: Sage.

Elias, N. (1998) 'The changing functions of etiquette', in Mennell, S. and Goudsblom, J. (eds), *On Civilisation, Power and Knowledge*. Chicago: University of Chicago Press.

Ellen, R.F. (1984) *Ethnographic Research: A Guide to General Conduct*. London: Academic Press.

Elliott, J. (2007) 'Imagining a gendered future: combining qualitative and quantitative approaches to the analysis of children's essays', *Children and the Lifecourse*. London: Centre for Longitudinal Studies, Institute of Education.

Elliott, J. and Morrow, V. (2007) 'Imagining the future: preliminary analysis of NCDS essays written by children at age 11', London: Centre for Longitudinal Studies. http://tinyurl.com/39ancg

Emerson, R.M., Fretz, R.I. and Shaw, L.L. (1995) *Writing Ethnographic Fieldnotes*. Chicago: University of Chicago Press.

Emmison, M. and Smith, P. (2000) *Researching the Visual: Images, Objects, Contexts and Interactions in Social and Cultural Inquiry*. London: Sage.

Empey, L. and Erickson, M. (1966) 'Hidden delinquency and social status', *Social Forces*, 44: 546–54.

Entman, R.M. and Rojecki, A. (2002) *The Black Image in the White Mind: Media and Race in America*. Chicago: University of Chicago Press.

Epstein, D., Boden, R. and Kenway, J. (2005) *Writing for Publication*. London: Sage.

Erben, M. (1993) 'The problem of other lives: social perspectives on written biography', *Sociology* 27(1): 15–26.

Erikson, K. (1967) 'A comment on disguised observation in sociology', *Social Problems*, 14: 366–73.

ESRC (2005) *Research Ethics Framework*. London: ESRC. http://tinyurl.com/2jzc7f

Ess, C. and AoIR Ethics Working Committee (2002) *Ethical Decision-Making and Internet Research: Recommendations from the AoIR Ethics Working Committee*. http://tinyurl.com/2qvobb

European Commission (2005) *Special Eurobarometer Report 224. Europeans, Science and Technology*, Brussels: European Commission. http://tinyurl.com/3369d7

Evans, J. and Hall, S. (1999) *Visual Culture: The Reader*. London: Sage Publications in association with the Open University.

Evans, M. (1993) 'Reading lives: how the personal might be social', *Sociology* 27(1): 5–14.

Fairclough, N. (1989) *Language and Power*. London: Longman.

Fairclough, N. (1995) *Critical Discourse Analysis*. London: Longman.

Fairclough, N. and Wodak, R. (1997) 'Critical discourse analysis', in van Dijk, T. (ed.), *Discourse Studies: A Multidisciplinary Introduction* (vol. 2, pp. 258–84). London: Sage.

Ferri, E., National Children's Bureau, City University, Social Statistics Research Unit, and Economic and Social Research Council. (1993) *Life at 33: The Fifth Follow-up of the National Child Development Study*. London: National Children's Bureau.

Festinger, L. (1964) *When Prophecy Fails*. New York: Harper and Row.

Fetterman, D.M. (1998) *Ethnography: Step by Step* (2nd edn). London: Sage.

Fichter, J.H. (1973) *One-Man Research: Reminiscences of a Catholic Sociologist*: New York: Wiley.

Fielding, J., Burningham, K., Thrush, D. and Catt, R. (2007) 'Public response to flood warnings', in Environmental Agency Science Report SC020116. http//:tinyurl.com/342n58

Fielding, J.L. and Gilbert, N. (2006) *Understanding Social Statistics* (2nd edn). London: Sage.

Fielding, N. (1981) *The National Front*. London: Routledge and Kegan Paul.

Fielding, N. (1982) 'Observational research on the National Front', in Bulmer, M. (ed.), *Social Research Ethics: An Examination of the Merits of Covert Participant Observation* (pp. 80–104). London: Macmillan.

Fielding, N. (1988) *Joining Forces*. London: Routledge.

Fielding, N. (1990) 'Mediating the message: affinity and hostility in research on sensitive topics', *American Behavioral Scientist*, 33(5): 608–20.

Fielding, N. and Fielding, J.L. (1986) *Linking Data: The Articulation of Qualitative and Quantitative Methods in Social Research*. London: Sage.

Fielding, N. and Lee, R. (eds) (1991) *Using Computers in Qualitative Research*. London: Sage.

Fielding, N. and Lee, R. (eds) (1993) *Using Computers in Qualitative Research* (2nd edn). London: Sage.

Fielding, N. and Lee, R.M. (1998) *Computer Analysis and Qualitative Research*. London: Sage.

Fielding, N. and Macintyre, M. (2006) 'Access grid nodes in field research', *Sociological Research Online* 11(2). http://tinyurl.com/355uty

Fielding, N. and Schreier, M. (2001) 'Introduction: on the compatibility between qualitative and quantitative research methods' *Forum Qualitative Sozialforschung/Forum: Qualitative Social Research*, 21(1): 1–10.

Filmer, P. (1998) 'Analysing literary texts', in Seale, C. (ed.), *Researching Society and Culture*. London: Sage.

Filstead, W.J. (1970) *Qualitative Methodology: Firsthand Involvement with the Social World*: Chicago, Markham Pub. Co.

Fink, A. (2004) *Conducting Research Literature Reviews: From the Internet to Paper* (2nd edn). London: Sage.

Fishbein, M. and Ajzen, I. (1975) *Belief, Attitude, Intention and Behavior*. Reading, MA: Addison-Wesley.

Fisher, M. (1997) *Qualitative Computing: Using Software for Qualitative Data Analysis*. Aldershot: Ashgate.

Foddy, W.H. (1993) *Constructing Questions for Interviews and Questionnaires: Theory and Practice in Social Research*. Cambridge: Cambridge University Press.

Foot, K.A. and Schneider, S.M. (2006) *Web Campaigning*. Cambridge, MA: MIT Press.

Ford, R., Marsh, A. and Finlayson, L. (1998) *What Happens to Lone Parents: A Cohort Study, 1991–1995*. London: The Stationery Office.

Foss, C. and Ellefsen, B. (2002) 'The value of combining qualitative and quantitative approaches in nursing research by means of method triangulation', *Journal of Advanced Nursing*, 40(2): 242–8.

Foster, C.G. (2001) *The Ethics of Medical Research on Humans*. Cambridge: Cambridge University Press.

Foucault, M. (1977) *Discipline and Punish: The Birth of the Prison*. Harmondsworth: Allen Lane.

Fox, A.J., Goldblatt, P.O. and Jones, D.R. (1985) 'Social class mortality differentials: artefact, selection or life circumstances', *Journal of Epidemiology and Community Health*, 39: 1–8.

Fox, S. and Livingston, G. (2007) *Latinos Online*. Washington, DC: Pew Internet and American Life Project and Pew Hispanic Center. http://tinyurl.com/yttn3f

Frank, A.W. (1995) *The Wounded Storyteller: Body, Illness, and Ethics*. Chicago: University of Chicago Press.

Frank, A.W. (2000) 'The standpoint of storyteller', *Qualitative Health Research*, 10(3): 354–65.

Frank, R. and Kerouac, J. (1958) *The Americans*. New York: Pantheon Books.

Frankham, J. (2006) *Partnership Research: Negotiating User Involvement in Research Design* (End of Award Report): ESRC. http://tinyurl.com/2w3b2n

Frankland, J. and Bloor, M. (1999) 'Some issues arising in the systematic analysis of focus group materials', in Barbour, R.S. and Kitzinger, J. (eds), *Developing Focus Group Research: Politics, Theory and Practice*. London: Sage.

Freeman, D. (1999) *The Fateful Hoaxing of Margaret Mead: A Historical Analysis of Her Samoan Researches*. Boulder, CO: Westview Press.

Frye, M. (1983) *The Politics of Reality: Essays in Feminist Theory*. Berkeley, CA: Crossing Press.

Fullagar, S. (2003) 'Wasted lives: the social dynamics of shame and youth suicide', *Journal of Sociology*, 39(3): 291–307.

Fussell, P. (1975) *The Great War and Modern Memory*. Oxford: Oxford University Press.

Fussell. P. (1989) *Wartime: Understanding and Behavior in the Second World War*. Oxford: Oxford University Press.

Game, A. and Metcalfe, A. (1996) *Passionate Sociology*. London: Sage.

Gammon, L. and Marshment, M. (1988) *The Female Gaze: Women as Viewers of Popular Culture*. London: Women's Press.

Garfinkel, H. (1967a) *Studies in Ethnomethodology*. Englewood Cliffs, NJ: Prentice-Hall.

Garfinkel, H. (1967b) '"Good" organizational reasons for "bad" clinical records', in Garfinkel, H. (ed.), *Studies in Ethnomethodology* (pp. 186–207). Englewood Cliffs, NJ: Prentice Hall.

Garton, L., Haythornthwaite, C. and Wellman, B. (1997) 'Studying online social networks', *Journal of Computer Mediated Communication*, 3(1). http://tinyurl.com/3daue3

Gaskell, G., Allum, N.C., Bauer, M.W., Durant, J., Allansdottir, A., Bonfadelli, H., et al. (2000) 'Biotechnology and the European public', *Nature Biotechnology*, 18(9): 935–8.

Geertz, C. (1975) *The Interpretation of Cultures: Selected Essays*. New York: Basic Books.

Gerbner, G., Gross, L., Eleey, M.E., Jackson-Beeck, M., Jeffries-Fox, S. and Signorielli, N. (1977) 'Television violence profile no. 8: the highlights', *Journal of Communication*, 27: 171–80.

Gerrish, K. (1999) *Practice Development: Criteria for Success: An Evaluation of the Practice Development Programme Offered by Centre for the Development of Nursing Policy and Practice, University of Leeds*. Leeds: School of Healthcare Studies, University of Leeds.

Gibbs, G.R., Friese, S. and Mangabeira, W. (2002) 'The use of new technology in qualitative research', *FQS*, 3(2). http://tinyurl.com/4sttl

Giddens, A. (1976) *New Rules of the Sociological Method*. London: Hutchinson.

Giddens, A. (1984) *Constitution of Society: Outline of a Theory of Structuration*. Cambridge: Polity Press.

Gilbert, G.N. and Mulkay, M. (1984) *Opening Pandora's Box: A Sociological Analysis of Scientists' Discourse*. Cambridge: Cambridge University Press.

Gill, R. (1996) 'Discourse analysis: practical implementation', in Richardson, J.T.E. (ed.), *Handbook of Qualitative Research Methods for Psychology and the Social Sciences* (pp. 141–56). Hove: The British Psychological Society.

Glaser, B. (1992) *Basics of Grounded Theory Analysis: Emergence Versus Forcing*. Mill Valley, CA: Sociology Press.

Glaser, B. and Strauss, A. (1965) *Awareness of Dying*. New York: Aldine.

Glaser, B. and Strauss, A. (1967) *The Discovery of Grounded Theory: Strategies for Qualitative Research*. London: Weidenfeld and Nicholson.

Glass, G.V., McGraw, B. and Smith, M.L. (1981) *Meta-analysis in Social Research*. London: Sage.

Gobo, G. (2001) 'Best practices: rituals and rhetorical strategies in the "initial telephone contact"', *FQS (Forum: Qualitative Social Research)* (2):1. http://tinyurl.com/2s3bzb

Goffman, E. (1961) *Asylums: Essays on the Social Situation of Mental Patients and Other Inmates*. Garden City, NY: Anchor Books.

Goffman, E. (1969) *The Presentation of Self in Everyday Life*. Harmondsworth: Penguin.

Goffman, E. (1971) *Relations in Public: Microstudies of the Public Order*. New York: Basic Books.

Goffman, E. (1979) *Gender Advertisements*. London: Macmillan.

Goldthorpe, J., Lockwood, D., Bechhofer, F. and Platt, J. (1968) *The Affluent Worker: Industrial Attitudes and Behaviour*. Cambridge: Cambridge University Press.

Gombrich, E.H. (1960) *Art and Illusion: A Study in the Psychology of Pictorial Representation; the A.W. Mellon Lectures in the Fine Arts, 1956, National Gallery of Art, Washington*. London: Phaidon.

Gombrich, E.H. (1972) 'The visual image', in *Scientific American* (ed.), *Communication* (pp. 46–60). San Francisco: W.H. Freeman and Company.

Goodley, D. and Hove, G. van. (2005) *Another Disability Studies Reader?: People with Learning Difficulties and a Disabling World*. London: Garant.

Gorden, R.L. (1980) *Interviewing: Strategy, Techniques, and Tactics* (3rd edn). Homewood, IL: Irwin-Dorsey Ltd.

Graham, J., Grewal, I. and Lewis, J. (2007) *Ethics in Social Research: The Views of Research Participants*: London: HM Treasury, Government Social Research Unit.

Gray, J.N., Lyons, P.M. and Melton, G.B. (1995) *Ethical and Legal Issues in AIDS Research*. Baltimore, MD: Johns Hopkins University Press.

Green, J. and Hart, L. (1999) 'The impact of context on data', in Barbour, R.S. and Kitzinger, J. (eds), *Developing Focus Group Research: Politics, Theory and Practice*. London: Sage.

Greenbaum, T.L. (2000) *Moderating Focus Groups: A Practical Guide for Group Facilitation*. Thousand Oaks, CA: Sage.

Greene, J., Benjamin, L. and Goodyear, L. (2001) 'The merits of mixing methods in evaluation', *Evaluation*, 7(1): 25–44.

Greene, J.C. and Caracelli, V.J. (1997) *Advances in Mixed-Method Evaluation: The Challenges and Benefits of Integrating Diverse Paradigms*. San Francisco: Jossey-Bass Publishers.

Greene, J., Caracelli, V.J. and Graham, W.F. (1989) 'Toward a conceptual framework for mixed-method evaluation designs', *Educational Evaluation and Policy Analysis*, 11(3): 255–74.

Grene, D. (ed.) (1959) *Thucydides' History of the Peloponnesian War*. New York: Cape.

Griffiths, M. (2007) 'Distinction: consumption and identity in the People's Republic of China'. mbgriffiths@gmail.com

Gross, L., Katz, J.S. and Ruby, J. (1988) *Image Ethics: The Moral Rights of Subjects in Photographs, Film, and Television*. Oxford: Oxford University Press.

Groves, R., Fowler, P., Floyd, J., Couper, M., Lepkowski, J.M., Singer, E. and Tourangeau, R. (2004) *Survey Methodology*. New Jersey: John Wiley & Sons, Ltd.

Gulli, A. and Signorini, A. (2005) 'The indexable web is more than 11.5 billion pages', paper presented at the 14th International World Wide Web Conference, Chiba, Japan. http://tinyurl.com/b3yyo

Gumilev, L.N. (1987) *Searches for an Imaginary Kingdom: The Legend of the Kingdom of Prester John*. Cambridge: Cambridge University Press.

Guttman, L. (1944) 'A basis for scaling qualitative data', *American Sociological Review*, 9: 139–50.

Hagan, J., Hirschfield, P. and Shedd, P. (2002) 'First and last words: apprehending the social and legal facts of an urban high school shooting', *Sociological Methods and Research*, 31(2): 218–54.

Halle, D. (1993) *Inside Culture: Art and Class in the American Home*. Chicago: University of Chicago Press.

Hammersley, M. and Atkinson, P. (2007) *Ethnography: Principles in Practice* (3rd edn). London: Routledge.

Hammersley, M. and Open University Principles of Social and Educational Research Course Team (1993) *Social Research: Philosophy, Politics and Practice*. London: Sage.

Haraway, D. (1991) *Simians, Cyborgs and Women: The Reinvention of Nature*. London: Free Association Books.

Harding, A. (1990) *Dynamic Microsimulation Models: Problems and Prospects*. London: Welfare State Programme, Suntory-Toyota International Centre for Economics and Related Disciplines.

Hargens, L.L. (1988) 'Scholarly consensus and journal rejection rates', *American Sociological Review*, 53: 139–51.

Harper, D. (1979) 'Life on the road', in Wagner, D. (ed.), *Images of Information: Still Photography in the Social Sciences* (pp. 25–42). London: Sage.

Harper, D.A. (1982) *Good Company*. Chicago: University of Chicago Press.

Hart, C. (1999) *Doing a Literature Review: Releasing the Social Science Research Imagination*. London: Sage.

Hart, C. (2001) *Doing a Literature Search*. London: Sage.

Hart, E. and Bond, M. (1995) *Action Research for Health and Social Care*. Buckingham: Open University Press.

Hartnoll, R. (1991) 'Epidemiological approaches to drug misuse in Britain', *Journal of Addictive Diseases*, 11(1): 33–45.

Haslam, C. and Bryman, A. (1994) *Social Scientists Meet the Media*. London: Routledge.

Have, P. ten. (1999) *Doing Conversation Analysis: A Practical Guide*. London: Sage.

Hawkes, T. (1992) *Structuralism and Semiotics*. London: Routledge.

Heath, C. (1986) *Body Movement and Speech in Medical Interaction*. Cambridge: Cambridge University Press.

Henry, M. (1999) *IT in the Social Sciences: A Student's Guide to the Information and Communication Technologies*. Oxford: Blackwell.

Hepburn, A. (2003) *An Introduction to Critical Social Psychology*. London: Sage.

Herbert, A.P. (1977) *Misleading Cases in the Common Law*. London: Eyre Methuen.

Heritage, J. (1984) *Garfinkel and Ethnomethodology*. Cambridge: Polity Press.

Heritage, J. and Greatbatch, D. (1986) 'Generating applause: a study of rhetoric and response at party political conferences', *American Journal of Sociology*, 92(1): 110–57.

Hindess, B. (1973) *The Use of Official Statistics in Sociology*. London: Macmillan.

Hine, C. (2000) *Virtual Ethnography*. London: Sage.

Hine, C. (ed.) (2005) *Virtual Methods: Issues in Social Research on the Internet*. Oxford: Berg.

Hochschild, A. (1983) *The Managed Heart: The Commercialization of Human Feeling*. Berkeley, CA: University of California Press.

Hodkinson, P. (2002) *Goth: Identity, Style, and Subculture*. New York: Berg.

Hodkinson, P. (2005) 'Insider research in the study of youth cultures', *Journal of Youth Studies*, 8(2): 131–49.

Hodkinson, P., Biesta, G., Gleeson, D., James, D. and Postlethwaite, K. (2005) 'The heuristic and holistic synthesis of large volumes of qualitative data: the TLC experience', paper presented at RCBN Annual Conference, Cardiff.

Holland, J., Women, Risk and AIDS Project and Men, Risk and AIDS Project (1998) *The Male in the Head: Young People, Heterosexuality and Power*. London: Tufnell.

Hollis, M. (2002) *The Philosophy of Social Science: An Introduction* (rev. edn). Cambridge: Cambridge University Press.

Holsti, O.R. (1969) *Content Analysis for the Social Sciences and Humanities*. Reading, MA: Addison-Wesley.

Homan, R. (1991) *The Ethics of Social Research*. London: Pearson Education.

Hope, K. and Waterman, H. (2003) 'Praiseworth pragmatism? Validity and action research', *Journal of Advanced Nursing*, 44(2): 120–7.

Hudson, J.M. and Bruckman, A. (2004) 'Go away? Participant objections to being studied and the ethics of chatroom research', *Information Society*, 20(2): 127–39.

Hughes, J.A. (1976) *Sociological Analysis: Methods of Discovery*. London: Nelson.

Humphrey, C. (1983) *Karl Marx Collective: Economy, Society and Religion in a Siberian Collective Farm*. Cambridge: Cambridge University Press.

Humphreys, L. (1970) *Tearoom Trade*. Chicago: Aldine.

Hutchby, I. and Wooffitt, R. (1998) *Conversation Analysis: Principles, Practices and Applications*. Cambridge: Polity.

Hyman, H.H. (1954) *Interviewing in Social Research*. Chicago: University of Chicago Press.

Illingworth, N. (2001) 'The Internet matters: exploring the use of the Internet as a research tool.' *Sociological Research Online*, 6(2). http://tinyurl.com/2lf9ec

International Telecommunications Union (2006) *World Information Society Report 2006*. Geneva: International Telecommunications Union. http://tinyurl.com/32pkym

Irving, B.L. and McKenzie, I.K. (1988) *Regulating Custodial Interviews: The Effects of the Police and Criminal Evidence Act 1984*. London: Police Foundation.

Janis, I.L. (1982) *Groupthink: Psychological Studies of Policy Decisions and Fiascoes* (2nd edn). Boston: Houghton Mifflin.

Jencks, C. (1973) *Inequality: A Reassessment of the Effect of Family and Schooling in America*. London: Allen Lane.

Jewitt, C. (1997) 'Images of men: male sexuality in sexual health leaflets and posters for young people', *Sociological Research Online* (2): 2. http://tinyurl.com/2mo7zw

Jhally, S. (1990) *Dreamworlds* (video): *Desire, Sex, and Power in Music Video*. Amherst, MA: University of Massachusetts at Amherst.

Johns, M.D., Chen, S.-L.S. and Hall, G.J. (eds) (2004) *Online Social Research: Methods, Issues, and Ethics*. New York: Peter Lang.

Johnson, S. (1997) *Interface Culture: How New Technology Transforms the Way We Create and Communicate*. New York: Basic Books.

Joinson, A. (2005) 'Internet behaviour and the design of virtual methods', in Hine, C. (ed.), *Virtual Methods: Issues in Social Research on the Internet* (pp. 21–34). Oxford: Berg.

Jones, S. (ed.) (1999) *Doing Internet Research: Critical Issues and Methods for Examining the Net*. Thousand Oaks, CA: Sage.

Jowell, R. and Centre for Comparative Social, Surveys (2007) *Measuring Attitudes Cross-Nationally: Lessons from the European Social Survey*. London: Sage.

Jowell, R., Curtice, J., Park, A., Thomson, K., Brook, L. and Bryson, C. (eds) (1998) *British – and European – Social Attitudes: The 15th Report*. Aldershot: Gower.

Jowell, R., Witherspoon, S. and Brook, L. (1989) *British Social Attitudes: Special International Report*. Aldershot: Gower.

Kalton, G. (1983) *Introduction to Survey Sampling*. London: Sage.

Katz, J., Capron, A.M., Glass, E.S. and Russell Sage Foundation (1972) *Experimentation with Human Beings: The Authority of the Investigator, Subject, Professions, and State in the Human Experimentation Process*: New York: Russell Sage Foundation.

Kelle, U. (1997) *Capabilities for Theory Building and Hypothesis Testing and in Software for Computer Assisted Qualitative Data Analysis*. http://tinyurl.com/32t8dz

Kelle, U. (2001) 'Sociological explanations between micro and macro and the integration of qualitative and quantitative methods', *FQS (Forum: Qualitative Social Research)* (2): 1. http://tinyurl.com/2s3bzb

Kelly, G.A. (1970) 'A brief introduction to personal construct theory', in Bannister, D. (ed.), *Perspectives in Personal Construct Theory*. London: Academic Press.

King, G., Keohane, R.O. and Verba, S. (1994) *Designing Social Enquiry: Scientific Inference in Qualitative Research*. Princeton, NJ: Princeton University Press.

Kitsuse, J.I. and Cicourel, A.V. (1963) 'A note on the uses of official statistics', *Social Problems*, 11: 131–9.

Knodel, J. (1993) 'The design and analysis of focus group studies: a practical approach', in Morgan, D. (ed.), *Successful Focus Groups: Advancing the State of the Art*. Newbury Park, CA: Sage Publications.

Krathwohl, D. (1998) *Methods of Educational and Social Science Research: An Integrated Approach*. Harlow: Longman.

Krathwohl, D. (2006) *Methods of Educational and Social Science Research* (2nd edn). New York: Waveland Pr. Inc.

Kress, G.R. and Van Leeuwen, T. (2006) *Reading Images: The Grammar of Visual Design* (2nd edn). London: Routledge.

Krippendorf, K. (2004) *Content Analysis* (2nd edn). London: Sage.

Krueger, R.A. (2000) *Focus Groups: A Practical Guide for Applied Research*. Newbury Park, CA: Sage.

Kuhn, T.S. (1970) *The Structure of Scientific Revolutions* (2nd edn). Chicago: University of Chicago Press.

LaPiere, R.T. (1934) 'Attitudes vs actions', *Social Forces*, 13: 230–7.

Labov, W. (1972) 'The transformation of experience in narrative syntax', in Labov, W. (ed.), *Language in the Inner City*. Philadelphia, PA: University of Philadelphia Press.

Laslett, P. (1976) 'The wrong way through the telescope: a note on literary evidence in sociology and in historical sociology', *British Journal of Sociology*, 27(3): 319–42.

Latané, B., Williams, K. and Harkins, S.G. (1979) 'Many hands make light work: the causes and consequences of social loafing', *Journal of Experimental Social Psychology*, 37: 822–32.

Latour, B. (1992) 'Where are the missing masses? The sociology of a few mundane artefacts', in Bijker, W. and Law, J. (eds), *Shaping Technology/Building Society*. Cambridge, MA: MIT Press.

Latour, B. (2005) *Reassembling the Social: An Introduction to Actor-Network-Theory*. Oxford: Oxford University Press.

Law, A. and McNeish, W. (2007) 'Contesting the new irrational actor model', *Sociology*, 41(3): 439–56.

Layder, D. (1993) *New Strategies in Social Research*. Cambridge: Polity.

Layder, D. (1998) *Sociological Practice*. London: Sage.

Lee, R. and Stanko, B. (eds) (2003) *Researching Violence: Essays on Methodology and Measurement*. London: Routledge.

Lee, R.M. (1993) *Doing Research on Sensitive Topics*. London: Sage.

Lee-Treweek, G. and Linkogle, S. (2000) *Danger in the Field: Risk and Ethics in Social Research*. London: Routledge.

Lees, S. (1993) *Sugar and Spice: Sexuality and Adolescent Girls*. London: Penguin.

Leeuwen, T. van and Jewitt, C. (2000) *The Handbook of Visual Analysis*. London: Sage.

Lemert, C. (2005) *Social Things: An Introduction to the Sociological Life* (2nd edn). Oxford: Rowman and Littlefield.

Lewin, K. (1946) 'Action research and minority problems', *Journal of Social Issues*, 2: 34–46.

Lewins, A. and Silver, C. (2007) *Using Software in Qualitative Research: A Step-by-Step Guide*. London: Sage.

Ley, D. (1996) *The New Middle Class and the Remaking of the Central City*. Oxford: Oxford University Press.

Lieblich, A., Tuval-Mashiah, R. and Zilber, T. (1998) *Narrative Research: Reading, Analysis, and Interpretation* (Vol. 47). Thousand Oaks, CA: Sage.

Likert, R. (1932) 'A technique for the measurement of attitudes', *Archives of Psychology*, 140.

Littler, C. (1982) *The Development of the Labour Process in Capitalist Societies*. London: Heinemann.

Lofland, J. (1971) *Analyzing Social Settings: A Guide to Qualitative Observation and Analysis*. Belmont, CA: Wadsworth.

Lofland, J. and Lofland, L.H. (1995) *Analyzing Social Settings: A Guide to Qualitative Observation and Analysis* (3rd edn). London: Wadsworth.

Lurie, A. (1967) *Imaginary Friends*. London: Heinemann.

Macdonald, K.M. (1989) 'Building respectability', *Sociology*, 23(1): 55–80.

Madge, C. and O'Connor, H. (2002) 'Online with the E-mums: exploring the Internet as a medium for research', *Area*, 34: 92–102.

Maney, M. and Oliver, P.E. (2001) 'Finding collective events: sources, searches, timing', *Sociological Methods and Research*, 30(2): 131–69.

Mann, C. and Stewart, F. (2000) *Internet Communication and Qualitative Research: A Handbook for Researching Online*. London: Sage.

Marin, L. (1983) 'Discourse of power – power of discourse: Pascalian notes', in Montefiore, A. (ed.), *Philosophy in France Today*. Cambridge: Cambridge University Press.

Market Research Society (2006) *Questionnaire Design Guidelines*. London: Market Research Society. http://www.mrs.org.uk/standards/quant.htm

Marsh, A. (2000) 'The DSS/PSI programme of research into lone-income families (PRILIF)', *Data Archive Bulletin*, 73: 5–9.

Marsh, C. (1988) *Exploring Data: An Introduction to Data Analysis for Social Scientists*. Cambridge: Polity.

Marsh, C., Skinner, C., Arber, S., Penhale, B., Openshaw, S., Hobcraft, J., et al. (1991) 'The Case for a sample of anonymised records from the 1991 Census', *Journal of the Royal Statistical Society, Series A*, 154(2): 305–40.

Marshall, G. (1980) *Presbyteries and Profits: Calvinism and the Development of Capitalism*. Edinburgh: Edinburgh University Press.

Marshall, G. (1982) *In Search of the Spirit of Capitalism: An Essay on Max Weber's Protestant Ethic Thesis*. London: Hutchinson.

Marx, K. (1976) *Capital: A Critique of Political Economy*. Harmondsworth: Penguin.

Marx, K. and Engels, F. ([1848] 1948) *The Communist Manifesto*. London: Socialist Party of Great Britain.

Mason, J. (2006) 'Mixing methods in a qualitatively driven way', *Qualitative Research*, 6(1): 9–25.

May, T. (2001) *Social Research: Issues, Methods and Process* (3rd edn). Maidenhead: Open University Press.

McCall, G.J. and Simmons, J.L. (1969) *Issues in Participant Observation: A Text and Reader*: Reading, MA: Addison-Wesley.

McPherson, J.M. and Smith-Lovin, L. (1986) 'Sex segregation in voluntary associations', *American Sociological Review,* 51: 61–79.

McRobbie, A. (1978) *Jackie: An Ideology of Adolescent Femininity.* Birmingham: Centre for Contemporary Cultural Studies.

McRobbie, A. (1991) *Feminism and Youth Culture: From Jackie to Just Seventeen.* London: Macmillan.

Merton, R. (1967) *On Theoretical Sociology.* New York: Free Press.

Merton, R.K. (1965) *On the Shoulders of Giants: A Shandean Postscript.* New York: Harcourt Brace Jovanovich.

Merton, R.K. (1968) *Social Theory and Social Structure.* New York: The Free Press.

Merton, R.K. and Kendall, P.L. (1946) 'The focused interview', *American Journal of Sociology,* 51: 541–57.

Meyer, J. (2001) 'Action research', in Fulop, N., Allen, P., Clarke, A. and Black, N. (eds), *Studying the Organisation and Delivery of Health Services.* London: Routledge.

Middlebrook, M. (1978) *The Kaiser's Battle.* Harmondsworth: Penguin.

Middlebrook, M. (1983) *The Schweinfurt-Regensburg Mission.* Harmondsworth: Penguin.

Miles, M.B. and Huberman, A.M. (1994) *Qualitative Data Analysis: An Expanded Sourcebook* (2nd edn). London: Sage.

Miller, D. and Slater, D. (2000) *The Internet: An Ethnographic Approach.* Oxford: Berg.

Mirzoeff, N. (1999) *An Introduction to Visual Culture.* London: Routledge.

Mishler, E.G. (1986) *Research Interviewing: Context and Narrative.* Cambridge, MA: Harvard University Press.

Mitchell, W.J. (1992) *The Reconfigured Eye: Visual Truth in the Post-Photographic Era.* Cambridge, MA: MIT Press.

Modood, T., Berthoud, R., Lakey, J. and Policy Studies, Institute (1997) *Ethnic Minorities in Britain: Diversity and Disadvantage: The Fourth National Survey of Ethnic Minorities.* London: Policy Studies Institute.

Moran, R.A. and Butler, D.S. (2001) 'Whose health profile?' *Critical Public Health,* 11(1): 59–74.

Moran-Ellis, J., Alexander, V.D., Cronin, A., Dickinson, M., Fielding, J., Sleneny, J., et al. (2004) 'Following a thread: an approach to integrating multi-method data sets', paper presented at the ESRC Research Methods Programme, Methods Festival Conference, Oxford, 1–2 July.

Moran-Ellis, J., Alexander, V.D., Cronin, A., Dickinson, M., Fielding, J., Sleneny, J., et al. (2006) 'Triangulation and integration: processes, claims and implications', *Qualitative Research,* 6(1): 45–59.

Moran-Ellis, J. and Fielding, N.G. (1996) 'A national survey of the investigation of child sexual abuse', *British Journal of Social Work,* 26: 337–56.

Morgan, D.L. (1997) *Focus Groups as Qualitative Research.* London: Sage.

Morrow, V. (2001) 'Using qualitative methods to elicit young people's perspectives on their environments: some ideas for community health initiatives', *Health Education Research,* 16(3): 255–68.

Morse, J.M. (1991) 'Approaches to qualitative-quantitative methodological triangulation', *Nursing Research,* 40(2): 120–3.

Mortensen, T. and Walker, J. (2002) 'Blogging thoughts: personal publication as an online research tool', in Morrison, A. (ed.), *Researching ICTs in Context* (pp. 249–79). Oslo: InterMedia Report.

Moser, C.A. and Kalton, G. (1971) *Survey Methods in Social Investigation* (2nd edn). Aldershot: Gower.

Mulkay, M. (1985) *The Word and the World.* London: Allen and Unwin.

Munck, R. and Rolston, W. (1987) *Belfast in the 30's: An Oral History.* Belfast: Blackstaff Press.

Nash, R. (2002) 'Numbers and narratives: further reflections in the sociology of education', *British Journal of Sociology of Education,* 23(3): 397–412.

Netemeyer, R.G., Bearden, W.O. and Sharma, S. (2003) *Scaling Procedures: Issues and Applications.* London: Sage.

Neuman, W.L. (2000) *Social Research Methods; Qualitative and Quantitative Approaches* (4th edn). Boston: Allyn and Bacon.

Newman, I. and Benz, C.R. (1998) *Qualitative-Quantitative Research Methodology [Electronic Resource]: Exploring the Interactive Continuum.* Carbondale, IL: Southern Illinois University Press.

Norris, M. (1983) *A Beginner's Guide to Repertory Grid.* Department of Sociology, University of Surrey.

Norusis, M. (2006) *SPSS 14.0 Guide to Data Analysis.* Upper Saddle River, NJ: Prentice Hall.

Norusis, M. (2007) *SPSS 15.0 Statistical Procedures Companion.* Upper Saddle River, NJ: Prentice Hall.

O'Leary, Z. (2004) *The Essential Guide to Doing Research.* London: Sage.

O'Neill, F.H. and Silver, C. (2002) 'Improving patients' hospital experience: team-working and the integration of non-clinical and clinical roles', *Practice Development in Healthcare,* 1(2): 98–103.

OFCOM (2006) *Media Literacy Audit: Report on Media Literacy Amongst Adults from Minority Ethnic Groups.* London: OFCOM. http://tinyurl.com/38xd3e

Office of National Statistics (2000a) *Standard Occupational Classification 2000,* Volume 1: *Structure and Descriptions of Unit Groups.* London: The Stationery Office.

Office of National Statistics (2000b) *Standard Occupational Classification 2000,* Volume 2: *Coding Index.* London: The Stationery Office.

Office of National Statistics (2005) *Living in Britain: Results from the 2004 General Household Survey.* London: HMSO.

Oliver, M. (1996) *Understanding Disability: From Theory to Practice.* Basingstoke: Palgrave Macmillan.

Oppenheim, A.N. (1992) *Questionnaire Design, Interviewing and Attitude Measurement* (2nd edn). London: Pinter Publishers.

Orgad, S.S. (2005) *Storytelling Online: Talking Breast Cancer on the Internet.* New York: Peter Lang.

Page, S., Allsopp, D. and Casley, S. (1998) *The Practice Development Unit: An Experiment in Multidisciplinary Innovation.* London: Whurr Publishers.

Page, S. and Hamer, S. (2002) 'Practice development: time to realise the potential', *Practice Development in Healthcare,* 1(1): 2–17.

Park, A. (2004) *British Social Attitudes: The 23rd Report: Perspectives on a Changing Society.* London: Sage.

Parker, H., Aldridge, J. and Measham, F. (1998) *Illegal Leisure: The Normalisation of Adolescent Recreational Drug Misuse.* London: Routledge.

Parker, I. (1989) *The Crisis in Modern Social Psychology: And How to End It.* London: Routledge.

Parker, I. (1990) 'Discourse: definitions and contradictions', *Philosophical Psychology,* 3(2): 189–204.

Parker, I. (1992) *Discourse Dynamics: Critical Analysis for Social and Individual Psychology.* London: Routledge.

Parker, I. (1994) 'Discourse analysis', in Banister, P., Bruman, E., Parker, I., Taylor, M. and Tindall, C. (eds), *Qualitative Methods in Psychology* (pp. 92–107). Buckingham: Open University Press.

Patashnick, J.L. and Rich, M. (2005) 'Researching human experience: Video Intervention/ Prevention Assessment (VIA)', *Australasian Journal of Information Systems*, 12(2): 103–11.

Patton, M.Q. (1987) *How to Use Qualitative Methods in Evaluation*. London: Sage.

Patton, M.Q. (1998) 'Paradigms and pragmatism', in Fetterman, D.M. (ed.), *Qualitative Approaches to Evaluation in Education: The Silent Scientific Revolution* (pp. 116–37). New York: Praeger.

Patton, M.Q. (2002) *Qualitative Evaluation and Research Methods*. Newbury Park, CA: Sage.

Pawson, R. (1995) 'Quality and quantity, agency and structure, mechanism and context, dons and cons', *BMS, Bullétin de Méthodologie Sociologique*, 47: 5–48.

Pearson, G. (1983) *Hooligan*. London: Macmillan.

Peirce, C.S. (1958) *Selected Writings*, ed. P. Wiener. New York: Dover Press.

Petticrew, M. and Roberts, H. (2006) *Systematic Reviews in the Social Sciences: A Practical Guide*. Malden, MA: Blackwell Publishing.

Phillips, E. and Pugh, D.S. (2005) *How to Get a PhD: A Handbook for Students and Their Supervisors* (4th edn). Maidenhead: Open University Press.

Pinch, T.J. and Clark, C. (1986) 'The hard sell: "patter merchanting" and the strategic (re)production and local management of economic reasoning in the sales routines of market pitchers', *Sociology*, 20(2): 169–91.

Pink, S. (2007) *Doing Visual Ethnography: Images, Media, and Representation in Research* (2nd edn). Thousand Oaks, CA: Sage Publications.

Platt, J. (1981) 'Evidence and proof in documentary research', *Sociological Review*, 29(1): 31–66.

Plummer, K. (1983) *Documents of Life: An Introduction to the Problems and Literature of a Humanistic Method*. London: Allen and Unwin.

Plummer, K. (1995) *Telling Sexual Stories: Power, Change, and Social Worlds*. London: Routledge.

Polsky, N. (1971) *Hustlers, Beats and Others*. New York: Anchor Books.

Pomerantz, A.M. (1986) 'Extreme case formulations: a way of legitimizing claims', in Button, G., Drew, P. and Heritage, J. (eds), *Human Studies* (Vol. 9, Special Issue on Interaction and Language Use), pp. 219–29.

Potter, J. (1996) *Representing Reality: Discourse, Rhetoric and Social Construction*. London: Sage.

Potter, J. (2000) 'Post-cognitive psychology', *Theory and Psychology*, 10(1): 31–7.

Potter, J. and Wetherell, M. (1987) *Discourse and Social Psychology: Beyond Attitudes and Behaviour*. London: Sage.

Power, C., Manor, O., Fox, J. and City University Social Statistics Research Unit (1991) *Health and Class: The Early Years*. London: Chapman and Hall.

Prosser, J. (1998) *Image-Based Research: A Sourcebook for Qualitative Researchers*. London: Falmer.

Puchta, C. and Potter, J. (2004) *Focus Group Practice*. London: Sage.

Punch, K. (2005) *Introduction to Social Research: Quantitative and Qualitative Approaches* (2nd edn). London: Sage.

Punch, M. (1986) *The Politics and Ethics of Fieldwork*. London: Sage.

Putnam, R. (1995) 'Bowling alone: America's declining social capital', *Journal of Democracy*, 6(1): 65–78.

Quinney, R. and Wilderman, J. (eds) (1977) *The Problem of Crime* (2nd edn). New York: Harper and Row.

Rabinow, P. and Sullivan, W.M. (1979) *Interpretive Social Science: A Reader*. Berkeley, CA: University of California Press.

Rees, P., Martin, D.J. and Williamson, P. (2002) *The Census Data System*. Chichester: John Wiley & Sons, Ltd.

Rich, M., Lamola, S., Amory, C. and Schneider, L. (2000) 'Asthma in life context: video intervention/prevention assessment (VIA)', *Pediatrics*, 105(March): 469–77.

Rickman, H.P. (1961) *Meaning in History: William Dilthey's Thought on Society and History*. London: Allen and Unwin.

Riessman, C.K. (1990) *Divorce Talk: Women and Men Make Sense of Personal Relationships*. New Brunswick, NJ: Rutgers University Press.

Riessman, C.K. (1993) *Narrative Analysis*. London: Sage.

Ritzer, G. and Goodman, D. (2007) *Sociological Theory* (7th edn). Boston: McGraw-Hill.

Robb, J.H. (1954) *Working-Class Anti-Semite: A Psychological Study in a London Borough*. London: Tavistock.

Roberts, C.M. (2004) *The Dissertation Journey: A Practical and Comprehensive Guide to Planning, Writing, and Defending Your Dissertation*. Thousand Oaks, CA: Corwin Press.

Robertson, A. and Cochrane, R. (1976) 'Attempted suicide and cultural change: an empirical investigation', *Human Relations*, 29(9): 863–83.

Rocco, T.S., Bliss, L.A. Gallagher, S. and Pérez-Prado, A. (2003) 'Taking the next step: mixed methods research in organization systems', *Information Technology, Learning, and Performance Journal*, 21(1): 19–29.

Rock, P. (1979) *The Making of Symbolic Interactionism*. London: Macmillan.

Rogers, A. and Nicolaas, G. (1998) 'Understanding the patterns and processes of primary care use: a combined quantitative and qualitative approach', *Social Research Online* (3): 4. http://www.socresonline.org.uk/socresonline/3/4/5.html

Rorty, R. (2000) *Philosophy and Social Hope*. Harmondsworth: Penguin.

Rose, D. (1995) 'Official social classifications in the UK', *Social Research Update* 9. http://tinyurl.com/2jtpbj

Rose, D. and ESRC Research Centre on Micro-Social (1992) *Micro-Social Change in Britain: Current and Future Research Using the British Household Panel Survey*. Colchester: ESRC Research Centre on Micro-Social Change.

Rose, D. and O'Reilly, K. (eds) (1997) *Constructing Classes: Towards a New Social Classification for the UK*. Swindon: ESRC/ONS.

Rose, D. and Pevalin, D.J. (2003) *A Researcher's Guide to the National Statistics Socio-Economic Classification*. London: Sage.

Rose, G. (2006) *Visual Methodologies: An Introduction to the Interpretation of Visual Materials* (2nd edn). London: Sage.

Rosenhan, D.L. (1973) 'On being sane in insane places', *Science*, 179(January 19): 250–8.

Rosenweld, G.C. and Ochberg, R.L. (1992) *Storied Lives: The Cultural Politics of Self-Understanding*. New Haven, CT: Yale University Press.

Rothon, C. and Heath, A. (2003) 'Trends in racial prejudice', in Park, A., Curtice, J., Thomson, K., Jarvis, L. and Bromley, C. (eds), *British Social Attitudes: The 20th Report – Continuity and Change over Two Decades*. London: Sage.

Rubin, H.J. and Rubin, I. (1995) *Qualitative Interviewing: The Art of Hearing Data*. London: Sage.

Rustin, M. (2000) 'Reflections on the biographical turn in social science', in Chamberlayne, P., Bournat, J. and Wengraf, T. (eds), *The Turn to Biographical Methods in Social Science* (pp. 33–52). London: Routledge.

Sacks, H. (1963) 'Sociological description', *Berkeley Journal of Sociology*, 8: 1–16.

Sacks, H. (1992) *Lectures on Conversation*. 2 vols. Oxford: Blackwell.

Sale, J.E.M., Lohfeld, L.H. and Brazil, K. (2002) 'Revisiting the quantitative-qualitative debate: implications for mixed-methods research', *Quality and Quantity*, 36(1): 43–53.

Saussure, F. de ([1915] 1959) *Course in General Linguistics*. New York: Philosophical Library.

Schegloff, E. (1972) 'Notes on a conversational practice: formulating place', in D. Sudnow (ed.), *Studies in Social Interaction* (pp. 75–119). New York: The Free Press.

Schneider, S.J., Kerwin, J., Frechtling, J. and Vivari, B.A. (2002) 'Characteristics of the discussion in online and face-to-face focus groups', *Social Science Computer Review*, 20(1): 31–42.

Schneider, S.M. and Foot, K.A. (2004) 'The Web as an object of study', *New Media and Society*, 6(1): 114–22.

Schudson, M. (1992) *Watergate in American Memory: How We Remember and Reconstruct the Past*. New York: Basic Books.

Schur, E.M. (1971) *Labeling Deviant Behaviour*. New York: Harper and Row.

Schutt, R.K. (2004) *Investigating the Social World: The Process and Practice of Research* (4th edn). Thousand Oaks, CA: Pine Forge Press.

Scott, J. (1990) *A Matter of Record: Documentary Sources in Social Research*. Cambridge: Polity Press.

Scott, J. (ed.) (2006) *Documentary Research*. London: Sage.

SCPR (1982) *Public Attitudes Towards Industrial, Work-related and Other Risks*. London: SCPR.

Seale, C. (1999) *The Quality of Qualitative Research*. London: Sage.

Seale, C. and Filmer, P. (2004) 'Doing social surveys', in Seale, C. (ed.), *Researching Society and Culture* (2nd edn). London: Sage.

Sellin, T. and Wolfgang, M.E. (1964) *The Measurement of Delinquency*. New York: John Wiley & Sons, Ltd.

Selltiz, C. and Jahoda, M. (1962) *Research Methods in Social Relations* (Rev. edn). New York: Holt, Rinehart and Winston.

Seymour-Smith, M. (1990) *Rudyard Kipling*. London: Papermac.

Shapiro, S. and Eberhart, J. (1947) 'Interviewer differences in an intensive survey', *International Journal of Opinion and Attitude Research*, 2.

Sharrock, W., Francis, D. and Cuff, E. (2005) *Perspectives in Sociology* (5th edn). London: Routledge.

Shively, J. (1992) 'Cowboys and Indians: perceptions of Western films among American Indians and Anglos', *American Sociological Review*, 57: 725–34.

Short, J. Jr and Nye, F.I. (1958) 'Extent of unrecorded juvenile delinquency: tentative conclusions', *Journal of Criminal Law and Criminology*, 49: 296–302.

Shove, E. (2003) *Comfort, Cleanliness and Convenience: The Social Organization of Modernity*. Oxford: Berg.

Sica, A. (1998) *What Is Social Theory? The Philosophical Debates*. Oxford: Blackwell.

Sieben, I. and de Graaf, P.M. (2004) 'Schooling or social origin? The bias in the effect of educational attainment on social orientations', *European Sociological Review*, 20(2): 107–22.

Silver, C. (2002) *The Development of School-Based Sex Education in the Netherlands and England and Wales: Culture, Politics and Practice*. Surrey: University of Surrey, UK.

Silverman, D. (1985) *Qualitative Methodology and Sociology: Describing the Social World*. Aldershot: Gower.

Silverman, D. (1998) *Harvey Sacks: Social Science and Conversation Analysis*. Cambridge: Polity Press.

Silverman, D. (2006) *Interpreting Qualitative Data: Methods for Analyzing Talk, Text and Interaction* (3rd edn). London: Sage.

Silvey, J. (1975) *Deciphering Data: The Analysis of Social Surveys*. London: Longman.

Simmel, G. (1950) *The Sociology of Georg Simmel*. Glencoe, IL: The Free Press.

Singer, E., Frankel, M. and Glassman, M. (1983) 'The effect of interviewer characteristics and expectations on response', *Public Opinion Quarterly*, 47(1): 68–83.

Sismondo, S. (2003) *An Introduction to Science and Technology Studies*. Oxford: Blackwell.

Slater, D. (1998) 'Analysing cultural objects: content analysis and semiotics', in Seale, C. (ed.), *Researching Society and Culture*. London: Sage.

Smith, D. (1996) 'Women's perspective as a radical critique of sociology', in Keller, E.F. and Longino, H. (eds), *Feminism and Science*. Oxford: Oxford University Press.

Smith, D.E. (1978) '"K is mentally ill": the anatomy of a factual account', *Sociology*, 12: 23–53.

Smith, M.J. (2005) *Philosophy and Methodology of the Social Sciences*. London: Sage.

Smith, N. and Williams, P. (1986) *Gentrification of the City*. Boston: Allen and Unwin.

Sociology (1993) 'Special issue: auto/biography in sociology', *Sociology* 27(1).

Speller, G.M. (2000) *A Community in Transition: A Longitudinal Study of Place Attachment and Identity Processes in the Context of an Enforced Relocation*. Surrey: University of Surrey, UK.

Spiegelberg, S. (1980) 'Phenomenology and observation', in Glassner, B. (ed.), *Essential Interactionism*. London: Routledge and Kegan Paul.

Sproston, K. and Primatesta, P. (eds) (2003) *Health Survey for England 2003* (Vol. 1: Cardiovascular Disease). London: The Stationery Office.

SPSS (2006) *SPSS Base 15.0 User's Guide*. Chicago: SPSS Inc.

Stacey, M. (1969) *Methods of Social Research* (1st edn) New York: Pergamon Press.

Stacey, M. and British Sociological Association and Social Science Research Council (1969) *Comparability in Social Research*. London: Heinemann Educational Books.

Stanley, L. and Wise, S. (1990) 'Method, methodology and epistemology in feminist research processes', in Stanley, L. (ed.), *Feminist Praxis: Research, Theory and Epistemology in Feminist Sociology*, London: Routledge.

Stasz, C. (1979) 'The early history of visual sociology', in Wagner, J. (ed.), *Images of Information* (pp. 119–36). Ann Arbor, MI: UMI Books on Demand [London: Sage].

Stewart, D.W., Shamdasani, P.N. and Rook, D.W. (2007) *Focus Groups: Theory and Practice* (2nd edn). Thousand Oaks, CA: Sage.

Stewart, K. and Williams, M. (2005) 'Researching online populations: the use of online focus groups for social research', *Qualitative Research*, 5(4): 395–416.

Stinchcombe, A.L. (1968) *Constructing Social Theories*. Chicago: University of Chicago Press.

Strauss, A. (1987) *Qualitative Analysis for Social Scientists*. Cambridge: Cambridge University Press.

Strauss, A. and Corbin, J. (1994) 'Grounded theory methodology: an overview', in Denzin, N.K. and Lincoln, Y.S. (eds), *Handbook of Qualitative Research*. Thousand Oaks, CA: Sage.

Strauss, A. and Corbin, J. (1998) *Basics of Qualitative Research: Techniques and Procedures for Developing Grounded Theory* (2nd edn). London: Sage.

Sturken, M. and Cartwright, L. (2001) *Practices of Looking: An Introduction to Visual Culture*. Oxford: Oxford University Press.

Sudman, S. and Bradburn, N.M. (1974) *Response Effects in Surveys: A Review and Synthesis*. Chicago: Aldine Pub. Co.

Sudman, S. and Bradburn, N.M. (1982) *Asking Questions: A Practical Guide to Questionnaire Design*. San Francisco: Jossey-Bass.

Summers, G.F. (1977) *Attitude Measurement*. London: Kershaw.

Swift, J. and Motte, B.D. (1726) *Travels into Several Remote Nations of the World: In Four Parts*. London: printed for Benj. Motte, at the Middle Temple-Gate in Fleet-Street.

Tashakkori, A. and Teddlie, C. (1998) *Mixed Methodology: Combining Qualitative and Quantitative Approaches.* London: Sage.

Tashakkori, A. and Teddlie, C. (2003) *Handbook of Mixed Methods in Social and Behavioral Research.* London: Sage.

Taylor, S. (1982) *Durkheim and the Study of Suicide.* London: Macmillan.

Taylor, S. (1988) *The Sociology of Suicide.* New York: Longman.

Tesch, R. (1990) *Qualitative Research: Analysis Types and Software Tools.* London: Falmer.

Thelwall, M. (2004) *Link Analysis: An Information Science Approach.* Amsterdam: Elsevier.

Thody, A. (2006) *Writing and Presenting Research.* London: Sage.

Thomas, G. and James, D. (2006) 'Reinventing grounded theory: some questions about theory, ground and discovery', *British Educational Research Journal,* 32(6): 767–95.

Thomas, H. (2003) 'Pregnancy, illness and the concept of career', *Sociology of Health and Illness,* 25(5): 383–407.

Thomas, W.I. and Znaniecki, F. (1958) *The Polish Peasant in Europe and America.* New York: Dover Publications.

Thompson, P.R. (1992) *The Edwardians: The Remaking of British Society* (2nd edn). London: Routledge.

Thompson, P.R. (2000) *Voice of the Past: Oral History* (3rd edn). New York: Oxford University Press.

Thurlow, C., Lengel, L. and Tomic, A. (2004) *Computer Mediated Communication: Social Interaction and the Internet.* London: Sage.

Thurston, L.L. (1928) 'attitudes can be measured', *American Journal of Sociology,* 33: 529–54.

Todhunter, C. (2001) 'Undertaking action research: negotiating the road ahead', *Social Research Update* (34). http://tinyurl.com/2nlpjf

Tonkiss, F. (2004) 'Analysing discourse', in Seale, C. (ed.), *Researching Society and Culture* (pp. 367–82). London: Sage.

Turner, B. (1981) 'Some practical aspects of qualitative data analysis: one way of organising the cognitive processes associated with the generation of grounded theory', *Quality and Quantity,* 15: 225–47.

Twine, F.W. (2006) 'Visual ethnography and racial theory: family photographs as archives of interracial intimacies', *Ethnic and Racial Studies,* 29(3): 487–511.

van Dijk, T. (1993) 'Principles of critical discourse analysis', *Discourse and Society,* 4: 249–83.

Van Maanen, J. (1982) *Varieties of Qualitative Research.* Beverly Hills, CA: Sage.

Van Maanen, J. (1988) *Tales of the Field: On Writing Ethnography.* Chicago: University of Chicago Press.

Wadsworth, M. and National Survey of Health and, Development (1991) *The Imprint of Time: Childhood, History, and Adult Life.* Oxford: Clarendon Press.

Wadsworth, M.E.J. (1986) 'Serious illness in childhood and its association with later-life achievement', in Wilkinson, R.G. (ed.), *Class and Health: Research and Longitudinal Data.* London: Tavistock.

Wagner, J. (1979) *Images of Information: Still Photography in the Social Sciences.* London: Sage.

Waldfogel, J. (1993) *Women Working for Less: A Longitudinal Analysis of the Family Gap.* London: Suntory-Toyota Centre for Economics and Related Disciplines, London School of Economics.

Walliman, R. (2006) *Social Research Methods.* London: Sage.

Warwick, D.P. (1982) 'Types of harm in social research', in Beauchamp, T.L., Faden, R.R., Wallace, R.J. and Walter, L. (eds), *Ethical Issues in Social Science Research* (pp. 101–24). Baltimore, MD: Johns Hopkins University Press.

Weaver, T. (ed.) (1973) *To See Ourselves: Anthropology and Modern Social Issues*. Glenview, IL: Scott Foresman.

Webb, E.J., Campbell, D.T., Schwartz, R.D. and Sechrest, L. (1966) *Unobtrusive Measures: Non Research in the Social Sciences*. Chicago: Rand McNally.

Weber, M. (1930) *The Protestant Ethic and the Spirit of Capitalism* (trans. T. Parsons). London: George Allen and Unwin.

Weber, R.P. (1990) *Basic Content Analysis* (2nd edn). Newbury Park, CA: Sage.

Weitzman, E. and Miles, M. (1995) *Computer Programs for Qualitative Data Analysis: A Software Source Book*. Thousand Oaks, CA: Sage.

Wellings, K. and National Survey of Sexual Attitudes and Lifestyles (1994) *Sexual Behaviour in Britain: The National Survey of Sexual Attitudes and Lifestyles*. London: Penguin Books.

Wengraf, T. (2001) *Qualitative Research Interviewing: Biographic Narrative Methods and Semi-Structured Methods*. London: Sage.

WHO (2005) http://tinyurl.com/37xzsh

Widdicombe, S. and Wooffitt, R. (1995) *The Language of Youth Subcultures: Social Identity in Action*. Hemel Hempstead: Harvester Wheatsheaf.

Wikipedia (2006) 'The answer to life, the universe, and everything'. http://tinyurl. com/3yecml

Williams, G. (1984) 'The genesis of chronic illness: narrative reconstruction', *Sociology of Health and Illness, 6*(2): 175–200.

Williams, M. (2007) 'Avatar watching: participant observation in graphical online environments', *Qualitative Research, 7*(1): 5–24.

Williamson, J. (1995) *Decoding Advertisements: Ideology and Meaning in Advertising*. London: Marion Boyars.

Willig, C. (2001a) 'Foucauldian discourse analysis', in C. Willig, *Introducing Qualitative Research in Psychology* (pp. 106–24). Buckingham: Open University Press.

Willig, C. (2001b) *Introducing Qualitative Research in Psychology*. Buckingham: Open University Press.

Willis, P.E. (1977) *Learning to Labour: How Working Class Kids Get Working Class Jobs*. Farnborough: Saxon House.

Willis, P.E. (1980) 'Notes on method', in Hall, S., Hobson, D., Lowe, A. and Willis, P.E. (eds), *Culture, Media, Language: Working Papers in Cultural Studies, 1972–79*. London: Hutchison.

Wittgenstein, L. (1953) *Philosophical Investigations*. Oxford: Blackwell.

Wodak, R. and Meyer, M. (2001) *Methods of Critical Discourse Analysis*. London: Sage.

Wolcott, H.F. (2001) *Writing up Qualitative Research* (2nd edn). London: Sage.

Wooffitt, R. (1992) *Telling Tales of the Unexpected: The Organization of Factual Discourse*. Hemel Hempstead: Harvester Wheatsheaf.

Wooffitt, R. (2005) *Conversation Analysis and Discourse Analysis: A Comparative and Critical Introduction*. London: Sage.

Wright Mills, C. (1959) *The Sociological Imagination*. Oxford: Oxford University Press.

Yin, R.K. (2003) *Case Study Research: Design and Methods* (3rd edn). London: Sage.

Zimmerman, D. and Pollner, M. (1973) 'The everyday world as a phenomenon', in Douglas, J. (ed.), *Understanding Everyday Life: Towards the Reconstruction of Sociological Knowledge*. London: Routledge.

INDEX

intra-class correlation (rho) 177, 513
introduction 492, 495–6, 500
  focus groups 238–9
  literature review 77
introductory letters 203
INTUTE 74, 342
Irving, B. L. 258
item non-response 172

Jahoda, M. 260
James, D. 92, 93, 94
Janis, I. L. 239
Jefferson, G. 443
Jencks, C. 368
Jewitt, C. 463, 465
Jewkes, R. 118
Jhally, S. 468
Johnson, S. 463
Joinson, A. 310
journals 71, 487–9, 490, 491–500
Jowell, R. 378, 383

Katz, J. 151
Kedrowski, K. M. 289
Kelle, U. 127, 128, 131–2
Kelly, G. A. 407
Kendall, P. L. 237, 247, 260
key questions, focus groups 239
keywords 75
King, G. 167
Kipling, R. 290
Kitsuse, J. I. 32
Kitzinger, J. 232, 233, 234, 242
Knodel, J. 242
Krathwohl, D. 335
Kress, G. R. 465
Krippendorf, K. 295
Krueger, R. A. 230, 240, 242
Kuhn, T. 7–8, 34
KWALITAN 398

Labour Force Survey (LFS) 377, 378, 386
labour process 298–9
Labov, W. 434, 435–6
Lahelma, E. 384
langue 465–6, 509
LaPiere, R. T. 208–9
Latané, B. 235
Latour, B. 12–13, 14
Law, A. 36–7
Layder, D. 93, 400–1
lay theories 16–17

leading questions 195
Lee, R. 87, 92, 155, 156, 397
Lees, S. 155
Level of Living Survey 384
levels of analysis 355, 509
Lewin, K. 103–4
Lewins, A. 347, 394–419
Ley, D. 30
library, literature review 69, 70–1
Lieblich, A. 433, 434
life history interview 248
life-story research 430
Likert scaling 212–14, 218, 509
Lincoln, Y. S. 128, 278
literature review 2, 59, 63–79, 84, 90–1, 96, 97, 509
Littler, C. 299
Livingston, G. 307
Lofland, J. 87, 92, 247, 253–4, 271, 274, 278–9
Lofland, L. H. 87, 92, 247, 253–4, 271, 274, 278–9
longitudinal research 36, 37, 373–4, 377, 509
  ethics 156
  narrative analysis 430–1
  surveys 380–1
Longitudinal Study of Ageing 382
Longitudinal Survey (LS) 379–80
Lurie, A. 153

McCall, G. J. 270, 280
Macdonald, K. M. 285–303, 467, 471, 474
Macintyre, M. 270
Mckenzie, I. K. 258
McLeish, W. 36–7
McNaughton, 242
McPherson, J. M. 494–500, 501
McRobbie, A. 295
Madge, C. 311
magnitude estimation 215–16
Maney, M. 300
Mann, C. 253, 311
mapping, CAQDAS 405–6, 413
Marcus, G. 278
marginal frequency distributions 356, 361, 367, 509
Marin, L. 449
Marsh, A. 381
Marshall, G. 297–8
Marsh, C. 379
Marshment, M. 426

Marxism 10, 448, 509
Marx, K. 12, 45, 298–9
Mason, B. 475
Mason, J. 128, 131, 136, 139
matrix theory 221
MAXdictio 398
MAXqda 92, 396–7, 398, 399, 404, 412–13, 415
May, T. 93
Mead, M. 282
mean 168–71
meaning
  documents 294–6, 297–8
  ethnography 269–70
  visual materials 476–7
measurement theory 33, 34, 38, 509
media
  documents 289–90
  ethics 154
  narrative analysis 432
  social context 300
medical discourse 450
Meehl, P. E. 217
memories 446–7
memos 89, 98, 348–9, 402
Merton, R. K. 8, 149, 237, 247, 260–1, 489, 496
meta-analysis 67, 68, 509
meta-theories 138, 464, 510
Metcalfe, A. 47
methodological triangulation 510
methodology 510
  grounded theory 83
  literature review 66
  participatory approaches 116–17
methods 21–40, 496–7, 501
  design 22
micro-data 374, 379–80
Middlebrook, M. 290
middle-range theory 8, 22, 496, 510
Middleton, D. 446
Miles, M. 97, 279, 395, 397
Millennium Cohort Study (MCS) 377, 381
Miller, D. 313
Mills, 45
MiMeG 121
Mind Manager 405–6
Minitab 354
Mirzoeff, N. 463